DIRECTORY
OF LIBRARY
CONSULTANTS

DIRECTORY OF LIBRARY CONSULTANTS

EDITED BY JOHN N. BERRY III

Introduction by
Ralph Blasingame, Jr.

R. R. BOWKER COMPANY, NEW YORK & LONDON   1969

Z
681.5
B46

Published by the R. R. Bowker Co. (A XEROX COMPANY)
1180 Avenue of the Americas, New York, N.Y. 10036
Copyright © 1969 by the Xerox Corporation.

All rights reserved including those to reproduce this
book or parts thereof in any form.

Standard Book Number: 8352-0210-0
Library of Congress Card Number: 75-79425

Printed and bound in the United States of America

CONTENTS

PREFACE   VII

INTRODUCTION   IX

LIST OF LIBRARY CONSULTANTS   1

SPECIALTY INDEX   121

GEOGRAPHICAL INDEX   139

PREFACE

This first edition of the DIRECTORY OF LIBRARY CONSULTANTS is frankly experimental. It attempts, with limited success, to provide, for the first time in one place, a listing of most of the active consultants in the library and related professions in the U.S. For each consultant or firm listed sufficient information is provided to enable a potential employer to make, at least, the initial inquiries and to determine some of the background and experience of the consultant in question. The DIRECTORY is not complete, indeed, it is doubtful that any such directory could ever make that claim. Its compilation was difficult, and took nearly three years.

Problems of definition were great. It was difficult to determine just who should be called a consultant, and what criteria should determine which consultants would be listed. Our working rule was to err on the side of inclusion, listing any individual who indicated that he or she had served, with compensation, in a consultative status on any library project.

THE DIRECTORY OF LIBRARY CONSULTANTS *does not* endorse nor recommend those persons and firms listed in it. Neither does it claim that only those listed are competent or available. We are certain that other library consultants of at least equal competence to those included are available, some of whom asked not to be listed. This DIRECTORY is not in any way an attempt to provide an accredited list of library consultants. It is merely a listing of those individuals and firms which responded to our published calls for information and who completed our questionnaire. No judgments were made as to the expertise of the individuals or firms included nor of the validity of the information they reported. We merely rearranged the information supplied by each consultant to make it more compact and consistent with the other entries in the book. In short, the DIRECTORY is designed to provide a place where the library consultant can "hang out his shingle," announce to his colleagues that he is available, and indicate to them some of his qualifications to serve them.

The specialties listed were provided by the individual under whose name they are listed. The material has not been changed except for clarification, and it remains as it was reported to us.

Consultants and firms were required to limit the consultantships they reported to the five most recent in the hope that this information would be sufficiently up-to-date to serve both as a record of their recent experience and as references for those interested in obtaining their services. It is recommended to potential employers that the previous employers of consultants listed be contacted for further information regarding a given consultant or firm.

The entries are arranged alphabetically, and there are specialty and geographic indexes. Each entry begins with the consultant's name, followed by his date of birth, current title and position, home address, education, professional positions held, other honorary or organizational positions held, memberships, no more than five of his recent publications, his five most recent consultantships, and his specialties by numerical code. The key to the consulting specialties is given at the bottom of each two-page spread.

In short, THE DIRECTORY OF LIBRARY CONSULTANTS is designed to provide, through this and subsequent editions, a continuing source for those institutions and individuals who have a problem to solve and desire consultative services toward the solution. It is also a place where the individual consultant or consulting firm can make their qualifications known to the library world. It is our hope that future editions will be more complete, and we welcome additional names as well as suggestions for the expansion or improvement of the information provided, and hope that readers will contact the editor with such suggestions.

The editor is most grateful to the director, Elizabeth W. Cattell, and staff of the Jaques Cattell Press without whose expert aid and fine work this DIRECTORY could not have been published. Special thanks are due to Mrs. Joyce Howell, Mrs. Dorothy Hancock, and Miss Margie Hackett at Jaques Cattell Press for their meticulous attention to the style, arrangement, and completeness of the biographies, and for seeing them into print.

To Miss Carole Collins, Mr. Robert Landau, and Miss Rona Morrow, of Bowker's Book Editorial Department, our thanks for help in the initiation of the DIRECTORY and editing of the data, and for their moral support through its endless delays. Thanks too, to Mrs. Anne J. Richter, Editor-in-Chief of the Book Editorial Department at Bowker, for her guidance throughout the entire project.

JNB

INTRODUCTION
by RALPH BLASINGAME, JR.

PURPOSE OF A CONSULTANT:

The use of consultants to solve problems large and small in libraries has become commonplace. Behind the best and most successful of state planning there is the work of a consultant and a report in which he pulls together his observations and makes his recommendations. One of the first steps which a librarian or board of trustees often takes in order to renovate an old building or plan a new one, to rejuvenate a faltering organization or to plan the distant future of a presently satisfactory organization is to employ a person or firm with experience in organization, management, financing, community relations, and related matters. Development of a county library service plan often starts with the work of a consultant. Expansion of colleges, universities, and other educational institutions very often requires either forming or updating a library or library system. For these and many other purposes the consultant is often a valuable member of the team, worth far more than the fee he claims. Many times, as for example in the case of problems involving automation, the consultant brings to an organization knowledge and skill which it could not possibly duplicate from within its own staff. The consultant may represent, then, a shortcut to new, expanded or up-dated facilities and programs. At the same time, the consultant does not weigh down the organization permanently with a high salary.

On the other hand, the work of a consultant is often not productive. The number of reports which have been filed away without action is legendary. Some of these reports are perfectly sound but were not picked up by the progressive administrator, board of trustees, college president, or other responsible agent. Some of the reports are really not sound. They are incomplete, leaving out recommendations on such significant items as the operating costs of the proposed program or other information which would permit one to visualize fully the impact of the recommended course of action. A consultant may give most of his consideration to one part of a problem. It is possible, for instance, for the consultant to occupy himself with size and location of buildings when the central problem is one of adequacy of services or collections.

One matter to be given serious consideration, then, is what the consequences may be if the consultant's report is unacceptable, or not acted upon for various reasons. How long will it be before another study can be done? What other consequences, for example, to the reputation of the librarian may ensue? Sometimes these consequences are more important than is gaining the solution to a particular problem.

SELECTING A CONSULTANT:

There is, then, no telling in advance what problems will be solved by the consultants; which reports will be useful and which will not; what solutions will be acceptable. How, then, does one know when it is appropriate to hire a consultant and when it may not be? Some criteria are:

First, is the problem at hand one on which the librarian may reasonably seek outside help or is it really one to which he should apply his own expertise and authority, even at the risk of incurring the irritation of the public or governing authority?

Second, has the problem been defined carefully enough to make sure that its solution requires knowledge and skill which do not exist within the organization?

Third, does it seem likely that consultants are available who can make useful recommendations, in general line with the institution's overall goals?

Fourth, is there the temper and will in the organization and community to put into action recommendations requiring major commitment of energy and funds?

Fifth, is there the prospect of obtaining enough money to hire an expert of the required ability for the necessary period of time?

If some criteria are not established in advance, it may be assumed that a rational end result will not ensue. It is not uncommon to find in reports of major studies such recommendations as, "The public libraries of this state should strive to reach American Library Association standards as rapidly as possible." Perhaps they should, but this statement will not be of real help unless it is supported by clear factual evidence that the libraries do not meet reasonable standards and by recommended steps by which standards may be achieved.

It is appropriate to hire a consultant either to make a study and make certain recommendations or to consult periodically with the management of the organization or with one of its operating units where there is full recognition that a problem exists, where there is desire to achieve a solution and where the desire is backed up by the necessary supply of energy and will. The periodic employment of a consultant to serve as a general advisor and sounding board for an organization or organizational unit is uncommon in this field. Many consultants in librarianship are practitioners spending a relatively small part of their time on consulting, or are members of library school faculties with full-time commitments to teaching and research. These consultants, of course, owe their first consideration to their principal employers. Thus it is difficult to find a person who could spend one day per month, or even one day every two months, with an organization. In time, this type of consulting may become more common. There are many potential advantages in having such a consultant to aid not only in the solution of specific problems but to bring into the organization a continuous supply of fresh ideas, unfettered by the traditions and limitations of the past. The great variety of problems on which reports have been made by library consultants suggests the great range of skills and knowledge which may reside in consultants.

The publication of this DIRECTORY represents a major step forward. It has often been difficult in the past to get the names of several consultants whose backgrounds fit them for a particular investigation. Selecting the consultant has been often a catch-as-catch-can matter. Furthermore, where only a few choices are open to the person or organization wishing to hire a consultant, it is rather uncommon for there to be any systematic check on the consultant's competence. A few people (and firms) have national reputations; a great number of individuals active as consultants are not well-known outside their home area. In the first case one hires the person or firm on the basis of national reputation, and in the second case, the individual is often hired because his price is right. In either case, the result may be disappointing.

It is not difficult to think of criteria which might be used to decide what kind of consultant ought to be hired and then to select among several persons or firms offering services. No consultant, for example, should be offended if the agency interested in hiring him requires him to supply references from persons or organizations for whom work has previously been done. In following up on a reference, it would be well to describe as closely as possible the work that is to be done to see whether or not the previous employer had a problem of the same general type and scope. It is entirely reasonable, also, to ask a consultant to supply copies of previous reports or of reports of studies to which he or his firm has made substantial contributions. It would be foolish to ask for such evidence and then not have it read carefully to see whether or not the consultant's general attitude and approaches are acceptable. Most consultants also expect to appear personally in order both to discover the local circumstances and to offer the prospective employer an opportunity to make his own estimate of the consultant's personal qualities. Very often, the consultant, especially one operating on an occasional basis, will ask that this time be paid for. Most consultants will require payment of expenses if this interview trip involves any great distance or staying away from home for several days.

THE CONSULTANT CONTRACT:

When thinking about selecting a consultant, it will also be necessary to think through the process of who should be involved in selection and who should sign the contract or letter of agreement which may result. If the chief librarian is to do this, he must have obtained previous permission to do so from his board of trustees, college administrator, school board or other responsible body. If a board of trustees or committee is to select the consultant, they must establish for themselves some procedures to be followed, questions to be asked and so forth. Unless there is some regularity in this process, the final selection may be based on incomplete information.

Of course, it would be foolish on the part both of the employer and the consultant to fail to obtain a copy of the necessary resolution, letter, or other authorizing legal document. This process need not be particularly elaborate, but there should be an exchange of letters, a signed contract or other evidence which will both support the payment of necessary costs and outline the work that is to be done. It is well to remember that a contract with an individual who does not operate or serve as a part of a larger organization will be valueless if the person becomes incapacitated. A contract with a consultant firm, while not a guarantee that the work will be done, at least assures some continuity of action. Of course, if one employs a firm on the basis that a particular individual will perform the consulting assignment, the same problems apply as with an individual not connected with a firm.

Many consultants often receive very generally worded requests for assistance. In fact, it is almost axiomatic that the first inquiry to a consultant will be so vaguely worded that the nature and scope of the work to be performed are not at all clear. From one point of view, this uncertainty may be helpful — at least, it does not tie the organization or the consultant to a preconceived description of the problem or the outline of a solution. At the same time, a vague statement of the matter under consideration opens up the possibility that the consultant will really prescribe what is to be done. On the one hand, this is part of the consultant's responsibility. However, one is on thin ice if one puts too much in the hands of the consultant. The consultant may describe the problem according only to his own personal biases; he may word parts of his proposal in such fashion that it will be difficult to insist upon proper performance of the work; or he may intentionally or unintentionally neglect to mention certain aspects of a problem.

It is common practice for a consultant to look at the situation at first hand, or talk for some period of time with the librarian or other individual directly concerned and then to make a detailed proposal. This proposal very often contains a brief statement of problem, a statement of the work to be done, a deadline for a final report, or other timetable of events, and a fee. The fee is very often stated as a set amount of money, but it can also be stated as an estimate of a total sum with provision for payment for certain specific expenses, including fees for services. The fixed cost contract is becoming increasingly common.

Before a consultant can reasonably make an estimate, he should be informed of any deadline which is of importance to the client. Similarly, the client should review the consultant's statement carefully to make sure that it is complete and to assure himself that any work which he may be required to do can be done in a reasonable time. Of course, the responsible officer of the contracting organization should be absolutely certain that he can, in fact, make the payments required and meet the payment schedule of the consultant. It is not unusual for clients, especially governmental agencies, to experience long delays in paying consultant fees. All consultants who have worked for government understand this, but all unnecessary delays should certainly be avoided.

The letter of agreement or contract should be reviewed both by the client and the consultant. It should be absolutely certain, for example, that the person signing the letter or contract has indeed authority to do that. There is nothing formidable about this process. In fact, many consultants have worked on enough contracts and letters of agreement so that they feel quite able to handle the matter without the assistance of an attorney. If the consultant is to subcontract some parts of the work, this should be agreeable to the client and it is generally advisable to have this fact mentioned in the contract or letter of agreement. When dealing with large governments, or in any situation where lines of authority are complicated or not clear, several clearances may be necessary before work is begun. In general, it is illegal for the consultant to charge a fee for work which was performed prior to the contract date. It will also be necessary to clear any questions of conflict of interest which might arise because, for example, of the consultant's previous employment or present commitments. All special conditions should be spelled out. For example, if the work to be performed requires access to records or to offices, that fact should be noted and the agreement as to responsibility for gaining access spelled out. If the study is to be done under the advice of one or more committees, that must be agreed to in advance and the relationship of the consultant to the committee(s) indicated in the contract. It will also be well to indicate a schedule for claiming payments for work accomplished.

THE CONSULTANT REPORT:

The contract between a consultant and his client should specify what report or reports are to be made and, as nearly as possible, it should answer other major questions about the report. Is the report to be oral or written, or will there be a written report presented orally one or more times? Will the report be printed and given general distribution, or is it to be considered as a staff report of concern only within the organization? If the client chooses not to publish the report, is the consultant free to do so on his own initiative or to use the data in other publications? What are the interests of various parties in the report — consultant, administrator, college president, board of trustees? (The interests of all should be considered in establishing the method and distribution of the report in advance.) In certain instances, consultants will not accept assignments unless the report is to be made public. In other cases, the consultant may summarize the report in a separate publication, or authorize someone else to do so. Seldom is it acceptable for the client to publish excerpts from the report without the consultant's prior, specific approval. The opportunities for intentional or unintentional misrepresentation are obvious. It is quite common among business and industrial organizations for the consultant to give only one or two copies of his report to a particular individual. It is then management's prerogative to keep the report secret, to broadcast it, or to take some position between. However, it still is dangerous to issue excerpts without the consultant's knowledge. In general, the consultant's report should be published, or made generally available to the persons and/or organizations which may be interested, as quickly as possible, unless some agreement to the contrary has been reached.

The report ideally is related to the contract. That is to say, if the contract specified that "personnel" should be studied and present and future action recommendations be given, one should be able to locate a "personnel" section in the report and to compare it with the contract agreement as to scope and depth.

It is seldom wise for the consultant to be brought into an organization to make a study without giving some attention to how his presence should be recognized. Where the consultant is studying a part of an organization, the individuals who may be immediately affected should be notified and given as much information as is feasible. Adequate announcement and explanation of the study should also be given to other staff members so that the normal uneasiness which accompanies such a visit can be kept to a minimum.

Where the consultant is to be concerned broadly with the development of the library, it is ordinarily well to use his visits and the study as a whole as publicity devices. Especially where one of the points of the study may be to modify opinions on the part of the public or the faculty of a college, attention should be given to announcing the study with due dignity and to making an explanation of the circumstances. If the study is to result in long term recommendations, the process of consent-building must begin soon and must be carried through the course of the study, building toward some climax.

It is sometimes advisable to form a special committee to work with the consultant to give members at large of the community some feeling of identification with the study from beginning to end. Another reason for having a lay advisory body is to make sure that the recommendations of the study are based on real conditions. An advisory committee which has no particular axe to grind and whose members have no personal gain to look forward to can often be much more free and frank in its comments than will people who are closely concerned with the problem at hand. Dealing with such devices requires considerable knowledge of local conditions. Within a state, one must gain some sense of the political temper; within all academic institutions one must know something of the power structure. In short, one should not rush into the creation either of a citizens committee or the process of consent building without having first given some study to the general atmosphere and temper of the times.

Sometimes the use of a study as a publicity device can backfire. Not all instances of the hostility which may result can be anticipated. Furthermore, not all conflict is to be feared. Indeed, conflict can, if properly handled, be a most valuable device in publicizing a study or a set of long-term recommendations of significance. Handled badly, however, the hostility which results from rushing publicity can be very harmful.

It is also important to know whether or not to have the consultant present his study and to ask him to aid in the promotion of the recommendations. Ordinarily, it will be best if local people do the promoting, calling upon the consultant only when he seems especially well-suited to appearing in a program. For example, a librarian of national standing reasonably could speak before meetings of librarians, trustees, faculty and other persons who may be expected to have a major interest in libraries. It would probably be unwise to attempt to get a consultant of this type to speak to a local service club. First off, it is a waste of his time and of your money, but such organizations in all likelihood would pay more attention to someone whose base is closer home. Again, all of these considerations are modified by knowledge of local conditions.

It is, of course, entirely reasonable and proper to broadcast the qualifications of the consultant if it appears that this will add weight to his recommendations.

ETHICS:

As the amount of money going into libraries increases and as we turn more and more to several levels of government for financing of library activities, questions of ethical conduct, particularly of conflict of interest, will arise. Librarians are generally not accustomed to dealing with these problems and often do not think in these terms. Consequently, some unfortunate incidents have occurred, most of which have not been publicized, and surely there will be many more. A complicating factor here, too, is that a growing number of individuals are entering the consulting field and there is yet no general agreement among them on basic issues such as who may work for whom and what fees are reasonable for all concerned. It is likely that some of these individuals have not taken time to study the conflict of interests statutes and regulations with the care which they might have.

The person who wishes both to hold a full-time job carrying heavy responsibility and to do consulting work should obtain the agreement of his full-time employer. Preferably, this agreement should be obtained before the appointment is accepted. It is possible to do consulting work during vacation or evenings but the work, properly done, is wearing and often takes more hours than one estimates will be required. Inevitably such work affects one's ability to perform on a regular job. The profession has not yet settled on any guideline on this score. A full, up-to-date statement of professional ethics is in order.

One last word: it is not ordinarily ethical or wise to "use" a consultant to rid an organization of incompetent persons. That is the job of the chief administrator or governing board. Where the consultant is asked to estimate the ability of persons to perform their jobs, either at present or in some future condition, that should be clearly stated in advance. Then the outsider is on notice as to what his job really is. Neither is it ethical for a consultant to attempt to blame all the problems of an organization on the law, local custom or an individual. His findings should be sufficiently clear and well supported to allow the legally authorized person or body to make such determinations if they are justified.

ABBREVIATIONS

AASL—American Association of School Librarians
acad—academic, academy
ACRL—Association of College and Research Libraries
admin—administration, administrative
adminstr—administrator
adv—adviser, advisory
agr—agricultural, agriculture
AHIL—Association of Hospital and Institution Libraries
Ala—Alabama
ALA—American Library Association
Alta—Alberta
ALTA—American Library Trustee Association
Am—America, American
anal—analysis
anthrop—anthropological, anthropology
Apr—April
Apt—Apartment
archaeol—archaeological, archaeology
archit—architectural, architecture
Ariz—Arizona
Ark—Arkansas
ASD—Adult Services Division (of ALA)
ASL—American Association of State Libraries

Asn—Association
assoc(s)—associate(s), associated
asst—assistant
Aug—August
Ave—Avenue

B.C—British Columbia
bd—board
bibliog—bibliographic, bibliographical, bibliography
bldg(s)—building(s)
Blvd—Boulevard
br—branch
Bull—Bulletin
bus—business

Calif—California
Can—Canada, Canadian
Cath—Catholic
cent—central
cert—certificate, certified
chap—chapter
chmn—chairman
cmn(s)—commission(s)
cmnr—commissioner
cmt(s)—committee(s)
co—companies, company
co-auth—co-author
col(s)—college(s)
Colo—Colorado
commun—communication(s)
conf—conference
Conn—Connecticut
consol—consolidated, consolidation
consult—consultant, consultantships, consulting
contrib—contributing, contributor
corp—corporation
coun—council, councilor
CSD—Children's Services Division (of ALA)

D.C—District of Columbia
Dec—December
Del—Delaware
del—delegate, delegation
dept—department
develop—development
dir(s)—director(s)
dist—district
div—division
document—documentation
Dr—Doctor, Drive

E—East
East—Eastern
econ—economic(s)
ed—edition, editor, editorial
educ—education, educational
elem—elementary
emer—emeritus
ESEA—Elementary and Secondary Education Act
eval—evaluation
exec(s)—executive(s)
exp—experiment, experimental

Feb—February
fed—federal

fedn—federation
fel(s)—fellow(s), fellowship(s)
Fla—Florida
Found—Foundation
Ft—Fort

Ga—Georgia
gen—general
gov—governor(s)
govt—government, governmental
grad—graduate

hist—historical, history
hon—honorary
hosp(s)—hospital(s)
hq—headquarters

Ill—Illinois
Inc—Incorporated
Ind—Indiana
info—information
inst(s)—institute(s), institution(s)
instnl—institutional
int—international
ISAD—Information Science and Automation Division (of ALA)

J—Journal
Jan—January
jr—junior

Kans—Kansas
Ky—Kentucky

La—Louisiana
lab(s)—laboratories, laboratory
LAD—Library Administration Division (of ALA)
lectr—lecturer
LED—Library Education Division (of ALA)
legis—legislation, legislative
libr—libraries, library
librn(s)—librarian(s)
lit—literary

Ltd—Limited

mag—magazine
Mar—March
Mass—Massachusetts
math—mathematic(s), mathematical
Md—Maryland
med—medical, medicine
mem—member, memorial
metrop—metropolitan
mgr—manager
mgt—management
Mich—Michigan
mid—middle
Minn—Minnesota
Miss—Mississippi
Mo—Missouri
Mont—Montana
Mt—Mount

N—North
NASA—National Aeronautics and Space Administration
nat—national
N.C—North Carolina
N.Dak—North Dakota
NDEA—National Defense Education Act
Nebr—Nebraska
Nev—Nevada
New Eng—New England
New York—New York City
N.H—New Hampshire
N.J—New Jersey
N.Mex—New Mexico
North—Northern
Northeast—Northeastern
Northwest—Northwestern
Nov—November
N.Y—New York State

Oct—October
Okla—Oklahoma
Ont—Ontario
oper(s)—operation(s), operational, operative
Ore—Oregon
orgn—organization(s), organizational

Pa—Pennsylvania
Pac—Pacific
Phila—Philadelphia
PLA—Public Library Association
P.O—Post Office
prep—preparation
pres—president
prfnl—professional
proc—proceedings
prof—professor, professorial
pub—public
publ—publication(s), publisher, publishing

Quart—Quarterly
Que—Quebec

Rd—Road
R.D—Rural Delivery
rep—representative
res—research
rev—revised
R.I—Rhode Island
R.R—Rural Route
RSD—Reference Services Division (of ALA)
RTSD—Resources and Technical Services Division (of ALA)

S—South
Sask—Saskatchewan
S.C—South Carolina
sch(s)—school(s)
sci—science(s), scientific
S.Dak—South Dakota
sec—secondary
sect—section
secy—secretary
Sept—September
serv—service(s)
SLA—Special Libraries Association
soc—social, society
sociol—sociological, sociology
South—Southern
Southeast—Southeastern
Southwest—Southwestern

spec—special
sr—senior
St—Saint, Street
statist—statistical, statistics
subcmt—subcommittee
suppl—supplement
supt—superintendent
supv—supervising,
  supervision
supvr—supervisor
supvry—supervisory
symp—symposium(s)
syst—system

tech—technical,
  technological, technology

Tenn—Tennessee
Tex—Texas
theol—theological, theology
transl—translation(s),
  translator
treas—treasurer
TV—television

U.K—United Kingdom
UN—United Nations
UNESCO—United Nations
  Educational, Scientific
  and Cultural
  Organization
univ(s)—universities,
  university

U.S—United States

Va—Virginia
vol(s)—volume(s)
v.pres—vice president
Vt—Vermont
W—West
Wash—Washington
West—Western
Wis—Wisconsin
W.Va—West Virginia
Wyo—Wyoming

YASD—Young Adult
  Services Division
  (of ALA)

LIST OF LIBRARY CONSULTANTS

A

ACETO, VINCENT JOHN, Feb. 5, 32; Associate Professor, School of Library Science, State University of New York at Albany, Albany, N.Y. 12203. Home: 2392 Rosendale Rd, Schenectady, N.Y. 12309. A.B, 53; M.A, 54; M.L.S, 59. Hist. teacher, Scotia-Glenville Cent. Schs, Scotia, N.Y, 56-57; high sch. librn. & chmn, Burnt Hills-Ballston Lake Cent. Schs, Burnt Hills, N.Y, 57-59; dir, Ballston Community Libr, Burnt Hills, 58-60; assoc. prof, sch. libr. sci, State Univ. N.Y. Albany, 59- Other: Chmn, cent. processing cmt, N.Y. Libr. Asn, 61-63; Fulbright prof, Univ. Dacca, E. Pakistan, 64-65; v.pres, Hudson-Mohawk Libr. Asn, 64-66; mem, cmt. on revision of sch. libr. standards, N.Y. State Educ. Dept, 66- Mem: ALA; N.Y. Libr. Asn; Hudson-Mohawk Libr. Asn; Pakistan Libr. Asn; E. Pakistan Libr. Asn; Kappa Phi Kappa; Phi Delta Kappa. Publ: Panacea or Pandora's Box—A Look at Central Processing in New York State, Libr. J, 1/15/64; Reading Habits of Librarians of the Pakistan Library Association, Proc. Pakistan Libr. Asn. Conf, Lahore, 65; The Function of the College Library, East. Librn, 9/66; Children's Librarian-Passive Provider or Active Agent for Change, Res. Quart, winter 67; Opening New Doors to Film Literacy, Film Libr. Quart, summer 68. Consult: 1) Amsterdam Pub. Schs, Amsterdam, N.Y, develop. of Title II spec. purpose grant for sch. libr, Sept-Oct. 65; 2) Albany Pub. Schs, Albany, N.Y, plan for develop. & construction of instructional materials center, Title I & II proposal, Feb-May 66; 3) Niskayuna Pub. Schs, Schenectady, N.Y, libr. adv. on successful Title III project for independent study program, 66; 4) Libr. Develop. Div, N.Y. State Educ. Dept, Albany, construction of questionnaire on libr. manpower needs & preliminary anal. of returns, Apr-June 66 & Jan. 67. Specialties: 1c, 1e, 1f; 2d (films); 5b, 5d (manpower surveys); 7b, 7c; 8f.

ACKERMAN, PAGE, June 30, 12; Associate University Librarian, University Library, University of California, Los Angeles, Calif. 90024. Home: 310 20th St, Santa Monica, Calif. 90402. B.A.(English), 33; B.S.(libr. sci), 40. Asst. univ. librn, Univ. Calif, Los Angeles, 54-65; assoc. univ. librn, 65- Other: Regional rep, recruitment cmt, ALA. Mem: ALA; Calif. Libr. Asn. Publ: Druid Hills Freshmen Buy Books for the Library, Educ. Method, 12-39; A Survey of Education for Librarianship in California, Calif. Librn, 7/61. Consult: 1) Univ. Fla, Gainesville, Gen. personnel & budget problems, 66. Specialties: 5a, 5b, 5c, 5d (commun. & staff morale); 9 (gen. budget techniques).

ADAMOVICH, SHIRLEY, May 8, 29, Film Consultant (Coordinator), contract basis with states of N.H, Vt. & Maine. Home: 14 Thompson Lane, Durham, N.H. 03824. B.A, 54; M.S, Simmons Col, 55. Regional librn, Free Pub. Libr. Serv, Vt, 55-57; state supvr. of Fed. Libr. Programs, Vt, 57-58; head librn, East. Gas & Fuel Asn, Boston, Mass, 59-60; cataloger, Bentley Col, Boston, 61-62; dist. libr. consult, N.H. State Libr, 65-66. Mem: N.H. Libr. Asn; New Eng. Libr. Asn; ALA; Kappa Delta Pi. Publ: The Film Reviews, N. Country Libr. Consult: 1) Nathaniel Hawthorne Col, Antrim, N.H, advice on bldg. a collection for a small liberal arts col, 64-66; 2) St. Joseph's Seminary, Peterborough, N.H, cataloging, classifying, arranging high sch. libr. (20,000 vols) in seminary, 65-66; 3) Hancock Pub. Libr, Hancock, N.H, weeding & bldg. collection, Aug. 66. Specialties: 2a, 2b, 2c; 3a, 3f (cataloging Cath. collections, music & phono-records).

ADAMS, SCOTT, Nov. 20, 09; Deputy Director, National Library of Medicine, Bethesda, Md. 20014. Home: 4621 High St, Chevy Chase, Md. 20015. A.B, Yale Col, 30; M.L.S, Columbia Univ, 40. Librn, Nat. Inst. Health, 50-59; program dir. foreign sci. info, Nat. Sci. Found, 59-60; deputy dir, Nat. Libr. Med, 60- Other: Past pres, Am. Document. Inst; pres, Med. Libr. Asn, 67-68. Mem: ALA; SLA; Am. Soc. Info. Sci; Med. Libr. Asn; D.C. Libr. Asn. Publ: MEDLARS: Progress and Prospects, In: Toward a National Information Service; The Scientific Revolution and the Research Library, Col. & Res. Libr; Hospital Libraries, Hospitals, 6/16/64; The National Library of Medicine's Role in Biomedical Communication, Bioscience, 9/65; Bibliographic Organization in the Biomedical Sciences, Wilson Libr. Bull, 4/66. Consult: 1) Agency Int. Develop, Washington, D.C, develop. of acad. med. libr. in Korea & Viet Nam, 66; 2) Icelandic Ministry of Educ. & Icelandic Med. Asn, Reykjavik, Iceland, advice on organizing a single nat. med. libr, 12/66; 3) UNESCO, Paris, France, mem, Int. Adv. Cmt. on Document, Libr. & Archives, 67- Specialties: 2d (biomed. sci); 4b; 7a, 7c; 8a, 8b, 8c, 8g (int. functions).

ALEXANDER, ESTHER MONA, Aug. 3, 18; State Library Consultant, ESEA Title II, Kansas State Department of Public Instruction, Topeka, Kans. 66612. Home: 120 E. Tenth, Topeka, Kans. 66614. B.A, 39; M.L.S, 63. Teacher & librn, Stanley High Sch. & Elem. Sch, 54-60; librn, Lenexa Elem. Sch, Lenexa, Kans, 60-66. Other: Pres, Tri-Dist. Teachers Asn. Johnson County, Kans, 65; dir. dist. I, Kans. Asn. Sch. Librns, 66, mem. coun. & standards cmt. Mem: Dept. Audiovisual Instruction; KAVCO; Kans. Libr. Asn; ALA; AASL; Mt. Plains Libr. Asn. Publ: Kans. Asn. Sch. Librns. Newsletter, (co-ed); Filmstrip Selection Aid for Junior High and High School Libraries, Kans. State Dept. Pub. Instruction, 66; See the Demonstration Libraries in Action, Kans. State Dept. Pub. Instruction, 66-67; Selection Aids for Elementary, Junior High and Senior High School Libraries, Kansas, 66, 67. Consult: 1) Kans. State Teachers Col, Emporia, Kans, consult. for Cooperative Processing for Sch. Libr. Workshop, Mar. 67; 2) Kans. State Teachers Col, consult. for Inst. for Sch. Adminstr. & Librns, Apr. 67; 3) Kans. State Dept. Pub. Instruction, 120 E. Tenth, Topeka, Kans, planning & assisting in 12 workshops, Where the Action Is—The Media Center, Oct. 67. Specialties: 1c; 2b, 2c, 2d (reading, English, math, sci); 3a, 3d; 5a; 6d (info. bull, inserv. insts. & workshops); 7a, 7b; 8a, 8d, 8f.

ALLEN, JAMES W; Coordinator of Library Service & Resource Consultant, Kings County Superintendent of Schools, 1144 W. Lacey Blvd, Box C, Hanford, Calif. 93230 & Tulare County Superintendent of Schools, 202 County Civic Center, Visalia, Calif. 93277. Home: 11400 12th Ave, Hanford, Calif. 93230. B.A, 49; M.S, 56; M.A, 64. Gen. libr. consult. & sch. librn, Redondo Beach City Sch. Dist, 60-64; dist. libr. & audiovisual coordinator, Cypress Sch. Dist, Cypress, Calif, 64-66; sch. libr. consult, bureau audiovisual & sch. libr. educ, State Dept. Educ, Sacramento, Calif, 66-67; coordinator libr. serv. & resource consult, Kings County Supt. Schs, Hanford, Calif, 67- & Tulare County Supt. Schs, Visalia, Calif, 68- Other: Ad hoc Title II cmt. mem, State of Calif, 67-68. Mem: Calif. Asn. Sch. Librns; Audio-Visual Educ. of Calif; ALA; Dept. Audiovisual Instruction; Nat. Educ. Asn; Calif. Teachers Asn; Phi Delta Kappa. Publ: Contrib, Calif. Sch. Libr, 68. Consult: 1) Visalia Unified Sch. Dist, 200 S. Dollner St, Visalia, Calif, program on sch. libr. facilities, Nov. 67; 2) Coronado Unified Sch. Dist, 706 W. Sixth St, Coronado, Calif, developed libr. program for new high sch. libr, May 68. Specialties: 1c, 1e, 1f; 4b; 6a; 7a.

ALLEN, KENNETH S, Dec. 7, 20; Associate Director University Libraries, University of Washington, Seattle, Wash. 98105. Home: 7016 28th N.E, Seattle, Wash. 98115. B.A, 49; B.L.S, 51. Head librn. sci. reading room, Univ. Wash, Seattle, Wash, 53-56, asst. head, acquisitions div, 57-58, head, acquisitions div, 59-60, admin. asst. to dir. libr, 60, assoc. dir. libr, 61- Other: Chmn. nominating cmt, Pac. Northwest Libr. Asn, 61-62; mem. statewide book catalog cmt, Wash. Libr. Asn, 61-62, mem. develop. cmt, 62-63; treas, Faculty Men's Club, Univ. Wash, 63-65. Mem: Pac. Northwest Libr. Asn; Wash. Libr. Asn. Publ: Management Methods in Libraries, Bull. Med. Libr. Asn, 10/61; Bookbinding at the University of Washington, Seattle, Wash, 62; Library Planning for Automation (ed), Macmillan, London, 65. Consult: 1) Boeing Co, Seattle, Wash, gen. bldg. & orgn, 56-60; 2) United Control Co, Bellevue, Wash, planning bldg, orgn, staff & collection develop, 63-64. Specialties: 1b, 1d, 1e, 1f, 1g; 2e; 3b, 3c, 3d, 3e; 4a, 4b; 5a, 5b, 5c; 6d (faculty relations); 7a, 7b; 8b, 8c, 8f; 9 (budget develop).

ALLEN, LOREN H, Oct. 3, 09; Director Learning Resources, Illinois Central College, P.O. Box 2400, East Peoria, Ill. 61611. Home: 603 Devonshire Rd, Washington, Ill. 61571. B.Ed, 37; B.S. in L.S, 38; M.S. in L.S, 50. Instructional materials consult, Dept. Pub. Instruction, State of Ill, 60-61; dir. instructional materials, Richwoods Community High Sch, 61-66; dir. instructional materials & libr. serv, Sauk Valley Col, Dixon, Ill, 66-68; dir. learning resources, Ill. Cent. Col, 68- Other: Bd. mem, Ill. Reading Serv, 50-57; bd. mem, Ill. Asn. Sch. Librns, 54-58. Mem: ALA; AASL; Nat. Ed. Asn; Dept. Audiovisual Instruction; Ill. Ed. Am; Ill. Libr. Asn. Publ: Launching a Successful Audiovisual Program, Educ. Screen & Audiovisual Guide 11/62; Consult: 1) Instructional Materials, Dept. Pub. Instruction, State of Ill, consult. to Ill. pub. schs. on libr. bldgs, libr. admin. collections & recruiting, June 60-July 61; 2) Sullivan High Sch, Sullivan, Ill, eval. of libr. orgn, books & materials with recommendations, Mar. 66; 3) Windsor Consolidated Schs, Windsor, Ill, eval. of high sch. elem. libr. programs with recommendations for collections & serv, Apr. 66. Specialties: 1c; 2b; 4b; 7a; 8c.

ALVAREZ, DR. ROBERT S, June 7, 12; Library Administration, South San Francisco, 840 W. Orange Ave, South San Francisco, Calif. 94080. B.S. in L.S, 35; Ph.D, 39. Dir, Nashville Pub. Libr, Nashville, Tenn, 46-59; dir, Berkeley Pub. Libr, Berkeley, Calif, 59-61; librn, Montclair, Calif, 65-66; v.pres, Tolos

---

KEY TO CONSULTING SPECIALTIES: 1) ARCHITECTURE AND BUILDINGS, 1a) public libraries, 1b) academic libraries, 1c) school libraries, 1d) special libraries, 1e) library interiors, 1f) furnishings, 1g) site and location, 1h) other architectural; 2) COLLECTIONS: SELECTION, EVALUATION, WEEDING, 2a) adults, 2b) young adults, 2c) children, 2d) subject specialty, 2e) O.P. searches, 2f) rare books, 2g) appraisals, 2h) others; 3) TECHNICAL PROCESSES, 3a) cataloging, 3b) classification systems, 3c) acquisitions, 3d) materials processing, 3e) work flow and cost studies, 3f) others, 4) AUTOMATION, 4a) applications of data processing equipment, 4b) information storage and retrieval systems, 4c) systems analysis, 4d) others

Assocs, Palo Alto, Calif, 66; libr. adminstr, South San Francisco, Calif, 66- Other: Pres, Nashville Libr. Club, 48; pres, Tenn. Libr. Asn, 51; treas, Southeast. Libr. Asn, 52; pres, Sequoia Club, 56; pres, Glendale Club, 59; ed. & publ, Aviation Digest & Admin. Digest, 65- Mem: ALA; Calif. Libr. Asn. Publ: Qualifications of Heads of Public Libraries, Edwards, 43; contrib, Libr. J, ALA Bull. & Wilson Libr. Bull; columnist, Library Lookout. Consult: 1) Mobile Pub. Libr, Mobile, Ala, survey of facilities & serv. with report, 53; 2) Columbus Pub. Libr, Columbus, Ga, survey of libr. serv. with report, 56; 3) Montgomery County Bd. Educ, Rockville, Md, survey of book acquisition processes with report & recommendations, Oct-Dec. 61; 4) MERI, Palo Alto, Calif, study of needs of firm for co. libr. with report, Mar. 66; 5) Ames Res. Center, Moffett Field, Calif, study of oper. of two NASA libr, with Tolos Assocs, Apr. 66. Specialties: 1a, 1g; 2a; 3c; 6c; 7a; 8c.

ANDERSON, DOROTHY J, June 19, 34; Library Career Consultant, Illinois State Library. Home: 1709 N. Crilly Court, Chicago, Ill. 60614. B.A, 58; M.L.S, 61. Children's librn, Seattle Pub. Libr, 58-62; asst. to exec. secy, CSD & YASD, 62-64; libr. career consult, Ill. State Libr, 65- Other: Mem. int. relations cmt, CSD, 61, mem. bd. dirs, 68-; lectr. children's literature, Roosevelt Univ, 64; mem. recruitment cmt, Ill. Libr. Asn, 65-, mem. scholarship cmt, 66- Mem: ALA; Ill. Libr. Asn. Publ: Seattle Images (with Don Aylard), Hansen, 61; New Girl in a Strange Town, Chicago Sun Times, 10/63; Ice-Age Librarian and the Space Age Child, Ill. Libr, 12/65; Land of Lincoln Recruits Librarians, ALA Bull, 11/66. Consult: 1) Clarendon Hills Pub. Libr, Clarendon Hills, Ill, consult. on storytelling technique & programming, Sept. 65; 2) Wis. Libr. Asn, Wis. Libr. Cmn, Madison, Wis, demonstrated libr. recruitment at col. level, with Myrl Ricking, Sept. 65. Specialties: 2b, 2c, 2d (storytelling); 5b; 6a, 6b.

ANDERSON, FRANK J, Jan. 29, 19; Librarian, Wofford College Library, Spartanburg, S.C. 29301. B.A.(English & Am. literature), Univ. Ind; M.S. in L.S, Syracuse Univ, 51. Librn, Kans. Wesleyan Univ, Salina, 52-56; librn. in charge of Baring Ave. Br, E. Chicago Pub. Libr, Ind, 56-57; dir, Submarine Libr, Groton, Conn, 57-60; librn, Kans. Wesleyan Univ, 60-66; librn, Wofford Col. Libr, Spartanburg, S.C, 66- Other: V.pres, Mountain Plains Libr. Asn, 63-65, pres, 65-67; ed, Geography & Map Div. Bull, SLA, 65-; prop. of Kitemang Press. Mem: ALA; SLA; S.C. Libr. Asn; Southeast. Libr. Asn; Beta Phi Mu. Publ: Regular reviewer, Libr. J, 54-; Submarines, Submariners and Submarining (a bibliog), Shoe String Press, 63; H.L. Abbot's: Beginnings of Modern Submarine Warfare...A Facsimile Reprint of the Original 1881 Pamphlet with biographical, bibliographical Appendices and an Index, Shoe String, 66; contrib. to prfnl. journals. Consult: 1) U.S. Naval Submarine Sch, Submarine Base, New London, Conn, advised on orgn. of hist. & tech. libr, prepared manual for staff use & devised classification scheme, May-June 59; 2) Kans. Wesleyan Univ, Salina, planning of a 20,000 square foot expansion of libr. bldg, wrote program for architects, with Wilson & Co, Engineers, especially Gil Geary, Architect, 64; 3) Minn. State Col. Bd, Minneapolis, preliminary advice on bldg. design & problems of establishing a new state col. (Southwest. Minn. State Col) in Marshall, Minn, Dec. 64; 4) Kans. Higher Educ. Facilities Cmn, Topeka, space survey of institutions of higher educ. in Kans. (Ft. Hays State, McPherson & Bethany Cols), under direction of Robert B. Downs, May-June 65; 5) Morris Col, Sumter, S.C, advised on orgn, collections, policy & bldg, 67-68. Specialties: 1b, 1d; 2d (submarines, naval, ships & sea), 2e, 2h (hist. of printing); 3c; 5b, 5c; 6a, 6b; 8f.

ANDERSON, LE MOYNE W, Aug. 16, 23; Director of Libraries, Colorado State University, Fort Collins, Colo. 80521. Home: 2000 Orchard Place, Fort Collins, Colo. 80521. B.A. & B.S.L.S, 48; M.S, 51. Head reference dept, Univ. Ill, Chicago, 55-57; dir. libr, Colo. State Univ, Ft. Collins, 57- Other: Assoc, Am-Scandinavian Asn, 52-; treas, Chicago Libr. Club, 54; mem. coun, ALA, 59-63; mem. exec. bd, Colo. Libr. Asn, 59-63; pres, Ft. Collins Lions Club, 63-64; pres, Bibliog. Center for Res, Denver, Colo, 63-65. Mem: ALA; Mountain-Plains Libr. Asn; Colo. Libr. Asn; Colo. Coun. Librns; Bibliog. Center for Res. Publ: Let Freedom Ring, ALA Bull, 11/53; Human Relations Training for Librarians?, Col. & Res. Libr, 5/58; Cooperation in Colorado, Mountain-Plains Libr. Quart, summer 61; Report of a Survey of the Western Washington State College Library (with E.W. Erickson), ALA, 62; The Classification Game as Played at C.S.U, Colo. Acad. Libr, summer 64; Bucks for Books, Mountain-Plains Libr. Quart, 5/66. Consult: 1) West. Wash. State Col, Bellingham, gen. survey of libr, with E.W. Erickson, 62; 2) Bemidji State Col, Bemidji, Minn, bldg. critic, 65; 3) Mesa Col, Grand Junction, Colo, libr. bldg, 65-66; 4) Casper Jr. Col, Casper, Wyo, libr. bldg, 65-66. Specialties: 1b, 1e, 1f, 1g; 2g; 3c, 3d, 3e; 4a, 4c; 5a, 5b, 5c; 7a; 8c.

ANDREWS, JAMES C, Apr. 18, 21; Director, Library Services Department, Argonne National Laboratory, 9700 S. Cass Ave, Argonne, Ill. 60440. Home: 320 S. La Grange Rd, La Grange, Ill. 60525. B.S.(physics), 46; B.S.L.S, 47; M.S.L.S, 49. Head tech. info. serv, DuPont Savannah River Lab, Aiken, S.C, 50-58; libr. dir, Argonne Nat. Libr, Argonne, Ill, 59- Other: SLA rep, ALA Interlibr. Loan Cmt, 62-;

---

5) PERSONNEL AND RECRUITING, 5a) job evaluation and description, salary recommendations, 5b) recruitment of professionals and management personnel, 5c) administrative organization, 6) PUBLIC RELATIONS, 6a) publications, 6b) publicity programs, 6c) public opinion surveys, 6d) others, 7) SERVICES, 7a) evaluation of current program, 7b) studies of service to special publics, e.g., students, handicapped, aged, etc., 7c) programs for the implementation of new laws, program proposals to governments, 7d) others, 8) COMMUNITY, REGIONAL, STATE PLANNING, 8a) legislative programs, 8b) area analyses, 8c) centralized systems, cooperative arrangements, 8d) development of standards, 8e) state libraries and extension agencies, 8f) regional and statewide surveys, 8g) others, 9) OTHERS.

first chmn. nuclear sci. sect, SLA, 63; mem. mechanization cmt, Ill. Libr. Asn, 66- Mem: SLA; Am. Soc. Info. Sci; Ill. Libr. Asn. Consult: 1) Gaertner Sci. Co, Chicago, Ill, orgn, placement & oper. of a co. libr, 66; 2) Univ. El Salvador, Ciudad de Universitaria, San Salvador, consult. for Ford Found. on libr. oper. & orgn, equipment for new libr, Oct-Dec, 66; 3) Nat. Autonomous Univ. Honduras, Tegucigalpa, new libr. bldg. & personnel for oper. of new bldg, Nov-Dec. 66; 4) Nat. Univ. Nicaragua, Leon, libr. equipment & operating policy of the libr, Nov. 66. Specialties: 1b, 1d, 1f; 2d (sci); 3a, 3b, 3c, 3d, 3e; 4a; 5c.

ARCHER, DR. H. RICHARD, Sept. 13, 11; Librarian, Chapin Library, Williams College, Williamstown, Mass. 01267. Home: Sabin Dr, Williamstown, Mass. 01267. B.A, Univ. Calif, 40, cert. librarianship, 41, M.A, 43; Ph.D, Univ. Chicago Grad. Libr. Sch, 54. Res. asst, Univ. Chicago Grad. Libr. Sch, 42-44; supv. bibliographer, Clark Mem. Libr, Univ. Calif, Los Angeles, 44-52, curator spec. collections, 52-53, librn, R.R. Donnelley & Sons, Chicago, Ill, 53-57; librn. & lectr. graphic arts, Chapin Libr, Williams Col, Williamstown, Mass, 57- Other: Mem. coun, ALA, 63-66, chmn. rare book sect, 64-65, mem. adv. cmt. libr. tech. project, 65-; visiting lectr, libr. schs, Univ. Okla, 56, Univ. South. Calif, 60, Univ. Mich, 62, Simmons Col, 65 & State Univ. N.Y. Albany, 68. Mem: ALA; ACRL; New Eng. Col. Librns. Publ: The Chapin Library After Thirty-Five Years, Book Club of Calif. Quart. News Letter, summer 58; Private Presses and Collector's Editions, Libr. Trends, 7/58; Display and Exhibit Cases, Libr. Trends, 4/65; Rare Book Collections: Some Theoretical and Practical Suggestions for use by Librarians and Students (ed), ACRL Monograph 27, ALA, 65; The Private Press, In: Modern Fine Printing, Clark Mem. Libr, Univ. Calif, 68. Consult: 1) Emma Willard Sch, Troy, N.Y, advice on weeding & preservation of collections, with Wyllis E. Wright, 61. Specialties: 1b, 1f; 2f, 2h (preservation, conservation); 3c; 6a, 6d (exhibitions).

ARCHER, JOHN H, July 11, 14; University Archivist, Douglas Library and Professor of History, Queen's University, Kingston, Ont, Can. Home: 119 Earl St, Kingston, Ont, Can. B.S, 46; M.A, 48; B.L.S, 49. Legis. librn. Sask, 51-64; dir, McGill Univ. Libr, Montreal, Que, Can, 64-67. Other: Mem, Sask, Archives Bd, 51-64; mem. bd. dirs, Sask. Jubilee Corp, 53-55; pres, Regina Libr. Asn, 57-58; provincial archivist of Sask, 57-62; mem. ed. bd, Sask, Hist, 57-64; mem. adv. ed. bd, Americana Corp.(for Can), 58-; pres, Sask. Libr. Asn, 59-60; Sask. rep, Can. Centenary Cmt, 63-65; mem. bd. dirs, Can. Centenary Coun, 64-; pres, Can. Libr. Asn, 66-67. Mem: Can. Libr. Asn; ALA; Que. Libr. Asn; Asn. Can. Bibliothécaires Langue Française; Bibliog. Soc. Can. Publ: Historic Saskatchewan, Jr. Chamber Commerce, Saskatoon, 48; The Hudson's Bay Route (with A.M. Pratt), Kings Printer, 53; Saskatchewan: the History of a Province (with Alex M. Derby), McClelland & Stewart, 55; The Public Records in Saskatchewan, J. Soc. Archivist, 4/60; Acquisition of Canadian Provincial Government Documents, Libr. Resources & Tech. Serv, winter 61; Footprints in Time: A Source Book on the History of Saskatchewan (with C.B. Koester), House of Grant, 66. Consult: 1) Project officer, Royal Cmn. Govt. Orgn, survey of libr. & archives in fed. govt. of Can, with Willard E. Ireland, 61-62; 2) Univ. Sask, examination of documents & records center for proposed libr, 62; 3) Chmn, Cmt. Continuing Educ. for Province of Sask, survey of orgn. & develop. of univ. & provincial govt. libr. serv. to support adult educ. & extension program, 62. Specialties: 1h (archives, Can. collections & govt. documents); 5c; 7a; 8a, 8d, 8e; 9 (archival & govt. document programs).

ARMSTRONG, RODNEY, Mar. 5, 23; Librarian, Davis Library, Phillips Exeter Academy, Exeter, N.H. 03833. Home: 27 Front St, Exeter, N.H. 03833. A.B, Williams Col, 48; M.S, Columbia Univ, 50. Librn, Phillips Exeter Acad, 50- Other: Mem. coun, N.H. Libr. Asn, 51-52; v.pres, New Eng. Sch. Libr. Asn, 52; trustee, Thomas Bailey Aldrich Mem, Portsmouth, N.H, 55-; trustee, Kensington Soc. Libr, N.H, 57-; dir, Manuscript Soc, 64-; mem. coun, New Eng. Hist. Genealogical Soc, 65- Mem: ALA; N.H. Libr. Asn; New Eng. Sch. Libr. Asn. Consult: 1) Deerfield Acad, Deerfield, Mass, libr. program, staff, bldg, 64-; 2) Portsmouth Priory Sch, Portsmouth, R.I, libr. program, staff, bldg, 65-; 3) Foxcroft Sch, Middleburg, Va, libr. program, staff, bldg, 66-; 4) Middlesex Sch, Concord, Mass, bldg, 67-; 5) St. Mark's Sch, Southboro, Mass, bldg, 68- Specialties: 1c, 1e, 1f; 2b, 7a, 7b.

ASH, LEE, Sept. 15, 17; Library Consultant, 31 Alden Rd, New Haven, Conn. 06515. Columbia Univ, 32-37; cert, Pratt Inst, 36; grad. libr. sch, Univ. Chicago, 39-41. Librn, Carnegie Endowment for Int. Peace, 53-57; ed, Libr. Journal, 57-59; res. dir, Yale's Selective Book Retirement Program, 59-63; libr. consult, 63- Other: Mem. coun, Ala, 59-63; ed. & publ, Am. Notes and Queries, 62-; assoc. prof, grad. libr. sch, Drexel Inst. Tech, 63-65; ed, New Eng. Libr. Asn. Newsletter, 69- Mem: ALA; SLA; Med. Libr. Asn; New Eng. Libr. Asn; Conn. Libr. Asn; N.Y. State Libr. Asn; New York Libr. Club; Archons of Colophon; Grolier Club; Bibliog. Soc. Am; Am. Asn. Hist. Med; Hist. Sci. Soc; Modern Language Asn; Soc. Indexers, London; Scott Inst. Polar Res, Cambridge, Eng; Torch. Publ: Subject Collections (compiler), Bowker, 58, 2nd ed, 61, 3rd ed, 67; Serial Publications Containing Medical Classics, 61; Yale's Selective Book Retirement Program, 63; Interlibrary Request and Loan Transactions Among Medical Libraries of the Greater N.Y.

KEY TO CONSULTING SPECIALTIES: 1) ARCHITECTURE AND BUILDINGS, 1a) public libraries, 1b) academic libraries, 1c) school libraries, 1d) special libraries, 1e) library interiors, 1f) furnishings, 1g) site and location, 1h) other architectural; 2) COLLECTIONS: SELECTION, EVALUATION, WEEDING, 2a) adults, 2b) young adults, 2c) children, 2d) subject specialty, 2e) O.P. searches, 2f) rare books, 2g) appraisals, 2h) others; 3) TECHNICAL PROCESSES, 3a) cataloging, 3b) classification systems, 3c) acquisitions, 3d) materials processing, 3e) work flow and cost studies, 3f) others, 4) AUTOMATION, 4a) applications of data processing equipment, 4b) information storage and retrieval systems, 4c) systems analysis, 4d) others

Area, 66; Who's Who in Library Service (ed), 4th ed, 66, 5th ed, 70; Taste in the Design of Library Interiors (co-auth), 70. Consult: 1) Yale Univ. Libr, New Haven, Conn, res. dir, Yale's Selective Book Retirement Program, 59-63; 2) N.Y. Acad. Med, 2 E. 103rd St, New York, N.Y, project dir, survey of med. libr. resources of Greater New York, 63-66; 3) Harvard Med. Libr, Boston, Mass, sorting, weeding, disposal & develop. planning, to combine collections of the Boston Med/Harvard Med. Libr, 64-66; 4) Toronto Pub. Libr, College & St. George Sts, Toronto, Ont, Can, eval. of the reference collections, with recommendations for collections & personnel, 65-; 5) Queens Borough Pub. Libr, N.Y, cent. libr. eval. of res. collections, 69- Specialties: 1d, 1e, 1f, 1g; 2a, 2d (all spec. collections; hist, literature, med. particularly), 2e, 2f, 2g; 3a, 3b, 3c; 5a, 5b, 5c, 5d (trustee recruitment); 6a, 6b, 6c, 6d (develop. of Friends orgns); 7a, 7b, 7d (develop. of spec. subject & rare book collections); 8b, 8c, 8d, 8f; 9 (rare books & spec. collections—content eval, develop. programs, monetary appraisals).

ASHEIM, DR. LESTER, Jan. 22, 14; Director, Office for Library Education, American Library Association, 50 E. Huron, Chicago, Ill. 60611. Home: 253 E. Delaware Place, Chicago, Ill. 60611. B.A, 36; B.A.L.S, 37; M.A.L.S, 41; Ph.D, 49. Dean & assoc. prof, grad. libr. sch, Univ. Chicago, 52-61; dir. int. relations office, ALA, 61-66. Mem: ALA; Ill. Libr. Asn; SLA. Publ: Forum on the Public Library Inquiry (ed), Columbia Univ, 50; The Core of Education for Librarianship, ALA, 54; The Future of the Book (ed), Univ. Chicago, 55; The Humanities and the Library, ALA, 57; Persistent Issues in American Librarianship (ed), Univ. Chicago, 61; Librarianship in the Developing Countries, Univ. Ill, 66. Consult: 1) Univ. Brasilia, Brasilia, Brazil, survey of libr. needs, with Charles Gosnell, David Clift & German Garcia, autumn 63; 2) Univ. Indonesia Libr. Sch, Djakarta, Indonesia, survey of libr-educ. needs with recommendations, autumn 64; 3) Am. Univ. Beirut, Beirut, Lebanon, survey of libr. admin. orgn. with report & recommendations, Oct. 65; 4) Univ. Mich. Dept. Libr. Sci, Ann Arbor, Mich, survey of program & admin. orgn, with L. Quincy Mumford, Robert Downs & Raynard Swanks, 68. Specialties: 5b; 9 (libr. educ, int. librarianship, commun. study, accreditation, procedures & standards).

ATHERTON, PAULINE, Dec. 2, 29; Associate Professor, Syracuse University, School of Library Science, Syracuse, N.Y. 13210. Home: 126 Jamesville Ave, Apt. K-3, New York, N.Y. 13210. A.B, 51; M.S. in L.S, 54. Asst. prof. libr. sci, Chicago Teachers Col, 56-61; cross reference ed, World Book Encyclopedia, 58; program dir. AIP/UDC, Am. Inst. Physics, New York, N.Y, 61-68. Other: Mem. classification cmt, ALA-RTSD-CCS, 60-66; mem. cmt, FID-CR, 62-; treas, Am. Document. Inst, 63-65. Mem: ALA; SLA; Am. Soc. Info. Sci; N.Y. Libr. Asn; Phi Beta Kappa. Publ: Classification Research (ed), Proceedings of Elsinore Conference, Munksgaard, 65; Is Compatibility of Authority Files Practicable?, In: Information Systems Compatibility, Spartan, 65; Ranganathan's Classification Ideas: An Analytico-Synthetic Discussion, Libr. Resources & Tech. Serv, fall 65. Consult: 1) Rodfei Zedek Congregation Libr, Chicago, cataloging-reclassification project, with Henrieta Schultz, 59-60; 2) Syst. Develop. Corp, ed. consult on Nat. Abstracting & Indexing report, 67; 3) Westat Survey Inc, Bethesda, Md, info. retrieval project, 69- Specialties: 3a, 3b, 3e; 4a, 4b, 4c; 7a, 7b; 8c, 8d.

B

BADTEN, JEAN MARGARET, June 26, 32; State Supervisor of Learning Resources Services, Office of State Superintendent of Public Instruction, Box 527, Olympia, Wash. 98501. Home: 3800 Elizabeth Ave, 59B, Lacey, Wash. 98501. B.A.(soc. studies), Seattle Pac. Col, 54; M.L.S, Univ. Wash, 62. Librn, Highline Pub. Schs, Seattle, Wash, 58-62; libr. coordinator, Fed. Way Schs, King County, 62-66; asst. libr. supvr, Office State Supt. Pub. Instr, Olympia, Wash, 66, state supvr. libr. serv, 66- Other: Secy, Wash. State Asn. Sch. Librns, 64, ex-officio mem. exec. bd; chmn, AASL-Nat. Libr. Week Cmt, 67, mem. nat. bd, AASL & dir. region nine; mem, Title IV LSCA Adv. Cmt, 68; mem, Cmt. Regional Gov. Conf. on Libr, 68; mem. recruitment materials cmt, ALA, 68. Mem: ALA; Wash. State Asn. Sch. Librns; Dept. Audiovisual Instruction; Wash. State Dept. Audiovisual Instruction. Publ: The Secondary School Libraries in Washington State, Knapp Sch. Libr. Project, 3/67; Has Your Library Considered Pre-Cataloging? (co-auth), The Instructor, 11/67; Library Skills Charts, Transparencies, Guidelines, Worksheets (co-auth), Ideal Sch. Supply Co, 67; The Elementary and Secondary School Libraries of Washington State: a Survey (co-auth), 68. Consult: 1) Selah Pub. Schs, Box 398, Selah, Wash, ESEA Title III, 66, 68; 2) Port Angeles, 216 E. Fourth, Port Angeles, Wash, ESEA Title II spec. purpose grant, establishing elem. libr, with Nancy Motomatsu & Thomas Hannan, 67; 3) Mukilteo Pub. Schs, Mukilteo, Wash, bldg. planning, with Thomas Hannan, 67-68; 4) Puyallup Pub. Schs, 109 E. Pioneer, Puyallup, Wash, eval. of programs, with Nancy Motomatsu, 68; 5) Northshore Pub. Schs, 9816 N.E. 183rd St, Bothell, Wash, program planning, with Thomas Hannan, 68. Specialties: 1c; 2b, 2c; 3a, 3b, 3c, 3d; 5a, 5b, 5c; 7a, 7b, 7c; 8c, 8d, 8f.

BAER, DR. KARL A, Dec. 1, 06; Chief Librarian, National Housing Center, 1625 L St. N.W,

---

5) PERSONNEL AND RECRUITING, 5a) job evaluation and description, salary recommendations, 5b) recruitment of professionals and management personnel, 5c) administrative organization, 6) PUBLIC RELATIONS, 6a) publications, 6b) publicity programs, 6c) public opinion surveys, 6d) others, 7) SERVICES, 7a) evaluation of current program, 7b) studies of service to special publics, e.g., students, handicapped, aged, etc., 7c) programs for the implementation of new laws, program proposals to governments, 7d) others, 8) COMMUNITY, REGIONAL, STATE PLANNING, 8a) legislative programs, 8b) area analyses, 8c) centralized systems, cooperative arrangements, 8d) development of standards, 8e) state libraries and extension agencies, 8f) regional and statewide surveys, 8g) others, 9) OTHERS.

Washington, D.C. 20036. Home: 5111 Saratoga Ave. N.W, Washington, D.C. 20016. LL.B, Univ, Heidelberg, 28; LL.D, 31; B.L.S, Pratt Inst, 41. Chief librn, Nat. Housing Center, Wash, D.C, 55- Other: Chmn. biological sci. div, SLA, 53-54, chmn. planning, bldg, housing sect, 66-67, approved SLA prfnl. consult; lectr, Cath. Univ. Am. Libr. Sch, 53-62; pres, Wash, D.C. chap, SLA, 57-58, chmn. consultation cmt, 58-; pres. spec. libr. sect, Int. Fedn. Libr. Asn, 63- Mem: SLA; Am. Soc. Info. Sci; D.C. Libr. Asn. Publ: Founders of Neurology (ed. with Webb Haymaker), 53; Establishing an Association Library, Am. Soc. Asn. Execs. J, 10: 9-13; Bibliographical Methods in the Biological Sciences, Spec. Libr, 2/54; Relationship of Technical Writing and Library Functions, Spec. Libr, 1/58; Special Librarianship, In: Training and Education of Information Specialists, Wiley, 67. Consult: 1) Am. Inst. Architects, 1735 New York Ave. N.W, Wash. D.C, advice on physical plant of libr. to be part of new bldg, Feb. 65; 2) U.S. Army Personnel Res. Office, Wash, D.C, expansion of libr. & serv, with Lillian Hamrick & Fenton Kennedy, Aug. 65; 3) Commun. Workers Am, AFL-CIO, 1925 K St. N.W, Wash, D.C, classification, cataloging & housing of expanding collection, with Lillian Hamrick, Nov. 65; 4) Logetronics Inc, 500 E. Monroe, Alexandria, Va, assistance in establishing new info. center, with Lillian Hamrick & Logan Cowgill, Aug, 66; 5) Welex Electronics, 2431 Linden Lane, Silver Spring, Md, establishment of a tech. libr, with John Sherrod & Lillian Hamrick, Oct. 66. Specialties: 1d, 1e, 1f, 1g; 2d (sci, tech); 3a, 3b; 5a, 5b; 7a.

BAILEY, J. RUSSELL, Oct. 19, 05; Partner, Bailey & Gardner, Architects, P.O. Box 229, Orange, Va. 22960. Home: 278 Caroline St, Orange, Va. 22960. B.A, Park Col, 28; B.S, Univ. Mich, 32. Other: Mem. libr. lighting cmt, Illuminating Engineering Soc. Mem: ALA; Tau Sigma Delta. Publ: The Library as Part of the Learning Center, Am. Inst. Architects J, 6/63; Mr. Architect, Listen, Libr. J, 12/1/65. Consult: 1) Univ. Va. Med. Libr, Charlottesville, Va. program & site selection, Feb. 64-Dec. 67; 2) Miss. State Univ, State College, Miss, alterations & addition to libr. bldg, July 65-; 3) Union Theol. Seminary, Richmond, Va, program statement, planning & furnishings, Oct. 65-; 4) Med. Col. Va, Richmond, program statement, 67; 5) James M. Duncan Libr, Alexandria, Va, program, statement & planning, Mar. 68. Specialties: 1a, 1b, 1c, 1d, 1e, 1f, 1g..

BAILLIE, DR. STUART, Jan. 28, 14; Director of Libraries, San Jose State College, 250 S. Fourth St, San Jose, Calif. 95114. Home: 2444 Fairglen Dr, San Jose, Calif. 95125. B.A, Wash. Univ.(St. Louis), 35, M.A, 39, Ed.D, 61; B.S. in L.S, George Peabody Col. Teachers, 41. Librarianship teacher, univ. col. & engineering librn, Wash. Univ, St. Louis, Mo, 47-53; dir. libr, Univ. Denver, 53-66, dir. grad. sch. librarianship & prof. librarianship, 55-66; dir. libr. & prof. librarianship, San Jose State Col, Calif, 66- Other: V.pres. & pres-elect, Mo. Libr. Asn, 52-53; pres, Mountain Plains Libr. Asn, 63-65. Mem: ALA; Mountain Plains Libr. Asn; Nebr. Libr. Asn; Colo. Libr. Asn; SLA; Calif. Libr. Asn. Publ: Library School and Job Success, Studies in Librarianship 3, Univ. Denver Sch. Librarianship, 63. Consult: 1) Idaho State Libr, Boise, survey, 63; 2) Univ. Autonoma de Guadalajara, Guadalajara, Mex, new univ. libr. bldg, 63, 64 & 65; 3) Pub. Libr, Cheyenne, Wyo, survey, with Claude Settlemire, 64; 4) New Col, Sarasota, Fla, admin. problems, May-June 65; 5) Aspen Inst, Aspen, Colo, establishment of high sch. libr, coordinated its program with Aspen Inst. Libr, July 66. Specialties: 1a, 1b, 1c, 1g; 2d (col. & univ); 5a, 5b, 5c; 7a, 7c; 8e; 9 (educ. programs, accreditation problems).

BALLOU, HUBBARD W, Jan. 26, 17; Head, Photographic Services, Columbia University Libraries, 535 W. 114th St, New York, N.Y. 10027. Home: 90 Morningside Dr, New York, N.Y. 10027. A.B, Yale Univ, 39; B.S, Columbia Univ. Sch. Libr. Serv, 47. Head, photographic serv, Columbia Univ, N.Y, 48-, lectr. photoreproduction, sch. libr. serv, 50- Other: Secy, sect. cmt, PH5, U.S. Am. Standards Inst, 57-; assoc. ed. Am. Document, Am. Soc. Info. Sci, 58-60, U.S. correspondent on document reprod. to Fedn. Int. Document, 61-; assoc. ed. Nat. Micro-News, Nat. Microfilm Asn, 59-67, dir, 65-68; chmn, photoduplicating order forms cmt, ALA, 60-63; sect. ed. on Copying & Copying Equipment, Abstracts Photographic Sci. & Engineering, Soc. Photographic Scientists & Engineers, 63-64. Mem: ALA; SLA; Am. Soc. Info. Sci; fel, Nat. Microfilm Asn. Publ: Microcopying..., In: Information Processing Equipment, Reinhold, 55; Photography and the Library, Libr. Trends, 10/56; Guide to Microreproduction Equipment (ed), Nat. Microfilm Asn, 59-; Photographic Literature (assoc. ed), Bowker, 62; Microphotography, In: Encyclopedia International, Grolier, 64; Copying Methods Notes, Libr. Resources & Tech. Serv, 8: 81-85. Consult: 1) United Bus. Publ, 200 Madison Ave, New York, N.Y, consult. on microrecording for Industrial Photography & Systems, 58-66; 2) Libr. Tech. Project, 50 E. Huron St, Chicago, Ill, choice of microfilm reading machines, 60; Univ. Khartoum microfilming, 62; adv. bd. on copying methods manual, 63-66; 3) Coun. on Libr. Resources, 1028 Connecticut Ave. N.W, Wash, D.C, survey of ways to prepare a new Shaw list, 60; preliminaries to the preparation of a copying methods manual, 63; 4) Wis. Libr. Asn, Wis. State Col, Oshkosh, workshop on microform reading facilities, May 63; 5) Queens Col. Libr, Flushing, N.Y, proposed reprographic serv, May 64. Specialties: 2d

KEY TO CONSULTING SPECIALTIES: 1) ARCHITECTURE AND BUILDINGS, 1a) public libraries, 1b) academic libraries, 1c) school libraries, 1d) special libraries, 1e) library interiors, 1f) furnishings, 1g) site and location, 1h) other architectural; 2) COLLECTIONS: SELECTION, EVALUATION, WEEDING, 2a) adults, 2b) young adults, 2c) children, 2d) subject specialty, 2e) O.P. searches, 2f) rare books, 2g) appraisals, 2h) others; 3) TECHNICAL PROCESSES, 3a) cataloging, 3b) classification systems, 3c) acquisitions, 3d) materials processing, 3e) work flow and cost studies, 3f) others, 4) AUTOMATION, 4a) applications of data processing equipment, 4b) information storage and retrieval systems, 4c) systems analysis, 4d) others

(reprography, especially microreproduction), 2h (preservation); 3f (reprographic serv); 4b, 4d (microreproduction systs); 9 (microphotography, photoduplication).

BANISTER, JOHN R, Feb. 5, 12; Director of Libraries, Columbus, Ga. & 4-County Region, W.C. Bradley Memorial Library, Columbus, Ga. 31906. Home: 2952 Roswell Lane, Columbus, Ga. 31906. A.B, Univ. Mich, 36; B.S. in L.S, Univ. Ill, 37. Dir. libr, Columbus, Ga. & 4-county region (Muscogee, Marion, Chattahoochee & Stewart Counties), 51- Other: Mem. coun, ALA, 40-44, chmn, jr. mems. roundtable, 46; chmn, pub. libr. sect, Southeast. Libr. Asn, 48-49; first v.pres, Ga. Libr. Asn, 60-61; mem, L.S.A.C. Cmt. of Ga, 65- Mem: ALA; Southeast. Libr. Asn; Ga. Libr. Asn. Publ: Ed, Jr. Librn, 38-41; New Patterns for the Industrial Branch, Libr. J, 11/15/45; Subjective Survey of Florida's Public Libraries, Fla. Pub. Newsletter, 12/48; ed, Fla. Pub. Libr. Newsletter, 48-49; Does Your Library Deserve a Larger Appropriation?, Libr. J, 5/1/50; Accent on Gracious Service, Libr. J, 12/15/51. Consult: 1) Bradley Mem. Libr, Columbus, Ga, program, basic plans for Fourth Ave. br. libr, layout & interior arrangement, furniture & equipment, air-conditioning, with Bill Murphy, 52; 2) Manchester Pub. Libr, Manchester, Ga, site selection for headquarters, regional pub. libr, with Lila Rice, 65; 3) Albany Pub. Libr, Albany, Ga, program, plans for county pub. libr, complete air-conditioning, with Sim Fallis, 65; 4) Valdosta Pub. Libr, Valdosta, Ga, site selection, program, plans for headquarters pub. libr, bookmobile quarters, complete air conditioning, with Blake Ellis, 66. Specialties: 1a, 1g, 1h (program, basic layout); 3d; 9 (audio-visual equipment & layout; use of modern office equipment in pub. libr).

BARBER, RAYMOND WILLIAM, Feb. 25, 38; Coordinator of Instructional Media Services, University School, Kent State University, Kent, Ohio 44240. Home: 819 Saxon Ave, Akron, Ohio 44314. B.A, 60; M.S, 65. Head librn, West Jr. High Sch, Akron, Ohio, 60-67; coordinator of Learning Resource Centers, ESEA Title I, Akron, 67; coordinator, instructional media serv, univ. sch, Kent State Univ, 67- Other: Pres, Summit County Libr. Asn, 61; chmn. jr. high sch. librns, Ohio Sch. Libr. Asn. Mem: ALA; AASL; Ohio Libr. Asn; Ohio Sch. Libr. Asn; Dept. Audiovisual Instruction. Consult: 1) Cath. Newman Center, Univ. Ky, 320 Rose Lane, Lexington, Ky, bldg. & collection, 66-67. Specialties: 1c; 2b; 7a.

BARTOLINI, R. PAUL, July 21, 20; Library Director, Lake County Public Library, 221 W. Ridge Rd, Griffith, Ind. 46319. Home: 624 N. Oakwood Ave, Griffith, Ind. 46319. B.Ed, 42; B.S. in L.S, 46; M.S. in L.S, 47. Supvr, neighborhood & extension serv, Milwaukee Pub. Libr, Wis, 56-65; libr. dir, Lake County Pub. Libr, Griffith, Ind, 65- Other: Pres, Kans. Libr. Asn, 51-52; v.pres, Adult Educ. Coun. Metrop. Phila, 55-56; pres, Wis. Libr. Asn, 62-63; mem, Standards for Pub. Libr. Cmt, 65-69; mem. intellectual freedom cmt, Am. Libr. Trustees Asn, 65-69; chmn. cmt. pub. libr. develop, Ind. Libr. Asn, 66-67; mem. cmt. econ. status, welfare & fringe benefits, LAD, 66-69. Mem: Ind. Libr. Asn; ALA; Kappa Phi Kappa; Beta Phi Mu. Publ: The Position-Classification Plan for University Libraries, 10/48; The American Library Association Plan, In: Retirement for Librarians, ALA, 51; Double Header in Milwaukee, Libr. J, 12/1/64; Seven for Lake County, Libr. J, 12/1/66. Consult: 1) Mayville Pub. Libr, 105 N. Main St, Mayville, Wis, site selection & bldg. program, 64-65; 2) Fond du Lac Pub. Libr, 32 Sheboygan St, Fond du Lac, Wis, bldg. program, 65; 3) Wauwatosa Pub. Libr, 757 N. Broadway, Milwaukee, Wis, bldg. program, 67; 4) Bremen Pub. Libr, Bremen, Ind, site selection & bldg. prog, 68; 5) Greenville Pub. Libr, 414 W. Main St, Greenville, Ill, site selection & bldg. program, 68. Specialties: 1a, 1e, 1f, 1g; 2a, 2f, 2g; 4a; 5c; 8d.

BASCHE, JAMES R, JR, May 22, 26; Consultant, Nelson Associates, Inc, 845 Third Ave, New York, N.Y. 10022. B.S, Northwest. Univ; M.A, Columbia Univ. Found. staff mem. & univ. instructor int. relations, Soc. Sci. Found, Univ. Denver, Colo, 54-57; consult. adult educ. programs in world affairs, Foreign Policy Asn, 58-59; program officer in San Francisco & New York, asst. rep. in Bangkok & New York & acting rep. in Taipei & New York, Asia Found, San Francisco, Calif, 59-65; exec. dir, Greater New York Coun. for Foreign Students, Inc, 65-66. Consult: 1) Mich. State Libr, Lansing, survey of reference & res. libr. cooperation, in Mich, with David Watson, 66; 2) Wayne State Univ, Detroit, Mich, methods & procedures for measuring patron use & cost of patron serv. for the Detroit Metrop. Libr. Proj, 67; 3) Shenango Valley Libr. Study Cmt, Sharon, Pa, program of pub. libr. serv. for the Shenango Valley, 67; 4) Nassau County Dept. Pub. Works, N.Y, guidelines for construction of the Mitchel Field Libr, 67; 5) New Britain Inst. Libr, Conn, recommendations for future develop, 68. Specialties: 7a, 7c; 8a, 8b, 8c, 8d, 8e, 8f.

BEACH, CECIL P, July 12, 27; Director of Libraries, Tampa and Hillsborough County, 102 E. Seventh Ave, Tampa, Fla. 33602. Home: 305 Country Club Dr, Tampa, Fla. 33612. A.B, Univ. Chattanooga, 50; M.A, Fla. State Univ, 52. Dir, Piedmont Regional Libr, Winder, Ga, 54-61; dir, Gadsden Pub. Libr, Gadsden, Ala, 61-65; dir, Tampa & Hillsborough County Libr, Tampa, Fla, 65- Mem: ALA; Southeast. Libr. Asn; Fla. Libr. Asn; Ala. Libr. Asn. Consult: 1) Gadsden Pub. Libr, Gadsden, Ala, bldg. pro-

---

5) PERSONNEL AND RECRUITING, 5a) job evaluation and description, salary recommendations, 5b) recruitment of professionals and management personnel, 5c) administrative organization, 6) PUBLIC RELATIONS, 6a) publications, 6b) publicity programs, 6c) public opinion surveys, 6d) others, 7) SERVICES, 7a) evaluation of current program, 7b) studies of service to special publics, e.g., students, handicapped, aged, etc., 7c) programs for the implementation of new laws, program proposals to governments, 7d) others, 8) COMMUNITY, REGIONAL, STATE PLANNING, 8a) legislative programs, 8b) area analyses, 8c) centralized systems, cooperative arrangements, 8d) development of standards, 8e) state libraries and extension agencies, 8f) regional and statewide surveys, 8g) others, 9) OTHERS.

gram, site, furniture specifications & layout, 64; 2) Tampa Pub. Libr, Tampa, Fla, furniture specifications & layout, 65; 3) Macon Pub. Libr, Macon, Ga, survey of current program & recommendations, 67; 4) Sebring Pub. Libr, Sebring, Fla, bldg. program, site, furniture specifications & layout, 68; 5) St. Petersburg Beach Pub. Libr, St. Petersburg, Fla, bldg. program, site, furniture specifications & layout, 68. Specialties: 1a, 1e, 1f, 1g; 7a.

BEAN, DONALD ECKHART, Oct. 17, 00; President, Library Management & Building Consultants, Inc, Box 58, Evanston, Ill. 60204. Home: 1010 Golfview Rd, Glenview, Ill. 60025. A.B, Univ. Ill, 21. Libr. planning specialist on staff, Libr. Bureau, div. Remington Rand, 22-58; pres, Libr. Mgt. & Bldg. Consults, Inc, Evanston, Ill, 48-51, 58- Other: Trustee, Glenview Pub. Libr, Ill, 58-, pres, 61-63; mem. exec. bd, Ill. Libr. Trustees Asn, 60-61, pres, 65-; mem. exec. cmt, bldg. & equipment sect, LAD, 62-63; mem. exec. bd, Ill. Libr. Asn, 65-; mem. adv. cmt, libr. & industry study, Nat. Adv. Cmn. Libr, 67; mem. ad hoc cmt. physical facilities of libr, ALA. Mem: ALA; Ill. Libr. Asn. Publ: Modular Planning for College and Small University Libraries (with Ralph E. Ellsworth); Library Architecture, In: Grolier's Encyclopedia International; Survey of Library Buildings and Facilities, In: Library Surveys, Columbia Univ, 67. Manual of Library Equipment, ALA, 69. Consult: 1) Jefferson City & Cole County Libr, Jefferson City, Mo, survey of libr, bldg. program & review of plans, with William Chait & Frank Sessa, 66; 2) Can. Dept. Nat. Defence, Ottawa, Ont, survey for consolidation of 10-12 departmental libr, bldg. program & review of plans, with Foster E. Mohrhardt & Robert Severance, 66; 3) South. Methodist Univ, Dallas, Tex, bldg. program for libr. addition & review of plans, with Stephen A. McCarthy & Robert Muller, 66; 4) Pottsville Free Pub. Libr, Pottsville, Pa, preliminary bldg. program including some aspects of mgt. survey with Pottsville as dist. libr. center for surrounding libr, bldg. program & study of possibility of remodeling, with William Chait, Ernest I. Miller & Ralph Blasingame, 66; 5) Findlay Col, Findlay, Ohio, mgt. & bldg. survey, bldg. program & review of plans, with Maurice F. Tauber, Celianna Wilson & Robert Muller, 66. Specialties: 1a, 1b, 1c, 1d, 1e, 1f, 1g.

BEATON, MRS. MAXINE BAILEY, Apr. 13, 15; Medical Librarian, Presbyterian Medical Center, 19th at Gilpin Sts, Denver, Colo. 80218. Home: 1725 Albion St, Denver, Colo. 80220. B.S.(libr. sci), Simmons Col, 36. Librn, Presbyterian Med. Center, 51- Other: Pres, Colo. chap, SLA, 53-54, 62-63; secy. hosp. div, SLA, 54-55, v.chmn, 55-56, chmn 56-57; librn, Univ. Denver Sch. Nursing, Denver, Colo, 56-61, guest lectr. spec. libr. admin, grad. sch. librarianship, 63 & 66, SLA prfnl. consult. in hosp. libr, 62-; mem. Colo. Coun. Libr. Develop, 66. Mem: Colo. Libr. Asn; SLA. Consult: 1) Lutheran Hosp, Wheatridge, Colo, set up med. staff libr, 63; 2) Mental Health Inst, Mt. Pleasant, Iowa, reorganized med. libr, set up collection & procedures for nursing sch. libr, trained nonprfnl. in basic libr. tech. procedures, June 63; 3) W. Nebr. Gen. Hosp, Scottsbluff, Nebr, planning of new med-nursing libr, June 65; 4) Denver Med. Clinic, 701 E. Colfax Ave, Denver, Colo, set up med. staff libr, trained nonprfnl. in routine libr. serv, on retainer to furnish prfnl. libr. serv. as requested, 65-; 5) Med. Group Mgt. Asn, Metrop. Bldg, Denver, spec. indexing project, 66. Specialties: 1d; 2d (hosp. admin, med, nursing); 3a, 3b, 3c, 3d; 5a; 6a; 7a.

BEATTY, WILLIAM K, Feb. 5, 26; Librarian & Professor of Medical Bibliography, Northwestern University Medical School, 303 E. Chicago Ave, Chicago, Ill. 60611. Home: 1509 Forest Ave, Evanston, Ill. 60201. B.A, Columbia Univ, 51, M.S, 52. Asst. prof. med. bibliog, Univ. Mo, 56-57, assoc. prof, 58-62, med. librn, 56-62; librn. & prof. med. bibliog, med. sch, Northwest. Univ, Chicago, Ill, 62- Other: Ed, Transactions & Studies of Col. Physicians of Phila, 55-56; chmn. cmt. periodicals & serials publ, Med. Libr. Asn, 55-61, chmn. med. schs. group, 60, chmn. vital notes on med. periodicals, 61-, mem. bd. dirs, 66-69, chmn. 1969 convention prog. cmt; ed, Vital Notes on Med. Periodicals, 55-; chmn. hosp. div, SLA, 60-61, chmn. biological sci. div, 63-64, mem. bd. dirs, 64-67, v.pres. & pres-elect, Ill. chap, 68-69, prfnl. consult; ed. consult. med. literature, New Physician, 60-; mem. bd. dirs, AHIL, 62-64, pres. of asn, 65-66, chmn. 1963 conf. program cmt; chmn, Interasn. Hosp. Libr. Cmt, 63-64; mem. coun, Soc. Med. Hist. Chicago, 63-; chmn. Osler medal cmt, Am. Asn. Hist. Med, 65-66, mem. coun, 65-68; mem. cmt. selection, index medicus, Nat. Libr. Med, 65-, mem. manpower & training cmt, 66-; U.S. correspondent, libr. in hosps. subsect, Int. Fedn. Libr. Asn, 66-; chmn. Coun. Midwest Regional Health Sci. Libr. & Cooperative Info. Serv, 67-68; mem, Cmn. Educ. Commun, Sch. Dist, 65, Evanston, Ill, 67-68; mem. ed. bd, Familiar Med. Quotations, 68; chmn. cmt. hosp. & inst. libr, Ill. Libr. Asn, 68- Mem: ALA; Ill. Libr. Asn; Libr. Asn, Great Britain; Med. Libr. Asn; SLA. Publ: The New Medical Center Library, Bull. Med. Libr. Asn, 46: 514-518; Some Keys to the Literature, New Physician, 10: 313-315; A Historical Review of Bibliotherapy, Libr. Trends, 11: 106-117; Recently Build Medical School Libraries in the United States, J. Med. Educ, 38: 725-729; The Door to the Book, J. Am. Med. Asn; 200: 7-12; The Medical Library in the Community Hospital, Univ. Colo. Sch. Med. Collected

---

KEY TO CONSULTING SPECIALTIES: 1) ARCHITECTURE AND BUILDINGS, 1a) public libraries, 1b) academic libraries, 1c) school libraries, 1d) special libraries, 1e) library interiors, 1f) furnishings, 1g) site and location, 1h) other architectural; 2) COLLECTIONS: SELECTION, EVALUATION, WEEDING, 2a) adults, 2b) young adults, 2c) children, 2d) subject specialty, 2e) O.P. searches, 2f) rare books, 2g) appraisals, 2h) others; 3) TECHNICAL PROCESSES, 3a) cataloging, 3b) classification systems, 3c) acquisitions, 3d) materials processing, 3e) work flow and cost studies, 3f) others, 4) AUTOMATION, 4a) applications of data processing equipment, 4b) information storage and retrieval systems, 4c) systems analysis, 4d) others

Papers from the Hosp. Med. Staff Conf, 67. Consult: 1) Col. Med, Univ. Vt, Burlington, Vt, plans for new libr. quarters, 61; 2) Presbyterian-St. Luke's Hosp. Libr, Chicago, Ill, survey & program for expanded serv, 64-65; 3) Biomed. Libr, McMaster Univ, Hamilton, Can, plans for new bldg, 67-; 4) Health Center Libr, Univ. Okla, Oklahoma City, Okla, 67-; 5) Med. Sci. Libr, Univ. Utah, Salt Lake City, Utah, program for new integrated libr, with Donald Dean & Maurice Tauber, 67- Specialties: 1d, 1e; 2d (med. & related collections), 2f; 3c, 3e; 5c, 5d (training); 7a, 7b; 8b, 8c, 8d, 8f.

BENNETT, GORDON LATTA, May 20, 08; Director, Colorado State Library, 1362 Lincoln, Denver, Colo. 80203. Home: 5100 E. 17th Ave, Denver, Colo. 80220. B.A, Univ. Nebr, 31; B.S. in L.S, Univ. Denver, 37. Dir, Colo. State Libr, Denver, 56- Other: Pres, Jr. Mem. Round Table, Ark, 41; pres, Colo. Libr. Asn, 45-46, mem. exec. bd, 58-61; dir, PLD, 55-58; dir, Bibliog. Center for Res, Rocky Mountain Region, 58-59; dir, KRMA, Colo. Educ. TV Channel, Inc, 63- Mem: ALA; Mountain Plains Libr. Asn; Colo. Educ. Asn; Colo. Asn. Sch. Librns. Publ: Colorado Plan for Better Libraries, 1951, Colo. Dept. Educ, 51; Johnny Aspen and Suzy Columbine (series), Colo. Parent-Teacher Asn, 56-61; Education in Colorado, 1860-1954, Colo. Dept. Educ, 58; Colorado State Library, Self-Survey, Colo. Dept. Educ, 61; Colorado Plan for Library Development, Colo. Dept. Educ, 67. Consult: 1) Durango Pub. Libr, Durango, Colo, bldg. survey & gen. serv. consultation, with Lawrence V. Mott, 66; 2) Garfield County Pub. Libr, New Castle, Colo, construction, fiscal & gen. serv. consultation, with Denny Stephens, 66; 3) Las Animas Pub. Libr, Las Animas, Colo, libr. survey, with Denny Stephens, May 66; 4) Cortez Pub. Libr, Cortez, Colo, libr. survey, with Denny Stephens, Aug. 66; 5) Brush Carnegie Libr, Brush, Colo, complete survey of functions & orgn, 67- Specialties: 1a, 1e, 1f, 1g; 6a, 6b, 6c; 7a; 8a, 8e, 8f; 9 (finance, orgn).

BENSON, WILLIAM E, Feb. 25, 23; Principal, Benson Associates, Architects & Engineers, 2506 Howell St, Dallas, Tex. 75201. B.S. (archit. engineering), 47. Consult: 1) Jarvis Christian Col, Hawkins, Tex, layout & design of col. libr, all furnishings & equipment; 2) Dallas Pub. Libr, 1954 Commerce, Dallas, Tex, layout & design, furnishings & equip for br. libr. Specialties: 1a, 1b, 1e, 1f.

BERNINGHAUSEN, DAVID KNIPE, Feb. 5, 16; Director & Professor, Library School, University of Minnesota, Minneapolis, Minn. 55455. Home: 410 Groveland Ave. S, Minneapolis, Minn. 55403. B.A, Iowa State Teachers Col, 36; B.S.(libr. sci), Columbia Univ, 41; M.A. (English & philosophy), Drake Univ, 43. Librn, Cooper Union, 47-53; educ. fel, Harvard Univ, 50-51; dir. & prof, libr. sch, Univ. Minn, Minneapolis, 53- Other: Chmn, cmt. on intellectual freedom, ALA, 48-51, secy, 51-52, mem, cmt. on accreditation, 57-61, chmn, 60-61, mem. coun, 60-64; mem, cmn. for free pub. educ, Phi Delta Kappa, 51-52; Thomas Davidson Mem. lectr, Cooper Union, 52; pres, Minn. Libr. Asn, 57-58; pres, Asn. Am. Libr. Schs, 59-60; mem. bd. trustees, Citizens Orgn. for Responsible Govt. in Minneapolis & Hennepin County, 59-62; pres, Univ. Minn. chap, Am. Asn. Univ. Prof, 61-62; v.pres, Minn. br, Am. Civil Liberties Union, 61-62; mem. bd. dirs, Am. Religious Town Meeting of the Air, 61-62. Mem: ALA; Am. Asn. Libr. Schs; ACRL; Minn. Libr. Asn. Publ: Summary Reports of the Annual ALA Conference (ed), 54; Your Right to Read, In: Social Science and Freedom, Soc. Sci. Res. Center of Grad. Sch, Univ. Minn, 59; Undergraduate Library Education: Accreditation, Standards, Articulation (ed), Univ. Minn. Libr. Sch, 59; The Continuing Education of Librarians, ALA Bull, 4/62; Library Education in Taiwan, China Today, 2/63; An Exploratory Study of Juvenile Delinquency and the Reading of Sensational Books (with Richard Faunce), J. Exp. Educ, winter 64. Consult: 1) Veterans Hosp. Libr, Minneapolis, Minn, eval. of libr. serv. with recommendations, 56; 2) Minneapolis Sch. of Art, advice on bldg. a four-year col. libr. in a former prfnl. art sch, 60; 3) Nat. Taiwan Univ, Taipei, planning for libr. educ. in Taiwan, 62-63; 4) Regents of S.Dak, Pierre, survey of the seven insts. of higher educ. with recommendations for libr. improvement, with E.W. McDiarmid, Wesley Simonton, Raymond H. Shove & Lowell E. Olson; 5) State Libr. Cmn. of N.Dak, Bismarck, study & plan for libr. develop. in N.Dak, with Nancy Freeman, Muriel Fuller, Ernestine Grafton & James T. Dunn. Specialties: 1b, 1h (libr. educ; state libr. agencies); 5c; 7a; 8d, 8e, 8f.

BERRISFORD, PAUL DEE, Nov. 3, 25; Associate Professor & Assistant Director for Processing, University of Minnesota, Minneapolis, Minn. 55455. Home: 2245 Princeton Ave, St. Paul, Minn. 55105. B.A, 50; B.S. in Ed, 52; B.S.L.S, 52. Mem. descriptive cataloging cmt, cataloging & classification section, RTSD. Mem: ALA; Minn. Libr. Asn; Twin City Catalogers' Round Table. Consult: 1) Univ. Concepcion, Concepcion, Chile, consult. on the orgn. of a centralized cataloging syst. for Univ. Minn. & Ford Found. at Univ. Concepcion, with James Kingsley, Mar-June 65. Specialties: 3a.

BERRY, JOHN N, III, June 12, 33; Editor-in-Chief, Library Journal, R.R. Bowker Co, 1180 Ave. of the Americas, New York, N.Y. 10036. A.B, Boston Univ; S.M, Simmons Col. Youth-reference librn, Reading Pub. Libr, Reading, Mass, 58-60; reference librn, Simmons Col, Boston, Mass, 60-62, asst. dir. libr. & lectr. libr. sci, sch. libr. sci, 62-64; asst. ed, Libr.

---

5) PERSONNEL AND RECRUITING, 5a) job evaluation and description, salary recommendations, 5b) recruitment of professionals and management personnel, 5c) administrative organization, 6) PUBLIC RELATIONS, 6a) publications, 6b) publicity programs, 6c) public opinion surveys, 6d) others, 7) SERVICES, 7a) evaluation of current program, 7b) studies of service to special publics, e.g., students, handicapped, aged, etc., 7c) programs for the implementation of new laws, program proposals to governments, 7d) others, 8) COMMUNITY, REGIONAL, STATE PLANNING, 8a) legislative programs, 8b) area analyses, 8c) centralized systems, cooperative arrangements, 8d) development of standards, 8e) state libraries and extension agencies, 8f) regional and statewide surveys, 8g) others, 9) OTHERS.

Journal, 64-66; managing ed, new book projects, R.R. Bowker Co, New York, 66-68. Other: Mem. publ. cmt. & ed, Bay State Librn, Mass. Libr. Asn, 62-64; mem. exec. cmt, Libr. Pub. Relations Coun, 66-; publicity chmn, SLA convention, N.Y, 67, chmn. publ. div, SLA, 69; mem. exec. coun, New York Libr. Club, 67. Mem: ALA; SLA; Libr. Pub. Relations Coun; New York Libr. Club; Melvil Dui Chowder & Marching Soc. Publ: Editorials, Bay State Librn, 62-64; Demand for Dissent, Libr. J, 10/15/64; International by Definition, Libr. J, 11/15/64; Policy Making for Library Trustees, N. Country Libr, 9-10/65; An Education Pentagon, Libr. J, 1/15/66; A Regional Library Periodical for New England, Consultant Report, 9/66. Consult: 1) New Eng. Libr. Asn, Concord, N.H, study of feasibility, potential support, costs, mechanics of production & personnel for regional libr. periodical to be organ of the New Eng. Libr. Asn, Sept. 66; 2) Libr. Mail Serv, Grolier, Inc, New York, N.Y, advice on editorial & promotion; 3) Peter Kyle Studios, New York, consult. on mail promotion campaign to libr, 66. Specialties: 2d (soc. sci); 5a, 5b; 6a, 6b, 6c, 6d (asn. publ. programs); 9 (consult. to publishers on libr. market & promotion to it).

BERRY, JUNE, June 1, 25. Home: Route 1, Payson, Utah 84651. B.A, Brigham Young Univ, 47; M.S, Univ. Utah, 52. Librn. of lab. sch, Brigham Young Univ, Provo, Utah, 48-68, instructional materials specialist, summer workshops, 52-66; mem, Joint Coun. on Econ. Educ, 52- Other: Publ, chmn. Utah Congress, Parent-Teacher Asn, 61; pres. Provo br, Am. Asn. Univ. Women, 62-63; exec. secy, Utah Workshop on Econ. Educ, 62-; mem, selection of books & other materials cmt, YASD, 65-67; secy, Utah Reading Coun, 66. Mem: ALA; Utah Libr. Asn; Utah Educ. Asn; Brigham Young Univ. Libr. Asn. Publ: Services of School Libraries in Utah, Brigham Young Univ. Libr, 56; Library Service in Utah: A Graphic View, Utah State Div, Am. Asn. Univ. Women, 59; Using Your Library to Enrich Instruction, Education, 10/59; Librarians Are Executives Too, Bull. Nat. Asn. Sec-Sch. Principals, 10/61; Filing Miscellaneous Materials, Sch. Libr. J, 2/62; The IMC in the Continuous Progress School, Sch. Libr. J, 11/64. Consult: 1) Bassett Sch. Dist, Bassett, Calif, specifications for new libr. based on individualized instruction, 62; 2) Kane County Sch. Dist, Kanab, Utah, merging of high sch. libr. with town libr, suggestions on book selection, ordering, cataloging, weeding & arrangement, Feb. 64; 3) Kane County Sch. Dist, guidelines for establishing an instructional materials center with suggestions on furniture, equipment, arrangements & orgn. of sch. libr, Apr-May 65; 4) Granite Sch. Dist, eval. of total libr. facilities, arrangement, libr. use, instruction in libr. use & use by teachers, with Mrs. Heber C. Evans, Apr. 66; 5) Utah Coun. on Econ. Educ, Salt Lake City, instructional materials specialist for Utah workshop on econ. educ, with Glen F. Ovard, June 66. Specialties: 1c, 1d; 2b; 6a; 7b; 8d, 8f; 9 (genealogy libr. & res; econ. educ. materials for elem. & sec. schs).

BERTALAN, DR. FRANK J, Sept. 18, 14; Director, School of Library Science, University of Oklahoma, Norman, Okla. 73069. Home: 1608 Chestnut Lane, Norman, Okla. 73069. B.Ed, 38; B.S. in L.S, 39; M.S. in L.S, 45; Ph.D, 62. Head engineering info. br, U.S. Navy Bureau Aeronautics, 55-58, deputy exec. asst. sci. info, Office Naval Res, 58-62; asst. prof. libr. sci, Cath. Univ. Am, 62-63, deputy dir, Navy Office Sci. & Tech. Info, Office Naval Res, 63; chief emergency measures project team, Office Emergency Planning, Exec. Office President, 63-65. Other: V.chmn. & chmn-elect, libr. orgn. & mgt. section, LAD, 66-67; chmn. personnel & recruitment cmt, Am. Asn. Libr. Schs, 66-68; project dir, ESEA Title II program, U.S. Office Educ, 66-71; mem. joint cmt. govt. documents, ALA-SLA. Mem: SLA; ALA; Okla. Libr. Asn; Asn. Am. Libr. Schs. Publ: Books for Junior Colleges, ALA, 54, rev. ed, 66; Provisions of Federal Benefits for Veterans (Historical Analysis of Major Veterans' Legislation, 1862-1954), U.S. Govt. Printing Office, 55; A Proposed Acquisitions Policy for the (NASA) Goddard Space Flight Center, Mid-Atlantic Assocs, 63. Consult: 1) Mid-Atlantic Assocs, Inc, 1328 Galloway St. N.E, Wash, D.C, survey of Goddard Space Flight Center sci. & tech. personnel to determine policy for libr. develop, 62-63; 2) BRO-DART Found, BRO-DART Industries, Williamsport, Pa, planned & administered program for a new list of books for jr. col. libr, 64-65; 3) Lynchburg Col, Lynchburg, Va, plans for a new main libr. bldg, 65; 4) Univ. Okla. Res. Inst, Norman, prepared proposal to U.S. Office Ed. for state-wide admin. of ESEA Title II & a recommended state plan for the project, 66-68. Specialties: 1d; 2a, 2d (sci. & tech; libr. sci), 2h (jr. col. libr. collections); 5a, 5b; 7a, 7b, 7c; 8f.

BERTHEL, JOHN H, Mar. 27, 14; Librarian, Johns Hopkins University, Baltimore, Md. 21218. Home: 3701 Patterson Ave, Baltimore, Md. 21207. B.A, 38; M.A, 39; B.S, 41. Librn, Johns Hopkins Univ, 54- Other: Chmn, libr. review bd, U.S. Naval Acad, Annapolis, Md, 65-66; pres, Baltimore Bibliophiles, 65-66. Mem: ALA; ACRL. Consult: 1) Mt. St. Mary's Col, Emmitsburg, Md, libr. bldg, 55; 2) Am. Univ, Wash, D.C, libr. program, bldg. & orgn, 62; 3) Franklin & Marshall Col, Lancaster, Pa, consult. to pres. on libr, 65; 4) Bryn Mawr Sch, Baltimore, Md, libr, 66. Specialties: 1b, 1g; 5c; 7a; 8c; 9 (eval. teams).

BERUL, LAWRENCE H, Apr. 29, 34; Information Systems Consultant, Auerbach Corporation, 121 N. Broad St, Philadelphia, Pa. 19107. Home:

KEY TO CONSULTING SPECIALTIES: 1) ARCHITECTURE AND BUILDINGS, 1a) public libraries, 1b) academic libraries, 1c) school libraries, 1d) special libraries, 1e) library interiors, 1f) furnishings, 1g) site and location, 1h) other architectural; 2) COLLECTIONS: SELECTION, EVALUATION, WEEDING, 2a) adults, 2b) young adults, 2c) children, 2d) subject specialty, 2e) O.P. searches, 2f) rare books, 2g) appraisals, 2h) others; 3) TECHNICAL PROCESSES, 3a) cataloging, 3b) classification systems, 3c) acquisitions, 3d) materials processing, 3e) work flow and cost studies, 3f) others, 4) AUTOMATION, 4a) applications of data processing equipment, 4b) information storage and retrieval systems, 4c) systems analysis, 4d) others

1514 Pleasant Dr, Cherry Hill, N.J. 08034. B.S.(commerce), Drexel Inst. Tech, 57, M.B.A, 67; J.D, George Wash. Univ, 61. Patent examiner & systs. analyst, U.S. Patent Office, 57-60; staff attorney, C-E-I-R, Inc, 61; dir. Wash. opers, Info. Dynamics Corp, 62-63; info. systs. consult, Auerbach Corp, Phila, Pa, 63- Other: Session chmn, Second Annual Nat. Colloquium on Info. Retrieval, 65; program chmn, Fourth Annual Colloquium on Info. Retrieval, 67. Mem: Am. Document. Inst. Publ: Information Storage and Retrieval—A State of the Art Report, AD 630089 CFSTI, Auerbach Corp, 64; Output Printing for Library Mechanization (with D. Sparks & D. Waite), In: Proceedings of the Conference on Libraries and Automation, Libr. Congress, 64; DoD User Needs Study (et al), Phase I Final Report, Auerbach Corp, 1151-TR-3, Vol. I AD 615501 & Vol. II AD 615502 CFSTI, 65; Methodology and Results of the DoD User Needs Survey, In: Proceedings of the Special Libraries Association Workshop on the Report Literature, Western Publ, 66; An Evaluation of the Methodology of the DoD User Needs Study (with Allan Karson), In: Proceedings of the 1965 Congress-International Federation for Documentation, Spartan Books, 66; Whats Wrong With IR?, Machine Design, 7/66. Consult: 1) Sun Oil Co, Marcus Hook, Pa, feasibility study of employing microfilm for active storage of cent. tech. files & journals, 64; 2) Burlington Industries Cent. Tech. Libr, Greensboro, N.C, planning & design of a tech. info. syst, 66; 3) Nat. Libr. Med, Bethesda, Md, systs. anal. & design on MEDLARS syst. & libr. automation, an Auerbach Corp. project, with J. Dugan, J. Minker, N. Hardwick & H. Sternick, 66. Specialties: 3a, 3e; 4a, 4b, 4c, 4d (automated typesetting); 8c; 9 (microfilm systs).

BEVIS, LEURA DOROTHY, Apr. 19, 04; Associate Director & Professor, School of Librarianship, University of Washington, Seattle, Wash. 98105. Home: 4710 22nd N.E, Seattle, Wash. 98105. B.A, Pomona Col, 27; B.S. in L.S, Univ. South. Calif, 47; M.A, Univ. Wash. 51. Assoc. dir. & prof, sch. librarianship, Univ. Wash, Seattle, 47- Other: Chmn, Northwest Libr. Pub. Relations Coun, 48-51; mem, subscription books bull. cmt, ALA, 55-59, ALA rep. to Am. Standards Asn, 58 & 65; ALA coun-at-large, 65-68; asst. ed, Libr. Resources & Tech. Serv, 60-63; recording secy, LED, 61-63, mem, publ. cmt, 63-66; mem. ed. bd, Journal Educ. for Librarianship, 64-; past pres, Asn. Am. Libr. Schs. Mem: ALA; Pac. Northwest Libr. Asn; Wash. Libr. Asn; Asn. Am. Libr. Schs; WSASL; Beta Phi Mu. Publ: Night at Deepdene, Frederic Goudy, Inland Printer, 47; Changing Patterns of Reference Service, Univ. Wash, 50; Virginia Woolf: Symbol and Thought, Alan Swallow, 59; Rare Books in the College Library, ALA Bull, 59; Bibliographic Developments, Libr. Resources & Tech. Serv, 61, 62 & 63; Resources and Services of the Libraries of Washington State: A Survey, Wash. State Libr, 67. Consult: 1) U.S. Office Educ, Wash, D.C, consult. on undergrad. prerequisites for libr. educ, 63 & 66; 2) Escuela Interamericana, Medellin, Colombia, consult. on libr. educ, with Marietta Daniels Shepard, Sept. 65; 3) Wash. Libr. Asn, Wash. State Libr, Olympia, survey of libr. resources & serv. of State of Wash, 66-67; 4) Int. Relations Office, ALA, Wash, D.C, consult. on foreign libr. educ, spring 68. Specialties: 2a, 2f, 2g; 5b; 6a, 6b; 7a; 8d, 8f; 9 (libr. educ, evaluated according to the standards of the various levels).

BITNER, HARRY, July 22, 16; Law Librarian & Professor of Law, Cornell University, Ithaca, N.Y. 14850. Home: 406 Winthrop Dr, Ithaca, N.Y. 14850. LL.B, 39; A.B, 41; B.S.(libr. sci), 42. Librn, U.S. Dept. Justice, 54-57; law librn, Yale Univ, 57-65; law librn. & prof. law, Cornell Univ, 65- Other: Pres, Am. Asn. Law Libr, 62-63; v.chmn, Coun. Nat. Libr. Asns, 64- Mem: ALA; SLA; Am. Asn. Law Libr. Publ: Effective Legal Research (with Miles O. Price), Prentice-Hall, 53; Effective Legal Research, Student Edition (with Miles O. Price), Little, Brown & Co, 62. Consult: 1) Stanford Univ, Stanford, Calif, survey of law libr; orgn, admin. & collection, Aug-Sept, 51; 2) Cornell Univ, Ithaca, N.Y, survey of law libr; orgn, admin. & collection, with Miles O. Price, Nov. 60; 3) York Univ, Toronto, Ont, Can, survey of law libr: orgn, admin. & collection, Mar. 65. Specialties: 2d (law); 3c; 5c; 7a.

BIXLER, PAUL, Oct. 27, 99; Ford Foundation Library Consultant. Home: 1345 Rice Rd, Yellow Springs, Ohio 45387. A.B, 22; M.A, 24; B.L.S, 33. Librn, Antioch Col, Yellow Springs, Ohio, 35-65, emer. librn, 65- Other: Managing ed, Antioch Review, 43-58; exec. secy. & ed, Newsletter, intellectual freedom cmt, ALA, 52-56. Mem: Ohio Libr. Asn; ALA; ACRL. Publ: Book Selection and Acquisition & Selection & Acquisition of Special Types of Materials, In: Administration of the College Library, H.W. Wilson, 44; Freedom of Communication (ed), ALA, 53; Freedom of Book Selection (co-ed), ALA, 54; Libraries in the Far East (ed),& Burma: Ambivalence and Inner Conflict (auth), Libr. J, 11/15/62; Educational Overseasmanship: a Librarian in Asia, Teachers Col. Record, 12/63; The Mexican Library, Scarecrow, 68. Consult: 1) Bluffton Col, Bluffton, Ohio, consultation with faculty on libr. serv, new bldg, May 57; 2) Faculty Soc. Sci, Univ. Rangoon, Burma, advisor on new soc. sci. libr, personnel, book selection, libr. facilities, 58-60; 3) Wilmington Col, Wilmington, Ohio, libr. bldg, Mar. 61; 4) Faculty Exact & Natural Sci, Nat. Univ. Buenos Aires, Argentina, wrote a $225,000 program for book selection, personnel & new bldg. plans as libr. con-

---

5) PERSONNEL AND RECRUITING, 5a) job evaluation and description, salary recommendations, 5b) recruitment of professionals and management personnel, 5c) administrative organization, 6) PUBLIC RELATIONS, 6a) publications, 6b) publicity programs, 6c) public opinion surveys, 6d) others, 7) SERVICES, 7a) evaluation of current program, 7b) studies of service to special publics, e.g., students, handicapped, aged, etc., 7c) programs for the implementation of new laws, program proposals to governments, 7d) others, 8) COMMUNITY, REGIONAL, STATE PLANNING, 8a) legislative programs, 8b) area analyses, 8c) centralized systems, cooperative arrangements, 8d) development of standards, 8e) state libraries and extension agencies, 8f) regional and statewide surveys, 8g) others, 9) OTHERS.

sult. with Ford Found, 64-68; 5) Ford Found, survey of Mexican libr, with Carl M. White, 66-67. Specialties: 1b, 2a, 2e, 2g; 9 (foreign assignments in developing countries with attention to all aspects).

BLANCHARD, J. RICHARD, Mar. 3, 12; University Librarian, University of California Library, Davis, Calif. 95616. Home: 441 W. Eighth St, Davis, Calif. 95616. A.B.L.S, 33; A.B, 35; M.S, 53. Univ. librn, Univ. Calif, Davis, 51- Other: Pres, col, univ. & res. libr. sect, Calif. Libr. Asn, 53, pres, Golden Empire Dist, 54; mem. coun, ALA, 54-56, 60-63; chmn, pure & applied sci. sect, ACRL, 56; recipient, Oberly Mem. award for best bibliog. work in the natural sci. publ. in 58 & 59. Mem: ALA; SLA; Calif. Libr. Asn. Publ: Agricultural Research and the Exchange Problem, Col. & Res. Libr, 1/50; Report on the Policies and Programs of the United States Department of Agriculture Library, Agr. Libr. Sect, Asn. Col. & Ref. Libr, 51; Departmental Libraries in Divisional Plan University Libraries, Col. & Res. Libr, 7/53; Literature of Agricultural Research (with Harald Ostvold), Univ. Calif, Berkeley, 58; California's Problem Building Adds Wings, Libr. J, 12/1/64; Proceedings of the Third Life Sciences Librarianship Workshops, Japan Libr. Sch, Keio Univ, Tokyo, 64. Consult: 1) U.S. Dept. Agr. Libr, Wash, D.C, studied policies & programs of the libr, with Whiton Powell, Harlan C. Brown, Donald E. Thompson, Laura I. Makepeace & Irene Craft, Oct. 50; 2) San Jose State Col, Calif, accreditation cmt, 54; 3) Rockefeller Found, New York, N.Y, develop. of sci. libr. for Ministerio de Agr, Santiago, Chile, Mar-June 59; 4) Agency Int. Develop, U.S. State Dept, Wash, D.C, develop. of sci. libr. for Inst. Tech. Agropecuaria, Buenos Aires, Argentina, Nov-Dec. 62; 5) Univ. Ky, Lexington, assisted on survey of univ. libr, with David Kaser, Robert Muller, Donald Thompson & Robert Munn, Nov. 64. Specialties: 2d (sci. & agr); 9 (bibliog. of sci. & agr. & develop. of spec. libr. in sci. & agr).

BLASINGAME, RALPH, Oct. 9, 20; Professor, Graduate School of Library Service, Rutgers, The State University, New Brunswick, N.J. 08903. Home: 24 Pine Ridge Dr, East Brunswick, N.J. 08816. B.A, Pa. State, 42, B.S, 47; M.S, Columbia Univ, 50; D.Litt, St. Francis Col, 63. Pa. State Librn, 57-64; prof, Rutgers, 64- Other: Pres, LAD, 61-62, treas, ALA, 64-68. Mem: ALA; N.J. Libr. Asn; Am. Asn. Univ. Prof. Publ: Act 188: Retrospect and Prospect (The Pennsylvania Library Code of 1961), Pa. Libr. Asn. Bull, 2/63; Library Services in West Virginia: Present and Proposed, Libr. Cmn, Charleston, W.Va, 65; The Public Library in the Metropolitan Environment, In: The Changing Environment for Library Services in Metropolitan Areas, Univ. Ill. Grad. Sch. Libr. Sci, 65; How to Get Started and Keep Going, Proc. U.S. Office Educ. Conf, 9/65; Equalization of Opportunity, Libr. J, 3/1/65; Research on Library Services in Metropolitan Areas, Grad. Sch. Libr. Serv, Rutgers, 66. Consult: 1) W.Va. Libr. Cmn, Charleston, study of all types of libr. with recommendations for pub. libr. develop, with Thornton J. Ridinger, 64-66; 2) New Castle Free Pub. Libr, Pa, study of the libr. as a city libr. & dist. libr. center, & as a potential county libr, spring & summer, 65; 3) Bucknell Univ, Lewisburg, Pa, two-day session to advise faculty libr. cmt. on libr. develop, with Cameron & McKean, 65; 4) Pottsville Free Pub. Libr, Pottsville, Pa, to measure the impact of the pub. libr. in an area having suffered econ. reverses, 65-; 5) Ohio State Libr. Bd, Columbus, study of Ohio pub. libr, 66-68. Specialties: 2h (admin. aspects); 5c; 7a, 7c; 8a, 8b, 8c, 8d, 8e, 8f.

BLAUSTEIN, ALBERT P, Oct. 12, 21; Professor of Law & Law Librarian, School of Law, Rutgers, The State University, Camden, N.J. 08102. Home: 415 Barby Lane, Cherry Hill, N.J. 08034. A.B, Univ. Mich, 41; LL.B, Columbia Univ, 48. Assoc. prof. law, Rutgers Univ, Camden, N.J, 55-58, prof. law, 59-, law librn, 55- Other: Chmn. publ. cmt, Am. Asn. Law Libr. Publ: The American Lawyer, Univ. Chicago, 54; Fiction Goes to Court, Holt, 54 & Collier, 62; Desegregation and the Law, Rutgers Univ, 57 & Vintage, 62; Fundamental Legal Documents on Communist China, Rothman, 62; Manual on Foreign Legal Periodicals and Their Index, Parker Sch. Foreign & Comparative Law, Columbia Univ, 62; Civil Rights and the American Negro, Trident & Wash. Square, 68. Consult: 1) Haile Selassie I Univ, Addis Ababa, Ethiopia, prepared acquisitions lists and purchased books for law libr, set up initial orgn. & admin, 63-; 2) Int. Legal Center, 866 United Nations Plaza, New York, N.Y, law libr. consult. to SAILER Program, consult. on law book selections & acquisitions for various foreign schs. of law & gen. libr, 64-; 3) Vietnam Constituent Assembly, Nat. Assembly, Saigon, Vietnam, selected & purchased legal materials through U.S. Info. Serv. to guide drafting the 1967 Vietnamese Constitution, 66-67; 4) Vietnam Ministry of Justice, Saigon, surveyed libr. resources and made recommendations on acquisition of materials to aid in revising South Vietnamese legal syst. for U.S. Agency Int. Develop, 67. Specialties: 2d (law); 9 (advising on book selection of legal materials throughout the world for law schs. in developing countries, advising on setting up mechanics of new libr).

BLOOMQUIST, HAROLD, Oct. 27, 28; Acting Librarian, Francis A. Countway Library of Medicine, Harvard Medical School, 10 Shattuck St, Boston, Mass. 02115. Home: 650 Huntington Ave, Boston, Mass. 02115. A.B, 50; M.S, 54. Med. reference librn, Columbia Univ. Col. Physicians & Surgeons, 54-58; asst. librn. for

---

KEY TO CONSULTING SPECIALTIES: 1) ARCHITECTURE AND BUILDINGS, 1a) public libraries, 1b) academic libraries, 1c) school libraries, 1d) special libraries, 1e) library interiors, 1f) furnishings, 1g) site and location, 1h) other architectural; 2) COLLECTIONS: SELECTION, EVALUATION, WEEDING, 2a) adults, 2b) young adults, 2c) children, 2d) subject specialty, 2e) O.P. searches, 2f) rare books, 2g) appraisals, 2h) others; 3) TECHNICAL PROCESSES, 3a) cataloging, 3b) classification systems, 3c) acquisitions, 3d) materials processing, 3e) work flow and cost studies, 3f) others, 4) AUTOMATION, 4a) applications of data processing equipment, 4b) information storage and retrieval systems, 4c) systems analysis, 4d) others

resources & acquisitions, Harvard Med. Sch, 58-61, asst. librn, 61-66, assoc. librn, 66-67, acting librn, 67- Other: Mem, cmt. on continuing educ, Med. Libr. Asn; mem, sci. manuscripts cmt, Am. Asn. Dental Eds; mem. bd. dirs, Coun. on Res. in Bibliog, Inc; assoc. ed, Bull. Med. Libr. Asn. Mem: Med. Libr. Asn; SLA; Am. Asn. Dental Eds. Publ: Cataloging and Classification of Medical Library Materials: 1946-1956, Bull. Med. Libr. Asn, 47: 28-47; Attitudes Toward the Authorship of Manuscript Dealing with the Medical Sciences (with others), Miss. Valley Med. J, 81: 72-74; The Bibliographic Control of Supplements to Medical Periodicals: A Preliminary Study (with T.P. Fleming & J.B. Balkema), Bull. Med. Libr. Asn, 48: 299-307; The Status and Needs of Medical School Libraries in the United States, J. Med. Educ, 38: 145-163; Continuing Education in the Professions (with M.M. Kinney), Bull. Med. Libr. Asn, 51: 357-367; The Impact of the Behavioral Sciences on the Collecting Policy of Medical School Libraries (with R.C. MacKenzie), Bull. Med. Libr. Asn, 52: 220-233. Consult: 1) Survey of Med. Libr. Resources of Greater New York, N.Y, consult. on reader's use of interlibr. loans, Apr. 64; 2) Info. Dynamics Corp, Reading, Mass, consult. on materials for design study for U.S. med. libr. syst, June-Nov. 65; 3) Herner & Co, Wash, D.C, study of educ. for med. librarianship, with Irwin Pizer, Nov. 65; 4) Cornell Univ. Med. Col, New York, consult. to Ad Hoc Cmt. on the Libr, Mar. 66. Specialties: 1h (health sci); 2d (health sci); 6a; 7c.

BOAZ, DR. MARTHA, 1914; Dean, School of Library Science, Library School, University of Southern California, Los Angeles, Calif. 90007. Home: 1849 Campus Rd, Los Angeles, Calif. 90041. B.S; B.S. in L.S; M.A.(libr. sci); Ph.D. Dean & prof, sch. libr. sci, Univ. South. Calif, Los Angeles, 53- Other: Pres, Calif. Libr. Asn, 62; pres, Beta Phi Mu, 62; pres, South. Calif. Chap, Am. Document. Inst, 62; pres, Asn. Am. Libr. Schs, 62-63. Mem: ALA; Calif. Libr. Asn; SLA; Am. Soc. Info. Sci. Publ: Reviews in Library Book Selection (with L.C. Merritt & K.S. Tisdal), Wayne State Univ, 58; A Living Library (ed), Univ. South. Calif, 58; Modern Trends in Documentation (ed), Pergamon, 59; A Guide to General Booksellers in the U.S, Edwards Letter Shop, 60; Fervent and Full of Gifts, the Life of Althea Warren, Scarecrow, 61; The Quest for Truth (compiler), Scarecrow, 61. Consult: 1) Covina Unified Sch. Dist, Covina, Calif, survey of libr. of the dist. with recommendations, 60; 2) Ontario Pub. Libr, Ontario, Calif, survey of the pub. libr. with recommendations for new bldg. & staff, collections; 3) Security First Nat. Bank, Los Angeles, Calif, survey of libr, 63; 4) Los Angeles Pub. Libr, 630 W. Fifth St, Los Angeles, Calif, survey of 60 pub. libr. in South. Calif. with recommendations for a syst, with Lowell Martin &

Henry Reining, 64-65. Specialties: 1a, 1c, 1d; 2a, 2b, 2c, 2d (humanities); 5a, 5b, 5c; 6b; 7a; 8c, 8d, 8f.

BONN, GEORGE S, Sept. 19, 13; Visiting Professor, Dept. of Library Science, University of Delhi, Delhi 6, India. B.Ch.E, 35; M.S, 36; M.A.(libr. sci), 51. Chief sci. & tech. div, N.Y. Pub. Libr, 58-64; from asst. prof. to adjunct prof, grad. sch. libr. serv, Rutgers Univ, 56-65; prof. libr. studies & head sci-tech. reference & bibliog. serv, Univ. Hawaii, Honolulu, 65-67. Other: Fulbright res. scholar, Japan, 53-54; from v.chmn. to chmn. subject specialists sect, ACRL, 59-61, mem. bd, 59-62, chmn. libr. serv. cmt, 62-64, mem. cmt. accreditation, 62-65. Mem: ALA; Am. Document. Inst; SLA; Aslib; Am. Chemical Soc. Publ: Training Laymen in Use of the Library, Rutgers Univ. Grad. Sch. Libr. Serv, 60; The Aids of Selection, In: Collecting Science Literature for General Reading, Illini Bookstore, 61; Training and Education for Information Work, Am. Document, 7/62; Literature of Science and Technology, In: McGraw-Hill Encyclopedia of Science and Technology, McGraw-Hill, 2nd ed, 66; Science-Technology Literature Resources in Canada, Nat. Res. Coun, 66; Technical Information for California Business and Industry, Calif. State Libr, 67. Consult: 1) Syracuse Univ, Syracuse, N.Y, survey of engineering libr. collections, acquisitions, serv, facilities, June 59; 2) Worcester Polytech. Inst, Worcester, Mass, survey of libr. collections, acquisitions, serv. facilities, Jan. 60; 3) Univ. Pittsburgh Grad. Sch. Libr. & Info. Sci, Pittsburgh, Pa, survey of sci. & tech. literature available in west. Pa. libr, Oct-Dec. 64; 4) Nat. Res. Coun, Ottawa, Ont, survey of sci-tech. literature resources & serv. in Can. univs, res. coun. & pub. libr, May-June 65; 5) Calif. State Libr, survey of tech. info. resources & serv. in Calif. pub. libr, 68- Specialties: 2d (sci-tech); 7b, 7d (to scientists, engineers, res. staff); 9 (libr. educ, especially for sci. literature, document. work).

BOURNE, CHARLES P, Sept. 2, 31; Vice President, Programming Services, Inc, 999 Commercial St, Palo Alto, Calif. 94303. Home: 1619 Santa Cruz Ave, Menlo Park, Calif. 94025. B.S.E.E, Univ. Calif, 57; M.S.I.E, Stanford Univ, 62. Sr. res. engineer, Stanford Res. Inst, 57-66; lectr, Univ. Calif. Sch. Librarianship, 63-66; Other: Recipient, Annual Award of Merit, Am. Document. Inst, 65, mem. exec. coun. & ed. bd, ed, literature notes sect, Am. Document; mem. bd. dirs, info. sci. & automation div, ALA; mem. adv. bds. to Chem. Abstracts Serv, ADI Annual Review Info. Sci. & Tech, Document. Abstracts, Encyclopedia of Libr. & Info. Sci. & Wiley Book Series on Info. Sci; U.S. rep. to Int. Fedn. Document Study Cmt. on Theory of Machine Techniques & Systs; participant, Nat. Acad. Sci. Task Force to

---

5) PERSONNEL AND RECRUITING, 5a) job evaluation and description, salary recommendations, 5b) recruitment of professionals and management personnel, 5c) administrative organization, 6) PUBLIC RELATIONS, 6a) publications, 6b) publicity programs, 6c) public opinion surveys, 6d) others, 7) SERVICES, 7a) evaluation of current program, 7b) studies of service to special publics, e.g., students, handicapped, aged, etc., 7c) programs for the implementation of new laws, program proposals to governments, 7d) others, 8) COMMUNITY, REGIONAL, STATE PLANNING, 8a) legislative programs, 8b) area analyses, 8c) centralized systems, cooperative arrangements, 8d) development of standards, 8e) state libraries and extension agencies, 8f) regional and statewide surveys, 8g) others, 9) OTHERS.

study info. problems of biomed. researchers; participant, Engineers Joint Coun. Task Force to study info. problems of engineers. Mem: Am. Soc. Info. Sci; Inst. Electrical & Electronics Engineers. Publ: The World's Technical Journal Literature: An Estimate of Volume, Origin, Language, Field, Indexing, and Abstracting, Am. Document, 4/62; Methods of Information Handling, Wiley, 63; Cost Analysis and Simulation Procedures for the Evaluation of Large Information Systems (with D.F. Ford), Am. Document, 4/64; The Biomedical Information Complex Viewed as a System (Joint auth), Fedn. Proc, 9-10/64; Some User Requirements Stated Quantitatively in Terms of the 90% Library, In: Proceedings of the Conference on Electronic Information Handling, Spartan Books, 65; Evaluation of Indexing Systems, In: ADI Annual Review of Information Science and Technology, Wiley-Interscience, 66. Consult: 1) U.S. Patent Office, Wash, D.C, eval. of proposals for mechanized storage of the U.S. patent file, 66; 2) Houston Fearless Corp, 11801 W. Olympic Blvd, Los Angeles, Calif, design & eval. of mechanized microfilm equipment, Mar. 66-; 3) Libr. Congress, Wash, D.C, planning & eval. of the LC machine readable catalog project, Aug. 66-; 4) Redstone Sci. Info. Center, Huntsville, Ala, eval. of plans for libr. automation, Dec. 66- Specialties: 4a, 4b, 4c.

BOURNE, PHILIP W, Nov. 30, 07; Architect, 177 State St, Boston, Mass. 02109. Home: 93 Hale St, Beverly, Mass. 01915. Pres, Boston Soc. Architects, 64-65; chmn, Mass. Art Cmn, 65-; mem, designer selection bd, Commonwealth of Mass, 67; dir, Northeast Region, Am. Inst. Architects, 67-70. Mem: Fel, Am. Inst. Architects. Consult: 1) Pub. Libr, Salem, Mass, Gardner Maynard Jones Mem. Libr. (E. Br): planning review bldg. report, architect, 65; 2) Free Libr, Concord, Mass, planning report for libr. stacks, reading room for children, 66; 3) Pub. Libr, Salem, Mass, planning report for S. Br, 67; 4) Farnsworth Libr, Rockland, Maine, planning report for libr. & art museum, 68; 5) Libr, Concord, Mass, Fowler Br, furnishings, 69. Specialties: 1a, 1d, 1e, 1f, 1g.

BRAHM, WALTER T, Oct. 9, 10; State Librarian of Connecticut, Connecticut State Library, Hartford, Conn. 06115. Home: 96 Wildwood Rd, West Simsbury, Conn. 06092. A.B, 32; B.S. in L.S, 33. State librn, Ohio 42-64; state librn, Conn, 64- Other: Pres, Nat. Asn. State Libr, 55; recipient, Outstanding Librn. of Year award, Ohio Libr. Asn, 59; pres, ASL, 62. Mem: ALA; New Eng. Libr. Asn; Conn. Libr. Asn; SLA. Publ: Survey of Libraries of Pittsburgh & Allegheny County, Pennsylvania (with Mildred T. Sandoe), Columbus, 50; Survey of Meadville, Pennsylvania Public Library, Columbus, 50; State Libraries, Libr. Trends, 10/61; Survey of Monmouth County, New Jersey Libraries (with Mildred T. Sandoe),

Columbus, 62; A Plan for Library Service in the Harrisburg Area of Pennsylvania, Stoneman, 62; Suggested Plan for State-wide Library Service in Connecticut, Hartford, 66. Consult: 1) Community Develop, Pittsburgh, Pa, survey & plan of orgn. for libr. in Allegheny County, Pa, with Mildred T. Sandoe, 50; 2) Pub. Libr, Alliance, Ohio, survey on need for new bldg, 60; 3) Pub. Libr, Bellaire, Ohio, new bldg, program, layout & supv, 61; 4) Pub. Libr, Harrisburg, Pa, plan for libr. serv. in the Harrisburg area (four counties), with Mildred T. Sandoe, 62; 5) County Libr, Monmouth, N.J, survey of bldgs. & serv, with Mildred T. Sandoe, 62. Specialties: 1a, 1g; 3d, 3e; 4a; 5a, 5b, 5c; 6a; 7a, 7c; 8a, 8b, 8c, 8d, 8e, 8f.

BRANDON, ALFRED N, Sept. 10, 22; Director & Librarian, Welch Medical Library, Johns Hopkins University, 1900 E. Monument St, Baltimore, Md. 21205. Home: 6800 Liberty Rd, Apt. 1015, Baltimore, Md. 21207. Th.B, Atlantic Union Col, 45; B.S, Syracuse Univ, 48; M.S, Univ. Ill, 51; M.A, Univ. Mich, 56. Head librn, Univ. Ky. Med. Center, 57-63; dir. & librn, Welch Med. Libr, Johns Hopkins Univ, Baltimore, Md, 63- Other: Ed, Bull. Med. Libr. Asn, 61-; pres, Med. Libr. Asn, 65-66. Mem: Med. Libr. Asn; SLA; ALA. Publ: Checklist of Periodical Titles Currently Received in Medical Libraries in the Southern Region Univ. Ky, 60; Management Methods in Libraries: Space Management and Layout, Bull. Med. Libr. Asn, 10/61; Subject List of Journals Indexed in Index Medicus, Bull. Med. Libr. Asn, 7/62; The Development and Organization of a New Medical School Library, Bull. Med. Libr. Asn, 1/64; Selected List of Books and Journals for the Small Medical Library, Bull. Med. Libr. Asn, 7/65. Consult: 1) Temple Univ. Sch. Med, Broad St. at Ontario, Phila, Pa, planning for expansion of med. sch. libr, plans for new libr, June 1960 & May-June 1963; 2) Pan Am. Health Orgn, 525 23rd St. N.W, Wash, D.C, eval. of libr. serv. & planning for new libr. facility, May 1962; 3) Mich. State Univ, E. Lansing, plans for new med. sch. libr, Sept. 63; 4) Jefferson Med. Col. Libr, 1025 Walnut St, Phila, Pa, bldg. plans for new med. sch. libr, Mar. 65-; 5) Wash. Univ. Sch. Med. Libr, 4580 Scott Ave, St. Louis, Mo, advisor on planning new med. sch. libr. bldg, with Ralph T. Esterquest & Frank B. Rogers, June 1965. Specialties: 1d, 1h (med. libr); 2d (med); 7a; 9 (orgn. & admin. of new med. sch. libr).

BRANSCOMB, DR. LEWIS CAPERS, JR, Aug. 5, 11; Director of Libraries, Ohio State University Libraries, Columbus, Ohio 43210. Home: 1884 Coventry Rd, Columbus, Ohio 43212. A.B, 33; A.B.L.S, 39; A.M.L.S, 41; Ph.D, 54. Other: Secy-treas, Univ. Ill. chap, Am. Asn. Univ. Prof, 47-48, pres, Ohio State Univ. chap, 53-54, mem nat. coun, 52-55; chmn. col. & univ. sect,

---

KEY TO CONSULTING SPECIALTIES: 1) ARCHITECTURE AND BUILDINGS, 1a) public libraries, 1b) academic libraries, 1c) school libraries, 1d) special libraries, 1e) library interiors, 1f) furnishings, 1g) site and location, 1h) other architectural; 2) COLLECTIONS: SELECTION, EVALUATION, WEEDING, 2a) adults, 2b) young adults, 2c) children, 2d) subject specialty, 2e) O.P. searches, 2f) rare books, 2g) appraisals, 2h) others; 3) TECHNICAL PROCESSES, 3a) cataloging, 3b) classification systems, 3c) acquisitions, 3d) materials processing, 3e) work flow and cost studies, 3f) others, 4) AUTOMATION, 4a) applications of data processing equipment, 4b) information storage and retrieval systems, 4c) systems analysis, 4d) others

Ohio Libr. Asn, 52-53; dir, ACRL, 53-55, v.pres, 57-58, pres, 58-59, chmn. acad. status cmt, univ. libr. sect, 61-; dir, Midwest Inter-Libr. Corp, 53-65, mem. exec. cmt, 54-56, chmn. bd, 61-62; chmn. nominating cmt, ALA, 54-55; mem. exec. coun, Beta Phi Mu, 55-58; mem. bldg. cmt, Center Res. Libr, 61-, mem. acquisition cmt, 65- Mem: ALA; ACRL; Ohio Libr. Asn; Franklin County Libr. Asn; Am. Soc. Info. Sci; Beta Phi Mu. Publ: Ernest Cushing Richardson, 1860-1939, In: Pioneering Leaders in Librarianship, ALA, 53; Library Specialization through Institutional Specialization, In: Problems and Prospects of the Research Library; The Quest for Faculty Rank, In: The Status of American College and University Librarians, ACRL Monograph, 22, 58; Libraries in Larger Institutions of Higher Education, Libr. Trends, 10/61; Tenure for Professional Librarians on Appointment at Colleges and Universities, Col. & Res. Libr, 7/65. Consult: 1) Wesley Found, Ohio State Univ, Columbus, Ohio, bldg. collection, 57-59; 2) Methodist Theol. Sch. Ohio, Delaware, Ohio, on team to advise on libr. serv. & bldg, with John H. Lancaster, 58-60; 3) Trinity Methodist Church, 1581 Cambridge, Columbus, furnishings and layout for new libr, with Nancy Young, 61-62; 4) Cedarville Col, Cedarville, Ohio, study of bldg. improvements & relocation, July 63; 5) Punjab Agr. Univ. Libr, Ludhiana, Punjab, India, gen. consult, 67. Specialties: 1b, 1e, 1g; 5a, 5b, 5c, 5d (faculty rank for libr. staff); 7a; 8c.

BRINTON, HARRY, July 5, 16; Director of Libraries, Jacksonville Public Library System, 122 N. Ocean St, Jacksonville, Fla. 32202. Home: 1721 Dogwood Place, Jacksonville, Fla. 32210. A.B, Univ. Denver Libr. Sch, 38; M.S, Columbia Univ, Sch. Libr. Serv, 57. Chief, order dept, chief extension serv. & acting librn, Pub. Libr, Kansas City, Mo, 41-59; dir. libr, Jacksonville Pub. Libr. Syst, 59- Other: Past pres, Fla. Libr. Asn, past chmn, Pub. Libr. Div, chmn, local activities cmt; legis. chmn, Southeast. Libr. Asn; past pres, Mo. Libr. Asn. Mem: ALA; Fla. Libr. Asn; Southeast. Libr. Asn; Jacksonville Area Chamber Commerce; Civitan Club Jacksonville. Publ: Contrib. to libr. periodicals; past ed, Mo. Libr. Asn. Quart. Consult: 1) Suwannee River Regional Libr, Pine Ave, Live Oak, Fla, bldg. consult, Jan. 65-Feb. 66; 2) Ormond Beach Pub. Libr, Ormond Beach, Fla, bldg. consult, Mar. 65-; 3) Holly Hill Pub. Libr, Holly Hill, Fla, bldg. consult, Sept. 65-Apr. 66; 4) Edgewater Pub. Libr, Edgewater, Fla, bldg. consult, Mar. 66-; 5) Gainesville Pub. Libr, Gainesville, Fla, bldg. consult, July 66- Specialties: 1a, 1e, 1f, 1g; 3a, 3b, 3c, 3d, 3e; 5a, 5c; 7a; 8c, 8d.

BRODMAN, DR. ESTELLE, June 1, 14; Librarian and Professor of Medical History, Washington University School of Medicine, St Louis, Mo. 63110. Home: 4464 W. Pine Blvd, St. Louis, Mo. 63108. A.B, 35; B.S, 36; M.S, 43; Ph.D, 53. Chief reference div, Nat. Libr. Med, 49-61; lectr, Cath. Univ, 57; vis. prof. Japan Libr. Sch, Keio Univ, Tokyo, 62. Other: Pres, Med. Libr. Asn, 64-65; mem, President's Adv. Cmn. Libr, 66-68. Mem: ALA; SLA; Med. Libr. Asn; Bibliog. Soc. Am. Publ: Guidelines for Medical School Libraries, J. Med. Educ, 6/65; Computers in American Medical and University Libraries (Festschrift...), Libr. Sci, Tokyo, 65; Mechanization of Library Procedures in the Medium Sized Library, III: Acquisitions and Cataloging (with E.A. Moore & G. Cohen), Bull. Med. Libr. Asn, 7/65; Money Talks, But People Count, Bull. Med. Libr. Asn, 7/65; The Special Library as the Mirror of Its Society, J. Libr. Hist, 4/66; Bibliography: Current State and Future Trends, Part 2, Medicine, Libr. Trends, 4/67. Consult: 1) Rockefeller Found, New York, N.Y, surveyed Japanese med. sch. libr. with recommendations to China Med. Bd. for strengthening med. libr. in Japan, 62; 2) Nat. Inst. of Mental Health, Bethesda, Md, consult. to Mental Health Info. Clearinghouse, 64-68; 3) Southwest Tex. Med. Sch, San Antonio, new libr, 65; 4) Univ. Mich, Ann Arbor, consult. on new biomed. commun. center, 65; 5) Office of Sci. & Tech, Office of the President, Wash. D.C, consult. on nat. libr. systs, 65-66. Specialties: 1h (med); 2d (med); 5a, 5c, 5d (in med. libr. only); 7a, 7d (med. libr. only).

BROOK, JOHN B, 1914; President, J & J Brook Ltd, 4 New St, Toronto 5, Ont, Can. Home: 1394 Mount Pleasant Rd, Toronto 12, Ont, Can. B.Sc, Queen's Univ. Mem: Can. Libr. Asn; ALA. Consult: 1) Univ. Waterloo, Waterloo, Ont, Can, interior, Arts Libr. bldg, 64-65; 2) Queen's Univ, Kingston, Ont, Can, interior, Douglas Libr. bldg, 65. Specialties: 1e, 1f.

BROWN, ALBERTA L, Jan. 9, 94; Self-employed, 3234 Butternut Lane, Kalamazoo, Mich. 49007. A.B, 20. Head librn, Upjohn Co, Kalamazoo, Mich, 40-59; assoc. prof, dept. librarianship, West. Mich. Univ, Kalamazoo, 62-64; spec. rep. to legislature, Mich. Libr. Asn, 65- Other: Pres, SLA, 57-58. Mem: SLA; ALA; Mich. Libr. Asn. Publ: The Relation of the Librarian to Management, to the Patron and to the Library Staff, Bull. Med. Libr. Asn, 46: 82-89, Scientific and Technical Libraries: Their Organization and Administration (with L.J. Straus & I.M. Strieby), Interscience, 64; Special Libraries: Company Sponsored Units Aid Research and Development, Mich. Challenge, 5: 22-23. Consult: 1) Mich. State Libr, Lansing, Mich, planned health dept. libr, June 66; 2) Mich. State Libr, planning work of state agency libr, with Jean Legg, June 66. Specialties: 1d, 1e, 1f, 1g; 2d (sci, pharmaceuticals); 3a, 3b, 3c, 3d; 5c; 7c; 8a, 8c.

BROWN, GERALD G, Aug. 12, 32; Interior Design Consultant, 55 W. Snell Rd, Oshkosh, Wis.

---

5) PERSONNEL AND RECRUITING, 5a) job evaluation and description, salary recommendations, 5b) recruitment of professionals and management personnel, 5c) administrative organization, 6) PUBLIC RELATIONS, 6a) publications, 6b) publicity programs, 6c) public opinion surveys, 6d) others, 7) SERVICES, 7a) evaluation of current program, 7b) studies of service to special publics, e.g., students, handicapped, aged, etc., 7c) programs for the implementation of new laws, program proposals to governments, 7d) others, 8) COMMUNITY, REGIONAL, STATE PLANNING, 8a) legislative programs, 8b) area analyses, 8c) centralized systems, cooperative arrangements, 8d) development of standards, 8e) state libraries and extension agencies, 8f) regional and statewide surveys, 8g) others, 9) OTHERS.

54901. Archit. draftsman, 57-62, color coordinator, 62-65; interior designer, 65-68. Other: Mem. bd. dirs, Midwest Chap, Nat. Soc. Interior Designers, 67. Mem: Nat. Soc. Interior Designers. Consult: 1) Pub. Libr, Oshkosh, Wis, interior design, space planning, furnishings & equipment specifications, with Irion & Reinke, project architects, May 66; 2) Pub. Libr, Fond du Lac, Wis, interior design, space planning, furnishings & equipment specifications, with Stepnoski & Peterson, project architects, Feb. 67; 3) Pub. Libr, Libertyville, Ill, interior design, space planning, furnishings & equipment specifications, with Cone & Dornbusch, project architects, May 67; 4) Learning Resources Center, Wis. State Univ, Stevens Point, interior design, space planning, furnishings & equipment specifications, with Irion & Reinke, Sept. 67; 5) Polk Libr, Wis. State Univ, Oshkosh, interior design, with Irion & Reinke, Nov. 67. Specialties: 1e, 1f.

BRYAN, DR. JAMES E, July 11, 09; Director, Newark Public Library, Newark, N.J. 07101. Home: 666 Highland Ave, Newark, N.J. 07104. B.S, Lafayette Col, 31; B.L.S, Drexel Inst, 32; M.A, Am. Univ, 37; Litt.D, Rutgers Univ, 64. Asst. dir, Newark Pub. Libr, N.J, 43-58, dir, 58- Other: Pres, N.J. Libr. Asn, 52-54; pres, PLA, 59-60; pres, ALA, 62-63; chmn. adv. bd, Grad. Libr. Sch, Rutgers Univ. Mem: ALA; N.J. Libr. Asn. Publ: Contrib. to prfnl. journals. Consult: 1) Tulsa City-County Libr, Tulsa, Okla, main libr. bldg, program & serv, 62-65; 2) Monmouth County Libr, Freehold, N.J, bldg. requirements studies, East. Regional Libr, 64-68; 3) Lewis J. Crozer Libr, Chester, Pa, bldg. requirements study, main libr. & br. develop. & orgn, with Bernard Schein, 65-66; 4) Hackensack, N.J, area reference libr. bldg. program, 65-67; 5) Public Libr, White Plains, N.Y, bldg. program, 67-68. Specialties: 1a, 1g; 5c.

BRYANT, JACK W, Jan. 8, 26; Director, Worcester Public Library & Central Massachusetts Regional System, Salem Square, Worcester, Mass. 01608. Home: 29 Whitman Rd, Worcester, Mass. 01608. B.A, Univ. Calif, Los Angeles, 51, M.S.L.S, Univ. South. Calif, 52. Admin. asst. to librn, Hoover Libr, Stanford Univ, Stanford, Calif, 54-57; admin. asst, circulation & popular libr, Enoch Pratt Free Libr, Baltimore, Md, 57-60; dir, Crandall Libr, Glens Falls, N.Y, 60-62; dir, Greenwich Libr, Greenwich, Conn, 62-66; dir, Worcester Pub. Libr. & Cent. Mass. Regional Syst, Worcester, Mass, 66- Other: Exec. dir, Nat. Libr. Week, Conn, 62-63; program chmn, Conn. Libr. Asn, 64-65; mem, Conn. Libr. Res. Adv. Cmt, 65; chmn. pub. relations sect. goals & policies cmt, LAD, 65-66, chmn. trustee film cmt, LAD- Am. Libr. Trustee Asn, 65- Mem: N.Y. Libr. Asn; Conn. Libr. Asn; Westchester Libr. Asn; New Eng. Libr. Asn; Mass. Libr. Asn; ALA. Publ: Greenwich, Connecticut, Public Library Displays Books Like Diamonds from Tiffany's, Libr. J, 1/15/64; Planning Library Promotion: the Administrator's View, Wilson Libr. Bull, 2/65; Suburban Service, In: The Library Reaches Out, Oceana, 65; Greenwich Reading Time, Wilson Libr. Bull, 2/66. Consult: 1) Fairfield Pub. Libr, Fairfield, Conn, new br. & bldg. site, 65; 2) State Libr, Hartford, Conn, state res. adv. functions on cmt. to develop. state plan for Conn, with Charles Funk, 65-66; 3) Lancaster Pub. Libr, Lancaster, Mass, book collection & bldg. survey, 67; 4) Torrington Pub. Libr, Torrington, Conn, serv. & new wing survey, 68. Specialties: 1a, 1e, 1f, 1g; 5a, 5b, 5c; 6a, 6b, 6c; 7a, 7c; 8a, 8b, 8c, 8d, 8e, 8f.

BUCKINGHAM, BETTY JO, Aug. 6, 27; Library Consultant, State of Iowa, Department of Public Instruction, Grimes State Office Bldg, Des Moines, Iowa 50319. Home: Box 83, R.R. 2, Prairie City, Iowa 50228. B.A, State Col. Iowa, 48; M.S.(libr. sci), Univ. Ill, 53. High sch. librn, Ft. Madison, Iowa, 54-60; jr. high librn, Kurtz Jr. High, Des Moines, Iowa, 60-64; libr. consult, State of Iowa, Dept. Pub. Instruction, Des Moines, 64- Other: Pres, Iowa Asn. Sch. Librns, chmn. sch. libr. develop. cmt. & student assistants cmt. Mem: ALA; AASL; Iowa Libr. Asn; Nat. Educ. Asn; Iowa State Educ. Asn; Iowa Asn. Sch. Librns; Dept. Audiovisual Instruction; Audiovisual Educ. Asn. Iowa. Consult: 1) Keokuk Community Schs, Keokuk, Iowa, eval. of libr. program, kindergarten through 12th & recommendations, Mar. & May 67; 2) Sioux City Community Schs, Sioux City, Iowa, eval. of libr. program & recommendations in facilities, staff, budget & collection, May 67; 3) Carroll Community Schs, Carroll, Iowa, libr. serv. program including expansion of sec. libr, May 67; 4) Nesco Schs, Zearing, Iowa, utilization of space for enlargement of high sch. libr. with report, June 67. Specialties: 1c; 2b, 2c; 3f (application to sch. libr. serv); 4d (application to sch. libr. serv); 7a, 7b; 8c, 8d.

BUCKLEY, JOHN, Dec. 23, 20; School Librarian, Hyde Park High School (Boston Public Schools), Hyde Park, Mass. 02136. Home: 157 Aldrich St, Boston, Mass. 02131. A.B, Tufts Univ, 47; B.L.S, Columbia Univ, 47; M.Ed, State Col. at Boston, 68. Chief librn, Stonehill Col, N. Easton, Mass, 58-59; res. asst, Nursing Res. Index, Yale Univ. Sch. Nursing, 60; librn, Highland Cent. Sch, N.Y, 60-61; librn, Hyde Park High Sch, Boston, Mass, 62- Publ: Indexes for Chicago History, 1960, 1963 & 1967. Consult: 1) Keene State Col, Main St, Keene, N.H, assisted in planning moving of libr. to new quarters, July-Aug. 63; 2) New Eng. Mobile Book Fair Co, 70 Needham St, Newton Highlands, Mass, planned & operated cataloging cent. for ESEA Title II sch. libr. purchases, July-Nov. 66; 3) Info. Dynamics Corp, 80 Main St, Reading, Mass, assisted in making thesauri for Army Quartermaster res. for conversion to

---

KEY TO CONSULTING SPECIALTIES: 1) ARCHITECTURE AND BUILDINGS, 1a) public libraries, 1b) academic libraries, 1c) school libraries, 1d) special libraries, 1e) library interiors, 1f) furnishings, 1g) site and location, 1h) other architectural; 2) COLLECTIONS: SELECTION, EVALUATION, WEEDING, 2a) adults, 2b) young adults, 2c) children, 2d) subject specialty, 2e) O.P. searches, 2f) rare books, 2g) appraisals, 2h) others; 3) TECHNICAL PROCESSES, 3a) cataloging, 3b) classification systems, 3c) acquisitions, 3d) materials processing, 3e) work flow and cost studies, 3f) others, 4) AUTOMATION, 4a) applications of data processing equipment, 4b) information storage and retrieval systems, 4c) systems analysis, 4d) others

machine-readable indexing, Oct-Nov, 66; 4) Info Dynamics Corp, 80 Main St, Reading, Mass, assisted writing proposal for acquisitions—cataloging contract for NASA, Dec, 66. Specialties: 1c; 2b; 3c, 3d; 4b, 4d (technical thesauri for machine-readable use).

BURGESS, ROBERT S, Nov. 22, 17; Professor, School of Library Science, State University of New York at Albany, Albany, N.Y. 12203. Home: R.D. 1, Box 290A, Rensselaer, N.Y. 12144. A.B, 38; B.S. in L.S, 39; M.A, 42. Chmn. dept. librarianship, State Col, Albany, 48-59; vis. prof, Yonsei Univ, Seoul, Korea, 59-61; prof, Sch. Libr. Sci, State Univ. N.Y. Albany, 61- Mem: ALA; N.Y. Libr. Asn; hon. mem, Korean Libr. Asn. Consult: 1) Ministry of Educ, Seoul, Korea, advice on libr. sci. curriculum, supv. of transl. & selection of basic collection in libr. sci, with Ethel Swiger, Feb. 59-Aug. 61; 2) Sch. Syst, University City, Mo, survey & report on sch. libr. develop, Feb. 65; 3) Univ. Puerto Rico, Rio Piedras, San Juan, report on establishment of grad. program in libr. sci, Sept. 66. Specialties: 2d (libr. sci); 5a, 5b, 5c; 9 (libr. educ—curriculum, personnel & facilities).

BURKE, DR. JOHN EMMETT, Aug. 22, 08; Director of Library Service, East Texas State University Library, Commerce, Tex. 75428. Home: 1201 Earl St, Commerce, Tex. 75428. B.A, 30; B.S, 31; M.A, 36; B.L.S, 47; Ed.D, 57. Dir. libr. serv, E.Tex. State Univ, Commerce, Tex, 53- Other: Nat. membership chmn, Am. Asn. Res. Libr, 52; state rep, ALA, 65-66; mem. dist. legis. cmt, Tex. Libr. Asn, 65-66. Mem: ALA; ACRL; Tex. Libr. Asn; Nat. Educ. Asn. Publ: The School Librarian at Work, 54; Guideposts to Improved Library Service, 58; Planning the Modern Functional Library, 61; Specifications Covering Furniture and Equipment for the Library, 63; The Rising Tide—Research Libraries, E.Tex. State Univ, 66. Consult: 1) Univ. Dallas, Dallas, Tex, designed floor plan, furniture & equipment layout, 66; 2) DePaul Univ, Chicago, Ill, plans for new acad. center & libr, 63; 3) Sam Houston State Col, Huntsville, Tex, program for new libr, Oct-Nov. 65. Specialties: 1b, 1c, 1e, 1f, 1g; 2d (educ, hist, English); 3e; 5c; 6a, 6c; 7a; 8b, 8d; 8f.

BURKE, REDMOND A, C.S.V, Aug. 4, 14; Associate Director, Catholic University of America Press, 620 Michigan Ave. N.E, Washington, D.C. 20017. Home: 1212 Otis St. N.E, Washington, D.C. 20017. A.B. & A.M, Univ. Ill, 38, M.S.L.S, Cath. Univ. Am, 44, Ph.D, Univ. Chicago, 48. Dir, DePaul Univ. Libr, Chicago, Ill, 48-67; Other: Prof. libr. sci, Rosary Col, 44-52; vis. prof. libr. sci, Cath. Univ. Am, 62-63; mem. exec. bd, Cath. Libr. Asn, 62-67; chmn. book selection cmt, ALESCO; mem. literature cmt, Univ. Club of Chicago. Mem: ALA; Cath. Libr. Asn; Bibliog. Soc. Am; Chicago Libr. Club. Publ: What is the Index?; Culture and Communication Through the Ages; The CLA Booklist Annual (ed. biography sect); German Librarianship from an American Angle. Consult: 1) St. Mary's Seminary, Perryville, Mo, consult. on libr. planning, 52-54; 2) St. Thomas Seminary, 1300 S. Steele St, Denver, Colo, consult. on libr. planning, 56-57; 3) E. Tex. State Univ, Commerce, consult. on libr. planning, 57-59; 4) Col. of St. Scholastica, Atchison, Kans, libr. planning, 60-62; 5) Mundelein Col, 6353 Sheridan Rd, Chicago, Ill, prepared program statement, with Sister Mary Clara, B.V.M, 65-66. Specialties: 1b, 1e, 1f, 1h (seminary libr); 2a, 2d (theol. & philosophy, biography), 2f.

BURNS, LORIN R, July 22, 34; Supervisor Library Data Processing Services, Illinois State Library, Springfield, Ill. 62706. Home: 1913 Greentree Rd, Springfield, Ill. 62703. U.S. Army, 51-59; supvr. tech. process, Lake County Pub. Libr, 60-61, admin. asst, 61-65; supvr, libr. data processing serv, Ill. State Libr, Springfield, 65- Mem: Data Processing Mgt. Asn; ALA; Ill. Libr. Asn; Ind. Libr. Asn; Am. Mgt. Asn. Publ: Book Purchasing and Collection Control at Lake County Public Library, I.B.M. Corp; Automation of Library Operations, Univ. Ill; Illinois State Library Data Processing, Rosary Col; Library Data Processing, Ill. State Libr; Library Clerical Automation, Friden Corp; Paper Tape vs Punch Card for Library Data Processing Input, Rosary College. Consult: 1) Dearborn Pub. Libr, Dearborn, Mich, study of automation feasibility; 2) Ind. State Libr, Indianapolis, telecommun. consult. for state; 3) Hq. 3rd U.S. Army, Ft. McPherson, Ga, study of automation, personnel & bldg. needs for 3rd Army area processing center. Specialties: 1a, 1g; 3a, 3e; 4a, 4b, 4c, 4d (libr. systs. develop).

BURY, PETER P, Nov. 29, 27; Head Librarian, Glenview Public Library, 1930 Glenview Rd, Glenview, Ill. 60025. Home: 1537 Brandon Rd, Glenview, Ill. 60025. A.B, 48; M.A, 49; M.S, 55. Librn. II, Detroit Pub. Libr, 55-58; head librn, Glenview Pub. Libr, Glenview, Ill, 58-60; consult, Bureau Libr. Serv, State of Conn, 61-62; libr. dir, Glenview Pub. Libr, Glenview, Ill, 63- Other: Secy, Glenview Rotary Club, 60-61 & 65-67; pres, Libr. Administr. Coun. of North. Ill, 60-61; exec. dir. of Nat. Libr. Week in Ill, 64-65; chmn, local arrangement cmt, Ill. Libr. Asn, 65; ALA mem. chmn. for Ill, 65-67. Mem: Conn. Libr. Asn; Ill. Libr. Asn; ALA; Laconi. Publ: Michigan Bibliography, 1955, Mich. Hist, 9/56; Michigan Bibliography, 1956, Mich. Hist, 9/57; Publicity for Small Libraries, Ill. Libr, 2/61. Consult: 1) Gail Borden Pub. Libr, Elgin, Ill. critique of plans for new bldg, Apr. 66; 2) Worth Village Libr, Worth, Ill, eval. of several libr. sites with recommendations, with Edna Holland, Apr. 66; 3) W. Deerfield Township Libr, Deerfield, Ill, appraisal of libr, May 66; 4) Wilmington Township Libr,

---

5) PERSONNEL AND RECRUITING, 5a) job evaluation and description, salary recommendations, 5b) recruitment of professionals and management personnel, 5c) administrative organization, 6) PUBLIC RELATIONS, 6a) publications, 6b) publicity programs, 6c) public opinion surveys, 6d) others, 7) SERVICES, 7a) evaluation of current program, 7b) studies of service to special publics, e.g., students, handicapped, aged, etc., 7c) programs for the implementation of new laws, program proposals to governments, 7d) others, 8) COMMUNITY, REGIONAL, STATE PLANNING, 8a) legislative programs, 8b) area analyses, 8c) centralized systems, cooperative arrangements, 8d) development of standards, 8e) state libraries and extension agencies, 8f) regional and statewide surveys, 8g) others, 9) OTHERS.

Wilmington, Ill, report on possible use of church bldg. as libr, with Edna Holland, May 66; 5) Little Rock Township Pub. Libr, Plano, Ill, survey of libr. serv, bldg. problems & potential libr. sites, with Edna Holland, June 66. Specialties: 1a, 1g, 1h (critique of libr. plans & layout); 2a, 2b, 2d (hist); 3e; 5a, 5b, 5c, 5d (salary schedules & personnel policies & procedures); 6b, 6c; 7a, 7d (orgn. & creation of new libr); 8b, 8d.

BUTLER, EVELYN, Aug. 23, 15; Librarian, School of Social Work, University of Pennsylvania, Philadelphia, Pa. 19104. Home: 124 W. Queen Lane, Germantown, Philadelphia, Pa. 19144. A.B, 37; A.B.L.S, 38; A.M.L.S, 46. Librn, sch. social work, Univ. Pa, 46-. Other: Pres, Conn. chap, SLA, 46; secy, Spec. Libr. Coun. Phila, 48-49, dir, 58-60; chmn. soc. welfare section, soc. sci. div, SLA, 51, 60-63, chmn. soc. sci. div, 52-53. Mem: ALA; Pa. Libr. Asn; SLA; Conn. Libr. Found. Publ: Rule of the Thumb, Spec. Libr, 5-6/60; Building a Social Work Library, (joint compiler), Coun. Soc. Work Educ, 62. Consult: 1) Howard Univ, Washington, D.C, assisted in starting sch. of soc. work libr, 62; 2) Hunter Col, New York, N.Y, assisted in planning a soc. work libr, structural & orgn, 64; 3) Syracuse Univ, assisted in starting sch. of soc. work libr, 66-67. Specialties: 1b, 1d, 1e, 1f, 1g; 2d (soc. work); 5c.

BYERS, MRS. EDNA HANLEY, Mar. 30, 00; Librarian, Agnes Scott College, Decatur, Ga. 30030. Home: 226 E. Hancock St, Decatur, Ga. 30030. A.B, 23; A.B. in L.S, 27; A.M. in L.S, 34. Librn, Agnes Scott Col, Decatur, Ga, 32-; lectr. libr. sci, Univ. Mich, 57. Mem: Ga. Libr. Asn; Southeast. Libr. Asn; ALA. Publ: Work Rooms in College and University Buildings, Am. Sch. & Univ, 38; College and University Library Buildings, ALA, 39; Recent Trends in Small College Library Buildings, Libr. J, 12/15/43; College and University Library Buildings, Bibliographies, Col. & Res. Libr, 54 & 56; Robert Frost at Agnes Scott College, 63. Consult: 1) King Col, Bristol, Tenn, assisted writing bldg. program, 61. Specialties: 1b (small liberal arts cols).

C

CAMPBELL, HENRY CUMMINGS, Apr. 22, 19; Chief Librarian, Toronto Public Library, Toronto, Ont, Can. Home: 373 Glengrove Ave, Toronto 12, Ont, Can. B.L.S, 41; M.A, 47. Head, UNESCO Clearing House Libr, 51-56; chief librn, Toronto Pub. Libr, Toronto, Ont, Can, 56-. Other: Mem, Can. Nat. Cmn. for UNESCO, 58-60; pres, Ont. Asn. Continuing Educ, 66-. Mem: ALA; Can. Libr. Asn; Ont. Libr. Asn. Publ: UNESCO Bulletin for Libraries (ed. & contrib), 51-56; Metropolitan Public Library Planning Throughout the World, Pergamon, 66; How to Find Out About Canada, Pergamon, 67; Canadian libraries, Bingley, 69. Consult: 1) Ont. Asn. Curriculum Develop, leisure time adult educ. serv, Nov. 65; 2) UNESCO, Paris, planning of nat. libr. serv. in Latin Am, with Kenneth Roberts, Feb. 66; 3) Sci. Secretariat, Can. Govt, Ottawa, Ont, sci. & tech. info. study, Apr. 67-Sept. 68; 4) Can. Coun. Urban & Regional Res. Coun, Ottawa, Can. Urban Info. Syst, Aug. 68. Specialties: 2e; 7c; 8a, 8c, 8d, 8e, 8f; 9 (urban metrop. pub. libr. orgn, particularly for consolidations & mergers in both libr. & document. fields).

CARLSON, WILLIAM H, Sept. 5, 98; Director of Libraries Emeritus, Oregon State System of Higher Education, Corvallis, Ore. 97330. Home: 769 N. 11th St, Apt. 33, Corvallis, Ore. 97330. A.B, Univ. Nebr, 24; Cert, N.Y. State Libr, Sch, 26; A.M.L.S, Univ. Calif, Berkeley, 37. Librn, Ore. State Univ, Corvallis, 45-65; dir. libr, Ore. State Syst. Higher Educ, Corvallis, 45-65, libr. planning & res. assoc, 65-68. Other: Pres, ACRL, 47-48; pres, Pac. Northwest Libr. Asn, 52-53; pres, LED, 52-53; pres, Ore. State chap, Phi Kappa Phi, 55-56; mem, Ore. State Libr. Bd. Trustees, 55-63, chmn. bd, 57-59. Mem: ALA; ACRL; Pac. Northwest Libr. Asn; Ore. Libr. Asn; Can. Libr. Asn; Bibliog. Soc. Am. Publ: Development and Financial Support of Seven Western and Northwestern State University Libraries, Univ. Calif, Berkeley, 38; College and University Libraries and Librarianship (et al), ALA, 46; A Report of a Survey of the Library of Texas A&M College, October, 1949 to February, 1950, Tex. A&M Col, 50; Mobilization of Existing Library Resources, Libr. Trends, 1/58; Libraries and Library Service in the Portland (Oregon) High Schools, Portland Sch. Dist. 1, 59; The Holy Grail Evades the Search, Am. Document, 7/63. Consult: 1) Pac. Lutheran Univ, Tacoma, Wash, new libr. bldg. with Rodney K. Waldron, 64-66; 2) South. Ore. Col, Ashland, new libr. bldg, 64-; 3) Mt. Angel Col, Mt. Angel, Ore, new libr. bldg, 65-; 4) Mont. State Univ, Missoula, new libr. bldg, 66-; 5) Ariz. State Univ, Tempe, survey of total libr. complex of State of Ariz, with Bradley Simon, 66-. Specialties: 1b, 1f, 1g; 5a, 5b, 5c; 7a; 8a, 8b, 8c, 8d, 8e, 8f.

CARNOVSKY, DR. LEON, Nov. 28, 03; Professor, Graduate Library School, University of Chicago, Chicago, Ill. 60637. Home: 5805 Dorchester Ave, Chicago, Ill. 60637. A.B, Univ. Mo, 27; Ph.D, Univ. Chicago, 32. Prof, grad. libr. sch, Univ. Chicago, 32-; vis. prof, Univ. Calif, 37-39, Syracuse Univ, 56, Columbia Univ, 60, 64. Other: Mem. & chmn, Cmt. on Accreditation, ALA, 60-67; recipient, Melvil Dewey Medal for creative prfnl. achievement, 62. Mem: ALA; Asn. Am. Libr. Schs. Publ: Library Service in a Suburban Area (with E.A.Wight), ALA, 35; Libraries and Readers in New York (with D. Waples), Univ. Chicago, 39; A Metropolitan

---

KEY TO CONSULTING SPECIALTIES: 1) ARCHITECTURE AND BUILDINGS, 1a) public libraries, 1b) academic libraries, 1c) school libraries, 1d) special libraries, 1e) library interiors, 1f) furnishings, 1g) site and location, 1h) other architectural; 2) COLLECTIONS: SELECTION, EVALUATION, WEEDING, 2a) adults, 2b) young adults, 2c) children, 2d) subject specialty, 2e) O.P. searches, 2f) rare books, 2g) appraisals, 2h) others; 3) TECHNICAL PROCESSES, 3a) cataloging, 3b) classification systems, 3c) acquisitions, 3d) materials processing, 3e) work flow and cost studies, 3f) others, 4) AUTOMATION, 4a) applications of data processing equipment, 4b) information storage and retrieval systems, 4c) systems analysis, 4d) others

Library in Action (with C.B. Joeckel), Univ. Chicago, 40; The Library in the Community (joint ed), Univ. Chicago, 44; International Aspects of Librarianship, Univ. Chicago, 54; The Medium-Sized Public Library, Univ. Chicago, 63. Consult: 1) Vancouver Pub. Libr, Vancouver, B.C, survey, 56; 2) UNESCO libr. expert to Israel, survey libr. situation; plans for libr. sch. at Hebrew Univ, Jerusalem, 56; 3) UNESCO libr. expert to Greece, survey libr. situation; report & plan for libr. sch. for Greece, 60; 4) Chicago Schs. Survey, report on sch. libr, in final report of the Survey, 64; 5) Racine Pub. Libr, Racine, Wis, survey, 64-65. Specialties: 2a; 5c; 7a; 8b; 9 (educ. for librarianship, eval. of numerous programs).

CARPENTER, DR. RAY L, Dec. 1, 26; Associate Professor & Project Director, School of Library Science, University of North Carolina at Chapel Hill, Chapel Hill, N.C. 27514. Home: P.O. Box 484, Chapel Hill, N.C. 27514. A.B, 49, M.A, 51; M.S. in L.S, 58; Ph.D, 68. Libr. asst. extension dept, libr. Univ. N.C, Chapel Hill, 56-57, head searching sect. & order sect, 57-58, instructor, sch. libr. sci, 59-60, lectr, 60-68, assoc. prof, 68- Other: Asst. managing ed, Libr. Resources & Tech. Serv, 59-60; Libr. Binding Inst. scholarship, 60; South. fel, 60. Mem: ALA; Southeast. Libr. Asn; N.C. Libr. Asn; N.C. Libr. Asn; Asn. Am. Libr. Schs; Beta Phi Mu; Alpha Kappa Delta; Am. Sociol. Asn; Am. Asn. Univ. Prof. Publ: The Theatre Today, 1954-1957, Univ. N.C. Libr. monograph, 10/57; The Mission of the Librarian (transl. & ed. with James Lewis), Antioch Rev, summer 61 & monograph, G.K. Hall, 61; Current Research at the School of Library Science, University of North Carolina at Chapel Hill, Southeast. Librn, spring 65; Education for Librarianship in North Carolina, In: Resources of North Carolina Libraries, 65 & Southeast. Librn, fall 65; The Public Library Executive, USOE Monograph. Consult: 1) N.C. Gov. Cmn. Libr. Resources, P.O. Box 448, Raleigh, N.C, survey of libr. educ. in N.C, 64; 2) U.S. Office Educ, survey pub. libr. admin, 67. Specialties: 2d (soc. sci); 5c; 6c; 8a, 8b, 8c, 8d, 8e, 8f, 8g; 9 (educ. for librarianship).

CARRISON, DALE K, Apr. 29, 36; Chairman, Department of Library Science, Mankato State College, Mankato, Minn. 56001. Home: 104 Lillian Dr, Mankato, Minn. 56001. B.S, West. Ill. Univ, 57, M.S, 59; M.A.(libr. educ.), Univ. Denver, 62. Faculty asst. periodicals libr, West. Ill. Univ. Macomb, Ill, 57-58; high sch. librn. & adult bus. educ. instructor, United Township High Sch, East Moline, Ill, 58-61; part-time librn, Fed. Correctional Inst, Englewood, Colo, 61-62; asst. prof. libr. sci, West. Ill. Univ, 62-64; instructor libr. sci. & asst. to dean grad. sch. librarianship, Univ. Denver, Denver, Colo, 64-68, dir, NDEA Inst. Sch. Librns, summer 65-66 & assoc. dir, summer 67; chmn. dept. libr. sci, Mankato State Col, Mankato, Minn, 68- Other: Treas, Rock Island-Mercer-Henry County Sch. Librns. Asn, 60-62; chmn. publicity cmt, Ill. Asn. Sch. Librns, 61-62; mem. cmt, YASD, 63-64; chmn. cmt, LED, 65-; mem, Liaison Cmt. for Develop. of Libr. Sci. Curriculum for Metrop. State Col, Denver, 66-67; ed, Studies in Librarianship series, Grad. Sch. Librarianship, Univ. Denver, 66-68. Mem: Am. Asn. Univ. Prof; ALA; Am. Asn. Sch. Librns; Colo. Asn. Sch. Librns; Colo. Audio-Visual Asn; Colo. Libr. Asn; Mt. Plains Libr. Asn; Dept. Audiovisual Instruction; Beta Phi Mu; Phi Delta Kappa; Pi Omega Pi; PDK-AERA Spec. Interest Group Res. Instruction. Publ: Three syllabi for use in teaching basic library methods (cataloging, book selection, reference) to public librarians in Illinois, sponsored by the Libr. Training & Serv. Div, Ill. State Libr, 64; Literature for the Young Adult, a Compilation of Papers and Bibliographies from an NDEA Institute for School Librarians (ed), Studies in Librarianship series 7, Grad. Sch. Librarianship, Univ, Denver, 68. Consult: 1) Ill. State Libr, Springfield, Ill, develop. libr. sci. instruction program, fall 64; 2) Breckenridge Job Corp Center, Morganfield, Ky, survey & eval. of libr. collection, fall 65; 3) Boulder Valley Schools, Boulder, Colo, participated in develop. of planning grant for cooperative community educ. resources center, Mar-July 67. Specialties: 2a, 2b; 3a, 3c, 3d; 7a; 9 (libr. educ—programs & courses).

CARTER, MRS. OMA, Feb. 1, 13; Director, Library Consultant Service, 1912 South Blvd, Edmond, Okla. 73034. B.S, Abilene Christian Col, 52; M.S, Kans. State Teachers Col, 55. Librn, Okla. Christian Col, 59-64; librn, Edmond High Sch, Okla, 64-65, Edmond Sch. Dist, 65- Mem: ALA; Southwest. Libr. Asn; Okla. Libr. Asn; Nat. Educ. Asn; Am. Asn. Univ. Women. Publ: Contrib, Okla. Librn, Kans. Librn, Ark. Libr. J, AAUW, Tex. Libr. Asn. J, Okla. Teacher. Consult: 1) Edmond High Sch. & Sch. Dist, Edmond, Okla, anal. of the grade sch. purchases over a three year period, 64-65; 2) Southwest. Christian Col, Terrell, Tex, eval. & planning for expansion in services, redoing catalog, Nov. 67-Sept. 68; 3) El Reno Pub. Libr, El Reno, Okla, equipment for spec. services room, May 68; 4) Choctaw Sch. Dist, Choctaw, Okla, graded book list for teachers, Sept. 68; 5) Garland Rd. Church Libr, 10715 Garland Rd, Dallas, Tex, planning & orgn. of church libr. Specialties: 1b, 1c, 1e, 1f, 1h (jr. col); 2c, 2d (profile anal. of library); 3a, 3b, 3c, 3d, 3e, 3f (xerox card duplicating); 5c; 7a; 8c.

CASELLAS, ELIZABETH REED (BRANNON), Jan. 7, 25; Head, Business, Science & Technology Department, Orlando Public Library, Ten N. Rosalind, Orlando, Fla. 32801. Home: 1616 S. DeLaney, Orlando, Fla. 32806. M.A, Columbia Univ, 49, prfnl. diploma, 50, M.S, 64. Asst. Librn, J.M. Mathes, Inc, New York, 55-57; head librn, Commun. Counselors,

---

5) PERSONNEL AND RECRUITING, 5a) job evaluation and description, salary recommendations, 5b) recruitment of professionals and management personnel, 5c) administrative organization, 6) PUBLIC RELATIONS, 6a) publications, 6b) publicity programs, 6c) public opinion surveys, 6d) others, 7) SERVICES, 7a) evaluation of current program, 7b) studies of service to special publics, e.g., students, handicapped, aged, etc., 7c) programs for the implementation of new laws, program proposals to governments, 7d) others, 8) COMMUNITY, REGIONAL, STATE PLANNING, 8a) legislative programs, 8b) area analyses, 8c) centralized systems, cooperative arrangements, 8d) development of standards, 8e) state libraries and extension agencies, 8f) regional and statewide surveys, 8g) others, 9) OTHERS.

Inc, New York, 57-59; head librn, Cresap, McCormick & Paget, New York, 59-60; head librn, Stewart, Dougall & Assocs, New York, 60-65; asst. prof. grad. sch. libr. sci. & libr. specialist in bus, Univ. Hawaii, 65-66; head bus. sci. & tech. dept, Orlando Pub. Libr, Orlando, Fla, 66- Other: Lectr. advertising sources, Advertising Group, 58-; chmn. N.Y. chap, Social Sci. Group, 59-60; rep. McKinsey Found. Book Cmt, 64; prfnl. consult, SLA, 65-, chmn. Fla. group, S.Atlantic chap, 68- Mem: Hawaii Econ. Asn; SLA, ALA; ACRL; Fla. Libr. Asn; Kappa Delta Pi. Publ: Librarian's Role in a Public Relations Organization, Pub. Relations J, 7/59; Sources of Information for Electronic Product Engineers, IEEE Transactions on Product Engineering & Production, 9/63; Relative Effectiveness of the Harvard Business, Library of Contress and the Dewey Decimal Classifications for a Marketing Collection, Libr. Resources & Tech. Serv, fall 65; Specialized Services to Business and Industry in Florida Public Libraries, Fla. Libr, 3/68. Consult: 1) Case & Co, Inc, 600 Fifth Ave, New York, N.Y, appraisal of libr, 64. Specialties: 1d; 2d (bus. especially mgt. & marketing); 3a, 3b; 5a.

CASTAGNA, EDWIN, May 1, 09; Director, Enoch Pratt Free Library, 400 Cathedral St, Baltimore, Md. 21201. Home: 3815 Juniper Rd, Baltimore, Md. 21218. A.B, 35; Certificate in Librarianship, 36. City librn, Long Beach Pub. Libr, Long Beach, Calif, 50-60; dir, Enoch Pratt Free Libr, Baltimore, Md, 60- Other: Pres, Nev. Libr. Asn, 46-47; pres, Pub. Libr. Execs. Asn. South. Calif, 52; pres, Calif. Libr. Asn, 54; pres, ALA, 64-65. Mem: ALA; Md. Libr. Asn; Calif. Libr. Asn. Publ: Courage and Cowardice: The Influence of Pressure Groups on Library Collections, Libr. J, 2/63; The Development of Library Collections, In: Local Public Library Administration, Int. City Mgr. Asn, Chicago, 64; The Climate of Intellectual Freedom—Why is it Always so Bad in California?, ALA Bull, 1/65; Library Service of the Future—Some Guesses about What's Ahead, In: The Library Reaches Out (ed. with Kate Coplan), Oceana, 65; Three Who Meet the Challenge: Joseph L. Wheeler, Lawrence Clark Powell, Frances Clarke Sayers, Peacock, 65; Long, Warm Friendship: H.L. Mencken and the Enoch Pratt Free Library, Peacock, 66. Consult: 1) Ontario Pub. Libr, Ontario, Calif, bldg, serv. & orgn, with Dr. Martha Boaz, 59; 2) Santa Monica Pub. Libr, Santa Monica, Calif, new bldg, 59; 3) Palos Verdes Estates Pub. Libr, Palos Verdes Estates, Calif, libr. bldg. & serv, 59; 4) Chula Vista Pub. Libr, Chula Vista, Calif, libr. bldg, serv. & orgn, 60; 5) Municipal Govt, City of Culver City, Calif, survey of libr. serv. in Culver City with recommendations, with E. Caswell Perry, 65. Specialties: 1a, 1g; 2a; 5c; 6a; 7a, 7c; 8a, 8c, 8d; 9 (work simplification & methods improvement).

CAVAGLIERI, DR. GIORGIO, Aug. 1, 11; Architect, 250 W. 57th St, New York, N.Y. 10019 & Adjunct Professor, Pratt School of Architecture. Home: 75 Central Park W, New York, N.Y. 10023. Dr. Archit. Engineering, Sch. Engineering, Milan, 32; dipl. city planning, Sch. Archit, Rome, 34. Architect, 36-; adjunct prof, Pratt Sch. Archit, 56- Other: Secy, bd. trustees, Nat. Inst. Archit. Educ, 55-56, chmn, 56-58; v.pres, Archit. League, 60-62; secy, Municipal Art Soc, N.Y, 62-63, pres, 63-65; mem, Selection Panel Archit, 63. Publ: Outline for a History of City Planning, J. Soc. Archit. Historian, 7/47, 1/48, 1/49 & 7/49; People and Buildings, N.Y. Herald Tribune, 3/55; Designing a Union Headquarters, Serv. Employee, 4/57; Institute of Design and Construction, Brooklyn, N.Y, 51; contrib, prfnl. journals. Consult: 1) N.Y. City Dept. Pub. Works, Municipal Bldg, New York, N.Y, restoration of Jefferson Market Courthouse & conversion to libr, Manhattan, N.Y, 62-67; 2) N.Y. City Dept. Pub. Works, bldg. for Spuyten Duyvil Br. Libr, Bronx, N.Y, 66-68; 3) N.Y. City Dept. Pub. Works, bldg. for Kip's Bay Br. Libr, Manhattan, 67-68. Specialties: 1a, 1c, 1d, 1e, 1f, 1g.

CHAIT, WILLIAM, Dec. 5, 15; Director, Dayton & Montgomery County Public Library, Dayton, Ohio 45402. Home: 2931 Ensley Ave, Dayton, Ohio 45414. B.A, Brooklyn Col, 34; B.S.L.S, Pratt Inst, 35; M.S.L.S, Columbia Univ, 39. Dir, Kalamazoo Pub. Libr, 48-56; dir, Dayton & Montgomery County Pub. Libr, Dayton, Ohio, 56- Other: Pres, Mich. Libr. Asn, 55-56; pres, PLA, 64-65; pres, Ohio Libr. Asn, 64-65; vis. lectr, Univ. Ill. Grad. Sch. Libr. Sci, summers 64 & 66, Kent State Univ. Sch. Libr. Sci, summer 67. Mem: ALA; Ohio Libr. Asn. Publ: Survey of the Public Libraries of Asheville (City) and Buncombe County, North Carolina (with R.E. Warncke): ALA, 65; Survey of the Public Libraries of Norwalk, Connecticut (with Robert S. Ake), ALA, 66. Consult: 1) Cleveland Heights Pub. Libr, 2345 Lee Rd, Cleveland Heights, Ohio, survey of serv, staffing, work prodedures, bldg. program, bldg. campaign, bldg. plans, Dec. 64-; 2) Jefferson City & Cole County Libr, 210 Adams St, Jefferson City, Mo, survey of orgn, mgt, staffing, finances, serv. to neighboring counties & bldg. program, with Frank B. Sessa & Libr. Mgt. & Bldg. Consult, Inc, July 65-; 3) Ambler Pub. Libr, 209 Race St, Ambler, Pa, survey of serv, facilities & relations with other libr. in area, Mar-Apr. 66; 4) Montgomery County Free Libr, 400 Markley St, Norristown, Pa, survey of serv. & facilities with recommendations, Mar-May 66; 5) Pottsville Free Pub. Libr, Third & Market Sts, Pottsville, Pa, review of orgn. & serv. to mem. libr. in dist, bldg. program & recommendations on temporary bldg. changes, with Libr. Mgt. & Bldg. Consult, Inc, May 66- Specialties: 1a, 1g; 5a, 5b, 5c; 7a; 8b, 8c, 8f.

KEY TO CONSULTING SPECIALTIES: 1) ARCHITECTURE AND BUILDINGS, 1a) public libraries, 1b) academic libraries, 1c) school libraries, 1d) special libraries, 1e) library interiors, 1f) furnishings, 1g) site and location, 1h) other architectural; 2) COLLECTIONS: SELECTION, EVALUATION, WEEDING, 2a) adults, 2b) young adults, 2c) children, 2d) subject specialty, 2e) O.P. searches, 2f) rare books, 2g) appraisals, 2h) others; 3) TECHNICAL PROCESSES, 3a) cataloging, 3b) classification systems, 3c) acquisitions, 3d) materials processing, 3e) work flow and cost studies, 3f) others, 4) AUTOMATION, 4a) applications of data processing equipment, 4b) information storage and retrieval systems, 4c) systems analysis, 4d) others

CHAPIN, DR. RICHARD E, Apr. 29, 25; Director of Libraries, Michigan State University, East Lansing, Mich. 48823. Home: 614 Camelot Dr, East Lansing, Mich. 48823. A.B, 48; M.S, 49; Ph.D, 55. Assoc. librn, Mich. State Univ, East Lansing, 55-59, dir. libr, 59- Other: Chmn. univ. libr. sect, ACRL, 61; chmn. cmt. availability of resources, Asn. Res. Libr, 65-; pres, Mich. Libr. Asn, 66. Mem: ALA; Asn. Res. Libr; Mich. Libr. Asn. Publ: Libraries, In: Colliers Encyclopedia; Mass Communications, Mich. State Univ, 58; contrib. to prfnl. journals. Consult: 1) E. Lansing Pub. Libr, East Lansing, Mich, new bldg, with M.M. Jones, 60-61; 2) Nat. Agr. Libr, Wash, D.C, Project ABLE & its relationship to land-grant univs, 62; 3) U.S. Office Tech. Serv, Wash, D.C, study of distribution & use of tech. reports, 63; 4) Alma Col, Alma, Mich, 68; 5) EDUCOM, elements of libr. network, 68. Specialties: 1b; 3b, 3e; 4a, 4d (cost anal); 5c; 7a.

CHASE, WILLIAM D, Apr. 8, 22; Chief Librarian, Flint Journal, 200 E. First St, Flint, Mich. 48502. Home: 1113 Kensington Ave, Flint, Mich. 48503. B.A, Univ. Mich, 43, M.A, 53. Chief librn, Flint Journal, 49- Other: Owner & publ, Apple Tree Press, Flint, Mich; chmn. newspaper div, SLA, 57; pres, Flint Libr. Club, 64. Mem: SLA; Nat. Microfilm Asn; Am. Soc. Info. Sci. Publ: Newspaper Libraries (ed); G. Bernard Shaw's Last Will & Testament (ed), Apple Tree Press, 54; Chases' Calendar of Annual Events, Special Days, Weeks and Months (ed. & pub), 58- Consult: 1) Vietnam Press, 116 Hong Thap Tu, Saigon, Vietnam, organized libr. serv. & trained personnel & ed. staff under State Dept. grant, May-Aug. 66. Specialties: 2h (newspaper libr).

CHEN, DR. JOHN H.M, June 24, 21; Director of Library & Professor of Education and Library Science, Lynchburg College, Lynchburg, Va. 24501. Home: Box 2021, Lynchburg, Va. 24501. B.S, Kansu Univ, 46, Ph.D, 49; M.S, Va. Polytech. Inst, 57; M.S. in L.S, Columbia Univ, 62; M.A, N.Y. Univ, 64; Ed.D, Pa. State Univ, 68. Sr. consult, ICA, MSMC, 53-56; bibliographer & cataloger, Pa. State, 57-60; dir. libr. serv. & instructional materials center, SCCC, State Univ. N.Y, 63-65; dir. libr, prof. educ. commun. & foreign student adv, W.Va. Inst. Tech, 65-66; dir. libr. & prof. educ. & libr. sci, Lynchburg Col, Lynchburg, Va, 66- Other: Sr. consult, Univ. Circulation Serv, 58-; dir, Int. Friendship Serv, 60-; dir, Int. House Asn, 63-65. Mem: ALA; Cath. Libr. Asn; Nat. Educ. Asn; Asn. Higher Educ; Am. Asn. Univ. Profs. Publ: Audiovisual Materials, Pa. State, 59; Bibliotherapy, Central Islip, N.Y, 63; Library Handbook, W.Va. Polytech. Inst, 66; Periodicals Directory, W.Va. Polytech. Inst, 66; Book Collection According to the Library of Congress Classification, Lynchburg Col, 66- Consult: 1) State Univ. N.Y. Cols, develop. of libr. programs for cols. of State Univ. N.Y, 63-65; 2) W. New Eng. Col, Springfield, Mass, libr. programs & serv, 64-65; 3) State Univ. N.Y, Westchester Community Col, instructional materials & audiovisual programs & serv, 65; 4) W.Va. Libr. Asn. & W.Va. Univ, Morgantown, interlibr. cooperation, Union List of Periodicals, regional libr. develop, 65-66; 5) Lynchburg Col, Va, libr. bldg, automation, orgn. of libr. materials, LC classification, 66. Specialties: 1a, 1b, 1e, 1f, 1g; 2a, 2d; 3a, 3b, 3d, 3e; 4a, 4b; 5c; 6b; 7a, 7b; 8b, 8c, 8d; 9 (tech. info. center; Libr. Congress classification; microforms; libr. programs & develop).

CHERRY, SCOTT T, Nov. 21, 20; President, Institutional Interiors, Inc, 215 Stemmons Tower West, Dallas, Tex. 75207. Home: 7627 Rolling Acres Dr, Dallas, Tex. 75240. B.J, Univ. Mo, 42. Spec. rep, Libr. Bureau, St. Louis, Mo, 46-63, coordinator, Nat. Design & Planning Dept, N.Y, 63-66. Other: Chmn, St. Louis Libr. Club, 58-59. Mem: ALA; Mo. Libr. Asn. Consult: 1) Stephens Col. Libr. & Learning Center, Columbia, Mo, interior layouts, furnishings selections & design, 63; 2) Bowdoin Col, Brunswick, Maine, interior layout, equipment selection & design, 63-64; 3) Skidmore Col, Saratoga Springs, N.Y, interior layout, equipment selection & design, 65-66; 4) Univ. Wis, Milwaukee Campus, interior layout, equipment selection & design, with Edna E. Voigt, 65-66; 5) Tulane Univ. Libr, New Orleans, La, interior layout, equipment selection & design, 67. Specialties: 1a, 1b, 1c, 1d, 1e, 1f.

CHISHOLM, DR. MARGARET E, July 25, 21; Associate Professor of Education, University of New Mexico, Albuquerque, N.Mex. 87106. Home: 2909 Indiana N.E, Albuquerque, N.Mex. 87110. B.A, 57; M.L, 58; Ph.D, 66. Elem. librn, jr. high librn. & sr. high librn, 56-61; librn, Everett Community Col, 61-63; assoc. prof. librarianship, Univ. Ore, Eugene, 63-65; dir. instructional materials & media, Seattle Pub. Schs, Wash, 66-67; assoc. prof. educ, Univ. N.Mex, Albuquerque, 67- Mem: ALA; Dept. Audiovisual Instruction; N.Mex. Audiovisual Asn; N.Mex. Libr. Asn; Asn. Supv. & Curriculum Develop. Publ: Survey of Elementary, Junior, and Senior High School Libraries in Oregon, State Dept. of Educ, Salem, 65; Career Opportunities in Librarianship, Pac. Northwest Employment Directory, Craftsman, 66; Educational Technology: How Humane Can It Be?, Educ. Leadership, 12/67. Consult: 1) Reed-Belvedere Sch. Dist, San Francisco, Calif, evaluated sch. dist. libr. program, Oct. 64; 2) Anchorage, Alaska, in-serv. workshop for sch. faculty & admin, Mar. 65; 3) Fed. City Col, Wash, D.C, plans & budget for media center, 67; 4) Calif. State Dept. Educ, program eval. conf. for librn. & adminstr, Mar. 68. Specialties: 1c; 2c; 7b, 7c.

5) PERSONNEL AND RECRUITING, 5a) job evaluation and description, salary recommendations, 5b) recruitment of professionals and management personnel, 5c) administrative organization, 6) PUBLIC RELATIONS, 6a) publications, 6b) publicity programs, 6c) public opinion surveys, 6d) others, 7) SERVICES, 7a) evaluation of current program, 7b) studies of service to special publics, 7c) programs for the implementation of new laws, program proposals to governments, 7d) others, 8) COMMUNITY, REGIONAL, STATE PLANNING, 8a) legislative programs, 8b) area analyses, 8c) centralized systems, cooperative arrangements, 8d) development of standards, 8e) state libraries and extension agencies, 8f) regional and statewide surveys, 8g) others, 9) OTHERS.

CHITWOOD, JACK, June 1, 21; Director, Rockford Public Library & Northern Illinois Library System, 215 N. Wyman St, Rockford, Ill. 61101. Home: 2134 Oxford St, Rockford, Ill. 61103. B.A, 42; M.Mus, 48; M.A, 54. Coordinator, adult serv, Indianapolis Pub. Libr, 56-61 dir, Rockford Pub. Libr, Rockford, Ill, 61- Other: Chmn. standards cmt, ASD, 61-66; mem. libr. develop. cmt, Ill. Libr. Asn, 62-, pres. of Asn, 65-; mem. exec. bd, ASD, 63-66, pres, bldg. & equipment sect, 67; chmn. staff develop. cmt, LAD, 64-; mem. Rockford Rotary Bd, 65-66; pres, Unitarian Church, Rockford, 65-; mem. exec. bd, Rockford Civic Symphony, 65; chmn. subcmt. materials of standards cmt, PLA, 66; mem. bd, Rockford Area Chamber of Commerce, 66- Mem: ALA; Music Libr. Asn; Ill. Libr. Asn. Consult: 1) Dolton Pub. Libr, Dolton, Ill, bldg. consult, 65-66; 2) Fremont Township Pub. Libr, Mundelein, Ill, program developer & bldg. consult, 65-66; 3) Addison Township Pub. Libr, Addison, Ill, program developer & bldg. consult, 65-; 4) Crystal Lake Pub. Libr, Crystal Lake, Ill, program developer & bldg. consult, 65- Specialties: 1a, 1e, 1f, 1g; 2a, 2d (humanities); 3c, 3d; 5a, 5c; 7a, 7c; 8a, 8b, 8c, 8d.

CLARK, MRS. GERTRUDE M, Mar. 14, 15; Assistant Librarian, Medical Sciences Library, University of Utah, Salt Lake City, Utah 84112. A.B.(modern languages), Occidental Col, 40; B.S.(libr. sci), Univ. South. Calif, 41. Asst. chief librn. & chief librn, Los Angeles County Med. Asn, 51-57; chief librn, Stuart Co. Div, Atlas Chemical Industries, Inc, Pasadena, Calif, 59-68. Other: V.pres. & pres, Med. Libr. Group South. Calif, 54-56; registered prfnl. consult, SLA, 58-, publ. chmn, 65, chmn. biological div, 66. Mem: SLA; Am. Soc. Info. Sci; Calif. Libr. Asn; Med. Libr. Group South. Calif. Publ: Union List of Periodicals, Medical and Biological Sciences, Los Angeles Area (ed), 51; Some Secondary Tools in Reference Work, Bull. Med. Libr. Asn, 10/53; Symposium on Types of Medical Libraries: The Medical Society Library, Bull. Med. Libr. Asn, 4/55; Coordinate Indexing of Pharmaceutical Information, Bull. Med. Libr. Asn, 7/62; Union List of Periodicals in Southern California Libraries (ed), 63; The Biblioteca Mario Negri report from Milan, Spec. Libr, 2/65. Consult: 1) Dr. Alles Biochemical Labs, Arroyo Seco Parkway, Pasadena, Calif, orgn. of small libr, 44; 2) Mario Negri Inst. Pharmaceutical Res, Via Eritrea 62, Milan, Italy, establishment of libr. & coordinate indexing syst. (mechanized-IBM), with J. Walsh, Sept. 63-Mar. 64. Specialties: 1d; 2d (med, pharmacology, biochemistry); 3a, 3b, 3c; 4b.

CLARK, RHETA A, Feb. 18, 02; School Library Consultant, Connecticut State Department of Education, Hartford, Conn. 06115. Home: 131 Tyron St, South Glastonbury, Conn. 06073. A.B, Conn. Col, 23; M.A, Columbia Univ, 31, B.L.S, 41. Sch. libr. consult, Conn. State Dept. Ed, Hartford, 44- Other: Pres, Conn. Sch. Libr. Asn, 33-34; pres, New Eng. Sch. Libr. Asn, 40-42; mem. exec. bd, AASL, 42-45, v.chmn, 45-46, chmn, 46-47, dir. region I, 57-59; councilor-at-large, ALA, 66- Conn. Libr. Asn; Conn. Sch. Libr. Asn; Am. Asn. Childhood Educ. Int; Am. Asn. Univ. Women; Asn. Supvr. & Curriculum Develop; Conn. Educ. Asn; Delta Kappa Gamma; Nat. Coun. Teachers of English; Nat. Educ. Asn. Publ: Criteria for Service Personnel, Rooms, Budget and Book Selection of School Libraries, School Library Program, Minimum Library Facilities for the K-Six School, 1952-1958, Conn. State Dept. Educ. Consult: 1) Frederick R. Noble Sch, Willimantic, Conn, plan in-serv. workshop demonstrations for teachers from 40 sch. dists, with Sophie Jenkins, July 65-Feb. 66; 2) Lapham High Sch, New Canaan, Conn, libr. bldg, with Russell Capen, Jan. 66; 3) Danbury State Col, Danbury, Conn, plan in-serv. training workshop for classroom teachers in three demonstration elem. sch. libr, with Margaret Farquhar, Mar-May 66; 4) Mystic Oral Sch, Mystic, Conn, plan of libr. program for deaf children under ESEA, with Geraldine Garrison, Apr-July 66; 5) Fred D. Wish Sch, Hartford, Conn, demonstration elem. sch. libr. program in inner-city sch, June 66. Specialties: 1c; 2b, 2c; 5a; 7a; 8d.

CLARKE, DR. ROBERT FLANDERS, June 20, 32; Chief, Library Services, National Clearinghouse for Smoking & Health, 4040 N. Fairfax Dr, Arlington, Va. 22203. Home: 2710 Elsmore St, Fairfax, Va. 22030. B.S.(gen. engineering), U.S. Naval Acad, 54; M.L.S, Rutgers Univ, 61, Ph.D.(libr. serv), 63. Trainee, E. Orange Pub. Libr, East Orange, N.J, 60-61; fel, grad. sch. libr. serv, Rutgers Univ, 61-63; libr. systs. analyst, Nat. Libr. Med, 63-64, asst. to chief tech. serv. div, 64, deputy chief tech. serv. div, 64-65, spec. asst. to chief reference serv. div, 65-66. Other: Publicity chmn. Savannah region, Sports Car Club Am, 59-60; adv, Montgomery County Pub. Libr, Md, 64-66; mem. vital notes cmt, MLA, 65-66; membership cmt, Commissioned Officers Asn, Pub. Health Serv, 66-67; chmn. membership cmt, D.C. Libr. Asn, 66-67. Mem: ALA; Med. Libr. Asn; SLA; D.C. Libr. Asn; Beta Phi Mu. Publ: Sports Car Events, Arco, 59; Impact of Photocopying on Scholarly Publishing, Libr. J, 7/63; Recruiting of New Graduates from Library Schools, Wilson Libr. Bull, 2/64; Recent Trends of Biomedical Offprint Distribution, Bull. Med. Libr. Asn, 1/66; Your Charging System, Is It Thiefproof?, Libr. J, 2/66. Consult: 1) Mountainside Libr. Bd, Pub. Libr, Mountainside, N.J, survey for pub. & sch. libr. syst, 61; 2) Div. Water Pollution Control, Wash, D.C, advised on the establishment of libr. around U.S. for info. on water pollution, 64-65; 3) Nat. Clearinghouse for Smoking & Health, 8600 Wisconsin Ave, Bethesda, Md, advised on

---

KEY TO CONSULTING SPECIALTIES: 1) ARCHITECTURE AND BUILDINGS, 1a) public libraries, 1b) academic libraries, 1c) school libraries, 1d) special libraries, 1e) library interiors, 1f) furnishings, 1g) site and location, 1h) other architectural; 2) COLLECTIONS: SELECTION, EVALUATION, WEEDING, 2a) adults, 2b) young adults, 2c) children, 2d) subject specialty, 2e) O.P. searches, 2f) rare books, 2g) appraisals, 2h) others; 3) TECHNICAL PROCESSES, 3a) cataloging, 3b) classification systems, 3c) acquisitions, 3d) materials processing, 3e) work flow and cost studies, 3f) others, 4) AUTOMATION, 4a) applications of data processing equipment, 4b) information storage and retrieval systems, 4c) systems analysis, 4d) others

establishment of info. center for info. on smoking, tobacco & health, 65-66; 4) Temple Sch, 14th St. N.W, Wash, D.C, planned & established a program for teaching new libr. asst, 65-66. Specialties: 2h (med. subject fields); 3d, 3e, 3f (microfilm); 4c; 5c; 6a, 6b; 7a, 7b; 9 (new systs. planning & interlibr. loan syst. studies, photocopy syst. studies).

COCHRAN, JEAN D, July 12, 10; Director, Augusta-Richmond County Public Library, 902 Greene St, Augusta, Ga. 30902. Home: 2515 Parkway Dr, Augusta, Ga. 30904. A.B, Guilford Col, 32; B.S. in L.S, Univ. N.C, 41. Dir, Augusta-Richmond County Pub. Libr, 49- Other: Mem. bd, Augusta Players; mem. bd, Augusta Art Asn; trustee, scholarship fund, Pilot Club of Augusta; chmn, pub. libr. sect, Southeast. Libr. Asn; v.pres. & chmn. pub. libr. sect, Ga. Libr. Asn, pres. asn, 67-69; mem. bd, Y.W.C.A. Mem: ALA; Southeast. Libr. Asn; Ga. Libr. Asn. Consult: 1) Elberton Regional Libr, Elberton, Ga, bldg. program, site selection, preliminary drawings, floor plan, furniture, selection & specs, Aug. 64; 2) Northeast Ga. Regional Libr, Clarksville, Ga, bldg. program, site selection & preliminary drawings, Feb. 65; 3) Toombs County Pub. Libr, Vidalia, Ga, bldg. program, preliminary drawings, floor plan & furniture specifications, Apr. 65; 4) Athens Regional Libr, Athens, Ga, bldg. program, site selection, preliminary drawings, floor plan, Jan. 67; 5) Merritt Island, Fla, bldg. program, site approval, preliminary drawings, floor plan, Apr. 67. Specialties: 1a, 1e, 1f, 1g, 1h; 7a.

COHEN, AARON, Aaron Cohen, Architect, 165 W. 91st St, New York, N.Y, 10024. B.S. & B.Arch, 58; M.Arch, 61. Designer & project mgr, Edward D. Stone, 61-67. Other: Mem. bldg. cmt, Sephardic Jewish Brotherhood, 67; chmn. speakers' bureau, N.Y. chap, Am. Inst. Architects, 67-68. Consult: 1) Univ. Pa, studies for Pa. libr, with Ralph Blasingame, June 67; 2) Hudson Inst, Harmon-on-Hudson, N.Y, design & construction of libr. with Alfred Bush, current; 3) Bronx Community Col, 120 E. 184th St, Bronx, N.Y, consulting architect for libr, current. Specialties: 1a, 1b, 1c, 1d, 1e, 1g; 4c; 7a; 8b, 8c, 8d, 8e, 8f.

COHEN, DAVID, May 24, 09; High School Librarian, Plainview-Old Bethpage High School, Plainview, N.Y. 11803. Home: 68-71 Bell Blvd, Bayside, N.Y. 11364. B.S.S, City Col. New York, 30, M.S.E, 34; M.S.L.S, Columbia Univ, 39. Teacher elem. grades, New York, N.Y, 47-54; regional mgr, World Book Encyclopedia, 54-59; librn, Jonas Salk High Sch, Levittown, N.Y, 59-60; librn, Plainview High Sch, Plainview, N.Y, 60- Other: Instr. children's literature, Hofstra Univ; vis. prof. libr. sci, Miami Univ; pres, Nassau-Suffolk Sch. Libr. Asn. & chmn. freedom to read cmt; chmn. salary cmt, Plainview Fedn. Teachers; chmn, Long Island Intellectual Freedom Cmt.

Mem: ALA; Nassau-Suffolk Sch. Libr. Asn. Publ: NSSLA Freedom to Read Kit (compiler); Plainview Welcomes Paperbacks, Libr. J, 1/15/65; Recommended Paperback Books for the Elementary Schools (compiler), spring 66. Consult: 1) Stevenson Sch, 24 W. 74th St, New York, N.Y, reorganized libr. collection to meet govt. standards, July 47-June 48; 2) Book Fairs, Inc, 162 Atlantic Ave, Lynbrook, N.Y, consult. on book selection, processing for sch. libr, fall 64-; 3) Green Vale Sch, Glen Head, N.Y, eval. of libr. serv. & physical facilities, fall 66. Specialties: 1c; 2b, 2c, 2d (soc. sci), 2g (use of paperbacks in collection & book fairs); 3c, 3d; 5a, 5b; 6b; 7a; 8d; 9 (inserv. training through courses & workshops).

COHEN, MORRIS L, Nov. 2, 27; Law Librarian & Professor of Law, Law School, University of Pennsylvania, Philadelphia, Pa. 19104. Home: 2285 N. 51st St, Philadelphia, Pa. 19131. B.A, Univ. Chicago, 47; LL.B, Columbia Univ, 51; M.L.S, Pratt Inst, 59. Asst. law librn, law sch, Rutgers Univ, 58-59; asst. law librn, Columbia Univ, 59-61; law librn. & assoc. prof, State Univ. N.Y. Buffalo, 61-63; Biddle law librn. & prof. law, Univ. Pa, Phila, Pa, 63- Other: Lectr. libr. sci, Columbia Univ, 64-; lectr, Drexel Inst. Tech, 64- Mem: Am. Asn. Law Libr; ALA; Am. Bar Asn; Am. Soc. Info. Sci; Bibliog. Soc. Am. Publ: Legal Bibliography Briefed, Drexel Libr. Sch, 65; Legal Research in a Nutshell, West Publ, 68. Consult: 1) Phila. Bar Asn, City Hall, Phila, Pa, bldg. plans, collection & staff develop, 66-; 2) Faculty of Law, Univ. Toronto, Toronto 1, Ont, Can, bldg. program, 67; 3) Sch. Law, York Univ, Osgood Hall, Toronto 1, Ont, review of bldg. plans, 67; 4) Sch. Law, Emory Univ, Atlanta, Ga, bldg. program & plans, collection & staff develop, 67-; 5) Sch. Law, Hofstra Univ, Holland House, Hempstead, N.Y, bldg. program & plans, staff develop, 68- Specialties: 1h (law libr); 2d (law libr); 4d (automation in relation to legal bibliog); 5d (law libr).

COLE, DORIS M, Apr. 12, 05; Associate Professor, School of Library Science, Syracuse University, Syracuse, N.Y. 13210. Home: 212 Lockwood Rd, Syracuse, N.Y. 13214. A.B, 25; B.S. in L.S, 37; M.S.(educ), 41. Sch. libr. supvr, Massena, N.Y, 31-61; prof. libr. educ, State Univ. N.Y. Col. Geneseo, 57-58 & 61-62; assoc. prof, sch. libr. sci, Syracuse Univ, N.Y, 62- Other: Pres, sch. libr. sect, N.Y. Libr. Asn, 58-59, mem. coun, 59-61 & 65-67; pres. local chap, Delta Kappa Gamma, 59-61; mem. coun. ALA, 66-70; pres, N.Y. Libr. Asn, 67-68. Mem: N.Y. State Teachers Asn; N.Y. Libr. Asn; Am. Asn. Univ. Prof; ALA; Nat. Educ. Asn; Int. Reading Asn. Publ: Top of the News (ed), 61-63; The Reading of Children (ed), Syracuse Univ, 63; What Goes on Your Library Shelves? (ed), spec. suppl, The Instructor, 11/63. Consult: 1) LeRoy High Sch, LeRoy, N.Y, eval. of sch. libr-pub. libr. program, with

---

5) PERSONNEL AND RECRUITING, 5a) job evaluation and description, salary recommendations, 5b) recruitment of professionals and management personnel, 5c) administrative organization, 6) PUBLIC RELATIONS, 6a) publications, 6b) publicity programs, 6c) public opinion surveys, 6d) others, 7) SERVICES, 7a) evaluation of current program, 7b) studies of service to special publics, e.g., students, handicapped, aged, etc., 7c) programs for the implementation of new laws, program proposals to governments, 7d) others, 8) COMMUNITY, REGIONAL, STATE PLANNING, 8a) legislative programs, 8b) area analyses, 8c) centralized systems, cooperative arrangements, 8d) development of standards, 8e) state libraries and extension agencies, 8f) regional and statewide surveys, 8g) others, 9) OTHERS.

Rosemary Schiffli, Apr-May 56; 2) E. Syracuse-Minoa Pub. Schs, East Syracuse, N.Y, eval. of syst-wide sch. libr. program as part of reading program study, Jan-June 63; 3) Johnson City High Sch, Johnson City, N.Y, eval. of sch. libr. program as basis for planning a new bldg. & new program, Mar. 66; 4) Medina Pub. Schs, Medina, N.Y, eval. of libr. program & design of new sch, Nov. 66. Specialties: 1c; 2b, 2c; 5a, 5c; 6b; 7a, 7b, 7c.

COLE, GEORGIA (RANKIN), May 27, 26; Coordinator of Instructional Materials, Vigo County School Corporation, Terre Haute, Ind. 47803. Home: 216 Woodridge Dr, Terre Haute, Ind. 47803. A.B, 45; M.S.L.S, 53. Coordinator libr. serv, Dependents Schs, U.S. Air Force in Europe, 56-57; dir. div. sch. libr. & teaching materials, State Dept. Pub. Instruction, Indianapolis, Ind, 58-62; asst. prof, dept. libr. sci, Univ. Ky, 62-65; coordinator instructional materials, Vigo County Sch. Corp, Terre Haute, Ind, 66- Other: Chmn. prfnl. relations cmt, AASL, 59-62, secy. of Asn, 60-61, 2nd v.pres, 63-64; mem. intellectual freedom cmt, ALA, 66- Mem: ALA; AASL; Nat: Educ. Asn; Dept. Audiovisual Instruction; Asn. Supv. & Curriculum Develop; Ind. Libr. Asn; Ind. Sch. Librns. Asn; Ind. State Teachers Asn. Publ: Status of School Libraries at Elementary Level in Indiana, 1959-60, Ind. Dept. Pub. Instruction, 61; The Library Today, Ind. Architect, 9/61; Demonstration and the Creative Elementary School Library, Wilson Libr. Bull, 11/61; Activities of the Professional Relations Committee, Sch. Libr, 1/61; Controversial Areas in Library Materials, Bull. Nat. Asn. Sec. Sch. Principals, 1/66. Consult: 1) Mt. Vernon Schs, Mt. Vernon, Ind, consulted regarding establishment of elem. sch. libr, spring 62; 2) Elkhart City Schs, Elkhart, Ind, advised on establishing elem. sch. libr, 62; 3) Jefferson County Schs, Louisville, Ky, recommended plan for expansion of sch. libr, with Eleanor Simmons, spring 64. Specialties: 1c, 1h (cent. instructional materials centers for sch. systs); 2b, 2c; 3f (centralized cataloging & processing for sch. systs); 7a; 8c; 9 (instruction in use of libr).

COLE, MARY ELIZABETH, Aug. 4, 21; Director, Public Libraries Section, Tennessee State Library and Archives, Nashville, Tenn. 37219. B.S, Tenn. Polytechnic Inst; M.A. in L.S, George Peabody Col. Teachers. Regional librn, Blue Grass Regional Libr, Columbia, Tenn, 55-60; pub. libr. consult, Fla. State Libr, Tallahassee, 60-67. Other: Pres, Bus. & Prfnl. Women, Mt. Pleasant, Tenn, 55-56; exec. dir. Nat. Libr. Week, Tenn, 60 & Fla, 63, 64; secy, pub. libr. div, Southeast. Libr. Asn, 62-64; nat. treas. bldg. fund, Colonial Dames XVII Century, 63-65; secy, Fla. Libr. Asn, 64-65, exhibits chmn. Mem: Fla. Libr. Asn; Southeast. Libr. Asn; ALA. Publ: A Survey of Library Service in Pinellas County, Fla. State Libr, 63; A Survey of Library Service in Polk County, 65; A Survey of Library Service in Palm Beach County, 66. Consult: 1) Nat. Book Cmt, One Park Ave, New York, N.Y, survey of use of books in Community Action Programs of U.S. Office Econ. Opportunity, June 66. Specialties: 1a; 7a; 8c.

COMAN, EDWIN TRUMAN, JR, May 18, 03; University Librarian Emeritus, University of California, Riverside, Calif. 92502. Home: 5784 Bellevue Ave, La Jolla, Calif. 92037. B.A, Yale, 26; Cert. in Librarianship, Univ. Calif, 33; M.A, Claremont Univ, 34. Univ. librn, Univ. Calif, Riverside, 51-65. Other: Pres, San Francisco Bay Region chap, SLA, 49; pres, Calif. Libr. Asn, 49-50; mem. coun, ALA, 50-51; chmn. bldg. cmt, ACRL, 59-61. Mem: ALA; ACRL; Calif. Libr. Asn; SLA. Publ: The History of Business, Stanford Grad. Sch. of Bus. Bull, 3/46; Sources of Business Information, Prentice-Hall, 49; Time, Tide, and Timber (with H.M. Gibbs), Stanford Univ, 49; Review of The Beekmans of New York in Politics and Commerce 1647-1877, Am. Archivist, 7/58; Sources of Business Information, 2nd ed, Univ. Calif, Berkeley, 64; Economics, Libr. Trends, 67. Consult: 1) Calif. Baptist Col, Riverside, libr. collection, 63-65; 2) Bank of America, 100 S. Van Ness Ave, San Francisco, Calif, setting up libr. in Training Div, June 64; 3) Bank of Calif, 400 California St, San Francisco, plan for financial libr, July 65; 4) Claremont Univ, Claremont, Calif, study orgn. of Honnold Libr. and make recommendations, with Keyes D. Metcalf, Ernest C. Colwell, Andrew H. Horn & Tadashi Mayeda, Sept. 65; 5) Ore. State Libr, State Libr. Bldg, Salem, surv. of libr. resources & serv. to bus. & industry, Mar-May 66. Specialties: 1b, 1d, 1e, 1f, 1g; 2d (bus. & econ); 5a; 7a; 8b.

CONNOLLY, BRENDAN, S.J, Feb. 10, 13; Director of Libraries, Boston College, Chestnut Hill, Mass. 02167. B.A, 37; M.A, 38; S.T.L, 44; B.S.L.S, 46; Ph.D, 55. Librn, Weston Col, Mass, 51-59; dir. libr, Boston Col, Chestnut Hill, Mass, 59- Mem: Cath. Libr. Asn; ALA. Publ: Jesuit Library Beginnings, Libr. Quart, 60; The Catholic Library World: A Report and a Projected Discussion, Cath. Libr. World, 4/61. Consult: 1) W. Baden Col, West Baden, Ind, anal. of tech. processes, eval. & weeding for transfer to different site, Oct. 63; 2) Oblate Seminaries, Newburgh, N.Y. & Wash, D.C, gen. advice preparatory to accreditation, with Philip J. McNiff, Nov. 64; 3) Col. Holy Cross, Worcester, Mass, anal. of staff, bldg, budget & future growth, with Philip J. McNiff, Sept. 64-Nov. 65; 4) Ateneo de Manila Univ, Quezon City, Philippines, recommendations for unification of libr. staff, serv. & material, May 66; 5) Southeast. Mass. Tech. Inst, Dartmouth, advice to pres. on libr. bldg. plans, with Philip J. McNiff, 66- Specialties: 1b, 1c, 1g; 2a, 2d (English, theol, reference); 3b, 3c, 3d; 5a, 5c; 6c; 7a, 7b.

KEY TO CONSULTING SPECIALTIES: 1) ARCHITECTURE AND BUILDINGS, 1a) public libraries, 1b) academic libraries, 1c) school libraries, 1d) special libraries, 1e) library interiors, 1f) furnishings, 1g) site and location, 1h) other architectural; 2) COLLECTIONS: SELECTION, EVALUATION, WEEDING, 2a) adults, 2b) young adults, 2c) children, 2d) subject specialty, 2e) O.P. searches, 2f) rare books, 2g) appraisals, 2h) others; 3) TECHNICAL PROCESSES, 3a) cataloging, 3b) classification systems, 3c) acquisitions, 3d) materials processing, 3e) work flow and cost studies, 3f) others, 4) AUTOMATION, 4a) applications of data processing equipment, 4b) information storage and retrieval systems, 4c) systems analysis, 4d) others

COOLIDGE, COIT, Apr. 27, 06; Library Consultant, 965 35th St, Richmond, Calif. 94805. B.A, Stanford Univ, 28; M.L.S, Columbia Univ, 29; M.A, Univ. Calif, 34. City librn, Richmond, Calif, 40-66. Other: Pres, Calif. Libr. Asn, 45, chmn, cmt. to explore state aid for pub. libr, 49, chmn, libr. bldgs. cmt, 64; mem. adv. coun, Sch. Librarianship, Univ. Calif, Berkeley, 56-57; mem, state adv. cmt. on correctional libr, 60-62; elder, Presbyterian Church. Mem: ALA. Calif. Libr. Asn. Publ: Traveling Branch, Wilson Libr. Bull, 4/49; New California Library Reflects Community's Nature, Libr. J, 5/1/50; Service Relationships and Work Flow—The Small and Medium Sized Library, News Notes of Calif. Libr, 7/57; Dynamic Librarianship, Calif. Libm, 10/57; San Leandro's Community Library Center, Calif. Librn, 1/58; How Do We Measure Up? A Quick Look at the Public Library Needs for the San Francisco Bay Area and a Forecast for the Future, News Notes of Calif. Libr, summer 62. Consult: 1) San Leandro Community Libr, 300 Estudillo, San Leandro, Calif, wrote program for architect, recommended site chosen, estimated cost of oper, 56-57; 2) Great Falls Pub. Libr, Great Falls, Mont, wrote program for architect, advised on interior arrangements, with Mrs. Nancy P. Coolidge, 58-67; 3) Klamath Falls Pub. Libr. & Klamath County Libr, Klamath Falls, Ore, survey of city & county libr, with recommendations, with Mrs. Nancy P. Coolidge, July 62; 4) Livermore Pub. Libr, Livermore, Calif, wrote program for architects, with Mrs. Nancy P. Coolidge & Ratcliff, Slama, & Cadwallader, 64-65; 5) San Luis Obispo County Free Libr. & San Luis Obispo Pub. Libr, San Luis Obispo, Calif, libr. serv. plan for San Luis Obispo County with recommendations, with Mrs. Nancy P. Coolidge, 68. Specialties: 1a, 1e, 1f, 1g, 1h (how much to plan in relation to the community need); 8b, 8c, 8d, 8f.

COVEY, DR. ALAN DALE, Feb. 3, 17; University Librarian, Arizona State University Library, Tempe, Ariz. 85281. Home: 308 Loma Vista Dr, Tempe, Ariz. 85281. A.B, Univ. Calif, Berkeley, 40, Teaching Cert, 41, Cert. in Librarianship, 46; Ed.D, Stanford Univ, 55. Librn, Sacramento State Col, Calif, 52-62; univ. librn, Ariz. State Univ, Tempe, 62- Other: Pres, Calif. Libr. Asn, 60; chmn, Calif. State Col. Librns, Coun, 60-61; mem, adv. cmt. to Univ. Calif. Libr. Schs, 60-61; pres. univs. & cols. div, Ariz. State Libr. Asn, 65-66, chmn. conf. cmt, 66-67. Mem: Calif. Libr. Asn; Ariz. State Libr. Asn; ALA. Publ: From Program to Preliminary Planning, News Notes of Calif. Libr, 7/57; A Fine Contagion (ed. with Armine D. Mackenzie); Evaluation of College Libraries for Accreditation Purposes, Stanford Univ, 58; Fine Printing in California (ed), Calif. Libr. Asn, 60; Operation Libmation, Ariz. Librn, 22: 9-10; Library Survey Report Navajo Community College, Ariz. State Univ, 66. Consult: 1) Mesa Jr. Col, Mesa, Ariz, planning of new libr. bldg, Nov. 65-Apr. 66. Specialties: 1b, 1e, 1g; 3a, 3b, 3c, 3e, 3f (recataloging); 4a; 5b, 5c.

CRANFORD, THEODORE NELSON, May 9, 30; Library Research Analyst, Space & Information Systems Division, D/41-096, AJ01, North American Aviation, Inc, 12214 Lakewood Blvd, Downey, Calif. 90241. Home: 11931 Lakewood Blvd, Apt. 8, Downey, Calif. 90241. A.B, Univ. Wash, Seattle, 52, M.A.(librarianship), 53. Librn, Nat. Adv. Cmt. for Aeronautics, 54-57; tech. info. librn, Univ. Calif. Lawrence Radiation Lab, 57-62; libr. res. analyst, N. Am. Aviation, Inc, Downey, Calif, 62- Other: Mem. thesaurus cmt, SLA, 64; charter mem. spec. interest group in educ. for info sci, Am. Document. Inst. Mem: SLA; Am. Document. Inst. Publ: ERIC Guidelines for Abstracting and Indexing, SID66-991, N. Am. Aviation, Inc, 12/62; Training of Indexers for Consistency in a Technical Information Processing System, SLA Bull, spring 65. Consult: 1) U.S. Office Educ, 400 Maryland Ave, Wash, D.C, developed syst. for educ. res. info. center, bureau of res, with Judith Corin & William E. Nelson, May 66- Specialties: 3a, 3b, 3d, 3e, 3f (abstracting); 4a, 4b, 4c, 4d (educ. for info. sci).

CRAWFORD, HELEN, July 19, 06; Librarian & Associate Professor, University of Wisconsin Medical Library, Madison, Wis. 53706. Home: 1305 Chandler, Madison, Wis. 53715. B.A, Univ. N.Dak, 28; B.S.L.S, Simmons Col, 31. Librn. & assoc. prof. Univ. Wis. Med. Libr, Madison, 45- Other: Chmn. extension cmt, Med. Libr. Asn, 50-51, mem. by-laws cmt, 56-60, mem. med. sch. libr. group, 58, chmn. Midwest regional group, 58-59, mem. exec. bd, 60-63, mem. cert. cmt, 65-; secy, Univ. Wis. chap, Phi Beta Kappa, 53-61; recipient, Wis. State Med. Soc. Pres. Citation, 62. Mem: ALA; Med. Libr. Asn; Wis. Libr. Asn. Publ: Medical Library Extension Service, Bull. Med. Libr. Asn, 1/49; Planning a Better Medical School Library: Panel Discussion, Bull. Med. Libr. Asn, 4/61; The Pursuit of Flexibility, In: Problems in Planning Library Facilities, Proc. Libr. Bldgs. Inst, 63; Regional Plans for Medical Library Service: Proposal for an Expanded Medical Library Extension Service for Wisconsin, Bull. Med. Libr. Asn, 7/64; Centralization vs. Decentralization in Medical School Libraries, Bull. Med. Libr. Asn, 7/66; Preservation, In: Handbook of Medical Library Practice, 3rd ed. Consult: 1) Veterans Admin. Hosp, Madison, Wis, survey of libr, 55. Specialties: 1d; 2d (med), 2f; 3c; 8b.

CRAWFORD, PAUL RUSSELL, June 16, 19; Director, Ventura County Schools Library Services, Courthouse, Ventura, Calif. 93001. Home: 145 Stadium Ave, Ventura, Calif. 93003. B.A, 42; M.A, 49; B.L.S, 52. Asst. librn, Ventura Col, 54-61; dir, Ventura County Schs.

---

5) PERSONNEL AND RECRUITING, 5a) job evaluation and description, salary recommendations, 5b) recruitment of professionals and management personnel, 5c) administrative organization, 6) PUBLIC RELATIONS, 6a) publications, 6b) publicity programs, 6c) public opinion surveys, 6d) others, 7) SERVICES, 7a) evaluation of current program, 7b) studies of service to special publics, e.g., students, handicapped, aged, etc., 7c) programs for the implementation of new laws, program proposals to governments, 7d) others, 8) COMMUNITY, REGIONAL, STATE PLANNING, 8a) legislative programs, 8b) area analyses, 8c) centralized systems, cooperative arrangements, 8d) development of standards, 8e) state libraries and extension agencies, 8f) regional and statewide surveys, 8g) others, 9) OTHERS.

Libr. Serv, Ventura, Calif, 61- Other: Calif. state chmn, County Schs. Libr. Serv. Cmt, 63-67. ALA; Calif. Asn. Sch. Librns; Calif. Libr. Asn; Phi Alpha Theta. Consult: 1) Bureau Audio-Visual & Sch. Libr. Educ, Calif. State Dept. Educ, advised on and read fed. ESEA Title II projects, Nov. 66; 2) Santa Barbara County Sch. Dist, 4400 Cathedral Oaks Rd, Santa Barbara, Calif, advised local sch. dist. officers on proper procedures in preparing ESEA Title II projects, with Mrs. Lucile Gregor, Oct. 67; 3) San Luis Obispo County Sch. Dist, 2156 Sierra Way, San Luis Obispo, Calif, advised local sch. dist. officers on proper procedures in preparing ESEA Title II projects, with Mrs. Lucille Gregor, Oct. 67. Specialties: 1c; 2b, 2c, 2d (hist); 8d, 8f; 9 (intellectual freedom).

CRONIN, JOHN WILLIAM, Feb. 10, 05. Home: 2129 - 32nd Place, S.E, Washington, D.C. 20020. A.B.(govt), Bowdoin Col, 25; LL.B, Georgetown Law Sch, 29. Dir, Processing Dept, Libr. Congress, 52-68. Other: Recipient, Margaret Mann Citation, 61, Melvil Dewey Award, 64 & Libr. Congress Distinguished Serv. Award, 65. Mem: ALA; Bibliog. Soc. Am; Cath. Libr. Asn; D.C. Libr. Asn. Publ: Contrib. to prfnl. journals. Consult: 1) New York Pub. Libr, Fifth Ave. & 42nd St, New York, N.Y, consult. on future of card catalog of New York Pub. Libr. Specialties: 3a, 3b, 3c, 3d, 3e.

CURLEY, WALTER W, Mar. 29, 23; Director of Information Systems, Arthur D. Little, Inc, 20 Acorn Park, Cambridge, Mass. 02140. Home: 270 Pelham Island Rd, Wayland, Mass. 01778. B.S.(bus. admin), Northeast. Univ, 47; M.S.L.S, Simmons Col, 50. Reference librn, Providence Pub. Libr, Providence, R.I, 50-55, bus. mgr, 55-59, asst. dir, 59-61; dir, Suffolk Libr. Syst, Belport, N.Y, 61-68. Other: Pres, R.I. Libr. Asn, 55-57; pres, New Eng. Libr. Asn, 58; chmn, Libr. Develop. Cmt, New York, 64-66; mem. Gov. Cmt, N.Y, 66. Mem: ALA. Publ: Occasional Paper, Univ. Ill, 65; contrib. to, Sch. Libr. J. & Libr. J. Consult: 1) Sachem Pub. Libr, Sachem, N.Y, bldg. consult, 65; 2) Mich. State Libr, Lansing, syst. consult, surveyed jr. cols, with Nelson Assocs, 65. Specialties: 1a; 3d, 3e; 4a, 4c.

CURRIE, DOROTHY H, Supervisor of School Libraries & Audiovisual Instructional Materials, Board of Education, 138 S. Broadway, Yonkers, N.Y. 10701. B.A, 32; B.S, 42; M.S, 52. Other: Consult. for ESEA Title II, bur. sch. libr, N.Y. State Dept. Educ, 65- Mem: N.Y. Libr. Asn; Westchester County Sch. Libr. Asn. Publ: Making Dioramas and Displays, Owen, 62; Let's Learn about Language Labs, N.Y. State Dept. Educ, 62; Selected Reading on Programed Learning (Bibliography), N.Y. State Dept. Educ, 63; How to Organize a Children's Library, Oceana, 65. Consult: 1) N.Y. State Dept. Educ, Albany, workshop for non-pub. sch. staffs at St. John's Univ, spring 66; 2) N.Y. State Dept, Educ, implementing audiovisual and nonbook materials collections of Title II programs, spring 66; 3) Encyclopaedia Britannica, Inc, Chicago, Ill, consult. on educ. serv. of bus, Apr. 64. Specialties: 1c, 1e, 1f; 2b, 2c; 9 (city-wide sch. libr. orgn. & admin, nonbook materials—eval, selection, orgn, utilization).

D

DAILY, DR. JAY ELWOOD, June 17, 23; Professor of Library Science, Graduate School of Library and Information Sciences, University of Pittsburgh, Pittsburgh, Pa. 15213. Home: 709 S. Negley, Pittsburgh, Pa. 15232. B.A, N.Y. Univ, 51; M.S, Columbia Univ, 52; D.L.S, 57. Consult. librn, Office of Prime Minister, Rangoon, Burma, 57-59; adv. librn, Univ. Mandalay, Burma, 59-62; libr. consult, Franklin Book Programs, New York, N.Y, 62-65; asst. dir, Univ. Pittsburgh Libr; mem. ed. bd, Encyclopedia of Library and Information Science, 68- Mem: ALA; Pa. Libr. Asn; SLA; Am. Asn. Univ. Prof; Columbia Sch. Libr. Serv. Alumni Asn. Publ: Notation for Subject Retrieval Files, Am. Document, 7/56; Subject Headings and the Theory of Classification, Am. Document, 10/57; Search for Sample Books, Wilson Libr. Bull, 9/64; Oil for the Lamps of Knowledge, Libr. J, 11/15/64; Automation and Authority versus Autonomy, Libr. J, 10/15/67. Consult: 1) Coun. for Financial Aid to Educ, New York, N.Y, organized spec. libr, Dec. 53-May 57; 2) Ford Found, Rangoon, Burma, organized Univ. Mandalay Libr. Syst, including Main Libr, Med. Libr, Agr. Libr, Intermediate Col. Libr, AV Libr, July 59-Aug. 62; 3) Ford Found, Rangoon, organized libr. of the Inst. of Pub. Admin, May 57-July 59; 4) Ford Found, 477 Madison Ave, New York, survey of acad. libr. of Argentina & Chile, Aug-Oct. 63; 5) Univ. Pittsburgh-Agency Int. Develop, mem. of book survey team for Peru, with Seth Spaulding, Oct-Nov. 66. Specialties: 2d (language & literature): French, Italian, Spanish, Latin, English); 3a, 3b, 3c, 3d, 3e, 3f (preparation for automation); 4b, 4c, 4d (personnel training); 5c; 9 (design of subject heading lists, orgn. of spec. libr).

DALTON, JACK, 1908; Dean, School of Library Service, Columbia University, New York, N.Y. 10027. Home: 445 Riverside Dr, New York, N.Y. 10027. B.S, 30; M.S, 35. Dir, int. relations office, ALA, 57-59; dean, sch. libr. serv, Columbia Univ, 59- Mem: ALA; N.Y. Libr. Asn; Bibliog. Soc. Am; Bibliog. Soc, London. Consult: 1) Ford Found, New York, N.Y, consult. on role of Found. in libr. field & spec. projects, 60-; 2) Rockefeller Found, New York, consult. on role of Found. in libr. field & spec. projects, 60-; 3) Villanova Univ, Villanova, Pa, program in libr. educ, current; 4) Dalhousie Univ, Halifax, N.S, Can, program in

---

KEY TO CONSULTING SPECIALTIES: 1) ARCHITECTURE AND BUILDINGS, 1a) public libraries, 1b) academic libraries, 1c) school libraries, 1d) special libraries, 1e) library interiors, 1f) furnishings, 1g) site and location, 1h) other architectural; 2) COLLECTIONS: SELECTION, EVALUATION, WEEDING, 2a) adults, 2b) young adults, 2c) children, 2d) subject specialty, 2e) O.P. searches, 2f) rare books, 2g) appraisals, 2h) others; 3) TECHNICAL PROCESSES, 3a) cataloging, 3b) classification systems, 3c) acquisitions, 3d) materials processing, 3e) work flow and cost studies, 3f) others, 4) AUTOMATION, 4a) applications of data processing equipment, 4b) information storage and retrieval systems, 4c) systems analysis, 4d) others

libr. ed, current; 5) Univ. S.C, Columbia, program in libr. ed, current. Specialties: 9 (libr. schs. & libr. ed. programs).

DANTON, DR. J. PERIAM, July 5, 08; Professor of Librarianship, School of Librarianship, University of California, Berkeley, Calif. 94720. Home: 700 Grizzly Peak Blvd, Berkeley, Calif. 94708. B.A, 28; B.S, 29; M.A, 30; Ph.D, 35. Dean, Sch. Librarianship & prof. librarianship, Univ. Calif, Berkeley, 46-61, prof, 61- Other: Pres, Asn. Am. Libr. Schs, 49-50; Fulbright res. scholar, Germany, 60-61, Austria, 64-65; dir, U.S. Dept. State-ALA Multi-Area Group Librn. Program, 63-64. Mem: ALA; Asn. Am. Libr. Schs; ACRL; Bibliog. Soc. Am; Calif. Libr. Asn. Publ: Education for Librarianship: Criticisms, Dilemmas and Proposals, Columbia Univ. Sch. Libr. Serv, 46; Education for Librarianship (also French, Spanish & Arabic eds), UNESCO Pub. Libr. Manuals No. 1, 49; United States Influence on Norwegian Librarianship, 1890-1940, Univ. Calif, Berkeley, 57; The Climate of Book Selection: Social Influences on School and Public Libraries (ed), Univ. Calif. Sch. Librarianship, 59; New and Continuing Problems in an Expanding University (ed), Univ. Calif, 62; Book Selection and Collections: A Comparison of German and American University Libraries, Columbia Univ, 63. Consult: 1) San Francisco Theol. Seminary Libr, San Anselmo, Calif, space, bldg. & personnel, 59-60; 2) U.S. Dept. State, libr. expert, Ethiopia, summer 61; 3) Veterans Admin, San Francisco, Calif, libr. consult. on Veterans Admin. libr. in 11 states of Western area, 61-64; 4) Ford Found, 477 Madison Ave, New York, N.Y, nat. & univ. libr. in Southeast Asia, with R.C. Swank, summer 63; 5) UNESCO, libr. consult, Jamaica, summer 68. Specialties: 1b, 1g; 2g, 2h (acad. libr); 3c; 5a, 5b, 5c; 7a.

DARLING, LOUISE, Aug. 3, 11; Biomedical Librarian, University of California, Los Angeles, Calif. 90024. Home: 197 Beloit, Los Angeles, Calif. 90049. A.B, 33; M.A, 35; cert. librarianship, 36; spec. sec. credential, 40. Other: Mem. coun, Am. Asn. Hist. Med, 61-64; mem. bd. dirs, Med. Libr. Asn, 61-65, v.pres, 62-63, pres, 63-64. Mem: Med. Libr. Asn; Am. Asn. Hist. Med; ALA; Calif. Libr. Asn; Med. Libr. Group; SLA. Publ: Russian Contributions to an Understanding of the Central Nervous System and Behavior—A Pictorial Survey (with H.W. Magoun & Mary A.B. Brazier), In: Transactions of the First Conference on Central Nervous System and Behavior, 1958, Josiah Macy, Jr. Found, 59; Evolution of Man's Brain (with H.W. Magoun & Jack Prost), In: Transactions of the Third Conference on the Central Nervous System and Behavior, 1960, Josiah Macy, Jr. Found, 60; Reader's Impressions of the Subject Catalog (Subject Control of Medical Literature: A Symposium), Bull. Med. Libr. Asn, 1/61; Development of Training Programs in American Medical Libraries, Bull. Med. Libr. Asn, 7/63; Centralizing Medical Library Resources, Libri, 3: 258-267; MEDLARS Regional Center at UCLA, Bull. Med. Libr. Asn, 10/66. Consult: 1) Facultad de Ciencias Medicas, Univ. Nacional Honduras, Tegucigalpa, recommendations for Biblioteca Medica Nacional, July-Oct. 62; 2) U.S. Pub. Health Serv. Cmt. Sci. Publ, publ. consult, Dec. 62-June 65; 3) Univ. Hawaii, Honolulu, planned libr. facilities for biomed. sci. program, Dec. 63. Specialties: 1d; 2d (med, biology); 7a.

DAUME, MRS. MARY ROSSITER, July 10, 13; Director, Monroe County Library System, 102 E. Grove St, Monroe, Mich. 48161. Instructor in Library Science, Wayne State University, Detroit, Mich. 48202. A.B, Col. Wooster, 34; B.S. in L.S, West. Reserve Univ, 35. Dir, Monroe County Libr, Monroe, Mich, 47-62; dir, Monroe County Libr. Syst, 63-; instructor libr. sci, Wayne State Univ, Detroit, Mich, 66- Other: Chmn. Dist. II, Mich. Libr. Asn, 51, legis. chmn, 55-56, chmn, county & regional sect, 56, mem, membership cmt. & pub. relations cmt, 64-65; legis. chmn, Mich. Asn. Sch. Libr, 60-62; secy. A.V. round table, ALA, 54-56, mem. coun, 56-57, chmn. exhibits round table, 57-60 & 66-69; mem, Mich. State Bd. for Libr, 60-65, chmn, 64-65; Mich. membership chmn, ALTA, 63-, mem, Nat. Libr. Week cmt, 66-68. Mem: ALA; Mich. Libr. Asn; Mich. Asn. Sch. Libr; AASL; ALTA. Publ: Library Cooperation in Port Huron and the St. Clair County Area with Recommendations for Immediate Action and for Long Range Planning. Consult: 1) Jackson Jr. Chamber of Commerce, c/o Mrs. J.E. Blanchard, 2285 Maple Dr, Jackson, Mich, merger of city & county libr. & suggested methods of financial support, June 63; 2) Genesee County Libr. Bd, c/o Dr. Dorothea Wyatt, 224 E. Court St, Flint, Mich, problems of growth, demonstration of methods used in Monroe County, July 63; 3) Port Huron Pub. Schs, Port Huron, Mich, advisability of using data processing for cent. book & instructional materials catalog, June-July 64; 4) City of Port Huron & County of St. Clair, Auditor's Office, City-County Bldg, Port Huron, survey of libr. facilities with recommendations, Feb. 64-Mar. 65; 5) St. Mary Acad. Libr, Monroe, Mich, aid in preparation of application for Knapp funds & advice on layout, furniture, carpeting, Nov-Dec. 65. Specialties: 1a, 1c, 1e, 1f, 1g, 1h (instructional materials centers); 2d (local hist), 2g, 2h (phonograph records); 3c, 3d, 3e; 4c, 4d (keysort, etc); 5a, 5c, 5d (personnel relationships); 6d (libr-community relationships); 7a, 7b, 7c, 7d (sch-pub. libr. cooperation in serv); 8b, 8c, 8d, 8f, 8g (sch-pub. libr. cooperation in serv).

DAVIDSON, DR. DONALD C, Dec. 11, 11: University Librarian & Lecturer in History, University of California, Santa Barbara, Calif. 93106. Home: 3685 La Entrada, Santa Barbara, Calif. 93105. B.A, 33; M.A, 34; Ph.D, 37; cert.

5) PERSONNEL AND RECRUITING, 5a) job evaluation and description, salary recommendations, 5b) recruitment of professionals and management personnel, 5c) administrative organization, 6) PUBLIC RELATIONS, 6a) publications, 6b) publicity programs, 6c) public opinion surveys, 6d) others, 7) SERVICES, 7a) evaluation of current program, 7b) studies of service to special publics, e.g., students, handicapped, aged, etc., 7c) programs for the implementation of new laws, program proposals to governments, 7d) others, 8) COMMUNITY, REGIONAL, STATE PLANNING, 8a) legislative programs, 8b) area analyses, 8c) centralized systems, cooperative arrangements, 8d) development of standards, 8e) state libraries and extension agencies, 8f) regional and statewide surveys, 8g) others, 9) OTHERS.

librarianship, 41. Univ. librarian & lectr. hist, Univ. Calif, Santa Barbara, Calif, 47-, acting dean divs. applied arts & lib. arts, 56-59. Other: Mem. coun, ALA, 63-67, chmn-elect, bldgs. & equipment sect, 65-66; chmn. cmt. bldgs, Calif. Libr. Asn, 65-66; Fulbright visiting sr. res. fel, postgrad. sch. librarianship, Univ. Sheffield, 66-67. Mem: ALA; Calif. Libr. Asn. Publ: Relations of Hudson's Bay Company with the Russian American Company on the Northwest Coast, 1829-1867, B.C. Hist. Quart, 10/41; The Alaskan-Canadian Boundary, In: Greater America: Essays in Honor of Herbert Eugene Bolton, Univ. Calif, 45; Proceedings, 1953 Building Plans Institute (ed), ACRL Monograph 10, 53; Six College Libraries (report to Fund Advancement Educ), 64. Consult: 1) Calif. Acad. Sci, San Francisco, Calif, admin. anal, program writing, bldg. plan criticism, with Edwin T. Coman, Jr, 55-57; 2) Fund Advancement Educ, N.Y, gen. consult. to six south. Calif. cols, 63-64; 3) Univ. Alaska, College, Alaska, bldg. plans, 64-; 4) Univ. Calif, Davis, Calif, program eval, with Paul Miles, 65. Specialties: 1b; 9 (comprehensive surveys).

DAVIES, RUTH A, June 28, 15; Lecturer, Graduate School of Library Science, University of Pittsburgh, Pittsburgh, Pa. 15213. Home: 156 McIntyre Rd, Pittsburgh, Pa. 15237. B.A, 39; M.Litt, 40; B.S.L.S, 41. Mem. faculty, grad. sch. libr. sci, Carnegie Inst. Tech, 48-60; coordinator sch. libr, North Hills Sch. Dist, Pittsburgh, Pa, 50-66; lectr, grad. sch. libr. sci, Univ. Pittsburgh, Pittsburgh, 60- Other: Standards implementation chmn. for Pa, ALA, 60-63; mem. legis. cmt, AASL, 63-67; mem. exec. coun, Pa. Libr. Asn, 64-65; outstanding serv. to educ. citation, Pa. Dept. Pub. Instruction. Mem: ALA; Nat. Educ. Asn; Pa. Libr. Asn; Pa. State Educ. Asn; Dept. Audiovisual Instruction. Publ: Enrichment Reading Experiences, The Instructor, 11/61; Planning Together in the Instructional Materials Center, ALA Bull, 2/63; The School Library—First National Bank of Communication, Visucom, spring 63; The Elementary Teacher and the Instructional Materials Coordinator Plan Together, In: The School Library Materials Center, Univ. Ill, 64; The Use of Primary Sources in the Teaching of American History, Pa. Dept. Pub. Instruction Curriculum Bull, 66. Consult: 1) Shaker Heights Sch. Dist, Shaker Heights, Ohio, evaluated the study skill experimental libr. program, fall 64; 2) Pa. Dept. Pub. Instruction, mem. state eval. team for teacher educ, 65-66. Specialties: 1c; 2b, 2c, 2d (sch. libr. collections); 7a, 8d; 9 (sch. eval—includes all phases of the educ. & sch. libr. program).

DAVIS, CHARLOTTE (DOYLE), June 22, 08; Coordinator of Library Services, Santa Barbara County Schools Educational Service Center, 4400 Cathedral Oaks Rd, Santa Barbara, Calif. 93105. Home: 5595 W. Camino Cielo, Santa Barbara, Calif. 93105. B.A, Bradley Univ, 31; M.L.S, Univ. South. Calif, 50. Coordinator libr. serv, Santa Barbara County Schs, Santa Barbara, Calif, 50- Other: Mem. legis. cmt, Calif. Asn. Sch. Librns, co-chmn. filmstrip on elem. libr, state chmn, instructional materials cmt, 66; mem. elem. cmt, AASL; AASL rep, reading cmt, Nat. Coun. Teachers English. Mem: Calif. Asn. Sch. Librns; Calif. Libr. Asn; South Calif. Coun. Children's Literature. Publ: Contrib, National Educational Association Department of Elementary School Principals 35th Yearbook, Wash, 56; California School Supervisor's Association Harbors of California (co-auth), Melmont, 57; Administrative Leadership and the High School Library, Calif. J. Sec. Educ, 5/60; Issue on School Libraries (co-auth), Calif. J. Elem. Educ, 8/60. Consult: 1) Lucia Mar Unified Sch. Dist, Pismo Beach, Calif. overview & anal. of existing libr. or lack of libr. provisions in eight dist, spring 66. Specialties: 1c, 1e, 1f, 1g; 2b, 2c, 2d (children's literature); 3c; 4d (automated equipment); 5a, 5b, 5c; 7a, 7b, 7c; 8f; 9 (working with teachers & librns. on the libr. program & creative use of the sch. libr).

DAWSON, DR. JOHN M, July 4, 17; Director of Libraries, University of Delaware Library, Newark, Del. 19711. Home: 2 Bent Lane, Newark, Del. 19711. B.A, Tulane Univ, 40; B.S.L.S, La. State Univ, 41; Ph.D, Univ. Chicago, 56. Asst. dir, Univ. Chicago Libr, 48-58; dir. libr, Univ. Del, Newark, Del, 58- Other: Mem. equipment cmt, ALA, 55-56, mem. bd. on bookbinding, 56-58, mem. catalog code revision cmt, 56-60, chmn. heads of tech. serv. large univ. & res. libr, 57-58, mem. coun, 58-69, chmn. personnel sect, 63-64, mem. exec. bd, 65-69; mem. cmt. cooperative & centralized cataloging, Asn. Res. Libr, 57-59, mem. cmt. econ. impact of catalog code revision, 61-63; mem. exec. bd, RTSD, 58-62; pres, Del. Libr. Asn, 64-65; chmn. univ. libr. sect, ACRL, 66-67. Mem: ALA; ACRL; Del. Libr. Asn; Beta Phi Mu. Publ: Xerography in Card Reproduction, Col. & Res. Libr, 25: 57-60; The Acquisitions and Cataloging of Research Libraries, Libr. Quart, 27: 1-22; Departmental Interrelationships, Libr. Resources & Tech. Serv. 1: 154-158; A Brief History of the Technical Services in Libraries, Libr. Resources & Tech. Serv, 6: 197-204; Not Too Academic, Col. & Res. Libr, 27: 37-39. Consult: 1) Tulane Univ, New Orleans, La, gen. survey of libr. for selection of new librn, 59; 2) Washington & Lee Univ, Lexington, Va, confidential survey of libr, 61; 3) Del. Libr. Asn, survey of pub. libr. in Del, 62; 4) Howell Lewis Shay & Assocs, Packard Bldg, Phila, Pa, planning for libr. bldg. for three acad. libr, 63-65; 5) Asn. Res. Libr, 1755 Massachusetts Ave. N.W, Wash, D.C, res. project concerning feasibility of

---

KEY TO CONSULTING SPECIALTIES: 1) ARCHITECTURE AND BUILDINGS, 1a) public libraries, 1b) academic libraries, 1c) school libraries, 1d) special libraries, 1e) library interiors, 1f) furnishings, 1g) site and location, 1h) other architectural; 2) COLLECTIONS: SELECTION, EVALUATION, WEEDING, 2a) adults, 2b) young adults, 2c) children, 2d) subject specialty, 2e) O.P. searches, 2f) rare books, 2g) appraisals, 2h) others; 3) TECHNICAL PROCESSES, 3a) cataloging, 3b) classification systems, 3c) acquisitions, 3d) materials processing, 3e) work flow and cost studies, 3f) others, 4) AUTOMATION, 4a) applications of data processing equipment, 4b) information storage and retrieval systems, 4c) systems analysis, 4d) others

centralized cataloging, 64-66. Specialties: 1b, 1g; 3b, 3c, 3f (implementing conversion from Dewey to Libr. Congress—reclassification); 8f.

DEAHL, THOMAS F, Feb. 17, 30; Member of Technical Staff (Systems Analyst), Auerbach Information Inc, 121 N. Broad St, Philadelphia, Pa. 19107. Home: 815 Carpenter Lane, Philadelphia, Pa. 19119. B.A, 57. Teaching asst, Univ. Minn, 58-59; curator pub. commun, Minn. Hist. Soc, 60-66; mem. tech. staff, Auerbach Corp, Phila, Pa, 66– Other: V.pres. & pres-elect, Minn. chap, SLA, 66, mem. res. cmt, SLA, 66-; mem. planning cmt, Fourth Annual Nat. Colloquim on Info. Retrieval, 66-67; chmn, Nat. Microfilm Asn. Seminar, Indexing Disciplines for Microfilm Info. Syst, 67; managing ed, Auerbach Graphic Processing Reports. Mem: Am. Soc. Info. Sci; Nat. Microfilm Asn; Am. Sociol. Asn; Soc. Gen. Syst. Res; hon. mem, Minn. Newspaper Asn. Consult: 1) St. Paul Pub. Libr, St. Paul, Minn, design of newspaper indexing & article retrieval syst, 66; 2) N. St. Paul-Maplewood Schs, North St. Paul, Minn, project for improved storage & retrieval of instructional material by microfilm, 66. Specialties: 1h (microfilm lab. layout); 2d (mass media—newspapers, radio, TV), 2h (newspapers, radio, TV collections); 3f (archival microfilming, tech); 4a, 4b, 4c; 5b, 5c; 6c.

DEALE, H(ENRY) VAIL, May 14, 15; Director of Libraries & Chairman, Department of Library Science, Beloit College, Beloit, Wis. 53511. Home: 1427 Chapin St, Beloit, Wis. 53511. B.A, DePauw Univ, 36; M.L.S, Univ. Ill, 37; M.A, Drake Univ, 50. Dir. libr, Beloit Col, Beloit, Wis, 53- Other: Chmn, Midwest Acad. Librns. Conf, 57-59; pres, Wis. Libr. Asn, 60-61; chmn col. sect, ACRL, 64-65, chmn. grants cmt, 68-70; Wis. dir, Nat. Libr. Week; city chmn, Brotherhood Week & UN Citizens Cmt. Mem: ALA; Wis. Libr. Asn; Am. Asn. Univ. Prof. Publ: Marshall Plan Bibliography, 48; Public Relations of Academic Libraries, Libr. Trends, 10/58; Ten Years of MALC, Col. & Res. Libr, 65; Trends in College Libraries issue (ed), Libr. Trends, 7/69; contrib. to Libr. J, Wilson Libr. Bull, ALA Bull, Wis. Libr. Bull. & Col. & Res. Libr. Consult: 1) Milton Col, Milton, Wis, survey preliminary to accreditation, 58; 2) Tougaloo Col, Tougaloo, Miss, bldg. plans, Jan. 67; 3) Mt. St. Paul Col, Waukesha, Wis, survey for accreditation, Apr. 68. Specialties: 1b; 5c; 6a.

DEES, MARGARET (NYHUS), Mar. 5, 17; Coordinator of Libraries, Urbana Community Schools, 101 N. McCullough St, Urbana, Ill, 61801. Home: 2016 Boudreau Dr, Urbana, Ill. 61801. B.S, Univ. Ill, 39, M.A.(elem. educ), 49, M.S. (libr. sci), 57. Librn, Champaign Sr. High Sch, Champaign, Ill, 57-58; coordinator of libr, Urbana Community Schs, Urbana, Ill, 58- Other: Pres, Urbana Educ. Asn, 63-64; pres, Champaign County Asn. for Childhood Educ, 64-65; pres, Ill. Asn. Sch. Librna, 67-68; mem, ALA Recruitment Network & Ill. Libr. Develop. Cmt. Mem: ALA; AASL; Ill. Asn. Sch. Librns; Kappa Delta Pi; Beta Phi Mu; Delta Kappa Gamma. Publ: How Elementary School Teachers and Librarians Cooperate in Instruction (with Mary Lathrope), Ill. State Libr, 4/66; A Librarian Talks with the Elementary Principal, Ill. Elem. Principal, 5/66. Consult: 1) Office of Supt. of Pub. Instruction, Springfield, Ill, libr. consult. for ESEA Title II, with James A. Boula, Dec. 65-Aug. 66. Specialties: 1c; 2b, 2c; 3a, 3d; 5b; 7a, 7c, 7d (elem. sch. libr. programs); 8a, 8c.

DE GENNARO, RICHARD, Mar. 2, 26; Associate University Librarian for Systems Development, Harvard University Library, Cambridge, Mass. 02138. Home: 16 Bates Rd, Lexington, Mass. 02173. B.A, Wesleyan Univ, 51, M.A, 60; M.A.L.S, Columbia Univ, 56. Reference librn, N.Y. Pub. Libr. Reference Dept, 56-58; Asst. reference librn, Harvard Univ. Libr, 58-60, admin. asst, 61-62, asst. univ. librn, 63-65, assoc. univ. librn, 65-66. Other: Mem, Cmt. Libr. Automation, 65; Information Processing Cmt, Inst. Electrical & Electronics Engineers, 65- Mem: ALA; Am. Soc. Info. Sci. Publ: A Computer Produced Shelf List, Col. & Res. Libr, July 65; Widener Library Shelflist series (ed), 65-; A Strategy for the Conversion of Research Library Catalogs to Machine Readable Form, Col. & Res. Libr, 7/67; Development and Administration of Automated Systems in Academic Libraries, J. Libr. Automation, 3/68; Automation in the Harvard College Library, Harvard Libr. Bull, 7/68. Consult: 1) Radcliffe Col, Cambridge, Mass, program for new libr. study center, 64-65; 2) Univ. Mich, Ann Arbor, consult on health sciences information center, 65; 3) Mass. Inst. Tech, Cambridge, survey of space utilization and physical facilities, 66. Specialties: 1b, 1d; 3f (book catalogues); 4a, 4b.

DENIS, LAURENT-G, Feb. 21, 32; Director, Ecole de Bibliothéconomie, Université de Montréal, C.P. 6128, Montréal 3, Qué, Can. Home: 2515 boul. Edouard-Montpetit, Apt. 11, Montréal 26, Qué, Can. B.A, 54; B.L.S, McGill Univ, 55, M.L.S, 65. Asst. dir. libr, Col. Militaire Royal de Saint-Jean, Qué, Can, 56-61; dir, Ecole de Bibliothéconomie, Univ. Montréal, 61- Mem: ALA; Can. Libr. Asn; Qué. Libr. Asn; Asn. Can. Bibliothécaires Langue Francaise; Inst. Prfnl. Librns. of Ont. Publ: Planification des Bibliothéques Publiques en Régions Urbaines, Univ. Montréal, 66; Etude de la Gestion de Six Bibliothèques de Collèges Classiques du Québec, Asn. Can. Bibliothécaires Langue Francaise, 67. Consult: 1) Dept. Educ, Québec Govt, Can, study on combining pub. & sch. libr, 65. Specialties: 2a; 7a; 8b, 8f.

---

5) PERSONNEL AND RECRUITING, 5a) job evaluation and description, salary recommendations, 5b) recruitment of professionals and management personnel, 5c) administrative organization, 6) PUBLIC RELATIONS, 6a) publications, 6b) publicity programs, 6c) public opinion surveys, 6d) others, 7) SERVICES, 7a) evaluation of current program, 7b) studies of service to special publics, e.g., students, handicapped, aged, etc., 7c) programs for the implementation of new laws, program proposals to governments, 7d) others, 8) COMMUNITY, REGIONAL, STATE PLANNING, 8a) legislative programs, 8b) area analyses, 8c) centralized systems, cooperative arrangements, 8d) development of standards, 8e) state libraries and extension agencies, 8f) regional and statewide surveys, 8g) others, 9) OTHERS.

DE YOUNG, JULIA M, Sept. 14, 05; Retired. Home: 501 Leggatt St, Grand Haven, Mich. 49417. A.B, Nebr. State Teachers Col, Kearney, 39; B.S. in L.S, West. Reserve Univ, 43. Dir. sch. libr, Kearney, Nebr, 39-42; dir. sch. libr, Lansing, Mich, 44-46; sch. librn, Muskegon Pub. Schs, Muskegon, Mich, 50-58, dir. sch. libr, 58-61; instructor children's literature, Musgegon Community Col, 60; dir. instructional materials dept, Grand Haven Pub. Schs, Grand Haven, Mich, 61-68; instructor, dept. librarianship, West. Mich. Univ, summer 66. Other: Mem. elem. cmt, Dept. Pub. Instruction Curriculum Cmt, 55-57, mem. instructional materials cmt, 58-60; mem, City-Wide Cmt. for Study of Community Standards (Censorship), Muskegon, Mich, 59; chmn, Citizens' Curriculum Cmt. for Study of Sch. Libr, Muskegon, 59-60; dir, Student Libr. Asst. Workshop, West. Mich. Univ, summers 59 & 60; mem. joint cmt. for develop. of sch. libr, Mich. State Libr, 59-61; mem, Mayor's Area Libr. Citizens' Cmt, Grand Haven, Mich, 63-65; mem. bd. dirs. & corresponding secy, Mich. Asn. Sch. Librns, 64-66; chmn, Mich. sch. libr. supvr. sect, 64-66; mem, Loleta D. Fyan Outstanding Librn. Award Cmt, 64-66; pres, Spanish Am. War Auxiliary, Sherman S. Dickinson, Grand Haven, 64-; chmn. instructional materials sect, Mich. Educ. Asn, 65-66. Mem: Mich. Asn. Sch. Librns; Mich. Libr. Asn; Mich. Educ. Asn; Mich. Audio-Visual Asn; Nat. Educ. Asn; ALA; AASL; Alpha Kappa chap, Delta Kappa Gamma; Spanish Am. War Auxiliary. Publ: Cataloging Manual for Nonbook Materials in Learning Centers and School Libraries (with Judith Loveys Westhuis), Mich. Asn. Sch. Librns, 66, rev. ed, 67. Consult: 1) Aberdeen Pub. Schs, Aberdeen, S.Dak, organized elem. sch. libr. with centralized processing, Feb-May 49; 2) Title III Planning Project, Saginaw Area Audio-Visual Serv, Saginaw Intermediate Sch. Dist, 420 S. Warren Ave, Saginaw, Mich, planned centralized processing serv, Nov-Dec, 66. Specialties: 1c; 3a, 3d; 5a, 5c; 6a; 7a; 8c, 8d.

DIEHL, KATHARINE SMITH, May 16, 06; Research Fellow, American Institute of Indian Studies, 12/2 Swinhoe, Calcutta, 19, India. Home: 101 S. Penn, Manheim, Pa. 17545. B.R.E, 28; A.B.L.S, 38; M.A.L.S, 54. Auth, 53-56; librn, South Ga. Col, 56-57; assoc. prof. & head dept. libr. serv, Univ. Tenn, 58-59; Fulbright prof. libr. sci, Dacca Univ, E. Pakistan, 59-61; Lilly Endowment, bibliographer & adv, Carey Libr, Serampore, W. Bengal, India, 61-62; asst. prof, Rutgers Univ. Grad. Libr. Sch, 63-66; res. fel, Univ. Chicago, 67. Other: Pres, Women's Club, 52-53; mem. cmt, Am. Asn. Univ. Women, 55-56; mem. libr. cmt, sect. of microform, Am. Asn. Asian Studies, 65- Mem: ALA; Southeast. Libr. Asn; Am. Theol. Libr. Asn; Tex. Libr. Asn; ACRL; Asn. Am. Libr. Schs; Am. Asn. Asian Studies. Publ: Formal Bibliography in the Upper Division, Col. & Res. Libr, 10/55; One Librarian, Scarecrow, 56; Concerning Books, Pakistan Observer, 60-61; Early Indian Imprints, Scarecrow, 64; Hymns and Tunes, an Index, Scarecrow, 66; The Confused Tax Picture, Res. Quart, summer 66. Consult: 1) Knox County Libr, Knoxville, Tenn, asst. in in-serv. training for the librns, winter 58-59; 2) Govt. Col. of Commerce, Chittagong, E. Pakistan, set up the plan for catalog of libr. of West. books after doing preliminary cataloging, Nov. 59; 3) Serampore Col, Serampore, W. Bengal, India, catalog of entire Carey Libr, advised on future plans, advised on serv. of trained full-time librn, prepared several filmed & printed publ, with H.K. Sircar, Sept. 61-Dec. 62, Sept. 67- Specialties: 1b, 1d; 2a, 2d (Asian materials, religious materials, reference sources), 2f; 3c, 3d; 9 (subject work—the acquisition processing & reference works which pertain thereto).

DI MUCCIO, SISTER MARY-JO, June 16, 30; Head Librarian, Immaculate Heart College, Los Angeles, Calif. 90027. Home: 5515 Franklin Ave, Los Angeles, Calif. 90028. B.A, 53; M.A, 60. Asst. librn, Immaculate Heart Col, 60-62, head librn, 62- Other: Sect. chmn, Cath. Libr. Asn, 64-66, unit chmn, 66-69. Mem: ALA; Cath. Libr. Asn; Calif. Libr. Asn. Publ: Relationship Between Parents' Choices and Their Children's Choices in Children's Leisure Reading, Immaculate Heart Col, 60; Manual for School Libraries (restricted circulation), Libr. Info. Manual, Sisters of the Immaculate Heart, 62. Consult: 1) St. Mary's, Apple Valley, Calif, planning & organizing of new elem. sch. libr, 60; 2) St. Bartholomew, Long Beach, Calif, planning & organizing libr. procedure in grades 1-8, 61; 3) Our Lady of Lourdes, Northridge, Calif, planning & organization of sch. libr, 62; 4) Mt. Carmel, Santa Barbara, Calif, planning & bldg. of libr. collection & serv. procedure, 63-64; 5) Corpus Christi, Piedmont, Calif, study of best use of facilities, 66. Specialties: 1b, 1c; 2b, 2c; 3e; 5a.

DIVETT, DR. ROBERT T, Nov. 4, 25; Librarian & Associate Professor of Medical Bibliography, Library of the Medical Sciences, University of New Mexico, Albuquerque, N.Mex. 87106. Home: 3705 Mary Ellen N.E, Albuquerque, N.Mex. 87111. B.Sc, Brigham Young Univ, 53; M.A, George Peabody Col. Teachers, 55; Ed.D, Univ. Utah, 68. Mem. librn. & asst. prof. libr. sci, Univ. Utah, Salt Lake City, 56-62; librn. & assoc. prof, med. bibliog, Sch. Med, Univ. N.Mex, Albuquerque, 63- Other: Chmn. spec. libr. sect, Utah Libr. Asn, 60-62; chmn. membership cmt, Med. Libr. Asn, 64-65; chmn. nominating cmt, biological sci. div, SLA, 64-65, consult. officer, Rio Grande chap, 66-67. Mem: Med. Libr. Asn; SLA; Am. Document. Inst; Southwest. Libr. Asn; N.Mex. Libr. Asn;

KEY TO CONSULTING SPECIALTIES: 1) ARCHITECTURE AND BUILDINGS, 1a) public libraries, 1b) academic libraries, 1c) school libraries, 1d) special libraries, 1e) library interiors, 1f) furnishings, 1g) site and location, 1h) other architectural; 2) COLLECTIONS: SELECTION, EVALUATION, WEEDING, 2a) adults, 2b) young adults, 2c) children, 2d) subject specialty, 2e) O.P. searches, 2f) rare books, 2g) appraisals, 2h) others; 3) TECHNICAL PROCESSES, 3a) cataloging, 3b) classification systems, 3c) acquisitions, 3d) materials processing, 3e) work flow and cost studies, 3f) others, 4) AUTOMATION, 4a) applications of data processing equipment, 4b) information storage and retrieval systems, 4c) systems analysis, 4d) others

Albuquerque Libr. Asn. Publ: Utah's Special Libraries, Utah Libr, spring 62; selection of Serials for a New Medical School Library, The Reminder, summer 64; Mechanization in a New Medical School Library, Part I: Acquisitions and Cataloging, Bull. Med. Libr. Asn, 1/65; Annual Administrative Reviews: Library Service, Hospitals, 4/65; Mechanization in a New Medical School Library, Part II: Serials and Circulation (with L.M. Payne & L. Small); Bull. Med. Libr. Asn, 10/66; There's Nothing Like Pushing a Button, Bull. Med. Libr. Asn, 67. Consult: 1) Utah Valley Hosp, Provo, plans for hosp. libr. bldg, 58; 2) Tex. Med. Center Libr, Houston, plans for mechanization of libr, Jan. 66; 3) Univ. Tex. Grad. Sch. Biomed. Sci. & M.D. Anderson Hosp, Houston, plans for develop. of Univ. Tex. Houston Campus Libr, Feb. 66; 4) Presbyterian Hosp. & Univ. Okla. Med. Center, Oklahoma City, bldg. plans for Presbyterian Hosp, libr. automation, with Lester Gorsline Assocs, Inc, July 66; 5) Mayo Clinic, Rochester, Minn, plans for libr. automation, Jan. 68. Specialties: 1d, 1h (med. Libr); 2d (med); 3e; 4a; 7a; 8c.

DIX, DR. WILLIAM SHEPHERD, Nov. 19, 10; University Librarian & Lecturer in English, Princeton University, University Library, Princeton, N.J. 08540. Home: 94 McCosh Circle, Princeton, N.J. 08540. B.A, 31; M.A, 32; Ph.D, 46; LL.D, 67. Univ. librn. & lectr. English, Princeton Univ, 53- Other: Chmn, U.S Nat. Cmn. for UNESCO, 59-61; chmn, Asn. Res. Libr, 62-63; mem. bd. dirs, Coun. on Libr. Resources, 66-; pres-elect, ALA, 68-69. Mem: Asn. Res. Libr; ALA. Publ: The Amateur Spirit in Scholarship, West. Reserve Univ, 42; The International Role of the University Library, Univ. Tenn. Libr. Lectures, 63; Of the Arrangement of Books, Col. & Res. Libr, XXV: 85-90; New Challenges to University Libraries, University, fall 65; Centralized Cataloguing and University Libraries, Libr. Trends, XVI: 97-111; Centralized Cataloguing at the National and International Level (co-auth), Libr. Resources & Tech. Serv, XI: 27-49. Consult: 1) N.Y. Univ. Libr, New York, critique of bldg. plans, 65; 2) Wesleyan Univ. Libr, Middletown, Conn, bldg. planning, long range develop, 65-; 3) Univ. Ky. Libr, Lexington, critique of plans for bldg. expansion, 66; 4) Johns Hopkins Univ, Baltimore, Md, critique of gen. libr. opers, with Logsdon & McCarthy, 66; 5) Swarthmore Col, Swarthmore, Pa, gen. critique of libr. opers. for spec. cmt. on libr. policy, 66-67. Specialties: 1b; 2h (univ. & res. collections); 7a.

DODD, JAMES BEAUPRE, Sept. 21, 26; Chief, Technical Information Service, Price Gilbert Memorial Library, Georgia Institute of Technology, Atlanta, Ga. 30332. Home: 2898 Rockingham Dr. N.W, Atlanta, Ga. 30327. B.S. (educ), 48; M.S.(educ), 50; M.S. in L.S, 52. Asst. librn. & librn, Nat. Reactor Testing Station, U.S. Atomic Energy Cmn, Idaho Falls, Idaho, 52-55; head info. serv. sect, atomic energy div, Babcock & Wilcox Co, Lynchburg, Va, 55-62, asst. ed, The Generator, 59-60; instructor libr. sci, Univ. Va. Extension Div, Lynchburg, 61-62; sci. librn. & asst. prof, North. Ill. Univ, De Kalb, 62-67; grad. librn, Ga. Inst. Tech, Atlanta, 67-68; chief, tech. info. serv, Price Gilbert Mem. Libr, 68- Other: Mem, tech. info. panel, U.S. Atomic Energy Cmn, 57-62; ed, Metals Div, News, SLA, 58-61, v.chmn. & chmn-elect, metals div, 61-62, chmn, 62-63; sr. instructor, N.S. Savannah Deck Officers Training Program, operated by Babcock & Wilcox Co. for U.S. Maritime Admin, 59; mem, Va. State Cmt. for Nat. Libr. Week, 60 & 61; chmn, spec. libr. sect, Va. Libr. Asn, 60-61; chmn, Interim Cmt. for City-Wide Libr. Serv, Lynchburg, 61-62; secy, col. & res. libr. sect, Ill. Libr. Asn, 64-65, chmn, 65-66; prfnl. consult, SLA, 65-, chmn, duplicate exchange project, metals-materials div, 65-; assoc. ed, Ill. Libr, 66-67. Mem: Am. Asn. Univ. Prof; ALA; SLA; Ga. Libr. Asn; Southeast. Libr. Asn. Publ: The Babcock & Wilcox Company Technical Library, Va. Librn, 11/59; Directory of Libraries and Library Personnel in and Around Lynchburg, Virginia, Babcock & Wilcox Co, 60; Lynchburg Takes First Steps Toward Public Library System, Va. Librn, spring 61; Creative Organization: The Librarian as Manager, Part III, Spec. Libr, 10/64. Consult: 1) De Kalb Agr. Asn, De Kalb, Ill, planning & staffing co. libr, 65; 2) North. Ill. Gas Co, P.O. Box 190, Aurora, planning, staffing & physical orgn. of co. libr, 65-66; 3) Office of Supt. Pub. Instruction, State of Ill, Springfield, field consult, ESEA Title II, 66. Specialties: 1d, 1e, 1f, 1g; 2d (chemistry, physics, bus, atomic energy); 3a, 3b, 3d, 3e; 4a, 4c; 5a, 5b; 6a, 6b; 7a, 7d (State Tech. Serv, serv. to industry); 8b, 8c; 9 (interrelationships of various types of libr. within a geographical area).

DOMS, KEITH, Apr. 24, 20; Director, Carnegie Library of Pittsburgh, Pittsburgh, Pa. 15213. Home: 113 Washington Rd, Pittsburgh, Pa. 15221. B.A, 42; B.L.S, 47. Asst. dir, Carnegie Libr. of Pittsburgh, Pa, 56-62, assoc. dir, 62-63, dir, 64- Other: Chmn. libr. archit. cmt, Pub. Libr. Div, ALA, 54-57; chmn, bldgs. & equipment sect, LAD, 58-60, pres, Div, 63-64; chmn. adv. cmt, Libr. Tech. Project, 59-62; pres, Pa. Libr. Asn, 60-61; pres, Beta Phi Mu, 63-64; mem. exec. bd, ALA, 63-67. Mem: ALA; SLA; Pa. Libr. Asn. Publ: Guidelines for Library Planners (ed. with Howard Rovelstad), Proc. Libr. Bldgs. & Equipment Inst, ALA, 60; Public Library Buildings, In: Local Public Library Administration, Int. City Mgrs. Asn, 64; The Trustee and Building Problems, In: The Library Trustee, Bowker, 64. Consult: 1) Citizens Pub. Libr, Washington, Pa, gen. survey & bldg. consult, 57-65; 2) Pub. Libr, Union-

---

5) PERSONNEL AND RECRUITING, 5a) job evaluation and description, salary recommendations, 5b) recruitment of professionals and management personnel, 5c) administrative organization, 6) PUBLIC RELATIONS, 6a) publications, 6b) publicity programs, 6c) public opinion surveys, 6d) others, 7) SERVICES, 7a) evaluation of current program, 7b) studies of service to special publics, e.g., students, handicapped, aged, etc., 7c) programs for the implementation of new laws, program proposals to governments, 7d) others, 8) COMMUNITY, REGIONAL, STATE PLANNING, 8a) legislative programs, 8b) area analyses, 8c) centralized systems, cooperative arrangements, 8d) development of standards, 8e) state libraries and extension agencies, 8f) regional and statewide surveys, 8g) others, 9) OTHERS.

town, Pa, bldg. consult, 63-65; 3) Free Pub. Libr, Cherry Hill, N.J, bldg. program statement, 64; 4) Cambria Pub. Libr, Johnstown, Pa, site studies & bldg. program, with Jos. Falgione, 66; 5) Pub. Libr, Ligonier, Pa, bldg. & interiors consult, 66-67. Specialties: 1a, 1g; 7a, 7c.

DONOHUE, JOSEPH CHAMINADE, Nov. 26, 30; Information Systems Specialist, c/o Documentation Center, 10831 Magnolia Dr, Cleveland, Ohio 44106. Home: 3157 Kensington Rd, Cleveland Heights, Ohio 44118. B.A, 58; S.M, 60. Adult serv. librn, New York Pub. Libr, 60-61; reference librn, Gen. Electric Co. TEMPO, 61-64; asst. librn, Rand Corp, Santa Monica, Calif, 64-65; mem. tech. staff, Informatics, Inc Sherman Oaks, Calif, 65-, on leave as U.S. Office Educ. fel. in libr. educ. program, 67-69. Other: Chmn. educ. cmt, South. Calif. chap, SLA, 65-66; chmn. spec. cmt. on univ. extension courses, Los Angeles chap, Am. Document. Inst, 65-66. Mem: ALA; SLA; Am. Soc. Info. Sci. Publ: A Guide to the Basic Sources of Current Information on Industrial Relations, Gen. Electric Co. TEMPO SP-205, 62; Industrial Resource Allocation: Bibliography and Report of Literature Search, TEMPO SP-212, 63; The TEMPO Library Reference Guide, TEMPO, 63; Information Transfer in Educational Research (with Jules Mersel & William Morris), Informatics Inc, 66; Coming of Age in Academe, Am. Documentation, 7/66; Librarianship and the Science of Information, Am. Documentation, 7/66. Consult: 1) U.S. Office Educ, establishment of ERIC syst, 66; 2) McGraw-Hill Book Co, N.Y, anal. of needs for publ. in the field of info. sci. & planning prep. of same, 66; 3) U.S. Army Corps of Engineers, on Army Tech. Libr. Improvement Study (ATLIS), 67; 4) U.S. Dept. of Agriculture, on design of file syst. for Foreign Agricultural Serv, 67; 5) Univ. Md. & Enoch Pratt Free Libr, Baltimore, design of expanded info. serv, 68. Specialties: 2d (gen. res. & develop, software); 3c; 4c, 4d (liaison between libr. & programming personnel); 5d (integration of info. activity into managerial function); 6a, 6b; 7a, 7d (liaison with res. staff); 9 (develop. of info. syst. combining tech. & admin. data; tech. commun).

DOWNS, ROBERT B, May 25, 03; Dean of Library Administration, University of Illinois, Urbana, Ill. 61801. Home: 708 W. Pennsylvania, Urbana, Ill, 61801. A.B, Univ. N.C, 26; B.S, Columbia Univ, 27, M.S, 29. Dir. libr. & libr. sch, Univ. Ill, Urbana, 43-58, dean libr. admin, 58- Other: Pres, ACRL, 40-41; pres, ALA, 52-53; pres, Ill. Libr. Asn, 56-57. Mem: ALA; ACRL; Southeast. Libr. Asn; Bibliog. Soc. Am; Ill. Libr. Asn. Publ: American Library Resources, ALA, 51-62; Books that Changed the World, ALA, 56; The First Freedom, ALA, 60; Molders of the Modern Mind, Barnes & Noble, 61; Famous Books, Ancient and Medieval, Barnes & Noble, 64; How to Do Library Research, Univ. Ill, Urbana, 66. Consult: 1) Gov. Cmn. on Libr. Resources, Raleigh, N.C, survey of all types of libr. in state, 64; 2) City Univ. New York, N.Y, survey of personnel problems in libr, 65; 3) Mo. State Libr, survey of all types of libr. except. sch, 66; 4) Asn. of Univs. & Cols. of Can, survey of resources of Can. acad. & res. libr, 67-; 5) Purdue Univ, survey of libr, 67. Specialties: 2h (eval. of holdings, surveys of resources); 5a, 5c; 7a; 8c, 8f.

DUKE, WILLIAM RICHARD, Dec. 4, 33; Inspector of High Schools, Department of Education, Edmonton, Alta, Can. Home: 10423 52nd St, Edmonton, Alta, Can. B.Sc, 55; B.Ed, 56; M.Ed, 65. Sch. principal, Wainwright Sch. Dist, 56-58; sch. principal, County of Red Deer, 58-63, supt. schs, Dept. Educ, 63-65; inspector of high schs, Lethbridge, Alta, 65-68. Other: Dir, Sch. Libr. Coun, 63, v.pres, 64, mem. sr. high curriculum cmt, 65-; mem, Minister's Adv. Cmt. on TV in Educ; pres, Sch. Libr. Coun. Alta. Mem: Sch. Libr. Coun. Alta. Publ: The Training of School Librarians, A.T.A. Mag; Rural Libraries—Where to?, Alta. Sch. Libr. Rev; School Equipment Foundation Program, A.S.T.A. Mag. Alta; Canadian Books for Schools—A Centennial Booklist (joint ed). Consult: 1) Calgary Sch. Dist. 19, 412 Seventh St. S.W, Calgary, Alta, Can, evaluated sch. libr. serv. at all levels, also cent. serv, May 64; 2) Grande Prairie Sch. Dist. 2357, 10213 99th St, Grande Prairie, evaluated the jr. & sr. high sch. libr. serv, Apr. 65; 3) Lethbridge Sch. Dist. 51; 433 15th St. S, Lethbridge, surveyed elem, jr. high & sr. high libr, Oct. 65; 4) Edmonton Sch. Dist. 7, 10733 101st St, Edmonton, evaluated libr. serv. of nine sr. high schs, Feb. & Mar. 66; 5) Medicine Hat Sch. Dist. 76, 601 First Ave. S.W, & Medicine Hat Sch. Dist. 21, 73 Seventh St, S.E, Medicine Hat, evaluated jr. high sch. libr. serv, Apr. 66. Specialties: 1c; 5c; 7a, 7b, 7c; 8a, 8c; 9 (orgn. aspects of sch. libr. at the sch, sch. syst. & regional levels; relationship of orgn. to instructional serv).

DUNKLEY, GRACE S, July 31, 07; Coordinator of Curriculum Material & School Libraries, Bellflower Unified School District, Bellflower, Calif. 90706. Home: 1014 Valencia Mesa Dr, Fullerton, Calif. 92633. B.S, Utah State Univ, 43; M.S, Univ. South. Calif, 53. Other: Pres, Delta Kappa chap, Delta Kappa Gamma, 56-58; spec. lectr, Univ. South. Calif, Los Angeles, summer 64; pres, Beta Phi Mu, 65-66; state pres, Calif. Asn. Sch. Librns, 66-67; mem. adv. bd, Univ. South. Calif. Libr. Sch, 66-; mem. bd. dirs, dept. instructional media, Calif. State Col. at Long Beach, 68- Mem: Calif. Libr. Asn; ALA; Calif. Asn. Sch. Librns; Nat. Educ. Asn; Calif. Teachers Asn; Phi Kappa Phi.

KEY TO CONSULTING SPECIALTIES: 1) ARCHITECTURE AND BUILDINGS, 1a) public libraries, 1b) academic libraries, 1c) school libraries, 1d) special libraries, 1e) library interiors, 1f) furnishings, 1g) site and location, 1h) other architectural; 2) COLLECTIONS: SELECTION, EVALUATION, WEEDING, 2a) adults, 2b) young adults, 2c) children, 2d) subject specialty, 2e) O.P. searches, 2f) rare books, 2g) appraisals, 2h) others; 3) TECHNICAL PROCESSES, 3a) cataloging, 3b) classification systems, 3c) acquisitions, 3d) materials processing, 3e) work flow and cost studies, 3f) others, 4) AUTOMATION, 4a) applications of data processing equipment, 4b) information storage and retrieval systems, 4c) systems analysis, 4d) others

Publ: Contrib. to Sch. Libr. J. Consult: 1) Torrance Schs, Torrance, Calif, consult. serv. to West High Sch, 61; 2) Univ. South. Calif, Los Angeles, spec. consult. NDEA, 66; 3) Compton Elem. Schs, Compton, Calif, develop. of elem. libr, 66-67. Specialties: 1c; 2b, 2c.

DUNLAP, DR. LESLIE W, Aug. 3, 11; Director of Libraries, University of Iowa, Iowa City, Iowa 52240. Home: 326 Hutchinson Ave, Iowa City, Iowa 52240. B.A, 33; A.M, 38; B.S. in L.S, 39; Ph.D, 44. Assoc. dir. & prof. libr. sci, Univ. Ill. Libr, 51-58; dir. of libr. & prof. libr. sci, Univ. Iowa, Iowa City, 58- Other: Mem, libr. adv. bd, Colliers Encyclopedia, 59-; chmn. bd. dirs, Center for Res. Libr, 65-66; mem, Libr. Congress adv. bds. on Nat. Union Catalog of Manuscript Collections & on Photocopying Foreign Manuscripts, 65-; consult-examiner, N. Cent. Asn. Col. & Univs. Cmn, Chicago, Ill, 65- Mem: ALA; ACRL; Iowa Libr. Asn; Manuscript Soc. Publ: The Letters of Willis Gaylord Clark and Lewis Gaylord Clark (ed), New York Pub. Libr, 40; American Historical Societies, 1790-1860, 44; ed, issue of Libr. Trends, 10/54; Libraries, In: Colliers Encyclopedia, 56-; Alexandria, the Capital of Memory, 62. Consult: 1) Northwest. Col, Orange City, Iowa, prepared libr. program; suggested bldg. plan, prepared layouts & lists of furniture & equipment, 62-64; 2) St. Ambrose Col, Davenport, Iowa, prepared report on libr. program with recommendations & layouts for expansion & remodeling of libr, 63; 3) Mich. State Univ, East Lansing, panel on develop. of campus libr, with R.B. Downs, Verner Clapp & Jerrold Orne, 64; 4) Northwest Mo. Libr, Kirksville, St. Joseph, Mo, site visits & reports on col. & pub. libr. in area for Resources of Missouri Libraries, Mo. State Libr, with Robert B. Downs, 66. Specialties: 1b, 1d; 2d (Lincolniana, & other literary & hist. manuscripts); 5b, 5c; 7a.

DUNN, DR. OLIVER C, Aug. 10, 09; Associate Director of Libraries, Purdue University Library, Lafayette, Ind. 47907. Home: 105 Leslie Ave, West Lafayette, Ind. 47906. B.A, Stanford Univ, 30, M.A, 34; Ph.D, Cornell Univ, 37; B.L.S. Univ. Calif, 49. Asst. dir, Purdue Univ. Libr, 53-60, assoc. dir, 60- Other: Mem. cmt. visual arts, Purdue Univ, 55-59, 66-69, chmn, 56-58, mem. exec. coun, 59-62, mem. cmt. int. educ. programs, 66-69. Mem: ALA; ACRL. Consult: 1) Biblioteca Agrícola Nacional, Univ. Agraria, La Molina, Lima, Peru, libr. serv. programming & bldg. planning, Apr. 62-; 2) Indian Inst. Tech, Kanpur, India, libr. serv. programming & bldg. planning, July 62-; 3) Univ. del Valle, Cali, Colombia, bldg. planning, May 65-; 4) Heidelberg Col, Tiffin, Ohio, bldg. planning, with J.H. Moriarty, 65-66; 5) Univ. Nacional Bogotá, Colombia, bldg. planning, Jan. 67- Specialties: 1b, 1e, 1f; 7d (orgn. of libr. serv. for acad. insts).

E

EASTLICK, JOHN TAYLOR, Apr. 28, 12; Librarian, Denver Public Library, 1357 Broadway, Denver, Colo. 80203. Home: 1010 S. Adams St, Denver, Colo. 80209. A.B, 34; M.A, 39; B.L.S, 40. Librn, Denver Pub. Libr, Denver, Colo, 51- Other: Pres, Denver Coun. Educ. TV, 54-56; pres, PLD, 56-57; 2nd v.pres, ALA, 59-60; pres, Adult Educ. Coun. Metrop. Denver, 61-62; chmn. libr. develop. cmt, Colo. Libr. Asn, 64- Mem: ALA; Colo. Libr. Asn; Mountain-Plains Libr. Asn; Bibliog. Center for Res, Rocky Mountain Region, Inc; Adult Educ. Coun. Metrop. Denver. Publ: Denver Goes Modern, Libr. J, 56; The Challenge of Learning, Denver Pub. Libr, 56; The Challenge of Continual Crisis, Saturday Review, 57; The Sixties and After, LAD, 60; A Library Building Program—The Librarian's Greatest Challenge, N.Y. State Libr, Libr. Extension Div, 61. Consult: 1) Littleton Pub. Libr, Littleton, Colo, statement of bldg. program & space allocation, 61; 2) Yuma City-County Libr, Yuma, Ariz, statement of bldg. program for a new libr. bldg, 64; 3) Oklahoma City-County Pub. Libr, Oklahoma City, Okla, study of Oklahoma City Libr. & suburban pub. libr. for consolidations, 65; 4) Pikes Peak Regional Dist. Libr, 21 W. Kiowa St, Colorado Springs, Colo, survey of existing admin. orgn. & serv. programs, with Willard O. Youngs, 66; 5) Natrona County Pub. Libr, Casper, Wyo, study of existing bldg. orgn. & staffing, with Henry G. Shearouse, Jr, 66. Specialties: 1a, 1f, 1g; 5a, 5b, 5c; 7a; 8c, 8f.

EATON, DR. ANDREW JACKSON, July 5, 14; Director of Libraries, Olin Library, Washington University, St. Louis, Mo. 63130. Home: 21 Dwyer Place, St. Louis, Mo. 63124. A.B, Col. Wooster, 35; A.B.L.S, Univ. Mich, 36; Ph.D, Univ. Chicago, 44. Dir. libr, Washington Univ, St. Louis, Mo, 53- Other: Chmn. univ. libr. section, ACRL, 64-65; pres, Mo. Libr. Asn, 65-66; v.pres. & pres-elect, Asn. Res. Libr, 67. Mem: ALA. Consult: 1) Drury Col, Springfield, Mo, libr. bldg, 58; 2) Emory Univ, Atlanta, Ga, libr. bldg. program, 64; 3) Danforth Found, St. Louis, Mo, libr. collection & orgn, 65; 4) Southwest Mo. State Col, Springfield, advice on bldg, with Donald Bean & Stephen McCarthy, 65; 5) Southeast Mo. State Col, Cape Girardeau, advice on bldg, 65-66. Specialties: 1b, 1e, 1f, 1g; 5c; 7a.

EBERT, MYRL, Oct. 20, 13; Chief Librarian & Associate Professor of Librarianship, Division of Health Affairs, University of North Carolina, Chapel Hill, N.C. 27514. Home: Route 7, Box 98, Durham, N.C. 27707. B.S, 43; B.S. in L.S, 45; M.S. 51. Chief librn. & assoc. prof. librarianship, div. health affairs, Univ. N.C, 52- Other: Chmn. spec. libr. sect, N.C. Libr. Asn, 53-55, recording secy. & bd. mem, 57-59; secy, Med. Libr. Asn, 62-64, chmn. nominating

---

5) PERSONNEL AND RECRUITING, 5a) job evaluation and description, salary recommendations, 5b) recruitment of professionals and management personnel, 5c) administrative organization, 6) PUBLIC RELATIONS, 6a) publications, 6b) publicity programs, 6c) public opinion surveys, 6d) others, 7) SERVICES, 7a) evaluation of current program, 7b) studies of service to special publics, e.g., students, handicapped, aged, etc., 7c) programs for the implementation of new laws, program proposals to governments, 7d) others, 8) COMMUNITY, REGIONAL, STATE PLANNING, 8a) legislative programs, 8b) area analyses, 8c) centralized systems, cooperative arrangements, 8d) development of standards, 8e) state libraries and extension agencies, 8f) regional and statewide surveys, 8g) others, 9) OTHERS.

cmt, 66-67. Mem: Med. Libr. Asn; SLA; N.C. Libr. Asn; Asn. Am. Libr. Schs. Publ: Rise and Development of American Medical Periodical, 1797-1850, Bull. Med. Libr. Asn, 40: 243-276; Bibliography of Early Psychoanalytic Monograph Series (with I. Bry & H. Bayne), J. Am. Psychoanalytic Asn, 1: 519-525; Aperçu—for Collateral Reading, Univ. N.C. Sch. Med. Bull, 1: 67; Teachers Take Time to Share Knowledge, Univ. N.C. Sch. Med. Bull, 2: 32-33; Quandaries and Queries in Subject Control, Bull. Med. Libr. Asn, 49; 42-50; Introduction to the Literature of the Medical Sciences, Univ. N.C. Book Exchange, 2nd ed, 67. Consult: 1) Mecklenburg County Med. Soc, Charlotte, N.C, recommended reorgn. of physical plant, collections & serv, Feb-Oct. 64; 2) Univ. Saigon Med. Sch, Saigon, Vietnam, reorgn. of med. sch. libr, with Walter Wiggins, 66-67; 3) Nat. Libr. Med, Bethesda, Md, served on cmt. for selection of literature for MEDLARS program, with T.P. Fleming, May 66-; 4) Petersburg Gen. Hosp, Petersburg, Va, advice on reorgn. of nursing sch. & hosp. med. libr, Feb. 67; 5) N.C. State Bd. Health, Raleigh, eval. of collection, Feb-Mar. 67. Specialties: 1d; 2d (med, health sci. in gen), 2g; 3c; 5b, 5c; 7a; 8b.

EDWARDS, IDA MAY, June 11, 09; Consultant in Instructional Materials, Stanislaus County Department of Education, 2115 Scenic Dr, P.O. Box 1697, Modesto, Calif. 95354. Home: 3112 Bartley Lane, Modesto, Calif. 95353. B.A; B.A.L.A. Consult: instructional materials, Stanislaus County Dept. Educ, Modesto, Calif, 53- Other: Chmn. audio-visual cmt, north sect, Calif. Asn. Sch. Librns, 53-57, chmn. county sch. librns. cmt, 59-60, mem. prfnl. cmt, 60-61, chmn, 61-62, mem. membership cmt, 63-; treas. San Joaquin sect, Calif. Asn. Supv. & Curriculum Develop, 55-56, secy, 65-66, mem. state instructional materials cmt, 56-59 & 64-67, mem. state conf. program cmt, 66-67; chmn. state conf. program cmt, Audio-Visual Educ. Asn. Calif, 56-57, pres. San Joaquin sect, 56-57, secy, 58-59 & 60-61; chmn. state publicity cmt, Calif. Asn. Sch. Librns, 59-60, mem. state instructional materials cmt, 64-67, rep, Calif. Asn. Supv. & Curriculum Develop, 64-; mem, Region 6, Sch. Libr. Develop. Proj, 61-62. Mem: ALA; AASL; Calif. Asn. Sch. Librns. Publ: Instructional Materials Center, Sch. Libr. Asn. Calif. Bull, 3/54; The Stanislaus County Audio-Visual and Library Program (with Harold C. Francis), Calif. J. Elem. Educ, 2/56; contrib. to Calif. J. Elem. Educ, 8/60; Instructional Materials: Selection Policies and Procedures, Calif. Asn. Sch. Librns, 65. Consult: 1) Office of County Supt. of Schs, Merced County Courthouse, Merced, Calif, admin. & operative procedures for reorgn. of the county schs. libr, 54-56; 2) Office of County Supt. of Schs, 141 S. Lassen St, Willows, Calif, procedures in orgn, admin, distribution & eval. of materials, spring 55; 3) Office of County Supt. of Schs, Mono County Courthouse, Bridgeport, Calif, admin. & operative procedures for reorgn. of the county schs. libr. Specialties: 1c; 2b, 2c, 2d (reading, social sci, sci. language arts); 3a, 3b; 5c; 7a; 8d, 8f.

EISNER, JOSEPH, May 14, 29; Director, Association of New York Libraries for Technical Services, (ANYLTS). Home: 54 Nassau Ave, Plainview, N.Y. 11803. B.A, Syracuse Univ, 50; M.S.L.S, Columbia Univ, 54. Dir, Plainview-Old Bethpage Pub. Libr, Plainview, N.Y, 55-68; dir, Asn. N.Y. Libr. Tech. Serv, (ANYLTS), 68- Other: Chmn. legal problems cmt, Nassau County Libr. Asn, 56-59 & 61-63, pres. of asn, 59-61; mem. libr. standards & legis. cmt, N.Y. Libr. Asn, 58-63, chmn. fed-state libr. relations cmt, 60-61, chmn. legis. cmt, 64-; secy, Libr. Trustees Found, N.Y. State, 61-66; lectr, C.W. Post Libr. Sch, 61-; columnist, Trustee Talk, N.Y. Libr. Asn. Bull, 62-65. Mem: N.Y. Libr. Asn; ALA; Nassau County Libr. Asn. Publ: The Personnel Crisis, N.Y. Libr. Asn. Bull, 3/62; Write the Program Down, Wilson Libr. Bull, 3/62; Recovery of Overdue Books by Court Action, Wilson Libr. Bull, 2/63; Plainview Emphasizes Site, Libr. J, 12/1/64; Re-registration of Borrowers by Direct Mail, Odds & Bookends, spring 66; Handbook of Laws and Regulations Affecting Public Libraries in N.Y. State (compiler), Nassau County Libr. Asn, rev. ed, 66. Consult: 1) Ramapo Catskill Libr. Syst, 619 North St, Middletown, N.Y, survey of reference resources, with Stanley Crane, 64-65; 2) Wantagh Pub. Schs, Beltage Ave, Wantagh, N.Y, survey for centralized processing & instructional materials centers, 65; 3) Stenson Mem. Libr, Sea Cliff Ave, Sea Cliff, N.Y, draft bldg. program for LSCA grant, 66; 4) New City Free Libr, 31 Maple Ave, New City, N.Y, advise on layout & furniture, 66; 5) N.J. State Libr, Trenton, survey inter-libr. cooperative possibilities for LSCA Title III grant, 68. Specialties: 1a, 1f, 1g, 1h (evaluate programs); 7a; 8c.

ELLERBROCK, EDWARD J, 1921; Library Consultant & Representative, Library Bureau, 3420 Prospect Ave, Cleveland, Ohio 44115. Home: 7777 Wall St, Valley View, Ohio 44125. B.S, Ohio State Univ, 48. Ohio Libr. Asn; ALA. Consult: 1) Cleveland State Univ, layout consult, 64; 2) Mary Manse Col, Toledo, Ohio, layout & color, 65-66; 3) Findlay Col, Findlay, Ohio, layout consult, 66; 4) Case Western Reserve Univ, layout consult, 66; 5) Canton Pub. Libr, Canton, Ohio, layout & color, 66. Specialties: 1a, 1b, 1c, 1d, 1e, 1f, 1h (layout & color); 4a, 4b.

ELLSWORTH, DR. RALPH E, Sept. 22, 07; Director of Libraries & Professor of Bibliography, University of Colorado, Boulder, Colo. 80302. Home: 860 Willowbrook Rd, Boulder, Colo. 80302. A.B, Oberlin Col, 29; B.S. in L.S, West. Reserve Univ, 31; Ph.D, Univ. Chi-

---

KEY TO CONSULTING SPECIALTIES: 1) ARCHITECTURE AND BUILDINGS, 1a) public libraries, 1b) academic libraries, 1c) school libraries, 1d) special libraries, 1e) library interiors, 1f) furnishings, 1g) site and location, 1h) other architectural; 2) COLLECTIONS: SELECTION, EVALUATION, WEEDING, 2a) adults, 2b) young adults, 2c) children, 2d) subject specialty, 2e) O.P. searches, 2f) rare books, 2g) appraisals, 2h) others; 3) TECHNICAL PROCESSES, 3a) cataloging, 3b) classification systems, 3c) acquisitions, 3d) materials processing, 3e) work flow and cost studies, 3f) others, 4) AUTOMATION, 4a) applications of data processing equipment, 4b) information storage and retrieval systems, 4c) systems analysis, 4d) others

cago, 37. Dir. libr. & prof, Univ. Iowa, Iowa City, 43-58; dir. libr. & prof. bibliog, Univ. Colo, Boulder, 58- Other: Pres, Colo. Libr. Asn, 37, 38 & 64; mem. exec. bd, ALA, 46-50; pres, ACRL, 51-52 & 61-62; mem. exec. cmt, Asn. Res. Libr, 61-64. Mem: ALA; Asn. Res. Libr; Colo. Libr. Asn. Publ: Planning the College and University Library Building, Pruett, 60; Buildings: State of the Library Art, Rutgers Univ, 60; The American Right Wing, Pub. Affairs Press, 62; The School Library, Facilities for Independent Study, Educ. Facilities Labs, Inc, 63; The School Library, Center Applied Res. in Educ, 65. Consult: 1) Wash. Univ, St. Louis, Mo, consult. to architect, 57-58; 2) Beaver Col, Phila, Pa, planning, 61-64; 3) Temple Univ, Phila, Pa, planning, 61-65; 4) Univ. Utah, Salt Lake City, Utah, planning, 63- ; 5) Univ. Rochester, Rochester, N.Y, planning, 65- Specialties: 1b, 1c, 1h (concept planning).

ELROD, J. McREE, Mar. 23, 32; Head of Catalogue Division, University of British Columbia Library, Vancouver 8, B.C, Can. Home: 2012 Dollarton, North Vancouver, B.C, Can. A.B, 52; M.A, 53; M.A.C.L.T, 54; M.S.L.S, 60. Asst. librn, Belmont Col, 53-54; assoc. libr, Yonsei Univ, 55-60; vis. prof, Peabody Libr. Sch, 60; librn, Cent. Col, 61-63; catalog libr, Ohio Wesleyan Univ, Delaware, 63-67. Other: Chmn, constitutional revision cmt, Mo. Libr. Asn, 62; v.chmn. & chmn-elect, tech. serv. roundtable, Ohio Libr. Asn, 66-67. Mem: Can. Libr. Asn; B.C. Libr. Asn; ALA; Am. Asn. Univ. Prof; ACRL. Publ: The Classed Catalog in the Fifties, Libr. Resources & Tech. Serv, spring, 61; Divided Catalog, Libr. J, 5/1/62; An Index to English Language Periodical Literature Published in Korea 1890-1940, Nat. Assembly Libr, 65; A Korean Classified Catalog, Libr. Resources & Tech. Serv, fall 60; Staffing of Technical Processes, Libr. J, 5/1/66; Modern Library Practices, a Series of Programed Units, Educ. Methods, Inc, 66- Consult: 1) Defiance Col. Libr, Defiance, Ohio, tech. serv, div. of catalog & LC reclassification, 65-66; 2) Ashland Col. Libr, Ashland, Ohio, tech. serv. & div. of catalog, 66; 3) Developmental Libr, Scott Seed Co, Marysville, Ohio, cataloging & classification of the collection, 66; 4) Ashland Theol. Seminary Libr, Ashland, work flow of tech. serv, 66- ; 5) Heidelberg Col. Libr, Springfield, Ohio, div. of catalog, Jan. 67. Specialties: 3a, 3b, 3d, 3e, 3f (LC reclassification, catalog div, pub. shelf list, classed catalog).

ENGLEY, DONALD B, July 19, 17; Librarian, Trinity College Library, Hartford, Conn. 06106. Home: 123 Vernon St, Hartford, Conn. 06106. B.A, 39; B.L.S, 41; M.A, 47. Librn, Trinity Col, 51- Other: Mem, Conn. State Libr. Cmt, 59- ; chmn, Gov. Cmt. on Libr, 62-63. Mem: ALA; ACRL; Conn. Libr. Asn. Publ: George Brinley, Collector of Americana, Trinity Col. Libr. Gazette, 4/54; James Hammond Trumbull, Bibliographer of Connecticut, Bibliog. Soc. Am. Papers, 54. Consult: 1) Hobart & William Smith Cols, Geneva, N.Y, survey of program, Nov. 67; 2) Taft Sch, Watertown, Conn, bldg. planning, including site, 67. Specialties: 1b, 1c, 1e, 1g; 2a, 2d (liberal arts); 7a, 7b; 8a, 8b, 8c, 8f.

ERTEL, MRS. MARGARET P, Apr. 25, 07; Library Director, Camp Lejeune Dependents' Schools, Marine Corps Base Bldg. 855, Camp Lejeune, N.C. 28542. Home: 3326 Hagaru Dr, Tarawa Terrace, N.C. 28543. A.B, Salem Col. (N.C); M.A, Univ. N.C, Chapel Hill. Librn, Leicester High Sch, Leicester, N.C, 45-53; librn, Goldsboro Senior High Sch, Goldsboro, N.C, 53-61; libr. dir, Camp Lejeune Dependents' Schs, 61- Mem: ALA; N.C. Libr. Asn. Consult: 1) Salvation Army, Goldsboro, N.C, directing processing of books for children's libr, with Mrs. Dale Williams, June-Nov. 66. Specialties: 2a, 2b, 2c; 3a, 3c, 3d; 5a, 5c.

ESHELMAN, WILLIAM ROBERT, Aug. 23, 21; Editor, Wilson Library Bulletin, H.W. Wilson Co, 950 University Ave, Bronx, N.Y. 10452. Home: 592 Gail Court, Teaneck, N.J. 07666. A.B, 43; A.M, 50; B.L.S, 51. Asst. col. librn, Los Angeles State Col, 54-59, col. librn, 59-65; univ. librn. & prof. bibliog, Bucknell Univ, Lewisburg, Pa, 66-68. Other: Mem, Adv. Coun. on Educ. for Librarianship, Univ. Calif, 61-64, mem, Acad. Senate, Calif. State Cols, 64-65; pres, L.A.S.C. chap, Am. Asn. Univ. Prof, 64-65; mem. ed. cmt, ALA, 64-66; mem. publ. cmt, ACRL, 64-69; mem. ed. bd, Choice, 66-68. Mem: ALA; Calif. Libr. Asn; Pa. Libr. Asn. Publ: Notes on Astraea Redux, In: John Dryden, Works, Vol. I, Univ. Calif, 56; 8 editorials, Calif. Librn, 60-63; Adrian Wilson: Book Designer, Printer, and Publisher, Calif. Librn, 7/61; Preface to A Lady of Quality, by Crébillon fils, Brandon House, 64. Consult: 1) Whittier Col, Whittier, Calif, bldg. consult, 60; 2) Univ. Nev, Las Vegas, surveyed libr. serv. with recommendations, with Andrew H. Horn, 64; 3) Univ. W. Fla, Pensacola, preliminary planning for libr. serv, including AV, TV, radio, 64; 4) Alderson Broaddus Col, Phillippi, W.Va, plan to develop libr. serv, 66-67. Specialties: 1b; 2d (poetry in English; fine printing), 2e; 3c; 5a, 5b, 5c; 6a.

ETCHISON, ANNIE LAURIE, Dec. 5, 09; Staff Librarian, Third U.S. Army System, Hq. Third U.S. Army, Ft. McPherson, Ga. 30330. Home: Cana, N.C, RFD 5, Mocksville, N.C, 27028. B.A, 39; B.L.S, 40. Command libr, Dept. Air Forces, Alaska, 50-51; librn (RCMT), Dept. Army TAGO, Wash, D.C, 52-53; staff librn, Dept. Army, Korea, 54-55; librn, Dept. Navy, Wash, D.C, 56; chief librn, Ft. Bragg, N.C, 57-63; staff librn; Third U.S. Army, Ft. McPherson, Ga, 63- Other: Mem, Fed. Libr. Cmt, 65- ; command coordinator, Army Career

---

5) PERSONNEL AND RECRUITING, 5a) job evaluation and description, salary recommendations, 5b) recruitment of professionals and management personnel, 5c) administrative organization, 6) PUBLIC RELATIONS, 6a) publications, 6b) publicity programs, 6c) public opinion surveys, 6d) others, 7) SERVICES, 7a) evaluation of current program, 7b) studies of service to special publics, e.g., students, handicapped, aged, etc., 7c) programs for the implementation of new laws, program proposals to governments, 7d) others, 8) COMMUNITY, REGIONAL, STATE PLANNING, 8a) legislative programs, 8b) area analyses, 8c) centralized systems, cooperative arrangements, 8d) development of standards, 8e) state libraries and extension agencies, 8f) regional and statewide surveys, 8g) others, 9) OTHERS.

Program for Librns. Mem: ALA; SLA. Publ: Foreign Fiction in Translation, Wilson Libr. Bull, 39; American Spirit in Fiction, ALA, 41; Library Music Hour, Wilson Libr, Bull, 43; Books for the Soldier, Libr. J, 44; The Soldiers Read at Langley Field, N.Y. Herald Tribune, 44; Books and the Midnight Sun, The State, Columbia, S.C, 51. Consult: 1) Dept. Army, TAGO Educ. & Libr. Div, Wash, D.C, pilot model automated libr. syst, July 64-Aug. 68. Specialties: 1a, 1d, 1e; 4a, 4b, 4c; 5a, 5b, 5c.

EVANS, RICHARD A, Aug. 29, 23; Professor-Librarian, U.S. Naval Academy, Annapolis, Md. 21402. Home: 14315 Gaines Ave, Rockville, Md. 20853. B.A, 50; M.S.L.S, 51. U.S. Govt, Wash, D.C, 51-57; mgr. tech. info. center, HRB-Singer, Inc, State College, Pa, 57-63, libr. consult, 63-64; group supvr, cent. lab. libr. group, Johns Hopkins Univ. Applied Physics Lab, Silver Spring, Md, 63-67; prof-librn, U.S. Naval Acad, Annapolis, Md, 67- Other: Secy-treas, Wash. D.C. chap. document. group, SLA, 66-67. Mem: Am. Soc. Info. Sci; SLA. Publ: Recommentations for the Development of the Technical Library at the Singer Manufacturing Company, Central Research Laboratory, Denville, New Jersey, 62; Planning the New Library: Applied Physics Laboratory, The Johns Hopkins University, Spec. Libr, 10/63. Consult: 1) Adler Educ. Systs, College Park, Md, Recommendations for develop. of collection for training-oriented libr, with Theodore Hines, June 65. Specialties: 1d; 2d (sci. & tech); 4b; 5c; 7a; 9 (libr. admin).

F

FALGIONE, JOSEPH F, Oct. 4, 31; Coordinator of District Services, Carnegie Library of Pittsburgh, 4400 Forbes Ave, Pittsburgh, Pa. 15213. Home: 307 Burlington Rd, Pittsburgh, Pa. 15221. B.S, Duquesne Univ, 54; M.L.S, Carnegie Libr. Sch, 57. Roving asst, Free Libr. Phila, 57-59; head librn, Athens County Libr, Ohio, 59-61; reference asst, Carnegie Libr. Pittsburgh, Pittsburgh, Pa, 61-62, coordinator dist. serv, 63- Other: Mem, membership cmt, Pa. Libr. Asn, 62-63, chmn, tech. arrangements cmt. for convention, 64, chmn, pub. libr. sect, 66-67, chmn, Carnegie Libr. Staff Asn, 62-63; part-time instructor, Pa. State Univ. Extension Div, 65; mem. Allegheny County adv. cmt, War on Poverty, 65-66; chmn, Pittsburgh Libr. Club, 66-67. Mem: Pa. Libr. Asn. Consult: 1) Flenniken Mem. Libr, Carmichaels, Pa, preparation of program statement & floor plans for addition to existing libr. bldg, with Keith Doms, Dec. 65-Feb. 66; 2) Kingwood Pub. Libr, Kingwood, W.Va, site for new libr. bldg, program statement & floor plans, Jan-Apr. 66; 3) Cambria County Libr, Johnstown, Pa, study of libr. housing problems, with Keith Doms, June-Sept. 66; 4) Clarksburg Pub. Libr, Clarksburg, W.Va, study of bldg. problems & overall admin, Aug-Nov. 67; 5) Bowlby Pub. Libr, Waynesburg, Pa, preparation of program statement & floor plans for addition to bldg, Apr-Sept. 68. Specialties: 1a, 1e, 1g; 2a; 5a, 5c; 8c, 8d.

FARBER, EVAN IRA, June 30, 22; Librarian, Lilly Library, Earlham College, Richmond, Ind. 47374. Home: 331 College Ave, Richmond, Ind. 47374. A.B, Univ. N.C, 44, M.A, 51, B.S. in L.S, 53. Chief serials & binding div, Emory Univ. Libr, 55-62; librn, Lilly Libr, Earlham Col, Rochmond, Ind, 62- Other: Treas, Ga. Libr. Asn, 58-60; mem. cmt. non-west. resources, col. sect, ACRL, chmn. col. sect, 68-69; mem. LAD cmt, ALA; asst. ed, Explorations in Entrepreneurial Hist, 64-; chmn, Dist. IV, Ind. Libr. Asn, 66-67; co-ed, Earlham Review, 66- Mem: Southeast. Libr. Asn; Ind. Libr. Asn; ALA. Publ: Classified List of Periodicals for the College Library, F.W. Faxon Co, 4th ed, 57; Selection and Acquisition of Special Types of Materials (revision), In: Administration of the College Library, H.W. Wilson Co, 3rd ed, 61; General Periodicals, Libr. Trends, 1/62; Earlham's Considerate Library, Libr. J, 12/1/63; Attention to Details in Planning Makes a Most Considerate Library, Col. & Univ. Bus, 3/64; High School Students and the College Library, Libr. Occurrent, 9/64. Consult: 1) Austin Col, Sherman, Tex, collection & orgn, Feb. 65; 2) Glenville State Col, Glenville, W.Va, bldg. plans, 65; 3) Asbury Theol. Seminary, Wilmore, Ky, layout & furnishings, with Hubboch's Inc, 65-66; 4) Malone Col, Canton, Ohio, bldg. plans, 66- Specialties: 1b, 1e, 1f; 2d (undergrad), 2h (serials); 5c; 7a.

FAST, MRS. ELIZABETH T, Feb. 8, 31; Director of Library Services, Groton Public Schools, Groton, Conn. 06340. Home: 2 Chestnut Hill Square, Groton, Conn. 06340. A.B, Radcliffe Col, 52; M.L.S, Univ. R.I, 68. Elem. Sch. librn, Groton Pub. Schs, Groton, Conn, 62-65, dir. libr. serv, 65- Other: Mem. & pub. relations chmn, Groton Pub. Libr. Bd, 58-64; mem. bd, Conn. Sch. Libr. Asn, 62-; alternate, White House fel. Program, 65; mem. cmt. to revise books on Asia for children's list, CSD, 65-66; New Eng. regional rep, state assembly planning cmt, AASL, 65-68, mem, Britannica Awards Cmt, 66-68, chmn, 67-68, chmn, Nat. Libr. Week Cmt, 68-; mem. bd, Conn. chap, Alpha Delta Kappa, 68- Mem: ALA; New Eng. Libr. Asn; New Eng. Sch. Librns. Asn; Conn. Libr. Asn; Conn. Sch. Librns. Asn; Nat. Educ. Asn; Conn. Educ. Asn; Dept. Audiovisual Instruction; ASCD; Phi Beta Kappa; Alpha Delta Kappa. Publ: Report and Recommendations of the School Library Advisory Committee, Groton, Conn. Pub. Schs, annually, 60-; The Gifted Child, Radcliffe Quart, 11/57; Education in Our Era of the Knowledge Explosion, Conn. Parent-Teacher, 6/63; The Knapp Project Film—Something

---

KEY TO CONSULTING SPECIALTIES: 1) ARCHITECTURE AND BUILDINGS, 1a) public libraries, 1b) academic libraries, 1c) school libraries, 1d) special libraries, 1e) library interiors, 1f) furnishings, 1g) site and location, 1h) other architectural; 2) COLLECTIONS: SELECTION, EVALUATION, WEEDING, 2a) adults, 2b) young adults, 2c) children, 2d) subject specialty, 2e) O.P. searches, 2f) rare books, 2g) appraisals, 2h) others; 3) TECHNICAL PROCESSES, 3a) cataloging, 3b) classification systems, 3c) acquisitions, 3d) materials processing, 3e) work flow and cost studies, 3f) others, 4) AUTOMATION, 4a) applications of data processing equipment, 4b) information storage and retrieval systems, 4c) systems analysis, 4d) others

More Than a Movie, Sch. Libr, 10/65; Librarian and Students—Multimedia Team, The Instructor, 11/65; Teachers and Librarians: State Managers for the Learning Program, Childhood Educ, 10/66. Consult: 1) Mystic Oral Sch. for Deaf (State of Conn), Oral School Rd, Mystic, Conn, advised & assisted with Title II, ESEA, spring & summer 66; 2) North Stonington Elem. Sch. & High Sch, North Stonington, Conn, assisted with application for Title II, ESEA & made recommendations for materials to be ordered & helped plan high sch. libr. program, May 66-68; 3) NDEA Inst. for Sch. Libr. Supvr, Columbia Univ. Sch. Libr. Serv, gen. consult. & lectr, 67. Specialties: 2c, 2h (elem. sch. libr); 3a, 3b, 3c, 3d, 3e, 3f (processing center oper); 5a, 5b, 5d (use of volunteers in sch. libr. & their training); 6b; 7a, 7c; 8g (sch. libr. planning); 9 (drafting & planning programs for sch. systs. for ESEA, book fairs).

FIELD, MRS. CAROLYN W, Nov. 5, 16; Coordinator of Work with Children, Free Library of Philadelphia, Logan Square, Philadelphia, Pa. 19103. Home: 1A Manheim Gardens, Philadelphia, Pa. 19144. B.S, Simmons Col, 38. Coordinator of work with children, Free Libr. Phila, 53- Other: Instructor, grad. sch. educ, Univ. Del, 57-59; mem, Libr. Congress Adv. Cmt. on Selection of Children's Books for Blind & Physically Handicapped, 58-; pres, CSD, 60; instructor, grad. sch. libr. sci, Drexel Inst, 61- Mem: ALA; CSD; Libr. Pub. Relations Asn. Greater Phila. Publ: The Library Reaches Out (contrib), Oceana, 65; New Book of Knowledge Annual (contrib), 68. Consult: 1) New Book of Knowledge, New York, N.Y, rev. ed. of encyclopedia, 66; 2) Silver Burdett Co, Morristown, N.J, consult. for series—Folk Literature Around the World, 66-; 3) Imperial Book Co, Philadelphia, Pa, basic catalog of books for elem. & jr. high sch. libr, 68. Specialties: 2c; 9 (work with children in pub. libr, storytelling).

FILION, PAUL-EMILE, S.J, Aug. 9, 22; Chief Librarian, Laurentian University, Sudbury, Ont, Can. Home: Albanel Hall, Laurentian University Campus, Sudbury, Ont, Can. B.A, 48; L.Ph, 49; L.Th, 55; M.S. in L.S, 57. Chief librn, Col. Immaculée-Conception, Montreal, Que, Can, 57-60; chief librn, Laurentian Univ, Sudbury, Ont, 60- Other: Pres, sect. Montreal, Asn. Can. Bibliothécaires Langue Française; 59-60, pres, sect. bibliothèques univ. govt. & spécialisées, 63-64; mem. adv. coun, Nat. Libr Can, 64-67; mem. bd. dirs, Inst. Prfnl. Librns. Ont, 64-67, 2nd v.pres, 65-66; 2nd v.pres, Can. Libr. Asn, 65-66, mem. coun, 68-71. Mem: ALA; Can. Libr. Asn; Asn. Can. Bibliothécaire Langue Française; Inst. Prfnl. Librns. Ont; Cath. Libr. Asn; Am. Theol. Libr. Asn; Asn. Bibliothécaires Français. Publ: Newsletter (ed), Can. Asn. Col. & Univ. Libr, 64-; Une Enquête de Bibliothèque Universitaire, Colloque sur les Enquêtes de Bibliothèques et Leur Milieu-Inst. on Libr. & Community Surveys, Ecole Bibliothéconomie, 65. Consult: 1) Univ. Laval, Quebec 10, Que, Can, gen. survey of collections & serv. & follow-up review, with Edwin E. Williams, Oct. 62-Nov. 65; 2) Asn. Univs. & Cols. of Can. & Can. Asn. Col. & Univ. Libr, 151 Slater, Ottawa 4, Ont, Can, study of Can. col. & univ. libr, with Robert B. Downs, 66-67. Specialties: 1b, 2h (undergrad. collections); 3c; 5c; 8f.

FITZGERALD, MRS. LOUISE H, Library & Public Relations Consultant, Department of Education, Green Bay Diocese, Box 186, Green Bay, Wis. 54305. Home: 2702 Ravine Way, Green Bay, Wis. 54301. B.L.S, 38. Libr. & pub. relations consult, Dept. Educ, Green Bay Diocese, Green Bay, 65- Other: Publicity consult, Wis. Libr. Asn. Convention, 58 & 60; consult. to Univ. Wis. Extension Div. on developing programs for continuing educ. of women, 60. Mem: ALA; Cath. Libr. Asn; Wis. Libr. Asn; Wis. Cath. Libr. Asn. Publ: Contrib. to State Journal, Capital Times & Select Mag, Madison & Green Bay Press Gazette. Consult: 1) Madison Pub. Libr, Wis, pub. relations program for passage of bond issue, 58-61; 2) Kellogg Pub. Libr, Green Bay Wis, community relations & project consult, 61-65; 3) Sch. Libr. Center, Diocesan Dept. Educ, Box 186, Green Bay, consult. & adv. for encouraging & developing centralized libr. & collections in elem. & sec. schs, 65- Specialties: 1c; 2b, 2c; 3a, 3c, 3d, 3e; 6a, 6b, 6d (TV & radio publicity); 7a, 7b, 7c; 9 (nonpub. sch. libr. develop).

FITZGERALD, DR. WILLIAM A, Jan. 28, 06; Director of Libraries & Professor of Library Science, Marquette University Libraries, Milwaukee, Wis. 53233. Home: 1111 N. Astor St, B-3, Milwaukee, Wis. 53202. A.B, 27; M.A, 28; Ph.D, 34; B.S. in L.S, 38. Dir. & prof. libr. sci, libr. sch, George Peabody Col. Teachers, 48-63; dir. libr. & prof. libr. sci, Marquette Univ, Milwaukee, Wis, 64- Other: Pres, Cath. Libr. Asn, 39-41, pres. libr. educ. div, 56-57, chmn, 62-64; mem. bd. dirs, Center Res. Libr. Mem: ALA; Cath. Libr. Asn; SLA; Tenn. Libr. Asn; Wis. Libr. Asn; Med. Libr. Asn. Publ: Librarianship: American Profession, America, 7/51; Plans for the Future in Chinese Libraries, Bull. of Libr. Asn. of China, 10/57; Library Mission in Taiwan, ALA Bull, 4/59; Taiwan, Island of Refugees, Tenn. Librn, 4/60. Consult: 1) Republic of China, libr. consult to Ministry of Educ. & to Overseas Chinese Affairs Cmn. for all libr. & libr. training, 56-58; 2) Hong Kong, advised in amalgamation of refugee Chinese cols, 57; 3) Kingdom of Libya, libr. consult. for all libr. in country, 61-63; 4) Sierra Leone, libr. consult. to sec. schs, 62; 5) Liberia, libr. consult. to all libr, 63. Specialties: 2a, 2b; 5a, 5b, 5c; 7a; 8b, 8c, 8d, 8f.

---

5) PERSONNEL AND RECRUITING, 5a) job evaluation and description, salary recommendations, 5b) recruitment of professionals and management personnel, 5c) administrative organization, 6) PUBLIC RELATIONS, 6a) publications, 6b) publicity programs, 6c) public opinion surveys, 6d) others, 7) SERVICES, 7a) evaluation of current program, 7b) studies of service to special publics, e.g., students, handicapped, aged, etc., 7c) programs for the implementation of new laws, program proposals to governments, 7d) others, 8) COMMUNITY, REGIONAL, STATE PLANNING, 8a) legislative programs, 8b) area analyses, 8c) centralized systems, cooperative arrangements, 8d) development of standards, 8e) state libraries and extension agencies, 8f) regional and statewide surveys, 8g) others, 9) OTHERS.

FLANDERS, FRANCES VIVIAN, Sept. 18, 08; Head Librarian, Ouachita Parish Public Library, 1800 Stubbs Ave, Monroe, La. 71201. Home: 1703 N. Third St, Monroe, La. 71201. A.B, Northwest. State Col, La, 29; B.S.(libr. sci), La. State Univ, 36. Head librn, Ouachita Parish Pub. Libr, Monroe, La, 46- Other: Treas, La. Libr. Asn, 37-38, pres, 51, parliamentarian, 53-54, chmn, program cmt, 66-, former chmn, Modisette award, La. literary award, constitution & by-laws & adult educ. cmts. Mem: ALA; La. Libr. Asn. Publ: Contrib. to La. Libr. Bull. & Libr. J. Consult: 1) Fayetteville Pub. Libr, Fayetteville, Ark, consult. to architect, with Warren Seagraves, 60-62; 2) Rogers Pub. Libr, Rogers, Ark, consult. to architect, with Warren Seagraves, 62; 3) La. State Libr, bldg, 67- Specialties: 1a, 1e 1f; 2d (genealogy); 8d.

FLEISCHMAN, AL, Nov. 16, 40; Librarian, Merritt College, 5714 Grove, Oakland, Calif. 94609. Home: 142 Alvarado Rd, Berkeley, Calif. 94705. B.A, 62; M.L.S, 64. Res. dir, TRIAK, 60-64; verifier, G.T.U, 65; instructional media specialist, Oakland Pub. Schs, 66-67. Other: V.pres, Active Conservation Tactics, 65; mem. bd. dirs, Hiking Club, 66. Mem: Calif. Libr. Asn. Consult: 1) Camp Park Job Corps Center, Camp Parks, Calif, survey of libr. program & personnel needs, Nov-Dec, 65. Specialties: 2b, 2d (culturally deprived needs); 7a.

FOLCARELLI, RALPH JOSEPH, Oct. 5, 28; Associate Professor of Library Science, Graduate Library School of Long Island University, Greenvale, N.Y. 11548. Home: 117 Bay Dr, Huntington, N.Y. 11743. B.S, Kutztown State Col, 51; M.L.S, Rutgers Univ, 58. Coordinator of sch. libr, Pennsbury Schs, Fallsington, Pa, 54-59; head librn, Mansfield State Col, Pa, 59-61; libr. coordinator, Cold Spring Harbor Schs, Cold Spring Harbor, N.Y, 61-65; assoc. prof. libr. sci, grad. libr. sch. Long Island Univ, Greenvale, N.Y, 65- Other: Mem, standards for sch. libr. cmt, Pa. Dept. Pub. Instruction, 58; pres, Bucks County Sch. Libr. Asn, 59; mem. exec. bd, Suffolk County Libr. Asn, 64- Mem: N.Y. Libr. Asn; ALA; Suffolk County Libr. Asn; Nassau-Suffolk Sch. Libr. Asn; Nat. Educ. Asn. Publ: Chap, In: Successful Reading Techniques for Secondary Schools, Pennsbury Schs, 57; Why Close the Library One Day a Week?, Grade Teacher, 11/65; Not a School—But a Library, SCLA Data, winter 66; Individualized Reading Programs..., Grade Teacher, 11/66. Consult: 1) Emma Willard Sch, Troy, N.Y, planning of new libr, Feb. 64; 2) Mid. Country Schs. Centereach, Selden, N.Y, planning of libr, 65-66; 3) Bureau of Sch. Libr, State Educ. Dept, Albany, N.Y, definitive manual on sec. sch. libr, with Diana Lembo & John Gillespie, 66; 4) Three Village Sch. Dist, Stonybrook-Setauket, N.Y, planning of libr, 66; 5) North Shore Schs, Glen Head, N.Y, eval. of program, 68-69. Specialties: 1c, 1e, 1f, 1h (decentralized sch. libr); 2b, 2g; 3d; 7a, 7c; 8c, 8d.

FRANKLIN, ROBERT D, Sept. 15, 08; Director, Toledo Public Library, 325 Michigan, Toledo, Ohio 43624. Home: 2707 Manchester Blvd, Toledo, Ohio 43606. B.A, Univ. Tenn, 33; B.S. in L.S, Columbia Univ, 34. Asst. dir, Toledo Pub. Libr, Ohio, 46-55, dir, 55- Other: Pres, Ohio Libr. Asn, 55; lectr. pub. libr. admin, Univ. Toledo M.L.S. prog, spring semesters, 63-; v.pres, Toledo Rotary Club, 65-66. Mem: Ohio Libr. Asn; ALA. Publ: Contrib. to The Administrator and the Board, Libr. Trends, 7/62. Consult: 1) Lansing Pub. Libr, Lansing, Mich, site selection, with Al Trezza, 62; 2) Kendallville Pub. Libr, Kendallville, Ind, site & program consult, 62; 3) Port Clinton Pub. Libr, Port Clinton, Ohio, site selection, program & new bldg. planning, May 66-; 4) U.S. Virgin Islands Pub. Libr. Serv, survey, Nov. 67 & consult. on program & bldg. planning, 67-68; 5) Bellevue Pub. Libr, Bellevue, Ohio, site & bldg. program, 68. Specialties: 1a, 1g; 2a; 5c; 6d (gen. pub. relations & staff relations); 7a; 8a, 8f; 9 (slide talks on pub. libr. serv. & staff relations).

FRAREY, CARLYLE J, Apr. 1, 18; Assistant to the Dean, School of Library Service, Columbia University, New York, N.Y. 10027. Home: 39 Claremont Ave, Apt. 61, New York, N.Y. 10027. B.A, Oberlin Col, 39; B.S.(libr. serv), Columbia Univ, 47, M.S.(libr. serv), 51. Assoc. prof, sch. libr. sci, Univ. N.C, Chapel Hill, 54-64, acting dean, sch. libr. sci, 60-64; asst. to dean & sr. lectr, sch. libr. serv, Columbia Univ, New York, N.Y, 64- Other: Mem. coun, ALA, 53-57 & 59-65, mem. exec. cmt, div. cataloging & classification, 53-57, mem. exec. cmt, cataloging & classification sect, 67-69, chmn, 68; managing ed, Journal of Cataloging & Classification & Libr. Resources & Tech. Serv, 53-61; mem. exec. bd, Asn. Am. Libr. Schs, 62-66; v.chmn, Decimal Classification Ed. Policy Cmt, 63-66, chmn, 66-69. Mem: ALA; SLA; Am. Asn. Libr. Schs; Am. Asn. Univ. Prof; N.Y. Libr. Asn; N.C. Libr. Asn; Southeast. Libr. Asn; N.Y. Tech. Serv. Librns. Publ: Technical Services in Libraries (with M.F. Tauber & others), Columbia Univ, 54; The Processing Services of the Dallas Public Library: A Report on Their Organization, Operation, and Administration, Dallas Pub. Libr, 59; Subject Headings, Rutgers Univ. Grad. Sch. Libr. Serv, 60. Consult: 1) Dallas Pub. Libr, Dallas, Tex, study of the processing opers. with recommendations, June-Aug. 59. Specialties: 3a, 3b, 3c, 3d, 3e.

FRIEDLANDER, DR. MICHEL O, Feb. 15, 08; Retired. Home: 68-54 Selfridge St, Forest Hills, N.Y. 11375. LL.D, Univ. Vienna, 31; M.S.L.S, Carnegie Inst. Tech, 42. Dir, engineering libr, Grumman Aircraft Corp, Beth-

---

KEY TO CONSULTING SPECIALTIES: 1) ARCHITECTURE AND BUILDINGS, 1a) public libraries, 1b) academic libraries, 1c) school libraries, 1d) special libraries, 1e) library interiors, 1f) furnishings, 1g) site and location, 1h) other architectural; 2) COLLECTIONS: SELECTION, EVALUATION, WEEDING, 2a) adults, 2b) young adults, 2c) children, 2d) subject specialty, 2e) O.P. searches, 2f) rare books, 2g) appraisals, 2h) others; 3) TECHNICAL PROCESSES, 3a) cataloging, 3b) classification systems, 3c) acquisitions, 3d) materials processing, 3e) work flow and cost studies, 3f) others, 4) AUTOMATION, 4a) applications of data processing equipment, 4b) information storage and retrieval systems, 4c) systems analysis, 4d) others

page, N.Y, until 68. Other: Chmn, ASTI Coordinating Cmt, SLA, 59-63, chmn. aerospace div, 65-66. Mem: SLA; Am. Soc. Info. Sci. Publ: The Research Librarian in a Challenging Age, Spec. Libr, 1/64; Planning the New Library: Grumman Aircraft Engineering Library, Spec. Libr, 2/64; Inside the Company Library—What It Contains and How to Use It, Electronic Design, 9/64; Inside the Company Library—The Technical Report, Electronic Design, 10/64; Research & Report, Today's Secy, 3/65; The L Report and the Report Gap, Sci-Tech News, fall-winter 65. Consult: 1) Pall Corp, Glen Cove, N.Y, establishing new libr, fall 62; 2) Nassau County Air Pollution Dept, 240 Old Country Rd, Mineola, N.Y, establishing a new libr, fall 65. Specialties: 1d; 2d (sci, tech); 3a, 3b, 3c, 3d, 3e; 4a, 4b, 4c; 5a, 5b, 5c; 6a, 6c; 7a, 7c; 9 (document, transl).

FRY, ALDERSON, Mar. 26, 06; Librarian, Medical Center Library, West Virginia University, Morgantown, W.Va. 26506. Home: 212 Logan, Morgantown, W.Va. 26505. A.B, 28; B.S, 29; M.A, 35; M.L.S, 37. Librn, Health Sci. Libr, Univ. Wash, Seattle, 48-56; librn, Med. Center Libr, W.Va. Univ, Morgantown, 56- Other: Chmn. & mem. several cmts, Med. Libr. Asn, 47-66, mem. bd, 63-66. Mem: ALA; Med. Libr. Asn; SLA. Publ: Plan and Equipment of the Health Sciences Library, University of Washington, Bull. Med. Libr. Asn, 1/53; Problems in Establishing a Dental Library, Bull. Med. Libr. Asn, 1/56; Medical Library Architecture in the Past Fifty Years, Bull. Med. Libr. Asn, 10/57; Planning a Better Medical School Library: Panel Discussion, Bull. Med. Libr. Asn, 4/61; Random Thoughts about Medical Library Planning, Bull. Med. Libr. Asn, 7/65; Medical Library Planning and Equipment, In: Handbook of Medical Library Practice, ALA, 3rd ed, 69. Consult: 1) Med. Libr, Seth G.S. Med. Sch, Bombay, India, planned new libr, Nov 63-Feb. 64; 2) Dental Libr, Am. Dental Asn, Chicago, Ill, new dental libr, May 65; 3) Med. Libr, Georgetown Univ. Med. Sch, Wash, D.C, new libr. plans, 65-66; 4) Med. Libr, Med. Sch, Univ. Louisville, Louisville, Ky, new libr. plans, Oct. 65-Feb. 66; 5) Health Sci. Libr, Gen. Hosp, Port of Spain, Trinidad, West Indies, planned a libr, Mar-Apr. 66. Specialties: 1d, 1h (med. center libr).

FUSSLER, DR. HERMAN HOWE, May 15, 14; Director of Library & Professor, Graduate Library School, University of Chicago Library, Chicago, Ill. 60637. Home: 5844 Stony Island Ave, Chicago, Ill. 60637. A.B, Univ. N.C, 35, A.B.L.S, 36; M.A, Univ. Chicago, 41, Ph.D, 48. Dir. libr. & prof, grad. libr. sch, Univ. Chicago, Chicago, Ill, 48-, acting dean, grad. libr. sch, 61-63. Other: Mem. bd. dirs, Center Res. Libr, 50-, chmn. 60-61; Melvil Dewey medal, ALA, 54; mem. bd. dirs, Asn. Res. Libr, 62-65, chmn. cmt. libr. automation, 63-65; mem. bd. regents, Nat. Libr. Med,

63-67. Mem: ALA; Am. Document. Inst; fel. Am. Asn. Advancement Sci; Ill. Libr. Asn. Publ: Photographic Reproduction for Libraries, 42; Library Buildings for Library Service (ed), 47; The Function of the Library in the Modern College (ed), 54; The Research Library in Transition, Univ. Tenn. Libr. Lectures, 57; Patterns in the Use of Books in Large Research Libraries (with Julian Simon), Univ. Chicago Libr, 61. Consult: 1) Ford Found, New York, N.Y. & Paris, France, advised on bldg. of the Maison des Sciences de l'Homme, Paris, France, with Douglas Bryant, 60 & 63; 2) Ford Found, New York, N.Y. & São Paulo, Brazil, libr. bldg. & orgn. of Univ. São Paulo, Brazil, 62; 3) State Cols. Calif, Office of the Chancellor, Los Angeles, Calif, develop. of resources, tech. serv. & bldgs. & fiscal control of state col. libr, 63; 4) Univ. Calif. Berkeley & other campuses, orgn. problems & res. objectives Libr. Res. Inst, 64. Specialties: 1b; 2d (gen. resource problems of large res. libr. & cooperative facilities); 4a, 4b, 4c.

G

GALFAND, SIDNEY, Sept. 12, 15; Supervisor of Central Processing, School District of Philadelphia, 734 Schuylkill Ave, Philadelphia, Pa. 19146. Home: 725 Yale Rd, Cynwyd, Pa. 19004. B.S. in Ed, 36; B.S.(libr. sci), 38; M.Ed, 46. High sch. librn, 36-61; synagogue librn, Temple Adath Israel, 55-62 & Har Zion Temple, 62-; instr. libr. sci, Villanova Univ. & Drexel Inst. Tech, 61-; supvr. cent. processing, Sch. Dist. Phila, Phila, Pa, 61- Other: Past pres. & secy, Sch. Librns. Asn. Phila; founder, 1st pres. & permanent mem. exec. bd, Jewish Libr. Asn. Greater Phila; mem, Sch. Libr. Tech. Serv. Cmt, 61; pres, Asn. Prfnl. Supvr, 64-65; mem. supt. adv. cmt, Phila. Sch. Dist, 64-65; chmn. joint seminar Jewish librarianship, Drexel Inst. Tech-Jewish Libr. Asn; mem. exec. bd, Drexel Libr. Sch. Alumni Asn. Mem: ALA; Asn. Jewish Libr; Jewish Libr. Asn. Greater Phila; Sch. Librns. Asn. Phila; Spec. Libr. Asn. Phila; Pa. Libr. Asn; Phila. Area Tech. Serv. Librns. Asn; Cath. Libr. Asn; Drexel Libr. Sch. Alumni Asn; Schoolmen's Club; Pi Gamma Mu. Publ: The School Library (co-auth), In: Professional Growth, Crofts, 58; Organized Jewish Libraries, Libr. J, 1/1/61; Central Cataloging, Newsletter, Phila. Teachers Asn, 5/63. Consult: 1) Akiba Hebrew Academy, Merion, Pa, consult. on libr. orgn, 60. Specialties: 2b, 2c, 2d (Judaica in English); 3a, 3d; 9 (orgn. of synagogue libr, orgn. of sch. libr. processing centers).

GALICK, MRS. V. GENEVIEVE, Feb. 27, 13; Director, Massachusetts Bureau of Library Extension, 648 Beacon St, Boston, Mass. 02215. Home: 28 Travis Rd, Natick, Mass. 01760. B.S, Simmons Col, 34. Dir, Mass. Bureau Libr. Extension, Boston, 49- Other: Mem,

---

5) PERSONNEL AND RECRUITING, 5a) job evaluation and description, salary recommendations, 5b) recruitment of professionals and management personnel, 5c) administrative organization, 6) PUBLIC RELATIONS, 6a) publications, 6b) publicity programs, 6c) public opinion surveys, 6d) others, 7) SERVICES, 7a) evaluation of current program, 7b) studies of service to special publics, e.g., students, handicapped, aged, etc., 7c) programs for the implementation of new laws, program proposals to governments, 7d) others, 8) COMMUNITY, REGIONAL, STATE PLANNING, 8a) legislative programs, 8b) area analyses, 8c) centralized systems, cooperative arrangements, 8d) development of standards, 8e) state libraries and extension agencies, 8f) regional and statewide surveys, 8g) others, 9) OTHERS.

Lippincott Jury award cmt, ALA, 64, councilor-at-large, 66-70; chmn. nominating cmt, ALA-ASL, 65; mem. exec. bd, ASL, 66-70; v.pres. & pres. elect, New Eng. Libr. Asn, 67-68, pres, 68-69. Mem: ALA; New Eng. Libr. Asn; Mass. Libr. Asn; SLA; Cath. Libr. Asn. Publ: Contrib. to prfnl. journals. Consult: 1) Mass. Div. Civil Serv, Boston, developing position specifications & examinations, 49-66; 2) Bureau of Libr, Conn. Dept. Educ, Hartford, statewide libr. develop. plans, with L. Marion Moshier, 58; 3) Libr. Serv. Br, U.S. Office Educ, Wash, D.C, collection of pub. libr. statist, 60; 4) N.Y. State Civil Serv. Div. & Dept. Educ. Bureau of Personnel, Albany, examiner serv, 60 & 64; 5) Tex. Educ. Agency, Austin, ESEA Titles (sch. libr. resources & materials), May 66. Specialties: 5a, 5b, 5c; 7a, 7b, 7c; 8a, 8b, 8c, 8d, 8e, 8f.

GALVIN, HOYT R, Feb. 26, 11; Director, Public Library of Charlotte & Mecklenburg County, P.O. Box 20532, Charlotte, N.C. 28202. Home: 2259 Vernon Dr, Charlotte, N.C. 28211. B.A, Simpson Col, 32; B.S. in L.S, Univ. Ill, 33. Dir, Pub. Libr. Charlotte & Mecklenburg County, Charlotte, N.C, 40- Other: Pres, Ala. Libr. Asn, 38-39; pres, N.C. Libr. Asn, 39-43; pres, Rotary Club Charlotte, 49-50; chmn. bldgs. cmt, ALA, 50-54; chmn. educ. cmt, Charlotte Chamber Commerce, 53 & 63; pres, N.C. Adult Educ. Asn, 57; chmn. coun. librarianship, N.C. Libr. Asn-ALA Recruiting Project, 59-62; pres, Southeast. Libr. Asn, 62-64; mem, Am. Inst. Architects-ALA-Nat. Book Cmt. Libr. Bldg. Award Jury, 64 & 66; pres, LAD, 65-66. Mem: N.C. Libr. Asn; N.C. Adult Educ. Asn; Southeast. Libr. Asn; ALA. Publ: Films in Public Libraries, Bowker, 47; Planning a Library Building, the Major Steps (ed), ALA, 55; The Small Public Library Building (with Martin Van Buren), UNESCO, Paris, France, 59; Proposed Outline for Public Library Building Institutes and Workshops (auth. & ed), Libr. Serv. Br, U.S. Office Educ, 64; forty libr. bldg. programs & consult. reports, 58-68. Consult: 1) Augusta-Richmond County Pub. Libr, Augusta, Ga, develop plans for pub. libr. bldg, 60; 2) Granville County Libr, Oxford, N.C, develop. of plans for libr. bldg, 63; 3) Portsmouth Pub. Libr, Portsmouth, Va, develop. remodel plans for pub. libr. bldg, 63; 4) New Albany-Floyd County Pub. Libr, New Albany, Ind, develop. bldg. program & plans for pub. libr. bldg, 68; 5) Bryant Libr, Roslyn, N.Y, bldg. prog. & plans for pub. libr. bldg, 68. Specialties: 1a, 1b, 1e, 1f, 1g.

GALVIN, THOMAS JOHN, Dec. 30, 32; Director of Students & Associate Professor of Library Science, School of Library Science, Simmons College, Boston, Mass. 02115. Home: 30 Winter St, South Braintree, Mass. 02185. A.B, Columbia Univ, 54; S.M, Simmons Col, 56. Reference librn, Boston Univ, 54-56; chief librn, Abbot Pub. Libr, Marblehead, Mass, 56-59; asst. dir. libr. & lectr. libr. sci, Simmons Col, Boston, Mass, 59-62, acting dir, sch. libr. sci, 62-63, dir. students, 62-, asst. prof. libr. sci, 62-67, assoc. prof, 67- Other: Mem. exec. cmt, Mass. Pub. Libr. Film Cooperative, 57-59; chmn. membership cmt, Mass. Libr. Asn, 58-59, treas, 59-62, chmn. cmt. certification of librns, 60-62; exec. officer, Multi-National Seminar for Foreign Librns, ALA-U.S. Dept. State, 61-62; mem. joint cmt. to study content of reference courses, ALA-Asn. Am. Libr. Schs, 63-65; chmn. subscription books cmt, ALA, 64-66, mem. coun, 64-66; mem. regional planning cmt, New Eng. Libr. Asn, 64-, chmn. cmt. to establish a regional recruiting center for librarianship, 65-66; mem. publ. cmt, LED, 64-, legis. cmt, 68-; exec. officer, pub. libr. bldg. inst, Simmons Col, 65, exec. officer, inst. pub. libr. trustees, 66; mem. cmt. instruction, Asn. Am. Libr. Schs, 65-; dir-at-large, RSD, 67-; mem. standards develop. cmt, ASD, 68- Mem: ALA; Asn. Am. Libr. Schs; New Eng. Libr. Asn; Mass. Libr. Asn; Am. Asn. Univ. Prof; Phi Beta Kappa; Am. Soc. Info. Sci. Publ: The Case Technique in Education for Reference Service, J. Educ. for Librarianship, spring 63; Supply and Demand of Library Personnel in Massachusetts, Bay State Librn, 4/64; Regional Union Lists— Some Unanswered Questions, Libr. Resources & Tech. Serv, winter 64; Problems in Reference Service, R.R. Bowker, 65; Public Library Book Selection, North Country Libr, 1-2/66; Building a Strong Reference Collection, Choice, 6/66. Consult: 1) Vt. Tech. Col, Randolph, develop. of book collection, 64-65; 2) Groton Pub. Libr, Groton, Mass, survey of libr. bldg. & serv, with Kenneth R. Shaffer, Nov. 65-May 66; 3) State Street Bank & Trust Co, Boston, Mass, orgn. & staffing tech. libr, Mar-Apr. 66; 4) Architects Collaborative, Cambridge, Mass, orgn. & staffing tech. libr, Aug. 66; 5) Beacon Press, Inc, Boston, bibliog. adv, 66- Specialties: 2a, 2d (reference holdings of acad. & spec. libr), 2h (develop. of acad. & spec. libr. collections); 3c; 5a; 7a, 7b, 7d (acad. & spec. libr. serv—eval. & program develop); 9 (reference & subscription book publ).

GARRISON, DR. GUY, Dec. 17, 27; Dean & Professor, Graduate School of Library Science, Drexel Institute of Technology, Philadelphia, Pa. 19104. Home: 2280 N. 52nd St, Philadelphia, Pa. 19131. B.A, 50; M.S, 54; Ph.D, 60. Asst. librn, Oak Park Pub. Libr, Ill, 56-58; grad. fel, Univ. Ill, 58-60; head, Reader Serv, Kansas City Pub. Libr, Mo, 60-62; dir. libr. res. center & prof, grad. sch. libr. sci, Univ. Ill, Urbana, 62-68. Mem: ALA; Pa. Libr. Asn. Publ: Seattle Voters and Their Public Library, Ill. State Libr, 61; Voting on a Library Bond Issue, Libr. Quart, 7/63; Research Methods in Librarianship (ed), Libr. Trends, 7/64; A Statewide Reference System for Wisconsin Libraries, Univ. Ill, Urbana, 64; Some Recent Public Library Branch Location Studies by City Planners, Libr. Quart, 4/66; The Changing

---

KEY TO CONSULTING SPECIALTIES: 1) ARCHITECTURE AND BUILDINGS, 1a) public libraries, 1b) academic libraries, 1c) school libraries, 1d) special libraries, 1e) library interiors, 1f) furnishings, 1g) site and location, 1h) other architectural; 2) COLLECTIONS: SELECTION, EVALUATION, WEEDING, 2a) adults, 2b) young adults, 2c) children, 2d) subject specialty, 2e) O.P. searches, 2f) rare books, 2g) appraisals, 2h) others; 3) TECHNICAL PROCESSES, 3a) cataloging, 3b) classification systems, 3c) acquisitions, 3d) materials processing, 3e) work flow and cost studies, 3f) others, 4) AUTOMATION, 4a) applications of data processing equipment, 4b) information storage and retrieval systems, 4c) systems analysis, 4d) others

Role of State Library Consultants (ed), Univ. Ill, Urbana, 68. Consult: 1) D.C. Libr. Asn, Wash, D.C, proposal for study of libr. serv. to students, Oct. 64; 2) N. Country Reference & Res. Resources Coun, Canton, N.Y, survey of libr. resources, with Barbara Slanker, 65-66; 3) Pub. Libr, Dixon, Ill, libr. bldg, 66-67; 4) Pub. Libr, River Forest, Ill, bldg. & site eval, July 66; 5) Pub. Libr, Skokie, Ill, bldg. & site eval, Jan. 68. Specialties: 1a, 1g; 7c; 8b, 8c, 8e, 8f.

GAVER, MARY VIRGINIA, Professor, Graduate School of Library Service, Rutgers, The State University, New Brunswick, N.J. 08903. Home: 29 Baldwin St, New Brunswick, N.J. 08901. A.B, 27; B.S.(libr. sci), 32; M.S.(libr. sci), 38. Prof. Grad. Sch. Libr. Serv, Rutgers Univ, 54- Other: V.pres, N.J. Libr. Asn, 47-48, pres, 54-55, chmn, libr. develop. cmt, 52-54, co-chmn, 63-; pres, LED, 49-50; pres, AASL, 57-58; chmn. adv. cmt, Knapp Sch. Libr. Project, 63-66; pres, ALA, 66-67. Mem: ALA. Publ: The Research Paper (with Lucyle Hook), Prentice-Hall, 4th ed, 69; Effectiveness of Centralized School Library Services (Phase 1), Rutgers Univ, 2nd ed, 63; School Libraries of Puerto Rico (with Gonzalo Velasquez), 63; Libraries for the People of New Jersey (with Lowell Martin), 64; Patterns of Development of Elementary School Libraries Today, Encyclopaedia Britannica, 3rd ed, 69; The Elementary School Library Collection, Basic Materials (ed), Bro-Dart Found, annual plus suppl. Consult: 1) Baltimore County Libr, Towson, Md, eval. of collection & pattern for admin. of children's & young adult serv, with Lowell Martin, 58; 2) Bd. of Educ, La Grange, Ill, eval. of total program of high sch. & jr. col. libr, 61; 3) Coun. of Libr. Resources & Libr. Asn. of Puerto Rico, eval. of elem. & sec. sch. libr. resources & facilities, with Gonzalo Velazquez, 62; 4) N.J. Libr. Asn, co-author & co-chmn. of N.J. Libr. Asn. program for develop. of N.J. libr, with Lowell Martin & J.E. Bryan, 63- Specialties: 2b, 2c; 7a, 7b; 8d, 8f.

GEDDES, ANDREW, Oct. 2, 22; Director, Nassau Library System, Lower Concourse, Roosevelt Field, Garden City, N.Y. 11530. Home: 29 Patten Ave, Oceanside, N.Y. 11572. B.A.(hist), 50; M.L.S, Columbia Univ, 51. Admin. asst. to chief librn, Queens Borough Pub. Libr, 55-58, chief extension serv, 58-63; deputy dir, Nassau Libr. Syst, Hempstead, N.Y, 63-64, dir, 64- Other: Mem. liaison cmt. to Am. Textbook Pub. Inst, ALA, 62-67, chmn. regional rep. office for recruitment, 63-68; chmn. personnel admin. cmt, N.Y. Libr. Asn, 63-65, v.pres. & pres-elect, 65-67; chmn. statist. cmt, N.C. Libr. Asn, 64-66; chmn. cmt. certification of librns, LAD-PAS, 65-66. Mem: ALA; N.Y. Libr. Asn; N.J. Libr. Asn; Libr. Pub. Relations Coun; Archons of Colophons; Melville Dui Chowder & Marching Asn; N.Y. Libr. Club; Nassau County Libr. Asn; Columbia Alumni Asn; Hofstra Alumni Asn; Booksellers League. Publ: Survey of the Finkelstein Memorial Library, Spring Valley, New York (with Edgar Glick), 2/62; A Survey of Queens Communities with recommendation for Library Service, 5/63; Survey of the Cherry Hill (N.J) Public Library (with Edgar Glick), 3/64; Survey of the Gloucester City (N.J) Public Library, 11/64; Current Trends in Branch Libraries (spec. issue ed), Libr. Trends, 4/66; contrib. to prfnl. periodicals. Consult: 1) Queens Borough Pub. Libr, Jamaica, N.Y, study of br. & possible br. sites, May 63; 2) Cherry Hill Free Pub. Libr, Cherry Hill, N.J, study of serv, staffing, collections, budgeting & facilities, with Edgar A. Glick, Mar. 64; 3) Gloucester City Libr, Gloucester City, N.J, complete study of serv, staffing, collections, budgeting & facilities, Nov. 64; 4) Finkelstein Mem. Libr, Spring Valley, N.J, bldg. consult, June 66; 5) Morris County Free Libr, Morristown, N.J, study of serv, staffing, collections, budgeting & facilities, with William Ersfeld, Oct. 66. Specialties: 1a, 1g; 2a, 2b, 2c, 2g; 4a; 5a, 5b, 5c; 7a; 8b, 8c.

GELFAND, DR. MORRIS A, June 1, 08; Chief Librarian, Paul Klapper Library, Queens College, City University of New York, Flushing, N.Y. 11367. Home: Stone House, Post Dr, Roslyn Harbor, N.Y. 11576. B.S, 33; B.S. in L.S, 34; M.A, 39; Ph.D, 60. Supvr. reserve reading room, Wash. Square Libr, N.Y. Univ, 31-37; libr. asst, asst. librn. & chief librn, Queens Col, City Univ. New York, Flushing, N.Y, 37-, initiator & supvr. libr. educ. program, 54-64. Other: Libr. officer, U.S. Army Forces, Pac, 45-46; pres, N.Y. Libr. Club, 47; mem. eval. cmts, Mid. States Asn. Cols. & Sec. Schs, 49-; chmn, Wilson Indexes Cmt, 52-53, mem, 53-67; mem. cmt. relations with publ, ALA, 55-56, ALA rep, UN orgn, 62-65, mem. adv. cmt. for Univ. Brasilia Project, 63-; mem. cmt. standards, ACRL, 61-62, mem. cmt. libr. surveys, 62-65, mem. program cmt. for 1966 conf; mem. bd. trustees, New York Metrop. Reference & Res. Libr. Agency, Inc, 65; mem. bd. trustees, Coun. on Res. in Bibliog, Inc, 66; mem. bd. trustees, Bryant Libr, Roslyn, N.Y. Mem: ALA; ACRL; N.Y. Libr. Club, N.Y. Libr. Asn; Am. Asn. Univ. Prof; Bibliog. Soc. Am; Archons of Colophon. Publ: Techniques of Library Evaluators in the Middle States Association, Col. & Res. Libr, 7/58; Creating Personnel Policies to Attract and Retain Librarians, Educ. Record, 7/60; University Library Buildings and Equipment, UNESCO, 62; Cooperative Acquisition Schemes and the Developing Countries, UNESCO Bull. Libr, 11-12/65; Brazil's Library Law, Libr. J, 3/15/66; University Libraries for Developing Countries, UNESCO, Paris, 68. Consult: 1) Univ. Rangoon, Rangoon, Burma, survey of univ. libr, 58-59; 2) Nat. Libr. Burma, Rangoon, UNESCO program for proposed bldg, May-June 59; 3) Chulalongkorn Univ, Nat. Libr. Thailand,

5) PERSONNEL AND RECRUITING, 5a) job evaluation and description, salary recommendations, 5b) recruitment of professionals and management personnel, 5c) administrative organization, 6) PUBLIC RELATIONS, 6a) publications, 6b) publicity programs, 6c) public opinion surveys, 6d) others, 7) SERVICES, 7a) evaluation of current program, 7b) studies of service to special publics, e.g., students, handicapped, aged, etc., 7c) programs for the implementation of new laws, program proposals to governments, 7d) others, 8) COMMUNITY, REGIONAL, STATE PLANNING, 8a) legislative programs, 8b) area analyses, 8c) centralized systems, cooperative arrangements, 8d) development of standards, 8e) state libraries and extension agencies, 8f) regional and statewide surveys, 8g) others, 9) OTHERS.

Bangkok, Thailand, UNESCO libr. expert for reorgn. of Nat. Libr, plans for new nat. libr. bldg. & improvement of sch. & pub. libr. serv, May-July 62; 4) Univ. Brasilia, Brasilia, D.F, Brasil, admin. reorgn, preliminary estimates for new bldg, recommendations for strengthening faculty of libr. sci, Mar-May 66; 5) Univ. Delhi, Delhi 6, India, survey of dept. libr. sci. with recommendations, July-Sept. 66. Specialties: 1b; 5c; 7a.

GELLER, WILLIAM SPENCE, Mar. 31, 14; County Librarian, Los Angeles County Public Library System, P.O. Box 42272, Los Angeles, Calif. 90042. Home: 624 Knight Way, La Canada, Calif. 91011. A.B, Univ. South. Calif, 36, M.S, 37; B.L.S, Univ. Calif, Berkeley, 53. Asst. county librn, Los Angeles County Pub. Libr. Syst, Los Angeles, Calif, 56-63, county librn, 63- Other: Chmn. exhibits cmt, Calif. Libr. Asn, 54, chmn. constitution revision cmt, 55, mem. libr. develop. & standards cmt, 62, 63 & 66, chmn, finance cmt, 64-65, mem. legis. cmt, 65, v.pres. & pres-elect south. dist, 65, pres, 66, mem. exec. bd, 66; mem. cmt. pub. libr. standards, PLA, 55, mem. cmt. interlibr. cooperation, 63-67, chmn, 65-67, chmn. study pub. libr. systs, 66; secy, v.pres. & pres, Pub. Libr. Execs. South. Calif, 57-60; mem. equipment cmt, ALA, 58-65, chmn, 61-62, regional chmn. membership cmt, 61-62, mem. adminstr. large pub. libr, 63-; pres. alumni asn, Sch. Librarianship, Univ. Calif, Berkeley, 61; mem. adv. cmt, Calif. Statewide Survey Pub. Libr. Serv, 64-65; mem. libr. adv. cmt, County Supvr. Asn, 64-, v.chmn, 65, mem. electronic data-processing people cmt, 66; chmn. nominating cmt, LAD, 65; mem. adv. coun. educ. for librarianship, Univ. Calif, 65-68; mem. adv. coun, sch. libr. sci, Univ. South. Calif; mem. hist. landmarks cmt, County of Los Angeles; mem. adv. cmt, first dist. coun, Congress of Parents & Teachers. Mem: ALA; Calif. Libr. Asn; Pub. Libr. Execs. South. Calif; County Supvr. Asn; Pi Sigma Alpha. Publ: Duplicate Catalogs in Regional and Public Library Systems, Libr. Quart, 1/64; Gauging Progress, Libr. J, 9/15/66; The Rio Hondo Regional Library, Los Angeles County Public Library System (with Ben Bailey), News Notes of Calif. Libr, summer 66; The West San Gabriel Valley Regional Library, Los Angeles County Public Library System (with Ben Bailey), News Notes of Calif. Libr, summer 66. Consult: 1) Gardena Libr, Gardena, Calif; 2) Duarte Libr, Duarte, Calif; 3) Rio Hondo Regional Libr, Montebello, Calif; 4) West San Gabriel Regional Libr, Rosemead, Calif; 5) San Gabriel Libr, San Gabriel, Calif. Specialties: 1a, 1e, 1f, 1g; 5c; 7c, 7d (projected planning for serv. programs); 8b, 8c, 8f.

GEORGI, CHARLOTTE; Chief Librarian, Graduate School of Business Administration, University of California, Los Angeles, Calif. 90024. Home: 545 Kelton Ave, Los Angeles, Calif. 90024. B.A, Univ. Buffalo, 42, M.A, 43; M.S.L.S, Univ. N.C, 56. Chief librn, bus. admin. & soc. sci. div, Univ. N.C, 57-59; chief librn, grad. sch. bus. admin, Univ. Calif, Los Angeles, 59- Other: Secy. bus. & finance div, SLA, 61-62, v.chmn, 62-63, chmn, 63-64, mem. bd. dirs, 66-69. Mem: SLA; ALA; Calif. Libr. Asn. Publ: The Novel and the Pulitzer Prize, 1918-1958, Univ. N.C. Libr, 58; The Businessman in the Novel, Univ. N.C. Libr, 59; Sources of Commodity Prices (co-compiler), SLA, 60; Statistics Sources, Gale Res. Co, 62, 2nd ed, 65; The Literature of Executive Management, SLA, 63; contrib, prfnl. journals. Consult: 1) Arthur Young & Co, Los Angeles, Calif, consulted on local libr. resources in field of accounting, 62-63; 2) Training Develop. Program, Bank of Am, Los Angeles, consulted on setting up libr, set up the libr, trained & consulted with the librn. hired to maintain it, 66-67; 3) Cantor-Fitzgerald, Beverly Hills, Calif, consulting on setting up a financial libr, 67-; 4) Rogers, Cowan & Brenner, Beverly Hills, consulting on setting up a financial libr, 68-; 5) Librn. of Office of Econ. Production, Univ. Chile, Santiago, Chile, consultation, 66-67. Specialties: 1d; 2d (bus. & econ. liberal arts), 2f; 3c; 5a, 5c; 6a, 7a; 8c.

GERLACH, DR. ARCH C, May 12, 11; Chief Geographer, U.S. Geological Survey, Washington, D.C. 20242. Home: 5615 Newington Rd, Washington, D.C. 20016. B.A,(geography), San Diego State Col, 33; M.A.(geography), Univ. Calif, Los Angeles, 35; Ph.D.(geography), Univ. Wash, Seattle, 43. Chief, geography & map div, Libr. Congress, Wash, D.C, 50-67; chief geographer, U.S. Geological Survey, 67- Other: Mem, exec. bd, SLA, 57-60; pres, Asn. Am. Geographers, 62-63; v.pres, Int. Geographical Union, 64-68. Mem: SLA. Publ: Potential Uses of Government Libraries for Geographical Research, J. Geography, 1/53; Geography and Map Cataloging and Classification in Libraries, Spec. Libr, 5-6/61; Technical Problems in Atlas Making, In: International Yearbook of Cartography. Consult: 1) Univ. Mich, Ann Arbor, reorgn. of map libr, Sept. 57-Jan. 58. Specialties: 1d, 2h (geography & cartography).

GIBSON, FRANK E, May 30, 13; Director, Omaha Public Library, 1823 Harney, Omaha, Nebr. 68102. Home: 6802 N. 41st St, Omaha, Nebr. 68112. B.A, 48; B.S. in L.S, 49; M.A, 52. Asst. dir, Omaha Pub. Libr, Omaha, Nebr, 53-57, dir, 57- Other: Pres, Nebr. Libr. Asn, 56-57, coun, 63-66; mem. archit. cmt. for pub. libr, LAD, 56-62, chmn. libr. orgn. & mgt, budgeting, accounting & costs cmt, 60-62, chmn. sect. bldgs. & equipment, 63-64; spec. consult. libr. bldgs, Nebr. Pub. Libr. Cmn, 61- Mem: Nebr. Libr. Asn; ALA; Phi Beta Kappa. Consult: 1) Univ. City Pub. Libr, University City, Mo, site selection, with Robert H. Rohlf & Assocs, 64-65; 2) Millard

---

KEY TO CONSULTING SPECIALTIES: 1) ARCHITECTURE AND BUILDINGS, 1a) public libraries, 1b) academic libraries, 1c) school libraries, 1d) special libraries, 1e) library interiors, 1f) furnishings, 1g) site and location, 1h) other architectural; 2) COLLECTIONS: SELECTION, EVALUATION, WEEDING, 2a) adults, 2b) young adults, 2c) children, 2d) subject specialty, 2e) O.P. searches, 2f) rare books, 2g) appraisals, 2h) others; 3) TECHNICAL PROCESSES, 3a) cataloging, 3b) classification systems, 3c) acquisitions, 3d) materials processing, 3e) work flow and cost studies, 3f) others, 4) AUTOMATION, 4a) applications of data processing equipment, 4b) information storage and retrieval systems, 4c) systems analysis, 4d) others

Pub. Libr, Millard, Nebr, site selection, eval. of current program, written bldg. program, review of specifications, selection of furnishings & equipment, 65-; 3) Pierre Carnegie Libr, Pierre, S.Dak, site selection, eval. of current program, written bldg. program, with Henningson, Durham & Richardson, Engineers, Architects, 65-; 4) Yankton Pub. Libr, Yankton, S.Dak, site selection, eval. of current program, written bldg. program, with Henningson, Durham and Richardson, Engineers & Architects, 66-; 5) Columbus Pub. Libr, Columbus, Nebr, bldg. program, 66- Specialties: 1a, 1e, 1f, 1g; 7a, 7b, 7c; 8a, 8b, 8c, 8d, 8e, 8f.

GILBERT, CHRISTINE B, June 30, 09; Associate Professor, Graduate Library School, Long Island University, Greenvale, N.Y. 11548. Home: Post Apt. AE9, Greenvale, N.Y. 11548. B.A, Mt. Holyoke Col, 32; M.S, sch. libr. serv, Columbia Univ, 34, M.A, Teachers Col, 45. Dir. sch-community relations, Manhasset Pub. Schs, Manhasset, N.Y, 49-61, librn, Plandome Rd. Sch, 61-67; adjunct assoc. prof, grad. libr. sch, Long Island Univ. Other: Mem, Newbery-Caldecott selection cmt, ALA; mem. joint cmt, ALA-Children's Book Coun. Mem: ALA; Nat. Educ. Asn; N.Y. State Teachers Asn; N.Y. Libr. Asn; Nassau-Suffolk Sch. Libr. Asn. Publ: Gateways to Readable Books (with Ruth Strang & Margaret Scoggin), 1st ed, H.W. Wilson. Consult: 1) Field Enterprises, Chicago, Ill, revision of Childcraft Rev. Project, with Leland Jacobs, 65; 2) Childrens Book Coun, New York, N.Y, bibliog. of book selection aids, 65; 3) Westminster Press, Phila, Pa, manuscript readings, 65-; 4) Grolier Encyclopedia, New York, Book of Knowledge revision, 65-; 5) Silver Burdett, Morristown, N.J, primary grades series of soc. studies books, 66- Specialties: 1c; 2b, 2c, 2d (sch. curriculum areas); 3d; 7a, 7b; 9 (manuscript reading & advising on publ. of books suitable for sch. libr, particularly in regard to curriculum needs).

GITLER, DR. ROBERT L(AURENCE), May 1, 09; University Librarian & Professor of Library Science, University of San Francisco, San Francisco, Calif. 94117. Home: 222 Willard N, Apt. 102, San Francisco, Calif. 94118. B.A, 30; grad. cert. librarianship, 31; M.S, 39; hon. Ph.D, 56. Founding dir, prof. & consult, Japan Libr. Sch, Keio Univ, Tokyo, 51-56 & 61; exec. secy, LED & secy. cmt. accreditation, ALA, 56-60; dir. div. libr. educ, State Univ. N.Y. Col. Geneseo, 62-63; dir, Peabody Libr. Sch, George Peabody Col. Teachers, Nashville, Tenn, 64-67; univ. librn. & prof. libr. sci, Univ. San Francisco, Calif, 67- Other: Mem, Wash. State Cert. Bd. Librns, 45-51; mem. cmt. salaries, tenure, Pac. Northwest Libr. Asn, 47; mem. exec. bd, Am. Asn. Libr. Schs, 47-49; mem. libr. educ. standards cmt, Univ. Accrediting Asn, Japan, 54-56; mem. coordinating cmt, Am. Asn. Col. Teacher Educ, 56-60. Mem: ALA; ACRL; Southeast. Libr. Asn; Tenn. Libr. Asn; SLA. Publ: Library Science Education, In: Accreditation in the Profession (Higher Education), Govt. Printing Office, 59; Accreditation: Agencies, Practices and Procedures, J. Educ. for Librarianship, fall 60; Library Report—Education for Librarianship at the University of Hawaii, Univ. Hawaii, 61; Manpower, Wisdom and Understanding, The Bookmark, 12/62; Education for Librarianship: Japan, Libr. Trends, 10/63; Quo Vadimus, Library Education and New Directions, Peabody J. Educ, 9/65. Consult: 1) Japan Libr. Sch, Keio Univ, Mita, Minato-Ku, Tokyo, reviewed curriculum preparatory to establishing grad. program, with Takahisa Sawamoto & Ikuo Anzai, 61; 2) Univ. Hawaii East-West Center, Honolulu, survey of libr. educ. needs with recommendations, with Raynard Swank, 61; 3) Univ. San Francisco, Parker & Golden Gate Aves, San Francisco, Calif, curriculum & budget, sch. libr. curriculum program, proposed master's degree program, 61, 62 & 65; 4) Sch. Librarianship, Univ. Wash, Seattle, study of curriculum revision & space needs proposal, 62; 5) Kans. State Teachers Col. Dept. Librarianship), Emporia, curriculum, staff & criteria for ALA accreditation, 62 & 65. Specialties: 1b, 1d, 1h (libr. sch. libr); 2d (libr. educ. collections); 5a, 5d (recruitment); 6a; 7d (in libr. sch); 9 (libr. educ. consulting; served on col. & univ. libr. study teams).

GOLDSTEIN, DR. HAROLD, Oct. 3, 17; Dean, School of Library Science, Florida State University, Tallahassee, Fla. 32306. Home: 2324 Limerick Dr, Tallahassee, Fla. 32301. B.S, 42; B.S.L.S, 47; M.A, 48; Ed.D, 49. Dir, Davenport Pub. Libr, Davenport, Ia, 55-59; prof, grad. sch. libr. sci, Univ. Ill, 59-67; dean, sch. libr. sci, Fla. State Univ, Tallahassee, Fla, 67- Other: V.pres. & pres-elect, Iowa Libr. Asn, 59; pres, Ill. Libr. Asn, 67. Mem: ALA; Fla. Libr. Asn; Southeast. Libr. Asn. Publ: National Conference on the Implications of the News Media... (ed), 63; Changing Environment for Library Services in the Metropolitan Area (ed), 66; Library School Teaching Methods—Evaluation of Students (ed), 67. Consult: 1) Mo. State Libr, Jefferson City, Mo, audiovisual serv. for the state, 62; 2) N.Y. State Libr, Albany, N.Y, audiovisual serv. of the state libr, 63 & 67; 3) Franklin Park Pub. Libr, Franklin Park, Ill, serv, bldg. program, 66-67; 4) River Forest Pub. Libr, River Forest, Ill, bldg. program, 67; 5) Kans. State Libr, Topeka, Kans, state plan for libr. serv, 68. Specialties: 1a, 1b, 1g; 5c; 6b; 8d, 8e, 8f.

GOODBREAD, JUANITA W, Aug. 10, 11; Library Supervisor, Hillsborough County Board of Public Instruction, Tampa, Fla. 33602. Home: 7821 Pine Hill Dr, Tampa, Fla. 33610. B.S, 33; M.S, 53. Librn, Woodlawn Elem. Sch, Sebring, Fla, 55-62; libr. supvr, Hillsborough County Sch.

5) PERSONNEL AND RECRUITING, 5a) job evaluation and description, salary recommendations, 5b) recruitment of professionals and management personnel, 5c) administrative organization, 6) PUBLIC RELATIONS, 6a) publications, 6b) publicity programs, 6c) public opinion surveys, 6d) others, 7) SERVICES, 7a) evaluation of current program, 7b) studies of service to special publics, e.g., students, handicapped, aged, etc., 7c) programs for the implementation of new laws, program proposals to governments, 7d) others, 8) COMMUNITY, REGIONAL, STATE PLANNING, 8a) legislative programs, 8b) area analyses, 8c) centralized systems, cooperative arrangements, 8d) development of standards, 8e) state libraries and extension agencies, 8f) regional and statewide surveys, 8g) others, 9) OTHERS.

Syst, Tampa, Fla, 62- Other: Pres, Classroom Teachers Asn, 52; pres, Highlands County Educ. Asn, 57, Teacher of the Year, 59. Mem: Fla. Asn. Sch. Librns; Fla. Libr. Asn; ALA; Delta Kappa Gamma. Consult: 1) Univ. South Fla, Tampa, consult. for fed. project to build model libr. in new elem. sch, with Alice Smith, June 67. Specialties: 1c; 2b, 2c; 3a, 3b, 3c, 3d, 3e; 5b, 5c; 6b; 7a, 7c; 8a, 8d, 8f.

GORCHELS, CLARENCE CLIFFORD, Aug. 26, 16; Director of the Library, Oregon College of Education, Monmouth, Ore. 97361. Home: 342 Stadium Dr. S, Monmouth, Ore. 97361. B.S, Wis. State Univ, Oshkosh, 40; B.L.S, Univ. Wis, 45; M.S, Columbia Univ, 52. Acting asst. dir. libr, Wash. State Univ, 55-57; assoc. libr. serv, Columbia Univ, 59-60; dir. libr, Cent. Wash. State Col, 60-63; col. librn, Calif. State Col. Palos Verdes, Calif, 63-66. Other: Chmn. statist. cmt, ALA, 52-54 & 56-57, mem. coun, 56-57, chmn. budgeting, costs & accounting cmt, 65-; v.chmn, Pac. Northwest Libr. Asn, 56; mem. exec. bd, Wash. Libr. Asn, 61-63; chmn, Wash. State Higher Educ. Librns, 62-63; secy, Calif. Col. Librns, 64-65. Mem: ALA; Am. Asn. Univ. Prof; Ore. Libr. Asn; ACRL; Pac. Northwest Libr. Asn; Kappa Delta Pi; Phi Alpha Theta. Publ: UNESCO: Bibliographic Control in the Social Sciences, Libr. J, 9/55; Making Subject Specialists Available for Service, Col. & Res. Libr, 10/55; Library Acquisitions Policy Statements in Colleges of Education, Libr. Resources & Tech. Serv, spring 61; Centralized Services in New Central Washington Building, Col. & Res. Libr, 9/62; Of New Libraries and Futuristic Libraries, Col. & Res. Libr, 7/64. Consult: 1) Univ. Wash, Seattle, personnel classification, orgn. of libr. serv, Nov. 58-Mar. 59; 2) South Bay State Col, 2930 Imperial Highway, Inglewood, Calif, centralized acquisition of books & other materials, personnel, tech. processing, automation, integration of audiovisual serv, Feb-Mar. 63; 3) Libr. Develop. Cmt, Bd. Trustees, Calif. State Cols, 5670 Wilshire Blvd, Los Angeles, personnel, staffing, reduction of & automation of tech. processes, 64-65; 4) Univ. Tasmania, Hobart, Australia, advised program for grad. schs, personnel admin, classification of books & other materials & automation, Aug. 65. Specialties: 1b; 3b, 3c; 4a, 4b, 4c; 5a, 5b, 5c; 7a.

GORDON, BERNARD L, 1931; Assistant Professor, Department of Natural Science, Northeastern University, Boston, Mass. 02115. Home: 27 Heath St, Brookline, Mass. 02146. B.Sc, 55; M.Sc, 58. Antiquarian book dealer & appraiser, 52-; sec. sch. sci. teacher, 55-56; instructor biology, R.I. Col, 56-60; teaching fel, Boston Univ, 60-61; instructor, Northeastern Univ, Boston, Mass, 61-65, asst. prof, 65- Other: Dir, R.I. Wildlife Fedn, 59-62; participant, Am. Asn. Advancement Sci. meetings, 59 & Int. Oceanographic Congress, 66; marine sci. educ. consult, 60-; lectr, Munson Inst. Marine Hist, 62 & 63; nat. dir, nature educ. group, jr. div, Am. Littoral Soc, 62- Mem: Mass. Libr. Asn. Publ: Aquatic Science Handbook, Am. Littoral Soc, 64; Marine Fishes of Rhode Island, Book & Tackle; Anthology of Oceanographic Writings (ed); contrib. to: Natural Hist, Am. Biology Teacher, Grade Teacher, Sea Frontiers, Underwater Naturalist, Antiquarian Bookman. Consult: 1) Stonington Libr, Stonington, Conn, appraised books, 60-; 2) Mass. Dept. Educ, Boston, sci. educ. program in sec. schs, 63; 3) Hale Libr, Matunuck, R.I, appraised books, 64-; 4) N. Kingston Libr, North Kingston, R.I, appraised books, 66. Specialties: 2a, 2b, 2d (ocean sci, marine tech), 2e, 2f, 2g, 2h (programmed instruction); 3c; 6d (exhibits, displays); 7c; 9 (prepare bibliog. of books & films relating to ocean sci. & fresh water sci).

GORMLEY, MARK McGUIRE, Nov. 4, 24; Professor, Director of University Library & University Archivist, University of Wisconsin, 2500 E. Kenwood Blvd, Milwaukee, Wis. 53211. Home: 4764 N. Ardmore Ave, Milwaukee, Wis. 53217. B.S, Wis. State Univ, Superior, 51; M.A.L.S, Univ. Denver, 54. Asst. dir. libr. & assoc. prof. libr. sci, Colo. State Univ, 56-61; exec. secy, ACRL, 61-62; prof, dir. univ. libr. & univ. archivist, Univ. Wis, Milwaukee, 62- Other: Pres, Colo. Libr. Asn, 59-60; visiting prof, grad. sch. librarianship, Univ. Denver, summers, 62 & 65; chmn. cmt. grants, ACRL, 63-64, chmn. cmt. libr. surveys, 64-65, chmn. publ. cmt, 66-69. Mem: ALA; ACRL; Wis. Libr. Asn. Publ: The Sioux Falls College Library: A Survey, ALA, 61; Library Associates of UWM, Wis. Acad. Review, fall 63; Program Requirements for the Library at the University of Wisconsin-Milwaukee, Univ. Wis-Milwaukee, 63; Quotations Abbreviated from the Program Requirements for the Library of the University of Wisconsin-Milwaukee, In: Planning Academic and Research Library Buildings, McGraw-Hill, 65; ACRL Grants Program, Stechert-Hafner Book News, 3/65; Rapid Expansion: Building a Teacher's College Collection into a University Library, Univ. Wis-Milwaukee, 5/65. Consult: 1) Sioux Falls Col, Sioux Falls, S.Dak, survey of col. libr. serv, with Ralph H. Hopp, Oct. 61; 2) Macalester Col, St. Paul, Minn, survey of libr. serv, Dec. 66; 3) State Univ. N.Y. Col. Geneseo, Geneseo, N.Y, survey of libr. serv, Mar. 67; 4) Lawrence Univ, Appleton, Wis, survey of libr. serv, Sept. 67; Kenyon Col, Gambier, Ohio, survey of libr. serv, with Maurice Tauber, Mar. 68. Specialties: 1b; 3a, 3c, 3d; 4c; 7a.

GORSKI, LORRAINE K.M, Jan. 6, 21; Assistant Library Director, Services to Children & Schools, East Orange Board & Education & East Orange Public Library, East Orange, N.J.

KEY TO CONSULTING SPECIALTIES: 1) ARCHITECTURE AND BUILDINGS, 1a) public libraries, 1b) academic libraries, 1c) school libraries, 1d) special libraries, 1e) library interiors, 1f) furnishings, 1g) site and location, 1h) other architectural; 2) COLLECTIONS: SELECTION, EVALUATION, WEEDING, 2a) adults, 2b) young adults, 2c) children, 2d) subject specialty, 2e) O.P. searches, 2f) rare books, 2g) appraisals, 2h) others; 3) TECHNICAL PROCESSES, 3a) cataloging, 3b) classification systems, 3c) acquisitions, 3d) materials processing, 3e) work flow and cost studies, 3f) others, 4) AUTOMATION, 4a) applications of data processing equipment, 4b) information storage and retrieval systems, 4c) systems analysis, 4d) others

07018. Home: 188 Glenwood Ave, East Orange, N.J. 07017. B.A, 48; M.L.S, 51. Asst. libr. dir, serv. to children & schs, at E. Orange Pub. Libr, East Orange, N.J, 51- Other: Chmn, cmt. on human relations, N.J. Libr. Asn; mem, E. Orange Cmt. for Academically Able, 58-60. Mem: N.J. Libr. Asn. Publ: ABC Classification for Children Using School and Public Libraries, East Orange, 58. Consult: 1) Alanar, subsidiary of Bro-Dart Industries, Newark, N.J, selection of children's books to be purchased & processed, with Margery Quigley, 58-60. Specialties: 1c, 1e, 1f; 2b, 2c, 2h (curriculum-oriented collections, bookmobile collections & serv); 3b.

GOSNELL, DR. CHARLES F, July 7, 09; Director of the Libraries & Professor of Library Administration, New York University Library, Washington Square, New York, N.Y. 10003. Home: 11 Orchard Circle, Suffern, N.Y. 10901. A.B, 30; B.S, 32; M.S, 37; Ph.D, 43. State librn. & asst. cmnr. educ, N.Y. State, Albany, 45-62; dir. libr. & prof. libr. admin, N.Y. Univ, New York, 62- Other: Mem. coun, ALA, 39-41, 45-49, 53-56 & 63-, mem. exec. bd, 53-56; pres, Nat. Asn. State Libr, 47-50; chmn, Coun. Nat. Libr. Asn, 53; secy. cmt. records protection, Nat. Fire Protection Asn, 63-; pres, LAD, 66-67; pres, N.Y. Libr. Asn, 68-69. Mem: ALA; N.Y. Libr. Asn; Bibliog. Soc. Am; Am. Lodge of Res. Publ: Spanish Personal Names, Wilson, 38; Obsolescence of Books in College Libraries, 45; New York State Freedom Train Document Book, N.Y. State Libr, 50; Copyright Grab Bag, ALA, 66. Consult: 1) Univ. Brasilia, Brasilia, D.F, Brazil, develop. of libr. syst, with D.H. Clift & M.A. Gelfand, 63-68; 2) Rockland Community Col, Suffern, N.Y, gen. survey of libr. & cooperation with other libr. in county, Aug. 64; 3) Howard Univ, Wash, D.C, gen. survey, Sept. 65; 4) Conn. Gov. Cmt. on Res. Libr. Serv, gen. comment on program, Dec. 65; 5) Hawaii Gov. Cmt. Libr. Serv, gen. comment on program of libr. orgn. & develop, with J. Lorenz & R. Vosper, Mar. 66. Specialties: 1b, 1f, 1g; 2d (col. & univ), 2f, 2g; 5c; 6a, 6b, 6c; 7a, 7c; 8a, 8c, 8d, 8e, 8f; 9 (Latin Am. libr, Spanish & Portuguese).

GRAFTON, C(ONNIE) ERNESTINE, Jan. 17, 13; Director, Iowa State Traveling Library, Historical Building, E. 12th & Grand Ave, Des Moines, Iowa 50319. Home: 3215 St. Johns Rd, Des Moines, Iowa 50312. A.B, Trinity Univ, 33; A.B.(libr. sci), Univ. Okla, 34; M.A, Univ. Chicago, 40. Dir, Iowa State Traveling Libr, Des Moines, Iowa, 56- Other: Mem. planning cmt, ASL, 64-; coun. mem-at-large, ALA, 64-68; pres, Iowa Coun. Community Improvement, 65-; secy, Adult Educ. Asn, 66- Mem: ALA; Iowa Libr. Asn. Publ: Contrib, Iowa Libr. Quart. Consult: 1) N.Dak. Libr. Cmn, Bismarck, N.Dak, survey, summer 66. Specialties: 1a, 1e, 1g; 5a, 5c; 8a, 8b, 8c, 8d, 8e, 8f.

GRAHAM, MAE, Sept. 29, 04; Assistant Director, Division of Library Extension, Maryland State Department of Education, 301 W. Preston St, Baltimore, Md. 21201. Home: 4105 Bedford Rd, Baltimore, Md. 21207. A.B; B.S. in L.S; M.L.A. Supvr. sch. libr, Md. State Dept. Educ, Baltimore, Md, 48-68. Other: Mem. coun, ALA, 44-46 & 62-64, pres, div. libr. for children & young people, 50-51, mem. exec. bd, 52-56; pres, Md. Libr. Asn, 55; ed, Md. Libr, 60-62. Mem: ALA; Md. Libr. Asn; Nat. Ed. Asn; Md. State Teachers Asn. Consult: 1) CIE, SCAP, Tokyo, Japan, consult. for sch. libr, Feb-June 47. Specialties: 7b; 8d, 8e; 9 (sch. libr. programs).

GREER, DR. ROGER CLEMENT, Apr. 29, 28; Dean, School of Library Science, Syracuse University, Syracuse, N.Y. 13210. Home: 5011 Skyline Terrace, Syracuse, N.Y. 13215. B.A, 50; M.L.S, 56; Ph.D, 64. Instructor, grad. sch. libr. serv, Rutgers Univ, 60-64; dir. libr. serv, State Univ. N.Y. Col. Potsdam, 64-67; asst. dean & assoc. prof, sch. libr. sci, Syracuse Univ, 67-68, dean, 68- Other: Pres, N. Country Reference, Res. & Resources Coun, 64-67; vis. prof, grad. sch. libr. studies, Univ. Hawaii, summers 65-66; pres. bd. trustees, N. Country 3R Coun, 67; v.pres. & pres-elect, col. & univ. libr. sect, N.Y. Libr. Asn, 67-; mem. adv. bd, Mater Dei Col, N.Y. Mem: N.Y. Libr. Asn; ALA; SLA; Am. Soc. Info. Sci. Publ: National Bibliography, Libr. Trends, 1/67; Professional Aspects of Information Science and Technology (co-auth), In: Annual Review of Information Science and Technology, 68. Consult: 1) Syst. Develop. Corp, Santa Monica, Calif, consult. on acad. libr, 67-68; 2) Gaylord Bros, Syracuse, N.Y, gen. consult, 67- Specialties: 1b; 2d (reference); 5c; 7a; 8c, 8d, 8f.

GROPP, ARTHUR ERIC, Nov. 10, 02; Librarian, Columbus Memorial Library, Pan American Union, Washington, D.C. 20006. Home: 5113 Western Ave. N.W, Washington, D.C. 20016. B.S, 27; B.A, 30; M.A, 31. Librn, Columbus Mem. Libr, Pan Am. Union, Wash, D.C, 50- Other: Chmn, Cmt. on Libr. Cooperation with Latin Am, 36-41; dir, libr. sch, Univ. Montevideo, 43-48; mem, adv. bd. of sci. commun, Inter-Am. Inst. Agr. Sci, Turrialba, C.R, 50-56; mem. bd. dirs, D.C. Libr. Asn, 55-57; mem, ad hoc periodicals cmt, U.S. Info Agency, Jan-Feb. 67. Mem: ALA; D.C. Libr. Asn; Asn. Interam. Bibliotecarios & Documentalistas Agricolas; hon. mem, Uruguayan Asn. Librns. Publ: Rare Americana, New Orleans, 32; Manuscripts in the Department of Middle American Research, New Orleans, 33 & rev. ed, 34; Sixteenth Century Printing in New Spain, Bull. La. Libr. Asn, 6/40; Guide to Libraries and Archives in Central America and the West Indies, New Orleans, 41; Union List of Latin American Newspapers in Libraries in the United States, Wash, D.C, 53; Bibliografia

---

5) PERSONNEL AND RECRUITING, 5a) job evaluation and description, salary recommendations, 5b) recruitment of professionals and management personnel, 5c) administrative organization, 6) PUBLIC RELATIONS, 6a) publications, 6b) publicity programs, 6c) public opinion surveys, 6d) others, 7) SERVICES, 7a) evaluation of current program, 7b) studies of service to special publics, e.g., students, handicapped, aged, etc., 7c) programs for the implementation of new laws, program proposals to governments, 7d) others, 8) COMMUNITY, REGIONAL, STATE PLANNING, 8a) legislative programs, 8b) area analyses, 8c) centralized systems, cooperative arrangements, 8d) development of standards, 8e) state libraries and extension agencies, 8f) regional and statewide surveys, 8g) others, 9) OTHERS.

de Fuentes Archivisticas Relacionadas con Iberoamerica, Sevilla, 65. Consult: 1) U.S. Dept. State, Wash, D.C, consult. to librns. of Uruguay, Sept-Oct. 63; 2) U.S. Info. Agency, Wash, D.C, study of policy & practices relative to periodical subscriptions & distribution with James J. Kortendick & Helen R. Thompson, Jan-Feb. 67. Specialties: 9 (bibliog. libr, archives, librns. & organizational needs relative to Latin Am).

GROSCH, AUDREY N, Jan. 10, 34; Library Systems Coordinator, University of Minnesota Library, Minneapolis, Minn. 55455. Home: 3314 Kyle Ave. N, Minneapolis, Minn. 55422. B.A, Univ. Minn, 55, M.A, 56. Asst. librn. electronics div, Gen. Mills, Inc, 57-63, marketing res. librn, 64; libr. systs. coordinator, Univ. Minn. Libr, Minneapolis, 65- Other: Registered prfnl. consult, SLA, 64-; instructor, data processing in the libr, Univ. Minn. Libr. Sch, 65- Publ: Application of Uniform Coordinate Indexing to a Marketing Research Report Collection, Spec. Libr, 56: 303-311; The Special Librarians Link to Data Processing— a Communication Problem, Spec. Libr. Asn. Gen. Session Paper 1966 Convention. Consult: 1) Minister's Life & Casualty Co, Minneapolis, Minn, organized small libr, trained operational personnel, advised SDI program on firm's IBM 1401 computer, May 64; 2) Farmer's Union Cent. Exchange, South St. Paul, Minn, determine need for spec. libr. serv, draft mgt. proposal for facility, Jan. 65. Specialties: 1d, 1f, 1g; 3a, 3e, 3f (gen. records control & forms design); 4a, 4c, 4d (data collection & representation); 5a, 5b, 5c; 6a; 9 (procedure manuals syst. oper. manuals for libr. systs).

H

HAAS, ELAINE, July 27, 18; Director, Technical Library Service, 104 Fifth Ave, New York, N.Y. 10011. Home: 35-20 Leverich St, Jackson Heights, N.Y. 11372. A.B, 39; M.S, 63. Data analyst, Avien, Inc, Woodside, N.Y, 59-62; dir, Tech. Libr. Serv, New York, N.Y, 62- Other: Libr. aide, engineering libr, Columbia Univ, 62-63; asst. to librn, sci. libr, Queens Col, Flushing, N.Y, 64; literature searcher, Engineering Socs. Libr, New York, 64; instructor libr, Borough Manhattan Community Col, New York, 64, asst. prof, 65 & 67; librn, United Nuclear Corp, Elmsford, N.Y, 66-67. Mem: ALA; Am. Document. Inst; SLA; N.Y. Libr. Club. Consult: 1) Soc. for Advancement of Judaism, 32 W. 86th St, New York, N.Y, instructed & supervised libr. cmt. in cataloging 3000 vols, advised on acquisitions, tech. serv, user relations, Jan-Sept. 64; 2) Am. Power Jet Co, Ridgefield, N.J, improved acquisitions, cataloging, tech. serv, weeding, user relations, devised & installed manual indexing & retrieval syst, July-Nov. 64; 3) J.C. Penney Co, Inc, 1301 Ave. of Americas, New York, weeded collection, advised on acquisitions, aided in layout of new quarters, instructed clerk in libr. oper, advised on user relations, Sept. 64-July 65; 4) Explorers Club, 46 E. 70th St, New York, advised on cataloging spec. collection, improvement of subject headings, care of rare book collection, selection of prfnl. librn, on call for spec. assistance, Jan. 65-; 5) St. Alphonsus Church, 14 Thompson St, New York, instructed teachers in libr. oper, acquisition, tech. serv. & serv. to students, Oct. 65-Mar. 66. Specialties: 1b, 1d, 1e, 1f; 2d (sci. & tech, bus), 2e; 3a, 3b, 3c, 3d, 3e; 4a, 4b, 4c; 5a, 5b, 5c, 5d (personnel training); 7a; 9 (consult. to small bus. & industrial libr, specialist in current awareness serv. & literature res).

HAAS, WARREN J, Mar. 22, 24; Director of Libraries, University of Pennsylvania, Philadephia, Pa. 19104. Home: 730 Hazelhurst, Merion, Pa. 19066. B.A, Wabash Col, 48; B.L.S, Univ. Wis, 50. Asst. librn, Johns Hopkins Univ, 54-59; consult, coun. higher educ. Inst, New York, N.Y, 59-61; assoc. dir, Columbia Univ. Libr, 61-66; dir, Univ. Pa. Libr, 66- Other: Mem, Commissioner's Cmt. on Reference & Res. Libr, New York, 59-61. Mem: ALA. Publ: Cooperative Library Service for Higher Education, Coun. Higher Educ. Inst, N.Y, 61; A. Study of the Use of Metropolitan New York Libraries by Higher Education Students, Coun. Higher Educ. Inst, 61; Student Use of New York's Libraries, Libr. Trends, 4/62; Statewide and Regional Reference Service, Libr. Trends, 1/64. Consult: 1) Inst. Higher Educ, Teachers Col, Columbia Univ, N.Y, comprehensive survey of libr. in Negro cols, with Earl McGrath, 64; 2) State Univ. N.Y. Col. Buffalo, new bldg, with Perkins and Wills, 64; 3) U.S. Naval Acad, Annapolis, Md, mem. bd. of review on libr. to survey & make planning recommendations, with John H. Berthel, 65-66; 4) Univ. Mass, Amherst, bldg. new univ. libr, with Edward Durell Stone, Architect, 65-; 5) N.Y. State Libr, Albany, participation in planning new bldg. with Harrison & Abromowitz, architects, 66. Specialties: 1b, 1e; 3e; 5a, 5c; 8c, 8f.

HALL, ELVAJEAN, May 30, 10; Supervisor of Library Services, Division of Instruction, Newton Public Schools, 88 Chestnut St, West Newton, Mass. 02165. Home: 233 Commonwealth Ave, Boston, Mass. 02116. B.A, Oberlin Col, 30; dipl, Univ. Wis. Libr. Sch, 32; M.S, Columbia Univ, 41. Supvr. libr. serv, Newton Pub. Schs, West Newton, Mass, 46- Other: Nat. Recruitment chmn, AASL, 56; pres, Boston chap, Women's Nat. Book Asn, 57-58, mem. nat. bd, Women's Nat. Book Asn, 57-62, nat. secy, 60-62. Mem: ALA; NESLA; MSLA; AASL; Sch. Supvr. Group. Publ: Books to Build On, Bowker, 56; Land and People of Argentina, Lippincott, 60; Pilgrim Stories & Pilgrim Neighbors, Rand McNally, 62 & 64;

KEY TO CONSULTING SPECIALTIES: 1) ARCHITECTURE AND BUILDINGS, 1a) public libraries, 1b) academic libraries, 1c) school libraries, 1d) special libraries, 1e) library interiors, 1f) furnishings, 1g) site and location, 1h) other architectural; 2) COLLECTIONS: SELECTION, EVALUATION, WEEDING, 2a) adults, 2b) young adults, 2c) children, 2d) subject specialty, 2e) O.P. searches, 2f) rare books, 2g) appraisals, 2h) others; 3) TECHNICAL PROCESSES, 3a) cataloging, 3b) classification systems, 3c) acquisitions, 3d) materials processing, 3e) work flow and cost studies, 3f) others, 4) AUTOMATION, 4a) applications of data processing equipment, 4b) information storage and retrieval systems, 4c) systems analysis, 4d) others

Land and People of Norway, Lippincott, 63; Land and People of Czechoslovakia, Lippincott, 66; Hong Kong, Rand McNally, 67. Consult: 1) Chung Chi Col, Chinese Univ. Hong Kong, Ma Liu Shui, Hong Kong, program, bldg. reference collection, fall 62-winter 63; 2) Univ. Col, Dublin, Ireland, sch. libr. programs, July 67-July 68. Specialties: 1c; 2c, 2d (hist. & travel), 2h (relating trade books to sch. curriculum); 7b; 9 (book reviewing & eval. of nonbook materials).

HAMLIN, ARTHUR T, Feb. 8, 13; University Librarian & Professor of Bibliography, University of Cincinnati Library, Cincinnati, Ohio 45221. Home: 211 Greendale Ave, Cincinnati, Ohio 45220. A.B, Harvard Univ, 34; B.S.L.S, Columbia Univ, 39. Exec. secy, ACRL, 49-56; univ. librn. & prof. bibliog, Univ. Cincinnati Libr, Cincinnati, Ohio, 56- Other: Chmn. bldg. & equipment sect, LAD, 57-58; chmn. cmt. found. grants, ACRL, 56-58 & 64-66; Fulbright lectr, Univ. Pavia, Italy, 62, pres-elect, Ohio Libr. Asn, 65-66; Fulbright res. scholar, Univ. Birmingham, Eng, 66. Mem: ALA; Bibliog. Soc. Am; Ohio Libr. Asn; Am. Document. Inst; Grolier Club; Am. Asn. Univ. Prof. Publ: College and Research Library Contributions to Adult Education, Libr. Trends, 7/59; The Impact of College Enrollments of Library Acquisitions, Liberal Educ, 52: 204-210; The Libraries of the Universities of Italy, Libri, 15: 138-158; The Rise and Fall of a Library, ALA Bull, 4/66; The Libraries of Florence, ALA Bull, 2/67. Consult: 1) Lilly Found, Indianapolis, Ind, review & judge series of grant applications from Ind. cols. for improvement of their book collections, with Harvey Branscomb, Robert Downs & Newton McKeon, 59-60; 2) U.S. Office Educ, Wash, D.C, study and write detailed report on the needs of off-campus instructional programs for libr. resources, spring & summer 61; 3) Miles Col, Birmingham, Ala, report on book collections and gen. oper. of libr, Apr. 66; 4) Ball State Univ, Muncie, Ind, review of bldg. needs in relation to expanding grad. program, May 66; 5) ALA, 50 E. Huron St, Chicago, Ill, investigate & report on damage to Italian libr. in Nov. floods, Nov. 66. Specialties: 1h (bldg. program); 2d (col. & univ); 3c, 3e; 5a, 5b, 5c; 7a, 7b; 8c, 8e.

HARDAWAY, ELLIOTT, Jan. 1, 13; Vice-President for Administrative Affairs, University of South Florida, Tampa, Fla. 33620. Home: 11337 Oakleaf Ave, Tampa, Fla. 33612. B.A, Vanderbilt Univ, 35; M.A, Univ. Ill, 36, M.S. in L.S, 40. Asst. chief, Info. Centers Br, Tokyo, 47-50; chief tech. proc, La. State Univ, 50-53; assoc. dir, Univ. Fla, 53-57; dir. libr, Univ. S. Fla, 57-65, dean instructional serv, 65-67. Mem: ALA; Fla. Libr. Asn; Southeast. Libr. Asn. Consult: 1) Ruskin Pub. Libr, Ruskin, Fla, bldg. consult, Feb. 65-Feb. 66; 2) Temple Terrace Pub. Libr, Temple Terrace, Fla, bldg. consult, May 65-Mar. 66; 3) Fla. South. Col. Libr, Lakeland, bldg. consult, Sept. 65-Mar. 66; 4) Bradenton Pub. Libr, Bradenton, Fla, bldg. consult, May 66- Specialties: 1a, 1b, 1c, 1d, 1e, 1f, 1g.

HARDING, NELSON F, Sept. 19, 24; Director of Instructional Materials, Norwalk Public Schools, Board of Education, 105 Main St, Norwalk, Conn. 06851. Home: 49 Maher Dr, Norwalk, Conn. 06850. B.A, Am. Int. Col, 50; M.S. (educ), Univ. Wis, 52, M.S.(libr. sci), 59. High sch. librn, 56-59; jr. high librn, 59-65; dir. instructional materials, Norwalk Pub. Schs, 65- Other: Secy, Conn. Sch. Libr. Asn, 63-64, chmn. standards cmt, 64-66. Mem: ALA; Nat. Educ. Asn; Conn. Sch. Libr. Asn; Norwalk Teachers Asn. Publ: Contrib. to local sch. publ. Consult: 1) State Dept. Educ, Hartford, Conn, consult. for area on Title II funds, 65-67. Specialties: 1c; 2b, 2c; 3a, 3d; 5a, 5b, 5c; 6b; 7a, 7c; 8d.

HARLOW, NEAL, June 11, 08; Dean & Professor, Graduate School of Library Service, Rutgers, The State University, New Brunswick, N.J. 08903. Home: 896 River Rd, Piscataway, N.J. 08854. Ed.B, 32; M.A, 49. Univ. librn, Univ. B.C, Vancouver, Can, 51-61; dean & prof, grad. sch. libr. serv, Rutgers Univ, New Brunswick, N.J, 61- Other: Mem. coun, ALA, 52-63, mem. exec. bd, 59-63, mem. int. relations cmt, 62-67; pres, Can. Libr. Asn, 60-61; pres, ACRL, 63-64; mem, Cmt. Univ. Brasilia, 66-; mem. biomed. commun. study sect, Nat. Insts. Health, 66- Mem: ALA; N.J. Libr. Asn; Can. Libr. Asn; Asn. Am. Libr. Schs; Can. Bibliog. Soc; Am. Asn. Univ. Prof. Publ: Levels of Need for Library Service in Academic Institutions, Col. & Res. Libr, 9/63; Physical Housing and Equipment, In: Rare Book Collections, Some Theoretical and Practical Suggestions, ALA, 65; Misused Librarians, Libr. J, 4/1/65; A Study of the Need for Additional Facilities for the Education of Librarians in the University of California, Univ. Calif, 67; Planner to Architect, J. Educ. for Librarianship, summer 68; The Library in the Future of Higher Education, In: Festschrift for Jesse H. Shera. Consult: 1) Emmanuel Col, Victoria Univ, Toronto, Can, gen. consult. on behalf. of Am. Theol. Libr. Asn. Libr. Develop. Program, with Dr. Maria Grossman, Jan. 66; 2) Univ. Calif, Berkeley, Calif, report on need for additional facilities for the educ. of librns. in the univ, Oct. 66; 3) ALA, Chicago, Ill, report on libr. sch, Univ. Brasilia, confidential, July 67; 4) Univ. Montreal, Montreal, Can, recommendations on spec. collection, confidential, with Roy Kidman, Dec. 67; 5) Grad. Libr. Sch, Univ. R.I, Providence, R.I, report on develop. of inst. & program, confidential, Feb. 68. Specialties: 1b; 7a; 9 (grad. prfnl. educ. for librns).

---

5) PERSONNEL AND RECRUITING, 5a) job evaluation and description, salary recommendations, 5b) recruitment of professionals and management personnel, 5c) administrative organization, 6) PUBLIC RELATIONS, 6a) publications, 6b) publicity programs, 6c) public opinion surveys, 6d) others, 7) SERVICES, 7a) evaluation of current program, 7b) studies of service to special publics, e.g., students, handicapped, aged, etc., 7c) programs for the implementation of new laws, program proposals to governments, 7d) others, 8) COMMUNITY, REGIONAL, STATE PLANNING, 8a) legislative programs, 8b) area analyses, 8c) centralized systems, cooperative arrangements, 8d) development of standards, 8e) state libraries and extension agencies, 8f) regional and statewide surveys, 8g) others, 9) OTHERS.

HARNSBERGER, THERESE; Library Consultant, Researcher, Free-lance Writer, 2809 W. Hellman Ave, Alhambra, Calif. 91803. B.A, 52; M.S.L.S, 53. Educ, reference & fine arts librn, Los Angeles State Col, 56-59; jr. high & high sch. librn, Covina-Valley Unified Sch. Dist, Covina, Calif, 56-66, dist. librn, 64-66. Other: Mem. legis. cmt, chmn. legis. newsletter & mem. adv. coun, Calif. Asn. Sch. Librns, 65-66; secy. legis. cmt, Covina Unified Educ. Asn, 65-66. Mem: Calif. Libr. Asn; ALA; South. Calif. Coun. Literature for Children & Young People; Calif. Asn. Sch. Librns; Pi Lambda Theta. Publ: Publicizing Your New High School Library, Wilson Libr. Bull, 3/54; Tears, In: Annual California Chapparal Poetry Compilation, 59. Consult: 1) San Marino Hall, Atlantic & Huntington Dr, South Pasadena, Calif, cataloger of entire libr. & consult. on ordering books, reference collection, with Beatrice Clark Wright, 56-61. Specialties: 1c, 1f, 1h (innovations & short cuts in archit. & furniture); 2b, 2c, 2d (children's literature; Indians, especially Southwest occult), 2e; 3a, 3d, 3e, 3f (time studies; automation in libr); 4a, 4b, 4c, 4d (particular application to tech. processing); 5a, 5b, 5c, 5d (more flexibility; more use of allied personnel—art personnel); 6a, 6b, 6c, 6d (pub. contact; author rights); 7a, 7b, 7c, 7d (in-serv); 8a, 8b, 8c, 8d; 9 (correlation of libr. with other insts.—nat, state regional; help libr. become more dynamic).

HARRIS, WALTER H, Aug. 13, 20; Coordinator, Library Services & Publications, Contra Costa County Department of Education, 75 Santa Barbara Rd, Pleasant Hill, Calif. 94523. Home: 4651 Lincoln Dr, Concord, Calif. 94521. B.S. (elem. educ), Minot State Col, 52; M.Ed, Univ. Ore, 56; Libr. Credential, Univ. San Francisco. Travelling librn, Mt. Diablo Unified Sch. Dist, Concord, Calif, 56-59; consult, libr. serv, Contra Costa County Dept. Educ, Pleasant Hill, Calif, 59-66, coordinator, libr. serv. & publ, 66- Other: Mem, Citizens Adv. Cmt. on Adoptions, 60-67; mem, Concord City Park & Recreation Cmn, 62-65; mem. membership cmt. & chmn. county schs. librns, Calif. Asn. Sch. Librns. Mem: Calif. Teachers Asn; Nat. Educ. Asn; Dept. Elem. Sch. Principals; Calif. Asn. Sch. Librns; Asn. Children's Librns. Publ: Bookroom Bulletins (column), County Schs. Bull, 59-63; The County Instructional Materials Center in California, Calif. Sch. Libr, 11/62; Guidelines for Teaching Elementary Library Skills (booklet), 66; contrib. to Calif. Sch. Libr. Consult: 1) Alamo Elem. Sch. Dist, Stone Valley Rd, Alamo, Calif, developed libr. serv. in 3 schs, 60-63; 2) Pinole-Hercules Elem. Sch. Dist, Valley & Tennant Sts, Pinole, Calif, developed libr. in 9 elem. schs, 60-65; 3) Acalanes High Sch. Dist, Pleasant Hill Rd, Lafayette, Calif, survey of libr. serv. & staffing structure with recommendations, 60-65; 4) Sheldon Elem. Sch. Dist, Hillview Sch, El Sobrante, Calif, developed libr. in 4 elem. schs, 60-65. Specialties: 1c, 1e, 1f, 1g; 2b, 2c; 3a, 3b, 3c, 3d, 3e; 4b, 4c; 5a, 5b, 5c; 6a, 6b; 7a, 7b; 8a, 8b, 8c, 8d.

HART, DR. EUGENE D, Sept. 2, 08; Associate Professor, School of Library Science, University of Southern California, Los Angeles, Calif. 90007. Home: 516 E. Grace Ave, Apt. 3, Inglewood, Calif. 90301. B.S, 33; A.B, 34; M.A, 57; Ph.D, 58. Idaho state librn, 57-59; assoc. prof, Univ. South. Calif, 59- Other: Treas, Calif. Libr. Asn, 49; treas, South. Calif. Chap, SLA, 65, secy, 66. Mem: ALA; SLA; Calif. Libr. Asn; Idaho Libr. Asn. Publ: The Public Libraries of San Bernardino County, 66. Consult: 1) Commerce Pub. Libr, Commerce, Calif, advised on establishing free pub. libr, 61-63; 2) Black Gold Cooperative Libr. Syst, Ventura, Calif, plan for cooperation among 7 pub. libr, Dec. 63-Mar. 64; 3) San Bernardino County Libr, San Bernardino, Calif, plan for cooperation among 6 pub. libr, with Hans C. Palmer, Mar. 65-Feb. 66; 4) Buena Park Libr. Dist, Buena Park, Calif, re-location of new cent. bldg. & 2 br. libr, Feb-June 66. Specialties: 1a, 1g; 2a, 2g; 5a, 5c; 6a, 6b, 6c; 7a, 7c; 8c.

HARVEY, DR. JOHN FREDERICK, Aug. 24, 21; Professor, Graduate School of Library Science, Drexel Institute of Technology, Philadelphia, Pa. 19104. A.B, Dartmouth Col, 43; B.A. in L.S, Univ. Ill, 44; Ph.D, Univ. Chicago, 49. Head librn, prof. & chmn. dept. libr. sci, State Col, Pittsburg, Kans, 53-58; dir. libr, Drexel Inst. Tech, Phila, Pa, 58-62, dean grad. sch. libr. sci, 58-67, prof, 58- Other: Mem. statist. cmt, ALA, 53-55, mem. exec. bd. jr. mems. round table & chmn. libr. periodicals round table, 55-56, chmn. joint cmt. on librarianship as career, 55-58, mem. audiovisual cmt, 56-58, mem. coun, 57-61, 66-67, chmn. resolutions cmt, 62-63; chmn. audiovisual cmt, ACRL, 55-58, mem. bd. dirs, 57-61, mem. res. cmt, univ. libr. sect, 58-62, chmn. constitution cmt, 59-61, mem. nomination cmt, 65-67; mem. statist. cmt, LED, 58-59, chmn. res. cmt, 65-67; chmn. curriculum cmt, Asn. Am. Libr. Schs, 59-60; del. to corp, U.S. Book Exchange, 59-62; Pa. exec. dir, Nat. Libr. Week, 60-62; mem. exec. coun. & chmn. adv. bd, Am. Soc. Info. Sci, 62-64, chmn. student membership cmt, 65-67; pres, Pa. Libr. Asn, 64-65; dir, Drexel Press, 64-; recipient, Libr. Binding Inst. Silver Book Award, 65; conf. publicity dir, Med. Libr. Asn, 65; chmn. cert. policy cmt. & mem. bd. trustees, Am. Transl. Asn, 65-67; founder, Libr. Pub. Relations Asn. Phila, 66; Church & Synagogue Libr. Asn, 67; Fulbright grant & chmn. dept. libr. sci, Univ. Tehran, Iran, 67-69; Iran ed, East. Librn, 68- Mem: ALA; Am. Asn. Univ. Prof; Am. Chemical Soc; Am. Soc. Info. Sci; Am. Personnel & Guidance Asn; Am. Transl. Asn; Archons of Colophon; Asn. Am. Libr. Schs; ACRL; Dart-

KEY TO CONSULTING SPECIALTIES: 1) ARCHITECTURE AND BUILDINGS, 1a) public libraries, 1b) academic libraries, 1c) school libraries, 1d) special libraries, 1e) library interiors, 1f) furnishings, 1g) site and location, 1h) other architectural; 2) COLLECTIONS: SELECTION, EVALUATION, WEEDING, 2a) adults, 2b) young adults, 2c) children, 2d) subject specialty, 2e) O.P. searches, 2f) rare books, 2g) appraisals, 2h) others; 3) TECHNICAL PROCESSES, 3a) cataloging, 3b) classification systems, 3c) acquisitions, 3d) materials processing, 3e) work flow and cost studies, 3f) others, 4) AUTOMATION, 4a) applications of data processing equipment, 4b) information storage and retrieval systems, 4c) systems analysis, 4d) others

mouth Club Phila; Med. Libr. Asn; Melvil Dui Asn; Pa. Libr. Asn; Phi Kappa Phi; Philobiblon Club Phila; SLA. Publ: Drexel Information Science Series (ed), Spartan, 64-; Drexel Library School Students: Where Do They Come From and Where Do They Go?, Col. & Res. Libr, 3/65; Building and Equipment Trends (jr. col. libr), Libr. Trends, 1/65; The Library College (co-ed), Drexel Inst. Tech, 66; Guide to Library Education (issue ed), Drexel Libr. Quart, 1-4/67; Professional Aspects of Information Science, In: Annual Review of Information Science and Technology, Wiley, 67. Consult: 1) Holy Family Col, Phila, Pa, libr. bldg, plans, 65; 2) U.S. Office Educ, Wash. D.C, consult. on desirable guidelines of libr. res, 66; 3) Lipservice, Inc, Phila, libr. relationship problems of reference book distributor, 66; 4) Iranian Ministries of Foreign Affairs, Econ, Sci. & Higher Educ, Culture & Art, plan orgn. & senate, 67-68; 5) Iranian Govt, consult to nine Iranian cols. & univs, 67-68. Specialties: 1b; 2a; 4a, 4b; 5a, 5b, 5c; 6a, 6b; 9 (libr. educ; recruitment to the professions; comparative librarianship).

HARWELL, RICHARD, June 6, 15; College Librarian, Smith College Library, Northampton, Mass. 01060. Home: 8 College Lane, Northampton, Mass. 01060. A.B, Emory Univ, 37; A.B.L.S, 38; D.Lit, New Eng. Col, 66. Dir. of publ, Va. State Libr, 56-57; exec. secy, ACRL, 57-61, & assoc. exec. dir, ALA, 58-61; librn, Bowdoin Col, 61-68; librn, Smith Col, 68- Other: Exec. secy, Southeast. Libr. Asn, 53-54; mem. coun, ALA, 62-; bd. mem, Maine Hist. Soc, 63-; bd. mem, Tracy B. Kittredge Found, 65- Mem: ALA; Maine Libr. Asn; New Eng. Libr. Asn; Bibliog. Soc. Am; Bibliog. Soc. Univ. Va. Publ: Research Resources in the Georgia-Florida Libraries of SIRF, South. Regional Educ. Bd, Atlanta, 55; A Union List of Serial Holdings in Chemistry and Allied Fields, South. Regional Educ. Bd, 55; More Confederate Imprints, Va. State Libr, 57; The Arizona State University Library (with Everett T. Moore), ALA, 59; The War They Fought, McKay, 60; The Place of a Research Library in a Liberal Arts College, Bowdoin Col, 63. Consult: 1) Alma Col, Mich, gen. survey, published report, with Robert L. Talmadge, 57; 2) Ariz. State Univ, Tempe, gen. survey with published report, with Everett T. Moore, Nov. 59; 3) Franklin & Marshall Col, Lancaster, Pa, gen. survey with confidential written report, with Maurice F. Tauber, Mar. 65; 4) Univ. Jordan, Amman, Jordan, bldg. consult, Aug-Oct. 66; 5) Bates Col, Lewiston, Maine, gen. survey with confidential report, with Wyman Parker & Ellsworth Mason, Nov. 67.

HAWKEN, WILLIAM R, Feb. 25, 17; Owner & Director, William R. Hawken Associates, P.O. Box 796, Berkeley, Calif. 94701. Home: 2135-A Parker St, Berkeley, Calif. 94704. Head, libr. photographic serv, Univ. Calif, Berkeley, 47-59; independent consult. document reproduction, 59- Other: Nat. Sci. Found. travel grant, First Int. Congress Reprography, Cologne, Germany, 63; U.S. Bd. mem, Microfiche Found, Netherlands, 63- Mem: ALA; ACRL; Am. Document. Inst; fel, Inst. Reprographic Tech; fel. Nat. Microfilm Asn. Publ: Photocopying from Bound Volumes, Libr. Tech. Publ. 4, ALA, 62; Equipment and Methods in the Production of Full-Size Copy from Microtext, In: Proceedings—Library Furniture and Equipment Institute, ALA, 63; Equipment and methods in Photocopying, with Special Emphasis on Copying from Bound Volumes, In: Proceedings—Library Furniture and Equipment Institute, ALA, 63; Enlarged Prints from Library Microforms, Libr. Tech. Program Publ. 6, AHA, 63; Photocopying from Bound Volumes, supplements 1, 2 & 3, Libr. Tech. Program, ALA, 63-64; Copying Methods Manual, Libr. Tech. Program Publ. 11, ALA, 66. Specialties: 9 (microfilm, document reproduction).

HEALEY, JAMES S, July 14, 31; Assistant Professor of Library Science, University of Rhode Island Graduate Library School, Promenade and Gaspee Sts, Providence, R.I. 02908. Home: 30 Carriage Hill Rd, North Kingstown, R.I. 02852. A.B, 55; M.L.S, 58. Librn, Pub. Libr, Stoneham, Mass, 56-61; chief librn, Free Pub. Libr, New Bedford, Mass, 61-67; chief libr. extension serv, Dept. State Libr. Serv, R.I, 67-68. Other: Subscription books cmt, ALA, 61-65, 67-69; ASD-AHIL Joint Cmt. on Nat. Libr. Week, 66-68, chmn, 68-69; exec. dir, Nat. Libr. Week, R.I, 67-68. Mem: ALA; New Eng. Libr. Asn; R.I. Libr. Asn. Publ: Symphony Hall Comes to Stoneham, Bay State Librn. autumn 57; Splendid Headache, Libr. J, 9/15/62, Salt Spray and Sperm Whales, Wilson Libr. Bull, 3/63; Having a Ball, Wilson Libr. Bull, 3/64; On board in New Bedford, Wilson Libr. Bull, 11/65; Automated Library in New England, Wilson Libr. Bull, 12/66. Consult: 1) Somerset Pub. Libr, Somerset, Mass, bldg. program, 65; 2) Swain Sch. of Design, Hawthorn St, New Bedford, Mass, survey of serv, collection & facilities with recommendations, 65; 3) Cumberland Pub. Libr, Cumberland, R.I, survey of libr. serv. & facilities with recommendations, Jan-June 66; 4) Harris Inst, Woonsocket, R.I, survey libr. serv. & facilities with recommendations, Aug. 66-; 5) Area libr. survey encompassing Lincoln, Cumberland, Woonsocket, R.I, feasibility study with recommendations, Aug. 68. Specialties: 1a, 1b, 1f, 1g; 3d, 3e; 4a, 4c; 7a; 8c.

HEILIGER, EDWARD MARTIN, Dec. 14, 09; Professor of Library Science and Director, Center for Library Studies, School of Library Science, Kent State University, Kent, Ohio 44240. Home: 1571 Stratford Dr, Kent, Ohio 44240. A.B, Univ. of the Pac, 33; B.S. in L.S, Univ. Denver, 35, M.A, 41. Librn. & prof. libr. admin, Univ. Ill,

---

5) PERSONNEL AND RECRUITING, 5a) job evaluation and description, salary recommendations, 5b) recruitment of professionals and management personnel, 5c) administrative organization, 6) PUBLIC RELATIONS, 6a) publications, 6b) publicity programs, 6c) public opinion surveys, 6d) others, 7) SERVICES, 7a) evaluation of current program, 7b) studies of service to special publics, e.g., students, handicapped, aged, etc., 7c) programs for the implementation of new laws, program proposals to governments, 7d) others, 8) COMMUNITY, REGIONAL, STATE PLANNING, 8a) legislative programs, 8b) area analyses, 8c) centralized systems, cooperative arrangements, 8d) development of standards, 8e) state libraries and extension agencies, 8f) regional and statewide surveys, 8g) others, 9) OTHERS.

Chicago, 55-63; dir. libr. & info. retrieval serv. & prof. hist, Fla. Atlantic Univ, 63-67; sr. scientist, United Aircraft Corp, 67-68; prof. libr. sci. & dir, center libr. studies, Kent State Univ, 68- Other: Chmn, Sears Found. Project, ALA, 58; pres, Chicago Libr. Club, 58-59; del, U.S. Nat. Cmn. for UNESCO, 7th & 8th nat. conf, 61; chmn, document reproduction cmt, SLA, 63; chmn, info. retrieval cmt, RSD, 63-65; mem, AV cmt, ACRL, 64, chmn, cmt. on cooperative educ. & prfnl. orgn, 65; counsel to bd. regents, State of Fla, 65; mem. bd. dirs, Nat. Educ. Asn. for Res. & Develop, Inc, 65- Mem: ALA; SLA; Am. Soc. Info. Sci. Publ: Transl, Codigo Para Clasificadores, by Merrill, Ed. Kapelusz, Buenos Aires, 58; Advanced Data Processing in the University Library (co-auth), Scarecrow Press, 62; The Library As an Information System (co-auth), McGraw-Hill, (in prep); plus others. Consult: 1) Hofstra Univ, Hempstead, N.Y, accommodation of bldg. plans for future automation, Jan. 64; 2) Oxford Univ, Brasenose Col, Oxford, Eng, consult. at Anglo-Am. Conf. on Mechanization of Libr. Serv, June-July 66; 3) State Univ. N.Y, Stony Brook, consult. for libr. bldg. planning conf, with Robert Downs & Fred Wagman, 66; 4) Wofford Col, Spartanburg, S.C, planning for libr. automation, Feb. 67; 5) Wesleyan Univ, Middletown, Conn, consult. for univ. conf. on libr. tech, with Kilgour & deGennaro, Mar. 68. Specialties: 1b; 4a; 9 (int. libr. work).

HEILMANN, MARGARET AYERS, July 25, 14; Director of Library Services, Herricks Public Schools, New Hyde Park, N.Y. 11040. Home: 214-08 Hillside Ave, Queens Village, N.Y. 11427. B.S. in Ed; M.S. Dir. libr. serv, Herricks Pub. Sch, New Hyde Park, N.Y, 58-; asst. adjunct prof, grad. libr. sch, C.W. Post Campus, Long Island Univ, 62- Other: Mem. bd. sch. libr. sect, N.Y. Libr. Asn, 64-65, chmn. pub. cmt, 65-68; mem. YA cmt, ALA, 66-; past pres, Nassau-Suffolk Sch. Libr. Asn. Mem: N.Y. Libr. Club; ALA; AASL; N.Y. Libr. Asn; Nassau-Suffolk Sch. Libr. Asn; Nassau County Libr. Asn. Publ: Contrib. to prfnl. journals. Consult: 1) Shelter Rock Pub. Libr, Willis Ave, Alberton, N.Y, worked with parents & state orgn. plans, 60; 2) East Woods Schs, Yellow Cote Rd, Oyster Bay, N.Y, renovation of ballroom for libr, 64-65. Specialties: 1c, 1e, 1f; 2a, 2b, 2c; 3a, 3c, 3d; 5a, 5b, 5c; 6a; 7a, 7c; 8d.

HELLUM, BERTHA D, Nov. 2, 11; County Librarian, Alameda and Contra Costa County Libraries, 1750 Oak Park Blvd, Pleasant Hill, Calif. 94523. Home: 1917 Golden Rain Rd, Apt. 6, Walnut Creek, Calif. 94595. A.B, 33; cert, Univ. Calif, 34. County librn, Contra Costa County, Pleasant Hill, Calif, 54-, Alameda County Libr, 64- Other: Adv. mem, 32nd Dist. Parent-Teacher Asn, 56-; mem. bd. dirs, Contra Costa County Hist. Asn, 56-; part-time lectr, Univ. Calif. Sch. Librarianship, 58-; adv. mem. bd. mgr, Calif. Congress Parents & Teachers, 62-64; pres, Calif. Libr. Asn, 63; county librn, Alameda County Libr, 64-; part-time univ. librn, John F. Kennedy Univ, Martinez, Calif, 65-67; mem. bd. dirs, Contra Costa Park & Recreation Coun; hon. mem. bd. dirs, Friends of Libr. orgns. Mem: ALA; Calif. Libr. Asn. Publ: Contra Costa County Library Master Plan for Library Service, 57, rev. ed, 59 & 67; Friends of County Libraries, In: Friends of Libraries, ALA, 62; Contra Costa Library Construction, Calif. Librn, 1/63; Consult: 1) City of Concord, City Hall, Concord, Calif, bldg. planning, financing, gaining pub. support, organized Friends of Libr, drafting bldg. program, with John Powers Smith, architect, 56-59; 2) City of El Cerrito, City Hall, El Cerrito, Calif, bldg. consult, writing of program, working with architect, recommended furniture & equipment, 59-60; 3) County of Contra Costa, c/o County Administrator, Martinez, Calif, bldg. planning for six libr, 59-65; 4) City of Pittsburg, City Hall, Pittsburg, Calif, bldg. consult, application for fed. funds, writing of program, working with architect, selection of furniture & equipment, with Beland & Gianelli, architects, 64-; 5) County of Alameda, 1221 Oak St, Oakland, Calif, writing bldg. program, application for fed. funds, with Herbert G. Crowle & archit. firm of Ostwald & Kelley, 66- Specialties: 1a, 1e, 1f, 1g, 1h (legal & financial & pub. relations); 2d (California); 5a; 6d (organizing Friends of Libr. groups for pub. relations); 7a; 8a, 8c; 9 (starting new libr. systs, rehabilitating old libr. systs, libr. demonstration).

HENDERSON, JOHN D, Mar. 21, 03; Library Consultant, 27 Westminster Ave, Berkeley, Calif. 94708. A.B, Univ. Calif. Berkeley, 25, Cert. in Librarianship, 30. County librn, Los Angeles County Pub. Libr, 47-63; vis. prof, Univ. Calif. Libr. Sch, Los Angeles, summer 62; vis. prof, Univ. South. Calif. Sch. Libr. Sci, summers 63, 65, 66; prof, Univ. Ill. Grad. Sch. Libr. Sci, 64; lectr, sch. librarianship, Univ. Calif, 66-68. Other: Pres, Calif. Libr. Asn, 40-41; pres, Pub. Libr. Execs. Asn. South. Calif, 45; mem. coun. ALA, 48-52, pres. extension sect, 50-52, mem. cmt. intellectual freedom, 54-56; pres. south. dist, Calif. Libr. Asn, 49; chmn. hist. landmarks cmt, Los Angeles County, 58-63; coordinator, Ore. Libr. Asn. Pub. Libr. Bldg. Inst, Coos Bay, 65. Mem: ALA; Calif. Libr. Asn. Publ: The Regional Branch, In: Reaching Readers, Univ. Calif, 49; The Planning Team, In: A Living Library, Univ. South. Calif, 57; County and Regional Libraries, Libr. Trends, 10/61; County and Regional Libraries, In: The Future of Library Service, Univ. Ill. Grad. Sch. Libr. Sci, 62; The Book Catalogs of the Los Angeles County Public Library, In: Proceedings of the Graduate School of Library Science, Univ. Ill, 64; The Alameda County Library: A Report with Recommendations, 64, 67. Consult: 1) Pub. Libr. Santa

Cruz, Calif, program for new libr. bldgs, 63-67; 2) Pub. Libr, Astoria, Ore, program for new libr. bldg, including eval. of possible sites, spring 65; 3) Kings County & Hanford City Libr, Hanford, Calif, bldg. program for joint city-county serv, 65; 4) Minneapolis Pub. Libr. & Hennepin County Libr. Minn, study of city & county support, 66; 5) Mechanics Inst. Libr, San Francisco, Calif, review of opers. & policies. Specialties: 1a, 1e, 1g, 1h (procedure for selection of architect); 7a, 7c; 9 (reorganizing county libr. on regional basis & setting up geographical areas of serv; programming & planning br. & regional bldgs).

HENDERSON, MARY JANE, 1903; Home: 3465 Stanley St, Apt. 2, Montreal 2, Que, Can. & 98 Church St, Brockville, Ont, Can. B.A, 25; B.L.S, 26. Librn, Sun Life Assurance Co. of Can, Montreal, Que, to 58; librn, Montreal Trust Co.(spec. assignment), Montreal, 58-60. Other: 1st pres, Montreal SLA, 32, chmn. convention cmt, SLA, 36 & nominating cmt; dir, SLA New York, 3 years, mem, SLA Hall of Fame. Mem: Can. Libr. Asn; Que. Libr. Asn; SLA. Publ: List of Publications on Life Insurance Investments, 32; List of Publications on India, 33; Union List of Periodicals in Montreal Special Libraries, 1st ed, 33; Brief to the Royal Commission on National Development in the Arts and Sciences, Massey Cmn. Consult: 1) Montreal Bd. of Trade, Montreal, Que, Can, prepared report; 2) Murray Ballantyne Collection on Can. Hist, Montreal, catalogued, set up collection, spec. classification & subject heading list, with Mrs. H.G. Stockwell; 3) Univ. Club of Montreal, catalogued & set up libr. collection, with Mrs. Lawrence Short & Phoebe Prowse; 4) Carbec Mines Ltd. & Can. Matachewan Mines Ltd, organized records & prepared report & manual for mines in Can, Peru & Zambia, 67; 5) R.W. Howe, Engineer, Montreal, arranged libr. of mining, metallurgical, geological & other materials. Specialties: 1d; 2d (Can. bus. & econ, int. econ, investments, industry); 3a, 3b, 3c, 3d, 3e; 4a; 5a, 5d (arranged spec. courses for MSLA in job methods, job anal. & job eval. in cooperation with fed. govt. training plan); 7a, 7d (res); 8b; 9 (syst. for supvry. control of investment portfolios for a trust co, using computer & manual methods).

HENINGTON, DAVID M, Aug. 16, 29; Director, Houston Public Library, 500 McKinney, Houston, Tex. 77002. Home: 7611 Pagewood, Houston, Tex. 77042. B.A, Univ. Houston, 51; M.S.L.S, Columbia Univ, 56. Librn, Brooklyn Pub. Libr, 56-58; head, literature & hist. dept, Dallas Pub. Libr, Dallas, Tex, 58; dir, Waco Pub. Libr, Waco, Tex, 58-62; asst. dir, Dallas Pub. Libr, 62-67. Other: Second v.pres, Tex. Libr. Asn, 61-62, chmn. constitution cmt, 62-65, chmn. libr. develop. cmt, 65-66, v.pres. & pres-elect, 66-67. Mem: Tex. Libr. Asn; Southwest. Libr. Asn; ALA. Consult: 1) Richardson Pub. Libr, Richardson, Tex, eval. of current situation with recommendations, 64; 2) Nicholson Mem. Libr, Garland, Tex, libr. reorgn. & bldg. program, 65; 3) Fredricksburg Mem. Libr, Fredricksburg, Tex, bldg. consult, with Lillian M. Bradshaw, 66; 4) Liberty Pub. Libr, Liberty, Tex, bldg. Specialties: 1a, 1e, 1f, 1g; 5a, 5c; 6a, 6b; 7a; 8b, 8c, 8d.

HENKLE, DR. HERMAN H, Mar. 26, 00; Executive Director, John Crerar Library, 35 W. 33rd St, Chicago, Ill. 60616. Home: 4800 Chicago Beach Dr, 1702 N, Chicago, Ill. 60615. A.B, 28; M.A, 33; D.Litt, 61. Librn, John Crerar Libr, Chicago, Ill, 47-65, exec. dir, 63-; lectr, grad. libr. sch, Univ. Chicago, 50-66; adjunct prof, sci. info. serv, Ill. Inst. Tech, 65- Other: Pres, SLA, 45-46; pres, Am. Document. Inst, 57-58; treas, Joint Cmt. on Union List of Serials, 58-68; mem. metallurgical document. cmt, Am. Soc. Metals, 58-61. Mem: ALA; SLA; Am. Soc. Info. Sci; Med. Libr. Asn; Am. Asn. Libr. Schs. Publ: The History of Medical Libraries in Chicago, J. Int. Col. Surgeons, 12/63. Consult: 1) Univ. Wis, Madison, evaluated plans for new med. libr. bldg, with Louis Kaplan, Nov-Dec. 62; 2) Deere & Co, Moline, Ill, orgn. of space, furniture & equipment in libr. in new bldg, with Charlotte L. Anderson, Nov. 62-Jan. 63; 3) Mass. Inst. Tech, Cambridge, full-time participant in INTREX conf, Woods Hole, Mass, with Karl Overhage, July-Aug. 65; 4) UNESCO, Place de Fontenoy, Paris, France, sci. libr. in Pakistan, with A.R. Mohajir, July-Aug. 66. Specialties: 1b, 1d, 1e, 1g; 2d (bio-med. sci), 2f, 2h (sci. & tech); 3a, 3b, 3e; 5a, 5b, 5c; 7a, 7d (sci. info. serv).

HERON, DAVID W, Mar. 29, 20; Director of Libraries, University of Kansas, Lawrence, Kans. 66044. Home: 802 Tennessee St, Lawrence, Kans. 66044. B.A, 42; B.L.S, 48; M.A, 51. Asst. to dir, Stanford Univ. Libr, 55-57; asst. librn, Hoover Inst, 57-59; asst. dir, Stanford Univ. Libr, 59-61; dir. libr, Univ. Nev, 61-68; Univ. Kans, 68- Other: Pres, Univ. Calif. Libr. Sch. Alumni Asn, 61; mem. coun, ALA, 62-64, council-at-large 66-; pres, Nev. Libr. Asn, 64-66. Mem: ALA; Calif. Libr. Asn; Nev. Libr. Asn; Mountain Plains Libr. Asn. Publ: The Centrifugence of University Libraries, Col. & Res. Libr, 5/62; Winged Victory for Nevada (with Robert Alexander), Libr. J, 12/1/62; Libraries of the Ryukyus (with Eugene de Benko), UNESCO Bull. for Libr, 9-10/64; Photocopy and Interlibrary Loan, Res. Quart, Vol. 4, No. 3; Prospects for Library Telefacsimile (with J. Richard Blanchard), Libr. J, 8/66. Consult: 1) Univ. of the Ryukyus, Naha, Okinawa, advisor, Gen. Libr. Admin. & Libr. Educ, with Eugene De Benko, 60-61. Specialties: 1b, 1f, 1g; 2d (political sci); 4d (telefacsimile systs); 5a, 5b, 5c; 6a; 7a, 7b; 8b, 8c, 8f.

HERRICK, MARY DARRAH, Nov. 23, 08; Assistant Director for Bibliographic Organization,

---

5) PERSONNEL AND RECRUITING, 5a) job evaluation and description, salary recommendations, 5b) recruitment of professionals and management personnel, 5c) administrative organization, 6) PUBLIC RELATIONS, 6a) publications, 6b) publicity programs, 6c) public opinion surveys, 6d) others, 7) SERVICES, 7a) evaluation of current program, 7b) studies of service to special publics, e.g., students, handicapped, aged, etc., 7c) programs for the implementation of new laws, program proposals to governments, 7d) others, 8) COMMUNITY, REGIONAL, STATE PLANNING, 8a) legislative programs, 8b) area analyses, 8c) centralized systems, cooperative arrangements, 8d) development of standards, 8e) state libraries and extension agencies, 8f) regional and statewide surveys, 8g) others, 9) OTHERS.

Boston University Libraries, Boston, Mass. 02215. Home: 271 Dartmouth St, Boston, Mass. 02116. B.S, Simmons Col; B.A, Univ. Maine; M.S, Columbia Univ. Asst. dir. bibliog. orgn, Boston Univ. Libr, 48- Other: Mem. coun, ALA, 49-53 & 56-59, mem, catalog code revision cmt, 56-65. Mem: ALA. Publ: Index to the Classified Catalog of the Boston University Libraries: A Relative Index Based on the Library of Congress Classification (ed. & compiler), 2nd ed. rev, G.K. Hall, 2 vols, 64; Catalog of African Government Documents and African Area Index (ed. & compiler), 2nd ed. rev, G.K. Hall, 64. Consult: 1) Mass. Inst. Tech, Cambridge, Libr. Congress classification, Jan. 63; 2) Wellesley Col, Wellesley, Mass, Libr. Congress classification, Apr. 66; 3) Univ. R.I, Kingston, Libr. Congress classification; 4) Univ. Louisville, Ky, Libr. Congress classification, Apr. 67; 5) Middlebury Col, Vt, Libr. Congress classification, Aug. 67. Specialties: 3a, 3b.

HIATT, DR. PETER, Oct. 19, 30; Associate Professor, Graduate Library School & Public Library Consultant, Indiana State University, Bloomington, Ind. 47401. Home: 703 Gourley Pike, Apt. 199, Bloomington, Ind. 47401. B.A, Colgate Univ, 52; M.L.S, Rutgers Univ, 57, Ph.D, 63. Br. librn, Elizabeth Pub. Libr, Elizabeth, N.J, 57-59; instr, grad. sch. libr. serv, Rutgers Univ, 59-62; asst. prof, div. libr. sci, Ind. Univ, Bloomington, Ind, 63-66, assoc. prof, grad. libr. sch, 66-; pub. libr. consult, Ind. State Libr, 63-; dir, Ind. Libr. Studies, Bloomington, Ind, 68- Other: Secy, N.J. Libr. Asn, 59-60; chmn. reference div, Ind. Libr. Asn, 65-67, mem. program planning cmt, 66; mem. serv. to functionally illiterate cmt, ALA, 65-67, mem. reading improvement cmt, 65-68; chmn. centralized processing cmt, RTSD, 65-68; mem. program planning cmt, Ind. Sch. Librns. Asn, 66 & Ind. Adult Educ. Asn, 67; chmn. cmt. educ. state libr. personnel, ASL-LED, 68- Mem: ALA; SLA; Adult. Educ. Asn; Am. Soc. Info. Sci; Ind. Sch. Librns Asn; Ind. Libr. Asn. Publ: Urban Public Library Services for Adults of Low Education (with Henry Drennan), Libr. Quart, 4/65; The Monroe County Public Library: Planning for the Future (with Donald Thompson), Bloomington, Ind, 66; Public Library Service for the Functionally Illiterate: Survey of Practice (with Henry Drennan), ALA, 67; The Public Library Needs of Delaware County: The Community, Muncie Public Library and the Future (with Donald Thompson), Bloomington, 67; Cooperative Processing Centers for Public Libraries, Libr. Trends, 7/67; Automation and Hoosier Libraries & issue ed, Focus on Ind. Libr, 3/68. Consult: 1) Monroe County Pub. Libr, Bloomington, Ind, community survey with recommendations for programs, site location, bldg, with Donald Thompson, Nov. 65-June 66; 2) Batesville Pub. Libr, Batesville, Ind, need & procedure for community survey & bldg.

program, with Donald Thompson, July-Aug. 66; 3) Muncie Pub. Libr, Muncie, Ind, community survey & recommendations for serv, location of bldg, with Donald Thompson, fall 66-spring 67; 4) West. Interstate Compact for Higher Educ, Boulder, Colo, survey & program to achieve continuing educ. for personnel working in libr. in the 13 states served by WICHE, Apr. 67-; 5) Libr. Sch, Univ. Wis, Madison, Wis, consult. on design & implementation of res. project, Libr. Materials in Serv. to the New Adult Reader, U.S. Office Educ. project, with Mrs. Helen Lyman, Sept. 67- Specialties: 5d (inserv. educ. & training); 7a, 7b, 7d (basic programs of reader serv. to implement libr. objectives); 8b, 8c, 8f; 9 (continuing educ. of libr. personnel)

HICKS, WARREN B, July 25, 21; Director of Library Services, Chabot College, 25555 Hesperian Blvd, Hayward, Calif. 94545. Home: 1672 Orchard Way, Pleasanton, Calif. 94566. B.B.A, Univ. Denver, 48, M.B.A.(libr. sci), 50. Head librn, Union High Sch. Dist, Lodi, Calif, 53-61; supvr. libr, Unified Sch. Dist, Berkeley, Calif, 61-63; dir. libr. serv, Chabot Col, Hayward, Calif, 63- Other: Lectr. libr. sci, Univ, San Francisco, San Francisco, Calif, 58-; pres. north. sect, Calif. Asn. Sch. Librns, 61; mem. nat. cmt. standards, AASL, 63-66; chmn, Calif. State Sch. Libr. Standards Cmt, 63-67; mem, Calif. Jr. Col. Libr. Standards, 65-67. Mem: ALA; Calif. Asn. Sch. Librns; Calif. Libr. Asn. Publ: Preparation and Cataloging Time for School Libraries (with Anna Mary Lowrey), North Sect, Sch. Libr. Asn. Calif, 59; Cataloging and Labeling of Audiovisual Materials (with Lyndon Vivrette), Berkeley Unified Sch. Dist, 63; New School Library Standards, Calif. Educ, 10/64; Library in the Round, Calif. Librn, 10/66; Chabot Rounds Out Resources, Libr. J, 12/1/66. Specialties: 1b, 1c, 1e, 1f; 2a, 2b; 3c, 3d, 3e; 4a, 4b; 5a, 5b, 5c; 7a, 7c; 8c, 8d.

HILD, ALICE P, Dec. 24, 40; State School Library Consultant, State Department of Education, Cheyenne, Wyo. 82001. Home: 704 W. 31st St, Cheyenne, Wyo. 82001. A.B, Roanoke Col, 62; M.A.(librarianship), Univ. Denver, 63. Extension asst, extension div, Va. State Libr, 63-66; state sch. libr. consult, Wyo. State Dept. Educ, Cheyenne, Wyo, 66- Other: Mem. cmt. young adult lists, ALA-YASD Clearinghouse, 66-67, chmn, 67-; mem. Wyo. liason, ALA-JMRT, 66-; ex-officio mem, Title III LSCA Adv. Bd. for Wyo, 67- Mem: Am. Asn. Univ. Women; ALA; Wyo. Libr. Asn; Wyo. Educ. Asn; Mountain-Plains Libr. Asn. Consult: 1) LaGrange Sch, LaGrange, Wyo, eval. of elem. & high sch. serv, arrangement, usage of personnel with report to supt, Dec. 66; 2) Johnson County Rural Schs, Buffalo, Wyo, estimates on county bookmobile serv, with J. Andrew Fisher, Dec. 66-Jan. 67; 3) Burns Sch, Burns, Wyo, eval. of entire libr. program with report, Feb. 67; 4) Wyo. Pub. Schs, all areas

---

KEY TO CONSULTING SPECIALTIES: 1) ARCHITECTURE AND BUILDINGS, 1a) public libraries, 1b) academic libraries, 1c) school libraries, 1d) special libraries, 1e) library interiors, 1f) furnishings, 1g) site and location, 1h) other architectural; 2) COLLECTIONS: SELECTION, EVALUATION, WEEDING, 2a) adults, 2b) young adults, 2c) children, 2d) subject specialty, 2e) O.P. searches, 2f) rare books, 2g) appraisals, 2h) others; 3) TECHNICAL PROCESSES, 3a) cataloging, 3b) classification systems, 3c) acquisitions, 3d) materials processing, 3e) work flow and cost studies, 3f) others, 4) AUTOMATION, 4a) applications of data processing equipment, 4b) information storage and retrieval systems, 4c) systems analysis, 4d) others

of libr. program 66-2 and media program for Cedar Rapids, Sept. 67; 5) Wash. Elem. Sch, Laramie, Wyo, cataloging instruction, created cent. sch. libr, Oct. 67. Specialties: 1c, 1e, 1f; 2b, 2c; 3a, 3b, 3c, 3d; 5b; 7a, 7b, 7c; 8c, 8d.

HILL, LAURENCE G, May 4, 14; Director, Westchester Library System, 28 S. First Ave, Mt. Vernon, N.Y. 10550. Home: 55 Rockledge Rd, Bronxville, N.Y. 10708. A.B, 36; M.S, 39. Dir, Pub. Libr, New Bedford, Mass, 49-60; dir, Nioga Libr. Syst, Niagara Falls, N.Y, 60-67. Other: Mem. exec. cmt, Mass. Libr. Asn, 55-60; mem, Mass. Libr. Develop. Cmt, 58-60; pres. adult serv, New York Libr. Asn, 65-66; N.Y. State Regents Adv. Coun. on Libr, 67- Mem: N.Y. Libr. Asn; ALA. Consult: 1) Yarmouth Pub. Libr, Yarmouth, Mass, survey of serv. & bldg. requirements, report on proposed conversion of town offices bldg, July 56; 2) Dartmouth Pub. Libr, Dartmouth, Mass, layout, arrangement, equipment & furniture, cost estimates & specifications, July 58; 3) Herkimer Free Libr, Herkimer, N.Y, survey of serv, site study, bldg. space & personnel with recommendations, Feb-May 66; 4) South. Tier Libr. Syst, Corning, N.Y, consultation & report on bldg. & expansion plans for Syst. Headquarters, May 65 & June 66. Specialties: 1a, 1e, 1f, 1g; 2a; 3d, 3e; 5c; 7a; 8c.

HINES, DR. THEODORE C, Sept. 9, 26; Associate Professor, Columbia University School of Library Service, New York, N.Y. 10027. Rothines Associates, 28 Edgemont Ave, Summit, N.J. 07901. Home: 54 North Dr, East Brunswick, N.J. 08816. A.B, 50; M.L.S, 58; Ph.D, 60; A.L.A, British Libr. Asn, 60. Chief extension dept, Wash. Pub. Libr, Wash, D.C, 47-57; res. assoc, instr, asst. prof, Rutgers Univ. Libr, Sch, 57-63; spec. asst. to dean & asst. prof, Columbia Univ. Sch. Libr. Serv, New York, N.Y, 63-68. Other: Bibliog. & index adv, McGraw-Hill, 63-; chmn. N.Y. chap, Am. Document. Inst, 65, councilor-at-large, 66-; summer lectr, libr. sch, Univ. Calif, Los Angeles, 65; mem, JOG, Am. Document. Inst-SLA, 65-; mem. bd. trustees, East Brunswick Free Pub. Libr, 65-; mem. adv. cmt, URBANDOC, 66-; mem. publ. cmt, Boy Scouts Am, 66- Mem: ALA; The Libr. Asn; Soc. Indexers; Int. Asn. Documentalists; Am. Soc. Info. Sci; SLA; Am. Asn. Advancement Sci. Publ: Bibliography (transl), Scarecrow, 62; Documentation Systems: a Structural Outline, Rutgers Univ, 63; Computer Arrangement of Bibliographic, Index, and Catalog Entries (with J.L. Harris), Bro-Dart Found, 66; The Bookfinder, R. R. Bowker, 3rd ed, 66; McGraw-Hill Bibliography of Science and Technology (coordinating ed), McGraw-Hill, 66; Index design for American Negro Reference Book, Prentice-Hall, 66. Consult: 1) John R. Wiley & Sons, New York, N.Y, survey of the info. needs of the ed. staff, recommended syst. design to meet these needs, with Maurice F. Tauber, 65; 2) Farmingdale Pub. Sch, Farmingdale, N.Y, design & supv. of production of prototype machine-based book catalog for three jr. high schs. & production of a manual, with J.L. Harris, 65-; 3) Camden County Libr, Camden, N.J, survey of libr. serv. with recommendations, with Harold L. Roth, 66; 4) Hillside Pub. Libr, New Hyde Park, N.Y, survey of libr. needs for the sch. dist. area, with eval. of present serv. & twenty-year projections, with Harold L. Roth, 66; 5) Anne Arundel, Baltimore, Montgomery & Prince Georges Counties, Md, survey of possibilities for joint tech. serv, computer-based cataloging, with Pfefferle, 66- Specialties: 2c, 2d (sci, tech); 3a, 3b, 3d, 3e; 4a, 4b; 7a, 7c; 8c; 9 (indexing, consult. for publ. interested in the libr. market, publ. methods).

HINTZ, DR. CARL W, Oct. 14, 07; University Librarian, Professor of Librarianship & Director of Libraries, Oregon State System of Higher Education, University of Oregon Library, Eugene, Ore. 97403. Home: 2460 Pioneer Pike, Eugene, Ore. 94703. A.B, 32; A.B.L.S, 33; A.M.L.S, 35; Ph.D, 52. Univ. librn. & prof. librarianship, Univ. Ore, Eugene, 48-; dir. libr, Ore. State Syst. Higher Educ, 65- Other: Pres, Md. Libr. Asn, 41-43; pres, Ore. Libr. Asn, 55-56; pres, Pac. Northwest Libr. Asn, 57-58; Fulbright lectr. & consult, India, 61; pres, LED, 62-63, chmn, cmn. on nat. plan for libr. educ, ALA. Mem: ALA; ACRL; Pac. Northwest Libr. Asn; Ore. Libr. Asn. Publ: Museum Libraries in the U.S, Libr. Quart, 4/48; Notable Materials Added to North American Libraries, 1948-49, Libr. Quart, 7 & 10/51; Personnel Administration, PNLA Quart, 10/51; Libraries and Library Services in the Portland High Schools (with W. H. Carlson), Sch. Dist. 1, Multnomah County, Ore, 59; Academic Library and the Community, In: College, University and Special Libraries of the Pacific Northwest, Univ. Wash, 61; Education for Librarianship in India, Occasional Paper 73, Univ. Ill. Grad. Sch. Libr. Sci, 10/64. Consult: 1) Sch. Dist. 1, Multnomah County, Portland, Ore, survey of libr. & libr. serv. with reference to suitability for col-bound student, with William H. Carlson, Mar-June 59; 2) Univ. Alaska, Fairbanks, survey of libr. with recommendations, Apr. 59; 3) Mont. State Univ, Missoula, survey of bldg. needs, May-June 62; 4) Cleveland State Univ, Cleveland, Ohio, bldg. program, projections of libr. growth & develop, Oct. 65-Mar. 66; 5) Mt. Angel Abbey, Benedict, Ore, libr. bldg. consult, Nov. 65- Specialties: 1b; 7a, 7b; 8d, 8f.

HIRSCH, DR. FELIX EDWARD, Feb. 7, 02; Librarian & Professor of History, Trenton State College, Trenton State College Library, Trenton, N.J. 08625. Home: 14 Pershing Ave, Trenton, N.J. 08618. Ph.D.(hist), Univ. Heidelberg, 23; B.S. in L.S, Columbia Univ, 40. Librn. & prof. hist, Bard Col, 36-54, librn. & prof. hist, Trenton State Col, Trenton, N.J, 55-

---

5) PERSONNEL AND RECRUITING, 5a) job evaluation and description, salary recommendations, 5b) recruitment of professionals and management personnel, 5c) administrative organization, 6) PUBLIC RELATIONS, 6a) publications, 6b) publicity programs, 6c) public opinion surveys, 6d) others, 7) SERVICES, 7a) evaluation of current program, 7b) studies of service to special publics, e.g., students, handicapped, aged, etc., 7c) programs for the implementation of new laws, program proposals to governments, 7d) others, 8) COMMUNITY, REGIONAL, STATE PLANNING, 8a) legislative programs, 8b) area analyses, 8c) centralized systems, cooperative arrangements, 8d) development of standards, 8e) state libraries and extension agencies, 8f) regional and statewide surveys, 8g) others, 9) OTHERS.

Other: Mem. coun, ALA, 53-57, chmn, cmt. on standards, ACRL, 57-63; pres, col. & univ. sect, N.J. Libr. Asn, 59-60; mem, Notable Books Coun, 60-63; vis. prof. hist, Tech. Univ. Karlsruhe, Germany, 62 & Univ. Heidelberg, 65; adjunct prof. libr. sci, Drexel Inst. Grad. Libr. Sch, 63-64, 67, 68; chmn-elect, hist. sect, RSD, 67-68; chmn, N.J. Coun. State Col. & Univ. Librn, 68-69. Mem: ALA; N.J. Libr. Asn; Am. Hist. Asn; Am. Asn. Univ. Prof. Publ: Gustav Stresemann, Patriot and European, Göttingen, 64; contrib. to prfnl. journals. Consult: 1) Md. State Cols, Towson, Coppin, Frostburg, Salisbury & Bowie, developed long range plans for personnel & collections, with Sarah Jones, Elizabeth Simkins, Frank N. Jones, Bernardine Handy & William Williamson; 2) Hunter Col, New York, N.Y, reevaluation of City Univ. of New York, Oct. 66. Specialties: 1b; 2a, 2d (hist, polit. sci. & world affairs); 3c; 5c; 7b; 8d.

HOLLEY, DR. EDWARD GAILON, Nov. 26, 27; Director of Libraries & Professor, University of Houston, Houston, Tex. 77004. Home: 4837 Briarbend, Houston, Tex. 77035. B.A, 49; M.A, 51; Ph.D, 61. Educ, philosophy & psychology librn, Univ. Ill, 57-62; dir. libr. & prof, Univ. Houston, 62- Other: Vis. lectr, libr. sch, Univ. Wis, Madison, summer 68. Mem: ALA; Tex. Libr. Asn; Southwest. Libr. Asn; Tex. Asn. Col. Teachers; Kappa Delta Pi; Phi Kappa Phi; Beta Phi Mu. Publ: Effective Librarian-Faculty Relationships, Ill. Libr, 12/61; Charles Evans, American Bibliographer, 63; The Trend to L.C: Thoughts on Changing Library Classification Schemes, La. State Univ. Libr. Lectures, 66; Raking the Historic Coals, 67; Resources for Research in Urban Areas, Wilson Libr. Bull, 1/67; Resources of Texas Libraries (co-auth), 68. Consult: 1) Sam Houston State Col, Huntsville, Tex, bldg. consult, 64-65; 2) Univ. St. Thomas, Houston, Tex, use of ACRL grant for libr. resources, Dec. 66; 3) Southwest Tex. Col, San Marcos, bldg. consult, Apr. 67; 4) Coordinating Bd, Tex. Col. & Univ. Syst, Austin, survey of libr. resources for master plan for higher educ. in Tex, with Donald D. Hendricks, Alfred J. Coco, David A. Kronick & Marie Harvin, 67-68. Specialties: 1b; 2a, 2b, 2c, 2e, 2f, 2g; 3b; 8b, 8f.

HOLT, RAYMOND M, June 3, 21; City Librarian, Pomona Public Library, 625 S. Garey Ave, Pomona, Calif. 91766. Home: 1841 Westwood Place, Pomona, Calif. 91767. B.A, Univ. Redlands; B.S. in L.S, Univ. South. Calif. Mem: Calif. Libr. Asn; ALA. Publ: Contemporary Public Library Buildings, 62; Concepts in Dynamic Cultural Education: A Preliminary Program for Pomona's Cultural Center, 63; Building Program for Boise Public Library, Boise, Idaho, 64; The Community Library in an Age of Change: A Case Study of Public Libraries in San Gabriel Valley, 65; Community Libraries to Match Community Needs, 66.

Consult: 1) Arcadia Pub. Libr, 20 W. Duarte Rd, Arcadia, Calif, survey of libr. resources & serv, leading to reorgn. of serv. & libr. bldg. program, 59; 2) Boise Pub. Libr, 815 Washington St, Boise, Idaho, study of serv. & use, resulting in program & recommendations for new libr. bldg, 64; 3) Chula Vista Pub. Libr, Memorial Way, Chula Vista, Calif, feasibility & growth study, program & recommendations for new libr. bldg, 67; 4) Corona Pub. Libr, 805 S. Main St, Corona, Calif, program for new libr. bldg, 68; 5) Burlingame Pub. Libr, 480 Primrose, Burlingame, Calif, community survey, study of libr. collections & serv, site study, bldg. program, plans for interim expansion & design for new libr. bldg, 68. Specialties: 1a, 1g; 7a, 7c; 8b, 8c, 8d, 8f; 9 (master planning of libr, integrated with other cultural insts. such as museums & art galleries).

HOPE, ARLENE, Apr. 12, 13; Library Services Program Officer, U.S. Office of Education, J.F. Kennedy Fed. Bldg, Boston, Mass. 02203. Home: 255 Beacon St, Apt. 61, Boston, Mass. 02116. B.S, Simmons Col, 39; M.A, Boston Univ, 44; M.S. in L.S, Univ. Mich, 55. Consult, Calif. State Libr, 56-61, principal librn, consult. serv, 61-63; regional dir, Cent. Mass. Regional Libr. Syst, 63-64; libr. serv. program officer, U.S. Office Educ, 65- Mem: ALA; SLA; New Eng. Libr. Asn; Beta Phi Mu. Publ: The San Leandro Public Library, Calif. State Libr, Sacramento, 59; A Study of Library Services in Norwalk (co-auth), Calif. State Libr, 59; Mill Valley Public Library, Calif. State Libr, 62; The Santa Cruz Library System, Sacramento, 62; Recommendations for a San Joaquin Valley Library System, Fresno, 63; Westport, Massachusetts, a Site Study, 64. Consult: 1) Santa Cruz County Libr, Santa Cruz, Calif, anal. of merger possibilities with adjacent libr, full scale study of Santa Cruz bldg. needs, staffing & develop. program, 61-62; 2) Mill Valley Pub. Libr, Mill Valley, Calif, anal. of work program & recommendations for future space needs & staffing patterns, 62; 3) Fresno County Libr, Fresno, Calif, anal. of Fresno & adjacent counties as participants in a state-aid supported syst, Mar. 63; 4) Hudson Pub. Libr, Hudson, Mass, bldg. remodeling recommendations, 64; 5) Westport Pub. Libr, Westport, Mass, site study, July 64. Specialties: 1a, 1g; 3e, 3f (work simplification generally); 7a, 7c; 8b, 8c, 8f.

HOPP, DR. RALPH H, Oct. 24, 15; University Librarian, University of Minnesota Libraries, Minneapolis, Minn. 55455. Home: 1341 Keston St, St. Paul, Minn. 55108. B.S.(chemical engineering), Univ. Nebr, 43; M.S.(libr. sci), Univ. Ill, 50, Ph.D, 56. Prof. & univ. librn, Univ. Minn, Minneapolis, 53- Mem: ALA; Am. Asn. Univ. Prof; Minn. Libr. Asn. Publ: Survey of Sioux Falls College Library (with M.M. Gormley), ALA, 61; University Library

---

KEY TO CONSULTING SPECIALTIES: 1) ARCHITECTURE AND BUILDINGS, 1a) public libraries, 1b) academic libraries, 1c) school libraries, 1d) special libraries, 1e) library interiors, 1f) furnishings, 1g) site and location, 1h) other architectural; 2) COLLECTIONS: SELECTION, EVALUATION, WEEDING, 2a) adults, 2b) young adults, 2c) children, 2d) subject specialty, 2e) O.P. searches, 2f) rare books, 2g) appraisals, 2h) others; 3) TECHNICAL PROCESSES, 3a) cataloging, 3b) classification systems, 3c) acquisitions, 3d) materials processing, 3e) work flow and cost studies, 3f) others, 4) AUTOMATION, 4a) applications of data processing equipment, 4b) information storage and retrieval systems, 4c) systems analysis, 4d) others

Storage Problems, Col. & Res. Libr, 11/61; Extra-university Sources of Financial Support for Libraries, Col. & Res. Libr, 11/62; Survey of Faculty of Letters Libraries, Univ. Ankara, Dil ve Tarih Facultesi, 63; University of Minnesota: Program for the West Bank Library (with E.B. Stanford), Univ. Minn, 64. Consult: 1) Sioux Falls Col, Sioux Falls, S.Dak, survey of libr. serv, staff, collection, bldg. needs & function in col, with Mark M. Gormley, 61; 2) Univ. Ankara, Ankara, Turkey, survey of libr. resources, orgn. & serv, 62-63; 3) Gen. Beadle Col, Madison, S.Dak, bldg. consult, with Ralph Koch, 65; 4) N. Star Res. & Develop. Inst, Minneapolis, Minn, consult. on mgt. survey of Hill Reference Libr, 66; 5) Univ. Md. Libr, consult. on readers' serv, 66. Specialties: 1b, 1d; 2d (sci. & tech); 5c; 7a; 9 (readers' serv. in acad. libr).

HOUSEL, JAMES R, Feb. 16, 17; Head Librarian, Ontario City Library, Ontario, Calif. 91761. Home: 1253 College Way, Ontario, Calif. 91762. B.A, Univ. Wyo, 41; B.S.L.S, Univ. Calif, Berkeley, 48. Dir, First Regional Libr. of Miss, 52-56; head librn, Monterey Park Pub. Libr, 56-59; head librn, Ontario City Libr, 59- Other: Pres, Am. Legion Luncheon Club, 60; pres, West End Symphony Asn, 61; v.pres, Pomona Valley Writer's Club, 62. Mem: ALA; Calif. Libr. Asn; Calif. Alumni Asn. Publ: Staff Procedure Manual, 62. Consult: 1) Ellensburg Pub. Libr, Ellensburg, Wash, plan of serv. for regional libr, 52; 2) Northeast Regional Libr, Corinth, Miss, plan of serv. for multi-county libr, 55; 3) Monterey Park Pub. Libr, Monterey Park, Calif, plan of serv, with Arlene Hope, 56; 4) Downey Pub. Libr, Downey, Calif, bldg. consult, with John Perkins, 59; 5) Upland Pub. Libr, Upland, Calif, proposed cooperative libr syst, with Louise Franke, 66. Specialties: 1a, 1c; 2a; 3b, 3e; 5c; 6b, 6c; 7a; 8b, 8c.

HUMPHRY, JAMES, III, July 21, 16; Vice-President, H.W. Wilson Co, 950 University Ave, Bronx, N.Y. 10452. Home: 10 Ridge Rd, New Rochelle, N.Y. 10804. A.B, Harvard, 39; B.S. in L.S, Columbia Univ, 41. Librn. & prof. bibliog, Colby Col, 47-51, 54-57; chief librn, Metrop. Museum of Art, New York, N.Y, 57-68. Other: Mem, bookbinding cmt, ALA, 48-51, chmn, cmt. art index, RSD, 57-58 & cmt. Wilson indexes, 57-58, 61-66, coun, 59-63, mem, bldgs. cmt. col. & univ. libr, 59-63, mem, cmt. orgn, LAD, 63-65, subscription books cmt, 63-66; coordinator for ALA sponsored Libr. Serv. Bill, Maine Libr. Asn, 48-49, 55-57, ed. of Bull, 53-56, pres. of Asn. & chmn. exhibits cmt, 55-56; pres, Metrop. Museum Art Employees Asn, 58-60, mem, bd. gov, 58-68; chmn, arts cmt, N.Y. Libr. Club, 58-62, mem, coun, 59-, v.pres, 64-65, pres, 65-66; mem, bd. dirs, ACRL, 59-63, chmn, art subsect, Subj. Specialists Sect, 61-62, mem, planning & action cmt, 62-65, chmn, 66-67, v.chmn. & chmn, Subj. Specialists Sect, 64-66, v.pres. & pres-elect of Asn, 66-67; mem, cmt. copyright law rev, SLA, 61-65, chmn, museum group of N.Y. chap, 62-64, chmn. convention, N.Y, 67; convenor, Archons of Colophon, 63-64; mem, adv. cmt, St. John's Univ. Congress, 63-; chmn, libr. group, Am. Asn. Museums, 65; cor. mem, cmt. document, Int. Coun. Museums, Paris, 65-; mem, bd. dirs, H.W. Wilson Co, 66-; adv. bd, Libr. Presidential Papers, N.Y, 66-; mem. bd. trustees, Archives Am. Art, Detroit, 67- Mem: ALA; SLA; N.Y. Libr. Club; Am. Asn. Museums; Int. Coun. Museums; Metrop. Museum Art Employees Asn; Grolier Club; Archons of Colophon. Publ: Colby's Most Important Laboratory, Bull. Maine Libr. Asn, 11/49; The Library of Edwin Arlington Robinson, Colby Col, 50; The Nuremberg Chronicle, Colby Libr. Quart, 11/55; Fitzgerald's Rubaiyat, Centennial Edition (co-auth), Colby Col, 59; For Governor of Massachusetts: Long vs. Butler, Colby Libr. Quart, 6/61; Library Service in Delaware (with John A. Humphry), N.Y, 66; Library Service in Louisiana (with John A. Humphrey), N.Y, 68. Consult: 1) Greenwich Libr, Greenwich, Conn, report with recommendations for libr. program & bldg. expansion program, with John A. Humphry, 65-; 2) Libr. Cmn. for State of Del, Dover, state-wide survey for libr. serv. & facilities, including all types of libr, with John A. Humphry, 65-66; 3) R.I. Sch. of Design, Providence, report with recommendations for libr. program & new libr. bldg, with John A. Humphry, 65-66; 4) Henry Francis du Pont Winterthur Museum, Winterthur, Del, new libr. bldg, with John A. Humphry, 66-; 5) La. State Libr, Baton Rouge, state-wide libr. survey including libr. educ, with John A. Humphry, 66-68. Specialties: 1a, 1b, 1d, 1e, 1f, 1g; 2a, 2d (art, archaeol, archit), 2e, 2g; 3c, 3d, 3e; 4a, 4b; 5a, 5b, 5c; 6a; 7a, 7c; 8a, 8b, 8c, 8d, 8e, 8f.

HUMPHRY, JOHN AMES, July 21, 16; State Librarian & Assistant Commissioner for Libraries, State Education Department, Albany, N.Y. 12224. Home: 2316 Rosendale Rd, Schenectady, N.Y. 12309. A.B, Harvard Univ, 39; B.S.(libr. sci), Columbia Univ, 41. Dir, Springfield Libr, Springfield, Mass, 48-64, exec. dir, Springfield Libr. & Museums Asn, 60-64; dir, Brooklyn Pub. Libr, Brooklyn, N.Y, 64-67; state librn. & asst. cmnr. libr, State Educ. Dept, Albany, N.Y, 67- Other: Mem, Mass. Bd. Libr. Cmnrs, 57-64; dir, Forest Press, Inc, 65-; mem. adv. bd, Annual Congress for Librns, St. John's Univ, 65-; dir, Coun. Libr. Resources, Inc, Wash, D.C, 68- Mem: ALA; N.Y. Libr. Asn; Mass. Libr. Asn; N.Y. Libr. Club, Archons of Colophon; Melvil Dui Chowder & Marching Asn; West. Mass. Libr. Club. Publ: Library Cooperation, the Brown University Study of University-School-Community Library Coordination in the State of Rhode Island, Brown Univ, 63; A Study of the Newton (Massachusetts) Free Library (with Philip J. McNiff), 4/64; A Study of Public Library Service in

---

5) PERSONNEL AND RECRUITING, 5a) job evaluation and description, salary recommendations, 5b) recruitment of professionals and management personnel, 5c) administrative organization, 6) PUBLIC RELATIONS, 6a) publications, 6b) publicity programs, 6c) public opinion surveys, 6d) others, 7) SERVICES, 7a) evaluation of current program, 7b) studies of service to special publics, e.g., students, handicapped, aged, etc., 7c) programs for the implementation of new laws, program proposals to governments, 7d) others, 8) COMMUNITY, REGIONAL, STATE PLANNING, 8a) legislative programs, 8b) area analyses, 8c) centralized systems, cooperative arrangements, 8d) development of standards, 8e) state libraries and extension agencies, 8f) regional and statewide surveys, 8g) others, 9) OTHERS.

Niagara Falls, New York, 65; A Study of the Groton Public Library, Groton, Connecticut, 11/65; Library Service in Delaware (James Humphry, III), State Libr. Cmn, Dover, Del, 66 An Evaluation of the Library, Rhode Island School of Design (with James Humphry, III), 3/66. Consult: 1) Niagara Falls Pub. Libr, 1022 Main St, Niagara Falls, N.Y, study of serv. program & bldg. requirements, with Laurence G. Hill, 64-65; 2) Libr. Cmn. for State of Del, Dover, statewide libr. survey, with James Humphry, III, 65-66; 3) R.I. Sch. Design, Providence, serv. & bldg. program, with James Humphry, III, 65-66; 4) Greenwich Libr, Greenwich, Conn, study of bldg. expansion program, with James Humphry, III, Aug. 65-; 5) La. State Libr, Baton Rouge, statewide libr. study, including libr. educ, with James Humphry, III, Jan. 66-Apr. 68. Specialties: 1a, 1b, 1c, 1d, 1e, 1f, 1g; 2a, 2b, 2c; 3a, 3b, 3c, 3d, 3e; 5a, 5b, 5c; 7a, 7b, 7c; 8b, 8c, 8d, 8e, 8f; 9 (libr. equipment).

HUNT, DONALD H, Jan. 14, 20; Library Career Consultant, Graduate School of Library Science, Drexel Institute of Technology, Philadelphia, Pa. 19104. Home: 1530 Locust St, Philadelphia, Pa. 19102. B.A, 48; M.A.L.A, 50; M.A.L.A, 52. Admin. asst, Brooklyn Pub. Libr, 53-57; dir, Franklin Square Pub. Libr, 57-59; deputy dir, Nassau Libr. Syst, 59-62; libr. career consult, grad. sch. libr. sci, Drexel Inst. Tech, Phila, Pa, 62- Other: Pres, Pa. Libr. Asn; chmn. recruitment cmt, Coun. Nat. Libr. Asn. Mem: ALA; Cath. Libr. Asn; Pa. Libr. Asn; N.J. Libr. Asn; Am. Personnel & Guidance Asn. Publ: Ed, Drexel Libr. Quart; past ed, Odds and Book Ends; contrib. to prfnl. journals. Consult: 1) New Eng. Libr. Asn, N.H. State Libr, Concord, N.H, lecturing & consulting on establishment of regional recruitment program, Oct. 64; 2) Ill. Libr. Asn, lecturing & consulting on establishment of statewide recruitment program, Oct. 64; 3) Grad. Sch. Libr. Sci, Drexel Inst. Tech, Phila, Pa, dir. of conf. for nationwide recruitment planning, July 66; 4) Wis. Libr. Asn, Kellogg Pub. Libr, Green Bay, Wis, lecturing & consulting on establishment of statewide recruitment program, Sept. 66; 5) Mich. Libr. Asn, Flint, Mich, lecturing & consulting on establishment of statewide recruitment program, Oct. 66. Specialties: 5b.

HURLEY, RICHARD J, July 21, 06; Supervisor of Libraries, Fairfax County School Board, Fairfax, Va. 22030. Home: 10307 Beaumont St, Fairfax, Va. 22030. B.A, 32; B.S.L.S, 34; M.A. (educ), 36; A.M.L.S, 41. Asst. prof, dept. libr. sci, Cath. Univ. Am, 51-57; supvr. libr, Fairfax County Sch. Bd, Fairfax, Va, 57- Other: Pres, Cath. Libr. Asn; pres, Childrens Book League of Wash. Mem: ALA; AASL; Asn. Am. Libr. Schs; Va. Libr. Asn; Cath. Libr. Asn; Va. Educ. Asn. Publ: Key to the Out of Doors, H.W. Wilson; Your Library, Cath. Univ. Am;

Survey of Bay City Libraries, Univ. Mich; School Libraries, In: Encyclopedia of Educational Research. Consult: 1) Va. State Dept. Educ, Richmond, selection of new books on sec. sch. level, Oct. 66. Specialties: 2b, 2c; 7d (res. on sch. libr); 9 (local surveys).

I

ISLEY, DORIS NATELLE, Oct. 18, 29; Manager, Information Services Division, Mississippi Research & Development Center, Jackson, Miss. 39205. Home: 949 Morningside St, Apt. A-23, Jackson, Miss. 39202. B.A, 51; M.A, 52. Librn, sch. archit, Ga. Inst. Tech, Atlanta, 53-57; UNESCO tech. expert to Mid. E. Tech. Univ, Ankara, Turkey, 58-59; librn, sch. archit, Ga. Inst. Tech, 59-66, asst. prof, grad. program in city planning, 64-66 & res. asst, 65-66. Other: V.pres, Coun. of Planning Librns; mem. exec. cmt, Exchange Bibliog. Mem: Ga. Libr. Asn; Southeast. Libr. Asn; Miss. Libr. Asn. Publ: Civic and Cultural Centers: A Planning Bibliography (compiler with Leo J. Zuber), Metrop. Planning Cmn, Atlanta, 53; The Literature of Zoning, Ga. Local Govt. J, 5/55; Bibliography on the Control of Roadside Development, Ga. Inst. Tech, 55 & Supplement, 56; A Manual for Small Planning Agency Libraries, Ga. Inst. Tech, 66. Consult: 1) Del. State Planning Office, Dover, organized agency libr, 61; 2) E. Cent. Fla. Regional Planning Cmn, Titusville, organized agency libr, 65; 3) City of Atlanta Planning Dept, Ga, organized agency libr, 65; 4) Atlanta Region Metrop. Planning Cmn, organized agency libr, 65. Specialties: 2d (city planning); 8g (agency libr).

J

JACKSON, DR. WILLIAM VERNON, May 26, 26; Professor & Director, International Library Information Center, Graduate School of Library & Information Sciences, University of Pittsburgh, Pittsburgh, Pa. 15213. Home: 196 W. Kathleen Dr, Park Ridge, Ill. 60068. B.A, Northwest. Univ, 45; A.M, Harvard Univ, 48, Ph.D, 52; M.S.in L.S, Univ. Ill, 51. Assoc. prof. libr. sci, Univ. Ill, 58-62; assoc. prof. Spanish & Portuguese, Univ. Wis, 63-65; prof. libr. sci. & dir, Int. Libr. Info. Center, Univ. Pittsburgh, 66- Other: Pres, Beta Phi Mu (1955-56); chmn, int. relations round table, ALA, 65-66. Mem: ALA. ACRL; AALS; Theatre Libr. Asn; N.Y, Pa. & Ill. Libr. Asns; Bibliog. Soc. Am; Phi Beta Kappa, Beta Phi Mu, Phi Sigma Iota. Publ: Handbook of American Library Resources, 2nd ed, 62; Aspects of Librarianship in Latin America, 62; Latin America, Libr. Trends, 10/63; Library Guide for Brazilian Studies, 64; contrib. to prfnl. journals. Consult: 1) U.S. Info. Agency, Dept. of State, Wash. D.C, advisor on libr. in

KEY TO CONSULTING SPECIALTIES: 1) ARCHITECTURE AND BUILDINGS, 1a) public libraries, 1b) academic libraries, 1c) school libraries, 1d) special libraries, 1e) library interiors, 1f) furnishings, 1g) site and location, 1h) other architectural; 2) COLLECTIONS: SELECTION, EVALUATION, WEEDING, 2a) adults, 2b) young adults, 2c) children, 2d) subject specialty, 2e) O.P. searches, 2f) rare books, 2g) appraisals, 2h) others; 3) TECHNICAL PROCESSES, 3a) cataloging, 3b) classification systems, 3c) acquisitions, 3d) materials processing, 3e) work flow and cost studies, 3f) others, 4) AUTOMATION, 4a) applications of data processing equipment, 4b) information storage and retrieval systems, 4c) systems analysis, 4d) others

Latin Am, 56-; 2) Agency Int. Develop/ROCAP, Guatemala City, Guatemala, advisor on univ. libr, with Marietta D. Shepard & Carl W. Deal, 65-66; 3) N.Y. Pub. Libr, Reference Dept, N.Y, supvr. of guide to resources project, with Sam P. Williams, 65-; 4) Agency Int. Develop, Rio de Janeiro, Brazil, advisor on libr, Jan. 67. Specialties: 1b; 2d (Latin Am; libr. resources), 2h (univ; reference); 3c; 5d (educ. for librarianship); 7c; 8a, 8b, 8c, 8d, 8e, 8f; 9 (libr. develop. in Latin Am).

JACOBS, DR. JAMES WRILEY, July 25, 23; Director, Dept. of Educational and Managerial Information and Analysis, Montgomery County Public Schools, 850 N. Washington St, Rockville, Md. 20850. Home: 1 Central Ave, Gaithersburg, Md. 20760. B.S, 49; M.A, 52; Ed.D, 64. Jr. High principal, 56-60; Citizens Curriculum Study Cmt. Coordinator, 60-61; dir, Dept. Instructional Materials, 61-66, area dir, 66-67. Mem: Md. Libr. Asn; Md. Sch. Libr. Asn. Publ: Blueprint of an Idea, Sch. Libr, 10/63; The Summer Library Program for Montgomery County Schools, Md. Libr, fall 63; In-Service Education of Teachers in the Use of the School Library as a Materials Center, In: The School Library As a Materials Center, U.S. Office Educ, 63; The Organization and Administration of Instructional Materials Programs in School Systems Enrolling 25,000 or More Pupils, George Wash. Univ, 64. Consult: 1) Nat. Educ. Asn, Wash. D.C, on-site visitor for Educ. Media Inst. Eval. Project, with James W. Brown, 65-66; 2) Bossier Parish, Benton, La, media & tech, ESEA Title III, 66; 3) Md. State Dept. Educ, Baltimore, ESEA Titles II & III, 66; 4) U.S. Office Educ, Wash, D.C, ESEA Title III reader, 66-67; 5) Chenango County, Guillford, N.Y, gen. work pertaining to media & orgn, 66-67. Specialties: 1c; 3f (setting up processing serv); 4a, 4b; 7a, 8c; 9 (orgn. & admin. of comprehensive material programs).

JACOBSTEIN, J. MYRON, Jan. 27, 20; Law Librarian and Professor of Law, Law Library, Stanford University, Stanford, Calif. 94305. Home: 882 Cedro Way, Stanford, Calif. 94305. B.A, Wayne State Univ, 46; M.S.L.S, Columbia Univ, 50; LL.B, Chicago-Kent Col. Law, 53. Assoc. law librn, Columbia Univ, 55-59; law librn. & prof. law, Univ. Colo, 59-63; law librn & prof. law, Stanford Univ, 63- Other: Chmn, cmt. electronic data retrieval, Am. Asn. Law Libr, 60-63; mem. joint cmt. electronic data retrieval, Am. Bar Asn. & Am. Asn. Law Libr, 62- Mem: ALA; SLA; Am. Asn. Law Libr; Am. Document. Inst. Publ: Index to periodical articles related to law (ed), 58-; Legal Periodicals, Libr. Trends, 1/62; Law Library Administration, Libr. Trends, 1/63; Law Books in Print, Glanville Publ, 2 vols, 66. Consult: 1) Colo. Supreme Court, Denver, survey of Supreme Court Libr, Jan. 61; 2) Univ. Wyo, Law Libr, Laramie, survey of law libr, June 62; 3) Univ. Utah Sch. of Law, Salt Lake City, survey of law libr, Apr. 66. Specialties: 1h (law libr); 2d (law); 2h (law).

JAFFARIAN, SARA, Sept. 7, 15; Coordinator of Instructional Materials & Services, Lexington Public Schools, Lexington, Mass. 02173. Home: 58 Bateman St, Haverhill, Mass. 01830. A.B, Bates Col, 37; B.S, Simmons Col, 47; M.Ed, Boston Univ, 57. Dir. libr, Greensboro Pub. Schs, N.C, 53-60; supvr. libr, Seattle Pub. Schs, Wash, 60-61; coordinator libr, Lexington Pub. Schs, Mass, 61-65, coordinator instructional materials & serv, 65- Other: Dir, AASL, 54-56, recording secy, 56-57, chmn, sch. libr. supvrs, 64-65; mem, Newbery-Caldecott cmt, ALA, 59-60, mem. coun, 62-66; exec. dir, N.C. Nat. Libr. Week, 60; pres, Mass. Sch. Libr. Asn, 64-66; mem. bd. dirs, New Eng. Libr. Asn, 65. Mem: ALA. AASL; New Eng. Libr. Asn; Mass. Sch. Libr. Asn; Mass. Libr. Asn; Nat. Educ. Asn; Mass. & Lexington Teachers Asns; Asn. Supv. & Curriculum Develop; Dept. Audiovisual Instruction. Publ: Every School Needs a Library, New Eng. Sch. Develop. Coun, Harvard Univ, 52; The Library-centered School, In: Teaching in a World of Change, Harcourt, Brace & World, 66; contrib. to libr. & educ. journals. Consult: 1) Burlington Pub. Schs, Burlington, Mass, develop. of serv. program, plans & specifications for elem. schs. libr, 61-62; 2) Wellesley Pub. Schs, Wellesley, Mass, recommendations for serv. program, elem. schs. personnel, budgets, 63; 3) Brookline Pub. Schs, Brookline, Mass, interview personnel, recommendations for develop. of total serv. program, 66; 4) Dartmouth Pub. Schs, North Dartmouth, Mass, develop. of serv. program, plans & specifications for new & remodeled elem. & high sch. libr, 66; 5) Duxbury Pub. Schs, Mass, planning serv. in new mid. sch. instructional materials center, 68. Specialties: 1c, 1e; 2b, 2c; 3a, 3b, 3c, 3d; 5a; 7a, 7b, 7c; 8c, 8d; 9 (centralized purchasing & processing; sch. audiovisual programs).

JAMES, LOUISE, July 25, 22; Consultant, Riverside County Superintendent of Schools, Riverside County Schools, 4015 Lemon, Riverside, Calif. 92501. Home: 1405 Seventh St, Riverside, Calif. 92507. B.S.E, Univ. Ark, 49; M.A.(libr. sci), George Peabody Col. Teachers, 53; M.A. (instructional materials), Columbia Univ, 66. Dist. librn, Palm Springs Unified Schs, Palm Springs, Calif, 57-62; librn, Riverside City Schs, 62-63; consult, Riverside County Schs, Riverside, Calif, 63- Other: Chmn. south. sect. county sch. librns, & mem. south. sect. adv. bd, Calif. Asn. Sch. Librns; mem. instructional materials cmt, Calif. Asn. Supv. & Curriculum Develop. Mem: Calif. Asn. Sch. Librns; Calif. Asn. Supv. & Curriculum Develop. Consult: 1) Calif. State Dept. Educ, spec. consult. for ESEA, Title II for Riverside,

---

5) PERSONNEL AND RECRUITING, 5a) job evaluation and description, salary recommendations, 5b) recruitment of professionals and management personnel, 5c) administrative organization, 6) PUBLIC RELATIONS, 6a) publications, 6b) publicity programs, 6c) public opinion surveys, 6d) others, 7) SERVICES, 7a) evaluation of current program, 7b) studies of service to special publics, e.g., students, handicapped, aged, etc., 7c) programs for the implementation of new laws, program proposals to governments, 7d) others, 8) COMMUNITY, REGIONAL, STATE PLANNING, 8a) legislative programs, 8b) area analyses, 8c) centralized systems, cooperative arrangements, 8d) development of standards, 8e) state libraries and extension agencies, 8f) regional and statewide surveys, 8g) others, 9) OTHERS.

San Bernardino & Imperial counties, 65-; 2) Barstow Unified Sch, Barstow, Calif, survey of sch. libr. serv, Nov. 66. Specialties: 1c; 2b, 2c; 7a.

JANSEN, GUENTER A, Sept. 19, 30; Director, Suffolk Cooperative Library System, P.O. Box 187, Bellport, N.Y. 11713. Home: 2 Livingston Rd, Bellport, N.Y. 11713. A.B, Univ. Pa, 55; M.S. in L.S, Drexel Inst, 56. Head extension dept, Cedar Rapids Pub. Libr, Iowa, 58-60; asst. dir. & dir, Mobile Pub. Libr, Ala, 60-65; city librn, New Orleans Pub. Libr, 65-67; dir. Suffolk Cooperative Libr. Syst, N.Y, 67- Other: Mem, Insurance for Libr. Cmt, ISAD Adv. Cmt. & Pub. Relations Serv. to Libr. Cmt. Mem: ALA; SLA; N.Y. Libr. Asn; Libr. Pub. Relations Coun. Publ: Univac Electronic Data Processing in the Public Library Systems of Long Island, Univac Div, Sperry-Rand Corp, 68. Consult: 1) N. Babylon Pub. Libr, 1142 Deer Park Ave, North Babylon, N.Y, new main libr. bldg, Feb. 67-Dec. 68; 2) Nev. State Libr, Carson City, establishment of a statewide processing center & utilization of electronic data processing, May 67; 3) S. Huntington Pub. Libr, 31 Walt Whitman Rd, Huntington Sta, N.Y, new main libr. bldg, June 67-Sept. 68; 4) Port Jefferson Station-Terryville Pub. Libr, 33 Terryville Rd, Port Jefferson Sta, N.Y, new main libr. bldg, Jan-July 68; 5) Mid. Country Pub. Libr, Middle Country Rd, Selden, N.Y, new bldg, Sept. 68- Specialties: 1a, 1e, 1f, 1g; 3c, 3d, 3e, 3f (establishment of large processing centers); 4a.

JESSE, WILLIAM H, Sept. 16, 08; Director of Libraries, University of Tennessee, Knoxville, Tenn. 37916. Home: 518 Rockingham Dr, Knoxville, Tenn. 37919. B.A, Univ. Ky, 33; M.S, Columbia Univ, 38; M.A, Brown Univ, 45. Dir, Libr, Univ. Tenn, 43- Other: Pres, Southeast. Libr. Asn, 46-48; summer instructor, Univ. Ill, Columbia Univ, Fla. State Univ, 46, 48, 50-53, 55-56 & 62. Mem: ALA; ACRL; Southeast. Libr. Asn; Tenn. Libr. Asn; Asn. Southeast. Res. Libr; Asn. Res. Libr. Publ: Shelf Work in Libraries, ALA, 52; Staff Retention, Col. & Res. Libr, 3/58; Statement of Program for a New Library Building for the University of Concepcion, 62; Statement of Program for a New Library Building for Scarritt College, 63; Common Faults in Planning Library Buildings, Southeast. Librn, spring 64; New Library Buildings: Some Strengths and Weaknesses, Libr. J, 12/1/64. Consult: 1) Villa Madonna Col, Covington, Ky, study of existing facilities & programs with recommendations, with G.M. Abel, 64 & 65; 2) Eastern Ky. State Col, Richmond, study of existing facilities & programs with recommendations, with G.M. Abel, 64, 65 & 66; 3) Univ. Tampa, Tampa, Fla, study of existing facilities & programs with recommendations, 64 & 66; 4) Lincoln Mem. Univ, Harrogate, Tenn, on-the-spot observation, statement of program, 65; 5) Union Univ, Jackson, Tenn, study of existing facilities & programs with recommendations, with G.M. Abel, 65 & 66. Specialties: 1b, 1g, 1h (renovation & expansion); 7a, 7d (total libr. surveys).

JOHNSON, MRS. BARBARA COE, Jan. 19, 23; Director, Department of Libraries, Harper Hospital, 3825 Brush St, Detroit, Mich. 48201. Home: 2075 Hyde Park Rd, Detroit, Mich. 48207. B.A, Bryn Mawr Col, 44; B.L.S, Univ. Calif, Berkeley, 51; cert, Med. Libr. Asn, 59. Dir, dept. libr, Harper Hosp, Detroit, Mich, 56- Other: Cert. hosp. libr. consult, SLA, 59, treas. biological sci. div, 65-67; chmn. Midwest regional group, Med. Libr. Asn, 62-63, mem. bd. dirs, 68-, mem. by-law & publ. cmt; mem. ed. adv. bd, Int. Nursing Index, Am. Nurses' Asn, 64-; spec. rep, Coun. Nat. Libr. Asn-Joint Cmt. Hosp. Libr, 66-68; mem. cmt. revision standards for hosp. libr, AHIL, 66- Mem: Med. Libr. Asn; SLA. Publ: Integrated Library, Nursing Outlook, 7: 580-581; Integrated Hospital Library, Spec. Libr, 51: 440-443; Context of Reference Work in the Hospital Professional Library, Spec. Libr, 53: 141-144; The Librarian's Aid to Authors, Bull. Med. Libr. Asn, 50: 669-671; Purchasing for Hospital Libraries, Hosp. Progress, 10/63; A Step-By-Step Discard Program for a Hospital Library, Bull. Med. Libr. Asn, 7/68. Consult: 1) Am. Nurses' Asn, 10 Columbus Circle, New York, N.Y, feasibility study for Int. Nursing Index, 63-; 2) Med. Libr. Asn, 919 N. Michigan Ave, Chicago, Ill, consult. on revision of Handbook of Med. Libr. Practice, 63-; 3) Am. Hosp. Asn, 840 N. Lake Shore Dr, Chicago, manuscript eval. for Hospitals, June 66-; 4) Joint Cmn. Accreditation of Hosps, 645 N. Michigan Ave, Chicago, revision of Standards for prfnl. libr. in hosps, mem. adv. cmt, with Scott Adams, W.G. Dimond, Helen Yast & William Beatty, May 68. Specialties: 1d, 1h (hosp. libr); 2d (med, nursing), 2h (patient libr); 3a, 3b, 3c, 3d; 5a, 5c; 7a, 7b; 8c, 8d.

JOHNSON, DAVID L, May 10, 40; Director of Learning Resource Center, Robert Morris College, Carthage, Ill. 62321. Home: 723 Questover Dr, Carthage, Ill. 62321. B.S, East. Ill. Univ, 62; M.S. in L.S, Univ. Ill, 66. Librn. & audio-visual coordinator, Champaign Sr. High Schs, 62-65; supvr. instructional materials, office pub. instruction, State of Ill, 65-66. Other: Treas, Ill. Asn. Sch. Librns. Mem: Ill. Libr. Asn; ALA; Ill. Audiovisual Asn. Consult: 1) Hancock County Schs, Carthage, Ill, consult. for preparing an ESEA Title III project on sch. libr. develop, with Dr. McVean & Dr. Crawford, Dec. 67-May 68; 2) Hancock County Educ. & Cultural Enrichment Project, Carthage, libr. consult. for planning a multi-dist. sch. materials center, July 68. Specialties: 1c; 2b; 7a; 8c.

KEY TO CONSULTING SPECIALTIES: 1) ARCHITECTURE AND BUILDINGS, 1a) public libraries, 1b) academic libraries, 1c) school libraries, 1d) special libraries, 1e) library interiors, 1f) furnishings, 1g) site and location, 1h) other architectural; 2) COLLECTIONS: SELECTION, EVALUATION, WEEDING, 2a) adults, 2b) young adults, 2c) children, 2d) subject specialty, 2e) O.P. searches, 2f) rare books, 2g) appraisals, 2h) others; 3) TECHNICAL PROCESSES, 3a) cataloging, 3b) classification systems, 3c) acquisitions, 3d) materials processing, 3e) work flow and cost studies, 3f) others, 4) AUTOMATION, 4a) applications of data processing equipment, 4b) information storage and retrieval systems, 4c) systems analysis, 4d) others

JOHNSON, MRS. FRANCES KENNON, Nov. 1, 28; Assistant Professor of Library Education, School of Education, University of North Carolina at Greensboro, Greensboro, N.C. 27412. Home: 4310 Starmount Dr, Greensboro, N.C. 27410. A.B, Univ. S.C, 49; M.S.L, Univ. N.C, Chapel Hill, 54. Sch. libr. specialist, Baltimore City Schs, Baltimore, Md, 54-56; assoc. supvr. sch. libr. serv, N.C. State Dept. Pub. Instruction, 56-61; dir. sch. libr. develop. project, ALA, 61-62; instr, Univ. N.C, Greensboro, 62-66, asst. prof. libr. educ, 66- Other: Treas, Joint Cmt. Librarianship as Career, 57-59; mem, Grolier-Americana scholarship awards cmt, AASL, 58-59, mem. student asst. cmt, 59-62, mem. adv. bd, sch. libr. develop. project, 62-63, chmn. nominating cmt, 62-63, mem, 65-66, mem. publ. cmt, 62-64, mem. adv. cmt, Knapp Sch. Libr. project, 62-64, mem. bd. dirs, 66-68; secy. coun. librarianship, N.C. Libr. Asn, 58-61, mem. ed. bd, N.C. Libr, 63-; mem. jury for Scarecrow Press award libr. literature, ALA, 62-63, mem. ed. cmt, 63-, chmn, 65-, mem. publ. bd, 66-; mem. libr. educ. cmt, Southeast. Libr. Asn, 67- Mem: ALA; AASL; Southeast. Libr. Asn; N.C. Libr. Asn; N.C. Literary & Hist. Asn; Nat. Educ. Asn; N.C. Educ. Asn; Asn. Supv. & Curriculum Develop; Asn. Childhood Educ; Dept. Audiovisual Instruction; Phi Beta Kappa; Beta Phi Mu; Delta Kappa Gamma. Publ: Trends in Developing Elementary School Libraries, ALA Bull, 2/62; Planning School Library Development: A Report of the School Library Development Project (with Leila A. Doyle): ALA, 62; ed, School Libraries, Wilson Libr. Bull, 60-63; Planning School Library Quarters (guest ed. with Cora Paul Bomar), ALA Bull, 2/64; Evaluating Some Actual Experiences, The Instructor, 11/64; Educating School Librarians, Libr. J, 10/15/66. Consult: 1) U.S. Office Educ, Wash. D.C, read applications for NDEA insts. for sch. librns, Oct. 65; 2) N.C. Dept. Pub. Instruction, Raleigh, N.C, mem. adv. cmt. to develop. guidelines for col. & univ. curriculum materials center, 66-; 3) N.C. Dept. Pub. Instruction, mem. adv. cmt. to revise certification standards & guidelines, 66-; 4) Reidsville City Schs, Reidsville, N.C, libr. serv. for ESEA Title I project schs. & ESEA Title II project, 66-; 5) Lexington City Schs, Lexington, N.C, libr. serv, ESEA Title III project planning grant for model mid. sch. featuring instructional materials center, 66-67. Specialties: 1c; 2b, 2c; 7b, 7c; 8d.

JOHNSON, LEONARD L, July 5, 31; Director of Libraries, Greensboro Public Schools, 712 N. Eugene St, Greensboro, N.C. 27401. Home: 4310 Starmount Dr, Greensboro, N.C. 27410. B.S, 54; M.A, 55. Coordinator libr, High Point Pub. Schs, High Point, N.C, 55-59; libr. supvr, N.C. Dept. Pub. Instruction, Raleigh, N.C, 59-61; dir. libr, Greensboro Pub. Schs, Greensboro, N.C, 61- Other: Mem. instructional materials cmt, AASL, 63-68; mem. libr. standards cmt, South. Libr. Asn, 65; chmn. standards cmt, N.C. Asn. Sch. Librns, 66-67; treas, N.C. Libr. Asn, 66-69. Mem: ALA; Southeast. Libr. Asn; N.C. Libr. Asn; Greensboro Libr. Club. Publ: Useful Bibliographies in Developing Parallel Reading Lists—Secondary School, N.C. Dept. Pub. Instruction, 62; Manual on Central Cataloging, Greensboro Pub. Schs, 67; Books for Greensboro Students, a Bibliography for Young Adults (dir), Friends of Greensboro Pub. Libr, 63; Administrative Practices That Tend to Improve the Use of the School Library, Southeast. Librn, spring 64. Consult: 1) N.C. Advancement Sch, Winston-Salem, N.C, bldg. renovation, furnishing & program, 64-65; 2) U.S. Office of Educ, Wash, D.C, eval. & nomination of projects for NDEA Libr. Insts, with Frances Henne, Oct. 65. Specialties: 1c, 1e, 1f, 1h (educ. specifications); 2b, 2c, 2d (soc. studies), 2h (educ. books); 3a, 3c, 3d, 3f (cent. ordering, cataloging & processing of libr. & audiovisual materials); 5a, 5b, 5c; 7a, 7b, 7c; 8c, 8d; 9 (sch. libr. consult. work with State Educ. Dept).

JONES, FRANK N(ICHOLAS), Nov. 19, 06; Chief Librarian, Southeastern Massachusetts Technological Institute, North Dartmouth, Mass. 02747. Home: 635 Elm St, South Dartmouth, Mass. 02748. A.B, Harvard Univ, 30, A.M, 41; B.S. in L.S, Columbia Univ, 41. Dir, Peabody Inst. Libr, Baltimore, Md, 57-66; chief librn, Southeast. Mass. Tech. Inst, North Dartmouth, Mass, 66- Other: Pres, Ohio Libr. Asn, 53-54; pres, Md. Libr. Asn, 61-62; mem. coun, ALA, 64-66, mem. membership cmt; mem. subject specialists sect, ACRL; mem. copying methods sect, RTSD. Mem: Fel. Am. Geographical Soc; ALA; Mass. Libr. Asn; ACRL. Publ: Atlases on Parade, 64; George Peabody and the Peabody Institute, 65; Roads Through History, 66. Consult: 1) Nelsonville Pub. Libr, 46 Public Square, Nelsonville, Ohio, adv. on various phases of libr. orgn, especially the develop. of serv. to Athens County, 50-56; 2) Wilmington Col, Wilmington, Ohio, weeding & rejuvenation of book collections, spring 53; 3) Albert S. Cook Libr, Towson State Col, Towson, Md, survey of book collections & plan for expanded purchasing, with Felix E. Hirsch, Mar. 63; 4) Swain Sch. Design, 19 Hawthorne St, New Bedford, Mass, advice on new quarters, accessions policy & personnel appointment, Mar. 67; 5) Boston Col, Chestnut Hill, Mass, preliminary discussions of planning new bldg. for libr, Apr. 68. Specialties: 1a, 1b, 1e; 2a, 2d (hist, literature, sci. & tech), 2h (maps & cartography collections); 5c; 6b, 6d (exhibitions & displays in libr); 7a; 8d, 8f.

JONES, HAROLD D, June 26, 11; Assistant Professor, Library Department, Brooklyn College Library, Brooklyn, N.Y. 11210. Home: 160 Henry St, Brooklyn, N.Y. 11201. A.B, 33;

---

5) PERSONNEL AND RECRUITING, 5a) job evaluation and description, salary recommendations, 5b) recruitment of professionals and management personnel, 5c) administrative organization, 6) PUBLIC RELATIONS, 6a) publications, 6b) publicity programs, 6c) public opinion surveys, 6d) others, 7) SERVICES, 7a) evaluation of current program, 7b) studies of service to special publics, e.g., students, handicapped, aged, etc., 7c) programs for the implementation of new laws, program proposals to governments, 7d) others, 8) COMMUNITY, REGIONAL, STATE PLANNING, 8a) legislative programs, 8b) area analyses, 8c) centralized systems, cooperative arrangements, 8d) development of standards, 8e) state libraries and extension agencies, 8f) regional and statewide surveys, 8g) others, 9) OTHERS.

B.S.(libr. sci), 35; M.A, 40. Asst. to librn, Brooklyn Col. Libr, Brooklyn, N.Y, 52-61, asst. librn, 61-65, asst. prof, libr. dept. & chmn. libr. bldg. planning cmt, 65- Other: Pres, Libr. Asn. of City Univ. New York, 64-66; vis. prof. libr. sci, South. Conn. State Col, summer, 66; mem. bldg. cmt, N.Y. Libr. Asn, 67. Mem: ALA; ACRL; Am. Asn. Univ. Prof; Bibliog. Soc. Am; N.Y. Libr. Club; Gutenberg Soc. Publ: Faculty, Students Helped Plan This Library, Libr. J, 3/16/51; College Library for West Virginia, Col. & Univ. Bus, 8/53; Brooklyn College Library, Brooklyn, N.Y. (Proposed Extension), ACRL Monograph 10, 56; Automation in the Library: A Librarian's View, ACRL Monograph 17, 56; American College Libraries, Inst. Int. Educ. News Bull, 5/59; The Development of Reference Services in Colleges of Teacher Education, 1929-1958, ACRL Microcard Series 139, 63. Consult: 1) Coun. for Advancement of Small Cols, Inc, 1818 R St. N.W, Wash, D.C, prepared & set up acad. libr. bldgs. exhibit, Jan. 60; 2) Mitchel Col, Long Island Univ, Westbury, N.Y, survey & report with recommendations on book, periodical resources & catalog policy, Mar. 63; 3) Mitchel Col, survey & report with recommendations on orgn, personnel, physical facilities & procedures of tech. serv. dept, Mar. 64; 4) New Sch. Soc. Res, New York, N.Y, develop. of plans for new libr, 67; 5) Briarcliff Col, Briarcliff Manor, N.Y, bldg. planning, 68. Specialties: 1b; 2d (soc. sci. educ); 5c; 7c; 8a.

JONES, JAMES VICTOR, May 14, 24; Director of Libraries, Case Western Reserve University, Cleveland, Ohio 44106. Home: 2841 Berkshire Rd, Cleveland, Ohio 44118. B.S, 49; M.S. in L.S, 50. Librn, sch. commerce & finance, St. Louis Univ, 50-52, asst. dir. libr, 52-55, dir, 55-66; dir. libr, Cleveland State Univ, Cleveland, Ohio, 66-68. Other: Secy. col. & univ. div, Mo. Libr. Asn, 55-56, v.chmn, 56-57, chmn, 57-58, v.pres. of Asn, 58-59, pres, 59-60, chmn. nominating cmt, 62-63, mem. col. & univ. develop. cmt, 65-66, mem. col. & univ. libr. survey cmt, 65-66; mem. exec. bd, Greater St. Louis unit, Cath. Libr. Asn, 55-57, v.chmn, 57-59, chmn, 59-61, mem. adv. coun. Asn, mem. cmt, Cath. Periodical Index—Guide to Cath. Lit, 56-63, chmn. scholarship cmt, 58-63; mem. coun, ALA, 57-61, chmn. cmt. purpose, program & by-laws, libr. orgn. & mgt. sect, 60-62; mem. adv. cmt. librns, Center Res. Libr, 57-65, mem. bd. dir, 60-63, mem. coun, 65-66; mem. duplicates exchange union, RTSD, 59-64, chmn, 61-63, mem. nominating cmt, copying methods sect, 64-65; mem. exec. cmt, St. Louis Univ. chap, Am. Asn. Univ. Prof, 61-64; mem. cmt. relations with accrediting agencies, ACRL, 62-67, mem. cmt. urban univ. libr, 64-66, chmn. cmt. liaison with accrediting agencies, 65-67; convention chmn, SLA, 64, mem. exec. bd, Greater St. Louis chap; mem. adv. cmt, Cath. Family Serv, St. Vincent de Paul Soc, 64-66; secy, Jesuit Libr. Conf, 64-66; mem. libr. cmt, Higher Educ. Coordinating Coun. St. Louis, 64-66; mem. bd. gov, Case West. Reserve Univ, 65-67, chmn. visiting cmt, sch. libr. sci, 66, mem. bd. overseers, Univ, 67-68; mem. adv. cmt, Mo. State Librn, 65-66; mem. bd. dirs, San Val, Inc. & Lloyd Hampe, Inc, 65-; charter mem. bd. dirs, Harry S. Truman Libr. Inst, mem. cmt. relations with univs. & hist. socs; past v.pres. & pres, Greater St. Louis Libr. Club. Mem: ALA; SLA; Cath. Libr. Asn; Mo. Libr. Asn. Publ: The Library..., Nat. League for Nursing, 60; Ozanam, Cath. Charities Review, 60; Vending Library Makes Progress, Vending Times, 61; Selected Annotated Books, 62-; contrib, Libr. Trends, 65; Manuscripta (adv. ed). Consult: 1) North. Ariz. Univ, Flagstaff, survey of libr. orgn. & mgt, 64; 2) McKendree Col, Lebanon, Ill, libr. renovation, 64; 3) Univ. Dayton, Dayton, Ohio, survey of libr. orgn. & mgt, 64-65, bldg. program & layout, 67-69; 4) Univ. Ark, Fayetteville, libr. orgn. & mgt, 66; 5) Gannon Col. Libr, Erie, Pa, site location & bldg. program, 68-69. Specialties: 1b; 2h (col. & univ. eval); 3d; 4d (gen. applicability); 5c; 7a.

JONES, WYMAN, Dec. 17, 29; Director, Ft. Worth Public Library System, Ft. Worth Public Library, Ninth and Throckmorton Sts, Ft. Worth, Tex. 76102. Home: 4224 Lanark, Ft. Worth, Tex. 76109. B.A, 56; M.L.S, 58. Head sci. & industry dept, Dallas Pub. Libr, Dallas, Tex, 58-60, chief of br. serv, 60-64; dir, Ft. Worth Pub. Libr. Syst, Ft. Worth, Tex, 64- Other: Pres, pub. libr. div, Tex. Libr. Asn, 67; v.chmn. & chmn-elect, Southwest. Libr. Asn, 67. Mem: ALA; Tex. Libr. Asn; Southwest. Libr. Asn. Publ: Making of the Vote, Libr. J, 3/1/62; On the Grindstone, Libr. J, 1/12/64; Foursome for Dallas, Libr. J, 12/1/64; Administrative Conscience, Libr. J, 9/15/65; Penetrating the Neighborhoods of a Community, In: The Library Reaches Out, Oceana, 65; Role of the Branch Library in the Program of Metropolitan Library Service, Libr. Trends, 4/66. Consult: 1) New Orleans Pub. Libr, 219 Loyola Ave, New Orleans, La, br. bldg. consult, 63; 2) Arlington Pub. Libr, 106 W. Main St, Arlington, Tex, survey of extension agency needs, 67; 3) Haltom City Pub. Libr, 5024 Broadway Ave, Haltom City, Tex, consult for main libr, 67; 4) Deer Park Pub. Libr, 2222 Kingsdale, Deer Park, Tex, consult. for main libr, 67; 5) Rapides Parish Pub. Libr, 400 Washington St, Alexandria, La, site selection for projected br, 67. Specialties: 1a, 1e, 1f, 1g.

JORDAN, ROBERT THAYER, Aug. 3, 22; Director of Media Services, Federal City College, Washington, D.C. 20001. A.B, Antioch Col, 47; M.L.S, Univ. Calif, 57. Head librn, Taft Col, Taft, Calif, 57-60; sr. staff mem, Coun. Libr. Resources, Inc, Wash, D.C, 60-68; dir. media serv, Fed. City Col, 68- Other: Mem. exec. bd,

---

KEY TO CONSULTING SPECIALTIES: 1) ARCHITECTURE AND BUILDINGS, 1a) public libraries, 1b) academic libraries, 1c) school libraries, 1d) special libraries, 1e) library interiors, 1f) furnishings, 1g) site and location, 1h) other architectural; 2) COLLECTIONS: SELECTION, EVALUATION, WEEDING, 2a) adults, 2b) young adults, 2c) children, 2d) subject specialty, 2e) O.P. searches, 2f) rare books, 2g) appraisals, 2h) others; 3) TECHNICAL PROCESSES, 3a) cataloging, 3b) classification systems, 3c) acquisitions, 3d) materials processing, 3e) work flow and cost studies, 3f) others, 4) AUTOMATION, 4a) applications of data processing equipment, 4b) information storage and retrieval systems, 4c) systems analysis, 4d) others

Potomac Tech. Processing Librns, 62-64; mem, Ad Hoc Cmt. Copyright Law Revision, 63-; mem. libr. lighting cmt, Illuminating Engineering Soc, 63-; mem. cmt. standards & criteria, Jr. Col. Libr. Sect, ACR, 63-65; mem. title II adv. coun, U.S. Off. Educ. Higher Educ. Act, 65; mem. corp. representing Am. Document. Inst, U.S. Book Exchange, 65-; chmn. joint cmt. hospitality to visiting foreign librns, SLA-D.C. Libr. Asn, 65-67. Mem: Am. Soc. Info. Sci; ALA; D.C. Libr. Asn; Dept. Audiovisual Instruction; Southeast. Libr. Asn; SLA; Va. Libr. Asn. Publ: Re-Evaluation of Microfilm as a Method of Book Storage Verner W. Clapp), Col. & Res. Libr, 1/63; Library Characteristics of Colleges Ranking High in Academic Excellence, Col. & Res. Libr, 9/63; Lighting in University Libraries, UNESCO Bull. for Libr, 11-12/63; ed-in-chief, The Library-College Newsletter, 64-67; Quantitative Criteria for Adequacy of Academic Library Collections, Col. & Res. Libr, 9/65; The Library-College, (with Louis Shores & John Harvey), Drexel Inst. Tech, 66. Consult: 1) Oakland Univ. Rochester, Mich, review of univ. libr. & prospects for automation & book catalogs, spring 64; 2) Academy for Acad. Develop. (for Ohio Bd. Regents), Columbus, Ohio, libr. portion of state-wide master plan in higher educ, with Verner W. Clapp, spring & summer, 64; 3) Union for Res. & Experimentation in Higher Educ, Antioch Col, Yellow Springs, Ohio, assist in proposal writing, prepare booklet on innovation in higher educ, prepare directory of innovative cols, prepare proposal for regional cooperative res. libr, winter 66; 4) Center for Alcohol Studies, eval, 66; 5) Swarthmore Col. Libr, educ. initiatives, 67. Specialties: 1h (lighting); 2a; 3b, 3e, 3f (book catalogs, adhesive bindings); 4d (automatic shelving & retrieval); 8c, 8d, 8f; 9 (educ. initiatives by the acad. libr, delivery systs, microcopy, storage).

JOSEY, E.J, Jan. 20, 24; Chief, Bureau of Academic & Research Libraries, Division of Library Development, New York State Library, Albany, N.Y. 12224. Home: 13C Old Hickory Dr, Apt. 1A, Albany, N.Y. 12204. A.B, 49; M.A, 50; M.L.S, 53. Librn. I, Free Libr. Phila, Pa, 53-54; instructor soc. sci, Savannah State Col, Ga, 54-55; librn. & asst. prof, Del. State Col, 55-59; librn. & assoc. prof, Savannah State Col, 59-66; acad. & res. libr. consult, acad. & res. libr. bureau, div. libr. develop, N.Y. State Libr, Albany, 66-68. Other: Mem. bd. mgrs, Savannah Pub. Libr, 62-; mem. exec. bd, Chatham County Mental Health Asn, 62-66; mem. exec. bd, col. sect, ACRL, 64-; chmn. cmt. on community use of acad. libr, cmt. on develop, ALTA, 64- Mem: ALA; Southeast. Libr. Asn; ACRL; ALTA; N.Y. Libr. Asn; Ga. Libr. Asn. Publ: The College Library and Reading, Education, 3/60; Negro College Libraries and ACRL Standards, Libr. J, 9/1/63; Enhancing and Strenghtening Faculty-Library Relationships, J. Negro Educ, 4/64; A New Clarification of a Old Problem: Book Selection for College Libraries, Choice, 4/65; Negro Students, Reading and the Great Society, Quart. Review Higher Educ. Among Negroes, 7/65; Systems Development for Reference and Research Library Service in New York State: The 3 R's, B.C. Libr. Quart, 4/68. Consult: 1) Boggs Acad, Keysville, Ga, planning of new libr. & collection, June 65; 2) Mather Jr. Col, Beaufort, S.C, expansion of libr. & improvement of gen. libr. serv, May 66; 3) Tex. South. Univ, survey of libr, Nov. 67. Specialties: 1c, 1f, 1g; 2b, 2d (col. libr); 5a, 5c; 6c; 7a, 7b.

K

KANTOR, DAVID, Nov. 2, 15; Director of Libraries, Volusia County Public Libraries, City Island, Daytona Beach, Fla. 32014. Home: 7 Silk Oaks Dr, Ormond Beach, Fla. 32074. B.S, 38; Licentiate, Univ. Brussels, 39; B.S.L.S, 41. Librn, Calif. State Prison at Folsom, 49-62; dir, Extension Serv, Volusia County, 62-64, dir, libr, 64- Other: Pres, hosp. & insts. cmt, Calif. Libr. Asn, 53, pres, Golden Empire Dist. & mem. bd, dirs, 58. Mem: ALA; Fla. Libr. Asn; Southeast. Libr. Asn. Publ: Value of Library in a Correctional Institution, (Annals American Prison Assn, 54); A Survey of Public Library Services in Volusia County (with Elizabeth Cole), Fla. State Libr, Tallahassee, 64; Survey of Libraries and Library Services in State Institutions of Florida, Fla. State Libr, 67. Consult: 1) Fla. State Libr, Tallahassee, survey of libr. serv. in state correctional & mental insts, Jan-Apr. 67; 2) City of Hawthorne, Fla, libr. bldg, 68-; 3) Fla. Coun. for the Blind, Daytona Beach, Fla, libr. bldg, 68-; Clay County Bd, Green Cove Springs, Fla, libr. bldg, 68- Specialties: 1a, 1e, 1f, 1g, 1h (correctional inst. libr); 2a; 5a; 7a, 7b, 7d (evaluation of libr. serv. in correctional insts); 8d.

KASER, DR. DAVID, Mar. 12, 24; Director, Cornell University Libraries, Ithaca, N.Y. 14850. Home: 116 Crest Lane, Ithaca, N.Y. 14850. A.B, 49; M.A, 50; A.M.L.S, 52; Ph.D, 56. Chief of acquisitions, Wash. Univ. Libr, St. Louis, Mo, 56-58, asst. dir, 58-60; dir, Joint Univ. Libr, Nashville, Tenn, 60-68; dir, Cornell Univ. Libr, Ithaca, N,Y, 68- Mem: ALA; Southeast. Libr. Asn; Tenn. Libr. Asn; Am. Asn. Univ. Prof; Bibliog. Soc. Am. Publ: Messrs, Carey & Lea of Philadelphia, Univ. Pa, 57; Col. & Res. Libr. (ed), 62-; Joseph Charless, Printer in the Western Country, Univ. Pa, 63; Cost Book of Carey & Lea, Univ. Pa, 63; Books in America's Past, Univ. Press of Va, 66. Consult: 1) Univ. Ky, Lexington, libr. survey, with Robert H. Muller, Donald Thompson, Robert Munn & Richard Blanchard, 65; 2) Carson-Newman Col, Jefferson City,

---

5) PERSONNEL AND RECRUITING, 5a) job evaluation and description, salary recommendations, 5b) recruitment of professionals and management personnel, 5c) administrative organization, 6) PUBLIC RELATIONS, 6a) publications, 6b) publicity programs, 6c) public opinion surveys, 6d) others, 7) SERVICES, 7a) evaluation of current program, 7b) studies of service to special publics, e.g., students, handicapped, aged, etc., 7c) programs for the implementation of new laws, program proposals to governments, 7d) others, 8) COMMUNITY, REGIONAL, STATE PLANNING, 8a) legislative programs, 8b) area analyses, 8c) centralized systems, cooperative arrangements, 8d) development of standards, 8e) state libraries and extension agencies, 8f) regional and statewide surveys, 8g) others, 9) OTHERS.

Tenn, bldg. consult, 66; 3) Nebr. Wesleyan Univ. Lincoln, libr. survey, 66; 4) Hendrix Col, Conway, Ark, bldg. consult, 66; 5) Univ. Wis, Green Bay, bldg. consult, 67. Specialties: 1b; 2h (acad. libr. collections); 5c; 7a; 8c.

KATZ, BEATRICE, Oct. 13, 18; Resource and Reference Specialist and Consultant on Information Services and Libraries, Wayne County Intermediate School District. Home: 25881 Greenfield, Southfield, Mich. 48075. B.A, Wayne State Univ, 40, M.A, 57. Dir. sch. libr. serv, Oak Park Sch. Dist, Oak Park, Mich, 54-67; resource & reference specialist & consult. info. serv. & libr, Wayne County Intermediate Sch. Dist, 67- Other: Instructor, Wayne State Univ, Detroit, Mich; consult, Oakland County Bd. Educ; former chmn, sch. & children's sect, Mich. Libr. Asn. Mem: ALA; Mich. Libr. Asn; Mich. Asn. Sch. Librns. Publ: Contrib. to Wilson Libr. Bull. Consult: 1) Oakland Intermediate Sch. Dist, Pontiac Mich, set up & directed program for Title II, ESEA, 65-66. Specialties: 1c; 2b, 2c; 3a, 3c, 3d; 5c; 7a; 8g (schs).

KEMPER, DR. ROBERT E, Apr. 8, 36; Assistant Professor, School of Librarianship, University of Oregon, Eugene, Ore. 97403. Home: 2125 Birchwood, Eugene, Ore. 97401. B.A, 58; M.A.(librarianship), 63; D.B.A, 67. Pub. sch. teacher, Hayden & Meeker Pub. Schs, 59-62; asst. dir. & acquisitions librn, Ft. Hays, Kans. State Col, 62-64; asst. prof, sch. librarianship, Univ. Ore, Eugene, Ore, 66- Other: Mem. exec. cmt, Kans. Libr. Asn, 63, publicity dir, 63. Mem: ALA; Pac. Northwest Libr. Asn; Dept. Audiovisual Instruction; Ore. Asn. Sch. Librns; Ore. Libr. Asn; OIMA; Am. Asn. Univ. Prof; Am. Mgt. Asn. Consult: 1) Vancouver Gear Works, 975 Vernon Dr, Vancouver 6, B.C, Can, personnel policy & guidelines program review, Apr. 67; 2) Vancouver Gear Works, develop. of & negotiation for Wash. Sales Program with hiring of dist. sales mgr, June 67; 3) Ore. State Libr, State Libr. Bldg, Salem, Ore, dir. & chief consult. on Phase II of Ore. state-wide plan for libr, with Bureau Bus. & Econ. Res, June 68-June 69; 4) Vancouver Gear Works, long-range planning program, Feb. 68- Specialties: 3d, 3e; 4a, 4c; 5a, 5b, 5c; 6a, 6b, 6c; 7a, 7b, 7c; 8a, 8b, 8c, 8d, 8e, 8f; 9 (long-range planning, instructional materials systs. for sch. libr).

KEOUGH, FRANCIS P, Apr. 2, 17; Director, Springfield City Library, 220 State St, Springfield, Mass. 01103. Home: 16 Oxford St, Springfield, Mass. 01108. B.S.L.S, Columbia Univ, 47. Dir, Framingham Pub. Libr, Framingham, Mass, 51-64. Other: Chmn. publ. cmt, Mass. Libr. Asn, 51-53; v.pres. & program chmn, 57-58, pres, 58-59; chmn, W. Metrop. Boston Sub-Regional Libr. Center, 62-64; mem. exec. bd. & dir. headquarters libr, West Regional Pub. Libr. Syst, 64-; chmn. adv. cmt. on certification, Commonwealth of Mass, 65-, mem. adv. cmt. on minimum standards to Bd. Libr. Cmnrs, 66; dir. & mem. program cmt, Springfield Adult Educ. Coun; secy. & treas, Phillips Lecture. Mem: ALA; New Eng. Libr. Asn; Mass. Libr. Asn; West. Mass. Libr. Asn. Consult: 1) Jones Libr, Amherst, Mass, community libr. survey, gen. renovation & alteration program, with Alderman & MacNeish, 65; 2) Town of Dartmouth Libr, Dartmouth, Mass, community libr. survey, bldg. program & site selection, 65-66; 3) Medfield Pub. Libr, Medfield, Mass, community libr. survey & bldg. program, with Harry Gulesian & assocs, 65-66; 5) Agawam Pub. Libr, Agawam Center, Mass, community libr. survey, bldg. program & site selection, 66; 5) Lewiston Pub. Libr, Lewiston, Maine, bldg. program, develop. of preliminary & working drawings & selection of equipment & furniture, with The Architects Collaborative, 67-68. Specialties: 1a, 1c, 1e, 1f, 1g; 2a, 2b, 2c; 3e; 5a, 5c; 7a; 8b, 8c, 8d.

KINNEY, MARGARET MARY, May 27, 12; Administrative Librarian, Veterans Administration Hospital, 130 W. Kingsbridge Rd, Bronx, N.Y. 10468. B.A, 34; B.S.L.S, 37; M.S.L.S, 52. Admin. librn, Veterans Admin. Hosp, Bronx, N.Y, 47- Other: Pres, hosp. & nursing sect, SLA, 50; v.pres, div. hosp. libr, ALA, 51, pres, 52, pub. relations coordinator, AHIL, 52-55, mem, bibliotherapy cmt, 65-70; consult. ed, Mental Health Book Review Index, 56-60, 64-; mem. coun, ALA, 58-64, mem. exec. bd, 61-64; mem, Z-39 subcmt. on periodical abbreviations, U.S. Am. Standards Inst, 62-; mem, continuing educ. cmt, Med. Libr. Asn, 63-65; secy-treas, Coun. Nat. Libr. Asns, 64-, trustee, 68-69; coun, New York Libr. Club, 67-68, v.pres. & pres-elect, 68-70. Mem: ALA; SLA; Med. Libr. Asn; N.Y. Libr. Club; N.Y. State Libr. Asn; Coun. Nat. Libr. Asns. Publ: Bibliotherapy and the Librarian, Spec. Libr, 7-8/46; Medical Care Second to None (co-auth), Spec. Libr, 7-8/47; Hospital Libraries: Objective and Standards (co-auth), Joint Cmt. on Standards Hosp. Libr, ALA, 53; The Attitudes of Patients Regarding the Efficacy of Reading Popular Psychiatric and Psychological Articles and Books (co-auth), Mental Health, 1/59; The Bibliotherapy Program: Requirements for Training, Libr. Trends, 10/62; The Patient's Library in a Psychiatric Setting, AHIL Quart, winter 66. Consult: 1) Boston State Hosp, Boston, Mass, survey of med. libr, June 66. Specialties: 1d; 2a, 2d (med, nursing, gen. hosp); 3b; 5a; 7a, 7b, 7c; 8a, 8d.

KLEMPNER, DR. IRVING M, Nov. 28, 24; Associate Professor, School of Library Science, State University of New York at Albany, Albany, N.Y. 12203. Home: 864 Whitney Dr, Schenectady, N.Y. 12309. B.A, 51; M.S. in L.S, 52; D.L.S, 67. Prfnl. librn, Libr. Congress, 53-57; supvry. librn, Naval Applied Sci. Lab, 57-

KEY TO CONSULTING SPECIALTIES: 1) ARCHITECTURE AND BUILDINGS, 1a) public libraries, 1b) academic libraries, 1c) school libraries, 1d) special libraries, 1e) library interiors, 1f) furnishings, 1g) site and location, 1h) other architectural; 2) COLLECTIONS: SELECTION, EVALUATION, WEEDING, 2a) adults, 2b) young adults, 2c) children, 2d) subject specialty, 2e) O.P. searches, 2f) rare books, 2g) appraisals, 2h) others; 3) TECHNICAL PROCESSES, 3a) cataloging, 3b) classification systems, 3c) acquisitions, 3d) materials processing, 3e) work flow and cost studies, 3f) others, 4) AUTOMATION, 4a) applications of data processing equipment, 4b) information storage and retrieval systems, 4c) systems analysis, 4d) others

58; mgr. info. serv, United Nuclear Corp, 58-67. Other: Chmn. sci-tech. group N.Y, SLA, 64-65, chmn. document. div, 65-66, chmn. spec. libr. cmt, 67-68. Mem: Am. Soc. Info. Sci; ALA; New York Libr. Asn; SLA; Westchester Libr. Asn. Publ: The Influence of Photoreproduction on Library Operations, Libr. Resources & Tech. Serv, summer 63; Methodology for Comparative Analysis of Information Storage and Retrieval Systems, Am. Document, 7/64; Diffusion of Abstracting and Indexing Services for Government Sponsored Research, Scarecrow, 68. Consult: 1) Gen. Applied Sci. Labs, Inc, Westbury, N.Y, eval. of libr. serv. for sci. & tech. clientele, June 65; 2) Smith, Barney & Co, 20 Broad St, New York, N.Y, study of feasibility of producing & publ. new abstracting & indexing serv, Jan-June 67; 3) United Nuclear Corp, IR syst, anal, Sept. 67-June 68. Specialties: 3a, 3b, 3d; 4a, 4b, 4c; 7a, 7c.

KOPECH, GERTRUDE, Dec. 27, 23; Consultant in Communications of Biomedical and Physical Sciences, 105-25 65th Ave, Forest Hills, N.Y. 11375. A.B, Brown Univ, 41; B.S. in L.S, Columbia Univ, 42. Consult, Tissue Culture Bibliog, 56-66. Mem: SLA. Publ: A Bibliography of the Research in Tissue Culture: The Literature of the Living Cell Cultivated in Vitro (with Margaret R. Murray), Acad. Press, 2 vols, 53; Current Tissue Culture Literature: A Key to the World Periodical and Abstract Indexes (with Margaret R. Murray), October House, Vol. V, 65. Consult: 1) Eastern States Farmers Cooperative, West Springfield, Mass, established & introduced modern techniques streamlined holdings & set up standards for staff of agricultural libr, Sept-Dec. 55; 2) Austenal Labs, Inc, Dover, N.J, organized & designed technical libr. to serve res. staff of co. specializing in dental materials, instruments & equipment, Aug-Dec. 56; 3) Raymond Concrete Pile Co, 140 Cedar St, New York, N.Y, designed libr, selected collection, organized co. file syst. to serve various branches of construction engineering, May-Nov. 59. Specialties: 1d, 1e, 1f; 2d (biology, chemistry, engineering, agr, med); 3a, 3b, 3c, 3d; 4b, 4c, 4d (IBM/360 COBAL, BAL, FORTRAN programmer); 5a; 7a; 9 (subject bibliog).

KUHLMAN, A(UGUSTUS) F(REDERICK), Sept. 3, 89; Director Emeritus, Joint University Libraries, Nashville, Tenn. 37203. Home: 1908 Blakemore Ave, Nashville, Tenn. 37212. B.S, N.Cent. Col(Ill), 16; M.A, Univ. Chicago, 22, Ph.D, 29. Dir, joint univ. libr, Nashville, Tenn, 36-60; prof. libr. sci, George Peabody Col, 36-68, prof. emer, 68- Other: Pres, Nashville Libr. Club, 53-54; pres. Tenn. Libr. Asn, 54-55; chmn. Asn. Southeast. Res. Libr, 57-59; mem, Joint Cmt. Union List Serials, 58-66. Mem: ALA; Nashville Libr. Club; Tenn. Libr. Asn; Southeast. Libr. Asn; ACRL. Publ: A Guide to Material on Crime and Criminal Justice, H.W. Wilson Co, 29; College and University Library Service (ed), ALA, 38; Report of a Survey of the University of Mississippi Library for the University of Mississippi (with Icko Iben), Univ. Miss, 40; Development of Library Resources and Graduate Work in the Cooperative University Centers of the South (ed. with Phillip G. Davidson), Joint Univ. Libr, 44; Survey of Cooperation in Library Development and in Higher Education in St. Paul: A Preliminary Report, 52; Survey of the Libraries of the Arkansas Foundation of Associated Colleges, 58. Consult: 1) Vanderbilt Univ. Law Sch, Nashville, Tenn, planned, directed, supervised new libr. bldg. program, schedules, installation, 61-63; 2) Mid. E. Tech. Univ, Ankara, Turkey, UNESCO consult. for new libr, 63; 3) E. State Univ. Libr, Johnson City, Tenn, planned addition to libr, 63-66; 4) N. Greenville Jr. Col, Tigersville, S.C, prepared program, floor plans for new libr. bldg, 66; 5) Univ. Center, Atlanta, Ga, survey of six libr, 66- Specialties: 1b, 1e, 1f; 2g (acad); 5a, 5c; 7a, 7b.

KURTH, WILLIAM H, July 4, 17; Associate Director of Libraries, Washington University Libraries, St. Louis, Mo. 63130. Home: 7008 Kingsbury Blvd, University City, Mo. 63130. A.B.(philosophy), 41; M.S.(libr. sci), 58. Asst. chief, Order Div, Nat. Libr. Med, 50-59, chief, circulation div, 59-62; head, acquisitions dept, Univ. Calif, Los Angeles, 63-65; asst. dir, Wash. Univ. Libr, St. Louis, Mo, 65-67, assoc. dir, 67- Mem: ALA; Mo. Libr. Asn. Publ: A Proposed Cost of Books and Cost of Periodicals Index, Col. & Res. Libr, 10/55; Books in the Americas: A Study of the Principal Barriers to the Booktrade in the Americas (with Peter S. Jennison), Pan Am. Union, 60; Survey of the Interlibrary Loan Operation of the National Library of Medicine, U.S. Dept. Health, Educ. & Welfare Pub. Health Serv, 62; Moving a Library (with Ray Grim), Scarecrow, 66. Consult: 1) Veterans Admin, San Francisco, Calif, periodic eval. med. & patients' libr. in Veterans Admin. centers in Calif. & Ore, 63-65; 2) Nat. Book Cmt. Inc, survey of book industry & libr. of Brasil for Agency Int. Develop, with Ranald Hobbs & Ernest Schwehr, July 66. Specialties: 1h (logistics of moving libr— equipment & book collections); 2d (Latin Am; collection bldg. for res. libr. & for area studies programs); 3c, 3d, 3e; 4c; 7a; 8c.

L

LANCOUR, DR. HAROLD, June 27, 08; Dean and Professor of Library Science, Graduate School of Library and Information Sciences, University of Pittsburgh, Pittsburgh, Pa. 15213. Home: 429 Morrison Dr, Mt. Lebanon, Pa. 15216. A.B, 31; B.S. in L.S, 36; M.S. in L.S, 41; Ed.D, 48. Assoc. dir, Univ. Ill. Grad. Libr. Sch, 47-61; ed, Library Trends, 52-62. Other: Mem.

---

5) PERSONNEL AND RECRUITING, 5a) job evaluation and description, salary recommendations, 5b) recruitment of professionals and management personnel, 5c) administrative organization, 6) PUBLIC RELATIONS, 6a) publications, 6b) publicity programs, 6c) public opinion surveys, 6d) others, 7) SERVICES, 7a) evaluation of current program, 7b) studies of service to special publics, e.g., students, handicapped, aged, etc., 7c) programs for the implementation of new laws, program proposals to governments, 7d) others, 8) COMMUNITY, REGIONAL, STATE PLANNING, 8a) legislative programs, 8b) area analyses, 8c) centralized systems, cooperative arrangements, 8d) development of standards, 8e) state libraries and extension agencies, 8f) regional and statewide surveys, 8g) others, 9) OTHERS.

cmt. accreditation, ALA, 53-58, mem. ed. cmt, 61-63, mem. cmt. orgn, 64-66; pres, Asn. Am. Libr. Schs, 54-56, mem. publ. cmt, 58-; ed. J. Educ. for Librarianship, 60-64. Mem: ALA; Pa. Libr. Asn; ACRL; Asn. Am. Libr. Schs. Publ: American Art Auction Catalogues, 1785-1944, 44; Issues in Library Education, Council Libr. Asns, 49; The School Library Supervisor, ALA, 56; Libraries in British West Africa, Univ. Ill. Occasional Papers, 58; Nebraska Libraries Face the Future, Nebr. Libr. Cmn, 62; Bibliography of Ship Passenger Lists, 1538-1825, New York Pub. Libr, 3rd ed, 63. Consult: 1) Nebr. State Libr. Cmn, Lincoln, state-wide survey of libr. leading to state plan, with Harold Goldstein & Kathryn Gesterfield, 60-61; 2) Joliet Pub. Libr, Joliet, Ill, admin. survey & consult. on bldg. & site, with Harold Goldstein, 63; 3) Univ. San Carlos, Guatemala City, Guatemala, survey of libr. & libr. sci. dept, with Edward Fremd, Aug. & Dec. 65, Nov. 67; 4) Agency Int. Develop, survey of libr. in Chile & Iran, June-July & Oct-Nov. 66; 5) Kent State Univ, Sch. Libr. Sci, Kent, Ohio, evaluation of program, faculty, curriculum & advice on future develop, Dec. 66-Feb. 67. Specialties: 1a, 1b, 1c, 1g; 2a, 2b; 5a, 5b, 5c; 6a, 6b, 6c; 7a; 8a, 8b, 8c, 8d, 8e, 8f; 9 (libr. educ, admin, curriculum & programs).

LANE, SISTER M. CLAUDE, O.P, Feb. 7, 15; Archivist, Catholic Archives of Texas, Box 1828, Austin, Tex. 78767. Home: St. Pius X High School Library, 811 Donovan St, Houston, Tex. 77018. B.A, 53; M.L.S, 61. Teacher & librn, 56-60 & 61-64; archivist, Cath. Archives Tex, Austin, Tex, 60- Other: Libr. coordinator, Cath. Office Educ, Diocese of Austin, 65-67; mem. res. cmt, Tex. Old Missions Restoration Asn, 65-67; chmn, Austin Diocesan Unit, Cath. Libr. Asn, 65-67; mem. hospitality cmt, First Tex. Gov. Conf. Libr, 66. Mem: Cath. Libr. Asn; Austin Diocesan Unit, Cath. Libr. Asn; Tex. Libr. Asn; AASL; ALA. Publ: Catholic Archives of Texas: History and Preliminary Inventory, Sacred Heart Dominican Col, 61; The Development of the Catholic Library In Texas, Cath. Libr. World, 3/66; Catholic Archives of Texas, Tex. Cath. Hist. Soc. Consult: 1) St. Mary's Schs, Taylor, Tex, supervised separating 1-12 grade libr. into a 1-8 grade level, with Sister M. Beatrice, O.P, spring & summer 66; 2) Sacred Heart Sch, 5901 Reicher Dr, Austin, plans for converting large classroom into cent. libr, furnishing & arrangement with future expansion suggested, summer 66; 3) Cath. Off. Educ, 2501 N. Lamar, Box 1472, Austin, plans for setting up Diocesan Libr. Center, 66-67; 4) San Jose Sch, 2435 Oak Crest, Austin, furnishings, processing books, 66-67. Specialties: 1c, 1e, 1f; 2b, 2c, 2d (hist. documents), 2f; 3a, 3b, 3c, 3d; 5c, 5d (lay volunteer program); 6a, 6d (state meetings); 7a, 7c, 7d (workshops for training nonprfnl. personnel & volunteers); 8a, 8b, 8d, 8f; 9

(implementing Titles I & II in parochial schs, evaluating libr. collections, arranged Knapp Found. sch. libr. visits).

LANE, DR. MARGARET E, see CHISHOLM, DR. MARGARET E.

LEATHERS, JAMES A, Jan. 21, 31; Director of Libraries, Mid-Continent Public Library Services, 605 N. High, Independence, Mo. 64050. Home: 1100 Highway 71 Bypass N, Independence, Mo. 64050. B.A, Columbia Col, M.S, Sch. Libr. Serv, Columbia Univ. Librn, New York Pub. Libr, N.Y, 55-61; county librn, Jackson County Pub. Libr, Independence, Mo, 61-65; dir. libr, Mid-Continent Pub. Libr. Serv, 65- Other: Chmn. legis. cmt, Mo. Libr. Asn, 61- Mem: Mo. Libr. Asn; ALA; Am. Mgt. Asn. Consult: 1) Rolling Meadows Pub. Libr, Rolling Meadows, Ill, bldg. consult, July 65- Specialties: 1a, 1e, 1f, 1g; 3c, 3d, 3e; 8a, 8c, 8e, 8f.

LEE, DR. ROBERT ELLIS, Sept. 7, 24; Chairman, Department of Librarianship, Kansas State Teachers College, Emporia, Kans. 66801. Home: 1744 Trowman Way, Emporia, Kans. 66801. B.A, Guilford Col, 50; B.S.L.S, Univ. N.C, 51, M.F.A, 54; Ph.D, Univ. Chicago, 63. Asst. reference librn, 51-52; head, adult educ. dept, Greensboro Pub. Libr, Greensboro, N.C, 52-54; field worker & consult, ALA, 54-58; res. assoc. & dir. res. projects, educ-industry div, Univ. Chicago Industrial Relations Center, 58-63; chmn. dept. librarianship, Kans. State Teachers Col, Emporia, 63- Other: Chmn. publ. cmt, adult serv. cmt, ALA, 60-62, chmn, libr. binding inst. scholarship award jury, 64-65, mem. coun, 68-71, mem. cmt. accreditation, 67-72, pres, LED, 65-66; chmn, bookmanship cmt, Kans. Libr. Asn, 66-; bd. mem, bibliog. center, Rocky Mountain Region, Inc, 66- Mem: ALA; Kans. Libr. Asn; Adult Educ. Asn. U.S.A; Kans. Asn. Sch. Librns; Nat. Asn. Pub. Sch. Adult Educators; Ill. Adult Educ. Asn. Publ: Getting the Most Out of Discussion, ALA, 56; The Library-Sponsored Discussion Group, ALA, 57; Consumption and Savings (with William Mason), In: How Americans Obtain Goods and Services, Univ. Chicago Industrial Relations Center, 61; Recruitment of New Librarians, Kans. Libr. Bull, 3/64; Building Institute for Public Libraries, Kans. Libr. Bull, 12/64; Continuing Education for Adults through the American Public Library, ALA, 66. Consult: 1) Univ. N.Dak, Grand Forks, libr. educ. program, Apr. 66. Specialties: 7a, 7b, 7d (leadership training, community study); 9 (libr. educ—eval; design of libr. res. studies; libr. use studies; res. proposals).

LEGGETT, DR. STANTON F, May 8, 17; Partner, Engelhardt, Engelhardt & Leggett, Educational Consultants, Purdy Station, N.Y. 10578. Home: Somers, N.Y. 10589. A.B, Columbia Univ, 38, M.A, 39, Ph.D, 49. Educ.

KEY TO CONSULTING SPECIALTIES: 1) ARCHITECTURE AND BUILDINGS, 1a) public libraries, 1b) academic libraries, 1c) school libraries, 1d) special libraries, 1e) library interiors, 1f) furnishings, 1g) site and location, 1h) other architectural; 2) COLLECTIONS: SELECTION, EVALUATION, WEEDING, 2a) adults, 2b) young adults, 2c) children, 2d) subject specialty, 2e) O.P. searches, 2f) rare books, 2g) appraisals, 2h) others; 3) TECHNICAL PROCESSES, 3a) cataloging, 3b) classification systems, 3c) acquisitions, 3d) materials processing, 3e) work flow and cost studies, 3f) others, 4) AUTOMATION, 4a) applications of data processing equipment, 4b) information storage and retrieval systems, 4c) systems analysis, 4d) others

consult. & partner, Engelhardt, Engelhardt & Leggett, Educ. Consults, Purdy Station, N.Y, 47- Mem: Am. Asn. Sch. Adminstrs; Nat. Educ. Asn. Publ: Auth. & co-auth, An Analysis of Some Factors Associated with a High Level of Stability of Profession Personnel in a Large City School System, The Importance of Tax Leeway in Financing City School Systems in New York State, Planning Secondary School Buildings, Planning Elementary Schools & School Planning and Building Handbook. Consult: 1) Beverly Hills High Sch, Beverly Hills, Calif, libr. bldg, with Rowland H. Crawford, 66-; 2) Evanston Township High Sch, Evanston, Ill, libr. bldg, with Perkins & Will, 66-; 3) Scarsdale High Sch, Scarsdale, N.Y, libr. bldg, with Perkins & Will, 66-; 4) Springside Sch. for Girls, Chestnut Hill, Phila, Pa, libr. bldg, with Perkins & Will, 66-; 5) Univ. North Carolina at Charlotte, libr. bldg, with A.G. Odell, 67. Specialties: 1a, 1b, 1c, 1d, 1e, 1f; 4b.

LEMBO, MRS. DIANA L, Feb. 22, 25; Associate Professor, Palmer Graduate Library School, C.W. Post Campus, Long Island University, Greenvale, N.Y. 11548. Home: 96 Forest Ave, Locust Valley, N.Y. 11560. B.S, 46; M.S.(educ), 59; M.S.(libr. sci), 61. Librn, Locust Valley Elem. Sch, 57-59; head librn, Cent. Sch. Dist. 3, Brookville, N.Y, 59-65; assoc. prof, Palmer Grad. Libr. Sch, Long Island Univ, Greenvale, N.Y, 65- Other: Pres, Nassau-Suffolk Sch. Libr. Asn, 62-63; mem. planning cmt. joint meeting on instructional materials center, NSSLA-NPLA-LIECC, 66. Mem: Nassau-Suffolk Sch. Libr. Asn; N.Y. Libr. Asn; ALA; N.Y. Libr. Club; Dept. Audiovisual Instruction; N.Y. State Audiovisual Asn. Publ: Reading for Joy, Ideas for Teachers, 61-62; the Research Paper... (with Bishop, Copeland & Eggers), Kinnikat Press, 64; Index to the Masterplots and Masterpieces Series, Locust Valley High Sch. Libr. Club, 65; Your Library Can be the Exciting Nerve Center of Your School, Grade Teacher, 11/65; Juniorplots (with John Gillespie), R.R. Bowker, 66; Screenings, column in Sch. Libr. J, 67- Consult: 1) Bureau of Sch. Libr. Serv, N.Y. State Educ. Dept, Albany, N.Y, consult. & writer on handbook, The Secondary School Library—A Media Center, with Folcarelli & Gillespie, 66. Specialties: 1c; 2b, 2c; 3f (schs—nonbook materials); 7a, 7b; 9 (schs—establishment of instructional materials centers).

LEONDAR, JUDITH C, Feb. 8, 31; Library Operations Supervisor, Squibb Institute for Medical Research, New Brunswick, N.J. 08903. Home: 734 Park Ave, Plainfield, N.J. 07060. B.A.(chemistry), 52; M.L.S.(libr. serv), 60. Res. librn, Ethicon, Inc, Somerville, N.J, 56-61; sci. info. officer, Inst. Naval Studies, Cambridge, Mass, 61-65; res. assoc. & asst. prof, bur. info. sci. res, Rutgers Univ, New Brunswick, N.J, 65-66; sr. info. res. scientist, Squibb Inst. Med. Res, 66-68, libr. opers. supvr, 68- Other: V.chmn, New Eng. chap, Am. Document. Inst, 62-64; chmn. sci-tech. div, Boston chap, SLA, 63-65, prfnl. consult, SLA, 65-, chmn. engineering div, 66-67, v.pres, N.J. chap, 66-68, pres, N.J. chap, 68- Mem: SLA; Med. Libr. Asn; ALA; Am. Soc. Info. Sci; Am. Chemical Soc. Publ: Bibliography of Research Relating to the Communication of Scientific and Technical Information, Rutgers, 67; Subject-Index Standards, In: Proceedings of the American Documentation Institute, 10/67; Reproduction Literature and Sources of Information (Proceedings of a workshop held Apr. 5, 67), Spec. Libr, 2/68; mem. ed. bd, Current Contents, Physical Sciences, 68- Consult: 1) Tenneco Chem, Inc, Piscataway, N.J, planning for move of libr. to new location, 66; 2) Hudson-Champlain Water Pollution Control Project, U.S. Dept. Interior, Metuchen, N.J, planning new libr. layout, orgn. of materials, recommendations for acquisition, cataloging, info. storage & retrieval, training of libr. staff, 66-67. Specialties: 1d, 1e, 1f; 2d (sci. & tech, med); 3e; 4c; 7a, 7d (spec. libr); 9 (planning & orgn. of spec. libr. & info. centers).

LEOPOLD, MRS. CAROLYN CLUGSTON, Feb. 21, 19; Curriculum Laboratory Librarian, Board of Education, Montgomery County Public Schools, Rockville, Md. 20850. Home: 5705 Springfield Dr, Washington, D.C. 20016. B.A, Univ. Md; M.S. in L.S, Cath. Univ. Am. Librn, Upper Sch, Maret Sch, D.C, 59-60; librn, Mid. & Upper Schs, Holton-Arms Sch, D.C, 60-64; librn, Upper Sch, St. Albans Sch, Wash, D.C, 64-66. Mem: ALA; SLA; D.C. Libr. Asn; Beta Pi Mu. Publ: Real Child or Counterfeit Adult?, Libr. J, 1/1/63; The St. Albans Library— Opportunity and Challenge, St. Albans Bull, 5/65; Education for Decision, Libr. J, 1/1/66; What the Librarian Expects of the School Head, Independent Sch. Bull, 12/66; Helping the School Librarian Help Your Students, Croft Educ. Serv. Prof. Growth for Teachers, jr. high ed, 1st quarter ed, 67-68. Consult: 1) St. John's Church, 6701 Wisconsin Ave, Bethesda, Md, prepared spec. word classification syst. & supervised the complete reclassifying & recataloging of libr, 58-59; 2) Nature Conservancy, 1522 K St. N.W, Wash, D.C, prepared spec. word classification syst. & set up procedures & reference collection for new libr, 66; 3) Solomon Schecter Sch, East West Highway, Bethesda, Md, advised on procedures for setting up libr, 67. Specialties: 1c, 1f; 2b, 2c, 2d (sci—earth, water, pollution, children's literature, educ), 2e, 2f; 3a, 3b; 5c.

LIBRARY DESIGN ASSOCIATES, Suite 303 Parkland Plaza, 2121 S. Columbia Ave, Tulsa, Okla. 74114. Consult: 1) Univ. Okla. Undergrad. Libr, Norman, program, with Shaw & Shaw, Feb. 66; 2) Glendale Pub. Libr, Glendale, Ariz,

---

5) PERSONNEL AND RECRUITING, 5a) job evaluation and description, salary recommendations, 5b) recruitment of professionals and management personnel, 5c) administrative organization, 6) PUBLIC RELATIONS, 6a) publications, 6b) publicity programs, 6c) public opinion surveys, 6d) others, 7) SERVICES, 7a) evaluation of current program, 7b) studies of service to special publics, e.g., students, handicapped, aged, etc., 7c) programs for the implementation of new laws, program proposals to governments, 7d) others, 8) COMMUNITY, REGIONAL, STATE PLANNING, 8a) legislative programs, 8b) area analyses, 8c) centralized systems, cooperative arrangements, 8d) development of standards, 8e) state libraries and extension agencies, 8f) regional and statewide surveys, 8g) others, 9) OTHERS.

bldg. consult—review & recommendation of architect's preliminaries, Mar. 66; 3) Moore Libr, Moore, Okla, bldg. consult, 66-; 4) Warr-Acres Libr, Oklahoma City, Okla, bldg. consult, 66-; 5) Rosenberg Libr, Galveston, Tex, bldg. consult, 68- Specialties: 1a, 1b, 1c, 1d, 1e, 1f, 1g.

LIBRARY MANAGEMENT & BUILDING CONSULTANTS, INC, Box 58, Evanston, Ill. 60204. Consult: 1) Pub. Libr. of Ft. Wayne & Allen County Pub. Libr, Ft. Wayne, Ind, statement of program & reviews of plans for new main bldg, with Ernest I. Miller, William Chait, John I. Eastlick & Donald E. Bean, 64-65; 2) Can. Dept. Nat. Defence, Ottawa, Ont, statement of program for expanded libr. facilities in new bldg. with recommendations for reorgn. of libr. serv. among Can. defense agencies, with Foster E. Mohrhardt, Robert Severance & Donald E. Bean, 66; 3) Findlay Col, Findlay, Ohio, mgt. study & statement of program for new libr. bldg. & review of plans, with Maurice F. Tauber, Robert H. Muller & Donald E. Bean, 66; 4) Jefferson City & Cole County Libr, Jefferson City, Mo, mgt. study & statement of program for new cent. libr. bldg. with reviews of plans to follow, with William Chait, Frank Sessa, Ernest I. Miller & Donald E. Bean; 5) South. Methodist Univ, Dallas, Tex, statement of program for remodeling of & addition to main libr. bldg. & reviews of plans to follow, with Stephen A. McCarthy, Robert H. Muller & Donald E. Bean, 66. Specialties: 1; 2; 3; 4; 5; 6; 7; 8.

LINDAUER, DINAH, May 25, 26; Coordinator, Programs and Services, Nassau Library System, Lower Concourse, Roosevelt Field Shopping Center, Garden City, N.Y. 11530. Home: 81 Marion Ave, Merrick, N.Y. 11566. B.A, Hunter Col, 47; M.L.S, Columbia Univ, 49. Asst. coordinator work with young adults, Brooklyn Pub. Libr, 51-57; instructor, Pratt Libr. Sch, Brooklyn, N.Y, 58; dir. pub. libr. & sch. relations project, Nassau Libr. Syst, Hempstead, N.Y, 65-68. Other: Mem. adv. cmt, ESEA Title II & adv. cmt. revision sch. libr. standards in N.Y. State, N.Y. State Educ. Dept; pres. bd. trustees, Merrick Libr, Merrick, N.Y. Mem: ALA; N.Y. Libr. Asn; Nassau County Libr. Asn; Nassau-Suffolk Sch. Libr. Asn. Consult: 1) Encyclopaedia Britannica, Chicago, Ill, libr. consult. spec. traveling exhibit, with Don Cash, 63; 2) Educ. Coun. Sch. Res. & Develop, 131 Mineola Blvd, Mineola, N.Y, consult. libr. serv. anal. on $400,000 ESEA Title III, with Jack Tanzman, Apr. 66-June 67. Specialties: 2b; 7b, 7c, 7d (ESEA Titles II, III).

LINFORD, ARTHUR JOHN, JR, June 13, 36; Information Systems Librarian, Ohio State University Libraries, Columbus, Ohio 43210. Home: 181 Marion St, P.O. Box 37, Dublin, Ohio 43017. B.S.(psychology), Utah State Univ,

58; M.S.(libr. sci), West. Reserve Univ, 61. Tech. abstractor, indexer & writer, Thiokol Chemical Corp, Brigham City, Utah, 58-60; head librn, Hercules Power Co, Salt Lake City, Utah, 61-63; librn, project mgr. & book catalog rep, Document. Inc, Bethesda, Md, 63-66; info. systs. librn, Ohio State Univ. Libr, Columbus, Ohio, 66- Other: Chmn. info. sci. educ. inst, Cent. Ohio chap, Am. Document. Inst, 67-68. Mem: Am. Document. Inst; ALA; NMA. Publ: A Technical Proposal for a Book Catalog Program for the Public Libraries of North Carolina (with Finlayson, McCarren & Rebholz), Document. Inc, 65; Ford Foundation Study: Findings and Recommendations, Document. Inc, 66. Consult: 1) Cath. Univ. Am, Wash, D.C, mechanized aids to the indexing of the New Cath. Encyclopedia, with Donald Hummel, Aug. 64-June 66; 2) Engineering Resources Info. Center, U.S. Corps Engineers, Wash, D.C, design & assistance in implementation of ERIC Data Bank of bibliog. info, with Richard Potocko & Wulff Kuebler, Nov. 64-June 65; 3) Ford Found, New York, N.Y, recommendations for & initial implementation of improvements in found. libr, Aug-Sept. 66. Specialties: 4a, 4b, 4c, 4d (book catalogs).

LOGSDON, DR. RICHARD H, June 24, 12; Director of University Libraries, Columbia University, 535 W. 114th St, New York, N.Y. 10027. A.B, 33; B.S. in L.S, 34; Ph.D, 42. Librn, Adams State Col, 34-39; librn, Madison Col, 39-43; dir. libr. sci. dept, Univ. Ky, 43-45; chief librn, U.S. Off. Educ, 45-47; asst. dir. tech. serv, Columbia Univ, New York, N.Y, 47-48, assoc. dir, 48-53, dir. libr, 53- Other: Mem, Bd. Educ. for Librarianship, 46-51, chmn. 50-51; mem. cmn. higher insts, Mid. Atlantic States Asn, 51-57; mem. bd, Asn. Res. Libr, 62-65, chmn, 64. Publ: Columbia University Libraries (with Tauber, et al), Columbia Univ; Library Careers (with Mrs. Logsdon), Walck, 63; McGill University Libraries (a survey) (with Stephen McCarthy), 64. Consult: 1) McGill Univ, Montreal, Que, Can, gen. survey of all aspects of the univ. libr. syst, with Stephen McCarthy, 63-64; 2) Queens Univ, Kingston, Ont, Can, gen. survey of the univ. libr, 64-65; 3) Dartmouth Col, Hanover, N.H, orgn. pattern for future develop. of the col. libr, 64-65; 4) Univ. Alta, Edmonton Alta, Can, gen. survey of orgn. & staffing, with Stephen McCarthy, 65-66; 5) Univ. Man, Winnepeg, Man, Can, gen. survey of orgn. & staffing, with Stephen McCarthy, 66. Specialties: 3a, 3b, 3c, 3d, 3e; 5a, 5b, 5c; 6a, 6b, 6c; 7a, 7b, 7c; 9 (program planning; orgn, admin, staffing, personnel programs, faculty interrelationships in univ. libr).

LOHRER, ALICE, Jan. 29, 07; Professor of Library Science, Graduate School of Library Science, University of Illinois, Urbana, Ill, 61801. Home: 1905 N. Melanie Lane, Champaign, Ill. 61820. Ph.B, 28; B.S.L.S, 37; A.M, 44. Prof.

KEY TO CONSULTING SPECIALTIES: 1) ARCHITECTURE AND BUILDINGS, 1a) public libraries, 1b) academic libraries, 1c) school libraries, 1d) special libraries, 1e) library interiors, 1f) furnishings, 1g) site and location, 1h) other architectural; 2) COLLECTIONS: SELECTION, EVALUATION, WEEDING, 2a) adults, 2b) young adults, 2c) children, 2d) subject specialty, 2e) O.P. searches, 2f) rare books, 2g) appraisals, 2h) others; 3) TECHNICAL PROCESSES, 3a) cataloging, 3b) classification systems, 3c) acquisitions, 3d) materials processing, 3e) work flow and cost studies, 3f) others, 4) AUTOMATION, 4a) applications of data processing equipment, 4b) information storage and retrieval systems, 4c) systems analysis, 4d) others

libr. sci, Univ. Ill, Urbana, 41- Other: Pres, Ill. Asn. Sch. Librns, 40-41; pres, Ill. Libr. Asn, 46-47; pres, Beta Phi Mu, 54-55; mem. coun, ALA. Mem: Ill. Libr. Asn; Ill. Asn. Sch. Librns; ALA. Publ: A Planning Guide for High School Library Programs (with F. Henne & R. Ersted), ALA, 51; The Elementary School Library Planned as an Instructional Materials Center, In: Planning Library Buildings for Service, Libr. Bldg. & Equipment Inst, ALA, 64; School Library Materials Center, Its Resources and Their Utilization, Allerton Park Inst, Univ. Ill, 64; School Libraries in the U.S. Meet the Challenges of Today, Libr. Sci, Mita Soc. Libr. Sci, Tokyo, Japan, 65. Consult: 1) John Burroughs Sch, 755 S. Price Rd, Clayton, St. Louis, Mo, planned sch. libr, May 64; 2) Univ. Tehran, 78 Kennedy, Tehran, Iran, planned col. educ. libr, with M. Afzal & Mrs. Omid, 66-67; 3) McCluer High Sch, Ferguson-Florissant Sch. Dist, Florissant, Mo, IMC Proj, Aug. 68. Specialties: 1c; 2b, 2c.

LUCKER, JAY K, Feb. 23, 30; Associate University Librarian and Professor, Princeton University Library, Princeton, N.J. 08540. Home: 9 College Rd, Princeton, N.J. 08540. A.B, Brooklyn Col, 51; M.L.S, Columbia Univ, 52. First asst, sci. & tech. div, New York Pub. Libr, 57-59; asst. librn. for sci. & tech. & assoc. prof, Princeton Univ, Princeton, N.J, 59-68-, assoc. univ. librn. & prof, 68- Other: Chmn, subject specialists section, ACRL, 62-63; mem. libr. journal list cmt, RSD, 64-; mem, N.J. Libr. Resources Cmt. Mem: ALA. SLA; N.J. Libr. Asn. Publ: Bibliographic Index (assoc. ed), Wilson, 57-; Bibliography of Princeton Publications (ed), Princeton Univ. Conf, 59-; Science and Technology, In: Ulrich's Periodicals Directory, Bowker, 9th ed, 59, 10th ed, 63; The Phonograph is Now Perfect, Princeton Univ. Libr. Chronicle, spring 64; Survey of Library Resources in New Jersey, In: A Look at New Jersey's Research & Development Problems, N.J. Coun. for Res. & Develop, 63. Consult: 1) Inst. for Defense Analyses, Communications Res. Div, Von Neumann Hall, Princeton, N.J, designed libr, set up libr. procedures, established spec. classification list & subject headings, working on machine indexing & retrieval of documents collection, Nov. 59-; 2) Ingersoll-Rand Inc, Montgomery Rd, Rocky Hill, N.J, design of company library, established library routines and procedures, assisted in searching for librn, 63-65; 3) Stevens Inst. Tech, Hoboken, N.J, program, design & develop. of proposed new libr, 63-68; 4) Univ. Ill. at Chicago Circle, Chicago, developed program for mathematics dept. libr, June 66. Specialties: 1b, 1d, 1h (departmental libr. in univ. libr, especially in sci. & tech); 2d (sci. & engineering, mathematics); 3b, 3c; 4b; 7a, 7b.

LUTE, HARRIET, Jan. 30, 14; Supervisory Consultant, Nebraska Public Library Commission. Home: 921 E. Fourth St, North Platte, Nebr. 69101. B.A, Nebr. State Teachers Col, Kearney, 39; M.A, Univ. Denver, 54. Sch. libr. supvr, N. Platte Pub. Schs, 50-60; supvry. consult, Nebr. Pub. Libr. Cmn, 60- Other: Mem, Nebr. Libr. Develop. Cmt, 58-; pres, Nebr. Libr. Asn, 59-60. Mem: ALA; Nebr. Libr. Asn; Mountain-Plains Libr. Asn. Consult: 1) West. Plains Regional Syst, Sidney, Nebr, develop. of two-county regional syst, 61-67; 2) Pub. Libr, Sidney, construction & equipment to serve regional syst, 64-66; 3) Pub. Libr, Ogallala, Nebr, eval. & recataloging of book collection, weeding, acquisition of new materials, develop. of new serv. & new routines, 65; 4) Pub. Libr, Kimball, Nebr, construction & equipment, 65-66; 5) Pub. Libr, Lodgepole, Nebr, construction & equipment, 66. Specialties: 1a; 2a, 2b, 2c; 8c.

LYBECK, PAULINE, July 7, 29; Director of Information Systems, Interpublic Group of Companies, Inc, 1271 Ave. of Americas, New York, N.Y. 10020. Home: 225 E. 79th St, New York, N.Y. 10021. B.A, Tufts Univ, 50; M.S. in L.S, Columbia Univ, 51. Dir. info. serv, Papert, Koenig, Lois, Inc, 62-67; assoc. dir. ed. res. & libr, Cowles Commun, Inc, 67; head info. & microfilm centers, Batten, Barton, Durstine & Osborn, 68; dir. info. syst, Interpub. Group Companies, Inc, 68- Other: Rep. to Nat. Libr. Week Program, 65-; John Cotton Dana lectr, 68; promotion mgr, Document. Abstracts, 68-; approved consult, SLA. Mem: SLA; Am. Women in Radio & TV; Am. Soc. Info. Sci; Asn. Computing Machinery; Libr. Pub. Relations Coun; New York Libr. Club; Phi Beta Kappa. Publ: What's New in Advertising and Marketing (ed), 59-60; Advertising, Today, Yesterday, Tomorrow (contrib. ed), McGraw, 63; Guidelines for Standards for Advertising Agency Libraries, Spec. Libr, 64. Consult: 1) New York Times, 229 W. 43rd St, New York, N.Y, set up & directed pilot news res. project for editors & reporters; administered survey for design of automated info. retrieval syst, Oct. 57-Feb. 68; 2) Pandex, 135 W. 50th St, New York, marketing recommendations, 67; 3) Inst. for Training & Res. in Child Mental Health, 119 W. 57th St, New York, develop. of an info. program, 68; 4) F. & M. Schaefer Brewing Co, 430 Kent Ave, Brooklyn, N.Y, establishment of an info. center for the Pub. Relations Dept, outlined serv, wrote job description with salary recommendations & initiated recruiting for prfnl, 68; 5) N.Y. State Coun. on the Arts, 250 W. 57th St, New York, program of info. serv. & criteria for establishment of a small info. center, 68. Specialties: 1d; 2d (advertising & marketing; bus); 4b; 5a, 5b, 5c; 6b; 7a, 7b.

LYLE, GUY R, Oct. 31, 07; Director of Libraries, Emory University Library, Atlanta, Ga. 30322. Home: 2229 Tanglewood Rd, Decatur, Ga. 30033. A.B, Univ. Alta, 27,

5) PERSONNEL AND RECRUITING, 5a) job evaluation and description, salary recommendations, 5b) recruitment of professionals and management personnel, 5c) administrative organization, 6) PUBLIC RELATIONS, 6a) publications, 6b) publicity programs, 6c) public opinion surveys, 6d) others, 7) SERVICES, 7a) evaluation of current program, 7b) studies of service to special publics, e.g., students, handicapped, aged, etc., 7c) programs for the implementation of new laws, program proposals to governments, 7d) others, 8) COMMUNITY, REGIONAL, STATE PLANNING, 8a) legislative programs, 8b) area analyses, 8c) centralized systems, cooperative arrangements, 8d) development of standards, 8e) state libraries and extension agencies, 8f) regional and statewide surveys, 8g) others, 9) OTHERS.

LL.D, 64; B.S, Columbia Univ, 29, M.S, 32. Dir. libr, Emory Univ, Atlanta, Ga, 54- Other: Rockefeller Found. lecture series appointee, Japan Libr. Sch, Keio Univ, Tokyo, 57; chmn, Asn. Southeast. Res. Libr, 65-66; chmn. libr. adv. bd, Univ. Center of Ga, 65-67. Mem: ALA; ACRL; Southeast. Libr. Asn; Ga. Libr. Asn. Publ: Bibliography of Christopher Morley, Scarecrow, 52; The Launching, Phi Kappa Phi J, 10/53; Administration of the College Library, H.W. Wilson, 3rd ed, 61; The President, the Professor and the College Library, H.W. Wilson, 63; The Librarian's Role in Society, In: Sixth Annual Mary C. Richardson Lectures, State Univ. N.Y. Col. Geneseo, 63; Origin and Evolution of Library Survey, In: Library Surveys, Columbia, 66. Consult: 1) Adrian Col, Adrian, Mich, report seeking grant for book funds from the Kellogg Found, Nov. 61; 2) Episcopal Theol. Seminary of the Southwest, Austin, Tex, relationships to libr. cmt. & gen. serv. of the libr, Nov. 63; 3) Manchester Col, North Manchester, Ind, program & critique of plans, Feb-Aug. 64; 4) Mitchell Col, Statesville, N.C, program & critique of plans, 64 & 65; 5) Montreat-Anderson Col, Montreat, N.C, program for new bldg. & criticism of preliminary plans, June 66. Specialties: 1b; 2h (acad. libr—journals, reference books); 5c; 7a.

M

McADAMS, MRS. NANCY REEVES, July 28, 29; Architecture Librarian, School of Architecture, University of Texas, Austin, Tex. 78712. Home: 2607 Great Oaks Parkway, Austin, Tex. 78756. B. of Archit, 51; M.L.S, 66. Archit. practice, 56-61; staff architect, Page-Southerland-Page, Architects, Engineers & Consultants, 61; archit. librn, Univ. Tex, 65- Other: Registered architect, 56- Mem: Tex. Libr. Asn; ALA; SLA; Coun. Planning Librns. Publ: Selecting an Architect for the Library, Tex. Libr. J, summer 65; Super-Librarian and Sub-Architect, Libr. J, 12/1/66. Consult: 1) Tex. Women's Univ, Denton, interior planning & equipment layout of libr. addition, Kelly R. McAdams, Feb. 67; 2) Scott & White Found, Temple, Tex, interior planning & equipment layout for res. libr, Dec. 66-Mar. 67. Specialties: 1a, 1b, 1d, 1g; 2d (archit. & urban planning).

McANALLY, DR. ARTHUR M, Jan. 4, 11; Director of Libraries & Professor of Library Science, University of Oklahoma Library, Norman, Okla. 73069. Home: 1027 S. Berry Rd, Norman, Okla. 73069. B.A, 33; B.A. in L.S, 35; M.A, 36; Ph.D, 51. Dir, Univ. N.Mex. Libr, 45-49; asst. dir. reader's serv, Univ. Ill. Libr, 49-51; dir. libr, Univ. Okla, Norman, 51- Other: Pres, Southwest. Libr. Asn, 60-62; Fulbright & Ford Found. vis. prof, Ankara Univ. Libr. Sch, Ankara, Turkey, 63-64. Mem: ALA; ACRL; Southwest. Libr. Asn; Okla. Libr. Asn. Publ: The Dynamics of Securing Academic Status, Col. & Res. Libr, 9/57; Departmentation in University Libraries, Libr. Trends, 1/59; Social Pressures and Academic Librarianship, ALA Bull, 2/62; Privileges and Obligations of Academic Status, Col. & Res. Libr, 3/63; Budgets by Formula: a Study of Budgeting Practices of State Boards of Higher Education, Libr. Quart, 4/63. Consult: 1) Little Rock Univ, Little Rock, Ark, planning libr. develop, 58-59; 2) Wichita Univ, Wichita, Kans, planning new libr. bldg, 60-61; 3) Univ. San Marcos, Lima, Peru, planning cent. libr. bldg, July 63; 4) Univ. Ala, University, bldg. addition, 65-66; 5) Kans. State Teachers Col, bldg. addition, 67. Specialties: 1b; 9 (acad. libr. programs & mgt).

McCARTHY, DR. STEPHEN A, Oct. 7, 08; Executive Director, Association of Research Libraries, 1527 New Hampshire Ave. N.W, Washington, D.C. 20036. A.B, 29; M.A, 30; B.L.S, 32; Ph.D, 41. Dir. libr, Cornell Univ, Ithaca, N.Y, 46-67; exec. dir, Asn. Res. Libr, Wash, D.C, 67- Other: Pres, Nebr. Libr. Asn, 40; pres, N.Y. Libr. Asn, 51-52; Fulbright lectr. in Egypt, 53-54; exec. secy, Asn. Res. Libr, 60-62. Mem: ALA; ACRL; N.Y. Libr. Asn; Am. Asn. Univ. Prof. Consult: 1) Hunter Col, New York, N.Y, survey of bldg. needs & preparatory report for program, June-Dec, 64; 2) Dalhousie Univ, Halifax, Nova Scotia, Can, bldg. consult, Sept. 65-; 3) Univ. Alberta, Edmonton, Alberta, Can, survey of libr, with Richard H. Logsdon, Jan-May 66; 4) Winterthur Museum Libr, Wilmington, Del, bldg. consult, with James Humphry, Feb-May, 66; 5) Pa. State Univ, State College, bldg. consult, July 66- Specialties: 1b, 1g; 3a, 3b, 3c, 3d; 5c; 7a, 7b.

McCLARREN, ROBERT R, Mar. 15, 21; System Director, North Surburban Library System, 5814 Dempster St, Morton Grove, Ill. 60053 Home: 1560 Oakwood Place, Deerfield, Ill. 60015. A.B, Muskingum Col, 42; M.A, Ohio State Univ, 51; M.S, Columbia Univ, Sch. Libr. Serv, 54. Head librn, Crawfordsville Pub. Libr, Crawfordsville, Ind, 55-58; head librn, Cabell-Huntington Pub. Libr. & West. Counties Regional Libr, Huntington, W.Va, 58-62; dir. Ind. State Libr, Indianapolis, 62-67; syst. dir, N. Surburban Libr. Syst, Morton Grove, Ill, 67- Other: Pres, W.Va. Libr. Asn, 60-61; secy, ASL, 64-65; secy, ASD, 64-66; pres, Adult Educ. Asn. of Ind, 65-66; coun, ALA, 66-70, treas, 67-71. Mem: Ill. Libr. Asn; Ind. Sch. Librns. Asn; Am. Soc. Info. Sci; ALA; Beta Phi Mu. Publ: A Neglected Question: What About Publishers' Library Bindings?, The Rub-Off, 9-10/62; Emphasis on Research, Libr. J, 1/1/63; Libraries Can Assist in Community Recreation Planning, Libr. Occurrent, 3/65; Volunteer for the Cavalry, Libr. J, 5/1/65; Priority in Indiana, ALA Bull, 10/66; Planning and Constructing a New Library Building; An Outline and Checklist (with Donald E. Thomp-

---

KEY TO CONSULTING SPECIALTIES: 1) ARCHITECTURE AND BUILDINGS, 1a) public libraries, 1b) academic libraries, 1c) school libraries, 1d) special libraries, 1e) library interiors, 1f) furnishings, 1g) site and location, 1h) other architectural; 2) COLLECTIONS: SELECTION, EVALUATION, WEEDING, 2a) adults, 2b) young adults, 2c) children, 2d) subject specialty, 2e) O.P. searches, 2f) rare books, 2g) appraisals, 2h) others; 3) TECHNICAL PROCESSES, 3a) cataloging, 3b) classification systems, 3c) acquisitions, 3d) materials processing, 3e) work flow and cost studies, 3f) others, 4) AUTOMATION, 4a) applications of data processing equipment, 4b) information storage and retrieval systems, 4c) systems analysis, 4d) others

son), Libr. J, 12/1/66. Consult: 1) Huntington Pub. Libr, Huntington, W.Va, study of possible sites for location of main libr. with recommendations, Apr. 63; 2) Hanover Col, Hanover, Ind, survey of present col. libr. bldg. & serv. with recommendations, with Virginia Clark & James F. Holley, Feb. 65; 3) Cmt. to Study Libr. Needs of the State, Legis. Adv. Cmn, Ind. Gen. Assembly, Indianapolis, study libr. needs of libr. in the State & of citizens of Ind. with recommendations, with legislators & an adv. cmt, June 65-Sept. 66; 4) Dept. of Correction, State of Ind, Indianapolis, survey of libr. materials, serv. & facilities in the State's correctional insts. with recommendations, with C. Ray Ewick, June-Aug. 66. Specialties: 1a, 1g, 1h (integrated art); 2d (local hist); 7a, 7b; 8a, 8b, 8c, 8e, 8f.

McCONKEY, THOMAS W, July 26, 13; Chief, Administrative Services, Free Library of Philadelphia, Logan Square, Philadelphia, Pa. 19144. Home: 408 W. Price St, Philadelphia, Pa. 19144. B.A, Univ. Pittsburgh, 35; M.A, Univ. Pa, 56. Chief, admin. serv, Free Libr. of Phila, Pa, 53- Mem: Pa. Libr. Asn. Publ: Products and Equipment Column (ed), Libr. J, 56-; Library Buying Guide (ed), Libr. J, 56- Consult: 1) Grundy Mem. Libr, Bristol, Pa, interior shelving & equipment layout, with specifications, 65-66; 2) Jeanes Mem. Libr, Plymouth Meeting, Pa, site selection, financial feasibility & budgets, archit. program, 65-66; 3) Lansdale Pub. Libr, Lansdale, Pa, develop. of regional plan of libr. serv, 65-66; 4) Hazelton Pub. Libr, Hazelton, Pa, archit. program, 65-66; 5) Upper Darby Pub. Libr, Upper Darby, Pa, community libr. program, 66. Specialties: 1a, 1f, 1g; 5a, 5c; 7a, 7c.

McCOY, DR. RALPH E, Oct. 1, 15; Director of University Libraries, Southern Illinois University, Carbondale, Ill. 62901. Home: 1902 Chautauqua St, Carbondale, Ill. 62901. A.B, 37; B.S.L.S, 39; M.S, 50; Ph.D, 56. Dir. univ. libr, South. Ill. Univ, Carbondale & Edwardsville, Ill, 54-, spec. asst. to v.pres. planning, 63-64. Other: Chmn, Joint Cmt. Libr. Serv. to Labor, 53-54; pres, Ill. Libr. Asn, 56-57, outstanding contribution to librarianship award, 61; mem. adv. cmt, Collected Works of John Dewey, 63-, pres, ACRL 66-67. Mem: ALA; Ill. Libr. Asn; Bibliog. Soc. Am; Caxton Club; Beta Phi Mu. Publ: Personnel Administration in Libraries, ALA, 53; History of Labor and Unionism: a Bibliography, Inst. Labor & Industrial Relations, Univ. Ill, 53; Personnel in Circulation Services, Libr. Trends, 7/57; The Ordeal of a University Library, Libr. J, 5/1/60; Computerized Circulation Work: a Case Study of the 357 Data Collection System, Libr. Resources & Tech. Serv, winter 65; Freedom of the Press: a Bibliography, South. Ill. Univ, 68. Consult: 1) Ark. Agr, Mechanical & Normal Univ, Pine Bluff, Ark, survey of libr, with A.P. Marshall & Inez Boddy, Feb. 67; 2) Miami Univ, Oxford, Ohio, survey of libr, with G. Flint Purdy, Apr. 67; 3) Carnegie Inst. Tech, Pittsburgh, Pa, consultation on libr. resources, May 67; 4) Auburn Univ, survey of libr, with Robert W. Orr & Ralph H. Parker; May 67; 5) Northeast. Ill. Univ, Chicago, Ill, consultation on bldg. & tech. serv, with Robert L. Talmadge, July 67. Specialties: 1b, 1e; 2a, 2f; 3c; 4a, 4c; 5c; 8f; 9 (col. libr. budgeting).

McDANIEL, RODERICK D, Aug. 25, 27; Vice President, Professional Services, Xerox/Professional Library Services, 2200 E. McFadden Ave, Santa Ana, Calif. 92705. Home: 2051 Via Madonna, Lomita, Calif. 90717. B.A, Univ. South. Calif, 51, Ed.D, 67; M.A, Calif. State Col. at Long Beach, 59. Asst. principal, Walteria Elem. School, Torrance, Calif, 56-58; dir, educ. materials, Torrance Unified Sch. Dist, 58- Other: Mem, libr. & audiovisual standards cmt, Calif. Asn. Sch. Libr. & Audiovisual Educ. Asn. Calif, 64-65; coord. elem. teacher training, Univ. South. Calif, 65-66. Mem: Audiovisual Educ. Asn. Calif. Consult: 1) Temple City Unified Sch. Dist, 9516 Langdon St, Temple City, Calif, survey of instructional materials Resources with recommendations, with Ray Denno, June 65; 2) Calif. State Dept. Educ, oper. instructional material catalogs, 67; 3) Colton Unified Sch. Dist, Colton, Calif, survey, May 68. Specialties: 1h (educ. materials centers); 5c; 7a; 8c.

McDIARMID, DR. ERRETT WEIR, July 13, 09; Professor & Director, Graduate School Fellowship Office, University of Minnesota Library School, 3 Walter Library, Minneapolis, Minn. 55455. Home: 1473 Fulham St, St. Paul, Minn. 55108. A.B, 29; M.A, 30; A.B.(libr. sci), 31; Ph.D, 34. Univ. librn. & dir. div. libr. inst, Univ. Minn, Minneapolis, Minn, 43-51, dean col. sci, literature & arts, 51-63, prof. & dir. grad. fel. office, 63-, chief of party, Univ. Concepcion-Univ. Minn. Cooperative Program, Concepcion, Chile, 65-67. Other: Mem. coun, Am. Asn. Univ. Prof, 41-44; trustee, J.J. Hill Reference Libr, 46-; pres, ALA, 48-49; pres, Asn. Minn. Cols, 63-64. Mem: ALA; ACRL; Am. Asn. Univ. Prof; Minn. Libr. Asn. Publ: The Library Survey, ALA, 40; College and Research Libraries (managing ed), 41-43; Administration of the American Public Library (with John McDiarmid), Univ. Ill, 43; A University Library Personnel Program, In: Personnel Administration in Libraries, Univ. Chicago, 46; Current Concepts in Library Administration, Libr. Trends, 1/59. Consult: 1) U.S. Veterans Admin, Wash, D.C, survey of libr. programs of the Spec. Serv. Div, with Mrs. E.B. Stanford, 46; 2) Am. Found. for Blind, New York, N.Y, survey of libr. serv. to the blind, with F.R. St. John, I. Lieberman, E. Wilson & P.N. Rice, 57; 3) Regents for Higher Educ, Pierre, S.Dak, survey of libr. of insts. of higher educ, with D.K. Berninghausen, W. Simonton & R.H. Shove, 63-64; 4) Ford Found, New York, review

---

5) PERSONNEL AND RECRUITING, 5a) job evaluation and description, salary recommendations, 5b) recruitment of professionals and management personnel, 5c) administrative organization, 6) PUBLIC RELATIONS, 6a) publications, 6b) publicity programs, 6c) public opinion surveys, 6d) others, 7) SERVICES, 7a) evaluation of current program, 7b) studies of service to special publics, e.g., students, handicapped, aged, etc., 7c) programs for the implementation of new laws, program proposals to governments, 7d) others, 8) COMMUNITY, REGIONAL, STATE PLANNING, 8a) legislative programs, 8b) area analyses, 8c) centralized systems, cooperative arrangements, 8d) development of standards, 8e) state libraries and extension agencies, 8f) regional and statewide surveys, 8g) others, 9) OTHERS.

of proposals for cooperative program between the Univ. Minn. and the Univ. Concepcion, Concepcion, Chile, with F. Verbrugge & W.M. Myers, 64-65; 5) Va. Cmn. Higher Educ, Richmond, Va, survey of libr. of pub. insts. of higher educ, with John Dale Russell, 64-65. Specialties: 5a, 5b, 5c; 6a, 6b, 6c; 7a, 7b; 8b, 8c, 8f.

McDONALD, JOHN PETER, Oct. 17, 22; Director of Libraries, University of Connecticut, Storrs, Conn. 06268. Home: 18 Westwood Rd, Storrs, Conn. 06268. A.B, Univ. Va, 46; M.S.L.S, Drexel Inst, 51. Asst. to dir, Wash. Univ. Libr, 56-58, asst. dir. readers serv, 58-60, assoc. dir. libr, 60-63; dir. libr, Univ. Conn, Storrs, 63- Other: Carnegie Corp. fel, 58; mem. adv. cmt. cooperation with educ. & prfnl. orgn, ACRL, 61-65, chmn, 66-, mem. urban univ. libr. cmt, univ. libr. section, 61-63, mem. res. & develop. cmt, 63-65; mem. bd. dir, LAD, 62-66; mem. coun, ALA, 62-66; treas, East. Col. Librns. Conf, 64; Libr. Bldg. Consults. Inst, Univ. Colo, 64; v.chmn. & chmn, col. & univ. libr. sect, Conn. Libr. Asn. 65-67; mem. shared cataloging cmt, Asn. Res. Libr. Mem: Bibliog. Soc. Am; ALA; Conn. Libr. Asn. Publ: The Rutgers University Library: A Study of Current Problems of Organization and Service in a Decentralized University, In: Studies in Library Administrative Problems, Rutgers Univ, 60. Consult: 1) Westchester Community Col, Valhalla, N.Y, site selection, bldg. planning & interior layout, 64-65; 2) Marymount Col, Tarrytown, N.Y, site selection, bldg. planning & interior layout, 64-66; 3) Annhurst Col, Woodstock, Conn, interior planning, 65; 4) Fordham Univ, Lincoln Center Libr, 67. Specialties: 1b, 1e, 1f.

McDONOUGH, ROGER H, Feb. 24, 09; Director, New Jersey State Library, New Jersey Department of Education, 185 W. State St, Trenton, N.J. 08608. Home: 270 Spruce St, Princeton, N.J. 08540. A.B, Rutgers Univ, 34; B.S, Columbia Univ, 36. Dir, N.J. State Libr, Trenton, N.J, 47- Other: Secy, N.J. Tercentenary Cmt, 60-64; secy, Cmt. to Study Arts in N.J, 63-66; v.pres, Am. Libr. Trustee Asn, 66-; pres, ALA, 68-69. Mem: ALA; Am. Libr. Trustee Asn; N.J. Libr. Asn; SLA; Nat. Asn. State Libr. Publ: Government Interests in Libraries, Libr. Trends, 4/56; Federal Aid to Libraries—Challenge and Opportunity, Libr. J, 9/1/57; Twenty Years A-Growing: the Library Services Branch in 1958, ALA Bull, 1/58; Depository Library—Privilege or Responsibility, Libr. Resources & Tech. Serv, fall 63. Consult: 1) U.S. Office Educ, Wash, D.C, assisted libr. serv. br. in initial phases of Libr. Serv. Act, preparing guidelines, etc, 56; 2) U.S. Off. Educ, surveyed & reported on Libr. Serv. Act programs in five south. states; Fla, S.C, Ga, Miss. & La, 62-63; 3) Conn. State Libr, Hartford, surveyed & reported on orgn. structure of state libr. serv. at state level for future orgn. pattern, with Mrs. Mildred McKay, 64; 4) Fla. State Libr, Tallahassee, plans for new state libr. bldg, 65-66; 5) Maine Cultural Cmn, consult, libr-archives-museum bldg, 66- Specialties: 1a, 1b, 1g; 5c; 7a, 7b, 7c; 8a, 8e, 8f.

McELDERRY, STANLEY, Oct. 19, 18; Dean, Graduate School of Library Science, University of Texas, Austin, Tex. 78712. Home: 2615 Pembrook Trail, Austin, Tex. 78731. A.B, Univ. South. Calif, 40, B.S. in L.S, 41. Asst. dir. libr. & assoc. prof, Univ. Okla, 52-55; visiting lectr, Univ. Tex, 54, 55, 65 & Univ. South. Calif, 58, 62, 67; col. librn, San Fernando Valley State Col, 57-68; dean, grad. sch. libr. sci, Univ. Tex, Austin, 68- Other: Mem, in-serv. training cmt, personnel admin. sect, LAD, 59-60, mem, recruiting cmt, ALA, 62; pres, col, univ. & res. libr. sect, Calif. Libr. Asn, 64 & chmn, south. dist. Mem: ALA; Calif. Libr. Asn. Publ: The Effect of Enrollment Increases on College Library Resources and Services, Calif. Librn, 7/61. Consult: 1) Chapman Col, Orange, Calif, design & layout of libr. bldg, 65; 2) Trustees of Calif. State Cols, 5670 Wilshire Blvd, Los Angeles, budget, personnel & bldgs. coordinator of libr. serv. for 18 campuses of Calif. State Cols, 66-68; 3) Pasadena Col, Pasadena, Calif, design & layout of libr. bldg, 68. Specialties: 1b; 5c; 8a, 8c, 8d.

McFARLAND, KAY R, Apr. 11, 24; Director, Dept. of Library Science, Shippensburg State College, Shippensburg, Pa. 17257. Home: R.D. 2, Newville, Pa. 17241. B.S, Northwest. State Col. of La, 58; M.A. in librarianship, Univ. Denver, 59. Acquisitions librn, Univ. Denver, Colo, 58-59; acquisitions librn, Univ. Tulsa, Okla, 59-62; dir, dept. libr. sci, Shippensburg State Col, Shippensburg, Pa, 62- Other: Pres, sch. libr. sect, Pa. Libr. Asn, 63-64; pres, Capital Area Libr. Asn, Harrisburg, Pa, 64-65; teaching asst, Columbia Univ, N.Y, 65-66; regional chmn, PLA, 66-67. Mem: ALA; Pa. Libr. Asn; Pa. Sch. Librns. Asn; Capital Area Libr. Asn; Pa. State Educ. Asn; Am. Asn. Univ. Prof. Consult: 1) Cumberland Valley Sch. Dist, Mechanicsburg, Pa, planning & supv. students in model intermediate sch. with instructional materials center, with Samuel Sanzotto, 66-68. Specialties: 2b, 2h (sch. libr, libr. sci. collections); 5d (sch. libr. admin); 6b, 6d (recruiting from high sch. students); 7a, 7d (plan & organize workshops for teacher-librns); 8b, 8f.

McGOWAN, FRANK M, Dec. 29, 31; Assistant Chief, Overseas Operations Division, Library of Congress, Washington, D.C. 20540. Home: 10521 Bucknell Dr, Silver Spring, Md. 20902. B.A, 53; M.S. in L.S, 54. Acquisitions librn, Am. Univ. of Beirut, Lebanon, 54-57; univ. bibliographer, Univ. Pittsburgh, 57-60, head librn, Grad. Sch. Pub. & Int. Affairs, 60-65; asst. coordinator overseas programs, Libr.

KEY TO CONSULTING SPECIALTIES: 1) ARCHITECTURE AND BUILDINGS, 1a) public libraries, 1b) academic libraries, 1c) school libraries, 1d) special libraries, 1e) library interiors, 1f) furnishings, 1g) site and location, 1h) other architectural; 2) COLLECTIONS: SELECTION, EVALUATION, WEEDING, 2a) adults, 2b) young adults, 2c) children, 2d) subject specialty, 2e) O.P. searches, 2f) rare books, 2g) appraisals, 2h) others; 3) TECHNICAL PROCESSES, 3a) cataloging, 3b) classification systems, 3c) acquisitions, 3d) materials processing, 3e) work flow and cost studies, 3f) others, 4) AUTOMATION, 4a) applications of data processing equipment, 4b) information storage and retrieval systems, 4c) systems analysis, 4d) others

Congress, 66-68. Other: Chmn, Near & Middle E. Cmt, Int. Rels. Roundtable, ALA, 64- Mem: ALA. Publ: A Selected List of U.S. Readings on Development (with Saul Katz), Agency Int. Develop, Wash, D.C, 63. Consult: 1) Inst. of Admin, Zaria, Nigeria, orgn. study of libr, May 63; 2) Inst. Nat. Planning, Cairo, United Arab Republic, orgn. study & staff training for Document. Centre, June 63; 3) Univ. Central, Quito, Ecuador, orgn. study & staff training of libr. for faculty of econ. & admin, Feb-Mar. 65. Specialties: 1d; 2d (pub. admin; int. rels); 3c.

MACK, MRS. SARA R, Nov. 20, 21; Assistant Professor of Library Science, Kutztown State College, Kutztown, Pa. 19530. Home: 61 E. Centre Ave, Topton, Pa. 19562. B.S, Kutztown State Col, 43; M.S, Columbia Univ, 55. Librn, Mt. Penn-Lower Alsace Jr-Sr. High Sch, 49-58; asst. prof. libr. sci, Kutztown State Col, Kutztown, Pa, 58- Other: Secy, Pa. Sch. Librns. Asn, 60-62, v.pres, 62-64, pres, 64-66; mem, student asst. cmt, AASL, 60-64; recipient, pres. award for superior teaching, Kutztown State Col, 62; mem, Nat. Libr. Week cmt, Pa. Libr. Asn, 64, mem, recruiting cmt, 65-68; founder, Pa. Student Libr. Asst. Asn; sponsor, Alpha Beta Alpha. Mem: ALA; Pa. Libr. Asn; Pa. Sch. Librns. Asn. Publ: Reading List for Elementary Grades, Berks County Sch. Bull, 9/60; Grass-roots Recruiting, Pa. Libr. Asn. Bull, winter 62; The Function of the Elementary Library in the Curriculum, Recent Faculty Research, Kutztown State Col. Bull, 62; Inspirational Readings for Elementary Grades, Kutztown Publ. Co, 64; Pennsylvania Student Library Assistants Association—Progress Report, Pa. Libr. Asn. Bull, 8/64; Recruiting in Pennsylvania, Pa. Libr. Asn. Bull, 8/68. Consult: 1) Abington Sch. Dist, Abington, Pa, discussed teacher use of elem. sch. libr, Feb. 62; 2) Parkland Sch. Dist, Orefield, Pa, consult. on teacher & the elem. sch. libr, Mar. 62; 3) South. Jr. High Sch, Reading, Pa, discussed use of sec. sch. libr. with faculty, Nov. 64; 4) Kennett Square High Sch, Kennett Square, Pa, discussed use of sch. libr. with high sch. faculty, Dec. 64; 5) Hellertown Sch. Dist, Hellertown, Pa, teacher use of sch. libr, Nov. 65. Specialties: 1c; 2a, 2b, 2c, 2d (storytelling, book reviewing); 7a; 9 (sch. libr. relationship to the curriculum & serv. to teachers).

McKEON, NEWTON F, Dec. 21, 04; Director, Amherst College Library, Amherst, Mass. 01002. Home: 32 Hitchcock Rd, Amherst, Mass. 01002. B.A, Amherst Col, 26. Dir, Amherst Col. Libr, 39- Other: Dir, Hampshire Inter-Libr. Center, 51-, secy, 52-53, 55-57, treas, 58-59, 60-; mem. eval. cmt, New Eng. Asn. Cols. & Sec. Schs, 53-63; mem. coun, ALA & dir, ACRL, 59-62. Mem: ALA; ACRL; Bibliog. Soc. Am; Am. Asn. Univ. Profs; Grolier Club; Phi Beta Kappa. Publ: Amherst Massachusetts Imprints, 1825-1876 (ed), 46; The Place of the Library in a University (contrib), Harvard Col. Libr, 50; College Libraries Working Together, In: The College Library in a Changing World, Goucher Col, 53; The Nature of the College-Library Book Collection, In: The Function of the Library in the Modern College, Univ. Chicago Grad. Libr. Sch, 54. Consult: 1) Lilly Endowment, Indianapolis, Ind, adv. cmt. on grants to Ind. cols. for the strengthening of their collections (Butler, DePauw, Earlham, Evansville, Hanover, Wabash), with Harvie Branscomb, Robert B. Downs & Arthur T. Hamlin, Apr. 59; 2) Lilly Endowment, Indianapolis, adv. cmt. on grants to Ind. cols; inspection visits to the libr. of Anderson, Goshen, Ind. Cent, Manchester Cols, Rose Polytechnic Inst. & Valparaiso Univ, with Robert B. Downs & Arthur Hamlin; 3) Dickinson Col. Libr, Carlisle, Pa, new bldg. plans, Nov. 64; 4) Bucknell Univ. Libr, Lewisburg, Pa, survey of present state & recommendations for future develop, with Ralph Blasingame & Donald F. Cameron. Specialties: 1b; 2h (col. libr. collections).

MACLACHLAN, BRUCE, Consultant, Nelson Associates, Inc, 845 Third Ave, New York, N.Y. 10022. Home: 890 West End Ave, New York, N.Y. 10025. B.A, Univ. Fla, 58, M.B.A, 64. Res. assoc, Hammer, Greene, Siler & Assocs, 65; consult, Nelson Assocs, Inc, 65- Publ: Needs for Higher Education in the Evansville Area to 1980, 66; A study of Factors Related to Change in Freshmen Enrollment at Private Colleges in New York State, 61-66, 67. Consult: 1) Ohio State Libr, survey of present programs and future prospects, with Robert Goldberg & David Watson, 67; 2) Nat. Adv. Cmn. Libr, position paper on sch. libr. in the U.S, with Eugene Vorhies, 67; 3) Nat. Adv. Cmn. Libr, position paper on undergrad. & jr. coll. libr. in U.S, with Eugene Vorhies, 68; 4) Info. Syst. Off, Libr. Congress, survey of user needs, nat. serials data program, with James R. Basche, Jr, 68; 5) Div. Blind & Physically Handicapped, Libr. Congress, Survey of reader interests and study of circulation syst. in regional libr, 69. Specialties: 3c, 3d, 3e; 4c; 7a, 7b, 7c; 8c, 8e, 8f.

McMULLAN, THEODORE N, June 25, 08; Director of the Library, Louisiana State University, Baton Rouge, La. 70803. Home: 544 Magnolia Woods, Baton Rouge, La. 70808. B.S.(engineering), 31; M.S.(engineering), 32; B.S. in L.S, 34. Acting dir. libr, La. State Univ, Baton Rouge, 55-56, assoc. dir. libr, 56-61, dir. libr, 61- Other: Pres, La. Libr. Asn, 58; chmn, collections & reference sect, SLA, 64-65; 2nd v.pres, Southwest. Libr. Asn, 65-66; ed, Southwest. Newsletter, 65-66; La. rep. to ALA coun, 66-, mem, resolutions cmt, ALA. Mem: La. Libr. Asn; South. Libr. Asn; Am. Libr. Asn; Southeast. Libr. Asn. Publ: Newspaper Files in Louisiana State University, 61; Louisiana Newspapers 1794-1961, La. State

5) PERSONNEL AND RECRUITING, 5a) job evaluation and description, salary recommendations, 5b) recruitment of professionals and management personnel, 5c) administrative organization, 6) PUBLIC RELATIONS, 6a) publications, 6b) publicity programs, 6c) public opinion surveys, 6d) others, 7) SERVICES, 7a) evaluation of current program, 7b) studies of service to special publics, e.g., students, handicapped, aged, etc., 7c) programs for the implementation of new laws, program proposals to governments, 7d) others, 8) COMMUNITY, REGIONAL, STATE PLANNING, 8a) legislative programs, 8b) area analyses, 8c) centralized systems, cooperative arrangements, 8d) development of standards, 8e) state libraries and extension agencies, 8f) regional and statewide surveys, 8g) others, 9) OTHERS.

Univ. Libr, 65; The Dream Becomes Reality, La. State Univ. Alumni News, 31: 15-17; The Concept of a Library, La. State Univ. Alumni News, 31: 24-25; Louisiana State University Library, ALA-ACRL Bldg. Cmt. Fifth & Sixth Libr. Bldg. Plans Inst; New Library Buildings in Louisiana Colleges, La. Libr. Asn. Bull, 24: 12-16. Consult: 1) Univ. Southwest. La, Lafayette, consult. to architects, 65-66; 2) Univ. S. Ala, Mobile, consult. to architects, with Guy R. Lyle & Orwin Rush, Feb. 66; 3) La. State Univ, Shreveport, consult. to architect, spring 66; 4) La. State Univ, Eunice, consult. to architect, spring 66; 5) Grad. Facilities Br, Div. Grad. Programs, Bureau of Higher Educ, U.S. Office Educ, libr. consult, 66-69. Specialties: 1b, 1e, 1f; 2d (univ), 2f, 2g; 5c.

McNEAL, DR. ARCHIE L, Sept. 3, 12; Director of Libraries, University of Miami, Coral Gables, Fla. 33124. Home: 1414 Certosa Ave, Coral Gables, Fla. 33146. B.S, Memphis State Univ, 32; B.S. in L.S, George Peabody Col. Teachers, 36; Ph.D, Univ. Chicago, 51. Dir. libr, Univ. Miami, Coral Gables, Fla, 52- Other: Mem. coun, ALA, 55-65, chmn. intellectual freedom cmt, 59-64, mem. exec. bd, 61-65, 2nd v.pres, 68-69; summer visiting prof, Univ. N.C, 59 & 61; pres, LAD, 60-61; summer visiting prof, Columbia Univ, 64, 67; pres, ACRL, 64-65; pres, Southeast. Libr. Asn, 64-66; mem, Fla. State Libr. Cmn. Mem: ALA; Southeast. Libr. Asn; Fla. Libr. Asn. Publ: Financial problems of University Libraries, Col. & Res. Libr, 15: 407-410; Ratio of Professional to Clerical Staff, Col. & Res. Libr, 5/56; Academic and Research Libraries in India, Col. & Res. Libr, 5/59; Integrated Service in Southern Public Libraries, Libr. J, 6/1/61; The Library in the South: Socioeconomic and Cultural Aspects, Wilson Libr. Bull, 6/65. Consult: 1) Boston Univ, Boston, Mass, critic & reader-adv. on plans & report, represented L.B.C, with William H. Jesse, Maurice Tauber & Donald Bean, May-June 60; 2) S. Miami Pub. Libr, 6130 Sunset Dr, South Miami, Fla, site & methods of providing libr. serv, advised on decision to become part of larger syst, Dec. 64-May 65; 3) Biscayne Col, 16400 N.W. 32nd Ave, Miami, Fla, planning new libr. bldg, 65-67; 4) Memphis State Univ, Memphis, Tenn, consult. on needs in support of new Ph.D. programs, met with architects & reviewed plans for bldg. addition, Jan. 66; 5) Atlanta Univ. Center, Atlanta, Ga, libr. problems of the cols. & Atlanta Univ, plans for proposed addition to Atlanta Univ. Libr. & for separate new undergrad. libr, with A.F. Kuhlman & F.G. Clark, 68. Specialties: 1b, 1g; 5c.

McNIFF, PHILIP J, Feb. 10, 12; Director, Boston Public Library, 101 Waban Hill Rd, Chestnut Hill, Mass. 02167. A.B, Boston Col, 33; B.S, Columbia Univ, 40. Assoc. librn. & mem. faculty arts & sci, Harvard Univ, 56-65, Archibald Cary Coolidge bibliographer, 62-65: dir, Boston Pub. Libr, Boston, Mass, 65- Mem: ALA; Asn. Res. Libr; New Eng. Libr. Asn; Mass. Libr. Asn; Cath. Libr. Asn. Publ: Catalogue of the Lamont Library, Harvard Univ, 52; A List of Book Dealers in Underdeveloped Countries, ALA Resources & Tech. Serv. Div. 63. Consult: 1) Newton Free Libr, Newton, Mass, libr. survey, with John A. Humphry, 64; 2) Southeast. Mass. Tech. Inst, North Dartmouth, bldg. consult, with Brendan C. Connolly, S.J, 65-66; 3) Villanova Univ, Villanova, Pa, bldg. consult, 65-66; 4) Merrimack Col, North Andover, Mass, bldg. consult, 65-66; 5) Providence Col, Providence, R.I, bldg. consult, 66. Specialties: 1a, 1b, 1e, 1g; 2a, 2b, 2e, 2f, 2g; 3c; 5c; 8a, 8b, 8c, 8d, 8e, 8f.

McPHERSON, KENNETH F, Sept. 9, 25; Director, Morris County Library, 40 E. Hanover Ave, Whippany, N.J. 07981. Home: Pitney Dr, Brookside, N.J. 07926. B.A, 47; B.L.S, 49. Asst. dir, Bloomfield Pub. Libr, 54-59, dir, 59-67. Other: Pres, Libr. Pub. Rels. Coun, 61-62; chmn, Essex County Dirs. Group, 63-64; pres, N.J. Libr. Asn, 64-65. Mem: ALA; N.J. Libr. Asn; Libr. Pub. Rels. Coun. Consult: 1) Easton Pub. Libr, Sixth & Church Sts, Easton, Pa, bldg. requirements survey, 64-66; 2) Madison Pub. Libr, Madison, N.J, bldg. requirements survey, 64-66; 3) Little Falls Pub. Libr, Warren & Stevens Sts, Little Falls, N.J, bldg. requirements study, 65-66; 4) Mountainside Pub. Libr, New Providence Rd. & State Hwy, Route 22, N.J, bldg. requirements study, 65-66; 5) Nassau Libr. Syst, 320 Fulton Ave, Hempstead, N.Y, survey of 10 smaller mem. libr. with recommendations, with Ben E. Grimm, Feb. 66-Dec. 66. Specialties: 1a, 1b, 1c, 1d, 1e, 1f, 1g; 2a, 2b, 2c; 5a, 5c; 7a.

MAPP, EDWARD CHARLES; Chief Librarian, New York City Community College, 300 Jay St, Brooklyn, N.Y. 11201. Home: 1350 New York Ave, Brooklyn, N.Y. 11203. B.A, City Col. New York, 53; M.S, Columbia Univ, 56. Teacher of libr, New York City Bd. Educ, 57-64; reference librn, info. div, N.Y. Pub. Libr, summer 62. Other: Mem. libr. cmt, United Fedn. Teachers, 62-63; faculty adv. student publ, Alexander Hamilton High Sch, 62-63; mem. ad hoc cmt. on use of audiovisual materials in vocational high schs, New York City Bd. Educ, 64; mem. eval. teams, Mid. States Asn, 65-; book reviewer, Libr. J, 66-; mem. prfnl. cmt, New York City Sch. Librns, Asn. Mem: New York City Sch. Librns, Asn; N.Y. Libr. Club; Downtown Brooklyn Cooperating Libr; Acad. Libr. Brooklyn. Publ: Instructor-Librarian Collaboration in a Community College, Jr. Col. J, 3/58; The Library in a Community College, Col. & Res. Libr, 5/58; How We Publicize Our Library, Libr. J, 3/15/59; Library Education for the Educators, High Points, 11/60. Consult: 1) State Univ. N.Y. Albany, helped develop plan to improve the current status of prfnl. librns. in the univ. with recommendations, with

KEY TO CONSULTING SPECIALTIES: 1) ARCHITECTURE AND BUILDINGS, 1a) public libraries, 1b) academic libraries, 1c) school libraries, 1d) special libraries, 1e) library interiors, 1f) furnishings, 1g) site and location, 1h) other architectural; 2) COLLECTIONS: SELECTION, EVALUATION, WEEDING, 2a) adults, 2b) young adults, 2c) children, 2d) subject specialty, 2e) O.P. searches, 2f) rare books, 2g) appraisals, 2h) others; 3) TECHNICAL PROCESSES, 3a) cataloging, 3b) classification systems, 3c) acquisitions, 3d) materials processing, 3e) work flow and cost studies, 3f) others, 4) AUTOMATION, 4a) applications of data processing equipment, 4b) information storage and retrieval systems, 4c) systems analysis, 4d) others

Robert Deilly, May 66; 2) Col. Center, City Univ. New York, 250 Livingston St, Brooklyn, N.Y, orgn. of libr. to serve liberal arts students, June 66. Specialties: 1b, 1c; 2a, 2b, 2d (mass commun, theatre, films), 2h (Negro hist. & literature); 5c; 6a, 6b, 6c; 7a.

MARKE, JULIUS J, Jan. 12, 13; Law Librarian & Professor of Law, New York University, 40 Washington Square S, New York, N.Y. 10003. Home: 4 Peter Cooper Rd, New York, N.Y. 10010. B.S.S, 34; LL.B, 37; B.S. in L.S, 42. Other: Pres, Am. Asn. Law Libr, 62-63; v.pres, Coun. Nat. Libr. Asns, 63-64; chmn, Joint Cmt. Libr. Educ, 63- Mem: Am. Asn. Law Libr; Am. Asn. Law Schs; Am. Bar Asn. Publ: A Catalogue of the Law Collection at New York University with Selected Annotations, Law Center, N.Y. Univ, 53; Dean's List of Recommended Reading for Prelaw and Law Students, Oceana, 58; Bender's Legal Forms, Edward Thompson, Co, 61; Holmes Reader: The Life, Writings, Constitutional Decisions..., Oceana, 64; Vignettes of Legal History, Fred B. Rothman Co, 65; The Law in the United States of America: A Selected Bibliographical Guide (with Charpentier, Andrews & Stern), N.Y. Univ, 65. Consult: 1) Columbia Univ. Sch. Law, New York, N.Y, archit. plans for law libr, 62-63; 2) Univ. Puerto Rico, Río Piedras, complete survey of all law libr. serv. with recommendations, May 65, May 68; 3) Ohio North. Univ. Col. Law Libr, Ada, complete survey of libr. serv, book collection, personnel & role of libr. in law sch. activities, with Dean Ritchie, Nov. 65; 4) Fund for Advancement of Educ, New York, consult. copyright problems as they relate to pub. domain, libr, educ, Apr. 66-; 5) Queen's Univ. Law Libr, Kingston, Ont, Can, complete survey of libr. serv, book collection, personnel, with recommendations, Jan. 68. Specialties: 1e, 1h (law libr); 2d (law); 3a, 3b; 4b; 5a, 5b, 5c; 6a; 7a; 8a.

MARSHALL & BROWN, INC, Architects & Engineers, 920 Main, Suite 1730, TenMain Center, Kansas City, Mo. 64105. Consult: 1) Mid-Continent Pub. Libr. Serv, 605 N. High St, Independence, Mo, preliminary study for multi-million dollar libr. facilities program, 64-65; 2) Mid-Continent Pub. Libr. Serv, consult. to Inst. for Community Studies, Kansas City, Mo, for site selection, bldgs, as part of Metrop. Libr. Study, with Robert H. Rohlf, 67- Specialties: 1a, 1b, 1c, 1d, 1e, 1f, 1g; 4a, 4c; 7a.

MARTIN, ALLIE BETH, June 28, 14; Director, Tulsa City-County Library System, 400 Civic Center, Tulsa, Okla. 74103. Associate, Library Design Associates, Suite 303, 2121 S. Columbia, Tulsa, Okla. 74114. Home: 120 E. 26th, Tulsa, Okla. 74114. B.A, Ark. Col, 35; B.S. in L.S, George Peabody Col. Teachers, 39; M.L.S, Columbia Univ, 49. Head children's & extension depts, Tulsa Pub. Libr, Okla, 49-61; head extention div, Tulsa City-County Libr, 62-63, dir. libr, 63-; spec. lectr. libr. sci, libr. sch, Univ. Okla, 58-; assoc. Libr. Design Assocs, Tulsa, 65- Other: Pres, Ark. Libr. Asn, 46; pres, Okla. Libr. Asn, 56; mem. exec. bd, CSD, 59-61; coun, ALA, 59-61 & 65-; mem. exec. bd, PLA, 65-; mem, Okla. Gov. Coun. Libr, 65-; cert. of award, Okla. State Univ. Mem: ALA; Okla. Libr. Asn; Ark. Libr. Asn; Southwest. Libr. Asn. Publ: Ed. & contrib, Okla. Librn. & Ark. Libr; Triple for Tulsa, Libr. J, 12/1/64; Tulsa in Orbit, Libr. J, 12/1/65. Consult: 1) Rankin Mem. Libr, Neodesha, Kans, bldg. & interior, 65-66; 2) Glendale Pub. Libr, Glendale, Ariz, surveyed present bldg, evaluated recommendation for remodeling & proposed future bldg. develop, with Libr. Design Assocs, 66; 3) Moore Pub. Libr, Pioneer Multi-County Syst, Moore, Okla, new bldg, 66; 4) Pub. Libr, Okla. County Syst, Warr-Acres, Okla, new bldg, with Libr. Design Assocs, 66; 5) Houston Area Survey, Rosenberg Libr, Houston Pub. Libr. & Harris County Libr, Galveston, Tex, survey of the collections with recommendations, with Francis R. St. John, 67- Specialties: 1a, 1e, 1f, 1g; 2a, 2b, 2c; 7a; 8c, 8d, 8f.

MASON, DR. ELLSWORTH, Aug. 25, 17; Director of Library Services, Hofstra University, Hempstead, N.Y. 11550. Home: 71 Meadow St, Garden City, N.Y. 11530. B.A, Yale, 38, M.A, 42, Ph.D, 48. Reference librn, Colo. Col, Colo. Springs, 54-58, librn, 58-63; dir. libr. serv. & prof, Hofstra Univ, Hempstead, N.Y, 63- Other: Pres. South. Dist, Colo. Libr. Asn, 60-62; v.pres. & pres-elect, Bibliog. Center for Res, Denver, 61-63; mem. coun, ALA, 61-65; mem. cmt. on standards, ACRL, 62-; chmn, Colo. Coun. for Libr. Develop, 62-63; Mem: ALA; N.Y. Libr. Asn; Nassau County Libr. Asn. Publ: The Early Joyce: The Book Reviews, 1902-03, Mamulujo Press, 55; The Critical Writings of James Joyce (ed. with Richard Ellmann), Viking, N.Y, Faber & Faber, London & Macmillan of Can, 59, paperback ed, Compass Books, 64; The College Library, Third Invitational Conf. Col. Bldgs. Report, Albany, 64; The Beinecke Siamese Twins: An Objective Review of Yale's New Rare Book Library Building, Col. & Res. Libr, 5/65; A Coast Range Gem: The Los Gatos High School Library, ALA Bull, 3/66; Portrait of an Unborn Child (the new Hofstra Univ. Libr), Hofstra Review, 4/66. Consult: 1) N.Y. Inst. Tech, Westbury, writing program & estimating space needs & audio-visual needs for new libr, Mar. 65-; 2) Fieldston Sch, N.Y, defining libr. needs, writing program, estimating space requirements, analyzing & revising floor plans, Sept. 66-Aug. 67; 3) Elmira Col, Elmira, N.Y, estimating audiovisual needs, estimating space needs, analyzing new curriculum develop. in libr. terms, Jan. 66-; 4) Inter-Am. Univ. of Puerto Rico, San German, writing program, estimating

---

5) PERSONNEL AND RECRUITING, 5a) job evaluation and description, salary recommendations, 5b) recruitment of professionals and management personnel, 5c) administrative organization, 6) PUBLIC RELATIONS, 6a) publications, 6b) publicity programs, 6c) public opinion surveys, 6d) others, 7) SERVICES, 7a) evaluation of current program, 7b) studies of service to special publics, e.g., students, handicapped, aged, etc., 7c) programs for the implementation of new laws, program proposals to governments, 7d) others, 8) COMMUNITY, REGIONAL, STATE PLANNING, 8a) legislative programs, 8b) area analyses, 8c) centralized systems, cooperative arrangements, 8d) development of standards, 8e) state libraries and extension agencies, 8f) regional and statewide surveys, 8g) others, 9) OTHERS.

space needs, estimating audiovisual needs, June 66-; 5) Sarah Lawrence Col, Bronxville, N.Y, writing program, analyzing & revising floor plans, May 67-Apr. 68. Specialties: 1b, 1c; 2d (English literature).

MERRITT, DR. LeROY C, Sept. 10, 12; Dean, School of Librarianship, University of Oregon, Eugene, Ore. 97403. Home: 3935 Mill St, Eugene, Ore. 97405. B.A, 35; Ph.D, 42. Prof. librarianship, Univ. Calif, 46-66; dean, sch. librarianship, Univ. Ore, Eugene, 66- Other: Ed, Newsletter on Intellectual Freedom, ALA, 62-; pres, Asn. Am. Libr. Schs, 66. Mem: ALA; ACRL. Publ: The United States Government as Publisher, Univ. Chicago, 43; The Pattern of Modern Book Reviewing, In: Reviews in Library Book Selection, Wayne State Univ, 58. Consult: 1) Hayward Pub. Libr, Hayward, Calif, survey of resources, serv. & future develop, with E.A. Wight, 55; 2) Oakland Pub. Libr, Oakland, Calif, admin. survey, with E.A. Wight, 55; 3) Arcadia Pub. Libr. Arcadia, Calif, gen. survey, report published, with E.A. Wight, 55; 4) Pac. Grove Pub. Libr, Pacific Grove, Calif, admin. survey, with E.A. Wight, 57; 5) Vallejo Pub. Libr, Vallejo, Calif, admin. survey, report published, with J.P. Danton, 60. Specialties: 2a, 2b, 2c; 3c.

MERSKY, ROY MARTIN, Sept. 1, 25; Professor of Law & Director of Research, University of Texas School of Law Library, Austin, Tex. 78705. Home: 1419 Gaston, Austin, Tex. 78703. B.S, Univ. Wis, 48, LL.B, 52, M.A.L.S, 53. Asst. librn, chief readers' & reference serv, Yale Law Libr, 54-59; dir, Wash. State Law Libr, 59-63; exec. secy. judicial coun. & cmnr. for Wash. court reporters, State of Wash, 59-63; prof. law & law librn, Univ. Colo, 63-65; prof. law & dir. res, Univ. Tex, Austin, 65- Other: Book review ed, Law Libr. Journal, 60- Mem: ALA; ASL; SLA; Colo. Libr. Asn; Am. Asn. Law Libr; Southwest. Wash. Libr. Asn; Order of Coif. Publ: Law Books for Public Libraries, Libr. J, Part I, 7/59, Part II, 8/60; Application of Mechanical and Electronic Devices to Legal Literature, Libr. Trends, 1/63; Libraries in the United States: Library Laws, In: Encyclopedia Americana, 63; Introductory Essay on the Literature of Future Interests, Vanderbilt Law Review, 10/64; Water Law Bibliography, 1847-1965: Source Book on U.S. Water and Irrigation Studies—Legal, Economic, and Political (Compiler with J. Myron Jacobstein), Wash, Jefferson Law Book Co, 66; Special Issue on Law Library Architecture (ed), Law Libr. J, spring 67. Consult: 1) Lawyers Cmt. for Civil Rights under the Law, 1875 Connecticut Ave. N.W, Wash, D.C, established libr. in br. office in Jackson, Miss, Apr. 65; 2) Nat. Col. State Trial Judges, Univ. Nev, Reno, set up libr. doing ordering of books, selections & recommendation of some of the personnel, July 65-; 3) Univ. Houston, Houston, Tex, design & construction of new law sch. bldg. & libr, Nov. 65-; 4) Office of Econ. Opportunity, Wash, D.C, set up legal serv. office in neighborhood areas, July 66- Specialties: 1d; 2d (law), 2f, 2g; 3c; 4b; 5c; 7c; 8a, 8g (establish county law libr).

METCALF, DR. KEYES D, 1889; Library Consultant, 68 Fairmont St, Belmont, Mass. 02178. B.A, Oberlin Col, 11, Litt.D, 39; L.H.D, Yale Univ, 46; LL.D, Harvard Univ, 51, Univ. Toronto, 54; Marquette Univ, 58, St. Louis Univ, 59, Grinnell Col, 59, Univ. Notre Dame, 64; Litt.D, Brandeis Univ, 59, Bowdoin Col, 65. Adjunct prof, Rutgers Univ, 55-58; Fulbright lectr, Australia, 58-59; Fulbright distinguished scholar, Queen's Univ, Belfast, 66; lect, Inst. Advanced Archit. Studies, York, Eng, 66. Other: Pres, ALA, 42-43; exec. secy, Asn. Res. Libr, 38-41. Mem: ALA; Bibliog. Soc. Am; British Bibliog. Soc; Asn. Res. Libr; ACRL; Mass. Libr. Asn. Publ: Planning Academic Libraries, McGraw-Hill, 65; Cooperation for Libraries in Maine, 61. Consult: 1) Nat. Libr. of Australia, new bldg, 61-65; 2) Tulane Univ, New Orleans, La, new univ. libr, 64-66; 3) Joint Univ, Nashville, Tenn, libr. bldg. additions, 65-66; 4) Notre Dame Univ, Notre Dame, Ind, study of orgn, 65-66; 5) N.Y. Pub. Libr, New York, N.Y, study of cataloging problems, 65-66. Specialties: 1b, 1e, 1f, 1g; 2a; 3a, 3c; 5c; 7a; 8c, 8f.

MICHNIEWSKI, HENRY J, Dec. 25, 29. Coordinator, LSCA, New Jersey State Library, Trenton, N.J. 08608. Home: 500 Maple Ave, Trenton, N.J. 08648. M.L.S, Rutgers Univ. Adult serv. specialist, Brooklyn Pub. Libr, Brooklyn, N.Y, 55-57; head, gen. reading dept, Flint Pub. Libr, Flint, Mich, 57-62; coordinator, LSCA, N.J. State Libr, Trenton, 62- Other: Mem, planning cmt, Mich. Libr. Asn; mem, libr. develop. cmt, N.J. Libr. Asn; mem, ALA/CLA cmt, ALA. Mem: N.Y. Libr. Asn; Mich. Libr. Asn; N.J. Libr. Asn; ALA. Consult: 1) S. Huntington Pub. Libr, South Huntington, N.Y, site selection, with Edwin Beckerman, 65; 2) Tredyffrin Township, Pa, Plan for libr. develop, site selection, 65; 3) Bradford, Wyo, Sullivan County Libraries, Troy, Pa, survey with plan for growth, 66. Specialties: 1g; 2a; 7a, 7b, 7c; 8b, 8c, 8d.

MILCZEWSKI, MARION A, Feb. 12, 12; Director of Libraries, University of Washington Library, Seattle, Wash. 98105. Home: 3621 N.E. 100th St, Seattle, Wash. 98125. A.B, 36; B.S.L.S, 38; M.S, 40. Asst. univ. librn, Univ. Calif. Libr, Berkeley, 49-60; dir. libr, Univ. Washington Libr, Seattle, 60- Other: Chmn, int. relations cmt, ALA, 64-68, mem. coun, 64- & councilor-at-large, 66-67. Mem: ALA; Pac. Northwest Libr. Asn; Wash. Libr. Asn; Latin Am. Studies Asn. Publ: Libraries of the Southeast (with L.R. Wilson), Univ. N.C, 49; A

KEY TO CONSULTING SPECIALTIES: 1) ARCHITECTURE AND BUILDINGS, 1a) public libraries, 1b) academic libraries, 1c) school libraries, 1d) special libraries, 1e) library interiors, 1f) furnishings, 1g) site and location, 1h) other architectural; 2) COLLECTIONS: SELECTION, EVALUATION, WEEDING, 2a) adults, 2b) young adults, 2c) children, 2d) subject specialty, 2e) O.P. searches, 2f) rare books, 2g) appraisals, 2h) others; 3) TECHNICAL PROCESSES, 3a) cataloging, 3b) classification systems, 3c) acquisitions, 3d) materials processing, 3e) work flow and cost studies, 3f) others, 4) AUTOMATION, 4a) applications of data processing equipment, 4b) information storage and retrieval systems, 4c) systems analysis, 4d) others

Report of a Survey and Proposals for Libraries of Universidad del Valle, Univ. del Valle, Colombia, 62; Report and Recommendations for Libraries of Universidad de Oriente, Venezuela, Univ. Wash. Libr, 63; Libraries of the Universidad Javeriana, Their Present State and Some Recommendations for the Future, Pontificia Univ, Javeriana, Colombia, 64; Structural Organization of Latin American University Libraries, Pan Am. Union, 66. Consult: 1) Univ. del Valle, Cali, Colombia, consult. on libr. for Rockefeller Found, July-Aug. 62, July 68; 2) Univ. de Oriente, Cumana, Venezuela, consult. on libr. syst. for Ford Found, July 63; 3) Whitworth Col, Spokane, Wash, consult. on libr, Oct. 63; 4) Pontificia Univ. Javeriana, Bogota, Colombia, consult. on libr. orgn. for Ford Found, June 64; 5) Univ. de Los Andes, Bogota, Colombia, consult. on libr. orgn. for Ford Found, June 64. Specialties: 1b; 5c; 8f; 9 (orgn. of acad. libr).

MILES, PAUL M, Mar. 14, 17; Assistant University Librarian, University of California, Los Angeles, Calif. 90024. Home: 18824 Ingomar St, Reseda, Calif. 91335. B.A, Univ. Denver, 40; M.A, Univ. Calif, Berkeley, 57, M.L.S, 50. Bus. admin. librn, Univ. Calif, Los Angeles, 54-59, asst. univ. librn, 59-, on leave as libr. coordinator, Univ. Calif-Univ. Chile Exchange Program, 65-67. Other: Mem. bldgs. & equipment cmt, Calif. Libr. Asn, 64-65; pres, Univ. Calif. Libr. Schs. Alumni Asn, 65. Mem: ALA; Calif. Libr. Asn. Publ: Industrial Relations Theses and Dissertations (ed), 55-58; Bibliotecas de la Universidad Nacional de Colombia, Bogota, 62; Bibliotecas de la Universidad de Chile, Santiago, 65; UCLA in Three Stages, Libr. J, 10/1/64. Consult: 1) Nat. Univ. Colombia, Bogota, Colombia, survey of libr. with recommendations for reorgn, 62; 2) Ariz. State Univ, Tempe, Ariz, survey, site recommendation & reorgn. of collections & serv. between old & new bldg, 62; 3) Univ. Calif, Irvine, Calif, libr. bldg. consult, new main libr, Jan. 63; 4) Univ. Calif, Davis, Calif, libr. bldg. consult, addition to main libr, with Donald C. Davidson, June 63; 5) Univ. Chile, Santiago, Chile, survey of libr. with recommendations for reorgn. & integration, 65-67. Specialties: 1b, 1e, 1f, 1g; 3d, 3f (photographic methods).

MILLER, ERNEST I, Feb. 27, 07; Director, Public Library of Cincinnati, Cincinnati, Ohio 45202. Home: 6955 Nolen Circle, Cincinnati, Ohio 45227. A.B, Elmhurst Col, 31; B.L.S, Univ. Ill, 32; M.A, Univ. Tenn, 41. Dir, Pub. Libr. Cincinnati, Ohio, 55- Other: Past pres, Mich. & Ohio Libr. Asns; chmn. libr. archit. cmt, ALA, 44-47; chmn. bldg. cmt, pub. libr. div, 47-49. Mem: ALA; Ohio Libr. Asn. Consult: 1) Coral Gables Pub. Libr, Coral Gables, Fla, bldg. program, with Libr. Bldg. Consults, Inc, 61; 2) Nashville Pub. Libr, Nashville, Tenn, bldg. program, with Harry Peterson & Libr. Bldg. Consults, Inc, 63; 3) Ft. Wayne Pub. Libr, Ft. Wayne, Ind, bldg. program & plan review, with Libr. Bldg. Consults, Inc, 64-65; 4) Hillside Pub. Libr, Hillside, Ill, bldg. program, with Libr. Bldg. Consults, Inc, 66; 5) Harvey Pub. Libr, Harvey, Ill, bldg. program, site review, with Libr. Bldg. Consults, Inc, 66. Specialties: 1a, 1g.

MILLER, (J) GORMLY, Jan. 5, 14; Assistant Director of Libraries & Professor, School of Industrial & Labor Relations, Cornell University, Ithaca, N.Y. 14850. Home: 401 Turner Place, Ithaca, N.Y. 14850. A.B, Univ. Rochester, 36; B.S.(libr. serv), Columbia Univ, 38. Librn, N.Y. State Sch. Industrial & Labor Relations, Cornell Univ, Ithaca, N.Y, 46-64, prof, 56-, asst. dir. personnel & budget, Cornell Univ. Libr, 62- Other: Cmnr, Ithaca Civil Serv. Cmn, N.Y, 64- Mem: SLA; ALA; N.Y. Libr. Asn; Industrial Relations Res. Asn. Consult: 1) Dept. Labor Relations of INSORA, Univ. Chile, Santiago, recommendations for develop. of libr. program, Dec. 62; 2) Int. Labour Office, Geneva, Switzerland, survey of libr. & review of its program, Apr-May 64; 3) U.S. Dept. Labor, Wash, D.C, preparation of report on proposed space program for U.S. Dept. Labor Libr, July-Aug. 65; 4) Puerto Rico Dept. Labor, San Juan, report on proposed establishment of labor libr. & info. center, Aug. 65; 5) U.S. Dept. Labor, recommendations concerning expanded program of libr. serv. & develop. of specialized libr. resources, 65- Specialties: 1b, 1d; 2d (labor & related fields); 7a, 7b, 7c, 7d; 8a, 8c; 9 (all aspects of document. & libr. sources related to materials & serv. in the labor & manpower field).

MILLER, MRS. MELISSA, Oct. 6, 08; Library Consultant, Warren Consolidated Schools and Head Librarian, Warren High School Library, 5460 Arden, Warren, Mich. 48092. Home: Norfolk Farm, Romeo, Mich. 48065. B.Sc, 61; M.A.L.S, 65. Librn, Fuhrmann Jr. High Sch, 61-62; head librn, Warren Consolidated Cent. AV Libr. & High Sch. Libr, Warren, Mich, 62-66, libr. consult, Warren Consolidated Schs. & head librn, high sch. libr, 66- Other: Mem, supv. training librn. cmt, Wayne State Univ, 64; chmn, Warren Sec. Librns, 64-65; hostess, Mich. Asn. Sch. Librns, 66. Mem: ALA; Mich. Asn. Sch. Librns; Univ. Mich. Libr. Sci. Alumni Asn. Publ: The Library at School, Educ. Courier, Toronto, 4/34. Consult: 1) Butcher & Hartzig Jr. High Schs, Warren, Mich, archit, interiors & furnishings, 62-63; 2) Warren Woods High Sch, Warren Woods, Mich, libr. collection reference, 62-63; 3) Clintondale High Sch, Mt. Clemens, Mich, consult. on archit, site location, interior, 63-64. Specialties: 1c, 1d, 1e, 1f; 2b; 3c, 3d, 3e; 4a, 4b; 5b; 6a; 7a, 7b; 8c, 8d, 8f.

MILLER, DR. ROBERT A, Apr. 19, 07; Director of Libraries, Indiana University Libraries, Bloomington, Ind. 47401. Home: 1316 Nancy St,

Bloomington, Ind. 47401. B.A, 29; B.L.S, 30; Ph.D, 36. Dir. libr, Indiana Univ, 42- Consult: 1) Ind. Univ, Bloomington, new bldg. survey, design, interiors, equipment, 63-68; 2) Univ. Mo, Kansas City, new bldg. survey & design, 65-68; 3) S.Dak. Sch. Mines & Tech, Rapid City, new bldg. survey & design, 67-68; 4) Mid. Tenn. State Univ, Murfreesboro, new bldg. survey, design & interiors, 68; 5) North. Ill. Univ, De Kalb, new bldg. survey, 68. Specialties: 1b; 3a, 3c; 5c.

MILLS, JESSE C, Feb. 13, 21; Undergraduate Librarian, University of Tennessee, Knoxville, Tenn. 37916. Home: 2001 Emoriland Blvd, Knoxville, Tenn. 37917. B.S, Harvard Univ, 42; M.A, Univ. Tenn, 49; M.S.L.S, Rutgers Univ, 60. Head circulation dept, Univ. Pa. Libr, Phila, 56, head serv. div, 57-63, asst. dir. libr, 63-66. Other: Mem. senate, Univ. Tenn, chmn. univ. cmt. to organize sch. libr. sci. Mem: Tenn. Libr. Asn; ACRL. Publ: Pennsylvania's Sandwich, Libr. J, 12/1/62; Catalog of Misfortune, Libr. J, 12/1/67. Consult: 1) Charles Patterson Van Pelt Libr, Univ. Pa, Dietrich Graduate Center, bldg. consult, 58-62, 64-67; 2) Phila. Col. Art, Broad & Pine Sts, Phila, Pa, critique of drawings & plans for new libr, advice on preparation of program, Dec. 65-Jan. 66; 3) Morristown-Hamblen Pub. Libr, Morristown, Tenn, preparation of preliminary program for new pub. libr, orgn, collection, bldg. & staffing & budget, Jan-Feb. 66; 4) High Point Col. Libr, High Point, N.C, review & recommendations for libr. bldg. problems, Apr. 68-; 5) Morris Harvey Col. Libr, Charleston, W.Va, libr. bldg, Aug. 68- Specialties: 1a, 1b, 1d, 1e, 1f, 1g, 1h (programs & budgets); 2a, 2d (Am. literature), 2f, 2h (acad. res. collections); 4a, 4b; 5c; 6a, 6b; 7a; 8c.

MINDER, THOMAS L, Apr. 23, 25; Director, Pittsburgh Regional Library Center, Chatham College, Pittsburgh, Pa. 15232. B.S, Univ. Chicago, 54, M.A, 63. Math. & gen. sci. librn, Columbia Univ, 54-56; librn, res. div, Curtiss-Wright Corp, 56-58; data processing & col. engineering librn, Pa. State Univ, 58-64; systs. analyst, fed. systs. div, IBM Corp, 64-66; dir, Pittsburgh Regional Libr. Center, Chatham Col, Pittsburgh, Pa, 66- Other: Mem, info. systs. cmt, Am. Soc. Engineering Educ, 63-67; chmn. document. sect. Wash. & mem, govt. info. serv. cmt, SLA, 65-67. Mem: ALA; SLA; Fedn. Int. Document; Am. Soc. Info. Sci. Publ: On the Fundamental Theories of Bibliographic Organization, Am. Document, 1/57; A Review of the Engineers Joint Council Information Symposium and the Information Retrieval Program, J. Engineering Educ, 3/62; The Automation of the Penn State Library Acquisitions Department, Proc. 11th Annual Meeting Am. Document Inst, 64; Summary of the Dea's Colloquy on Recorded Information in Engineering Practice and Teaching, Spec. Libr, 2/64; Least Cost Searching Sequence,

Col. & Res. Libr, 3/64; Library Systems Analysis—A Job Description, Col. & Res. Libr, 7/66. Consult: 1) U.S. Govt, eval. of 4 EDP & ADP info. systs, 64-66; 2) Syracuse Univ, Syracuse, N.Y, eval. of the libr. automation program, 66. Specialties: 3a, 3c, 3d, 3e; 4a, 4c; 7a; 8c, 8d; 9 (libr. mgt, info. systs).

MINKER, DR. JACK, July 4, 27; Scientific Consultant, Auerbach Corporation, 1501 Wilson Blvd, Arlington, Va. 22209. Associate Professor of Computer Science, University of Maryland, College Park, Md. 20740. Home: 6913 Millwood Rd, Bethesda, Md. 20034. B.A.(math), 49; M.S.(math), 50; Ph.D.(math), 59. Mgr. info. tech, Radio Corp. Am, 57-63; dir. tech. staff, Auerbach Corp, Arlington, Va, 63- Other: Co-chmn, Nat. Conf. Info. Storage & Retrieval, Asn. Computing Machinery, 60, mem. program cmt, 1964 spring joint computer conf. & program chmn, 1967 nat. conf; mem. staff, grad. sch, Nat. Insts. Health, 65 & 66; mem. cmt. info. storage & retrieval, Inst. Electrical & Electronics Engineers, 66. Mem: Am. Soc. Info. Sci; Asn. Computing Machinery. Publ: Digital Simulation of Complex Traffic Problems in Communications Systems (with L. Brotman), Opers. Res, 10/57; A Multi-Level File Structure for Information Processing (with W.E. Shindle, L. Miller & W.G. Reed), Proc. West. Joint Computer Conf. San Francisco, Calif, 5/60; The Design and Simulation of an Information Processing System (with H. Gurk), J. Asn. Computing Machinery, 4/61; A Study of the Utility of Associative Memory Processors (with J. Dugan, R. Green & W.E. Shindle), In: Proceedings—Association of Computing Machinery National Meeting, 66; File and Data Management Systems (with J. Sable), In: Second ADI Annual Review of Information Science and Technology. Consult: 1) Nat. Libr. Med, Bethesda, Md, consulting on MEDLARS, with J. Dugan & N. Hardwick; 2) Rome Air Develop. Center, Griffiss Air Force Base, Rome, N.Y, study the utility of associative memory processors, with J. Dugan, W.E. Shindle, J. Mulford & R. Green; 3) Gen. Serv. Admin, Wash, D.C, tradeoff studies of digital equipment & microfilm store, with M. Dodge. Specialties: 3a, 3b, 3c, 3d, 3e; 4a, 4b, 4c, 4d; 8d, 8e.

MITCHELL, ELEANOR, Apr. 4, 07; 4421 Upland Dr, Alexandria, Va. 22310. B.A, Douglass Col, 28, hon. D.Lett, 68; B.S.L.S, Columbia Univ, 29; M.A, Smith Col, 36. Exec. dir. fine arts cmt, People-to-People Program, Wash, D.C, 57-61; secy. pro tem, Books for the People Fund, Inc, Wash, D.C, 61-62; biblio. asst, Int. Rice Res. Inst, Rockefeller Found. Bibliog. Project, Wash, D.C, 62-63; consult, Hispanic Found, Libr. Congress, 63; libr. consult, Universidad Católica del Ecuador, Quito, Ecuador (St. Louis Univ-USAID contract), 63-68. Other: Mem, visual methods cmt, ALA, 38-40, joint cmt. on educ. films & libr, 40-41, adv. cmt. on

---

KEY TO CONSULTING SPECIALTIES: 1) ARCHITECTURE AND BUILDINGS, 1a) public libraries, 1b) academic libraries, 1c) school libraries, 1d) special libraries, 1e) library interiors, 1f) furnishings, 1g) site and location, 1h) other architectural; 2) COLLECTIONS: SELECTION, EVALUATION, WEEDING, 2a) adults, 2b) young adults, 2c) children, 2d) subject specialty, 2e) O.P. searches, 2f) rare books, 2g) appraisals, 2h) others; 3) TECHNICAL PROCESSES, 3a) cataloging, 3b) classification systems, 3c) acquisitions, 3d) materials processing, 3e) work flow and cost studies, 3f) others, 4) AUTOMATION, 4a) applications of data processing equipment, 4b) information storage and retrieval systems, 4c) systems analysis, 4d) others

libr. cooperation with Latin Am, 42-44, int. relations bd, cmt. on libr. cooperation with Latin Am, 44-48; rep, int. exec. coun, Escuela Interamericana de Bibliotecología, Universidad de Antioquia, Medellín, Colombia, 56-65; mem, awards cmt, SLA, 47-48; mem, nat. adv. cmt, Educ. & Religious Radio & TV Asn, 60-63. Mem: ALA; ACRL; SLA. Publ: The Photograph Collection and Its Problems, Col. & Res. Libr, 3/42; Planning and Planting Your Garden (co-compiler), Bull. New York Pub. Libr, 5/50; Art and the People-to-People Program, Art Educ. Bull, 9/58; Contemporary Colombia: Its Bibliographic Present and Future, In: The Caribbean: Contemporary Colombia, Univ. Fla, 62; Books for the People Fund, Inc, D.C. Libr, 4/62; Ecuador: Pilot Project in the Andes, int. issue, Libr. J, 11/68. Consult: 1) Montclair Free Pub. Libr, Montclair, N.J, libr. collections & weeding, Apr-Sept, 55; 2) Biblioteca Pública Departmental, Cali, Colombia, U.S. specialist, Dept. of State Educ. Exchange Serv; reorgn. of collections, tech. processes, serv; conducted two in-serv. training courses for staff & other students; served as consult. to libr. of Centro Colombo-Americano, Barranquilla, Nov. 55-Nov. 56; 3) Escuela Interamericana de Bibliotecología, Medellín, Colombia, U.S. specialist, Dept. of State Educ. Exchange Serv; assisted in orgn. of libr. sch; planning prospectus, distribution of prospectus; promotion; planning sch. quarters, equipment, furnishings; program planning, Nov. 56-June 57; 4) Hispanic Found, Libr. of Congress, Washington, D.C, direction of preparation of catalog, Spanish & Portuguese Translations of U.S. Books, 1955-1962; assisted in preparation of directory of Latin Americanists, Apr-Aug. 63; 5) Universidad Católica del Ecuador, Quito, orgn. of univ. libr; remodeling of quarters; develop. of collections; reorgn. of routines & serv; in-serv. training courses for staff & other Ecuadorian univ. librns. & students; consult. to Universidad Cent, Binat. Centers, Oct. 63-Jan. 68. Specialties: 1a, 1b, 1c, 1d, 1e, 1f, 1g; 2a, 2b, 2c, 2d (art); 3a, 3b, 3c, 3d; 5a, 5b, 5c; 7a, 7b; 9 (gen. admin; Latin Am. area specialist; able to do consulting in Spanish, Italian, French).

MITCHELL, VERNON R, 1915, Independent Consultant, Particular Consulting Services, 412 N. Third St, Purcell, Okla. 73080. B.A, Okla. State Univ, 48; B.L.S, Univ. Okla, 69. Bus. consult, 58-64; pub. librn, 65-66; independent libr. consult, 65- Mem: ALA; SLA. Consult: 1) West. Savings and Loan Asn, 3030 N. Central Ave, Phoenix, Ariz, wrote specifications for furniture; cataloging & operating procedures, Feb. 66-Jan. 67; 2) First Nat. Bank, 411 N. Central Ave, Phoenix, Ariz, consolidated holdings of various depts, assessing objectives to enhance res. aspect of the collection, cataloging & acquisition, bldg. up collections in finance, statist, reference & industrial areas, Apr-Sept. 67; 3) Boysville Home for Boys, Austin Highway, San Antonio, Tex, surveyed elem. & high schs. serving students from this orgn, planning a libr. collection to supplement their serv; new bldg. construction, interior & furnishings, lighting; evaluated & culled old book stock, selected supplementary collection, with emphasis on occupational materials, Oct. 67-; 4) Okla. State Hq. Selective Serv, Leonhardt Bldg, 228 Robt. E. Kerr Ave, Oklahoma City, Okla, survey & feasibility study for cent. info. syst. to provide reference serv. to 77 county offices, May 68-; 5) McAllen Boys Club, 110 S. Tenth St, McAllen, Tex, complete reassessment of libr. facility, adequate lighting standards, sound-proofing insulation; culled collection, recommended modified cataloging, June-Aug. 68. Specialties: 1d, 1e, 1f; 2a, 2b, 2c, 2d (bus, finance, aviation, occupational); 3a, 3b; 4a, 4c; 7a, 7b; 9 (eval. & specification of libr. lighting requirements).

MOHRHARDT, CHARLES M, Aug. 3, 04; Interim Director, Detroit Public Library, Detroit, Mich, 48202. Charles M. Mohrhardt & Ralph A. Ulveling, Associated Library Building Consultants, 3996 Lincoln Dr, Birmingham, Mich. 48010. B.S.(mechanical engineering), Mich. State Univ, 26; B.S.(libr. sci), Columbia Univ, 28. Assoc. dir, Detroit Pub. Libr, Mich, 41-67. Other: Mem, libr. cmt, Engineering Soc. Detroit, 50-, chmn, 58 & 63; mem, Kresge-Hooker Sci. Libr. Assocs. Bd, 50-, pres, 65; mem, Libr. Archit. & Bldg. Planning Cmt, 51-54. Mem: ALA; Mich. Libr. Asn. Publ: Public Libraries, Archit. Record, 12/52; Buildings and Equipment, Libr. Trends, 4/53; American Memorial Library (Berlin, Germany), Libr. J, 3/15/54; A Building Programme for a Public Library, UNESCO Pub. Libr. Manual 7, Pub. Libr. for Asia, 56; Medillíns (Colombia) Pilot Library, Libr. J, 11/15/56; Automation in the Detroit Public Library, ALA Bull, 10/65. Consult: 1) Buffalo & Erie County Pub. Libr, Buffalo, N.Y, planning & layout of new bldg, with Ralph A. Ulveling, 56-65; 2) Tufts Libr, Weymouth, Mass, planning & layout of new bldg, with Ralph A. Ulveling, 61-65; 3) Elyria Pub. Libr, Elyria, Ohio, planning & layout of new bldg, with Ralph A. Ulveling, 62-66; 4) Bethlehem Pub. Libr, Bethlehem, Pa, planning & layout of new bldg, with Ralph A. Ulveling, 63-66; 5) Dearborn Pub. Libr, Dearborn, Mich, planning & layout of new bldg, with Ralph A. Ulveling, 63-66. Specialties: 1a, 1f, 1g.

MOLOD, SAMUEL E, Aug. 27, 21; Associate State Librarian, Connecticut State Library, Hartford, Conn. 06106. Home: 47 Huntington Dr, West Hartford, Conn. 06117. B.S, 43; M.A, 46; M.A.L.S, 53. Consult, Mich. State Libr, 53-62; dir, James V. Brown Libr, Williamsport, Pa, 62-66; assoc. state librn, Conn. State Libr, 66- Mem: ALA; Conn. Libr. Asn. Consult: 1) Mifflin County Libr, Lewistown, Pa, complete libr. survey, 65; 2) Montoursville Pub. Libr, Montoursville, Pa, bldg. construction, 65; 3) Muncy Pub. Libr,

---

5) PERSONNEL AND RECRUITING, 5a) job evaluation and description, salary recommendations, 5b) recruitment of professionals and management personnel, 5c) administrative organization, 6) PUBLIC RELATIONS, 6a) publications, 6b) publicity programs, 6c) public opinion surveys, 6d) others, 7) SERVICES, 7a) evaluation of current program, 7b) studies of service to special publics, e.g., students, handicapped, aged, etc., 7c) programs for the implementation of new laws, program proposals to governments, 7d) others, 8) COMMUNITY, REGIONAL, STATE PLANNING, 8a) legislative programs, 8b) area analyses, 8c) centralized systems, cooperative arrangements, 8d) development of standards, 8e) state libraries and extension agencies, 8f) regional and statewide surveys, 8g) others, 9) OTHERS.

Muncy, Pa, services, 65; 4) Hughesville. Pub. Libr, Hughesville, Pa, services, 65-66; 5) Norwich, Conn, libr. serv, 68. Specialties: 1a; 2a, 2b, 2c; 5a, 5b, 5c; 6a, 6b, 6c; 7a, 7b, 7c; 8a, 8b, 8c, 8d, 8e, 8f.

MONTGOMERY, JAMES W, Mar. 7, 25; Associate Librarian (Medicine), New York State Psychiatric Institute Library, 722 W. 168th St, New York, N.Y. 10032. Home: Apt. 7A, 245 W. 107th St, New York, N.Y. 10025. B.A, 48; B.Mus, 48; M.A, 49; M.S, 59; med. libr. cert, 62. Asst. librn, N.Y. State Psychiatric Inst. Libr, New York, N.Y, 59-61, sr. librn, 62-68, assoc. librn.(med), 68- Other: Med. librn, Hillside Hosp, Glen Oaks, N.Y, 61-62; asst. dept. psychiatry, Columbia Univ. Col. Physicians & Surgeons, 62- Mem: Med. Libr. Asn; ALA; SLA; Music Libr. Asn; New York Libr. Asn. Consult: 1) Hillside Hosp, P.O. Box 38, Glen Oaks, N.Y, plans for new psychiatric libr. in existing bldg, retained as consult. to both the prfnl. (psychiatric) & the patient libr, 62-; 2) New York City Community Mental Health Bd, 93 Worth St, New York, N.Y, determined space requirements & proposed budget needs for new libr, recommended serial & monograph acquisitions, recommended libr. equipment, 65; 3) Postgrad. Center for Mental Health, 124 E. 28th St, New York, recommended budget figures, engagement of prfnl. librn, acquisitions program, space expansion, 65; 4) Inst. for Basic Res. in Mental Retardation, Staten Island, N.Y, recommended libr. furnishing & equipment, prepared detailed floor plan, 65-66; 5) Washington Heights-West Harlem Comprehensive Community Mental Health Center, New York, prepared preliminary program of requirements for res. & patient libr, 67. Specialties: 1h (mental hosp. res. & patient libr); 2d (psychiatry, psychoanalysis, neurology); 4d (IBM 1050 syst); 7d (serv. to psychiatrists & allied prfnl. & student clientele).

MORAN, VIRGINIA L, Research Project Librarian, Research Foundation, New York State Department of Mental Hygiene, Kings Park State Hospital, Kings Park, N.Y. 11754. Home: 107 Unqua Rd, Massapequa, N.Y. 11758. A.B, Mt. St. Vincent Col; Sc.B.(libr. serv), Columbia Univ; A.M, N.Y. Univ. Dir, Massapequa Pub. Libr, 54-59; dist. librn, Syosset Pub. Schs, 59-60; dir, Half Hollow Hills Community Libr, 60-64; dir, Seaford Pub. Libr, Seaford, N.Y, 64-68. Other: Mem. bd. dirs, Nassau County Libr. Asn, 56-58 & 63-64; mem. bd. dirs, Suffolk County Libr. Asn, 61-64; ed, Odds & Bookends, 64- Mem: ALA; Nassau County Libr. Asn; N.Y. Libr. Asn; Suffolk County Libr. Asn; Am. Asn. Sch. Adminstr; Nat. Educ. Asn. Publ: Portrait, College Library Study, Libr. J, 9/15/52; Public Library Study (with others), Libr. J, 10/1/53; Massapequa's New Addition (with George J. Dippell), Libr. J, 9/1/55; What Good Public Relations did at Massapequa, Odds & Book Ends, winter 56; Seaford Finances a Library Building, Odds & Bookends, winter 67. Consult: 1) N.Y. State Libr, Albany, N.Y, survey of col. libr, teachers col. libr, pub. libr, with Charles Gosnell, Mason Tolman, 51, 52 & 53; 2) City Sch. Dist. New Rochelle, North Ave, New Rochelle, N.Y, established curriculum libr. in new bldg, organized book collection, serv. & did layout, 62-63; 3) St. William the Abbott Elem. Sch, Jackson Ave, Seaford, N.Y, assisted in establishment of elem. sch. libr, trained volunteers, with Mother Virginia, 64. Specialties: 1a, 1c; 2a, 2b, 2c, 2d (educ, literature); 3d; 6b; 8g (planned serv. of community libr. for adults, young adults & children).

MORELAND, CARROLL C, Dec. 20, 03; Librarian, Cromwell Library, American Bar Foundation, 1155 E. 60th St, Chicago, Ill. 60637. Home: 20617 Promethian Way, Olympia Fields, Ill. 60461. A.B, 24; LL.B, 27; B.S.(libr. sci), 37. Librn, Univ. Pa. Law Sch, 46-62; libr. adv, inst. pub. & bus. admin, Univ. Karachi, 59-61; vis. prof. libr. sci, Univ. Dacca & libr. adv. to Pakistan rep, Asia Found, 62-64; assoc. librn, Cromwell Libr, Am. Bar Found, Chicago, Ill, 64-66, librn, 66- Other: Pres, Am. Asn. Law Libr, 55-56; mem. adv. cmt, SLA, 51-53 & 56-58; mem. cmt. court facilities, Am. Bar Asn, 66-; dir, Nat. Seminar on Role of Libr. in Nat. Develop, Rawalpindi, Pakistan, Nov. 67. Mem: SLA; Am. Asn. Law Libr; Pakistan Libr. Asn. Publ: Legal Research (co-auth), Practising Law Inst, N.Y, 46; Research in Pennsylvania Law (co-auth), Oceana, 53; Equal Justice Under Law, Oceana, 57; The Legislative History of Statutory Revision in Pennsylvania, Am. J. Legal Hist, 1: 197-211; Pennsylvania's Statutory Imbroglio (co-auth), Univ. Pa. Law Review, 108: 1093-1123. Consult: 1) San Diego County Law Libr, San Diego, Calif, survey of collection & facilities, develop. of plans for future growth, June-July 66; 2) Memphis & Shelby County Law Libr, Courthouse, Memphis, Tenn, survey of holdings with recommendations, suggested arrangement of materials & space allocations, Nov. 66; 3) Baltimore County Law Libr, Towson, Md, plans for space allocation, arrangement of materials, facilities, 68. Specialties: 1d, 1h (law); 2d (law); 3a, 3c; 5c; 7a, 7b.

MORGAN, JOHN F, June 17, 23; Independent Consultant, P.O. Box 854, Point Lookout, N.Y. 11569. B.A, N.Y. Univ, 49; M.S.(libr. sci), Columbia Univ, 50. Asst. librn, Republic Aviation Corp, Farmingdale, N.Y, 56-58; librn, Filtron Co, Flushing, N.Y, 59-61; sr. librn, reference dept, East Meadow Pub. Libr, 61-62; libr. supvr, Fairchild Stratos, Wyandanch, N.Y, 62-63. Publ: Appraisal of Information Retrieval Systems for Engineering Libraries: State of the Art Report, Republic Aviation Corp, 57. Consult: 1) Cam Develop. & Micro. Components, Inc, New Canaan, Conn, gen. libr. con-

---

KEY TO CONSULTING SPECIALTIES: 1) ARCHITECTURE AND BUILDINGS, 1a) public libraries, 1b) academic libraries, 1c) school libraries, 1d) special libraries, 1e) library interiors, 1f) furnishings, 1g) site and location, 1h) other architectural; 2) COLLECTIONS: SELECTION, EVALUATION, WEEDING, 2a) adults, 2b) young adults, 2c) children, 2d) subject specialty, 2e) O.P. searches, 2f) rare books, 2g) appraisals, 2h) others; 3) TECHNICAL PROCESSES, 3a) cataloging, 3b) classification systems, 3c) acquisitions, 3d) materials processing, 3e) work flow and cost studies, 3f) others, 4) AUTOMATION, 4a) applications of data processing equipment, 4b) information storage and retrieval systems, 4c) systems analysis, 4d) others

sult, 67- Specialties: 1d, 1g; 2a, 2d (engineering, electronics, med, physical sci); 3a, 3b, 3c, 3d, 3f (handling of govt. documents); 4b; 5c; 6a, 6c; 7a; 8d; 9 (control of classified documents for govt. contractors).

MORIARTY, JOHN H, Nov. 9, 03; Director of Libraries & Audio-Visual Center, Purdue University Libraries, Lafayette, Ind. 47907. Home: 168 Drury Lane, West Lafayette, Ind. 47906. B.A, 26; B.S. in L.S, 34; M.S. in L.S, 38. Dir. libr. & audio-visual center, Purdue Univ, Lafayette, Ind, 44- Other: Pres, Ind. chap, SLA, 47-48; coun, ALA, 47-49 & 64-67; pres, Ind. Libr. Asn, 52-53; chmn. engineering sch. librns. cmt, Am. Soc. Engineering Educ, 54-55; pres, Univ. Film Producers Asn, 58-60. Mem: ALA; SLA; Am. Soc. Info. Sci; Univ. Film Producers Asn; Am. Soc. Engineering Educ. Publ: Directory Information Material (printed) for N.Y. City Residents, 1626-1786. New York Pub. Libr. Bull, 10/42; Hoosiers Sell Best, Ind. Quart. for Bookmen, 1/47; Needed Reference Services for American Agriculture, Col. & Res. Libr, 10/48; How the Library Can Serve Engineering Students, J. Engineering Educ, 5/52; Plea for Management Study of Partial Reclassification Problems, J. Cataloging & Classification, 1/56; Special Librarians and the Community, In: Papers Presented, Institution Channels of Communication for Special Libraries, April 22-23, 1960, Ind. Univ, 61. Consult: 1) Hofstra Univ, Hempstead, N.Y, review of audio-visual instructional program & bldg. area to be assigned to it, May-June 63; 2) Heidelberg Col, Tiffin, Ohio, review of libr. program & new bldg. plans, with Oliver C. Dunn, Oct. 64-Oct. 65; 3) U.S. Nat. Libr. Agr, Wash, D.C, relations of Nat. Libr. Agr. with land-grant univ. librns, with Richard Chapin, Apr. 65; 4) N.Y. State Libr, Albany, review audio-visual div. serv. & new bldg. area plans, with David F. Moses, Apr, May & July 66-; 5) Rose Polytech. Inst, Terre Haute, Ind, review of libr. program & new bldg. plan, with Oliver C. Dunn, June 66- Specialties: 1b, 1d, 1h (audio-visual facilities areas); 2d (engineering, agr); 7a, 7d (audio-visual serv).

MORIN, WILFRED LAURIER, Dec. 1, 11; Director, Freeport Memorial Library, Freeport, N.Y. 11520. Home: 9 New York Ave, Freeport, N.Y. 11520. B.A, 34; B.S. in L.S, 46; M.P.A, 56. Sr. pub. libr. supvr, N.Y. State Educ. Dept, 49-57; libr. extension specialist, U.S. Office Educ, 57-60; dir, Freeport Mem. Libr, Freeport, N.Y, 60- Other: Mem. legis. cmt, N.Y. Libr. Asn. Mem: ALA; D.C. Libr. Asn; Cath. Libr. Asn; SLA; N.Y. Libr. Asn; Nassau County Libr. Asn. Publ: Library Service in Alaska, Libr. J, 4/15/59; Interstate Library Cooperation, Wilson Libr. Bull, 5/59; NLW and My Home Town—1959, N. Country Libr, 1/60; American Laws Governing State Aid to Public Libraries, Libr. Trends, 7/60; State Library Extension Services: A Survey of Resources and Activities of State Library Administrative Agencies: 1955-66 (with Nathan Cohen), U.S. Office Educ, OE 15009, 60. Consult: 1) Alaska Territorial Libr, worked with Territorial libr. staff to qualify for fed. aid & prepared agency for state libr. serv, 57-60; 2) State of N.J, Trenton, worked with state agency staff & Libr. Asn. cmts. on developing state plans for recently enacted fed. aid, 57-60; 3) Pa. State Libr, Harrisburg, worked with the state libr. staff in presenting state plan for extension of libr. serv. under the fed. statutes, 57-; 4) State of R.I, Providence, worked with state agency staff & Libr. Asn. cmts. on pub. libr. serv. develop. in accordance with state & fed. statutes, 57- Specialties: 1a, 1e, 1f, 1g; 2a, 2b, 2c, 2d (humanities); 3e; 5b, 5c; 6a; 7a, 7b, 7c; 8a, 8b, 8c, 8e, 8f.

MORRIS, DR. RAYMOND PHILIP, Mar. 16, 04; Librarian, Divinity Library & Professor of Religious Literature, Yale University Divinity School, 409 Prospect St, New Haven, Conn. 06511. Home: 159 Westwood Rd, New Haven, Conn. 06515. A.B, 26; B.D, 29; B.S, 30; M.S, 32; hon. M.A, 51; Litt.D, 52, D.D, 65. Librn, Garrett Biblical Inst, 31-32; asst. librn, Yale Univ. Divinity Libr, 32-34, librn, 34- Other: Pres, Am. Theol. Libr. Asn, 51-53, chmn. bd. microtext & libr. develop. program. Mem: Am. Church Hist. Soc; ALA; Am. Theol. Libr. Asn; Soc. Am. Archivists. Publ: Libraries of Theological Seminaries, In: A Survey of Theological Education, 34; A Theological Book List, 60. Consult: 1) Andover Newton Theol. Sch, Newton Centre, Mass, bldg. consult, with Donald E. Bean & Calvin H. Schmitt, 63-; 2) Grad. Theol. Union, Berkeley, Calif, program consult, 64-; 3) Garrett Theol. Seminary, Evanston, Ill, program consult, 65; 4) Lancaster Theol. Seminary, Lancaster, Pa, bldg. consult, with Donald E. Bean; 5) Concordia Seminary, St. Louis, Mo, bldg. consult. Specialties: 1b, 1d; 2d (theol); 9 (consult. for theol. libr. & programs especially).

MORSE, A. LOUIS, June 29, 17; Director of Libraries, East Meadow Public Schools, East Meadow, N.Y. 11554. Home: 3778 Lincoln St, Seaford, N.Y. 11783. A.B, Cath. Univ. Am, 39; M.A, Manhattan Col, 45; B.L.S, St. John's Univ, 49; M.S. in L.S, Columbia Univ, 54. Librn, East Meadow Pub. Schools, East Meadow, N.Y, 54-58, supvr. libr, 58-61, dir. libr, 61-; asst. prof. libr. sci, Long Island Univ, 60-63, assoc. prof, 63- Other: Chmn. cataloging & classification sect, Cath. Libr. Asn, 51-52, mem. adv. cmt. cataloging & classification, 53-55, mem. exec. coun, Metrop. Cath. Col. Librns, 53-55, rep. to Am. Standards Asn. Z-39 subcmt. on indexing, 60-63; chmn. directory cmt, Nassau-Suffolk Sch. Libr. Asn, 55-56, chmn. nominations cmt, 58, pres. of Asn, 59-60, mem. exec. bd, 60-61, chmn. publicity cmt, 60-63;

---

5) PERSONNEL AND RECRUITING, 5a) job evaluation and description, salary recommendations, 5b) recruitment of professionals and management personnel, 5c) administrative organization, 6) PUBLIC RELATIONS, 6a) publications, 6b) publicity programs, 6c) public opinion surveys, 6d) others, 7) SERVICES, 7a) evaluation of current program, 7b) studies of service to special publics, e.g., students, handicapped, aged, etc., 7c) programs for the implementation of new laws, program proposals to governments, 7d) others, 8) COMMUNITY, REGIONAL, STATE PLANNING, 8a) legislative programs, 8b) area analyses, 8c) centralized systems, cooperative arrangements, 8d) development of standards, 8e) state libraries and extension agencies, 8f) regional and statewide surveys, 8g) others, 9) OTHERS.

mem. adv. bd, St. John's Libr. Congress, 59, 60 & 63; mem. non-book materials cmt, sch. libr. sect, N.Y. Libr. Asn, 59-60, mem. bd. dirs, 62-64, publicity dir, 62-64, mem. publ. cmt. of Asn, 62-64; mem. sch-pub. libr. relations cmt, Nassau County Libr. Asn, 61-63, chmn, 65-; mem, Adv. Cmt. on Nassau County Reference Libr, 63-; mem, Cmt. Nat. Libr. Week, YASD, 63- Mem: ALA; Cath. Libr. Asn; N.Y. Libr. Asn; Nassau County Libr. Asn; Nassau-Suffolk Sch. Libr. Asn. Publ: How to Get Going with Federal Funds, Grade Teacher, 11/65. Consult: 1) Gaylord Brothers, 155 Gifford St, Syracuse, N.Y, preparation of selected guide headings for Cath. libr, Sept. 64; 2) N.Y. State Educ. Dept. Bureau Sch. Libr, Albany, consultation & advice on the develop. of a handbook for the sec. sch. libr, with Frank A. Stevens, Jan. 65; 3) N.Y. State Educ. Dept, consultation & advice in planning & preparing the guidelines for Title II ESEA, with Frank A. Stevens, Apr. & June 65; 4) McGraw-Hill Book Co, 330 W. 42nd St, New York, N.Y, consultation to encyclopedia & subscription book div. on reference needs of sch. libr, Jan. & Aug. 66; 5) N.Y. State Educ. Dept, consultation & coordinating of LOIS Project, Feb-June 66. Specialties: 1c; 2b, 2c (English literature); 3a, 3b, 3d, 3e; 5a, 5c; 6a, 6b; 7a, 7b, 7c; 8a, 8d; 9 (in-serv. educ).

MOSTAR, ROMAN, June 14, 13; Assistant City Librarian & Head of Extension, Seattle Public Library, Fourth & Madison, Seattle, Wash. 98104. Home: 3502 N.E. 43rd St, Seattle, Wash. 98105. B.A, Univ. B.C, 39; B.A.(libr. sci), Univ. Wash, 40. Circulation librn, Univ. Wash, 46-60; asst. city librn. & head of extension, Seattle Pub. Libr, Wash, 60- Other: Libr. bldg. consult, State of Wash. Mem: ALA; Pac. Northwest Libr. Asn; Wash. Libr. Asn; Can. Libr. Asn. Publ: Contrib. to prfnl. journals. Consult: 1) Kirkland Pub. Libr, Kirkland, Wash, site selection, programming, planning, liaison between libr. bd, librn. & architect, 64-65; 2) Clallum County Regional Libr, Port Angeles, Wash, programming, planning, liaison between libr. bd, librn. & architect, 65; 3) Des Moines Pub. Libr, Des Moines, Wash, planning, programming, work with librn, city admin. & architect, 65; 4) Sno-Isle Regional Hq. Libr, Marysville, Wash, assisted librn. with programming & planning, liaison with bd, librn. & architect, 65-66; 5) Bellevue Pub. Libr, Bellevue, Wash, provided help with site selection, planning, selection of landscape architect & interior designer, liaison between city admin, bd, architect & librn, 66. Specialties: 1a, 1d, 1e, 1f, 1g; 9 (regional hq. bldgs).

MULLER, DR. ROBERT H, Mar. 12, 14; Associate Director, University Library, University of Michigan, Ann Arbor, Mich. 48104. Home: 1707 Dunmore Rd, Ann Arbor, Mich. 48103. B.A, Stanford Univ, 36; cert. in librarianship, Univ. Calif, 37; M.A, Univ. Chicago, 41; Ph.D, 42. Head librn, Bradley Univ, Peoria, Ill, 46-49; dir. libr, South. Ill. Univ, Carbondale, Ill, 49-54; asst. dir, Univ. Mich. Libr, 54-59, assoc. dir, 59- Other: Chmn. cmt. col. & univ. libr. bldg, ACRL, 49-53, chmn. cmt, res. & develop, univ. libr. sect, 59-63. Mem: ALA; Mich. Libr. Asn. Publ: College Library Buildings Self-Appraised, Col. & Res. Libr, 7/48; Library of Southern Illinois University, Ill. Libr, 4/51; Compact Storage Equipment: Where to Use It and Where Not, Col. & Res. Libr, 4/53; Evaluation of Campact Storage Systems, ACRL Bldg. Cmt. Third Libr. Bldg. Plans Inst, 53; The University Library and the Evolution of Its Physical Plant, Southeast. Librn, summer 60; The Economy of Compact Book Shelving, Libr. Trends, 4/65. Consult: 1) Loyola Univ, Chicago, Ill, libr. addition & downtown br. layout, 65-66; 2) Univ. Wis, Madison, col. libr. & agr. libr, 66; 3) South. Methodist Univ, Dallas, Tex, libr. bldg. program for libr. addition, with Stephen A. McCarthy, 67; 4) Miami Univ, Oxford, Ohio, long-range planning & bldg, chief consult, with John Berthel, 68; 5) North. Ill. Univ, DeKalb, grad. & undergrad. libr, chief consult, with Stephen A. McCarthy, Robert A. Miller, Donald E. Bean & Ralph E. Ellsworth, 68-69. Specialties: 1a, 1b, 1g; 3e; 5a, 5b, 5c; 7a; 9 (surveys of univ. or col. libr).

MUNN, R. RUSSELL, Sept. 7, 03; Retired. Home: 6860 Nanini Dr, Tucson, Ariz. 85704. B.A, Univ. B.C, 30; B.S, Columbia Univ, 32. Librn, Akron Pub. Libr, 44-67. Other: Pres, Ohio Libr. Asn, 47; trustee, Akron Art Inst. & secy, 45-61; treas, ALA, 49-52; pres, Adult Educ. Found. Akron, 51-53. Mem: ALA; Ariz. Libr. Asn. Publ: Library Service for Norfolk, Virginia (with Keith Doms), 58; Akron Completes Its Program, Libr. J, 12/1/59; Library Service for Raleigh and Wake County, North Carolina (with Geraldine LeMay), ALA, 60; On Losing and Winning a Bond Issue, Libr. J, 12/1/62. Consult: 1) Rodman Libr, Alliance, Ohio, plans and equipment layout, 60-61; 2) Wayne County Libr, Wooster, Ohio, plans & layout, 64-65; 3) Bowling Green Pub. Libr, Bowling Green, Ohio, site recommendations, 65-66; 4) Somerset County Libr, Sommerville, N.J, bldg. program, 66. Specialties: 1a, 1g.

MURPHY, LAVINIA ELLEN, Nov. 30, 39; Senior Supervisor of Education, School Library Development, Massachusetts Bureau of Library Extension, 648 Beacon St, Boston, Mass. 02215. Home: 152 Center St, Hanover, Mass. 02339. Elem. sch. librn, Marshfield Pub. Schs, 61-66; sr. supvr. educ, sch. libr. develop, Mass. Bureau Libr. Extension, Boston, 66- Other: Mem, Mass. Steering Cmt. for Sch. Libr, 62-; instructor, NDEA Inst. for Sch. Libr, Boston Univ, summer 65 & NDEA Inst. Educ. Media Specialists, summer 66. Mem: ALA; Dept. Audiovisual Instruction; New Eng. Libr. Asn; Mass. Sch. Libr. Asn; Mass. Audiovisual Asn. Publ: Contrib. to Mass. Elem. Sch. Principals

KEY TO CONSULTING SPECIALTIES: 1) ARCHITECTURE AND BUILDINGS, 1a) public libraries, 1b) academic libraries, 1c) school libraries, 1d) special libraries, 1e) library interiors, 1f) furnishings, 1g) site and location, 1h) other architectural; 2) COLLECTIONS: SELECTION, EVALUATION, WEEDING, 2a) adults, 2b) young adults, 2c) children, 2d) subject specialty, 2e) O.P. searches, 2f) rare books, 2g) appraisals, 2h) others; 3) TECHNICAL PROCESSES, 3a) cataloging, 3b) classification systems, 3c) acquisitions, 3d) materials processing, 3e) work flow and cost studies, 3f) others, 4) AUTOMATION, 4a) applications of data processing equipment, 4b) information storage and retrieval systems, 4c) systems analysis, 4d) others

Asn. publ. & Instructor Mag; regular column, Mass. Audiovisual Asn. Newsletter. Consult: 1) New Eng. Regional Lab. for Educ. Innovation, 55 Chapel St, Newton, Mass, design & guidance in developing a prfnl. libr. for educators, Jan. 66-; 2) Duxbury Mid. Sch, St. George St, Duxbury, Mass, design interior layout & collections to support instructional media program, with J. Baughman, Sept. 66-Feb. 67; 3) Lowell Fedn. Civic Orgns, c/o Mrs. Sidney Miezner, 375 Merrimack St, Lowell, Mass, designed sch. libr. space, facilities, personnel survey, Oct. 66-; 4) Marblehead Pub. Schs, Glover Sch, Marblehead, Mass, statist. & narrative visual program to initiate a sch. libr. program, Dec. 66-Apr. 67; 5) Project Bunker Hill, J.F. Kennedy Center, Charlestown, Mass, write & guide design for 4-unit IMC facility to support K-adult center, Feb. 67. Specialties: 1c, 1e, 1f, 1h (audiovisual facilities in libr); 2b, 2c, 2d (audiovisual materials); 4c; 5a, 5b; 6b, 6d (creation of visuals); 7a, 7c; 8e.

MURPHY, WALTER H, June 7, 33; Director, Flint River Regional Library, 210 S. Sixth St, Griffin, Ga. 30223. Home: 1454 Wesley Dr, Griffin, Ga. 30223. B.A, 55; M.L.S, 59. Asst. reference librn, Okla. City Libr, Okla, 57-59; admin. asst. to librn, Kans. City Pub. Libr, Mo, 59-60; dir. libr, Lakeland Pub. Libr, Lakeland, Fla, 60-66; instructor libr. sci, Fla. South. Col, 62-66; dir, Flint River Regional Libr, Griffin, Ga, 66- Other: Approved libr. bldg. consult, Fla, 64-; chmn, constitution cmt, Fla. Libr. Asn, 65; mem, Ga. Libr. Adv. cmt, 68- Mem: ALA; Ga. Libr. Asn; Southeast. Libr. Asn. Publ: A Letter by Emerson, Am. Liberature, 3/64; Nature's Gift to Literature, Fla. Naturalist, 4/64; Mobile Library Trailers in Florida, Fla. Libr, 3/65; Colorful Trailers Serve as Mobile Libraries, Am. City, 7/65; A Library for Lakeland, Fla. Libr, 3/67. Consult: 1) W.D. Grisso, private libr, Oklahoma City, Okla, cataloged private collection of Southwest Americana, 58; 2) Pub. Libr, Clayton County, Ga, site & location, bldg. program, with Clarence S. Paine, 66-67; 3) Cherokee Regional Libr, Lafayette, Ga, survey & eval, 68; 4) Pub. Libr, Chattooga County, Ga, site & location, bldg. program, 68. Specialties: 1a, 1e, 1f, 1g; 5a, 5c; 7a.

MURRAY, THOMAS B, Dec. 2, 12; Head Librarian, Diablo Valley College, Concord, Calif. 94523. Home: 776 North Rd, Lafayette, Calif. 94549. A.B, 46; B.L.S, 47; M.L.S, 53. Head librn, Diablo Valley Col, 50- Other: Pres, North. Sect, Sch. Libr. Asn. Calif, 51-52, state pres, 53-54; mem. ed. cmt, Calif. Libr. Asn, 66, chmn-elect, North. Div, Col, Univ. & Res. Libr. Sect, 67. Mem: Calif. Libr. Asn; ALA. Publ: An Evaluation of the Reference Collections in the Libraries of Seven San Francisco Bay Area Junior Colleges, ACRL Microcard Series, No. 10, 53. Consult: 1) Deep Springs Col, Deep Springs, Calif, survey of collection, financial & admin. problems, 53; 2) Contra Costa Col, San Pablo, Calif, design of libr. bldg, 60. Specialties: 1b, 1h (adaptation of existing bldgs. to libr. purposes); 3b, 3c; 5a, 5c; 9 (organizing jr. col. libr).

MUTSCHLER, HERBERT F, Nov. 28, 19; Director, King County Library System, 1100 E. Union, Seattle, Wash. 98122. Home: 5300 128th Ave. S.E, Bellevue, Wash. 98004. B.A, Jamestown Col, 47; M.A, West. Reserve Univ, 49, M.S.L.S, 52. Dir, Hamtramck Pub. Libr, Mich, 55-56; head pub. serv, Wayne County Libr, Mich, 56-59, asst. county librn, 59-63; dir, King County Libr. Syst, Seattle, Wash, 63- Other: Chmn. reference sect, Mich. Libr. Asn, 54; chmn. county sect, Mich. Libr. Asn, 57; mem. exec. bd, Wash. Libr. Asn, 64-, pres-elect, 65-67; pres, Wash. Libr. Asn, 68-69; coun-at-large, ALA, 69; chmn-elect pub. relations sect, LAD. Mem: Wash. Libr. Asn; Pac. Northwest Libr. Asn; ALA. Publ: Library in the Round, Libr, J, 12/1/60; Library Education and Talent Shortage, Libr. J, 4/1/66; King County Libr, Washington, HLA Journal, 6/66. Consult: 1) Wayne County, Wayne, Mich, planning & construction of 15 bldgs. plus hq, with Walter H. Kaiser, 56-62; 2) Des Moines Libr, Des Moines, Wash, program, bldg, with Roman Mostar, 65; 3) Kirkland Libr, Kirkland, Wash, bldg, layout, 65; 4) Bellevue Libr, Bellevue, Wash, program, bldg, plus 13 additional community libr, 65-66, 68; 5) Longview Libr, Longview, Wash, bldg, layout, Feb. 66-May 67. Specialties: 1a, 1e, 1f, 1g, 4a.

N

NEGRO, ANTOINETTE, Oct. 12, 33; Educational Media Specialist, Library Services Division, Department of Instructional Materials, Montgomery County Public Schools, Rockville, Md. 20850. Home: 104 Second St, Hackensack, N.J. 07601. B.S, Fordham Univ, 55; M.L.S, Rutgers Univ, 58; Ed.S, West. Mich. Univ, 67. Teacher, St. Cecilia High Sch, Englewood, N.J, 55-57; librn, Hanover Park High Sch, Hanover, N.J, 57-62; librn, U.S. Info. Agency, 62-63; sch. librn, Parsippany, N.J, 63-66; grad. assoc, 6th year specialist, West. Mich. Univ, Kalamazoo, 66-67; educ. media specialist, libr. serv. div, dept. instructional materials, Montgomery County Pub. Schs, Rockville, Md, 67- Other: Mem. exec. bd, N.J. Sch. Libr. Asn, 60-62 & 64-65, recruitment chmn, 65; instructor, Trenton State Col, 63 & Newark State Col, 64-65. Mem: ALA; N.J. Libr. Asn; AASL; N.J. Sch. Libr. Asn. Consult: 1) N.J. Sch. Libr. Asn, demonstrations of teacher-librn. cooperation, 61 & 64-65; 2) Johnson Pub. Libr, Hackensack, N.J, sch-libr. relations, develop. of children's serv, 63; 3) Parsippany Bd. Educ, Parsippany, N.J, spending of Title II funds to develop libr. programs, Jan-Mar. 66; 4) Fordham Univ, N.Y, resources for learning

---

5) PERSONNEL AND RECRUITING, 5a) job evaluation and description, salary recommendations, 5b) recruitment of professionals and management personnel, 5c) administrative organization, 6) PUBLIC RELATIONS, 6a) publications, 6b) publicity programs, 6c) public opinion surveys, 6d) others, 7) SERVICES, 7a) evaluation of current program, 7b) studies of service to special publics, e.g., students, handicapped, aged, etc., 7c) programs for the implementation of new laws, program proposals to governments, 7d) others, 8) COMMUNITY, REGIONAL, STATE PLANNING, 8a) legislative programs, 8b) area analyses, 8c) centralized systems, cooperative arrangements, 8d) development of standards, 8e) state libraries and extension agencies, 8f) regional and statewide surveys, 8g) others, 9) OTHERS.

master's student in-teacher training program, Dec. 66. Specialties: 1c; 2b; 4b; 5b, 5d (sch. libr. personnel); 7a, 7b, 7d (audiovisual); 8d; 9 (advisement of teacher training programs; libr. educ; coordinated instructional materials program).

NELSON ASSOCIATES, INC, 845 Third Ave, New York, N.Y. 10022. Consult: 1) N.Y. Pub. Libr, mgr. survey, 67; 2) N.J. county libr, plan for a regional syst. reorgn, 67; 3) Nat. Adv. Cmn. Libr, studies of Am. state libr. & state libr. agencies, pub. libr, sch. libr. & undergrad. & jr. col. libr, 68; 4) Nat. Serials Data Program, survey of user interests, 68; 5) Div. Blind & Physically Handicapped, Libr. Congress, user survey, 69. Specialties: 1a, 1b, 1e, 1g; 2a, 2b, 2c, 2d; 3a, 3b, 3c, 3d, 3e; 4a, 4b, 4c; 5a, 5b, 5c; 6c; 7a, 7b, 7c; 8a, 8b, 8c, 8d, 8e, 8f.

NELSON, CHARLES A, Dec. 21, 22; President, Nelson Associates, Inc, 845 Third Ave, New York, N.Y. 10022. Home: 1 Walworth Terrace, White Plains, N.Y. 10606. B.A, St. John's Col. (Md), 47. Pres, Nelson Assocs, New York, N.Y, 58- Other: Chmn. bd, Int. Sch. Serv; mem, bd. of visitors & gov, St. John's Col; charter mem. & dir, Soc. Prfnl. Mgt. Consult. Mem: N.Y. Libr. Asn. Publ: The University, The Citizen, and World Affairs, Am. Coun. on Educ, 56; Toward the Liberally Educated Executive, New Am. Libr, 59; Developing Responsible Public Leaders, Oceana, 63. Consult: 1) Queens Borough Pub. Libr, Brooklyn Pub. Libr. & New York Pub. Libr, N.Y, study to determine the feasibility of further centralizing tech. processing opers, with Eugene Vorhies, 66; 2) N.Y. State Libr, study of centralized processing activities of the N.Y. State libr. syst, with Davis Crippen & Cynthia Rice, 66; 3) Mich. State Libr, Lansing, statewide survey of reference & res. libr. cooperation with David Watson & James R. Basche, Jan-Oct. 66; 4) Detroit Pub. Libr, Detroit, Mich, design of instruments for measuring patron use & unit costs for metropolitan libr. demonstration, with James R. Basche, Aug. 66-Jan. 67; 5) Pub. Libr. Asn, 50 E. Huron St, Chicago, Ill, nationwide survey of multijurisdictional pub. libr. systs, Sept. 66-Oct. 67. Specialties: 2h (acquisition policy); 3a, 3b, 3c, 3d, 3e; 4a, 4b, 4c; 5a, 5c; 7a, 7b, 7c; 8a, 8b, 8c, 8d, 8e, 8f.

NESBIN, MRS. ESTHER WINTER, Aug. 5, 10; Director of Library Services, Palomar College, San Marcos, Calif. 92069. Home: P.O. Box 102, San Marcos, Calif. 92069. B.A, 31; libr. sci. cert, 32. Librn, Palomar Col. Libr, San Marcos, Calif, 47-65, dir. libr. serv, 65- Other: Secy, jr. col. librns. round table, Calif. Libr. Asn, 64, v.pres, 65, pres, 66. Mem: Calif. Libr. Asn; Calif. Asn. Sch. Librns; Calif. Teachers Asn; Delta Kappa Gamma. Publ: Shaker Literature in the Grosvenor Library: a Bibliography, Grosvenor Libr. Bull, Vol. 22, No. 4; Library Technology Manual for Library Technology Routines, Palomar Col. Libr, parts 1 & 2, 68. Consult: 1) Palos Verdes Jr. Col, Blythe, Calif, evaluation of collection, compiled titles for reference collection, Feb-Mar. 57; 2) Monterey Jr. Col, Monterey, Calif, floor plans for new libr, Sept. 58; 3) Camp Pendleton Legal Base Libr, Camp Pendleton, Calif, evaluation of current program, floor plan, cataloging syst, collection, May 64. Specialties: 1h (jr. col. libr); 2h (jr. col); 7a.

NIELSEN, ANDRE S, July 28, 09; 17306 Highway 101 W, Wayzata, Minn. 55391. B.B.A, Univ. Minn, 31, B.L.S, 38. Dir, Evanston Pub. Libr, 44-67. Other: Pres, Coun. Soc. Agencies, Evanston, 48; pres, Ill. Libr. Asn, 51; mem, headquarters bldg. cmt, ALA, 58-63; chmn, Regional Libr. Orgn. Cmt, N. Suburban, Ill, 65-66; mem. bd, Rotary Club, 8 years. Mem: ALA; Ill. Libr. Asn. Publ: Contrib. to libr. periodicals. Consult: 1) Little Rock Pub. Libr, Little Rock, Ark, program for new bldg, space relationships & libr. equipment, with Donald Bean & Libr. Bldg. Consults, 58; 2) Elgin Pub. Libr, Elgin, Ill, site eval, layout & plans, 64-65; 3) Waukegan Pub. Libr, Waukegan, Ill, layout & plans, 65; 4) Northbrook Pub. Libr, Northbrook, Ill, study of adequacy of present bldg. & serv. with recommendations, 65. Specialties: 1a, 1e, 1f, 1g, 1h (remodeling or enlarging bldgs); 8f.

NIKAS, MARY CREETY, Apr. 4, 27; President & Chief Designer, Interiors for Business, Inc, 1705 Commerce Dr. N.W, Atlanta, Ga. 30318. Home: 85 Avery Dr. N.E, Atlanta, Ga. 30309. B.F.A, 48. Interior designer, Becknell Assocs, Atlanta, Ga, 56-60; founder & chief designer, Interiors for Bus, Atlanta, 60-66, pres. & chief designer, Interiors for Bus, Heery & Heery, Architects, 66- Other: Charter mem. founding bd, Arts Festival of Atlanta, Inc, 52-, v.pres, 59-60, chmn. adv. & scholarship cmt. Consult: 1) Kelley Hill Br. Libr, Ft. Benning, Ga, layout, color scheme & selection of all furnishings & installation of same, 64-65; 2) Sandhill Libr, Ft. Benning, design for remodeling old bldg, renovation, 64-65 & 67; 3) Center Libr, Ft. Gordon, Ga, specifications & supv. of installation, 66; 4) Main Post Libr, Ft. Campbell, Ky, interior planning & specifications, 66; 5) Main Post Annex, Ft. Benning, design & specifications for new & remodeled areas, 66-67. Specialties: 1e, 1f, 1h (color consultation & spec. furniture design).

NORTON, ALICE, Apr. 20, 26; Library Public Relations, 392 Central Park W, New York, N.Y. 10025. B.A, Wellesley Col, 47; M.S.(libr. sci), Univ. Ill, 62. Pub. relations officer, Denver Pub. Libr, 55-61; pub. relations dir, Westchester Libr. Syst, Mt. Vernon, N.Y, 62-66; Wellesley Col. Stevens traveling fel, 66-67. Other: Mem, reading guide project cmt. on promotion, ASD, 61-63, mem, pub.

KEY TO CONSULTING SPECIALTIES: 1) ARCHITECTURE AND BUILDINGS, 1a) public libraries, 1b) academic libraries, 1c) school libraries, 1d) special libraries, 1e) library interiors, 1f) furnishings, 1g) site and location, 1h) other architectural; 2) COLLECTIONS: SELECTION, EVALUATION, WEEDING, 2a) adults, 2b) young adults, 2c) children, 2d) subject specialty, 2e) O.P. searches, 2f) rare books, 2g) appraisals, 2h) others; 3) TECHNICAL PROCESSES, 3a) cataloging, 3b) classification systems, 3c) acquisitions, 3d) materials processing, 3e) work flow and cost studies, 3f) others, 4) AUTOMATION, 4a) applications of data processing equipment, 4b) information storage and retrieval systems, 4c) systems analysis, 4d) others

relations in libr. cmt, ALA, 62-66, chmn, 62-63, chmn, pub. relations sect, 63-64, mem, office for recruitment materials cmt, 63-65, mem, John Cotton Dana publicity awards cmt, 64; v.pres. & pres-elect, Libr. Pub. Relations Coun, 68-69. Mem: ALA; N.Y. Libr. Asn; Libr. Pub. Relations Coun; Beta Phi Mu. Publ: The Westchester Library System Builds on Strength for Service (with Katharine M. Holden), The Bookmark, N.Y. State Libr, 11/63; guest ed, pub. relations issue, Wilson Libr. Bull, 3/64; Professional Publicity Services, a 1965 Checklist, Libr. J, 9/1/65; Public Relations, Information Sources, Mgt. Info. Guide Series, Gale Res. Co.(in prep). Consult: 1) Westchester Libr. Syst, 28 S. First Ave, Mt. Vernon, N.Y, radio-TV spot announcement libr. promotion, with pub. relations staff of metrop. N.Y. libr. systs. & radio-TV specialists Beth Blossom & Fred Hertz, 65-66, 68; 2) State Libr. of Ohio, 65 S. Front St, Columbus, Ohio, publ, 68; 3) Colo. State Libr, 231 Capitol Ave, Denver, Colo, speaker & discussion leader, pub. relations workshop, 68; 4) Ferguson Libr, Stamford, Conn, annual report; 5) Conn. State Libr, 231 Capitol Ave, Hartford, Conn, publ. & plan for statewide promotion of libr. serv, 68. Specialties: 6a, 6b, 6c, 6d (developing a pub. relations program; staff training in pub. relations; work with community orgns; conducting bond issue campaigns).

O

OBOLER, ELI M, Sept. 26, 15; University Librarian, Idaho State University Library, Pocatello, Idaho 83201. Home: 1397 Jane St, Pocatello, Idaho 83201. B.A, Univ. Chicago, 41; B.S. in L.S, Columbia, 42. Librn, Idaho State Col, Pocatello, to 63, univ. librn, Idaho State Univ, 63- Other: Pres, Idaho Libr. Asn, 50-53; ed, Idaho Librn, 50-54 & 57-58; chmn, Idaho periodicals roundtable, ALA, 52-53; Idaho Coun. to ALA, 53-59; pres, Pac. Northwest Libr. Asn, 55-56; ed, PNLA Quart, 58-67 (won H.W. Wilson-ALA libr. periodicals award, 65); guest prof. libr. sci, Utah State Univ, Logan, summers 60 & 66; chmn, col. sect, ACRL, 63-64; mem, intellectual freedom cmt, ALA, 65-69; mem. nat. adv. cmt. libr. training & res. project, U.S. Office Educ, 66-69. Mem: ALA; Pac. Northwest Libr. Asn; Idaho Libr. Asn; ACRL. Publ: Congress As Censor, Libr. J, 11/15/52; Faculty-Library Cooperation, Improving Col. & Univ. Teaching, spring 56; College and University Library Accreditation Standards (ed), ACRL, 58; Goodbye, Reference Librarian!, Reference Quart, 9/64; The Accuracy of Federal Academic Library Statistics, Col. & Res. Libr, 11/64; Machines and Libraries: The Parameters of Common Sense, Iconoclast, summer 66. Consult: 1) Idaho State Col. Libr, Pocatello, survey of entire libr, Mar. 49; 2) Idaho State Libr, 615 Fulton St, Boise, survey to recommend inter-city cooperation, spring 55; 3) Northwest Nazarene Col. Libr, Nampa, Idaho, survey for possible remodeling, improvement of collection, serv. & staffing changes, Apr. 56; 4) Col. Idaho Libr, Caldwell, survey of libr. for remodeling, collection & staffing, Apr. 56; 5) Northwest Nazarene Col. Libr, survey of collections, staffing & serv. with recommendations, spring 65. Specialties: 1b; 2h (col. libr); 3e; 5c; 6a; 7a; 8d, 8e.

O'BRIEN, JAMES M, July 1, 34; Director, Half Hollow Hills Community Library, 55 Vanderbilt Parkway, Dix Hills, Huntington Station, N.Y. 11746. Home: 5 Milburn Lane, Huntington, N.Y. 11743. B.A, Manhattan Col, 56; M.S.L.S, Syracuse, Univ. 58. Gen. asst, Great Neck Libr, 58-59; asst. dir, Huntington Pub. Libr, 60-62; dir, North Babylon Pub. Libr, 62-65; dir, Half Hollow Hills Community Libr, Melville, N.Y, 65- Other: Chmn, insurance for libr. cmt, ALA, 65-; pres, Suffolk County Libr. Asn, 65-66. Mem: ALA; New York Libr. Asn; Suffolk County Libr. Asn. Publ: Pricing Library Materials for Insurance Purposes, ALA Bull, 7-8/66. Consult: 1) Carnegie Pub. Libr, Paducah, Ky, eval. of amount of loss subsequent to fire & determination of requested insured value of loss, with Walter W. Curley, Jan. 65; 2) Deer Park Pub. Libr, 44 Lake Ave, Deer Park, N.Y, review of proposal & advice relative to insurance program, July-Sept. 66; 3) Center Moriches Libr, 529 Main St, Center Moriches, N.Y, advice on libr. insurance program, Jan. 67. Specialties: 9 (libr. insurance).

OLINER, STAN, June 13, 38; County Librarian, Laramie County Library, 2119 Capitol Ave, Cheyenne, Wyo. 82001. Home: P.O. Box 883, Cheyenne, Wyo. 82001. B.A, 60; M.A, 61. Bookmobile librn, Freeport, N.Y, 62-63; supv. librn. & area libr. supvr, Colorado State Libr, 63-65; county librn, Cheyenne, Wyo, 65- Other: Chmn. pub. libr. div, Colo. Libr. Asn, 65; mem. relations with state & local libr. asn. cmt, ALA, 65-; chmn. pub. libr. div, Wyo. Libr. Asn, 66; John Cotton Dana publicity award, 67. Mem: ALA; SLA; Colo. Libr. Asn; Wyo. Libr. Asn. Publ: Tramp Printer, 61- Consult: 1) Pitkin County Libr, Aspen, Colo, bldg. program for LSCA project, surveyed libr. serv. for ski resort area, 64-65; 2) Garfield County Libr, New Castle, Colo, planned three-county syst. including contracts for bookmobile serv, 64-65; 3) Durango Pub. Libr, Durango, Colo, wrote first phase of preliminary bldg. program, surveyed existing libr. facilities, May 65; 4) Crested Butte & Vail Pub. Libr, Crested Butte & Vail, Colo, established pub. libr. in previously unserved ski resort areas, 65; 5) Basalt Pub. Libr, Basalt, Colo, established pub. libr. serv. in previously unserved rural areas. Specialties: 1a; 2a, 2d (skis & skiing); 6a, 6d (Friends of the Library); 8c.

5) PERSONNEL AND RECRUITING, 5a) job evaluation and description, salary recommendations, 5b) recruitment of professionals and management personnel, 5c) administrative organization, 6) PUBLIC RELATIONS, 6a) publications, 6b) publicity programs, 6c) public opinion surveys, 6d) others, 7) SERVICES, 7a) evaluation of current program, 7b) studies of service to special publics, e.g., students, handicapped, aged, etc., 7c) programs for the implementation of new laws, program proposals to governments, 7d) others, 8) COMMUNITY, REGIONAL, STATE PLANNING, 8a) legislative programs, 8b) area analyses, 8c) centralized systems, cooperative arrangements, 8d) development of standards, 8e) state libraries and extension agencies, 8f) regional and statewide surveys, 8g) others, 9) OTHERS.

OLTMAN, FLORINE A, Nov. 13, 15; Chief, Bibliography Branch, Air University Library, Maxwell Air Force Base, Ala. 36112. Home: 219 E. Riding Rd, Montgomery, Ala. 36111. B.A, Southwest Tex. State Teachers Col, 37; B.S. in L.S, Univ. Denver, 42. Librn, Air War Col, 55-58; chief bibliographer, Reader Serv. Div, Air Univ. Libr, 58- Other: Secy. Mil. Div, SLA, 54, chmn, 59, pres, Ala. Chap, 56, chmn. adv. coun. & 2nd v.pres, 61-62; secy. Ala. Libr. Asn, 56. Mem: SLA. Consult: 1) Armed Forces Sch, Venezuelan Air Force, Caracas, Venezuela, classification of collection, admin. & policy, Nov. 60. Specialties: 1d; 2d (military); 5a, 5b, 5c; 6b; 7a.

ORNE, DR. JERROLD, Mar. 25, 11; University Librarian, University of North Carolina Library, Chapel Hill, N.C. 27514. Home: 529 Dogwood Dr, Chapel Hill, N.C. 27514. B.A, 32; M.A, 33; Ph.D, 39; B.S, 40. Dir. libr, Air Univ, Maxwell Air Force Base, Ala, 51-57; univ. librn, Univ. N.C, Chapel Hill, 57- Other: Bd. mem, SLA, 55-56, chmn, military libr. div, 57; bd. mem, N.C. State Libr, 57-; bd. mem, U.S. Book Exchange, 60-, chmn, 62-64; chmn, Asn. Southeast. Res. Libr, 62-64; chmn. Z-39 subcmt, U.S. Am. Standards Inst, 65- Mem: ALA; Southeast. Libr. Asn; N.C. Libr. Asn; Am. Asn. Univ. Prof; Asn. Southeast. Res. Libr. Consult: 1) Redstone Sci. Info. Center, Marshall Space Flight Center, Huntsville, Ala, opers. & program, with Robert Vosper & Joseph C. Shipman, 61 & Louis Shores, 66; 2) Mich. State Univ, East Lansing, libr. orgn. & planning, with Robert Downs, Verner W. Clapp & Leslie Dunlap, 64; 3) Gov. Cmn. on Libr. Resources, Raleigh, N.C, acad. libr, with R. B. Downs & Ben Powell, 64; 4) U.S. Dept. State, Wash, D.C, Adviser to Govt. of S. Vietnam on libr. & educ, proposed nat. libr. bldg. & new cent. univ. libr, June-Sept. 65; 5) Elon Col, Elon College, N.C, planning new col. libr, 65-66. Specialties: 1b, 1e, 1f, 1g; 2g; 3e, 3f (orgn); 4a, 4d (document handling); 5c; 7a, 7c, 7d (acad. orgn); 8c, 8d, 8e, 8f.

ORR, ROBERT WILLIAM, June 9, 05; Professor of Library Science, Iowa State University Library, Ames, Iowa 50010. Home: 919 Beach Ave, Ames, Iowa 50010. B.S, Iowa State Col, 30; M.S, Columbia Univ, 39. Prof, Iowa State Univ. Libr, 46-, dir. libr, 46-67. Other: Pres, Iowa Libr. Asn, 47-48, pres, ACRL, 56-57. Mem: ALA; ACRL; Iowa Libr. Asn. Publ: Contrib. to prfnl. journals. Consult: 1) Auburn Univ, Auburn, Ala, survey of libr, with Louis R. Wilson, Nov. 48-Mar, 49; 2) Texas A&M Col, State College, survey of libr, with William H. Carlson, Oct. 49-Feb. 50; 3) Tuskegee Inst, Ala, libr. consult. report, 56; 4) Mich. Tech. Univ, Houghton, survey of libr, with Melvin J. Voigt, May-July 60. Specialties: 1b.

ORTON, FLOYD EMORY, July 16, 10; Science Librarian, Washington State University, Pullman, Wash. 99163. B.S.(chemistry), 36, Libr. Sch. Cert, Univ. Minn, 37; A.M.L.S, Univ. Mich, 40. Sci. librn, Wash. State Univ, Pullman, Wash, 51- Mem: SLA; Am. Soc. Info. Sci; Int. Asn. Agr. Librns. & Documentalists. Consult: 1) Cath. Univ. of Chile, Santiago, consult. for engineering sch. libr, July 65-June 66. Specialties: 1d; 2d (sci. & tech); 3a, 3f (classified catalog); 5d (sci. & tech. staff); 9 (possibilities of cent. subject cataloging sci. books).

OSBORNE, FRED YANTIS, 1917; Head Librarian, Cabrillo College, 6500 Soquel Dr, Aptos, Calif. 95003. Home: 330 Kingsbury Dr, Aptos, Calif. 95003. A.B, Tex. Wesleyan Col, 40; M.A (hist), South. Methodist Univ, 47; M.A.(libr. sci), Univ. Denver, 50. Head librn, Long Beach City Col, Calif, 53-59; head librn, Cabrillo Col, 59- Other: Mem. bd. dirs, Calif. Libr. Asn. & pres, Jr. Col. Librns, 64-65. Mem: Calif. Libr. Asn; Calif. Asn. Sch. Librns; Friends of the Libr, Univ. Calif, Santa Cruz. Publ: Contrib. to Libr. J, Tex. Libr. J. Consult: 1) Baylor Univ, Waco, Tex, remodeling of bldg. & design of furniture, 51-52; 2) Paul Quinn Col, Waco, Tex, study of holdings, bldg, equipment & furniture with recommendations to meet accreditation standards, with Lulu Stine, 51-52; 3) Long Beach City Col, Long Beach, Calif, bldg. & furnishings plan, 57; 4) Cabrillo Col, Aptos, Calif, bldg. & furnishings, 59-60. Specialties: 1b, 1f, 1h (jr. col. libr).

OWENS, MRS. IRIS, Dec. 27, 08; Director, Educational Media, Bay County Schools, 1310 E. 11th St, Panama City, Fla. 32401. Home: 2619 W. Ninth St, Panama City, Fla. 32401. B.A, 49; M.A, 54. Other: Treas, Delta Kappa Gamma, 65-66; area chmn. & pres-elect, Fla. Asn. Sch. Librns, 67-68; Wash. County secy, Fla. Hist. Cmn; mem, Nat. Cmn. Teacher Educ. & Prfnl. Standards. Mem: ALA; Dept. Audiovisual Instruction; Beta Phi Mu; Fla. Asn. Sch. Librns; Fla. Audiovisual Asn; Bay County Sch. Libr. Asn. Consult: 1) Escambia County, Pensacola, Fla, sch. libr. eval, with William Malloy & Robert Latham, Apr. 64; 2) Wash. County, Chipley, Fla, sch. libr, with R.C. Lipscomb, May 65; 3) Wash. County, area film cooperative, with C.V. Williams & James Harbin, 65-66; 4) Walton County, De Funiak Springs, Fla, production of instructional materials, Aug. 66. Specialties: 1c; 2b, 2c; 3a, 3b, 3c, 3d; 5a; 7a; 8d.

P

PAINE, CLARENCE S, June 9, 08; Independent Library Consultant, Box 10445, Knoxville, Tenn. 37919. Home: Route 5, Box 192, Lenoir City, Tenn. 37771. A.B, 36; B.S. in L.S, 37; A.M, 37. Dir, Beloit Col. Libr, Beloit, Wis,

---

KEY TO CONSULTING SPECIALTIES: 1) ARCHITECTURE AND BUILDINGS, 1a) public libraries, 1b) academic libraries, 1c) school libraries, 1d) special libraries, 1e) library interiors, 1f) furnishings, 1g) site and location, 1h) other architectural; 2) COLLECTIONS: SELECTION, EVALUATION, WEEDING, 2a) adults, 2b) young adults, 2c) children, 2d) subject specialty, 2e) O.P. searches, 2f) rare books, 2g) appraisals, 2h) others; 3) TECHNICAL PROCESSES, 3a) cataloging, 3b) classification systems, 3c) acquisitions, 3d) materials processing, 3e) work flow and cost studies, 3f) others, 4) AUTOMATION, 4a) applications of data processing equipment, 4b) information storage and retrieval systems, 4c) systems analysis, 4d) others

38-48; dir. & bldg. interior design consult, Okla. City Libr, Okla, 48-59; chief librn. & bldg. consult, Lansing Sch. Dist. Libr, Mich, 59-65. Other: Mem, constitution & by-laws cmt, ALA, 40-45, mem, ed. cmt, 45-47, mem, microcard cmt, 47-55, mem. coun, 55-59, secy, exhibits round table, 58-59; pres, Wis. Libr. Asn, 43-44; Rockefeller Found. res. fel, West Range Cattle Industry Study, 45-46; chmn, Am. Red Cross, Beloit chap, 47; pres, Rotary Club, Beloit, 47; vis. lectr, Univ. Denver Grad. Sch. Librarianship, 48 & Cent. State Univ; Okla, 58; mem. bd. dirs, Great Books Found, 55-59; mem. exec. bd, Southwest. Libr. Asn, 56-59; conf. chmn, Mich. Libr. Asn, 62 & 64; mem. adv. cmt, dept. librarianship, West. Mich. Univ, 64-65. Mem: ALA; Southeast. Libr. Asn; Tenn. Libr. Asn. Publ: Microcards and Research Libraries (with Lucille M. Morsch), ALA Bull, 11/44; Materials of State and Local History in College Libraries, Col. & Res. Libr, 1/46; Microcard and the Future of the Public Library, Okla. State Libr. Bull, 4-6/48; Library, a Resource for Recreation, Recreation, 9/48; ...Drive-up Return System, Libr. J, 4/1/50; Planning in a Cube, In: Planning a Library Building, ALA Bldgs. Cmt, 55. Consult: 1) Lakeland Pub. Libr, Lakeland, Fla, bldg, interior design consult, 65-66; 2) East Orange, N.J. Pub. Libr, site, bldg, interior design, 66; 3) Clayton County, Ga, br. libr. site, bldg, interior, 66; 4) Peoples Libr, New Kensington, Pa, preliminary report for program of libr. serv. & bldg, 66-68; 5) City of Griffin, Spaulding County, Ga, site, 67. Specialties: 1a, 1e, 1f, 1g; 6a, 6b; 7a, 7b, 7c; 8b.

PALMER, DAVID C, Aug. 26, 25; Chief, Readers Services, New Jersey State Library, 185 W. State St, Trenton, N.J. 08625. Home: Box 438, R.D. 1, Lambertville, N.J. 08530. B.S, Johns Hopkins Univ; M.L.S, Rutgers Univ. Reference asst, Enoch Pratt Free Libr, Baltimore, Md, 56-57; exec. secy, Pa. Libr. Survey, 57-58; exec. dir, Gov. Cmn. on Pub. Libr. Develop. in Pa, 58-61; asst. dir. exten. div, Pa. State Libr, 61-63, head, standards & eval, 63-64, dir, libr. develop. div, 64-65; chief readers serv, N.J. State Libr, Trenton, 65-; instructor admin, grad. sch. libr. serv, Rutgers Univ, 65- Other: Chmn, statist. coordinating cmt. & statist. cmt. for state libr, ALA, 63-; chmn, planning cmt, ASL, 66-67. Mem: ALA; Pa. Libr. Asn; N.J. Libr. Asn; SLA. Publ: Summary of Recommendations of the Pennsylvania Library Survey, Pa. Libr. Bull, fall 58; Current Concepts in State Aid to Public Libraries (with E.E. Doerschuk), Libr. Trends, 7/60; A Study of the Kent-Caroline Public Libraries Association, Maryland (with Ralph Blasingame), The Asn, 2/65; chaps. on pub. & state libr, In: Library Statistics, A Handbook of Concepts, Definitions and Terminology, ALA, 66. Consult: 1) Baltimore County Libr, Towson, Md, res. asst. to Dr. Lowell A. Martin, 56; 2) Pa. State Libr, Harrisburg, Pa. libr. survey, with Lowell A. Martin, 57-58; 3) ALA, 50 E. Huron St, Chicago, Ill, pub. & state libr. statist. coordinating project, Nov. 63-Mar. 64; 4) Kent-Caroline Pub. Libr. Asn, Denton, Md, survey, with Ralph Blasingame, Oct. 64-Feb. 65; 5) New Castle Pub. Libr, New Castle, Pa, state aid, statist, with Ralph Blasingame, July 65. Specialties: 5c; 7a, 7b, 7c; 8a, 8b, 8c, 8d, 8e, 8f.

PARKER, DR. RALPH H, Apr. 21, 09; Dean, School of Library Science, University of Missouri, Columbia, Mo. 65202. Home: 1104 S. Glenwood, Columbia, Mo. 65201. B.A, 29; M.A, 30; Ph.D, 35. Univ. librn, Univ. Mo, 47-66. Mem: Mo. Libr. Asn; ALA. Publ: Missouri, Its Resources, People, Institutions (contrib), Univ. Mo, Columbia, 51; Library Applications of Punched Cards, ALA, 52; contrib. to prfnl. journals. Consult: 1) Ill. State Libr, Springfield, automation of libr. records, Sept. 64; 2) Cornell Univ. Libr, Ithaca, N.Y, automation of libr. records, Jan. 65; 3) Univ. Mich, Ann Arbor, automation of libr. records, June 65; 4) Ohio Col. Asn, design for computerized bibliog. network to serve col. & univ. libr. in Ohio, with Frederick Kilgour, Sept. 65-Mar. 66; 5) Dartmouth Col. Libr, Hanover, N.H, automation of libr. records, May 66. Specialties: 3d, 3e; 4a, 4b, 4c.

PARKER, WYMAN W, Oct. 31, 12; University Librarian, Olin Library, Wesleyan University, Middletown, Conn. 06457. Home: 330 Pine St, Middletown, Conn. 06457. B.S, 34; B.L.S, 35; M.A.(English), 39; hon. M.A, 57. Librn, Univ. Cincinnati, 51-56; librn, Wesleyan Univ, 56- Other: Pres, ACRL, 59-60; mem. adv. coun, Columbia Univ. Sch. Libr. Serv, 60- Mem: Conn. Libr. Asn; ALA; Bibliog. Soc, London; Bibliog. Soc. Am; Grolier Club; Columbiad Club; Am. Asn. Univ. Prof. Publ: Henry Stevens of Vermont, Amsterdam, 63; The Possibility of Extensive Academic Library Cooperation in Ohio: a Survey, Ohio Col. Asn, 63. Consult: 1) Ohio Col. Asn, c/o Ohio State Univ, Columbus, survey of the possibilities of acad. libr. cooperation, Jan-Mar. 63; 2) Vt. Coun. Acad. Libr, Vt. Pub. Libr. Serv, Montpelier, study toward correlation of acquisitions policies, July-Dec. 68. Specialties: 2f, 2g; 8c, 8f.

PARSONS, MRS. MARY DUDLEY, Mar. 21, 15; Permanent U.S. Address: c/o W.J. Boles, 2701 Pine Knoll Dr, Walnut Creek, Calif. 94595. Home: Cía. Agrícola de Río Tinto, La Lima, Cortés, Honduras. B.A, Univ. Calif. Berkeley, 36, cert. librarianship, 37. Head librn, Univ. Am, Mexico City, 55-62; prof. libr. admin. & orgn, Escuela Interamericana de Bibliotecología, Univ. Antioquia, Medellin, Colombia, 64- Mem: ALA; Asn. Mexicana de Bibliotecarios. Publ: The College Library: Laboratory or Store-

---

5) PERSONNEL AND RECRUITING, 5a) job evaluation and description, salary recommendations, 5b) recruitment of professionals and management personnel, 5c) administrative organization, 6) PUBLIC RELATIONS, 6a) publications, 6b) publicity programs, 6c) public opinion surveys, 6d) others, 7) SERVICES, 7a) evaluation of current program, 7b) studies of service to special publics, e.g., students, handicapped, aged, etc., 7c) programs for the implementation of new laws, program proposals to governments, 7d) others, 8) COMMUNITY, REGIONAL, STATE PLANNING, 8a) legislative programs, 8b) area analyses, 8c) centralized systems, cooperative arrangements, 8d) development of standards, 8e) state libraries and extension agencies, 8f) regional and statewide surveys, 8g) others, 9) OTHERS.

house?, In: Antología, MCC, 1956, Mexico City Col, 56; Directory of Mexico City Libraries (compiler, with R.A. Gordillo), Mexico City Col, 58; Descriptive List of Theses and Research Papers...(ed), Mexico City Col, 60; contrib. to Libr. J, ALA Bull. & Sci. of Man. Consult: 1) Escuela Nacional de Bibliotecarios & Archivistas, Durango 93, México, D.F, survey of orgn. of sch, curriculum, teaching methods, libr. resources with recommendations, Sept-Nov. 63; 2) Univ. Autónoma de Santo Domingo, Santo Domingo, Dominican Republic, reorgn. of libr. serv, survey of libr. facilities & planning for meeting of libr. experts, with Marietta Daniels Shepard, Mar-Apr. 65. Specialties: 1c; 2a, 2b; 3b, 3c, 3d; 5a, 5c; 7a, 7b; 8d.

PEASE, WILLIAM ARTIS, Jan. 28, 34; Librarian, Fackenthal Library, Franklin and Marshall College, Lancaster, Pa. 17604. A.B, Harvard, 59; M.S.L.S, Simmons Col, 61. Asst. librn, acquisitions dept, Univ. N.C, 61-62, undergrad. librn, 62-66; librn. designate, Franklin and Marshall College, Lancaster, Pa, 66-67, librn, 67- Mem: ALA; Pa. Libr. Asn. Publ: Words, Words, Words, Libr. J, 10/15/63; Robert B. House Undergraduate Library, N.C. Libr, winter 65; Opening-day Collection, Choice, 9-12/65; A List of Reference Works, an appendix to the Random House Dictionary of the English Language, 66. Consult: 1) E. Carolina Col, Greenville, N.C, book selection consult. for air force base acad. center, 63; 2) Random House, Inc, 501 Madison Ave, New York, N.Y, consult. to the Random House dictionary of the English language on major reference works, with Richard J. Lietz, 65-66. Specialties: 1b; 2h (acad).

PERREAULT, JEAN MICHEL, Jan. 6, 31; Director of the Library, University of Alabama, Huntsville, Ala. 35807. Home: 4009 Granada Dr. S.E, Huntsville, Ala. 35802. B.S, 52; M.A, 57; M.A. in L.S, 59. Librn. I & II, Milwaukee Pub. Libr, 59-63; chief cataloging, Fla. Atlantic Univ. Libr, 63-64, head, info. retrieval serv, 64-65; lectr, sch. libr. & info. serv, Univ. Md, College Park, Md, 65-68. Other: Corresponding mem, classification res. cmt, Fedn. Int. Document, 66-; mem. classification subcmt, cmt. Z-39, Am. Standards Asn, 66-; mem, info. retrieval cmt, ALA, 66-68, chmn, 68- Mem: ALA; U.S. Am. Standards Inst; affiliate, Fedn. Int. Document; Delta Epsilon Sigma. Publ: On Bibliography and Automation, or, How to Reinvent the Catalog, Libri, XV: 287-339; Categories and Relators; a New Schema, Revue Int. Document, XXXII: 136-144; Approaches to Library Filing by Computer, Clinic on Libr. Applications of Data Processing, Urbana, 66; Re-Classification; Some warnings and a Proposal, Ill. Grad. Sch. Libr. Sci. Occasional Paper 87; Proceedings of the International Symposium on Relational Factors in Classification (ed), Pergamon, Oxford, 67; Towards Explication of the Rules of Formation in UDC, FID/CR Report 4. Consult: 1) Bro-Dart Found, 57 Earl St, Newark, N.J, investigation of permissible compaction of descriptive bibliog. data & title entries, with T.C. Hines, Sept. 65-May 66; 2) Environmental Sci. Serv. Admin, U.S. Dept. Commerce, Wash. Sci. Center, Rockville, Md, survey of un-unified libr. systs, with J.C. Colson & K.M. Baker, Apr. 67-; 3) U.S. Pub. Health Serv. Nat. Center. Health Serv. Res. & Develop, participant in site visits, 67-; 4) Biological Sci. Commun. Project, George Washington Univ, develop. of computerized searchability of the UDC, with T. Caless, 67- Specialties: 2d (philosophy, bibliog); 3a, 3b; 4a, 4b.

PERRINE, RICHARD H, Jan. 2, 18; Reference Librarian & Architectural Consultant, Rice University Library, Houston, Tex. 77001. Home: 5701 Jackson, Apt. 105, Houston, Tex. 77004. B.F.A.(archit), Yale Univ, 40; M.L.S, Univ. Tex. 61. V.pres. & gen. mgr, Hawthorne Co, Houston, Tex, 53-58; libr. asst, Rice Inst. Libr, Houston, Tex, 58-60, reference librn, Rice Univ. Libr, 61- Other: Pres, RSD, 68-69. Mem: ALA; Tex. Libr. Asn. Publ: Problems of Urban Universities: Library Services for the High School Student (with Hardin Craig, Jr), Libr. Trends, 4/62; The 1965 Reference Librarians' Catalog Use Study, RQ, 66. Consult: 1) Huston-Tillotson Col, Austin, Tex. consult. for use of ACRL grant, Jan-Mar. 66; 2) Laredo Jr. Col, Laredo, Tex, new libr. bldg. & site, Oct. 66- Specialties: 1b.

PERRY, E. CASWELL, July 13, 12; Director, Public Library of Knoxville & Knox County. Home: 414 Forest Park Blvd, Knoxville, Tenn. 37917. A.B, Univ. Calif, Los Angeles, 38; B.L.S, Columbia Univ, 39. City librn, Burbank Pub. Libr, Burbank, Calif, 52-68; dir, Pub. Libr. Knoxville & Knox County, Tenn, 68- Other: Chmn. pub. relations cmt, Calif. Libr. Asn, 54; chmn. intellectual freedom cmt, 64 & 65; pres, Pub. Libr. Execs. Asn. South. Calif, 65; mem. intellectual freedom cmt, ALA, 68-70. Mem: ALA; Tenn. Libr. Asn; Southeast. Libr. Asn. Publ: Central Library, City of Burbank (with Eugene W. Fickes), Calif. Librn, 4/65; Library Services for the City of Culver City: a Report with Recommendations (with Edwin Castagna), 5/65; Site and Building Requirements for the Corona Public Library: a Study, 6/66; A Program for a New Public Library for Greene County, Tennessee, 6/68. Consult: 1) City of Culver City, Calif, feasibility study for establishing an independent city libr, with Edwin Castagna, 65; 2) Corona Pub. Libr, Corona, Calif, study & recommendation for new cent. bldg. & site, 66; 3) Green County Libr, Greeneville, Tenn, program for a county libr. bldg, June 68. Specialties: 1a, 1e, 1f, 1g; 2a, 2d (local & regional hist).

KEY TO CONSULTING SPECIALTIES: 1) ARCHITECTURE AND BUILDINGS, 1a) public libraries, 1b) academic libraries, 1c) school libraries, 1d) special libraries, 1e) library interiors, 1f) furnishings, 1g) site and location, 1h) other architectural; 2) COLLECTIONS: SELECTION, EVALUATION, WEEDING, 2a) adults, 2b) young adults, 2c) children, 2d) subject specialty, 2e) O.P. searches, 2f) rare books, 2g) appraisals, 2h) others; 3) TECHNICAL PROCESSES, 3a) cataloging, 3b) classification systems, 3c) acquisitions, 3d) materials processing, 3e) work flow and cost studies, 3f) others, 4) AUTOMATION, 4a) applications of data processing equipment, 4b) information storage and retrieval systems, 4c) systems analysis, 4d) others

PETERSON, HARRY N, Sept. 27, 07; Director, District of Columbia Public Library, Washington, D.C. 20001. Harry N. Peterson, Library Building & Management Consultant, 2000 Connecticut Ave. N.W, Washington, D.C. 20008. B.S, N.Y. Univ, 28; B.S.(libr. serv), Columbia Univ, 34. Dir, D.C. Pub. Libr, Wash, D.C, 47- Other: Mem. exec. bd, Tex. Libr. Asn, 39-41, 1st v.pres. & pres-elect, 42 & 46; mem. coun, ALA, 39-46, 49-52 & 55-63, mem. exec. bd, 61-62, 2nd v.pres, 62-63, mem. bd. dirs, LAD, 59-63; treas, Southwest. Libr. Asn, 40-42, 2nd v.pres, 46-47; temporary dir. & incorporator, U.S. Book Exchange, 48, mem. bd. dirs. & treas, 50; mem, libr. develop. cmt, PLA, 54-57, mem. coun, 55-59; mem, joint cmt. on reading develop, Am. Book Publ. Coun-ALA, 56-62; mem. bd. trustees, Wash. Educ. TV Asn, 57-; mem. exec. bd, D.C. Libr. Asn, 58-59. Mem: ALA; D.C. Libr. Asn; Wash. Educ. TV Asn; Cosmos Club. Publ: To Remodel or Not to Remodel, In: Guidelines for Library Planners: Proceedings of the Library Buildings and Equipment Institute, ALA, 60; Present and Future Library Service in Tarrant County, Texas, Ft. Worth Pub. Libr, 61; The Fort Lauderdale Public Library: A Survey, Wash, D.C, 63; Access to the D.C. Public Library (with Catherine M. Houck), D.C. Pub. Libr, rev. ed, 63; Public Library Organization & Public Library Management, In: Local Public Library Administration, Int. City Mgrs' Asn. (jointly sponsored with ALA), 64. Consult: 1) Aurora Pub. Libr, Aurora, Ill, complete Anal. of main libr. requirements, 62; 2) Glenview Pub. Libr, Glenview, Ill, statement of program for new main libr, 63; 3) Davenport Pub. Libr, Davenport, Iowa, site study, statement of program requirements, anal. of plans, 65; 4) D.C. Pub. Libr, Washington, D.C, program for new Downtown Cent. Libr, libr. consult. to Mies van der Rohe, 65-68; 5) East Orange Free Pub. Libr, East Orange, N.J, program for new libr, 68. Specialties: 1a, 1f, 1g; 7a; 9 (numerous surveys).

PITERNICK, GEORGE, Apr. 5, 18; Associate Professor of Librarianship, School of Librarianship, University of British Columbia, Vancouver 8, B.C, Can. Home: 1615 Vine St, Vancouver 9, B.C, Can. A.B, 39; B.L.S, 47. Cataloger, Univ. Calif. Libr, 47-54, catalog analyst, 54-58, libr. admin. analyst, 58-61; asst. dir. libr, Univ. Wash, Seattle, 61-65; assoc. prof. librarianship, Univ. B.C, Vancouver, 65- Mem: ALA; Can. Libr. Asn; Med. Libr. Asn; SLA; B.C. Libr. Asn; Pac. Northwest Libr. Asn; Asn. Am. Libr. Schs. Publ: Library Growth and Academic Quality, Col. & Res. Libr, 5/63; Duplicate Catalogs in University Libraries, Libr. Quart, 1/64. Consult: 1) Carleton Univ, Ottawa, Ont, Can, orgn. tech. serv, July 66. Specialties: 3a, 3d, 3e; 9 (acad. libr. admin. orgn).

POLLACK, ERVIN H, Apr. 19, 13; Professor of Law & Director of Research Services, Ohio State University College of Law Library, Columbus, Ohio 43210. Home: 1000 Urlin Ave, Columbus, Ohio 43212. LL.B, 39. Prof. law & law librn, Ohio State Univ, 54-59; prof. law & dir. res. serv, Ohio State Univ, 59- Other: Pres, Ohio Asn. Law Libr, 49-51; consult, Office of Econ. Stabilization, 51; pres, Am. Asn. Law Libr, 58-59; consult, Libr. Congress, 59-64; consult, U.S. Dept. State, 66- Mem: Am. Asn. Law Libr; Ohio Asn. Law Libr; Order of Coif. Publ: Ohio Court Rules Annotated, 49; Ohio Unreported Judicial Decisions Prior to 1823, 52; Brandeis Reader, 56; Fundamentals of Legal Research, 3rd ed, 67. Consult: 1) Univ. Houston Col. of Law Libr, Houston, Tex, surveyed Law Libr, 63; 2) Mahoning County Law Libr, Court House, Youngstown, Ohio, surveyed libr; & served as expert witness in law suit filed by Libr. Asn. against County Cmnrs, 64; 3) Tulane Univ. Sch. of Law, New Orleans, La, surveyed law libr, 65; 4) West. Reserve Univ. Law Libr, Cleveland, Ohio, survey of law libr, 66; 5) St. Louis County Law Libr, gen. consult, 68. Specialties: 1h (law libr); 2d (law); 9 (law libr).

POOLE, FRAZER G, Nov. 5, 15; Preservation Officer, Library of Congress, Washington, D.C. 20540. Home: 5410 Surrey St, Chevy Chase, Md. 20015. A.B, 37; B.L.S, 49. Asst. librn, Univ. Calif, Santa Barbara, 56-59; dir. libr. tech. project, ALA, 59-63; dir. libr, Univ. Ill, Chicago Circle, 63-67. Mem: Ill. Libr. Asn; Calif. Libr. Asn; Am. Document. Inst; ALA. Publ: Library Technology at Work, ALA Bull, 1/60; Library Furniture and Equipment (ed. with Edward Johnson & Alphonse Trezza), ALA, 63; Performance Standards and Specifications in the Library Economy, Libr. Trends, 4/63; The Library Environment, Aspects of Interior Planning (ed), ALA, 65; The Selection and Evaluation of Library Bookstacks, Libr. Trends, 4/65. Consult: 1) St. Benedict's Col, Atchison, Kans, bldg. planning, preparation of bldg. program, review & critique of architect's plans, recommendations & assistance in selection of architect, 64-67; 2) Monmouth Col, Monmouth, Ill, bldg. program, review & critique of architect's plans, 65-; 3) Iowa Wesleyan Col, Mt. Pleasant, review & critique of plans, furniture layout, & specifications, 65-; 4) Rosary Col, River Forest, Ill, bldg. program, review & critique of architect's plans, 66-; 5) Univ. Wis, Parkside Campus, Kenosha, Wis, bldg. program, review & critique of plans, 66- Specialties: 1b, 1e, 1f, 1g.

POPECKI, JOSEPH THOMAS, Nov. 25, 24; Director of the Library, St. Michael's College Library, Winooski, Vt. 05404. B.A, 45; B.S.L.S, 49. Lectr, sch. educ, Cath. Univ. Am, 50-67, asst. to dir. libr, 53-58, asst. dir. libr,

5) PERSONNEL AND RECRUITING, 5a) job evaluation and description, salary recommendations, 5b) recruitment of professionals and management personnel, 5c) administrative organization, 6) PUBLIC RELATIONS, 6a) publications, 6b) publicity programs, 6c) public opinion surveys, 6d) others, 7) SERVICES, 7a) evaluation of current program, 7b) studies of service to special publics, e.g., students, handicapped, aged, etc., 7c) programs for the implementation of new laws, program proposals to governments, 7d) others, 8) COMMUNITY, REGIONAL, STATE PLANNING, 8a) legislative programs, 8b) area analyses, 8c) centralized systems, cooperative arrangements, 8d) development of standards, 8e) state libraries and extension agencies, 8f) regional and statewide surveys, 8g) others, 9) OTHERS.

58-65, acting dir. libr, 65-67; dir. libr, St. Michael's Col, Winooski, Vt, 67- Other: Lectr, U.S. Dept. Agr. Grad. Sch, 50-67; past pres, Wash-Md. unit, Cath. Libr. Asn, 55-56, mem. adv. bd, 59-64; pres, Mid-Atlantic Assocs, Inc, Wash, D.C, 61-68; instnl. rep, Interuniv. Libr. Coun. Wash, D.C, 65-67. Mem: ALA; Cath. Libr. Asn; D.C. Libr. Asn; Am. Soc. Info. Sci. Publ: Near-Print Duplication and Photographic Reproduction, 54; Proposed Scope and Coverage of the Goddard Space Flight Center Library (with Frank J. Bertalan), 63; An Introduction to Bibliography, 64, A Thesaurus of Terms for the Coordinate Indexing of Nursing and Biomedical Literature, 66; A Union List of Serials of the University Libraries of Washington, D.C. (gen. ed), 67. Consult: 1) Dunbarton Col, 2935 Upton St. N.W, Wash, D.C, review of new libr. interior arrangement, furnishings, Sept-Oct. 65; 2) Am. Psychological Asn, 1700 18th St. N.W, Wash, D.C, new libr. design & furnishings, continuing consultation on info. serv. & index publ, 65-; 3) Computer Usage Corp, 7315 Wis. Ave. N.W, Wash. D.C, libr. technician on Nat. Libr. Med. proposal team, Feb-Mar. 66; 4) Naval Inst, Annapolis, Md, design of indexing system for centennial index of the Proceedings, Mar-Dec. 66. Specialties: 1b, 1c, 1e, 1f; 3f (forms design); 4a, 4b, 4d (automated production of indexes, bibliog); 6c; 7a; 8c.

PORTTEUS, ELNORA M, Directing Supervisor, School Libraries, Cleveland Public Schools, 1380 E. Sixth St, Cleveland, Ohio 44114. Home: 7357 W. Lake Blvd, Twin Lakes, Kent, Ohio 44240. B.S, 41; M.A. in L.S, 54. Librn, Findlay City Schs, Ohio, to 58; asst. prof. & sch. libr. specialist, sch. libr. sci, Kent State Univ, 58-65; directing supvr. libr, Cleveland Pub. Schs, Ohio, 65- Other: Pres, Ohio Asn. Sch. Librns, 58; chmn. serv. to schs. roundtable, Ohio Libr. Asn, 59, chmn. scholarship cmt, 65-; chmn, Midwest PATI-AASL Cmt, 63-66; consult. for children's books, Rand McNally & Co, 66-; vis. prof, Edinboro State Col, Univ. Tenn. & Appalachain State Univ; distinguished alumna award, Kent State Univ. Sch. Libr. Sci. Mem: ALA; AASL; Ohio Libr. Asn; Ohio Asn. Sch. Librns; Women's Nat. Book Asn; Delta Kappa Gamma. Publ: Aspects of Librarianship: When a Businessman Says Information Please, 53, School Library Budgets, 58 & Awards in the Field of Childrens' Books, 59, Kent State Univ; What to Buy First, Wilson Libr. Bull, 10/61; Focus on Libraries, Ohio Schs, 4/65; Handbook for Volunteer Service in Elementary Schools, Cleveland Pub. Schs, 65, 66. Consult: 1) Crestline Pub. Schs, Crestline, Ohio, elem. libr. planning, renovation of libr, 59 & 61; 2) East Liverpool Pub. Schs, East Liverpool, Ohio, weeding collections & remodeling of quarters, 60; 3) Warren Pub. Schs, Warren, Ohio, bldg. program, with Cooperative Educ. Serv, 60; 4) Mt. Gilead Pub. Schs, Mt. Gilead, Ohio, new bldg, planning, weeding of collection, personnel, 62; 5) Boardman Pub. Schs, Boardman, Ohio, instructional resources concept & quarters planning, personnel, with Cooperative Educ. Serv, 63. Specialties: 1c, 1f,,1h (remodeling); 2b, 2c, 2d (hist, soc. studies, older children's books—18th & 19th century); 3a; 5a, 5b, 5c; 6a, 6b; 8f (nat. survey, U.S. Office); 9 (integration of libr. in sch. curriculum).

PRICE, PAXTON P, June 18, 13; Chief, Library Services Branch, U.S. Office of Education, Washington, D.C. 20202. Home: 4420 41st St N, Arlington, Va. 22207. B.S, 37; B.S. in L.S, 41. State librn, Mo. State Libr, 49-64; Chief, Libr. Serv. Br, U.S. Office Educ, 64- Other: Pres, Nat. Asn. State Librns, 54; mem. coun, ALA, 59-63; pres, Mo. Libr. Asn, 60. Mem: D.C. Libr. Asn; ALA. Publ: State and Provincial Libraries in the U.S. and Canada, (ed), Libr. Trends, 4-56; Aspects of the Financial Administration of Libraries (co-ed), Libr. Trends, 4/63; Trustee and ALA Standards, In: The Library Trustee, 64; Financial Administration, In: Local Public Library Administration, 64; The California Partnership March to Meet the Challenge, News Notes Calif. Libr, fall 66; LSCA Amendments of 1966, Health, Educ. & Welfare Indicators, 9/66. Consult: 1) Biblioteca Nacional, Bogota, Colombia, S. Am, recommended staff training plan & plan for reorgn. of libr, Oct-Dec. 60; 2) U.S. expert at UNESCO Int. Conf. on Nat. Libr. Planning for Latin Am, Quito, Ecuador, 66. Specialties: 8e; 9 (nat. planning & financial mgt).

PRIDEAUX, B. ELIZABETH, Dec. 26, 14; Consultant on School Library Resources, State Department of Education, Salem, Ore. 97301. Home: Route 1, Box 318, Lyons, Ore. 97358. B.S, Ore. State Univ, 36, M. in Librarianship, Univ. Wash, 64. Librn, Stayton High Sch, Stayton, Ore, 60-66; consult. on sch. libr. resources, State Dept. Educ, Salem, Ore, 66- Other: Secy, Ore. Libr. Asn, 66; chmn. bd. trustees, Lyons Pub. Libr, 67- Mem: ALA; Nat. Educ. Asn; Dept. Audiovisual Instruction; Pac. Northwest Libr. Asn; Ore. Educ. Asn; Ore. Asn. Sch. Librns; Ore. Libr. Asn; Ore. Instructional Media Asn. Publ: ESEA Title II Handbook, State Dept. Educ, Salem, Ore, 66; Project Open Door: Demonstration School Library Programs, A Project of ESEA Title II, State Dept. Educ, Ore, 67; Open Door to Learning, Ore. Bd. Educ, 67. Consult: 1) Grants Pass Sch. Dist, 610 N.E. A St, Grants Pass, Ore, eval. of sch. libr. facilities, resources, program of all schs, 1-12 & recommendation for improved libr. program, with Phyllis Hochstettler, Jan. 67; 2) Eagle Point High Sch, Eagle Point, Ore, eval. of libr. facility, resources & program with recommendations, Mar. 67; 3) Villa St. Rose, 597 N. Dekum St, Portland, Ore, eval. of juvenile detention sch. facilities, resources & program with recommendations, May 67; 4) Rockwood Sch. Dist,

---

KEY TO CONSULTING SPECIALTIES: 1) ARCHITECTURE AND BUILDINGS, 1a) public libraries, 1b) academic libraries, 1c) school libraries, 1d) special libraries, 1e) library interiors, 1f) furnishings, 1g) site and location, 1h) other architectural; 2) COLLECTIONS: SELECTION, EVALUATION, WEEDING, 2a) adults, 2b) young adults, 2c) children, 2d) subject specialty, 2e) O.P. searches, 2f) rare books, 2g) appraisals, 2h) others; 3) TECHNICAL PROCESSES, 3a) cataloging, 3b) classification systems, 3c) acquisitions, 3d) materials processing, 3e) work flow and cost studies, 3f) others, 4) AUTOMATION, 4a) applications of data processing equipment, 4b) information storage and retrieval systems, 4c) systems analysis, 4d) others

740 S.E. 182nd, Portland, Ore, eval. of sch. libr. facilities, resources & program of 5 elem. schs. with recommendations, May 67; 5) Lincoln Sch, Pendleton, Ore, evaluated libr. program & resources, advised on improvements needed to qualify for a Spec. Projects grant, May 67. Specialties: 1a; 2b, 2c; 3a, 3b, 3c, 3d; 5a; 6a; 7a, 7b, 7c, 7d (ESEA Title II); 8b, 8c, 8f.

PROCTOR, MRS. MARGIA W, Mar. 8, 98; Independent Consultant, 151 Garrison Rd, Williamsville, N.Y. 14221. B.A, 20. Supvr. br, Buffalo & Erie County Pub. Libr, 52-57, deputy dir. libr, 57-66; consult. libr. bldgs, 66- Second v.pres, N.Y. Libr. Asn, 63, chmn. bldg. cmt, 65; leader, Libr. Bldg. Inst, N.Y, 66- Consult: 1) Lockport Pub. Libr, Lockport, N.Y, bldg. consult, study & recommendations on addition to and renovation of present bldg. and/or new bldg, spring 66; 2) North Tonawanda Pub. Libr, Tonawanda, N.Y, study and layouts for new bldg. & recommendations on addition to and renovation of present bldg. spring 66; 3) Patterson Libr, Westfield, N.Y, study & recommendations on renovation of libr. bldg, spring, 66; 4) Dunkirk Free Libr, Dunkirk, N.Y, study & recommendations on addition to & renovation of libr. bldg, spring 66; 5) Richmond Mem. Libr, Batavia, N.Y, study of present facilities & recommendations on site size & layout of new bldg, spring, 66. Specialties: 1a, 1e, 1f, 1g; 8b.

PULLEN, DR. WILLIAM R, Nov. 10, 19; Librarian, Georgia State College, Atlanta, Ga. 30303. Home: 2545 N. Druid Hills Rd. N.E, Atlanta, Ga. 30329. B.A, Univ. N.C, 42, B.S. in L.S, 47, M.A, 48, Ph.D, 51. Asst. librn, Univ. N.C. Libr, 57-58; librn, Ga. State Col, Atlanta, 59- Other: Fel, Carnegie Project in Advanced Libr. Admin, Rutgers Univ, 58; ed, Southeast. Librn, 61-64; secy, Ga. Libr. Asn, 65-67. Mem: ALA; Southeast. Libr. Asn; Ga. Libr. Asn. Publ: A Check List of Legislative Journals, ALA, 55; Selective Acquisitions at Yale, In: Studies in Library Administrative Problems, Rutgers Univ. Grad. Sch. Libr. Serv, 60; A Programmed Text on the Use of the Library for Georgia State College Students, Ga. State Col. Libr, 66. Consult: 1) Andrew Col, Cuthbert, Ga, wrote libr. bldg. program & consulted on preliminary plans, 65; 2) Young Harris Col, Young Harris, Ga, preliminary plans of libr. bldg, 65; 3) Atlantic Christian Col, Wilson, N.C, remodeling of existing libr. bldg, 65-66; 4) Campbellsville Col, Campbellsville, Ky, remodeling of existing libr. bldg, 67; 5) Mobile State Jr. Col, Mobile, Ala, preliminary plans for new libr. bldg, 67. Specialties: 1b, 1f; 2h (documents).

PUTNAM, HAMILTON S, Nov. 1, 10. Owner, Hamilton S. Putnam & Associates, 4 Park St, Concord, N.H. 03301. Home: 34 Ridge Rd, Concord, N.H. 03301. Accredited pub. relations counselor, Pub. Relations Soc. Am, 66. Publ: History, Wilton, New Hampshire, 39; History, Amphibious Forces, U.S. Navy, 45; History, New Hampshire Medical Society, 66. Consult: 1) State Librn, 20 Park St, Concord, N.H, full pub. relations counsel serv, 56- 2) State Libr, State House, Augusta, Maine, consult. to Creative Assocs, under Maine contract, 64- Specialties: 1a; 6a, 6b, 6c, 6d (planning); 7a, 7b, 7c; 8a, 8b, 8d, 8e, 8f.

R

RALEY, MRS. LUCILE W, Apr. 21, 07; Consultant in Library Services, Waco Independent School District, P.O. Drawer 27, Waco, Tex. 76703. Home: 4101 Grim Ave, Waco, Tex. 76710. B.A, 29; B.S.(libr. sci), 41. Libr. consult, Waco Independent Sch. Dist, Waco, Tex, 46- Other: Mem. elem. sch. libr. cmt, Asn. Sch. Libr, 52-54; chmn, Asn. Sch. Libr. Supvr, 56-57; mem. bd. consult, Standard Catalog for High Sch. Libr, 56-65; mem. adv. cmt, Univ. Tex. Grad. Sch. Libr. Sci; treas, AASL, 58-62; mem. bd. consult, Standard Catalog for Jr. High Sch. Libr, 65- Mem: ALA; Southwest. Libr. Asn; Tex. Libr. Asn; AASL; Am. Asn. Sch. Libr. Suprv; Friends of Libr; Nat. Educ. Asn; Tex. State Teachers Asn. Publ: Keeping Pace with Curriculum Development, Nat. Elem. Principal, 9/51; contrib, Saturday Review, 54-60; Texas TALA Convention, Sch. Libr, 5/56; Planning is a Family Affair in Waco, Libr. J, 2/15/60 & Jr. Libr, 2/60; Texas: Wilderness to Space Age (with William C. Pool & Claude Elliott), Naylor, 63; revised list of Books for Young Readers and Books for Older Readers, In: World Book Encyclopedia. Consult: 1) Highland Park Schs, Dallas, Tex, consult. in libr. serv. to help evaluate Highland Park Schs, with Tex. Educ. Agency Cmt, Oct. 64. Specialties: 1c, 1e, 1f; 2b, 2c; 3d; 5a, 5b; 6a, 6b; 7a, 7b, 7c; 8a, 8c, 8d.

RAMIREZ, WILLIAM LOUIS, Aug. 17, 25; Principal Librarian, Department of Rare Books & Special Collections, San Francisco Public Library, San Francisco, Calif. 94102. Home: 515 Vicente St, San Francisco, Calif. 94116. B.S, 48; B.L.S, 54. Head librn, bindery & book repair dept, San Francisco Pub. Libr. Syst, Calif, 56-59; principal librn, Richmond Br. Libr, 60-63, principal librn, dept. rare books & spec. collections, 63- Other: Mem, Calif. librn. advertising cmt, Calif. Libr. Asn, 57, mem, staff orgns. roundtable organizing cmt, 58-59, mem, Calif. libr. hist. cmt, 61, chmn, 63-64, mem, intellectual freedom cmt, 62; pres, San Francisco Pub. Libr. Staff Asn, 59-60, mem. bd. dirs, 60-61; mem. bd. dirs. & secy, Arguello Park Asn. San Francisco, 60-63; mem. bd. dirs, San Francisco Pub. Libr. Scholarship Fund, Inc, 64- Mem: Calif. Libr. Asn; ALA; San

---

5) PERSONNEL AND RECRUITING, 5a) job evaluation and description, salary recommendations, 5b) recruitment of professionals and management personnel, 5c) administrative organization, 6) PUBLIC RELATIONS, 6a) publications, 6b) publicity programs, 6c) public opinion surveys, 6d) others, 7) SERVICES, 7a) evaluation of current program, 7b) studies of service to special publics, e.g., students, handicapped, aged, etc., 7c) programs for the implementation of new laws, program proposals to governments, 7d) others, 8) COMMUNITY, REGIONAL, STATE PLANNING, 8a) legislative programs, 8b) area analyses, 8c) centralized systems, cooperative arrangements, 8d) development of standards, 8e) state libraries and extension agencies, 8f) regional and statewide surveys, 8g) others, 9) OTHERS.

Francisco Bay Area Reference Librns. Coun; San Francisco Pub. Libr. Staff Asn; Pub. Libr. Execs. Cent. Calif; Beta Phi Mu; Univ. Calif. Schs. Librarianship Alumni Asn. Publ: SCOWAH—The Schmulowitz Collection of Wit and Humor, Folklore & Folk Music Archivist, summer 63; Nat Schmulowitz, Calif. Librn, 4/66. Consult: 1) Salvation Army Officers Training Col, 1450 Laguna St, San Francisco, Calif, organized col. libr, with William A. Laughrey, 58-62; 2) Oakland Pub. Libr, 1457 Fruitvale Ave, Oakland, Calif, advise & recommend programs, materials & serv. for Spanish-speaking population of Oakland, Mar. 66- Specialties: 2a; 7a, 7b.

RAPHAEL, ANNE WAGNER, Apr. 12, 41; Library Systems Analyst, Programming Services, Inc, 999 Commercial St, Palo Alto, Calif. 94303. Home: 176 Osage Ave, Los Altos, Calif. 94022. B.A.(physiology), Mt. Holyoke Col, 62; M.L.S, Univ. Calif, Berkeley, 65. Libr. asst, Arthur D. Little, Inc, Cambridge, Mass, 62-64; reference librn, NASA, Ames Res. Center, Mountain View, Calif, 65-66; res. assoc, Programming Serv, Inc, 66- Mem: SLA; Am. Soc. Info. Sci; Beta Phi Mu. Consult: 1) Libr. of Congress, Wash, D.C, anal. of MARC project, including surveys of participating libr. & planning for expanded tape distribution of bibliog. data, with Charles Bourne, Oct. 66-Aug. 67; 2) ITT Semiconductors, 1801 Page Mill Rd, Palo Alto, Calif, anal. of small libr. collection, procedures & user needs, with Lisa Fajardo, Mar. 67-July 67; 3) Nat. Libr. Med, Bethesda, Md, anal. of an abstracting serv. in the field of pharmacology, Mar. 67-Aug. 67. Specialties: 2d (sci. & tech); 3a, 3b, 3c, 3d; 4a, 4b, 4c; 7c; 8c.

RATEAVER, DR. BARGYLA, Aug. 3, 16. Home: 8 Stadium Way, Kentfield, Calif. 94904. A.B. (botany), 43; M.S.(botany), Univ. Mich, 50, Ph.D, 51; M.S.L.S, Univ. Calif, Berkeley, 59. Organizer new libr, Dalmo Victor, 61; organizer new libr, Lockheed Calif. Co, 62; regional rep, J.W. Stacey, 63; automation analyst, N.Am. Aviation, Downey, Calif, 63-64; regional rep, McClelland & Stewart, Ont, 64-65; instr. libr. workshop, Calgary Sch. Bd. Adult Educ, 65; consult. sci-tech, Santa Rosa Pub. Libr, 66-67; organizer new libr, Loma Alta Schs, San Rafael, Calif, 67-68. Mem: Calif. Libr. Asn; ALA. Publ: Automation Primer, Systems and Procedures Manual, N.Am. Aviation. Consult: 1) Dalmo Victor, Belmont, Calif, proposal for setting up new libr, Nov. 61; 2) Hitco Co, Gardena, Calif, survey of existing facilities & methods with recommendations, fall 64; 3) Santa Rosa Pub. Libr, Third St, Santa Rosa, Calif, selection, acquisition & cataloging of new collection in sci. & tech, Oct. 66-Feb. 67. Specialties: 1d, 1e, 1f; 2a, 2b, 2c, 2d (sci. & tech); 3c; 4b, 4d (descriptions of automation systs, simplified explanations of automated systs);

6b; 9 (specialist in organizing new libr, consult. in sci. & tech, sci. books for children, training of nonprofessionals, course outlines & proposals).

READY, WILLIAM BERNARD, Sept. 16, 14; University Librarian & Professor of Bibliography, Mills Memorial Library, McMaster University, Hamilton, Ont, Can. Home: 170 Woodview Crescent, Ancaster, Ont, Can. B.A, Univ. Wales, 36, B.A, 38, dipl. paleography, 39; dipl. educ, Oxford Univ, 46; M.A, Univ. Manitoba, 48. Univ. librn. & assoc. prof. English, Marquette Univ, 56-61; univ. librn. & prof. bibliog, Sacred Heart Univ, 66; univ. librn. & prof. bibliog, McMaster Univ, Hamilton, Ont, Can, 66- Other: Chmn. publ. bd, ACRL, 54-58; secy, Libr. Resources Bd, 58-61; Thomas More Asn. award, 63; Clarence Day award, 64; mem, Libr. Booksellers Relations Bd, 64-; mem, Ont. Coun. Univ. Librns. Mem: ALA; Can. Libr. Asn; assoc. Libr. Asn, United Kingdom. Publ: The Great Disciple, New York, 51; The Poor Hater, Chicago, 59; The Reward of Reading, Bridgeport, 64; Tolkien Relation, Chicago, 68; contrib. to prfnl. journals. Consult: 1) Mundelein Col, Chicago, Ill, survey of bldg, future develop. & staff, 64-65; 2) U.S. Naval Acad, Annapolis, Md, survey of libr. staff, resources, bldgs, with John Berthol, Warren Hews & John McDonald, 65-66. Specialties: 1b; 2e; 3c; 4a, 4d; 6a; 8c.

REASON, DR. JOSEPH H, Mar. 23, 05; Director of University Libraries, Howard University, Washington, D.C. 20001. Home: 1242 Girard St. N.E, Washington, D.C. 20017. A.B, 28; A.B, 32; A.M, 33; B.S.L.S, 36; Ph.D, 58. Dir. univ. libr, Howard Univ, Wash, D.C, 46- Other: Mem. coun, ALA, 57-61, 2nd v.pres. & mem. coun. & exec. bd, 66-67; libr. adv, Univ. Rangoon, Burma, 61-62; exec. secy, ACRL, 62-63. Mem: ALA; ACRL; D.C. Libr. Asn. Publ: An Inquiry into the Structural Style and Originality of Chrestien's Yvain, Cath. Univ. Am, 58. Consult: 1) South. Asn. Cols, Atlanta, Ga, selections for paperback book project, with others, Feb. 66; 2) Coun. on Libr. Resources, Washington, D.C, studied serv, resources & facilities of the libr. of Va. Union Univ, Richmond, Va, Apr. 68; 3) New York Pub. Libr, New York, N.Y, serv. & resources of the Schomburg Collection, June 68. Specialties: 1b; 2a; 2d (French, Spanish, Negro in U.S); 7a.

REDMOND, DONALD A, May 19, 22; Chief Librarian, Queen's University Libraries, Kingston, Ont, Can. Home: 178 Barrie St, Kingston, Ont, Can. B.Sc, 42; B.L.S, 47; M.S. in L.S, 50. Librn, Nova Scotia Tech. Col, Halifax, Can, 49-60; sci. & engineering librn, Univ. Kans, Lawrence, Kans, 61-64; acting asst. dir. libr, 64-65; asst. dir. libr. reader serv, 65; chief librn, Queen's Univ, Kingston, Ont, 66- Other: Chmn. metal-materials div, SLA, 65-66, prfnl.

KEY TO CONSULTING SPECIALTIES: 1) ARCHITECTURE AND BUILDINGS, 1a) public libraries, 1b) academic libraries, 1c) school libraries, 1d) special libraries, 1e) library interiors, 1f) furnishings, 1g) site and location, 1h) other architectural; 2) COLLECTIONS: SELECTION, EVALUATION, WEEDING, 2a) adults, 2b) young adults, 2c) children, 2d) subject specialty, 2e) O.P. searches, 2f) rare books, 2g) appraisals, 2h) others; 3) TECHNICAL PROCESSES, 3a) cataloging, 3b) classification systems, 3c) acquisitions, 3d) materials processing, 3e) work flow and cost studies, 3f) others, 4) AUTOMATION, 4a) applications of data processing equipment, 4b) information storage and retrieval systems, 4c) systems analysis, 4d) others

consult, consultation serv. Mem: Can. Libr. Asn; SLA; ALA; Atlantic Provinces Libr. Asn; sr. mem. Chemical Inst. Can; Am. Soc. Engineering Educ; Soc. Tech. Writers & Publ. Publ: Small Technical Libraries: A Brief Guide, UNESCO Bull. Libr, 18: 49-79; After-Hours Access to Branch Libraries, Univ. Ky. Libr. Occasional Contribution 147, 64; Some Random Notes on International Expertise, Can. Libr, 11/65; Optimal Size: The Special Library Viewpoint, Sci-Tech News, 66. Consult: 1) Ceylon Inst. for Sci. & Industrial Res, 363 Bullers Rd, Colombo 7, Ceylon, tech. libr. adv, 57-58; 2) Mid. East Tech. Univ, Ankara, Turkey, dir. of the libr, planned expansion, 59-60; 3) Biblioteca Nacional Costa Rica, San Jose, Costa Rica, surveyed the Costa Rican collection catalogs of the Biblioteca Nacional Costa Rica & the libr. of the Banco Cent. Costa Rica with a view toward microfilming the catalogs for publ, Apr. 63. Specialties: 2d (sci-tech); 5a, 5b, 5c.

REICHMANN, DR. FELIX, Sept. 14, 99; Assistant Director for Development of Collections, Cornell University Libraries, Cornell University, Ithaca, N.Y. 14850. Home: 217 Willard Way, Ithaca, N.Y. 14850. Ph.D.(hist. of art, hist), Univ. Vienna, 23; M.A.(libr. sci), Univ. Chicago, 42. Asst. dir. tech. serv, Cornell Univ. Libr, 48-64, asst. dir. for develop. of collections & prof. bibliog, 64- Other: Fulbright prof. & Guggenheim fel. for study of medieval manuscript trade in Italy, 56-57. Mem: ALA. Publ: Gothische Wandmalerei in Niederoesterreich (sponsored by Vienna Acad. Sci); Amalthea Verlag, Wien, 25; German Printing in Maryland, a Check List 1768-1950, Baltimore Soc. for Hist. of Germans in Md, 50; Ephrata As Seen by Contemporaries (with E.E. Doll), German Folklore Soc, Phila, Pa, 53; Sugar, Gold, and Coffee: Essays on the History of Brazil, Cornell Univ, 59; Notched Cards, In: State of the Library Art, Rutgers Univ. Grad. Sch. Libr. Serv, 61; Library Survey of Eight Mid-Hudson Counties, 65. Consult: 1) Smithsonian Inst, Wash, D.C, libr. survey, 59; 2) Buffalo Pub. Libr, Buffalo, N.Y, libr. survey, with Maurice Tauber, 60; 3) State of N.Y, Dept. Educ, Albany, survey of eight mid-Hudson counties libr, with Joanne Rein, 65; 4) City Univ. New York, N.Y, survey of feasibility of centralized or cooperative procedures, with Irlene R. Stephens, June 66; 5) Hist. Soc. of Wis, Madison, survey of Libr, with Maurice Tauber & Irlene Roemer Stephens, 66. Specialties: 2a, 2d (humanities), 2f, 2g; 3a, 3b, 3c, 3d, 3e; 8c, 8f.

REMLEY, RALPH D, Aug. 23, 08; Self-employed, No. 209, 10400 Connecticut Ave, Kensington, Md. 20795. Home: Garrett Park, Md. 20766. B.S, 33. Asst. to dir, Bureau of Inspections, U.S. Civil Serv. Cmn, 56-61, asst. to chief, Classification Div, 61-66; alternate chmn, Canal Zone Bd. of Appeals, 59-66. Other: Mem, legis. & planning cmt, Md. Libr. Asn, 50-, chmn. & mem, trustee div, 58-; chmn. & mem, Montgomery County Libr. Bd, 50-64; mem, Md. Adv. Coun. Interlibr. Cooperation, 68- Mem: ALA; D.C. Libr. Asn; Md. Libr. Asn; ALTA. Consult: 1) Somerset County Libr, Somerville, N.J, survey of orgn. & personnel, with George B. Moreland & Norman Finkler, Sept-Dec. 66; 2) Annapolis & Anne Arundel County Libr, Annapolis, Md, job classification & pay study, Oct. 66-Jan. 67. Specialties: 5a, 5c; 8d, 8e, 8f.

RESCOE, A. STAN, Aug. 21, 10; Assistant Professor, Peabody Library School, George Peabody College for Teachers, Nashville, Tenn. 37203. Home: 812 Oxford House, 1313 21st. Ave. S, Nashville, Tenn. 37212. B.A, Cent. Mich. Univ, 49; M.A.(libr. sci), George Peabody Col. Teachers, 51. Asst. prof, Peabody Libr. Sch, George Peabody Col. Teachers, Nashville, Tenn, 51- Other: Pres, Nashville Libr. Club, 55; past pres, Nashville Catalogers, 57. Mem: ALA; Southeast Libr. Asn; Tenn. Libr. Asn; Alpha Psi Omega; Phi Beta Kappa; Phi Gamma Mu. Publ: Technical Processes, 52; Technical Processes Simplified, 56; Cataloging Made Easy, Scarecrow, 62. Consult: 1) Southern Baptist Convention, Ninth Ave. N, Nashville, Tenn, consultation in establishing & organizing libr for Baptist Sunday Sch. Bd, with Helen Conger, 54-; 2) Nashville Housing Authority, Nashville, Tenn, organized libr, cataloged collection of books & arranged pamphlet collection, 56-57; 3) Woman's Missionary Union, Birmingham, Ala, indexed the annual minutes from 1887-1957, with James Forester, 57-60; 4) Masonic Temple, Seventh at Broad, Nashville, Tenn, organized & cataloged collection, 58-59; 5) Charlotte Sch. Dist, Charlotte, Tenn, helped with application for Title II, 66. Specialties: 1d, 1f; 2a, 2d (pamphlets, pictures), 2f, 2h (bindings); 3a, 3b, 3d; 5a, 5c, 5d (guide lines for job anal); 7a, 7c, 7d (indexing); 8b, 8g (pilot resources center); 9 (bulletin bds, displays, exhibits).

RICE, CYNTHIA; Consultant, Nelson Associates, Inc, 845 Third Ave, New York, N.Y. 10022. Home: 166 E. 35th St, New York, N.Y. 10016. B.A, Rutgers Univ, 57. Planner, N.J. State Planning Bureau, 57-61; econ. researcher & statistician, Am. Petroleum Inst, 61-65; consult, Nelson Assocs, Inc, 65- Consult: 1) N.Y. State Libr, Albany, study of centralized processing activities with recommendations, with Davis Crippen, 66; 2) Temporary Adv. Coun. on Pub. Higher Educ, Seattle, Wash, planning for higher educ. needs in the State of Wash, Charles A. Nelson & with Robert L. Goldberg, 66; 3) N.Y. State Libr, Albany, evaluating pilot program in facsimile transmission of libr. materials, with Eugene Vorhies, 67-68; 4) N.Y. State Libr, Albany, evaluating pilot program in

---

5) PERSONNEL AND RECRUITING, 5a) job evaluation and description, salary recommendations, 5b) recruitment of professionals and management personnel, 5c) administrative organization, 6) PUBLIC RELATIONS, 6a) publications, 6b) publicity programs, 6c) public opinion surveys, 6d) others, 7) SERVICES, 7a) evaluation of current program, 7b) studies of service to special publics, e.g., students, handicapped, aged, etc., 7c) programs for the implementation of new laws, program proposals to governments, 7d) others, 8) COMMUNITY, REGIONAL, STATE PLANNING, 8a) legislative programs, 8b) area analyses, 8c) centralized systems, cooperative arrangements, 8d) development of standards, 8e) state libraries and extension agencies, 8f) regional and statewide surveys, 8g) others, 9) OTHERS.

expanded statewide interlibr. loan network, with Eugene Vorhies, 67-68; 5) Liaison Cmt, Pub. Libr. Bds, Lucas County, Ohio, developing a comprehensive, long-range plan for libr. serv. in the county, with Eugene Vorhies, 68. Specialties: 6c; 7a; 8c, 8e, 8f.

RICHARD, ST. CLAIR, Nov. 16, 10; Managing Partner, Halo House, Box 85, Larchmont, N.Y. 10538. Home: 60 The Boulevard, New Rochelle, N.Y. 10801. B.Lit.(journalism), Columbia Univ, 33. Pub. relations asst. to Westchester County Recreation Cmn, 59-60; asst. in municipal relations to Mayor of Mt. Vernon, N.Y, 62-63; press secy. to GOP state v.chmn, N.Y, 63-64; pub. relations dir, Westchester Libr. Syst. & pub. relations consult, Seelye, Stevenson, Valve & Knecht, at present. Other: Mem, Mayor's Cmt. on Nat. Shrine, Mount Vernon, N.Y, 57-64, exec. secy, Mayor's Adv. Cmt. on Urban Renewal, 62-63; v.chmn. bd, Cmt. for Nat. Shrine, St. Pauls, Eastchester. Mem: ALA; N.Y. Libr. Asn; Westchester Libr. Asn; N.Y. Libr. Pub. Relations Coun; N.Y. Libr. Club. Publ: Men of the Pulpit, N.Y. News, 56-58; Women in the News, 59-61; Do It Yourself Publicity, Anchora of Delta Gamma, spring 61 & Banta's Greek Exchange, 61; Women in Politics and Government, N.Y. Republican Cmt, 64; Drugs in Suburbia, N.Y. J. Am, 66. Consult: 1) County of Westchester, County Office Bldg, White Plains, N.Y, pub. relations, press relations, 60-61; 2) City of Mt. Vernon, City Hall, Mt. Vernon, N.Y, pub. relations, municipal relations, urban renewal community relations, 62-63; 3) Seelye, Stevenson, Valve & Knecht, 99 Park Ave, New York, N.Y, pub. relations, municipal relations, political relations, 62- Specialties: 6a, 6b, 6c, 6d (group dynamics; climate preparation; political & govt. liaison; news media relations).

RICHARDS, JAMES H, JR, Aug. 4, 18; Librarian, Carleton College, Northfield, Minn. 55057. Home: 219 Maple St, Northfield, Minn. 55057. B.A, Wesleyan Univ, 40, M.A, 41; B.S, Columbia Univ, 47. Librn, Carleton Col, Northfield, Minn, 52- Mem: ALA; ACRL; Minn. Libr. Asn. Consult: 1) Simpson Col, Indianola, Iowa, preliminary bldg. program, Feb. 56; 2) Centre Col, Danville, Ky, preliminary bldg. program, critique of basic plans, with Ralph Ellsworth, Apr. 63; 3) Concordia Col, Moorhead, Minn, survey of book collection with recommendations, Mar. 65-Mar. 66. Specialties: 1b; 2e; 8c.

ROBERTSON, BILLY O'NEAL, Mar. 27, 30; Director Media Network, Lincoln Public Schools, Box 200, Lincoln, Nebr. 68501. Home: 7310 S. Wedgewood Dr, Lincoln, Nebr. 68505. B.A, 59; M.A, 63. High sch. librn, 59-61; multi-sch. librn, 61-63; supvr. sch. libr, Greeley, Colo, 63-65; coordinator libr. serv, Lincoln Pub. Schs, Lincoln, Nebr, 65-68, dir. media network, 68- Other: Secy, SLD, Colo. Libr. Asn, 64-65; bd. mem, Colo. Asn. Sch. Librns, 64-65; coun. bd. mem, Lincoln Area Parent-Teacher Asn, 66-67; state chmn, Nat. Libr. Week, 67; mem. standing develop. cmt, Nebr. Sch. Librns. Mem: ALA; AASL; Mountain-Plains Libr. Asn; Nebr. Libr. Asn; Nat. Educ. Asn; NSEA; LEA; LLA; Dept. Audiovisual Instruction. Publ: Library Curriculum Manual, Greeley Pub. Schs, 65; Cooperative Efforts in Systems-Wide School Libraries, Mountain-Plains Libr. Asn. Quart, spring 66; Technical Services Handbook (A Manual of Job Descriptions and Procedures), Lincoln Pub. Schs, 67. Consult: 1) Kans. State Teachers Col, Emporia, cooperative cataloging syst, Feb. 66; 2) Lexington Pub. Schs, Lexington, Nebr, survey & eval. of serv. with recommendations, Mar. 66; 3) Nebr. State Dept. Educ, Lincoln, consult. on statist. for sch. libr. programs, Apr. 66. Specialties: 1c; 3a, 3d, 3e; 4a; 5a, 5b; 6b; 7a; 8d; 9 (statist. for sch. libr. programs, sch. media programs).

ROCHELL, CARLTON, Nov. 2, 33; Director, Atlanta Public Library, 126 Carnegie Way N.W, Atlanta, Ga. 30303. Home: 416 Beverly Rd. N.E, Atlanta, Ga. 30309. B.S.(math), George Peabody Col. Teachers, 59; M.S.L.S, Fla. State Univ, 60. Reference asst. & spec. asst. to dir, Nashville Pub. Libr, 57-61; dir, Hattiesburg Pub. Libr, Hattiesburg, Miss, 61-63; dir, Pub. Libr. Anniston & Calhoun County, Ala, 63-66; dir, Knoxville Pub. Libr, Knoxville, Tenn, 66-67. Other: Pres-elect pub. libr. div, Ala. Libr. Asn, 62; treas, Tenn. Libr. Asn, 67; mem. interlibr. cooperation cmt, PLA, 67-; mem. awards cmt, ALA, 68- Mem: Ga. Libr. Asn; Southeast. Libr. Asn; ALA. Consult: 1) Blount County, Maryville, Tenn, recommendations for establishment of county libr. syst, 66-68; 2) Tenn. State Libr, Nashville, Tenn, survey & program for serv. to insts. for blind & handicapped, with Marshall Stewart, Dave Palmer, Frank Sessa & Keith Doms, 67; 3) Sevier County Libr, Sevierville, Tenn, bldg. program, layouts, furniture & equipment specs, 67-68. Specialties: 1a, 1e, 1g; 5c; 7a; 7c, 7d (tax structures & larger units of serv); 8a, 8b, 8c, 8f; 9 (govt. tax structure, overlapping serv. & ways of cooperating or combining in larger units).

ROCKWELL, MRS. JEANETTE SLEDGE; Library Consultant, L-J-R Associates, 415 E. 52nd St, New York, N.Y. 10022. A.B, Univ. Calif, Berkeley, 37; B.L.S, Columbia Univ, 38. Chief librn, Standard-Vacuum Oil Co, 56-60; libr. mgr, Advanced Systs. Develop. Div, IBM Corp, 60-61; mgr. libr. serv, McKinsey & Co, 61-64. Other: Mem. ed. cmt, Spec. Libr, 62-64; SLA exhibit of info. storage & retrieval equipment, Int. Mgt. Congress, 63. Mem: SLA; ALA; N.Y. Libr. Club. Publ: Planning Inventory & A Suggested Checklist for Library Planning, Spec. Libr; How to Plan and Equip Them, SLA. Consult: 1) Va. Metal Products,

---

KEY TO CONSULTING SPECIALTIES: 1) ARCHITECTURE AND BUILDINGS, 1a) public libraries, 1b) academic libraries, 1c) school libraries, 1d) special libraries, 1e) library interiors, 1f) furnishings, 1g) site and location, 1h) other architectural; 2) COLLECTIONS: SELECTION, EVALUATION, WEEDING, 2a) adults, 2b) young adults, 2c) children, 2d) subject specialty, 2e) O.P. searches, 2f) rare books, 2g) appraisals, 2h) others; 3) TECHNICAL PROCESSES, 3a) cataloging, 3b) classification systems, 3c) acquisitions, 3d) materials processing, 3e) work flow and cost studies, 3f) others, 4) AUTOMATION, 4a) applications of data processing equipment, 4b) information storage and retrieval systems, 4c) systems analysis, 4d) others

Orange, Va, libr. planning & market consult, Jan. 68- Specialties: 1a, 1b, 1c, 1d, 1e, 1f, 1h (libr. equipment); 2d (gen. bus); 4b; 5a, 5b, 5c; 7a.

ROD, DONALD O, July 14, 15; Director of Library Services and Head Department of Library Science, University of Northern Iowa, Cedar Falls, Iowa 50613. Home: 2603 Iowa St, Cedar Falls, Iowa 50613. A.B, Luther Col. (Iowa), 38; A.B.L.S, Univ. Mich, 40. Dir, libr. serv. & head dept. libr. sci, Univ. North. Iowa, Cedar Falls, Iowa, 53- Other: Mem. bd. dirs, Iowa Libr. Asn, 56-59 & 61-65, pres, 57-58; mem. standards cmt, ACRL, 58-61 & 65-; state chmn, Iowa conf, Am. Asn. Univ. Prof, 60-61; mem. coun, ALA, 61-65; mem. equipment cmt, sect. bldgs. & equipment, LAD, 65-, mem. bldgs. cmt. col. & univ. libr. Mem: ALA; Iowa Libr. Asn. Consult: 1) Buena Vista Col, Storm Lake, Iowa, planning of new libr. bldg, 63-65; 2) Wisconsin State Univ, River Falls, planning of major addition to libr. bldg, 65-; 3) Wisconsin State Univ, Platteville, new libr. bldg, 66-; 4) Thiel Col, Greenville, Pa, planning of expanded libr. facilities, 66-; 5) Cent. Wash. State Col, Ellensburg, Wash, planning of new libr. bldg, 68- Specialties: 1b, 1e, 1f, 1g, 1h (specifications, especially equipment); 2h (evaluation of acad. libr. collections); 5c; 7a.

ROHLF, ROBERT HENRY, May 14, 28; Director of Administration, Library of Congress, Washington, D.C. 20540. Robert H. Rohlf Associates, 5400 Ridgefield Rd, Bethesda, Md. 20016. B.A, 49; B.S.L.S, 50; M.A, 53; cert. pub. admin, 55. Admin. asst. & new bldgs. officer, Minneapolis Pub. Libr, Minn, 56-58; dir, Dakota-Scott Regional Libr, West St. Paul, Minn, 59-66; coordinator bldg. planning, Libr. Congress, Wash, D.C, 66-68, dir. admin, 68- Other: V.pres, Minneapolis Jr. Chamber of Commerce, 56-57; dir, Judge Wright Fund, 56-59; pres, Minn. Libr. Asn, 58; dir, pub. libr. develop. project, Ill. Libr. Asn, 63; coun, ALA, 63-66; chmn, Minn. State Libr. Adv. Cmt, 65-66; chmn, archit. cmt. for pub. libr, LAD; chmn, standards cmt, PLA. Mem: ALA; Minn. Libr. Asn. Publ: A Plan for Public Library Development for Illinois, Ill. Libr. Asn, 63; bldg. program statements for: La Crosse, Wis, Minneapolis, Anoka County & St. Cloud, Minn, Manhattan, Kans. & others; contrib. to Libr. J, Libr. Trends, Col. & Res. Libr, Minn. Libr, Ill. Libr. & Kans. Librn. Consult: 1) LaCrosse Pub. Libr, Seventh & Main, La Crosse, Wis, bldg. program, plan review & revision, furniture & equipment specifications, with James L. Dorr & Del Westburg, 62-66; 2) Kans. City Pub. Libr, Sixth & Minnesota, Kansas City, Kans, bldg. program, plan review, furniture & equipment specifications & recommendations, with W. Dennis, 63-65; 3) Ramsey County Libr, Hamline & County Rd. B, St. Paul, Minn, bldg. program, plan review & revision, furniture &

equipment specifications & bid forms, with Joan Peters Rohlf, 63-65; 4) Wichita City Libr, Wichita, Kans, program review, plan review & revision, recommendations regarding furniture, 64-66; 5) Univ. City Pub. Libr, 613 Trinity, University City, Mo, site survey & recommendation, preliminary bldg. size & need statement, with Frank E. Gibson, 65-66. Specialties: 1a, 1b, 1e, 1f, 1g; 7a, 7c; 8a, 8b, 8c, 8d, 8f.

ROSENBERG, KENYON C, Sept. 9, 33; Assistant Professor, School of Library Science, Kent State University, Kent, Ohio 44240. Home: 608 Roosevelt Ave, Kent, Ohio 44240. B.A.(librarianship), Univ. Calif, Los Angeles, 59; M.S. (libr. sci), Univ. South. Calif, 61. Reference librn, Los Angeles County Law Libr, 58-60; Los Angeles librn, Calif. State Dept. Justice, 60-62; head reference, Atomics Int, 62; supvr, co. tech. document center, Hughes Aircraft Co, 62-65, head, tech. libr. serv, 65-66; dir. tech. info. serv, Ampex Corp, 66-68. Other: Mem. tech. info. adv. cmt. & chmn. info. anal. center task group, Nat. Security Industrial Asn, 65-; pres, San Francisco chap, Am. Soc. Info. Sci, 67-68. Mem: SLA; Am. Soc. Info. Sci; Am. Asn. Advancement Sci; Alpha Mu Gamma; Chi Delta Pi. Publ: Information Resources, DDC Document AD 622-056; A Comparison of the Relevance of Key-Word-In-Context Versus Discriptor Indexing Terms (with C.L.M. Blocher) Am. Document, 1/68. Consult: 1) Alaska State Court Syst, Anchorage, planned physical layout, collection, cataloging procedures & serials record, Apr-July 62; 2) Electronic Properties Info. Center, Hughes Aircraft Co, Culver City, Calif, adv. on indexing & automated info. retrieval, 63-65; 3) Electronics Lab. Libr, Ft. Huachuca, Ariz, reviewed plans for new facility, Feb. 66; 4) Career Guidance Center, Los Angeles, Calif, acted as Am. Document. Inst. consult. on libr. career exhibit, Feb. 66; 5) Col. San Mateo, Calif, consult, training program for libr. technicians, 68. Specialties: 1d, 1e, 1f; 2d (law, electronics); 3a, 3b, 3c, 3e; 4a, 4b, 4c; 5a, 5b, 5c; 6a, 6b.

ROTH, HAROLD LEO, Feb. 25, 19; Vice President, Library & Institutional Relations, Baker & Taylor Co, 1405 N. Broad, Hillside, N.J. 07205. Rothines Associates, 28 Edgemont Ave, Summit, N.J. 07901. B.A, N.Y. Univ, 48; M.S. in L.S, Columbia Univ, 50. Asst. dir, E. Orange Pub. Libr, East Orange, N.J, 54-57, dir, 57-66. Other: V.chmn, bldg. & equipment sect, LAD, 58-60, chmn, 60-61; treas, PLA, 61-62, chmn, cmt. to study accreditation pub. libr, 62-66; pres, N.J. Libr. Asn, 66-67. Mem: ALA; N.J. Libr. Asn; SLA; N.Y. Libr. Club; Libr. Pub. Relations Coun. Publ: New Jersey Public Libraries and Adult Education (with R. Jackson), N.J. Asn. for Adult Educ. Monograph 2, 12/61; Provision of Library Service to Scotch Plains, 63; Information Service for Interpace, a Survey Report (with T.C.

---

5) PERSONNEL AND RECRUITING, 5a) job evaluation and description, salary recommendations, 5b) recruitment of professionals and management personnel, 5c) administrative organization, 6) PUBLIC RELATIONS, 6a) publications, 6b) publicity programs, 6c) public opinion surveys, 6d) others, 7) SERVICES, 7a) evaluation of current program, 7b) studies of service to special publics, e.g., students, handicapped, aged, etc., 7c) programs for the implementation of new laws, program proposals to governments, 7d) others, 8) COMMUNITY, REGIONAL, STATE PLANNING, 8a) legislative programs, 8b) area analyses, 8c) centralized systems, cooperative arrangements, 8d) development of standards, 8e) state libraries and extension agencies, 8f) regional and statewide surveys, 8g) others, 9) OTHERS.

Hines), 63; Planning Library Buildings for Service (ed), ALA, 64; Education for Special Librarianship (ed), J. Educ. for Librarianship, 7: 3-20. Consult: 1) Ramsey Pub. Libr, Ramsey, N.J, site study, program & working with architect on plans for presentation to State for LSCA grant, with T.C. Hines, 63-66; 2) Elizabeth Pub. Libr, Elizabeth, N.J, changes in remodeling proposals, enlargement of main libr. structure to serve as community center & as regional reference center for grants in fed. aid program, furniture layout, revamping of all serv. areas, with T.C. Hines, 65-66; 3) Willingboro Pub. Libr, Willingboro, N.J, insurance adjustment after fire & extensive water & smoke damage, consult. on new libr. structure, placement in complex, develop. of program, layout & interior design, with T.C. Hines, 65-66; 4) Leonia Pub. Libr, Leonia, N.J, giving bd. & municipal officials direction in developing new pub. libr. facility, working with architect after developing program on preliminary plans designed to meet needs of community within framework of LSCA guidelines for aid, with T.C. Hines, 66-67; 5) Woodbridge Pub. Libr, Woodbridge, N.J, planning libr. for main libr. oper. in syst, programming, working with architect on plans, working drawings, developing layout & aiding in selection of furniture & equipment, with T.C. Hines, 67- Specialties: 1a, 1c, 1d, 1e, 1f, 1g, 1h (programming); 2a, 2d (reference—history), 2g; 5c; 6a, 6b; 7a, 7b; 8b, 8d; 9 (insuring of collections; adjusting of insurance losses).

ROTHINES ASSOCIATES, 28 Edgemont Ave, Summit, N.J. 07901. Consult: 1) City of E. Providence, R.I, survey & recommendations of existing five asn. libr. to be welded into one libr. syst, May 64; 2) Matawan Pub. Libr, N.J, Study of community, evaluation of existing libr, developing site location as part of recommendation for inclusion in master plans for joint serv. to township & borough, 65; 3) Greenburgh Pub. Libr, 280 Dobbs Ferry Rd, White Plains, N.Y, survey of community needs, relationship to County Libr, collection, admin. structure, site study & recommendation of size of libr, 65; 4) Union Free Sch. Dist. 5, Hillside Ave, New Hyde Park, N.Y, survey to evaluate libr. collections, bldg, serv. structure & relationship to other pub. libr. in area, 66; 5) Camden County Pub. Libr, Courthouse Annex, N.J, survey of county libr. serv, collection, admin. structure & potentials for growth, 66. Specialties: 1a, 1b, 1c, 1d, 1e, 1g, 1g; 2a, 2b, 2c, 2d (reference); 2g; 3a, 3b, 3c, 3d, 3e; 4a, 4b, 4c; 6a, 6b, 6c; 7a, 7b, 7c; 8b, 8c, 8d, 8e, 8f; 9 (insurance evaluation; relations with publishers; indexing; bibliography develop).

ROUNDS, GERTRUDE W; Librarian, State University of New York College at Oneonta, Oneonta, N.Y. 13820. Library Consultant, Walkerbilt Woodwork, Inc, Penn Yan, N.Y. 14527. Home: 6 Roosevelt Ave, Oneonta, N.Y. 13820. B.S. in L.S, Syracuse Univ; M.A, N.Y. Univ. Librn, State Univ. N.Y. Col. Oneonta, N.Y, 48- Other: Secy. teacher educ. libr. sect, ALA, 57-58, chmn, 58-59. Mem: ALA; N.Y. Libr. Asn. Consult: 1) Univ. Vermont, Burlington, furniture layout & planning of spec. equipment, with Roland M. Whittier, 62-63; 2) Oneonta Jr. High Sch, Oneonta, N.Y, furniture layout, planning of spec. furniture, with Myron A. Jordan, 65; 3) Phoenixville Pub. Libr, Phoenixville, Pa, furniture layout, planning of prfnl. areas, 66; 4) Port Chester Jr. High Sch, Port Chester, N.Y, furniture layout, 66; 5) Mastic Beach Sr. High Sch, Mastic Beach, N.Y, furniture layout, 66. Specialties: 1a, 1b, 1c, 1e, 1f.

ROVELSTAD, HOWARD, Mar. 5, 13; Director of Libraries & Professor Library Science, University of Maryland, College Park, Md. 20742. Home: 8530 Adelphi Rd, Hyattsville, Md. 20783. B.A, 36; M.A, 37; B.S.L.S, 40. Dir. libr. & prof. libr. sci, Univ. Md, 46- Other: Fel, City Col. N.Y. Libr, 39-40; mem, libr. bldgs. cmt, ACRL, 51-52, chmn, 52; chmn, Second Libr. Bldg. Plans Inst, 52; mem, bldgs. cmt, ALA, 52-56, chmn, 54-56, joint cmt. on Union List of Serials, 55-, chmn, 61-, mem, constitution & bylaws cmt, 59-66, chmn, 61-66, mem, coun, 61- Mem: ALA; SLA; Music Libr. Asn; Md. Libr. Asn; D.C. Libr. Asn; Am. Soc. Engineering Educ. Publ: Proceedings of the Third Library Building Plan Institute, ACRL (ed), 54; College and University Library Buildings, In: Contemporary Library Design (Frontiers in Librarianship, No. 1), Syracuse Univ, 58; The University and the Wise Man (ed), Univ. Md. Libr, 59; More Library for Your Building Dollar—the University of Maryland Experience, Col. & Res. Libr, 5/59; Guidelines for Library Planners (co-ed), ALA, 60. Consult: 1) Shepherd Col, Shepherdstown, W.Va, interior planning, furniture, equipment & book stack arrangement of new libr. bldg, 63-64; 2) U.S. Dept. of Housing & Urban Develop, 1626 K St. N.W, Wash, D.C, interior planning, furniture & book stack arrangement of libr. quarters in new bldg, 64-66; 3) Anne Arundel Community Col, Severna Park, Md, interior planning, furniture, equipment & book stack arrangement of new libr. bldg, 64-66; 4) St. Mary's Col. of Md, St. Mary's City, interior planning, furniture, equipment & book stack arrangement of new libr. bldg, 65-66; 5) Commonwealth Campuses of Pa, University Park, interior planning, furniture & equipment layout of new libr. bldgs. for several campuses, 65- Specialties: 1b, 1d, 1e, 1f, 1g.

ROWLAND, ARTHUR RAY, Jan. 6, 30; Librarian, Augusta College Library, 2500 Walton Way, Augusta, Ga. 30904. Home: 1339 Winter St, Augusta, Ga. 30904. A.B, 51; M.Ln, 52.

KEY TO CONSULTING SPECIALTIES: 1) ARCHITECTURE AND BUILDINGS, 1a) public libraries, 1b) academic libraries, 1c) school libraries, 1d) special libraries, 1e) library interiors, 1f) furnishings, 1g) site and location, 1h) other architectural; 2) COLLECTIONS: SELECTION, EVALUATION, WEEDING, 2a) adults, 2b) young adults, 2c) children, 2d) subject specialty, 2e) O.P. searches, 2f) rare books, 2g) appraisals, 2h) others; 3) TECHNICAL PROCESSES, 3a) cataloging, 3b) classification systems, 3c) acquisitions, 3d) materials processing, 3e) work flow and cost studies, 3f) others, 4) AUTOMATION, 4a) applications of data processing equipment, 4b) information storage and retrieval systems, 4c) systems analysis, 4d) others

Head, circulation dept, Auburn Univ, 56-58; librn. & assoc. prof, Jacksonville Univ, 58-61; librn. & assoc. prof, Augusta Col, Ga, 61- Other: Past v.pres. & pres, Cent. Savannah River Area Libr. Asn; past v.pres, Duval County Libr. Asn, Fla; pres. & curator, Richmond County Hist. Soc; v.pres, Ga, Libr. Asn, 65-67. Mem: ALA; Southeast. Libr. Asn; Ga. Libr. Asn; Cent. Savannah River Area Libr. Asn. Publ: Cataloging and Classification in Junior College Libraries, Libr. Resources & Tech. Serv, 7: 254-258, summer 63; Reference Services, Shoe String Press, 64; A Bibliography of the Writings on Georgia History, Archon Books, 66; Historical Markers of Richmond County, Georgia, Richmond County Hist. Soc, 66. Consult: 1) Candler Hosp, Savannah, Ga, orgn. of collection, procedures for ordering, cataloging, 55-56; 2) United Merchants Res. Center, Langley, S.C, orgn. of collection, systs. for cataloging, ordering & processing, Dec. 64-June 65; 3) Brenau Col, Gainesville, Ga, reorgn. of cataloging, set up inventory procedures, eval. & weeding of collection, Jan-June 66. Specialties: 2d (col. level); 3a, 3b, 3c, 3d.

RUNGE, DeLYLE P, Feb. 3, 18; Director of Libraries, St. Petersburg Public Library, 3745 Ninth Ave. N, St. Petersburg, Fla. 33713. Home: 4520 Cortez Way S, St. Petersburg, Fla. 33712. B.A, Sch. Commerce, Univ. Wis, B.L.S, Libr. Sch. Dir. libr, St. Petersburg Pub. Libr, St. Petersburg, Fla, 53- Other: Treas, Fla. Libr. Asn, 55, v.pres, 67, pres, 68, chmn, pub. libr. sect, 65. Publ: St. Petersburg at Lakeside, Libr. J, 12/1/64; Looking at Pelican Pete's New Library, Fla. Libr, 12/64. Consult: 1) Pub. Libr, Dunedin, Fla, libr. bldg. consult, 64; 2) Pub. Libr, Ocala, Fla, libr. bldg. consult, 66-67; 3) Pub. Libr, Coral Gables, Fla, libr. bldg, 68. Specialties: 1a.

RUSH, N. ORWIN, 1907; Director of Libraries, Florida State University Library, Tallahassee, Fla. 32306. Home: 427 Vinnedge Dr, Tallahassee, Fla. 32303. A.B, 31; B.S. in L.S, 32; M.S, 45. Dir. libr. & head libr. sci. dept, Univ. Wyo, 49-58; dir. libr, Fla. State Univ, Tallahassee, 58- Other: Pres, Maine Libr. Asn, 38-39; exec. secy, ACRL, 47-49; Fulbright scholar, 52-53; pres, Mountains-Plains Libr. Asn, 55-56. Mem: ALA; Southeast. Libr. Asn; Fla. Libr. Asn; ACRL. Publ: The Library—The Focus of the Classroom, Asn. Am. Cols. Bull, 10/50; The Library As a Teaching Agent, Sch. & Soc, 8/18/51; The British National Bibliography and Some Random Impressions of a Fulbrighter in England, Col. & Res. Libr, 10/53; Service to Readers of University Libraries, Libr. Asn. Record, 10/53; Central vs. Departmental Libraries, Mountain Plains Libr. Quart, summer 62; Special Collections, Col. & Res. Libr, 3/63. Consult: 1) Fla. Atlantic Univ, Boca Raton, mem, consult. team for planning new univ. libr, 60-61; 2) Univ. S. Ala, Mobile, libr. bldg. plans, with Guy Lyle & T.N.

McMullan, 66; 3) Fla. Mem. Col. St. Augustine, consult. on expenditure of ACRL grant for books, 66. Specialties: 1b, 1f, 1g; 2a; 3c; 5c.

S

ST. JOHN, FRANCIS R, 1908; Library Consultant, Francis R. St. John Library Consultants, 47 Sagamore St, Manchester, N.H. 03104. B.A, Amherst Col, 31; B.L.S, Columbia Univ, 32. Chief librn, Brooklyn Pub. Libr, 49-64; pres, Francis R. St. John Libr. Consult, Inc, 64- Other: Chmn. adv. cmt, libr. tech. project, ALA, 62-64. Mem: ALA; N.Y. Libr. Asn. Consult: 1) Ont. Libr. Asn, Toronto, Ont, Can, study of all types of libr. in Province & develop. of an integrated plan of serv, 65; 2) Pub. Libr, Norman, Okla, bldg. consult, 65; 3) Mid-West. Regional Libr, Fergus, Ont, Can, blueprint for regional libr. serv. in a four-county area & tax formula to implement, Sept. 65-June 66; 4) Fair Lawn Pub. Libr, Fair Lawn, N.J, personnel classification & methods survey including salary range, Dec. 65-June 66; 5) Tex. State Libr, Austin, six-county study, including book collection survey, personnel anal, pub. libr. outlets & plan for regional libr. serv, May 66-Feb. 67. Specialties: 1a, 1b, 1c, 1d, 1e, 1f, 1g; 2a, 2b, 2c, 2d, 2e, 2f, 2g; 3a, 3b, 3c, 3d, 3e; 4a, 4b, 4c; 5a, 5b, 5c; 6a, 6b, 6c; 7a, 7b, 7c; 8a, 8b, 8c, 8d, 8e, 8f; 9 (have also served as consult. to publishers & libr. suppliers; hire specialists in particular field when necessary).

SAMORE, THEODORE, July 27, 24; Professor, School of Library and Information Science, University of Wisconsin, Milwaukee, Wis. 53201. Home: 11300 N. Mulberry Dr, Mequon, Wis. 53092. B.A, 49; M.A, 52; M.A.L.S, 53. Asst. circulation librn, Univ. Mich. Law Libr, Ann Arbor, Mich, 55-57; periodical serv. librn, Ball State Univ, Muncie, Ind, 57-60; dir, sch. libr. serv, Livonia Pub. Schs, Livonia, Mich, 60-62; col. & univ. libr. specialist, U.S. Office Educ, 62-66. Other: Mem. statistics cmt. for cols. & univs, LAD, 62-; pres, Parent-Teacher Asn, Takoma Park, Md, 65-66; mem. standards cmt, ACRL, 65- Mem: ALA; Am. Document. Inst; ACRL; Phi Beta Kappa. Publ: Current Condition of American Academic Libraries, Higher Educ, 12/63; Libraries as Centers for Information on the United Nations: College and University Libraries, In: Teaching About the United Nations in the United States, January 1, 1960 through December 1963; Academic Library Buildings: Needs, Legislation, Inventory, Col. & Res. Libr, 7/64; Inventory of Academic Library Resources and Services: Needs and Prospects, ALA, 65; Library Resources and Services in White and Negro Colleges, Health, Educ. & Welfare Indicators, 7/65; Federal Legislation and Programs to Assist Academic Libraries, ALA Bull, 2/66. Consult: 1) West

---

5) PERSONNEL AND RECRUITING, 5a) job evaluation and description, salary recommendations, 5b) recruitment of professionals and management personnel, 5c) administrative organization, 6) PUBLIC RELATIONS, 6a) publications, 6b) publicity programs, 6c) public opinion surveys, 6d) others, 7) SERVICES, 7a) evaluation of current program, 7b) studies of service to special publics, e.g., students, handicapped, aged, etc., 7c) programs for the implementation of new laws, program proposals to governments, 7d) others, 8) COMMUNITY, REGIONAL, STATE PLANNING, 8a) legislative programs. 8b) area analyses, 8c) centralized systems, cooperative arrangements, 8d) development of standards, 8e) state libraries and extension agencies, 8f) regional and statewide surveys, 8g) others, 9) OTHERS.

Chester State Col. Libr, West Chester, Pa, planning of new libr. bldg, Oct. 62; 2) Millersville State Col, Millersville, Pa, planning of new libr. bldg, Dec. 62; 3) Shippensburg State Col. Libr, Shippensburg, Pa, planning of new libr. bldg, Jan. 63; 4) State Colleges of Wisconsin Libr, Madison, evaluation of admin. & orgn. of state & col. libr, Feb. 63; 5) State Cols. Wisconsin, Madison, recommendations & observations concering the State Colleges of Wis. libr, Mar. 63. Specialties: 1b; 2a, 2d (philosophy, psychology, sociology), 2f, 2g; 3a, 3b, 3c, 3d, 3e; 8a, 8c, 8d, 8f.

SATTLEY, HELEN R; Director, School Library Service, New York City Board of Education. Home: 433 W. 21st St, New York, N.Y. 10011. B.A, Northwestern Univ, 33, M.A, 34; B.S. in L.S, West. Reserve Univ, 36. Asst. prof, Columbia Univ, 47-50; assoc. prof, West. Reserve Univ, 50-53; dir. sch. libr. serv, New York City Bd. Educ, N.Y, 53- Other: Chmn. div. sch. librns, Ill. Libr. Asn, 41-42; mem. sch. libr. standards cmt, AASL, 54-59; chmn, City & County Sch. Libr. Supvr, 58-59; mem. joint cmt, ALA-Children's Book Coun, 60-65; chmn, Newbery-Caldecott Coun, 63-64; pres, CSD, 64-65. Mem: ALA; N.Y. Libr. Asn; N.Y. Libr. Club; Nat. Educ. Asn; Women's Nat. Book Asn. Publ: Shadow Across the Campus, Dodd, 57; The Credo of School Libraries, Saturday Review, 11/57; Reading Guidance for the Gifted Child, Brooklyn Teacher, 10/60 & TOP, 3/61; Annie, Dodd, 61; Elementary School Library Growth in New York City, ALA Bull, 6/64. Consult: 1) Univ. Denver, Denver, Colo, consult. sch. libr. supv, summer 62; 2) Asia Soc, New York, N.Y, consult. in children's books on India, spring & fall 66; 3) Asia Found, San Francisco, Calif, sch. libr. & children's literature consult. in Japan & Taiwan, summer 66; 4) N.Y. State Dept. Educ, consult. on ESEA Title II, automated regional processing centers, sch. libr. educ. training, 64- Specialties: 1c; 2b, 2c, 2d (children's books on India, Japan, Russia); 7b; 9 (sch. libr, sch. libr. supv, sch. libr. facilities).

SCARBOROUGH, RUTH ELLEN, Mar. 31, 17; Librarian, Centenary College for Women, Hackettstown, N.J. 07840. Home: 504 E. Valley View Ave, Hackettstown, N.J. 07840. B.S.(educ), 39; B.S. in L.S, 40. Librn, Centenary Col. for Women, Hackettstown, N.J, 46- Other: Secy. jr. col. libr. sect, ACRL, 49-50, v.chmn, 51-52, chmn, 52-53, dir, 54-57, dir-at-large, ACRL, 64-68; pres. col. & univ. sect, N.J. Libr. Asn, 51-52 & 62-63, secy, 57-58, secy. of asn, 55-56, corresponding secy, 61-62, mem-at-large exec. bd, 60-63, secy, N.J. Jr. Col. Sect, 63-64. Mem: ALA; ACRL; N.J. Libr. Asn. Publ: Library Handbook, Centenary Col. Women, 47-; Term Paper Manual, Centenary Col. Women, 48-65; Statistics for Junior College Libraries (compiler), Col. & Res. Libr, 1/56, 1/57 & 1/58; The Research Paper at Centenary College for Women (joint auth), 65. Consult: 1) Proposed Community Col. South. N.J, Atlantic City, planned layout, furniture & equipment, reference collection, proposed salaries, budget required for opening of libr, spring 59; 2) Villa Walsh Jr. Col, Morristown, N.J, book collection, 60; 3) Ocean County Community Col, Toms River, N.J, libr. bldgs. consult, planned interior of libr, arrangement & equipment, Feb. 65; 4) Assumption Jr. Col, Mendham, N.J, consult. in preparation for accreditation, spring 65; 5) Mt. St. Mary's Col, North Plainfield, N.J, preparation for accreditation, spring 67. Specialties: 1b, 1e; 2d (acad. libr, jr. col. libr); 5a; 7a.

SCHAFER, EMIL, July 20, 23; Information Systems Analyst, University of Southern California, Los Angeles, Calif. 90007. Home: 17210 Haas Ave, Torrance, Calif. 90504. B.S.(physics), 49; M.S.(libr. sci), 50. Head tech. info. center, atomic power dept, Westinghouse Electric Corp, Pittsburgh, Pa, 55-59; head tech. libr, gen. atomic div, Gen. Dynamics Corp, San Diego, Calif, 59-60, physicist, Convair Div, 60-61; tech. info. adminstr, Narmco Div, Telecomputing Corp, San Diego, 61-62; physicist & head electronic properties info. center, Hughes Aircraft Co, Culver City, Calif, 62-67; west coast mgr, Radioptics, Inc, 67. Other: Ed, Pittsburgh chap, SLA, 58, ed, South. Calif. chap, 64, recruitment chmn, 65; mem. bd. dirs, Los Angeles chap, Am. Document. Inst, 65-67. Mem: SLA; Am. Soc. Info. Sci; ALA. Publ: Polytrifluorochloroethylene Plastics, AD-413, 940, 6/62; Polytetrafluoroethylene Plastics, AD-413, 907, 6/62; Glossary of Electronic Properties, AD-816, 783, 1/65 & In: Electronic Materials Index, Plenum Press, 65; Some Indexing Problems, Fedn. Int. Documents. Conf, Wash, 65; Electronic Properties Information Center, 1965 Annual Report, AFML-TR-66-86, 5/66; EPIC System User Analysis, Am. Document. Inst. Convention, 10/66. Consult: 1) Univ. Calif, Berkeley, program in area of physics under the Calif. State Tech. Serv. Act, with H. Olkin, Aug. 66; 2) Optical Materials, Inc, indexing systs. & structures for solid state physics, Aug. 66; 3) Shock & Vibration Info. Center, Wash, D.C, anal. & structuring of sci. data for retrieval & data anal, Oct. 66; 4) Martin Co, Denver, Colo, admin. & direction of new info. anal. center for aerospace systs. safety, indexing & storage systs, Jan. 67; 5) Nat. Bureau Standards, Standard Reference Data Office, physical property data classification design, May-Sept. 67. Specialties: 3a, 3b, 3d, 3e; 4a, 4b, 4c, 4d; 6c; 7a, 7b, 7c; 8c; 9 (orgn. & mgt. of data & info. anal. centers & systs).

SCHEFTER, JOSEPH A, Mar. 20, 29; Director of Libraries, U.S. Dependent Schools in Europe, Directorate USDESEA, APO New York 09164. Home: 441 Lillian, Des Plaines, Ill. 60016. B.S, 56; M.A.(lib. sci), 62. Sch. librn,

KEY TO CONSULTING SPECIALTIES: 1) ARCHITECTURE AND BUILDINGS, 1a) public libraries, 1b) academic libraries, 1c) school libraries, 1d) special libraries, 1e) library interiors, 1f) furnishings, 1g) site and location, 1h) other architectural; 2) COLLECTIONS: SELECTION, EVALUATION, WEEDING, 2a) adults, 2b) young adults, 2c) children, 2d) subject specialty, 2e) O.P. searches, 2f) rare books, 2g) appraisals, 2h) others; 3) TECHNICAL PROCESSES, 3a) cataloging, 3b) classification systems, 3c) acquisitions, 3d) materials processing, 3e) work flow and cost studies, 3f) others, 4) AUTOMATION, 4a) applications of data processing equipment, 4b) information storage and retrieval systems, 4c) systems analysis, 4d) others

grades K-12, 56-58; librn. & audiovisual dir, grades K-12, 58-66; col. instructor, libr. & audiovisual courses (part-time), 62-66; dir. libr, U.S. Dependent Schs. Europe, 67- Other: Mem, sch. bd. Mem: ALA; SLA; Nat. Educ. Asn; Dept. Audiovisual Instruction; Nat. Microfilm Asn; Nat. Asn. Educ. Broadcasters. Publ: Developments in Audiovisual Instruction, Ill. Libr. J, 2/67. Consult: 1) School Dist. 59, Elk Grove, Ill, admin. orgn, 66; 2) Genesee Valley Regional Educ. Serv. Center, Rochester, N.Y, library-audiovisual coordination, bldg. design, in-serv. educ. of staff, 66-67. Specialties: 1c; 2d (audiovisual); 3d, 3e; 5c (Training Programs); 9 (audiovisual—admin. orgn).

SCHEIN, BERNARD, Nov. 16, 11; Deputy Director, Newark Public Library, 5 Washington St, Newark, N.J. 07101. Home: 405 Highland Ave, Newark, N.J. 07104. A.B, 39; B.L.S, 42; M.A, 46. Asst. dir, Newark Pub. Libr, 53-58, deputy dir, 58- Other: Chmn. cmt. certification, ALA, 56-57, mem 66-67; pres, N.J. Libr. Asn, 60-61; part-time faculty mem, Rutgers Univ. Grad. Libr. Sch, 62; part-time faculty mem, Drexel Inst. Tech. Grad. Libr. Sch, 63. Mem: ALA; N.J. Libr. Asn; Phi Beta Mu. Publ: Certification of Public Librarians in the United States, ALA Bull, 11/56; Certification (of Librarians), In: Encyclopedia Americana; The Modern Library and Its Services, In: The New Book of Knowledge. Consult: 1) Fairleigh-Dickinson Univ, Teaneck, N.J, study of book order procedures & personnel, Nov. 60; 2) Fairleigh-Dickinson Univ, study of classification systems used on the University's three campuses with recommendations, Mar. 61; 3) J. Lewis Crozer Libr, 11th & Edgemont Ave, Chester, Pa, provided plan of admin. & serv. orgn, position-classification & pay schedule, with James E. Bryan, Mar-June 66. Specialties: 5a, 5b, 5c; 7a, 7b; 8b, 8f.

SCHELL, HAROLD B, Oct. 28, 25; Assistant Director for Public Services & Building Planning, University Libraries, University of Pittsburgh, Pittsburgh, Pa. 15213. Home: 308 Carnegie Place, Pittsburgh, Pa. 15208. A.B, Wittenberg Univ, 55; M.S.L.S, Syracuse Univ, 57. Asst. catalog librn, Cornell Univ, 57-59, admin. asst. to dir. libr, 59-62, coordinator reader serv, 62-63, asst. to dir. libr, 64; asst. dir. libr, readers serv, Univ. Md, 64-66; asst. dir. for pub. serv. & bldg. planning, Univ. Pittsburgh, 66- Other: Mem. personnel admin. cmt, N.Y. Libr. Asn, 59-64, conf. program chmn, 63; adjunct assoc. prof. acad. libr. bldgs, grad. sch. libr. & info. sci, Univ. Pittsburgh, Pittsburgh, Pa, fall 66 & winter 67; mem. urban univ. cmt, ALA, 67-, chmn. conf. program, 68. Mem: ALA; Beta Phi Mu; Pa. Libr. Asn. Publ: Manual of Procedures (ed. with Robert B. Slocum & others), Catalog Dept, Cornell Univ. Libr, 59; Cornell Starts a Fire, Libr. J, 10/1/60; The John M. Olin Library, Cornell's New Research Library, Libr. J, 12/1/60. Consult: 1) N.Y. State Libr, Albany, tech. processes dept. bldg. planning, 66-; 2) Wright State Univ, Dayton, Ohio, planning new libr. bldg, 66-; 3) Grad. Sch. Libr. & Info. Serv, Univ. Md, gen. consult, 67-; 4) Univ. Miss, bldg, 66-67; 5) Edinboro State Col, Edinboro, Pa, bldg, 68- Specialties: 1b, 1d, 1f, 1g.

SCHICK, DR. FRANK L, Feb. 4, 18; Director, School of Library and Information Science, University of Wisconsin-Milwaukee, Chapman 303, Milwaukee, Wis. 53201. Home: 7460 N. Mohawk Rd, Milwaukee, Wis. 53217. B.A, Wayne State Univ, 46; B.L.S, Univ. Chicago, 47, M.A, 48; Ph.D.(libr. sci), Univ. Mich, 57. Asst. dir. libr. serv. br. & coordinator adult educ. & libr. statist, U.S. Office Educ, 58-66; dir. & prof, sch. libr. & info. sci, Univ. Wis-Milwaukee, 66- Other: Vis. prof, sch. libr. sci, Univ. N.C, summers 62 & 64; chmn. libr. statist. cmt, U.S. Am. Standards Inst, 62-67, mem. Sectional Cmt. Z39; chmn. libr. statist. cmt, Int. Standards Asn. TC46, 62-; mem. coun, ALA, 64-68, chmn, libr. educ. legis. cmt, LED, 66-, chmn. libr. educ. statist. cmt, LAD, 68-; fed. legis. liaison, Wis. Libr. Asn, 68- Mem: ALA; SLA; Wis. Libr. Asn; Int. Fedn. Libr. Asns; Int. Standards Orgn. TC46. Publ: The Paperbound Book in America, Bowker, 58; The Cost of Library Materials: Price Trends of Publications (co-auth), U.S. Office Educ, 61; The Future of Library Service: Demographic Aspects and Implications (ed), Univ. Ill. Grad. Sch. Libr. Sci, Urbana, 62; Research Libraries and Reference Services & Libraries in the United States, Types and Services, In: Encyclopedia Americana, 65 & 69; Survey of Special Libraries Serving the Federal Government, Nat. Center for Educ. Statist, HEW, 68; North American Library Directory (ed), ALA, 68. Consult: 1) Mathematica, Inc, Princeton, N.J, project On the Economics of Library Operations, prepared as a study for the Nat. Cmn. on Libr, Mar-Apr. 67; 2) R.R. Bowker Co, 1180 Ave. of the Americas, New York, N.Y, editorial & statist. consult. serv. on 1968 & 1969 editions of the Bowker Annual, 67-68; 3) ALA, 60 E. Huron St, Chicago, Ill, coordinating group of ALA-LAD Statist. Coordinating Project, develop. of a nat. Plan for Libr. Statist, with John Lorenz, Paul Howard, G. Flint Purdy, Richard Darling & Rose Vainstain; 4) Am. Med. Asn, 535 N. Dearborn St, Chicago, Ill, co-principal investigator for survey of U.S. health sci. libr, Nat. Inst. Health grant, with Susan Crawford & Ted Samore, 68-; 5) Wharton Sch, Univ. Pa, consult. to project dir. syst. anal. & info. sci. statist. data, 68. Specialties: 7a, 7c; 8a, 8d, 8f; 9 (libr. educ, libr. res. methodology, publ. hist. & statist, book binding).

SCHMUCH, JOSEPH J, Mar. 9, 28; Librarian, Belmont Memorial Library, Belmont, Mass. 02178. Home: 69 Lowell St, Reading, Mass. 01867. A.B, 48; M.A, 52; M.S, 58. Librn, Reading Pub. Libr, 57-61; librn, Belmont Mem.

5) PERSONNEL AND RECRUITING, 5a) job evaluation and description, salary recommendations, 5b) recruitment of professionals and management personnel, 5c) administrative organization, 6) PUBLIC RELATIONS, 6a) publications, 6b) publicity programs, 6c) public opinion surveys, 6d) others, 7) SERVICES, 7a) evaluation of current program, 7b) studies of service to special publics, e.g., students, handicapped, aged, etc., 7c) programs for the implementation of new laws, program proposals to governments, 7d) others, 8) COMMUNITY, REGIONAL. STATE PLANNING, 8a) legislative programs, 8b) area analyses, 8c) centralized systems, cooperative arrangements, 8d) development of standards, 8e) state libraries and extension agencies, 8f) regional and statewide surveys, 8g) others, 9) OTHERS.

Libr, 61- Other: Trustee, Reading Pub. Libr, 64-; pres, Mass. Pub. Libr. Adminstr, 65. Mem: ALA; Mass. Libr. Asn; New Eng. Libr. Asn. Consult: 1) Mem. Libr, Acton, Mass, libr. bldg. program, 63; 2) Pub. Libr, Burlington, Mass, libr. bldg. program, pub. rels & collection eval. & bldg, 63-64; 3) Scituate Libr, Scituate, Mass, eval. of serv. with recommendations, libr. bldg. program & recruitment of new chief librn, 64-65; 4) Pub. Libr, Walpole, Mass, bldg. expansion program & serv. recommendations, 65; 5) Pub. Libr, Wilmington, Mass, libr. bldg. expansion program, 67. Specialties: 1a, 1e, 1f, 1g; 2a; 6b; 7a.

SCHNEIDER, FRANK A, Mar. 14, 21; State Librarian, Library Commission for the State of Delaware, Loockerman St, Dover, Del. 19901. Home: 36 Konschak St, Dover, Del. 19901. B.A, 47; B.S. in L.S, 51; M.A, 53; Ed.D, 68. Librn, Phoenix Union High Sch. Dist, Phoenix, Ariz, 53-59; part-time instructor libr. sci, Ariz. State Univ, Tempe, 57-65, assoc. univ. librn, 60-64; dir, Mesa Pub. Libr, Mesa, Ariz, 64-68. Other: Pres, Ariz. State Libr. Asn, 58-59 & 65-66, pres, col. & univ. div, 61-62, Librn. of Year, 65-66; secy, tech. serv. sect, Southwest. Libr. Asn, 61-62; trustee, Tempe Pub. Libr, Ariz, 62-64. Mem: ALA; Ariz. State Libr. Asn; Southwest. Libr. Asn; Salt River Valley Librns. Asn; Del. Libr. Asn. Publ: A Student Guide to the Effective Use of the Matthews Library, Ariz. State Univ. 62; Publications of the Arizona State University Faculty, through 6/30/61 & 3 supplements 62-64; Crane Elementary District, Report of Survey June 1964 (with R. Merwin Deever & Howard K. Demeke, Ariz. State Univ. Bureau Educ. Res. & Serv, 64; Eloy Elementary Schools, Report of Survey April 1966 (with R. Merwin Deever & Howard J. Demeke, Ariz. State Univ. Bur. Educ. Res. & Serv, 66; Creighton Elementary Schools, Report of Survey May 1966 (with R. Merwin Deever & Harold K. Moore), Ariz. State Univ. Bureau Educ. Res. & Serv, 66; Arizona Public School Libraries: A Survey (with R. Merwin Deever & Harold K. Moore), Ariz. State Dept. Pub. Instruction, 67. Consult: 1) Ariz. State Libr. Survey, Ariz. State Dept. Libr. & Archives, develop, orgn. & presentation of data regarding survey of pub. sch. libr. of Ariz, assisted in develop. of survey forms for use with col, pub. & sch. libr. survey, Jan. 65; 2) City of Phoenix, Phoenix, Ariz, served on libr. Personnel Selection Cmt. evaluating candidates for prfnl. libr. positions, Nov. 65; 3) Eloy Sch. Dist, Eloy, Ariz, evaluated three sch. libr. collections, tech. processing, programs & personnel, with recommendations for instructional materials centers, Jan-Feb. 66; 4) Creighton Sch. Dist, Phoenix, Ariz, evaluated eight sch. libr. regarding book and non-book materials, processing procedures, libr. program and personnel with recommendations for future instructional materials centers, Feb-Mar. 66; 5) City of Scottsdale, E. Indian School Rd, Scottsdale, Ariz, served on Libr. Dir. Selection Bd. evaluating candidates for pub. libr. directorship, July 66. Specialties: 1a, 1b, 1c; 2a, 2b, 2d (educ, Am. hist, Am. literature, current fiction); 3d, 3e; 5a, 5b; 6a, 6c; 7a, 7c; 8b, 8c, 8e.

SCHORK, FRANCIS WILLIAM, Dec. 12, 24; University Librarian, American University, Washington, D.C. 20016. Home: 1641 19th St. N.W, Washington, D.C. 20009. A.B, Oberlin Col, 49; cert, Univ. Paris, 50; A.M, Johns Hopkins Univ, 51; A.M.L.S, Univ. Mich, 52. Librn, Mid. East Inst, 52-; librn, sch. advanced int. studies, Johns Hopkins Univ, 52-63; assoc. dir, East-West Center Libr, 63-64; univ. librn, American Univ, 64- Mem: ALA. Consult: 1) Nat. Defense Col, Tokyo, Japan, reorganized libr. according to Am. libr. standards, designed the new libr. bldg, Aug-Sept. 63; 2) Univ. Hawaii, Honolulu, recommendations in tech. processes reorgn. & new grad. libr. plans, Oct. 63-Apr. 64; 3) Univ. Wis, Madison, surveyed libr. to make recommendations concerning new bldgs, departmental libr. & eval. of present procedures, Apr. 64; 4) Univ. Wales, Aberystwyth, surveyed libr. to make recommendations for reorgn, May 66; 5) Univ. Va, Charlottesville, designed & installed automated circulation syst, Feb. 68. Specialties: 1b, 1d; 3a, 3b, 3c, 3d; 4a; 5c; 7a, 7b; 9 (to take over an indifferently-effective libr. & to reorganize it entirely; to plan new facilities or a new bldg; to devise more effective procedures in tech. processes).

SCHUTZE, GERTRUDE, June 5, 17; Consultant & Information Scientist, 7620 86th Ave, Woodhaven, N.Y. 11421. B.S, 39; M.S.L.S, 49. Mgr. info. serv, Grace Res. & Develop. Co, 53-59; mgr. libr. & info. serv, Standard & Poor's Corp, 59-60; chief librn, Union Carbide Res. Inst, 60-65; mgr. info. serv, Ayerst Labs. Division, Am. Home Products, Inc, 65- Other: Cert. prfnl. consult, SLA, 59- Mem: Am. Soc. Info. Sci; SLA; Am. Chemical Soc; Med. Libr. Asn. Publ: Documentation Digest (ed), 48-59; Bibliography of Guides to Science-Technical-Medical Literature, N.Y, 58, 63 & 67; supplement, 58-62 & 63-66; Guide to the Literature of Planning Libraries, In: Special Libraries; How to Plan and Equip Them, SLA, 63; Documentation Source Book, Scarecrow, 65; The Social Sciences: A Bibliography of Guides to the Literature, N.Y, 68; contrib, prfnl. periodicals. Consult: 1) Educ. & World Affairs, Inc, 522 Fifth Ave, New York, N.Y, design & orgn. of libr. systs. & serv, custom classification & cataloging, construction of thesaurus, machine application, 64-65; 2) Chas. Pfizer & Co, Inc, 235 E. 42nd St, New York, coding & indexing of med. literature, 66; 3) Long Island Univ, Brooklyn, N.Y, planned acquisitions policy, developed the acquisitions program, 66; 4) Pennie,

---

KEY TO CONSULTING SPECIALTIES: 1) ARCHITECTURE AND BUILDINGS, 1a) public libraries, 1b) academic libraries, 1c) school libraries, 1d) special libraries, 1e) library interiors, 1f) furnishings, 1g) site and location, 1h) other architectural; 2) COLLECTIONS: SELECTION, EVALUATION, WEEDING, 2a) adults, 2b) young adults, 2c) children, 2d) subject specialty, 2e) O.P. searches, 2f) rare books, 2g) appraisals, 2h) others; 3) TECHNICAL PROCESSES, 3a) cataloging, 3b) classification systems, 3c) acquisitions, 3d) materials processing, 3e) work flow and cost studies, 3f) others, 4) AUTOMATION, 4a) applications of data processing equipment, 4b) information storage and retrieval systems, 4c) systems analysis, 4d) others

Edmonds, Morton, Taylor & Adams, 330 Madison Ave, New York, N.Y, patent validity searches, with R. Kadel & S.T. Laurence, 67; 5) Am. Airlines, Inc, 633 Third Ave, New York, consolidation of tech. & econ. libr, cataloging & classification of entire collection, 67. Specialties: 1d; 2a, 2d (chemistry, tech, med), 2g; 3a, 3b, 3c, 3d; 4a, 4b; 6a, 6d (specialized abstracting & indexing publ); 7a, 7d (abstracting, indexing & bibliog. serv); 9 (design & organize spec. libr. & info. systs).

SEVERANCE, ROBERT W, Dec. 13, 07; Director, Air University Library, Maxwell Air Force Base, Montgomery, Ala. 36112. Home: 3743 Berkeley Dr, Montgomery, Ala. 36111. A.B, 28; A.M, 29; B.S. in L.S, 33. Deputy dir, Army Libr, Pentagon, Wash, D.C, 53-56; spec. asst. bldg. planning, Nat. Libr. Med, 56-57; dir, Air Univ. Libr, 57- Other: Pres, Fla. Libr. Asn, 38-40; pres, Tex. Libr. Asn, 47-48; pres, ACRL, 52-53; pres, Ala. Libr. Asn, 64-65. Mem: ALA; SLA; Southeast. Libr. Asn; Ala. Libr. Asn; fel. Royal Soc. Arts. Publ: Tex. Libr. J.(ed), 50-51. Consult: 1) U.S. Army Med. Serv. Sch, Ft. Sam Houston, Tex, eval. of libr. program, 59; 2) Le Moyne Col, Memphis, Tenn, libr. bldg. consult, 60-62; 3) Judson Col, Marion, Ala, libr. bldg. consult, 61; 4) Gulfport Col, Gulfport, Miss, libr. program & bldg. consult, 65; 5) Can. Dept. of Defence, Ottawa, Ont, eval. of libr. program, with Foster Mohrhardt & Donald Bean, 66. Specialties: 1b, 1d; 2d (military); 5a, 5b, 5c; 9 (fed. & military libr. serv).

SHAFFER, KENNETH R(AYMOND), June 5, 14; Director and Professor, School of Library Science, Simmons College, 300 The Fenway, Boston, Mass. 02115. Home: 1454 Beacon St, Apt. 541, Brookline, Mass. 02146. A.B, Butler Univ, 35; B.S. in L.S, Univ. Ill, 41. Dir. & prof, sch. libr. sci, Simmons Col, Boston, Mass, 46- Other: Trumbull lectr, Yale Univ, 54; trustee, Boston Center Adult Educ, 60-63; consult, U.S. Dept. State & Peace Corps & Am. specialist, U.S. Dept. State in Denmark, Holland, Germany & Yugoslavia, 62-63. Mem: ALA; SLA; Mass. Libr. Asn. Publ: Twenty-five Short Cases in Library Personnel Administration, 59; Cases in Executive-Trustee Relationships in Public Libraries, 60; The Book Collection, 61; Library Personnel Administration and Supervision, 63; contrib, Libr. J, Saturday Review Literature, Libr. Trends, Col. & Res. Libr, Wilson Libr. Bull. Consult: 1) The Town of South Windsor, Conn, survey of libr. facilities & bldg. program, 65; 2) City of Cranston, R.I, evaluative study with recommendations, 65; 3) State of Vermont Free Pub. Libr. Service, Montpelier, review of all applications for funds under Libr. Serv. & Construction Act, 65 & 66; 4) Bridgeport Pub. Libr, Bridgeport, Conn, study for re-use & renovation of cent. libr. bldg, 65-66; 5) Lexington Pub. Libr,

Lexington, Mass, study of programs & serv, 66. Specialties: 1a, 1b, 1d, 1e, 1f, 1g; 5a, 5c; 7a, 7b, 7c; 8a, 8b, 8c, 8f.

SHANK, DR. RUSSELL, Sept. 2, 25; Director of Libraries, Smithsonian Institution, Washington, D.C. 20560. Home: 1054 Dalebrook Dr, Alexandria, Va. 20560. B.S, 46; B.A, 49; M.B.A, 52; DLS, 66. Engineering-physical sci, librn, Columbia Univ, New York, N.Y, 53-59; asst. univ. librn, Univ. Calif, Berkeley, 59-64; sr. lectr, sch. libr. serv, Columbia Univ, 64-66, assoc. prof, 66-67- Other: Mem. exec. bd, personnel admin. sect, ALA, 57, v.chmn. & chmn, 64-66, mem, res. & develop. cmt, 66-, chmn, in-serv. training cmt, ALA, 59-64, mem. coun, 61-65, mem, policy & res. cmt, copying methods sect, 64-69, mem, policy & res. cmt, univ. libr. sect, 66-, mem, ad hoc cmt. on universal numbering syst. for publ, mem. sch. libr. manpower project adv. cmt, 67-70, pres. info. sci. & automation div, 68-69; mem. bd. dirs, ACRL, 61-65; mem, educ. cmt, SLA, 64-67, SLA rep. to ALA Cmn. on Nat. Plan for Libr. Educ. & to Coun. Nat. Libr. Asns. Joint Cmt. on Libr. Educ; mem, program planning cmt, Am. Document. Inst, 67 & mem. educ. spec. info. group on automation & networks. Mem: ALA; SLA; Am. Document. Inst. Publ: Scientific and Technical Book Publishing (with T.P. Fleming), Libr. Trends, 7/58; Year's Developments in California's Academic Libraries, Calif. Librn, 10/60, 1/62, 1/63 & 10/63; New Concepts in Indexing, Bull. Med. Libr. Asn, 7/65; Regional Access to Scientific and Technical Information, 7/68. Consult: 1) Univ. Calif. Berkeley, surveyed & designed classification & pay plan for libr. positions in state syst, with Page Ackerman & Katherine McNabb, 60-63; 2) U.S. Pub. Health Serv, Wash, D.C, site surveys for training grant proposals, 64-; 3) Nat. Sci. Found, Wash, D.C, review res. proposals, 64-; 4) New York Metrop. Reference & Res. Libr. Asn, 11 W. 40th St, New York, N.Y, survey & design project— sci. libr. & info. resources in New York region, 66-67; 5) Human Sci. Res, Inc, McLean, Va, consult. on info. handling & commun; libr. acquisition problems in sci, 66-67. Specialties: 2d (any sci); 3e; 4a, 4b; 5a, 5b, 5c, 5d (position classification & pay plans; in-serv. training); 7b; 8b, 8c, 8f; 9 (publ; educ. in info. sci).

SHAPIRO, MRS. LILLIAN L, Oct. 11, 13; Teaching Assistant, Columbia University School of Library Service, New York, N.Y. 10027. Home: 82-30 210th St, Hollis Hills, N.Y. 11427. B.A, 32; B.L.S, 40. Head librn, Woodrow Wilson High Sch, 48-62; acting asst. dir. sch. libr, high sch, New York, N.Y, 63-64; head librn, Springfield Gardens High Sch, Springfield Gardens, N.Y, 65-68; teaching asst, sch. libr. serv, Columbia, 68- Other: Pres, New York City Sch. Librns. Asn, 51-52; consult, sch. standards cmt, ALA, 57-60, mem, ad hoc cmt. revise

---

5) PERSONNEL AND RECRUITING, 5a) job evaluation and description, salary recommendations, 5b) recruitment of professionals and management personnel, 5c) administrative organization, 6) PUBLIC RELATIONS, 6a) publications, 6b) publicity programs, 6c) public opinion surveys, 6d) others, 7) SERVICES, 7a) evaluation of current program, 7b) studies of service to special publics, e.g., students, handicapped, aged, etc., 7c) programs for the implementation of new laws, program proposals to governments, 7d) others, 8) COMMUNITY, REGIONAL, STATE PLANNING, 8a) legislative programs, 8b) area analyses, 8c) centralized systems, cooperative arrangements, 8d) development of standards, 8e) state libraries and extension agencies, 8f) regional and statewide surveys, 8g) others, 9) OTHERS.

sch. libr. standards, 67-; coun. mem, v.pres. & pres, N.Y. Libr. Club. Mem: ALA; N.Y. Libr. Asn; New York City Sch. Librns. Asn; N.Y. Libr. Club. Publ: Contrib. to Wilson Libr. Bull. & Libr. J. Consult: 1) Woodhull Acad, Hollis, N.Y, outlining basic requirements for setting up new libr, 67. Specialties: 1c; 2b; 5a; 7a; 8a, 8d.

SHAW, THOMAS SHULER, Oct. 25, 06; Professor, Library School, Louisiana State University, Baton Rouge, La. 70803. Home: 835 Delgado Dr, Baton Rouge, La. 70808. B.A, George Wash. Univ, 30; B.S. in L.S, Columbia Univ, 46. Head, pub. reference sect, Libr. Congress, Wash, D.C, 54-62; prof, libr. sch, La. State Univ, Baton Rouge, 62- Other: Treas, ACRL, 49-52, chmn, educ. qualifications & preparation cmt, 52-53, chmn, conf. program cmt, 58-59, v.pres, 59-60 & 65-66, mem, L.J. list cmt, 62-64; summers, lectr, libr. sch, Univ. South. Calif, 52, vis. prof, sch. libr. serv, Univ. Calif, 61 & grad. sch. libr. sci, Univ. Ill, 62; mem, RSD-RTSD interdiv. cmt. on pub. documents, 61-65; mem, adv. cmt. to U.S. pub. printer on pub. documents, RSD, 62-, Mudge citation, 68; mem. coun, ALA, 62-65; mem. subscription books cmt, 67-, mem. subcmt. omnibus book reviews, 68-; mem, AALL-ALA-ACRL-SLA joint cmt. on govt. publ, 63-65; mem. res. cmt, Asn. Am. Libr. Schs, 66-; mem. legis. cmt, LED, 68. Mem: ALA; ACRL; La. Libr. Asn; Southwest. Libr. Asn; Baton Rouge Libr. Club. Publ: Index to Profile Sketches in the New Yorker Magazine, Faxon, 46; Syllabi for Government Publications, Basic Reference and Advanced Reference, La. State Univ, 62; ed, La. Libr. Asn. Bull, 64-65; issue of U.S. Govt. documents (ed), Libr. Trends, 7/66. Consult: 1) Libr. Congress, Washington, D.C, eval. & selection of books for White House Libr, with Donald Mugridge, 52 & 57; 2) Libr. Congress, eval. of the Delta Collection, 55; 3) Army & Navy Club, eval. of gen. collection, with Mary E. Shaw, 58. Specialties: 2a, 2d (reference, govt. publ, bibliog).

SHEEHAN, SISTER HELEN, 1904; Librarian, Trinity College Library, Washington, D.C. 20017. Home: Trinity College, Washington, D.C. 20017. B.A, Trinity Col, 24; B.S. in L.S, Simmons Col, 26. Librn, Trinity Col, Wash, D.C, 34- Other: Chmn, ed. bd, Choice, 66-; v.pres. & pres-elect, Catholic Libr. Asn, 67- Mem: ALA; ACRL; Cath. Libr. Asn; Libr-Col. Assocs. Publ: The Small College Library, Newman, 63; Trinity Caters to Taste: the New Library Building, Libr. J, 12/1/63; Breadth versus Depth & Architecture Report, In: The Library College, Drexel, 66; Experiments and the College Library, Md. Libr, fall 66; How to Spend $10,000,000, Cath. Libr. World, 10/66; Students and the Library, Proc. Drexel Conf. on the Library-College, 67. Consult: 1) Emmanuel Col, Boston, Mass, functional planning, 64-65; 2) Catholic Univ. Puerto Rico, Ponce, functional planning, 67. Specialties: 1b; 2h (col—basic collection); 3d; 5c; 7a.

SHEPARD, MRS. MARIETTA DANIELS, Jan. 24, 13; Associate Librarian, Pan American Union, 17th & Constitution Ave. N.W, Washington, D.C. 20006. Home: 3025 Ontario Rd. N.W, Washington, D.C. 20009. B.A, Univ. Kans, 33; M.A, Wash. Univ. (St. Louis), 45; B.S.L.S, Columbia Univ, 43. Assoc. librn, Pan Am. Union, Wash, D.C, 48- Other: Mem. coun, ALA, 56-57, 60-64 & 66-, mem. exec. bd, 68-; secy, Seminars on Acquisition of Latin Am. Libr. Materials, 56-; pres, int. exec. coun, Inter-Am. Libr. Sch, 56-; chmn, Books for the People Fund, Inc, 61- Mem: ALA; D.C. Libr. Asn; Asn. Int. Libr; Asn. Interam. Bibliotecarios & Documentalistas Agrícolas. Publ: La biblioteca pública en América, Bibliographic Series 34, Pan Am. Union, 51; Estudios y conocimientos en acción, Pan Am. Union, 59; The Seminars on the Acquisition of Latin American Library Materials, Estudios bibliotecarios 4, Pan Am. Union, 62; Public and School Libraries in Latin America, Estudios bibliotecarios 5, Pan Am. Union, 63. Consult: 1) Centro Interam. de Vivienda, Bogotá, Colombia, orgn. of sci. info. serv, including libr. & publ. program, Jan-Mar. 51; 2) Inst. Técnológico de Monterrey, Monterrey, Mex, survey of needs for reorgn, Aug. 57; 3) Univ. Puerto Rico Inst. of Caribbean Studies, Río Piedras, review of libr. needs, May 60; 4) Cent. Am. Univ. Libr, AID/ROCAP, Guatemala, survey of libr. with recommendations, with Carl Deal & William Jackson, July-Aug. 65; 5) Univ. Autónoma de Santo Domingo, Santo Domingo, Dominican Republic, survey of univ. libr. & recommendations for reorgn, Mar-Apr. 65. Specialties: 2a, 2d (Latin Am); 3c; 5c, 5d (training); 7c; 8a, 8b, 8c, 8f; 9 (univ. libr. reorgn, nat. planning, develop. of libr. schs).

SHEPHERD, GILES F. JR, Nov. 21, 12; Associate Director of Libraries, Cornell University Library, Ithaca, N.Y. 14850. Home: 101 Valley Rd, Ithaca, N.Y. 14850. A.B, 34; A.B.L.S, 36; M.A, 42. Asst. dir, Cornell Univ. Libr, Ithaca, N.Y, 47-66, assoc. dir, 66- Other: Chmn. intellectual freedom cmt, N.Y. Libr. Asn, 54-56, pres. col. & univ. sect, 59, second v.pres, 64, mem. cmt. on appointment of foreign librns, 66-68. Mem: ALA; N.Y. Libr. Asn; Bibliog. Soc. Am; Beta Phi Mu. Publ: Public Document Resources of the University Library, Univ. N.C. Bull, 47; Methods and Procedures, Libr. Trends, 7/57; Development in Copying Methods, Libr. Resources & Tech. Serv, spring 60. Consult: 1) Wells Col, Aurora, N.Y, review of bldg. program & sketches, Apr. 60; 2) Univ. Liberia, Monrovia, advising in the bldg, staffing & stocking, Nov. 62-Nov. 63; 3)

KEY TO CONSULTING SPECIALTIES: 1) ARCHITECTURE AND BUILDINGS, 1a) public libraries, 1b) academic libraries, 1c) school libraries, 1d) special libraries, 1e) library interiors, 1f) furnishings, 1g) site and location, 1h) other architectural; 2) COLLECTIONS: SELECTION, EVALUATION, WEEDING, 2a) adults, 2b) young adults, 2c) children, 2d) subject specialty, 2e) O.P. searches, 2f) rare books, 2g) appraisals, 2h) others; 3) TECHNICAL PROCESSES, 3a) cataloging, 3b) classification systems, 3c) acquisitions, 3d) materials processing, 3e) work flow and cost studies, 3f) others, 4) AUTOMATION, 4a) applications of data processing equipment, 4b) information storage and retrieval systems, 4c) systems analysis, 4d) others

South. Adirondacks Libr. Syst, Saratoga Springs, N.Y, survey of the reference serv, with Marion Mosher & Lucille Wickersham, Dec. 64-June 65; 4) Hampton Inst. Libr, Hampton, Va, advising on bldg, staffing, serv. & budget of the libr, with S.A.McCarthy, Jan. 66. Specialties: 1b, 1f, 1g; 5a, 5b, 5c; 7a, 7b; 8c, 8f.

SHORES, DR. LOUIS, Sept. 14, 04; Dean Emeritus, Library School, Florida State University, Tallahassee, Fla. 32306. Home: 2013 W. Randolph Circle, Tallahassee, Fla. 32303. A.B, Univ. Toledo, M.S, Columbia Univ; B.S. in L.S, Univ. Chicago; Ph.D, Peabody. Dean libr. sch, Fla. State Univ, 46-67, dean emer, 67- Other: Adv. ed, Compton's Pictured Encyclopedia, 34-41; adv. ed, Collier's Encyclopedia, N.Y, 46-59, ed. in chief, 60-; Fulbright fel, United Kingdom, 51-52; pres, Southeast. Libr. Asn. & Fla. Libr. Asn, 52; chmn. libr. adv. bd, Air Univ, Ala, 52-56; chmn. orgn. cmt, RSD; ALA Mudge award, 67; Beta Phi Mu award, 67. Mem: ALA; Am. Libr. Hist. Round Table; Southeast. Libr. Asn; Fla. Libr. Asn. Publ: Basic Reference Books, ALA, 2nd ed, 39; Challenges to Librarianship, 53; Basic Reference Sources, ALA, 54; Books, Libraries, and Librarians (co-auth), 55; Instructional Materials, 60; Mark Hopkins Log, 64. Consult: 1) Orlando Jr. Col, Orlando, Fla, bldg, 55; 2) Dallas Baptist Col, Dallas, Tex, bldg, June 67; 3) Johnson C. Smith Univ, Charlotte, N.C, libr. & educ. media program, with W. J. Quinly, July 67-June 68; 4) Bowling Green State Univ, Bowling Green, Ohio, libr. educ, Nov. 67; 5) Tex. State Libr, Austin, libr. technician educ, Nov. 67-Sept. 68. Specialties: 1b; 2h (acad. libr); 5d (prfnl. & semi-prfnl. educ); 6a; 7a, 7d (innovation); 8d; 9 (libr. educ, reference & info. serv, encyclopedia design, col. libr, jr. col. librarianship).

SIMMONS, JOSEPH M, Apr. 6, 21; Librarian, Chicago Sun-Times, 401 N. Wabash Ave, Chicago, Ill. 60611. Home: 1456 Oak Ave, Evanston, Ill. 60201. B.S.F.S, Georgetown Univ, 47; M.S.L.S, Columbia Univ, 53. Libr. specialist, libr. bureau, Remington Rand, N.Y, 53-60; librn, Chicago Sun-Times, Chicago, Ill, 60- Other: Pres, Ill. chap, SLA, 64-65; mem, Ill. State Librns. Adv. Cmt, 66-; part-time instructor, sch. libr. serv, Rosary Col. Mem: ALA; Cath. Libr. Asn; Ill. Libr. Asn; SLA; Soc. Am. Archivists; Am. Soc. Info. Sci. Publ: The Special Librarian as Company Archivist, Spec. Libr, 11/65. Consult: 1) DePaul Univ, Chicago, Ill, bldg. planning, 65; Mundelein Col, Chicago, bldg. planning & equipment, 68. Specialties: 1a, 1b, 1d, 1f; 2d (newspaper librs), 2h (archives in spec. libr); 3c, 3e; 5b, 5c; 6b.

SIMMONS, MARION L, May 20, 16; Assistant Executive Director, New York Metropolitan Reference & Research Library Agency, 11 W. 40th St, New York, N.Y. 10018. Home: 382 Central Park W, Apt. 20M, New York, N.Y. 10025. B.A, Elmira Col, 37; B.S. in L.S, Columbia Univ. 38. Pub. relations dir, Rochester Pub. Libr, Rochester, N.Y, 53-61; chief pub. relations office, New York Pub. Libr, 61-67; asst. exec. dir, New York Metrop. Reference & Res. Libr. Agency, New York, N.Y, 67- Other: Secy, pub. relations sect, ALA, 59-60, v.chmn, 60-61, chmn, 61-63, chmn. recruitment materials cmt, 66-68; alumnae trustee, Elmira Col, 60-62; ed, N.Y. Libr. Club Bull, 62-65; pres, Libr. Pub. Relations Coun, 64-65; chmn, ALA Local Conf. Arrangement Cmt. Publicity, 66. Mem: ALA; N.Y. Libr. Asn; Libr. Pub. Relations Coun; N.Y. Libr. Club. Publ: Rochester Offers Tests of Reading Skills, Libr. J, 10/1/56; Books Sandwiched In, Wilson Libr. Bull, 3/57; Rochester's Friends, Libr. J, 10/15/59; Television, Books and Ideas, Channel 13 Program Guide, 3/63; Technical Services Librarian—Image and Reality, N.Y. Libr. Asn. Bull, 7/63; The New Public Library, A Profile, Bookmark, 11/64. Consult: 1) Four-County Libr. Syst, 117 Court St, Binghamton, N.Y, advised local steering cmt. & pub. relations firm retained for LSCA funded Inter-Syst. Pub. Relations Project, with R. Edwin Berry, 66-68. Specialties: 5b; 6a, 6b, 6c.

SIMON, BRADLEY ALDEN, Mar. 9, 29; Director, Scottsdale Public Library, Civic Center, Scottsdale, Ariz. 85251. Home: 6738 E. Vernon Ave, Scottsdale, Ariz. 85251. B.S, 51; M.S. (libr. sci), 55. Asst. dir. libr, Pub. Libr. Charlotte & Mecklenburg County, Charlotte, N.C, 57-61; dir, Volusia County Pub. Libr, Daytona Beach, Fla, 61-64; part-time consult, M. Van Buren Inc, Charlotte, 64-65; head librn, Cent. Piedmont Col, Charlotte, 64-65; libr. bldgs. consult, Colo. State Libr, Denver, Colo, 65-66; coordinator, Ariz. Libr. Survey, Ariz. State Univ, Tempe, Ariz, 66. Other: Pres-elect, pub. libr. div, Ariz. State Libr. Asn, 68-70. Mem: ALA; Ariz. State Libr. Asn; Colo. Libr. Asn; Mt. Plains Libr. Asn; Southwest. Libr. Asn. Publ: Tailor-Made Charging System, Libr. J, 5/1/59; Charlotte—Builds Press Relations, Libr. J, 3/15/60; Arizona Library Survey, Ariz. Librn, summer 66. Consult: 1) Pitkin County Pub. Libr, Aspen, Colo, planning, layouts, archit. & construction consult, specifications, purchasing, systs. anal, 65-66; 2) Yuma Pub. Libr, Yuma, Colo, planning, layouts, archit. & construction consult, specifications, purchasing, systs. anal, 65-66; 3) Arvada Pub. Libr, Arvada, Colo, planning, layouts, archit. & construction, consult, specifications, purchasing, systs. anal, 65-66; 4) Steamboat Springs Pub. Libr, Steamboat Springs, Colo, planning, layouts, archit. & construction consult, specifications, purchasing, systs. anal, 65-66; 5) Scottsdale Pub. Libr, Civic Center, Scottsdale, Ariz, program, archit. consultation, layout, specification & selection of furnishings & equipment, interior design & function consult, Oct. 66- Specialties: 1a, 1b,

1c, 1d, 1e, 1f, 1g; 2a, 2b, 2c, 2h (intellectual freedom); 3b, 3d, 3e, 3f (circulation systs); 4a, 4b, 4c, 4d (automated book catalogs); 5a, 5c; 6a, 6b, 6c; 7a, 7c, 7d (art gallery & museum); 8a, 8b, 8c, 8d, 8e, 8f (consolidations).

SIMON, FANNIE, Apr. 15, 91; Librarian, Kristine Mann Library, 130 E. 39th St, New York, N.Y. 10016. Home: 201 E. 35th St, New York, N.Y. 10016. B.A, Smith Col, 14. Librn. & assoc. ed, McCall's Mag, 42-58; ref. librn, Am. Bible Soc, 59-61; librn, Agr. Develop. Coun, 61; asst. to dir, SLA, 61-62; librn, Kristine Mann Libr, 63- Other: Mem, Hall of Fame, SLA, pres, N.Y. chap, 45-46. Mem: SLA. Consult: 1) Files, Inc, New York, N.Y, advice about setting up picture file, 62; 2) New York City Temporary Finance Cmt, N.Y, set up filing syst, 64; 3) Nat. Cmt. for Child Day Care, 44 E. 23rd St, New York, made outline for libr, 64. Specialties: 6a; 9 (advertising).

SINCLAIR, DOROTHY, May 24, 13; Lecturer, School of Library Science, Case Western Reserve University, Cleveland, Ohio 44106. Home: 1820 Noble Rd, East Cleveland, Ohio 44112. A.B, Goucher Col, 33; B.S. in L.S, Columbia Univ, 42; M.A, Johns Hopkins Univ, 50. Libr. consult. & principal librn, field serv, Calif. State Libr, Sacramento, 55-60; coordinator adult serv, Enoch Pratt Free Libr, Baltimore, Md, 61-65. Other: Mem. spec. projects cmt, ASD, past pres, RSD. Mem: ALA; Ohio Libr. Asn; Adult Educ. Asn. U.S.A. Publ: Book Selection Policies and Procedures (ed), rev. ed, Enoch Pratt Free Libr, 61; Affiliated Libraries in California, News Notes of Calif. Libr, spring 62; Administration of the Small Public Libr, ALA, 65; Two Worlds of Reference, RQ, fall 65; Materials for Special Needs, Libr. Trends, 7/68. Consult: 1) Anne Arundel County Libr, Annapolis, Md, personnel structure, especially adult serv, materials selection, orgn. of large branches, staff-line relationships, 65; 2) East. Shore Area Libr, Wicomico County Libr, Salisbury, Md, studied opers. of area libr. & inter-libr. cooperation, Aug. 65; 3) Los Angeles County Pub. Libr, Los Angeles, Calif, prepared tentative plan of serv. for submission to state for funds & inter-libr. cooperation, 66; 4) Placer County Free Libr, Auburn, Calif, made recommendations for a libr. syst; 5) Tex. State Libr, Austin, Tex, survey of libr. in 36 counties in west cent. Tex, emphasis on interlibr. cooperation, 68-69. Specialties: 5c; 7a, 7c; 8c, 8f.

SKIPPER, DR. JAMES E, Dec. 10, 20; University Librarian, University of California, Berkeley, Calif. 94720. Home: 1910 Yosemite Rd, Berkeley, Calif. 94707. A.B, Univ. N.C, 43; B.S.L.S, Univ. Mich, 48, M.S.L.S, 49, Ph.D, 60. Asst. librn, Mich. State Univ, 56-59; dir. libr, Univ. Conn, 59-62; exec. secy, Asn. Res. Libr, Wash, D.C, 63-68. Other: Pres, Franklin County Libr. Asn, Ohio, 51; pres, col. sect, Mich. Libr. Asn, 57-58; chmn, copying methods sect, RTSD, 58-59, pres. of Div, 63-64; chmn, subcmt. on micropubl, ALA, 59-63, mem, statist. coordinating adv. cmt, 63-64; pres, col. sect, Conn. Libr. Asn, 62-63. Publ: Contrib. to prfnl. journals. Consult: 1) Univ. Tampa, Tampa, Fla, bldg. consult, 66-; 2) Morgan State Col, Baltimore, Md, bldg. consult, 66-; 3) Lincoln Univ, Pa, bldg, 67; 4) Briarcliff Col, Briarcliff, N.Y, bldg, 67; 5) Mercer County Community Col, N.J, bldg, 68. Specialties: 1b; 9 (libr. orgn. & admin).

SLOCUM, MRS. BETTY, Jan. 5, 24; Supervisor of Instructional Materials, Manatee County Board of Public Instruction, Bradenton, Fla. 33505. Home: P.O. Box 465, Bradenton, Fla. 33505. A.B, 45; M.S.L.S, 61. Elem. librn, 51-56; supvr. instructional materials, Manatee County Bd. Pub. Instruction, Bradenton, Fla, 57- Mem: Fla. Asn. Sch. Librns. Consult: 1) Sarasota Bd. Pub. Instruction, Hatton St, Sarasota, Fla, mem. ESEA Title III planning grant, media center, 65-66. Specialties: 2b, 2c; 3d.

SMITH, HANNIS S, June 23, 10; Director of Libraries, Library Division, State Department of Education, St. Paul, Minn. 55101. Home: 2083 Village Lane, St. Paul, Minn. 55116. M.A, Univ. Chicago Grad. Libr. Sch, 49. Pub. libr. consult, Wis. Free Libr. Cmn, Madison, 52-56; dir. libr, libr. div, State Dept. Educ, St. Paul, Minn, 56- Other: Pres, ASD, 58-59; chmn. nominating cmt, ALA, 63-64, chmn. cmt. on orgn, 64-66; pres, ASL, 66-67. Mem: ALA; Minn. Libr. Asn; SLA; Adult Educ. Asn. Publ: People Without Books, Univ. Miss, 49; Informal Education through Libraries (ed), Wis. Free Libr. Cmn, 54; Cooperative Approach to Library Service, Small Pub. Libr. Pamphlet 16, ALA, 64. Consult: 1) Miss. Libr. Survey, Miss. Libr. Cmn, Jackson, asst. dir. state survey, with Gretchen K. Schenk, June-Oct. 49; 2) Lake Geneva Pub. Libr, Lake Geneva, Wis, untangling conflicts concerning legacy for libr. bldg & bldg. consult. on new libr. bldg, with Ethel Brann, 52-54; 3) Legislative Coun, State of Tenn, State Capitol, Nashville, survey of pub. libr develop. program for State of Tenn, with report & recommendations, 58; 4) Dakota-Scott Regional Libr, 40 E. Emerson St, West St. Paul, Minn, negotiation of contract for formation of consolidated regional libr, with Emily L. Mayne, 58-65; plus eight others. Specialties: 1a, 1f, 1g; 4b; 7c; 8a, 8b, 8c, 8d, 8e, 8f; 9 (orgn. & admin. of new fed. programs).

SMITH, JAMES LeROY, July 6, 28; District Library Counselor & District Audio-Visual Counselor, Cicero Public Schools, 5110 W. 24th, Cicero, Ill. 60650. Home: 8700 S. Sproat Ave, Oak Lawn, Ill. 60453. B.Ed, 58; M.Ed.(libr. sci), 64. Teacher & teacher-librn, S. Stickney Pub. Schs, 54-64; dist. libr. counselor, Cicero Pub. Schs, Ill, 64- Other: Pres, Libra (elem.

KEY TO CONSULTING SPECIALTIES: 1) ARCHITECTURE AND BUILDINGS, 1a) public libraries, 1b) academic libraries, 1c) school libraries, 1d) special libraries, 1e) library interiors, 1f) furnishings, 1g) site and location, 1h) other architectural; 2) COLLECTIONS: SELECTION, EVALUATION, WEEDING, 2a) adults, 2b) young adults, 2c) children, 2d) subject specialty, 2e) O.P. searches, 2f) rare books, 2g) appraisals, 2h) others; 3) TECHNICAL PROCESSES, 3a) cataloging, 3b) classification systems, 3c) acquisitions, 3d) materials processing, 3e) work flow and cost studies, 3f) others, 4) AUTOMATION, 4a) applications of data processing equipment, 4b) information storage and retrieval systems, 4c) systems analysis, 4d) others

sch. libr. asn). Mem: ALA; Ill. Libr. Asn; Ill. Sch. Librns. Asn; Ill. Audiovisual Asn; Chicago Reading Roundtable, Chicago Teachers Librn. Asn. Consult: 1) Schaumberg Pub. Schs, 105 Audubon Place, Roselle, Ill, prepared recommended book list for initial purchase in setting up sch. libr, with Henry Boss, Mar-May 64; 2) Wilson Jr. Col, Chicago, Ill, training of para-professional personnel, two year col. program, 68. Specialties: 1c; 2c; 3a, 3b, 3c, 3d, 3e; 5c; 7a.

SMITH, MRS. JUNE SMECK, June 9, 17; Chairman, Department of Library Science, College of St. Catherine, St. Paul, Minn. 55116. Home: 2083 Village Lane, St. Paul, Minn. 55116. B.A, Wayne State Univ, 39; A.B.L.S, Univ. Mich, 40; M.A, Univ. Chicago, 51. Instructor, libr. sch, Col. St. Catherine, St. Paul, Minn, 56-57, readers' serv. librn. & asst. prof, 58-61, assoc. prof. & chmn. dept. libr. sci, 62- Other: Pres, Wis. Asn. Sch. Librns, 56; secy. children's sect, Minn. Libr. Asn, 61-62, recruiting chmn, 63-64; Minn. state recruiting chmn, ALA, 62-64, mem. H.W. Wilson recruitment award cmt, 65-66; mem. adv. coun, Cath. Libr. Asn, 62-; exec. bd. mem, Asn. Hosp. & Inst. Libr, 67-69. Mem: ALA; SLA; Cath. Libr. Asn; Minn. Libr. Asn; Minn. Asn. Sch. Librns; Am. Asn. Univ. Prof; League Women Voters. Publ: The Relationship Between Titles Circulated and Titles Held in Branches of a Metropolitan Library System, Detroit Pub. Libr, 53; The Library Staff, ALA, 62; contrib. to prfnl. journals. Consult: 1) Field Enterprises Educ. Corp, Chicago, Ill, eval. of five gen. encyclopedias, with Ralph Ulveling, Jan. 64; 2) Our Lady of Peace High Sch, St. Paul, Minn, eval. of the high sch. libr, Feb. 64; 3) Benilde High Sch, St. Louis Park, Minn, eval. of the high sch. libr, Feb. 65. Specialties: 2a, 2b, 2c; 5a, 5b, 5c; 7a, 7b, 7c.

SMITH, L. HERMAN, Aug. 14, 11; Dean of Community Services, Pasadena City College, Pasadena, Calif. 91106. Home: 925 E. Palm St, Altadena, Calif. 91001. B.A, 39; B.S. in L.S, 40; M.A, 49. Head librn, Pasadena City Col, Pasadena, Calif, 47-58, asst. dean extended day, 58-63, dean educ. serv, 63-67, dean community serv, 67- Other: Pres, South. Calif. chap, SLA, 45-46; pres, Pasadena Libr. Club, 55-56; pres, Sch. Libr. Asn. Calif, 56-57; mem state cmt. on develop. of criteria for librarianship credential programs, Calif. State Dept. Educ, 60-62; pres, Loyal Knights of Round Table, Pasadena Serv. Club, 63-65. Publ: Manuscript Repair in European Archives, Am. Archivist, 4/38; Pasadena Pioneers Building Planning, Libr. J, 12/5/48; Library Shortcuts, Pasadena City College, Sch. Libr. Asn. Calif. Bull, 5/51; The Junior College Library and the Community, Jr. Col. J, 5/52; Organizing and Training Student Assistants in a Junior College Library, Wilson Libr. Bull, 10/52; Exhibits and Displays in the Junior College Library, Jr. Col. J, 2/55. Consult: 1) El Camino Col, Calif, cataloging, personnel serv, reference, physical facilities, faculty-libr. relationships, with B. Lamar Johnson & Andrew Horn, May 66. Specialties: 1b, 1e; 2b, 2e, 2h (manuscripts); 3a, 3c, 3d; 7a; 8d.

SPRUG, JOSEPH W, Apr. 9, 22; Director of the Library, Loretto Heights College, 3001 S. Federal Blvd, Denver, Colo. 80236. Home: 2225 Dahlia, Denver, Colo. 80207. B.A, 46; B.S.L.S, 47; M.A, 49. Ed, Cath. Periodical Index, 52-61; head tech. processes, Fresno County Libr, 61-62; head tech. processes, St. Vincent Col, 62-64; dir. libr, Loretto Heights Col, Denver, Colo, 64- Other: Mem. cmt. cooperative indexing, Cath. Libr. Asn, 53-54 & 59-61, mem. exec. coun, 59-61. Mem: ALA; Cath. Libr. Asn; Colo. Libr. Asn. Publ: Cumulated Index to Vols. 1-30 of Worship (formerly Orato Fratres), Liturgical Press; Cumulated Index to 10 years of Bu-Docks Technical Digest, U.S. Navy BYD; Catholic Edition of Wilson Standard Catalog for High School Libraries (ed), 66-; Index to G.K. Chesterton, Cath. Univ. Am, 66. Consult: 1) U.S. Navy Bureau Yards & Docks, Wash, D.C, investigation of time & cost involved in making a conventional index to tech. documents, 58. Specialties: 1b, 2d (Cath. literature); 3a; 9 (indexing).

SPYERS-DURAN, PETER, Jan. 26, 32; Director of Libraries, Western Michigan University, Kalamazoo, Mich. 49001. Home: 1805 W. Grand, Kalamazoo, Mich. 49001. M.A, Univ. Chicago, 60. Reference librn, Chicago Pub. Libr, Ill, 59-60; head circulation librn, Univ. Wichita, Kans, 60-62; asst. to exec. secy, LAD, ALA, 62-63; assoc. dir. libr, Univ. Wis-Milwaukee, 62-67. Other: Chmn. cmt. on retirement homes, LAD; mem. standards cmt, ACRL. Mem: ALA. Publ: Moving Library Materials, ALA, 65; An ALA Sponsored Retirement Home: A Survey, ALA, 65; A Survey of Fringe Benefits, 66. Consult: 1) Athens Col, P.O. Box 175, Athens, Greece, bldg. consult, layout work, 62-63; 2) ALA, 50 E. Huron, Chicago, Ill, survey on moving libr. materials, 62-63; 3) ALA, Chicago, study need for a retirement home sponsored by ALA, 64-65; 4) ALA, Chicago, survey of specific fringe benefits offered to pub. librns, 66; 5) Wis. State Hist. Soc, Madison, suggested a method for improving tech. processes, card reproduction, 66. Specialties: 1a, 1b, 1c, 1d, 1e, 1f, 1g, 1h (layout); 2g; 3a, 3b, 3c, 3d, 3e, 3f (reclassification, card catalog production); 5a, 5b, 5c; 9 (moving & integrating libr. collections).

STEIN, THEODORE, Dec. 3, 24; Proprietor, Theodore Stein Co, 400 Madison Ave, New York, N.Y. 10002. Home: 389 Beechmont Dr, New Rochelle, N.Y. 10804. B.S.(physics), N.Y. Univ, 52. Tech. rep, Int. Bus. Machines, 54-59; independent data processing consult, 59-66. Publ: Automation and Library Systems, Libr. J. Consult: 1) N.Y. State Libr, State Univ. N.Y,

---

5) PERSONNEL AND RECRUITING, 5a) job evaluation and description, salary recommendations, 5b) recruitment of professionals and management personnel, 5c) administrative organization, 6) PUBLIC RELATIONS, 6a) publications, 6b) publicity programs, 6c) public opinion surveys, 6d) others, 7) SERVICES, 7a) evaluation of current program, 7b) studies of service to special publics, e.g., students, handicapped, aged, etc., 7c) programs for the implementation of new laws, program proposals to governments, 7d) others, 8) COMMUNITY, REGIONAL, STATE PLANNING, 8a) legislative programs, 8b) area analyses, 8c) centralized systems, cooperative arrangements, 8d) development of standards, 8e) state libraries and extension agencies, 8f) regional and statewide surveys, 8g) others, 9) OTHERS.

Albany, study of application of computer to a res. libr. network, 63; 2) N.Y. Pub. Libr, Fifth Ave. & 42nd St, New York, study of automation of cataloging, 66; 3) N.Y. State Libr, State Univ. N.Y, Albany, study of automation of libr. acquisitions procedures, 66. Specialties: 4a, 4c, 4g.

STEPHENS, DR. IRLENE ROEMER, Jan. 28, 28; Professor and Chief Librarian, Richmond, College, Staten Island, N.Y. 10301. Home: 15 Amherst Court, Maplewood, N.J. 07040. B.A, Rutgers Univ, 49, M.Ed, 52; M.S, Columbia Univ, 54, D.L.S, 66. Dir. libr, Celanese Corp. Am, Summit, N.J, 54-60; libr. dir, S. Orange Pub. Libr, South Orange, N.J, 63-65; assoc. in libr. serv, Columbia Univ, New York, N.Y, 65-66. Other: Chmn. cmt. tech. writing, Am. Chemical Soc, 54-60; summer instructor, sch. libr. sci, Univ. South. Calif, Los Angeles, 66, summer instructor, Univ. Calif, Berkeley, 68. Mem: Am. Soc. Info. Sci; ALA; Drug. Info. Asn; Med. Libr. Asn; Med. Writers' Asn; SLA. Publ: Technical Writing, In: Information and Communication Practice in Industry, Reinhold, 58; Searching for Theses, Dissertations and Unpublished Data, In: Searching the Chemical Literature (Advances in Chemistry Series 30), Am. Chemical Soc, 61; Southern California Library Study: Centralized Technical Processing (with Maurice F. Tauber), In: Strength Through Cooperation in Southern California Libraries (Los Angeles County, Orange County, Riverside County, San Bernardino County), Los Angeles, Calif, 65; Technical Services in 1965 (with Maurice F. Tauber), Libr. Resources & Tech. Serv, spring 66; Introduction: Recapitulation of Recommendations, In: The use of Printed and Audio-Visual Materials for Instructional Purposes (ed. with Maurice F. Tauber), U.S. Office Educ. Tech. Report, 66; Surveys of Technical Services in Libraries, In: Library Surveys (ed. with Maurice F. Tauber), Columbia Univ, 67. Consult: 1) N.Y. Genealogical & Biographical Soc, 122 E. 58th St, New York, libr. surv, 65; 2) Bridgeport Pub. Libr, Bridgeport, Conn, survey of the tech. serv, with Maurice F. Tauber, 65; 3) Mich. State Libr, Lansing, survey of tech. serv, with Maurice F. Tauber, 65; 4) Libr. Resources Develop. Program, survey of resources, opers. & serv. of libr. in west. Pa, with Maurice F. Tauber, 65; 5) City Univ. New York, N.Y, survey of tech. serv, with Felix Reichmann, June 66. Specialties: 1a, 1b, 1d, 1e, 1g; 2a, 2b, 2c, 2d (sci. & tech); 3a, 3b, 3c, 3d, 3e, 3f (orgn. & admin); 4a, 4b, 4c; 5a, 5c; 6a, 6c; 7a, 7b; 8a, 8b, 8c, 8d, 8f; 9 (admin. of libr. & info. centers).

STERN, DR. WILLIAM B, Mar. 12, 10; Foreign Law Librarian, Los Angeles County Law Library, 301 W. First St, Los Angeles, Calif. 90012. Home: 3030 Fernwood Ave, Los Angeles, Calif. 90039. Dr. iur. utr, Univ. Würzburg, 33. Foreign law librn, Los Angeles County Law Libr, Los Angeles, Calif, 39- Other: Ed, Law Libr, Journal, 53-54; mem. exec. bd, Am. Asn. Law Libr, 54-58, pres-elect, 68-69; chmn, Cmt. on Foreigh Law Indexing, 59-; secy, Int. Asn. Law Libr, 59-62, pres, 62-65; mem, cmn. de bibliothèque, Asn. Int. pour l'Enseignement du Droit Comparé, 62- Mem: Am. Asn. Law Libr; Int. Asn. Law Libr; Am. Foreign Law Asn; Am. Soc. Int. Law. Publ: Foreign Law in the Courts: Judicial Notice and Proof, Calif. Law Review, 57; A Proposed Program for Law Librarianship, Law Libr, J, 62; Comparative Law: The History of the Language Problem and the Use of Generic Terms, Law Libr. J, 62; Foreign Law in American Law Libraries, Libr. Trends, 63; Foreign Language Legal Dictionaries, Annual Meeting Am. Asn. Law Libr, 63; The Accessibility of Legal Developments Through the Legal Periodical Literature, 7th Int. Congress Comparative Law, spec. sect, Uppsala, 66. Consult: 1) Stanford Univ. Sch. of Law Libr, Stanford, Calif, report on survey of foreign law holdings & establishment & purposes of foreign law collections, Sept. 55; 2) Univ. Va. Sch. of Law Libr, Charlottesville, investigation of foreign law collection & advice to law librn, Apr. 64; 3) Facultad Derecho, Univ. Nacional Autónoma México, Ciudad Universitaria, México 20, D.F, survey of libr. of the Facultad de Derecho, July 65; 4) Faculté Int. pour l'Enseignement du Droit Comparé, Univ. Strasbourg, supplying book lists for libr. at European & Latin Am. institutions where the Faculté holds sessions, 66. Specialties: 2d (foreign law); 9 (programming foreign law collections & their use; programming Latin Am. univ. law collections & their housing & use).

STEVENS, NICHOLAS G, Sept. 30, 11; Director of Library Education, Kutztown State College, Kutztown, Pa. 19530. Home: 616 Highland Ave, Kutztown, Pa. 19530. A.B, Univ. Pittsburgh, 33, A.M.(hist), 40; A.M.L.S, Univ. Mich, 49. Assoc. prof. hist. & libr. educ, Kutztown State Col, Kutztown, Pa, 49-55, dir. libr. educ, 55- Other: Pres, Kutztown Lions Club, 58-59; mem, State Cmt. on New Standards for Pa. Sch. Libr, 60-61; sch. libr. consult, Dept. Pub. Instruction, Pa, 60-, recipient, Distinguished Educ. Award, 64; mem, Gov. Adv. Coun. on Libr. Develop, Commonwealth of Pa, 63-64; pres, Pa. Libr. Asn, 63-64; coun, ALA, 67-68. Mem: ALA; Pa. Libr. Asn; Pa. State Educ. Asn; Pa. Sch. Librns. Asn; Am. Asn. Univ. Prof; Phi Delta Kappa. Publ: School Libraries; How to Improve Them, School Libraries: How to Increase Their Use, The Elementary School Library: A Basic Beginning & Total Task of the School Librarian, Kutztown Bulletins; The School Instructional Materials Center and the Curriculum, Commonwealth of Pa. DPI Curriculum Publ, 62. Consult: 1) Mansfield State Col, Mansfield, Pa, eval. of new libr. educ. program, with Dr.

KEY TO CONSULTING SPECIALTIES: 1) ARCHITECTURE AND BUILDINGS, 1a) public libraries, 1b) academic libraries, 1c) school libraries, 1d) special libraries, 1e) library interiors, 1f) furnishings, 1g) site and location, 1h) other architectural; 2) COLLECTIONS: SELECTION, EVALUATION, WEEDING, 2a) adults, 2b) young adults, 2c) children, 2d) subject specialty, 2e) O.P. searches, 2f) rare books, 2g) appraisals, 2h) others; 3) TECHNICAL PROCESSES, 3a) cataloging, 3b) classification systems, 3c) acquisitions, 3d) materials processing, 3e) work flow and cost studies, 3f) others, 4) AUTOMATION, 4a) applications of data processing equipment, 4b) information storage and retrieval systems, 4c) systems analysis, 4d) others

Butterworth, Apr. 62. Specialties: 1b, 1c, 1g; 3c, 3e; 5c; 7a, 7b, 9 (methods of educ. & libr. res, libr. educ).

STEWART, DAVID MARSHALL, Aug. 1, 16; Director, Nashville Public Library, 222 Eighth Ave. N, Nashville, Tenn. 37203. Home: 6342 Torrington Rd, Nashville, Tenn. 37205. B.A, 38; B.S. in L.S, 39. Libr. consult, U.S. Govt, 47-60; dir, Nashville Pub. Libr, Tenn, 60- Other: Chmn, standards cmt, PLA, 64-65, pres, 66-67; pres, Tenn. Libr. Asn, 66-67. Mem: ALA; Tenn. Libr. Asn; Southeast. Libr. Asn. Consult: 1) Sumner County Pub. Libr, Gallatin, Tenn, bldg. consult, 65-67; 2) Robertson County Pub. Libr, Springfield, Tenn, bldg. consult, 66-67; 3) Athens Pub. Libr, Athens, Tenn, bldg. consult, 66-67. Specialties: 1a, 1e, 1f, 1g; 5a, 5c; 6b, 6d (gen. pub. relations for pub. libr); 7a; 8b, 8c, 8d.

STEWART, R.C, 1907; Associate Director, University Library, University of Michigan, Ann Arbor, Mich. 48104. Home: 765 Country Club Rd, Ann Arbor, Mich. 48105. A.B, 29; A.M, 30; A.B.L.S, 38; A.M.L.S, 40. Chief bibliographer & asst. dir. tech. processes, grad. libr, undergrad. libr. & non-sci, div. libr, Univ. Mich. Libr, Ann Arbor. Mem: ALA; Bibliog. Soc. London; Phi Kappa Phi. Publ: Undergraduate Library Shelf List, Univ. Microfilms, Inc, 59- Consult: 1) Univ. Calif, San Diego, develop. of new campuses' program, 64-65. Specialties: 2a, 2d (languages, literatures, philosophy, religion & soc. sci), 2f, 2g.

STOFFEL, LESTER L, 1920; Executive Director, Suburban Library System, 903 Burlington Ave, Western Springs, Ill. 60558. Home: 325 N. Grove Ave, Oak Park, Ill. 60302. B.A, 42; B.S.L.S, 46. Dir, Oak Park Pub. Libr, Ill, 55-67; exec. dir, Suburban Libr. Syst, Western Springs, Ill, 67- Other: Pres, Pa. Libr. Asn, 54-55; v.pres, Ill. Libr. Asn, 65; chmn, legislation cmt, PLA, 65-67; mem, Ill. State Libr. Adv. Cmt, 65-; mem, Ill. Libr. Serv. & Construction Act Adv. Coun, 65-; mem, adv. coun. instructional materials to Ill. Supt. Pub. Instruction, 68- Mem: ALA; Ill. Libr. Asn; Libr. Administrators Conf. North. Ill. Publ: The Role of the Librarian in Library Planning, In: Problems in Planning Library Facilities..., ALA, 64; Oak Park Public Library, Ill. Libr, 11/64; Scenic Showcase for Oak Park, Libr. J, 12/1/64; Building Issue of Ill. Libr.(assoc. ed), 12/66, 12/68; Public Library Development in Illinois, Libr. J, 1/15/67; Large City Library from the Viewpoint of the Suburban Library, Libr. Quart, 1/68. Consult: 1) Dundee Township Libr, West Dundee, Ill, community study leading to bldg. program recommendations & recommendations of site, Dec. 65-Aug. 66; 2) Champaign Pub. Libr, Champaign, Ill, assistance in bldg. program, selection of architect, site selection, referendum, furniture & equipment layout, specifications, book selection, Jan. 66-; 3) Chicago Heights Pub. Libr, Chicago Heights, Ill, assistance in bldg. program, planning, furniture layout, specifications, selection, referendum, July 66-; 4) T.B. Scott Pub. Libr, Wisconsin Rapids, Wis, assistance in bldg. program, Jan. 66-July 67; 5) Glencoe Pub. Libr, Glencoe, Ill, bldg. program, Apr. 68- Specialties: 1a, 1f, 1g, 1h (referendum); 5a, 5b, 5c; 7a; 8c.

STONE, DR. C. WALTER, June 25, 21; Director of University Libraries, University of Pittsburgh, Pittsburgh, Pa. 15213. Home: 47 Glen Ridge Lane, Pittsburgh, Pa. 15216. A.B, Columbia Univ, 46, B.S, 47, M.A, 48, Ed.D, 49. Prof. libr. sci, Univ. Ill, Urbana, 49-60; dir. educ. media br, U.S. Off. Educ, Wash, D.C, 59-62; prof. libr. sci. & educ. & dir. center libr. & educ. media studies, Univ. Pittsburgh, Pittsburgh, Pa, 62-, dir. libr, 65- Other: Mem. dept. audio-visual instruction, Nat. Asn. Educ. Broadcasters. Mem: ALA; Pa. Libr. Asn; Asn. Am. Libr. Schs; SLA; Educ. Media Coun. Publ: Instructional Television in Western Pennsylvania (ed), 64 & Professional Education for Media Service Personnel (ed), 64, Center Libr. & Educ. Media Studies, Univ, Pittsburgh; A Library Program for Columbia (project chmn. & ed), Coun. Libr. Resources, Wash, D.C, 65; Developmental Book Activities and Needs in the Republic of Korea (joint auth), 66, Developmental Book Activities and Needs in the Republic of Vietnam (joint auth), 66, Developmental Book Activities and Needs in the Philippines (joint auth), 66, Wolf Mgt. Serv-Agency Int. Develop. Consult: 1) Nat. Asn. Educ. Broadcasters, 1346 Connecticut Ave. N.W, Wash, D.C, educ. commun. systs. meetings, 64-66; 2) Educ. Media Coun, 1346 Connecticut Ave. N.W, Wash, D.C, educ. media index, 2/66; 3) Wolf Mgt. Serv, 30 E. 42nd St, New York, N.Y, book survey team, Agency Int. Develop. mission to the Philippines, Korea, Vietnam, with Stanley A. Barnet, David Kaser & Errol D. Michener, Apr-June 66; 4) McGraw-Hill Book Co, 330 W. 42nd St, New York, encyclopedic index, Nov-Dec. 66; 5) Wolf Mgt. Serv, 30 E. 42nd St, New York, book survey team, Agency Int. Develop. mission to Thailand, with Stanley A. Barnett, Emerson Brown & Austin McCaffrey, Jan-Feb. 67. Specialties: 1b, 1c, 1h (libr. planning); 2h (audiovisual materials); 7a, 7d (educ. media serv); 9 (educ. media res).

SUMMERS, F. WILLIAM, Feb. 8, 33; State Librarian of Florida, Florida State Library, Supreme Court Building, Tallahassee, Fla. 32303. Home: 1315 Lemond St, Tallahassee, Fla. 32303. B.A, Univ. Fla, 55; M.A, Rutgers Univ, 58. Librn, Jacksonville Pub. Libr, Jacksonville, Fla, 55 & 57; sr. librn, Linden Pub. Libr, Linden, N.J, 58-59; librn, Cocoa Pub. Libr, Cocoa, Fla, 59-61; dir, Providence, Pub. Libr, Providence, R.I, 61-65; assoc. librn.

5) PERSONNEL AND RECRUITING, 5a) job evaluation and description, salary recommendations, 5b) recruitment of professionals and management personnel, 5c) administrative organization, 6) PUBLIC RELATIONS, 6a) publications, 6b) publicity programs, 6c) public opinion surveys, 6d) others, 7) SERVICES, 7a) evaluation of current program, 7b) studies of service to special publics, e.g., students, handicapped, aged, etc., 7c) programs for the implementation of new laws, program proposals to governments, 7d) others, 8) COMMUNITY, REGIONAL, STATE PLANNING, 8a) legislative programs, 8b) area analyses, 8c) centralized systems, cooperative arrangements, 8d) development of standards, 8e) state libraries and extension agencies, 8f) regional and statewide surveys, 8g) others, 9) OTHERS.

& part-time lectr, Univ. R.I. Libr. Sch, 64-65. Other: V.pres, R.I. Libr. Asn, 64, pres, 65; mem. R.I. Bd. Libr. Cmnr, 64-65. Mem: ALA; Fla. Libr. Asn; Beta Phi Mu. Publ: Library Service in Pennsylvania (with Lowell Martin & others), Pa. State Libr, 58; Library Service in Missle-Land, Libr. J, 6/15/62; Recommendations for Improved Library Service in Somerset, Massachusetts, 64; Rhode Island's Legislative Program, In: Proceedings of the Legislative Workshop, Cmt. Legis, ALA, 65; Communications, a Survey of Ohio Libraries, 68. Consult: 1) Pa. State Libr, Harrisburg, Pa, res. asst, with Lowell Martin & others, 58; 2) Melrose Pub. Libr, Melrose, Mass, specifications for libr. furniture, 63; 3) Somerset Pub. Libr, Somerset, Mass, recommendations for improvement of libr. program & location of cent. libr, 64; 4) Ohio Libr. Survey, study of commun. & contrib. to gen. profile of Ohio libr, 68. Specialties: 5a, 5b, 5c; 7a, 7b, 7c; 8a, 8b, 8c, 8d, 8e, 8f.

SURRENCY, ERWIN C, May 11, 24; Professor of Law & Law Librarian, Law Library, Temple University, 1715 N. Broad St, Philadelphia, Pa. 19122. Home: 712 Pine Ridge Rd, Media, Pa. 19063. A.B, 57; M.A, 58; L.L.B, & M.A.L.S, 59. Law librn & prof. law, Sch. Law, Temple Univ, 50- Other: Visiting prof. law, Queens Univ, Belfast, N.Ireland, 63-64; mem. exec. bd, Am. Asn. Law Libr, 63-66. Mem: SLA; Am. Asn. Law Libr. Publ: American Journal of Legal History (ed), 57-; Guide to Legal Research, 59; Research in Pennsylvania Law, 65. Consult: 1) Am. Bar Asn. Found, Chicago, Ill, furnishings & construction, 57; 2) Queens Univ, Belfast, N. Ireland, book selection for law libr, 63-64; 3) Law Libr, Catholic Univ, 1323 18th St, N.W, Wash, D.C, furniture & furnishings, 65. Specialties: 1b, 1d, 1f; 2d (law, hist); 8d.

SWANK, DR. RAYNARD C, Dec. 20, 12; Dean & Professor, School of Librarianship, University of California, Berkeley, Calif. 94720. Home: 1800 Spruce St, Apt. 201, Berkeley, Calif. 94709. Dir. libr, Stanford Univ, 48-62; dean & prof, sch. librarianship, Univ. Calif, Berkeley, Calif, 62- Other: Dir. int. relations office, ALA, 59-61; mem, U.S. Nat. Cmn. UNESCO, 62-68; mem. adv. cmt. libr. res. & training projects, U.S. Office Educ, 66-68; mem. subcmt. joint use of libr, Calif. Coordinating Coun. Higher Educ, 68- Mem: ALA; Calif. Libr. Asn; SLA; Asn. Am. Libr. Schs. Publ: Soviet Libraries and Librarianship: Report of the Visit of the Delegation of U.S. Librarians to the Soviet Union, May-June, 61 ... (with Melville J. Ruggles), ALA, 62; The Midwest Inter-Library Center: Report of a Survey, May 1963 to June 1964 (with Stephen A. McCarthy), Chicago, 64; The Bibliographical Center for Research, Rocky Mountain Region, Inc, Report of a Survey, Denver, 66; Library Service for the Visually and Physically Handicapped: a Report to the California State Library, Sacramento, 67; Interlibrary Cooperation under Title III of the Library Services and Construction Act: a Preliminary Study for the California State Library, Sacramento, 6/67. Consult: 1) Bowling Green State Univ, Bowling Green, Ohio, consult. on orgn. & program of the univ. libr, Apr. 67; 2) Univ. Mich, Ann Arbor, Mich, eval. of libr. sch. program, with Lester Asheim, Robert Downs & Quincy Mumford, Nov. 67; 3) Ohio State Libr, Columbus, Ohio, consult. on serv. to the physically handicapped, Dec. 67; 4) Col. Wooster, Wooster, Ohio, consult. on orgn. and program of col. libr, Dec, 67; 5) Univ. Wis, Madison, Wis, advising on libr. sch. doctoral program, Apr. 68. Specialties: 1b; 3a, 3b, 3c, 3d, 3e; 5c; 7a, 7b; 8b, 8c, 8e, 8f; 9 (educ. for librarianship & info. sci, libr. & librarianship abroad).

T

TANIS, NORMAN EARL, Aug. 15, 29; Director of the Library & Professor of Library Science, Kansas State College, Pittsburg, Kans. 66762. Home: 306 W. Quincy, Pittsburg, Kans. 66762. A.B, Calvin Col, 51; M.A.L.S, Univ. Mich, 52; M.A, 56, M.A.(educ), 61. Reference & circulation librn, Henry Ford Community Col, Dearborn, Mich, 56-63, div. head libr. serv, 63-66; dir. libr. & prof. libr. sci, Kans. State Col, Pittsburg, 66- Other: Mem, notable books coun, ASD, 59-60; mem, standards cmt, ACRL, 59-61, chmn, 63-, chmn, standards criteria cmt, jr. col. libr. sect, 60-64, chmn. sect, 63-64, mem. bd. dirs, ACRL, 62-65, mem. ed. bd, Col. & Res. Libr, 63-, mem, cmt. on liaison with accrediting asn, 63-, mem, cmt. on appointments, 64-65; mem, intellectual freedom cmt, Mich. Libr. Asn, 59-62, chmn, jr. col. libr. sect, 62-63; pres, Henry Ford Community Col. chap, Am. Asn. Univ. Prof, 61-62; mem, spec. cmt. on interrelated libr. serv. to students, ALA, 62-64; chmn, liaison cmt, ALA-Am. Asn. Jr. Cols, 62-64, mem, ed. subcmt. on books for jr. col. libr, 63-, mem, joint cmt. on jr. col. libr, 64- Mem: ALA; Mich. Libr. Asn; Phi Kappa Phi. Publ: Implementing the Junior College Library Standards, Col. & Res. Libr, 3/61; The Library As a Part of Industrial Education, Industrial Arts & Vocational Educ, 4/61; The Departmental Allocation of Library Book Funds in the Junior College: Developing Criteria, Libr. Resources & Tech. Serv, fall 61; Guidelines for Establishing Junior College Libraries, Col. & Res. Libr, 11/63; Strengthening the College Library (with Karl J. Jacobs), Improving Col. & Univ. Teaching, spring 64; Strengthening the Junior College Library: The Application of Standards, Jr. Col. Libr. Occasional Report 8, 66. Consult: 1) Northwood Inst. Libr, Midland, Mich, survey of collection, assistance in accreditation problems, book selection, preliminary procedures for

---

KEY TO CONSULTING SPECIALTIES: 1) ARCHITECTURE AND BUILDINGS, 1a) public libraries, 1b) academic libraries, 1c) school libraries, 1d) special libraries, 1e) library interiors, 1f) furnishings, 1g) site and location, 1h) other architectural; 2) COLLECTIONS: SELECTION, EVALUATION, WEEDING, 2a) adults, 2b) young adults, 2c) children, 2d) subject speciaty, 2e) O.P. searches, 2f) rare books, 2g) appraisals, 2h) others; 3) TECHNICAL PROCESSES, 3a) cataloging, 3b) classification systems, 3c) acquisitions, 3d) materials processing, 3e) work flow and cost studies, 3f) others, 4) AUTOMATION, 4a) applications of data processing equipment, 4b) information storage and retrieval systems, 4c) systems analysis, 4d) others

undertaking bldg. program, Apr. 64; 2) Monroe Community Col, Monroe, Mich, planning of libr. bldg, spring 65; 3) Prince George Community Col, Suitland, Md, survey of libr, eval. of bldg. plans, Oct. 65; 4) Washentaw Jr. Col, Ann Arbor, Mich, recruitment of libr. personnel, Mar-Apr. 66; 5) North. Okla. Col, Tonkawa, Okla, survey of libr, Feb. 68. Specialties: 1b, 1f, 1g; 2a; 3c; 5a, 5b; 6a; 8d, 8e.

TAUBER, DR. MAURICE F, Feb. 14, 08; Melvil Dewey Professor of Library Service, School of Library Service, Columbia University, New York, N.Y. 10027. Home: 460 Riverside Dr, New York, N.Y. 10027. B.S, Temple Univ, 30, Ed.M, 39; B.S, Columbia Univ, 34; Ph.D, Univ. Chicago, 41. Prof, sch. libr. serv, Columbia Univ, 49-54, Melvil Dewey prof, 54- Mem: ALA; SLA; Am. Soc. Info. Sci; Am. Asn. Advancement Sci; N.Y. Tech. Serv. Librns; N.Y. State Libr. Asn; N.Y. Libr. Club; Am. Asn. Univ. Prof. Publ: Technical Services in Libraries, Columbia Univ, 54; The University Library (with L.R. Wilson), 2nd ed, Columbia Univ, 56; The Columbia University Libraries (with C.D. Cook & R.H. Logsdon), Columbia Univ, 58; Cataloging and Classification, In: State of the Library Art, Vol. 1, Part 1, Rutgers Univ, 61; Classification Systems (with Edith Wise), In: State of the Library Art, Vol. 1, Part 3, Rutgers Univ, 61; Book Catalogs (with R.E. Kingery), Scarecrow, 63. Consult: 1) Pa. State Univ. Libr, University Park, long range develop. plan, with William L. Locke & others, fall 64-Apr. 65; 2) Calif. Libr, Los Angeles, establishment of guidelines for centralized program, with Irlene Roemer Stephens, spring 65; 3) Franklin & Marshall Col. Libr, Lancaster, Pa, review of col. libr, with Richard B. Harwell, winter-spring 65; 4) John Wiley-Intersci. Publ, info. center, with Theodore C. Hines, 66; 5) Mich. State Libr, Lansing, tech. serv, with Irlene Roemer Stephens, fall 65-spring 66. Specialties: 1a, 1b, 1d, 1e, 1g; 2a, 2h (resources studies in all gen. surveys-archives as a part of collections); 3a, 3b, 3c, 3d, 3e, 3f (binding, photo-reproduction); 4a, 4b; 5a, 5b, 5c, 5d (classification & pay plans); 6a, 6b; 7a, 7b; 8b, 8c, 8e; 9 (spec. problems of spec. libr. & info. centers).

TAYLOR, ROBERT S, June 15, 18; Director Library, Hampshire College, Amherst, Mass. 01002. Home: Arnold Rd, R.F.D. 2, Amherst, Mass. 01002. B.A, 40; M.S, 50; M.A, 54. Assoc. librn, Lehigh Univ, Bethlehem, Pa, 57-67, dir. center info. sci, 62-67, assoc. prof. & head div. info. sci, 63-67. Other: Fulbright lectr, Technische Hogeschool, Delft, Holland, 56-57; mem. exec. coun, Am. Document. Inst, 58-60, pres-elect, 67; pres. Lehigh chap, Pa. Libr. Asn, 55-66; U.S. nat. rep, cmt. on training of documentalists, Int. Fedn. Documentalists, 66-69. Mem: ALA; Am. Soc. Info. Sci; Asn. Computing Machinery; Pa. Libr. Asn.

Publ: The Process of Asking Questions, Am. Document, 10/62; Toward an Educational Base for the Information Sciences and Information Engineering, In Proceedings, Symposium on Education for Information Sciences, Spartan, 65; Manual for the Analysis of Library Systems, Lehigh Univ. Center Info. Sci, 65; Information Management in Engineering Education, Proc. Conf, 66; Professional Aspects of Information Science and Technology, In: Annual Review of Information Science and Technology, Wiley, 66; The Interfaces between Librarianship and Information Science and Engineering, Spec. Libr, 1/67. Consult: 1) Nat. Sci. Found. Div. Grad. Educ. in Sci, Wash, D.C, review programs in educ. in the info. sci, Jan. 66-; 2) Syracuse Univ, Syracuse, N.Y, libr. systs, long-range libr. planning & libr. educ, Dec. 66-; 3) Hampshire Col, Amherst, Mass, planning & design of libr. for exp. col, including info. transfer exp, Jan. 67-; 4) Arthur D. Little Inc, Cambridge, Mass, libr. & info. syst. planning, Sept. 67- Specialties: 1b, 1e; 3c, 3d, 3e; 4b, 4c; 5c; 7d (long-range planning); 8c; 9 (educ. for librarianship & info. sci).

TECHNICAL LIBRARY SERVICE, 104 Fifth Ave, New York, N.Y. 10011. Consult: 1) Soc. for the Advancement of Judaism, 32 W. 86th St, New York, N.Y, directed the cataloging of approx. 3000 vols. by volunteer members, improved libr. space utilization, suggested pub. relations programs for members, Jan-Sept. 64; 2) Gen. Foods Corp, White Plains, N.Y, instructed secy-librn. in indexing & oper. of coordinate indexing syst, developed simple current awareness & intra-co. pub. relations programs, assisted in layout of new quarters, Mar-Apr. 64 & Jan. 65; 3) Am. Power Jet Co, Ridgefield, N.J, prepared procedures manual, spec. thesaurus, instituted coordinate indexing syst. & selective dissemination program, improved libr. space utilization, trained non-prfnl librn, July-Nov. 64; 4) J.C. Penny Co, Inc, 1301 Ave. of the Americas, New York, N.Y, advised on book selection, intra-co. pub. relations program, instructed clerk-librn. in libr. opers, advised on new libr. layout, Sept-Nov. 64 & July 65; 5) Explorers Club, 46 E. 70th St, New York, N.Y, prepared libr. policy, engaged book restorer, cataloged spec. collection, centralized control of Club's resources, aided in selection of prfnl. full-time librn, Jan-Apr. 65 & Jan-Feb. 66. Specialties: 1b, 1d, 1e, 1f; 2d (sci, tech, bus), 2d, 2e, 3a, 3b, 3c, 3d, 3e; 4a, 4b; 5a, 5b, 5c, 5d (personnel training); 6d (intra-orgn. programs); 7a; 9 (consulting serv. for small bus. & industry & researchers; specialized current awareness serv; literature searches).

THOMAS, HENRY, June 20, 23; Library Director, Free Public Library, 10-01 Fair Lawn Ave, Fair Lawn, N.J. 07410. Home: 16-18 Alden Terrace, Fair Lawn, N.J. 07410. A.B,

---

5) PERSONNEL AND RECRUITING, 5a) job evaluation and description, salary recommendations, 5b) recruitment of professionals and management personnel, 5c) administrative organization, 6) PUBLIC RELATIONS, 6a) publications, 6b) publicity programs, 6c) public opinion surveys, 6d) others, 7) SERVICES, 7a) evaluation of current program, 7b) studies of service to special publics, e.g., students, handicapped, aged, etc., 7c) programs for the implementation of new laws, program proposals to governments, 7d) others, 8) COMMUNITY, REGIONAL, STATE PLANNING, 8a) legislative programs, 8b) area analyses, 8c) centralized systems, cooperative arrangements, 8d) development of standards, 8e) state libraries and extension agencies, 8f) regional and statewide surveys, 8g) others, 9) OTHERS.

Kent State Univ, 49, M.A.L.S, 50. Dir, Rutherford Pub. Libr, N.J, 52-58; dir, Fair Lawn Pub. Libr, 59.- Consult: 1) Rutherford Pub. Libr, Rutherford, N.J, complete bldg. program, 60; 2) Upper Saddle River Pub. Libr, Upper Saddle River, N.J, complete bldg. program, 67; 3) East Paterson Pub. Libr, East Paterson, N.J, complete bldg. prog, 68. Specialties: 1a, 1e, 1f, 1g.

THOMPSON, DONALD EUGENE, July 10, 13; Librarian, Lilly Library, Wabash College, Crawfordsville, Ind. 47933. Home: 1103 W. Pike St, Crawfordsville, Ind. 47933. B.S, 35; B.S. in L.S, 37; M.A, 42. Librn, Wabash Col, 55-; bldg. consult, Ind. State Libr, 65- Other: Pres, Miss. Libr. Asn, 49-51; pres, Ind. Libr. Asn, 66-67. Mem: ALA; ACRL; Ind. Libr. Asn. Publ: A Self-survey of the University of Alabama Libraries, Col. & Res. Libr, 4/47; Planning a College Library, Ind. Architect, 9/61; Business and Economics Periodicals, Libr. Trends, 1/62; The Consultant's Role in the Preparation of the Library Building Program, Focus on Ind. Libr, 11/64; Education for Building, Libr. J, 12/1/65; The Monroe County Library: Planning for the Future (with Peter Hiatt), Ind. Univ, 66. Consult: 1) Ohio North. Univ, Ada, bldg. & Survey of libr. opers, 65; 2) Evansville Col, Evansville, Ind, survey of book & periodical collection, with A.F. Kuhlman, 65; 3) St. Joseph's Col, Rensselaer, Ind, Bldg. & site, 66; 4) Belhaven Col, Jackson, Miss, bldg, 66; 5) Park Col, Parkville, Mo, bldg. & survey of libr. opers, 66. Specialties: 1a, 1b, 1g; 2g; 7a; 9 (gen. survey of acad. libr. opers).

THOMPSON, DR. LAWRENCE S, Dec. 21, 16; Professor of Classics, University of Kentucky, Lexington, Ky. 40506. Home: 225 Culpepper, Lexington, Ky. 40502. A.B; M.A; Ph.D; A.B.L.S. Dir. libr, Univ. Ky, Lexington, 48-65, prof. classics, 56- Other: Mem. int. relations bd, ALA, 50-55; mem. bd. dirs, ACRL, 55-60, chmn. rare books sect, 67-68; pres, Ky. Folklore Soc, 64-65. Mem: Ky. Libr. Asn; Southeast. Libr. Asn; ALA; Bibliog. Soc. Am. Publ: The Kentucky Novel, Univ. Ky, 53; Die Handbuchbinderei in den Vereinigten Staaten von Nordamerika, Max Hettler, 55; Kentucky Tradition, Shoestring, 56; Boktryckarkonstens Uppkomst i Förenta Staterna, Gebers, 56; section on history of American Libraries, In: Handbuch der Bibliothekswissenschaft, Vol. III, Harrassowitz, 57; Printing in Colonial Spanish America, Archon, 62. Consult: 1) Turkish Ministry Educ, Ankara, gen. survey of Turkish res. libr, 51-52; 2) Caribbean Cmn, Port-of-Spain, Trinidad, survey of libr, 55; 3) Pikeville Col, Pikeville, Ky, gen. survey, 58; 4) Valparaiso Univ, Valparaiso, Ind, study of admin. orgn, 63; 5) Ohio Philosophical & Hist. Soc, Cincinnati, appraisal of manuscripts, 65. Specialties: 1b, 2f, 2g; 9 (qualitative anal. of collections of res. libr).

TREYZ, JOSEPH H, Nov. 23, 26; Assistant Director, University Library, University of Michigan, Ann Arbor, Mich 48104. Home: 3410 Woodlea Ave, Ann Arbor, Mich. 48103. B.A, Oberlin Col; M.S. in L.S, Columbia Univ. Asst. head catalog dept, Yale Univ. Libr, 55-61; head new campuses program, Univ. Calif. 61-65; asst. dir, Univ. Mich. Libr, Ann Arbor, 65- Other: Chmn. membership cmt, N.Y. Regional Catalog Group, 57-58; mem. pub. relations cmt, Conn. Libr. Asn, 57-58, mem. program cmt, 60-61; v.pres, N.Y. Tech. Serv. Librns, 58-59, pres, 59-60; mem. publ. cmt, RTSD, 59-60, mem. nominating cmt, cataloging & classification sect, 61-62, mem. exec. cmt, 64-67, mem. nominating cmt, copying methods sect, 65-66, mem. nat. libr. week cmt, 65-67, chmn. tech. serv. dirs. large res. libr, 67-68, chmn. cmt. coun. regional groups; chmn. program cmt, South. Calif. Tech. Processes Group, 61-62; RTSD rep, ALA Membership Cmt, 61-67; mem. Palomar dist. planning cmt, Calif. Libr. Asn, 62, secy, tech. processes round table, 62-63, v.pres. & pres-elect, 64-65, secy. col, univ, res. libr. sect, 63-64, mem. regional resources cmt, 63-65, mem. Palomar dist, Calif. ALA Membership Cmt, 62-66. Mem: ALA; ACRL; Am. Soc. Info. Sci; Bibliog. Soc. Am; Mich. Libr. Asn; Ann Arbor Libr. Club; Signature Club; Clements Libr. Assocs. Publ: The Xerox Process and its Application at Yale, Libr. Resources & Tech. Serv, 59; The Cards with Books Program, ALA Bull, 5/63; Equipment and Methods in Catalog Card Reproduction, Libr. Furniture and Equipment Proc. of a three-day inst, ALA, 63 & Libr. Resources & Tech. Serv, res. ed, 64; The Technical Services Librarian and the Profession (with F. Bernice Field), Libr. Resources & Tech. Serv, 65; The New Campuses Program (with M.J. Voigt), Libr. J, 5/15/65; The O.P. Market, Choice: Books for Col. Libr, 7-8/65. Consult: 1) Libr. Congress, Wash, D.C, univ. rep, consumer reaction team for cataloging-in-source, 59; 2) Libr. Tech. Project, ALA, 50 E. Huron St, Chicago, Ill, consult. to catalog card reproduction study, with George Fry & Assocs, 61; 3) Calif. State Col, San Bernardino, consult. for establishing two new state col. libr, 62; 4) Calif. State Col, Palos Verdes, establishing beginning collection of libr, 62; 5) Fordham Univ, New York, N.Y, surveyed tech. serv. depts, 67. Specialties: 2d (col. libr), 2h (opening a basic collection); 3a, 3b, 3c, 3d, 3e, 3f (catalog card reproduction, copying methods); 8g (centralized processing).

TREZZA, ALPHONSE F, Dec. 27, 20; Associate Executive Director for Administrative Sciences, American Library Association, 50 E. Huron St, Chicago, Ill. 60611. Home: 614 S. Arthur Dr, Lombard, Ill. 60148. B.S, Univ. Pa, 48, M.S, 50; librn. cert, Drexel Inst. Tech, 49. Ed, Cath. Libr. World, 56-60; assoc. exec. dir, ALA, Chicago, Ill, 60-, exec. secy, LAD,

---

KEY TO CONSULTING SPECIALTIES: 1) ARCHITECTURE AND BUILDINGS, 1a) public libraries, 1b) academic libraries, 1c) school libraries, 1d) special libraries, 1e) library interiors, 1f) furnishings, 1g) site and location, 1h) other architectural; 2) COLLECTIONS: SELECTION, EVALUATION, WEEDING, 2a) adults, 2b) young adults, 2c) children, 2d) subject specialty, 2e) O.P. searches, 2f) rare books, 2g) appraisals, 2h) others; 3) TECHNICAL PROCESSES, 3a) cataloging, 3b) classification systems, 3c) acquisitions, 3d) materials processing, 3e) work flow and cost studies, 3f) others, 4) AUTOMATION, 4a) applications of data processing equipment, 4b) information storage and retrieval systems, 4c) systems analysis, 4d) others

ALA, 60-67. Other: Page, Free Libr. Phila, 40-41 & 45-48, libr. asst, 48-49; cataloger & asst. reference librn, Villanova Univ, 49-50, instr, 56-60; head circulation dept, Univ. Pa. Libr, 50-56; lectr, Drexel Inst. Tech. Sch. Libr. Sci, 51-60; exec. dir, Cath. Libr. Asn, 56-60. Mem: ALA; Cath. Libr. Asn; Pa. Libr. Asn; Coun. Nat. Libr. Asns; Am. Asn. Univ. Prof; Kappa Phi Kappa. Consult: 1) Lansing Pub. Libr, Lansing, Mich, site selection, 62; 2) Lombard Pub. Libr, Lombard, Ill, advised on site selection, assisted in bond campaign, worked with architect on design of bldg, furniture & equipment, selection of new librn, 62-64; 3) Divine Savior Sch. Libr, Norridge, Ill, layout of libr, selection of furniture & equipment, selection of initial book collection & assisted in organizing the staffing of the libr, 63-65; 4) Lockport Pub. Libr, Lockport, Ill, bldg. program; layout of libr, selection of furniture & equipment, personnel matters, 64-66; 5) Clarke Col, Dubuque, Iowa, developing a bldg. program, planning a new libr, 65- Specialties: 1a, 1b, 1c, 1f, 1g; 5a, 5c.

TRINKNER, DR. CHARLES L, May 25, 20; Director of Library Services, Pensacola Junior College, Pensacola, Fla. 32504. Home: 2026 Peacock Dr, Pensacola, Fla. 32504. B.A.E, 50; M.E.D, 51; A.P.G, 52; M.S.L.S, 54; E.D.S, 56; Litt.D, 66; LL.D, 67. Librn, audio-visual specialist & teacher, State of Fla. Pub. Sch. Syst, 49-55; instructor, dept. libr. sci. & educ. bibliographer, N. Tex. State Univ, Denton, 55-56; reference & assoc. librn, Univ. Tex, Arlington, 56-57; libr. dir. & asst. prof. libr. sci, Ark. State Univ, 57-58; dir. libr. serv, libr. sci, instructor & FICUS libr. adminstr, Pensacola Jr. Col, Pensacola, Fla, 58- Other: Visiting prof. libr. sci, Tex. Woman's Univ, Denton, summer 55; consult. & res. librn, Appalachian State Univ, Boone, N.C, summer 60; visiting prof. libr. sci, dept. librarianship, Univ. Ore, Eugene, summer 63; pres, Pensacola chap, Kappa Delta Pi, 63-65; visiting lectr. libr. sci, Univ. Ill, Urbana, summer 64; dir. instructional materials workshop, Utah State Univ, Logan, summer 64; dir. libr. workshop, Univ. Mont, Missoula, 65; chmn. jr. col. sect, Fla. Libr. Asn, 64-66; mem, W. Fla. Libr. Bd, 64-67; dir, Libr. Educ. & Develop. Mem: ALA; Southeast. Libr. Asn; Fla. Libr. Asn; Fla. Sch. Libr. Asn; Southwest. Libr. Asn; Bibliog. Soc. Am; ACRL; Am. Asn. Univ. Prof; La. State Libr. Asn; Nat. Educ. Asn; Asn. Higher Educ; Fla. Educ. Asn; Am. Asn. State & Local Hist; Univ. Fla. Alumni Asn; Escambia Educ. Asn; Pensacola Hist. Soc; Fla. Hist. Soc; Am. Hist. Soc; South. Hist. Soc; Kappa Delta Pi; Psi Chi; Phi Delta Kappa; Alpha Phi Omega; Beta Phi Mu; Beta Alpha Beta; Alpha Kappa Delta; Gamma Iona X. Publ: Better Libraries Make Better Schools, Shoe String, 62; Basic Books for Junior College Libraries: 20,000 Vital Titles (gen. ed), Colonial Press, 63; Library Services for Junior Colleges (gen. ed), Am. South. Publ, 64; Trends in Junior College Libraries, Libr. Trends, 10/65; The Junior College Center: Library Buildings and Plans (gen. ed), Gull Point Press, 68; Teaching for Better Use of Libraries, Shoe String, 69. Consult: 1) Ark. State Col, Jonesboro, self-study eval. work, spring 57; 2) Appalachian State Univ, Boone, N.C, eval. project, July 60; 3) La. State Univ, Alexandria, libr. program, Apr. 64; 4) Paducah Jr. Col, Paducah, Ky, collection, bldgs, personnel, serv, Apr. 65; 5) El Centro Community Col, Dallas, Tex, eval, Apr. 68. Specialties: 1b, 1c, 1e, 1f, 1g; 2a, 2b, 2c, 2d (jr. col. collection); 3a, 3c, 3d; 4a; 5a, 5b, 5c; 6a, 6c; 7a, 7b, 7c; 8b, 8c, 8d, 8f.

TROKE, MRS. MARGARET KLAUSNER, Nov. 21, 11; Director of Library Services, Public Library, Stockton-San Joaquin County, 605 N. El Dorado, Stockton, Calif. 95202. Home: 825 W. Euclid St, Stockton, Calif. 95204. A.B, Univ. Denver, 39. Dir. libr. serv, Pub. Libr, Stockton-San Joaquin County, Stockton, Calif, 46-; adminstr, 49-99 Cooperative Libr. Syst, Calif, 66- Other: Second v.pres, Calif. Libr. Asn, 49, v.pres, 52, pres, 53, pres. pub. libr. sect, 59, v.chmn, liaison cmt. for Calif. Pub. Libr. Cmn; participant, conf. libr. standards, Minneapolis, ALA 54 & Chicago, 55, chmn. region II membership cmt, 57-58, mem. cmt. to develop revised costs pub. libr. serv, 59, mem. coun, 60, mem. adv. cmt. libr. tech. project, 60, mem. joint cmt, ALA & Cath. Libr. Asn, 65-66; mem. coun. sch. librarianship, Univ. Calif, 55-56; dir, Fifth Annual Inst. Workshop Planning Pub. Libr. Bldgs, Sacramento, 57; co-dir, Seventh Annual Inst. Libr. Systs, Bakersfield, 59; pres, PLA, 59-60; participant, Nat. Cmt. Revision Pub. Libr. Statist, Dept. Health, Educ. & Welfare, 60; mem, Calif. Pub. Libr. Develop. Bd, 63-71, chmn, 67, 68; mem. adv. cmt, Calif. Statewide Publ Libr. Serv. Survey, Sacramento, 64; chmn. cmt. orgn, LAD, 65; mem, Cmt. Develop Pub. Libr. Serv. Standards for Calif; mem. libr. adv. cmt, County Supvr. Asn. Calif, 68. Mem: ALA; Calif. Libr. Asn. Publ: Statement of Requirements for a New Central Library Building: Stockton Public Library, 51, rev. ed, 59; IBM Circulation Control: a Review and an Analysis of Use in Stockton Public and San Joaquin County Library, News Notes Calif. Libr, 7/55; Library Program—Its Purpose and Development, News Notes Calif. Libr, 7/57; Guideposts in Planning Public Library Buildings: an Outline of Some Criteria and Factors Useful in Preliminary Building Planning and Site Selection, News Notes Calif. Libr, 7/57; Statement of Requirements and a Preliminary Plan for a New Building: Watsonville Free Public Library Study, 58; Calaveras-Stockton-San Joaquin County Library Project, a Survey with Recommendations Prepared under Provisions of the Library Services and Construction Act (with Aurora West Gardner), 6/66. Consult: 1) Watsonville Pub. Libr, 310 Union

5) PERSONNEL AND RECRUITING, 5a) job evaluation and description, salary recommendations, 5b) recruitment of professionals and management personnel, 5c) administrative organization, 6) PUBLIC RELATIONS, 6a) publications, 6b) publicity programs, 6c) public opinion surveys, 6d) others, 7) SERVICES, 7a) evaluation of current program, 7b) studies of service to special publics, e.g., students, handicapped, aged, etc., 7c) programs for the implementation of new laws, program proposals to governments, 7d) others, 8) COMMUNITY, REGIONAL, STATE PLANNING, 8a) legislative programs, 8b) area analyses, 8c) centralized systems, cooperative arrangements, 8d) development of standards, 8e) state libraries and extension agencies, 8f) regional and statewide surveys, 8g) others, 9) OTHERS.

St, Watsonville, Calif, surveyed Watsonville situation, developed requirements for new bldg, planned layout & produced report, with Francis Joseph McCarthy, 58-; 2) Calaveras County Libr, P.O. Box 338, San Andreas, Calif, survey of serv, plan for future growth, renovation of present quarters & reorgn, equipping & furnishing bldg. for modern serv, develop. of adult & juvenile collections for current serv, with Aurora West Gardner, 65-66; 3) Amador County Libr, 530 Sutter St, Jackson, Calif, planned layout for new bldg, equipped, furnished & moved libr, with Mortensen & Hollstien, 65-66; 4) Tuolumne County Libr, 465 S. Washington St, Sonora, Calif, survey of libr. & county serv, plan for develop. & growth, remodel bldg. & adapt for libr. use, plan layout & secure equipment & furniture, plan move, reorgn. present serv. to fit new quarters, with Warren Wong, architect, 65-66. Specialties: 1a, 1e, 1f, 1g, 1h (moving plans); 2a; 5a, 5b, 5c; 6d (bond campaigns); 7a, 7c; 8b, 8c, 8d.

TROTIER, ARNOLD H, Dec. 25, 99; Director of Technical Departments & Professor of Library Administration Emeritus, University of Illinois Library, Urbana, Ill. 61801. Home: 2405 Hibiscus St, Saratoga, Fla. 33579. A.B, 25; A.M, 32. Dir. libr. tech. depts. & prof. libr. admin, Univ. Ill, Urbana, 47-66. Other: Chmn. catalog sect, ALA, 35-36, chmn. ed. cmt, 48-51, mem. catalog code revision steering cmt, 54-66, chmn. bookbinding cmt, 59-63; chmn. planning bd, Ill. Libr. Asn, 36-53; pres. of Asn, 41-42. Mem: Ill. Libr. Asn; ALA; ACRL. Publ: Organization and Administration of Cataloging Processes, Libr. Trends, 10/53; Mechanization in libraries (ed), Libr. Trends, 10/56; Doctoral Dissertations Accepted by American Universities, 1945-56 (ed); Cataloging and Classification, In: The Administration of the College Library, H.W. Wilson, 3rd ed, 61; American Library Binding Standards, In: The Bowker Annual, 1962, R.R. Bowker, 62. Consult: 1) Knox Col. Libr, Galesburg, Ill, surveyed cataloging and classification with recommendations, 36 & 46; 2) Ball State Col. Libr, Muncie, Ind, survey of tech. serv. with recommendations, with Robert A. Miller, Dec. 46; 3) Duke Univ. Libr, Durham, N.C, surveyed tech. serv. & made recommendations for improvement, with Robert A. Miller, Dec. 46. Specialties: 1b; 3a, 3b, 3d.

U

ULVELING, DR. RALPH A, May 9, 02; Professor, Dept. of Library Science, Wayne State University, Detroit, Mich. 48202. Charles M. Mohrhardt & Ralph A. Ulveling, Associated Library Building Consultants, 20434 Lichfield Rd, Detroit, Mich. 48221. Ph.B, DePaul Univ, 22; B.S.(libr. sci), Columbia Univ, 28; hon. L.H.D, Wayne State Univ, 56. Dir, Detroit Pub. Libr, Mich, 41-67, emer. dir, 67-; prof, dept. libr. sci, Wayne State Univ, Detroit, Mich, 68- Other: Pres, Mich. Libr. Asn, 37-38; pres, ALA, 45-46; mem. U.S. Nat. Cmn. for UNESCO, 46-49; mem. bd. trustees, Cranbrook Inst. Sci, 55- Mem: ALA; Mich. Libr. Asn. Publ: Public Libraries, Archit. Record, 12/52; The Library and Adult Education, ALA Bull, 4/54; Getting the Most for Your Money, In: Guidelines for Library Planners, ALA, 60; Problems of Library Construction, Libr. Quart, 1/63; Library (ed. adv), In: World Book Encyclopedia, Field Enterprises Educ. Corp; Metropolitan Areas Growing and Under Stress, Libr. Trends, 7/65. Consult: 1) Flint Pub. Libr, Flint, Mich, planning & layout, with Charles M. Mohrhardt, 55-58; 2) Buffalo & Erie County Pub. Libr, Buffalo, N.Y, planning & layout, with Charles M. Mohrhardt, 56-65; 3) Tufts Libr, Weymouth, Mass, planning & layout, with Charles M. Mohrhardt, 61-65; 4) Elyria Pub. Libr, Elyria, Ohio, planning & layout, with Charles M. Mohrhardt, 62-66; 5) Bethlehem Pub. Libr, Bethlehem, Pa, planning & layout, with Charles M. Mohrhardt, 63-66. Specialties: 1a, 1f, 1g.

USHER, MRS. ELIZABETH R; Chief Librarian, Metropolitan Museum of Art, New York, N.Y. 10028. Home: 5 Peter Cooper Rd, New York, N.Y. 10010. B.S, Univ. Nebr, 42; B.S.(libr. sci), Univ. Ill, 44. Asst. librn, Metrop. Museum of Art, 54-61, chief art reference libr, 61-68, chief librn, 68- Other: V.Chmn. & Bull. ed, museum div, SLA, 53-54, chmn, 54-55, pres. N.Y. chap, 57-58, dir, 63-65, chmn. nominating cmt, 59-60, mem, 62-63 & 65-66, mem, nomination cmt, SLA, 58-59, mem, cmt. constitution & by-laws, 58-60, mem, convention exec. cmt, 59, mem, cmt. develop. of promotion technique, 59-60, dir. of Asn, 60-63, mem, finance cmt, 61-63, chmn, awards cmt, 64-65, mem, spec. libr. cmt, 64-66, mem, H.W. Wilson Co. chap. award cmt, 65-66, pres-elect of Asn, 66-67, pres, 67-68; mem, New York City Libr. Adv. Cmt, 58; mem, libr. adv. & steering cmt, Coun. Higher Educ. Insts. New York City, 58-; mem, convention hospitality cmt, ALA, 66, mem, John Cotton Dana awards cmt. Mem: ALA; SLA; Am. Asn. Museums; New York Libr Club. Publ: Rare Books and the Art Museum Library, Spec. Libr, 1/61. Consult: 1) Nat. Asn. for Retarded Children, 386 Park Ave, New York, N.Y, survey of libr. serv. with recommendations, Jan-Feb. 60. Specialties: 1b, 1d, 1e, 1f, 1g; 2c, 2d (art, archaeology, archit, educ), 2e, 2g; 3a, 3b, 3c, 3d, 3e; 5a, 5b, 5c; 7a, 7b.

V

VAILLANCOURT, DR. PAULINE M, Consultant, P.O. Box 624, Lenox Hill Station, New York,

---

KEY TO CONSULTING SPECIALTIES: 1) ARCHITECTURE AND BUILDINGS, 1a) public libraries, 1b) academic libraries, 1c) school libraries, 1d) special libraries, 1e) library interiors, 1f) furnishings, 1g) site and location, 1h) other architectural; 2) COLLECTIONS: SELECTION, EVALUATION, WEEDING, 2a) adults, 2b) young adults, 2c) children, 2d) subject specialty, 2e) O.P. searches, 2f) rare books, 2g) appraisals, 2h) others; 3) TECHNICAL PROCESSES, 3a) cataloging, 3b) classification systems, 3c) acquisitions, 3d) materials processing, 3e) work flow and cost studies, 3f) others, 4) AUTOMATION, 4a) applications of data processing equipment, 4b) information storage and retrieval systems, 4c) systems analysis, 4d) others

N.Y. 10021. Home: 89-14 34th Ave, Jackson Heights, N.Y. 11372. B.S.(biology), St. John's Univ, 47; M.S. in L.S, Columbia Univ, 53; D.L.S, 68. Chief librn, Kings Park State Hosp, N.Y, 58-60; chief librn, Mem. Sloan-Kettering Cancer Center, 60-68; ed, Sci. Info. Notes, Sci. Assocs. Int, Inc, New York, 68-; adjunct assoc. prof, Long Island Univ, 69- Other: Chmn. biological sci. group, N.Y. Chap, SLA, 51-52, chmn, scholarship & student loan cmt, SLA, 54-55, asst. secy, N.Y. Chap, SLA, 55-56, secy, 56-57; vis. asst. prof, State Univ. N.Y. Albany, summer 60; chmn. post-grad. workshop, Med. Libr. Asn, 60-61; lectr, sch. libr. serv, Columbia Univ, spring 68; ALA rep. to nursing group at present. Mem: ALA; ACRL; AHIL; Med. Libr. Asn; SLA; Am. Soc. Info. Sci; New York Libr. Club; N.Y. Acad. Sci; Am. Asn. Advancement Sci. Publ: Periodical Checklist for Libraries in Catholic Schools of Nursing, Cath. Libr. World, 2/56; Hospital Nursing School Libraries, Bull. Med. Libr. Asn, 4/56; Basic List of Books for Hospital Libraries (co-auth), Libr. Extension Div, N.Y. State Libr, 10/60; Review of International Nursing Index, AHIL Quart, summer 66; reviews of Cros: L'Automatisation des recherches & Cardin: L'Organization de la documentation, Am. Documentation, 1/67; Bibliographic Control of the Literature of Oncology, 1800-1960, Scarecrow, 69. Consult: 1) Queensboro Tuberculosis & Health Asn, Jamaica, N.Y, selected books for selected schs. of nursing, 52-54; 2) United Hosp. Fund of N.Y, New York City, nursing sch. libr. specialist for Planning the Hospital Library, published by the Fund in 1955, with Jacqueline Felter, 54-55; 3) Cath. Med. Center of Brooklyn & Queens, 345 Adams St, Brooklyn & c/o Mary Immaculate Hosp, 152-11 89th Ave, Jamaica, N.Y, planning a cent. libr. with coordination of their 8 libr. in 5 present insts; planning for a 6th, Sept. 68-; 4) Countway Libr. med, Harvard Univ, coordinate a training inst. and follow-up, Nov. 68-Sept. 69. Specialties: 1d, 1h (med. & sci); 2d (med. & sci); 3f (med. & sci); 5d (med. & sci); 7d (med. & sci); 8g (regional med. programs, especially RMP & NLM).

VAN BUREN, MARTIN, Feb. 24, 21; President & Owner, M. Van Buren Inc, 725 Providence Rd, Charlotte, N.C. 28207. Home: 1628 Jameston Dr, Charlotte, N.C. 28209. B.S, Ga. Inst. Tech. Participant, Inst. Libr. Bldg. Consult, Univ. Colo. Educ. Facilities Labs, 64. Publ: The Small Library Building (co-auth), UNESCO, Paris, France; Layout Plans and Library Interiors, ALA, 60; Furniture Selection for the Library, ALA, 6/62; Procurement of Library Furnishings and Equipment, In: American School and University Yearbook, 63; Trends in Library Furniture, Libr. Trends, 65. Consult: 1) Silas Bronson Pub. Libr, Waterbury, Conn, interior planning, 63-64 & 65-66; 2) London Pub. Libr, London, Ont, Can, interior planning, 63-65; 3) Orlando Pub. Libr, Orlando, Fla, interior planning, 64-65; 4) Clemson Univ. Libr, Clemson, S.C, interior planning, 64-66; 5) Henry Ford Mem. Libr, Dearborn, Mich, interior planning, 65-66. Specialties: 1e, 1f, 1g.

VanJACKSON, WALLACE M, May 6, 00; Library Director, Johnston Memorial Library, Virginia State College, Petersburg, Va. 23803. Home: 41 Loyal Ave, Ettrick, Va. 23803. B.A. & B.L.S, 34; A.M.L.S, 35. Librn, Va. Union Univ, 27-39; prof, Atlanta Univ. Sch. Libr. Serv, 40-41, univ. librn, 41-47; pub. affairs officer, Am. Embassy, Monrovia, Liberia, 47-49; univ. librn, Tex. South. Univ, 49-54; libr. dir, Va. State Col, Petersburg, 54-62 & 64-; deputy dir, Nat. Libr. of Nigeria, 62-64. Other: Mem, UNESCO Summer Libr. Sch, London & Manchester, Eng, 49; mem, cmt. on intellectual freedom, ALA, 52-54, mem. coun, 57-60, mem, econ. programs cmt, 65- Mem: ALA; Va. Libr. Asn; Va. Teachers Asn; Tex. Libr. Asn. Publ: Discipline in the College Library, Fisk Univ. Libr. Conf. Proc, 30; The Role of the Library in Serving the Serious Student and Research Worker in Minority Groups, In: The Role of the Library in Collecting Information and Giving Service to the Serious Student and Research Worker, Univ. Tex, 54. Consult: 1) Ala. A&M Col. & Ala. State Col, Montgomery, acquisitions & bldg, planned expansion of bldgs, 52-54; 2) Claflin Col, Orangeburg, S.C, book acquisitions program, planned & directed reorgn. of program, staff & remodelling of libr. bldg, 57-58; 3) Morristown Col, Morristown, Tenn, planning, organizing & developing new libr. facility & program of acquisitions, 58; 4) Va. Union Univ, Richmond, request for ACRL grant, Oct. 66; 5) St. Paul's Col, Lawrenceville, Va, request for ACRL grant, Oct. 66. Specialties: 1b, 1e, 1f; 2a, 2d (soc. sci); 3c; 5c; 7a; 9 (developing collections on Africa & the Negro).

VAN VELZER, VERNA J, Jan. 22, 29; Head Librarian, Research Library, ESL, Inc, 495 Java Dr, Sunnyvale, Calif. 94086. Home: 4048 Laguna Way, Palo Alto, Calif. 94306. B.S. in L.S, 50; M.L.S, 57. Chief cataloger, Stanford Res. Inst. Libr, Menlo Park, Calif, 57-58; head librn, Tech. Libr, Gen. Electric Palo Alto Tube Oper, 58-64; head librn, Tech. Libr, Fairchild Semiconductor R&D Lab, Palo Alto, 64-65; head librn, Intelligence Libr, Sylvania Electric Products, Mt. View, Calif, 65-66. Other: Chmn. elections cmt, SLA, 63. Mem: SLA; Calif. Libr. Asn; Beta Phi Mu; Pi Lambda Sigma. Consult: 1) Children's Health Coun, 700 Willow Rd, Palo Alto, Calif, cataloged book collection & provided consultation training to employees, 58; 2) Stacey's, Inc, 2575 Hanover, Palo Alto, surveying of local needs for retail tech. bookstore & wholesale warehouse, 62; 3) SLA, Bay Region Chap, San Francisco, Calif, report on periodical acquisition & mgt. in tech. libr, with K. Johnson, 63. Specialties: 1d; 2d (elec-

---

5) PERSONNEL AND RECRUITING, 5a) job evaluation and description, salary recommendations, 5b) recruitment of professionals and management personnel, 5c) administrative organization, 6) PUBLIC RELATIONS, 6a) publications, 6b) publicity programs, 6c) public opinion surveys, 6d) others, 7) SERVICES, 7a) evaluation of current program, 7b) studies of service to special publics, e.g., students, handicapped, aged, etc., 7c) programs for the implementation of new laws, program proposals to governments, 7d) others, 8) COMMUNITY, REGIONAL, STATE PLANNING, 8a) legislative programs, 8b) area analyses, 8c) centralized systems, cooperative arrangements, 8d) development of standards, 8e) state libraries and extension agencies, 8f) regional and statewide surveys, 8g) others, 9) OTHERS.

tronics); 3a, 3b, 3c, 3d, 3f (security & classified document collection handling; serials); 5a, 5b, 5c, 5d (commun. with sci. personnel); 6a, 6c; 7a.

VEANER, ALLEN B, Mar. 17, 29; Assistant Director, Stanford University Libraries, Stanford, Calif. 94305. Home: 762 E. Charleston Rd, Palo Alto, Calif. 94303. B.A, 49; B.H.L, 51; Rabbi, 54; M.L.S, 60. Cataloger, Harvard Col. Libr, 57-59, chief photoduplication serv, Harvard Univ. Libr, 59-64; chief librn, acquisition div, Stanford Univ. Libr, Calif, 64-67. Other: Asst. ed, Libr. Resources & Tech. Serv, 63-; chmn. subcmt. on micropubl. projects, RTSD, 65. Mem: ALA; Am. Soc. Info. Sci; Phi Beta Kappa. Publ: Literature on Document Reproduction, Univ. Ill. Grad. Sch. Libr. Sci, 61, rev. ed, 63; European Report, Reprography Congress, Libr. Resources & Tech. Serv, 8: 199-204; Developments in Copying Methods and Graphic Communication, Libr. Resources & Tech. Serv, 10: 199-209; High Speed Reproduction of Library Cards Through Microreproduction Technique, Proc. Nat. Microfilm Asn, 13: 159-163; Microtext Materials in Libraries, J. Med. Educ, 40: 43-45; Bibliography of Copying Methods, In: Copying Methods Manual. Consult: 1) Ecole Pratique des Hautes Etudes, Maison des Sci. de l'Homme, 20 rue de la Baume, Paris, France, establishment of microreproduction lab. & publ. program, Oct. 63; 2) Micro Methods, Ltd, East Ardsley, Yorkshire, Eng, bibliog. & quality control in project to issue manuscripts in micropubl, Oct-Nov. 63; 3) Hebrew Union Col. Libr, Cincinnati, Ohio, recommendations on reproduction of libr. cards, paper prints & offset masters, July 65; 4) Libr. Tech. Program, c/o ALA, 50 E. Huron St, Chicago, Ill, compiled annotated bibliog. on copying res. materials, winter 65-spring 66; 5) R.A. Morgan Co, 3197 Park Blvd, Palo Alto, Calif, design & testing of bibliographer's camera for Coun. Libr. Resources, 67- Specialties: 3c, 3d; 4c, 4d (design of time-shared, real-time libr. info. systs); 9 (all phases of microreproduction, micropubl. & photoduplication, of scholarly & res. materials).

VEIT, DR. FRITZ, Sept. 17, 07; Director of Libraries, Chicago State College, 6800 S. Stewart Ave, Chicago, Ill. 60621. Home: 1716 E. 55th St, Chicago, Ill. 60615. Dr. Jur, Univ. Freiburg, 32; B.S. in L.S, Peabody Col, 36; Ph.D, Univ. Chicago, 41. Dir. libr, Chicago State Col. & Chicago City Col, Wilson Campus, 49-; vis. prof. libr. sci, Rosary Col, 50- Other: Supvr, John Marshall Law Sch. Libr, part-time, 49-57; assoc. ed, ACRL Monographs, 52-60; vis. prof, West. Mich. Univ, summer 59, Ariz. State Univ, 64-68; chmn, teacher educ. libr. sect, ACRL, 61; pres, Chicago Libr. Club, 64-65. Mem: ALA; Ill. Libr. Asn; Chicago Libr. Club; Ill. Educ. Asn. Publ: Reorganization of John Marshall Law School Library, Law Libr. J,

11/51; Education for School Librarianship at Chicago Teachers College (with George Butler), Ill. Libr, 3/58; Status of the Librarian According to Accrediting Standards of Regional and Professional Associations, Col. & Res. Libr, 21: 127-135; reviews, Libr. Quart, 1/61 & 4/64; Book Order Procedures in the Publicly Controlled Colleges and Universities of the Midwest, Col. & Res. Libr, 23: 33-40; Personnel for Junior College Libraries, Libr. Trends, 10/65. Consult: 1) John Marshall Law Sch. Libr, Chicago, Ill, survey & reorganized libr, 49; 2) Rodfei Zedek Temple Libr, Chicago, surveyed libr, 59; 3) Aquinas Inst. of Philosophy Libr, River Forest, Ill, surveyed libr, 65; 4) Chicago City Col, Wilson Campus, bldg, 68; 5) Thornton Jr. Col, Thornton, Ill, bldg, 68. Specialties: 1b; 5a, 5b, 5c; 7a; 9 (gen. survey of whole libr. oper—acad. & res. libr. field).

VERSCHOOR, DR. IRVING A, Dec. 27, 12; Dean, College of General Studies, State University of New York at Albany, Albany, N.Y. 12203. Home: Star Route, Ravena, N.Y. 12143. B.Sc, 36; M.A, 38; M.S, 49; LL.D, 60; D.L.S, 67. Dir, div. libr. extension, N.Y. State Educ. Dept, 56-61; dean, sch. libr. sci, State Univ. N.Y. at Albany, 61-66, dean, col. of gen. studies, 66- Other: Pres, ASL, 62. Mem: ALA; New York Libr. Asn; Am. Asn. Univ. Prof. Publ: Manual for Resistance Forces, 44; contrib. to Technical Services in Libraries, Major Problems in Education of Librarians, Survey of Library Service on State Level & Handbook of Laws and Regulations Affecting Public Libraries in New York. Consult: 1)N.Y. State Educ. Dept, Albany, personnel consult. & examiner, 61-66; 2) State Dept. Educ, Mass, personnel consult. & examiner, 61-66; 3) State Univ. N.Y, Albany, evaluate tech. insts. for libr. resources, 63; 4) Div. Libr. Extension, State Dept. of Educ, Mass, survey of pub. & regional libr, with Mary Lee Bundy, 64; 5) State of Vt, Montpelier, libr. survey of Vt, with S.G. Prentiss, 65-66. Specialties: 7c; 8a, 8b, 8c, 8d, 8e, 8f; 9 (non-prfnl. training, libr. law—legis. programs).

VOIGT, EDNA E, May 4, 01; Library Planning Consultant, 2207 Beech St, Wantagh, N.Y. 11793. Libr. planning consult, design & planning dept, Libr. Bur. of Remington Rand, 23-66; libr. planning consult, 66- Mem: ALA; N.Y. Libr. Club. Consult: 1) Bowling Green State Univ, Bowling Green, Ohio, preliminary study for bldg, dept. locations & functions, equipment layouts, color scheme, Feb. 64-Feb. 65; 2) Hayden Burns Pub. Libr, Jacksonville, Fla, furniture layouts, technical equipment some design & some material selection, Feb. 64-Nov. 65; 3) Ohio Univ, Athens, equipment layouts, color schemes, furniture design & selection, equipment specifications, Apr. 65-Aug. 68; 4) Peoria Pub. Libr, Peoria, Ill, bldg. plans, furniture layouts, selected furniture de-

---

KEY TO CONSULTING SPECIALTIES: 1) ARCHITECTURE AND BUILDINGS, 1a) public libraries, 1b) academic libraries, 1c) school libraries, 1d) special libraries, 1e) library interiors, 1f) furnishings, 1g) site and location, 1h) other architectural; 2) COLLECTIONS: SELECTION, EVALUATION, WEEDING, 2a) adults, 2b) young adults, 2c) children, 2d) subject specialty, 2e) O.P. searches, 2f) rare books, 2g) appraisals, 2h) others; 3) TECHNICAL PROCESSES, 3a) cataloging, 3b) classification systems, 3c) acquisitions, 3d) materials processing, 3e) work flow and cost studies, 3f) others, 4) AUTOMATION, 4a) applications of data processing equipment, 4b) information storage and retrieval systems, 4c) systems analysis, 4d) others

sign & color scheme, May 65-Mar. 66; 5) Univ. Wisconsin, Milwaukee, furniture layouts for bldg, color scheme, July 65-Feb. 66. Specialties: 1e, 1f.

VOIGT, MELVIN J, Mar. 12, 11; University Librarian, University of California, San Diego, La Jolla, Calif. 92037. Home: 8402 La Jolla Shores Dr, La Jolla, Calif. 92037. A.B, 33; A.B.L.S, 36; A.M.L.S, 38. Asst. librn, Univ. Calif, Berkeley, 52-59; librn, Kans. State Univ, 59-60; univ. librn, Univ. Calif, San Diego, 60- Other: Fulbright res. scholar, Univ. Copenhagen, 58-59; pres, RTSD, 60-61; pres, LED, 63-64. Mem: ALA; Am. Chemical Soc; Am. Soc. Info. Sci, SLA; Am. Asn. Advancement Sci; Calif. Libr. Asn. Publ: Subject Headings in Physics, ALA, 44; The Trend Toward Mechanization of Libraries, Libr. Trends, 5: 193-205; Scientists' Approaches to Information, ACRL Monograph 24, ALA, 61; Computer Processing of Serial Records (with George Vdovin, David Newman & Clay Perry), Libr. Resources & Tech. Serv, 7: 71-80; LC and Automation, Libr. J, 89: 1022-1025; The New Campuses Program (with Joseph Treyz), Libr. J, 90: 2204-2208. Consult: 1) UNESCO, Docomputation Centre, Cairo, U.A.R, Mar-Apr. 63; 2) Northwest. Univ, Evanston, Ill, data processing, with Robert Hayes, Apr-June 65; 3) UNESCO, Paris, France, planning for new Dept. of Document, with Jean Gardin & B.S. Kesevan, July 65; 4) State Univ. N.Y, Stony Brook, expansion of libr. collections & serv, Oct. 65; 5) Nat. Libr. Med, Bethesda, Md, bldg. & regional libr, 66- Specialties: 1b, 1d; 2d (col, univ, sci. & tech); 3a, 3b, 3c, 3d, 3e, 3f (serials); 4a, 4c.

VOOS, DR. HENRY, Aug. 10, 28; Associate Professor, Graduate School of Library Services, Rutgers, The State University, New Brunswick, N.J. 08903. Home: 28 Wenonah Ave, Rockaway, N.J. 07866. B.A, 48; M.A. & M.S.L.S, 53; Ph.D, 65. Librn, Int. Ladies Garment Workers Union, 53-56; chief tech. processing sect, Picatinny Arsenal Sci. & Tech. Info. Br, Dover, N.J, 56-68. Other: Mem. educ. & recruitment cmt, N.J. Spec. Libr. Asn, 58, mem. program cmt, 66; mem. Joint Atomic Weapons Tech. Info. Group, 58- Mem: SLA; ALA. Publ: The Role of a Technical Information Section in a Governmental Research and Development Organization (with M.A. Costello), Spec. Libr, 48: 327-331; Preparation of an Information Bulletin, Spec. Libr, 50: 454-457; Automated Circulation at a Government R&D Installation (with M.A. Costello), Spec. Libr, 55: 77-80; Standard Times for Certain Clerical Activities in Technical Processing (with I. Haznedari), Libr. Resources & Tech. Serv, 10: 223-227; Revision of Current LC Catalog Card, Libr. Resources & Tech. Serv, 67. Consult: 1) Rutgers Univ, New Brunswick, N.J, bibliog. on internal commun, July 66; 2) Army Engineer Dist, Savannah, Ga, proposal for user survey of Engineering Dist, 68. Specialties: 2d (any collection), 2e; 3a, 3b, 3c, 3d, 3e, 3f (automation); 4a, 4b, 4c, 4d (SDI); 5a; 7a; 9 (dissemination systs).

VORHIES, EUGENE, President, Nelson Associates, Inc, 845 Third Ave, New York, N.Y. 10022. Home: 440 E. 23rd St, New York, N.Y. 10010. B.S, Mass. Inst. Tech, 62; M.B.A, Univ. Pa, 64. Syst. analyst, Equitable Life Assurance of U.S, 61; analyst, syst. & data processing dept, W.R. Grace & Co, 64-65. Specialties: 3a, 3b, 3c, 3d, 3e; 4a, 4b, 4c; 5a, 5b, 5c; 7a; 8c, 8e, 8f.

VORMELKER, ROSE L, 1895; Chief, Library & Information Service, Center for Urban Regionalism, Kent State University, Kent, Ohio 44240. Home: 12700 Shaker Blvd, Cleveland, Ohio 44120. Cert. Libr. Sci, West. Reserve Univ, 19. Head bus. info. bureau, Cleveland Pub. Libr, 28-55, asst. dir, 55-56; libr. dir, Plain Dealer, Cleveland, Ohio, 56-62; chief libr. & info. serv, center urban regionalism & asst. prof, sch. libr. sci, Kent State Univ, Kent, Ohio, 63- Other: Pres, SLA, 48-49, consult, Cleveland chap, 56-; v.pres. & pres-elect, LED, 66-67, pres, 67-68. Mem: ALA; Ohio Libr. Asn; SLA; Asn. Am. Libr. Schs. Publ: Special Library Resources (ed), 2 vols, 40 & 46; Community Research Resources (ed), 63. Consult: 1) Libby-Owens Ford, Toledo, Ohio, establishment of co. bus. libr, 61-62; 2) Home News, New Brunswick, N.J, reorgn. of newspaper reference room, 63; 3) The Oregonian, Portland, Ore, merging & reorganizing two newspaper libr, 63; 4) Industrial Furnace Co, Salem, Ohio, organization of co. tech. libr, 63; 5) B.F. Goodrich Co, Akron, Ohio, organization of archives libr, 64- Specialties: 1d; 2a, 2d (bus. & finance newspapers, urban res); 6d (libr. publ).

VREELAND, ELEANOR P, Mar. 21, 30; Product Manager, Collier Macmillan Library Services, 866 Third Ave, New York, N.Y. 10022. Home: 51-15 Van Kleeck St, Elmhurst, N.Y. 11373. Asst. advertising, publicity & promotion, Peck & Peck, 47-58; pub. relations adv, Brooklyn Pub. Libr, 60-65; pub. relations adv, Queens Borough Pub. Libr, 65; v.pres, Francis R. St. John Libr. Consult, Inc, 65-68; product mgr, Collier Macmillan Libr. Serv, New York, N.Y, 68- Other: Secy, Libr. Pub. Relations Coun, 63-65, pres, 65-66; regional chmn, ALA Membership Cmt, 64; secy, Pub. Relations Officers, 65-66. Mem: ALA; N.Y. Libr. Asn; N.Y. Libr. Club. Consult: 1) Mid-York Libr. Syst, Rome, N.Y, complete survey of serv, systs, pub. relations & program for syst. hq. location & serv, with Thomas Tennyson, Oct. 64-Oct. 65; 2) Ginn & Co, New York, N.Y, promotion, fall 65; 3) Grolier & Co, New York, market res. for fed. program, spring 66; 4) Elecompak,

---

5) PERSONNEL AND RECRUITING, 5a) job evaluation and description, salary recommendations, 5b) recruitment of professionals and management personnel, 5c) administrative organization, 6) PUBLIC RELATIONS, 6a) publications, 6b) publicity programs, 6c) public opinion surveys, 6d) others, 7) SERVICES, 7a) evaluation of current program, 7b) studies of service to special publics, e.g., students, handicapped, aged, etc., 7c) programs for the implementation of new laws, program proposals to governments, 7d) others, 8) COMMUNITY, REGIONAL, STATE PLANNING, 8a) legislative programs, 8b) area analyses, 8c) centralized systems, cooperative arrangements, 8d) development of standards, 8e) state libraries and extension agencies, 8f) regional and statewide surveys, 8g) others, 9) OTHERS.

Inc, 200 Park Ave, New York, promotion advice, develop. of specialized mailing list, May-July 66; 5) Robbins Mem. Libr, Arlington, Mass, site & bldg, serv. anal, July 66-Jan. 67. Specialties: 2a, 2b, 2c; 5b, 5c; 6a, 6b, 6c; 7c; 8a, 8d, 8f.

W

WAGMAN, DR. FREDERICK H, Oct. 12, 12; Director, University Library, 209 General Library Building, University of Michigan, Ann Arbor, Mich. 48104. Home: 1407 Lincoln Ave, Ann Arbor, Mich. 48104. A.B, Amherst Col, 33, L.H.D, 58; A.M, Columbia Univ, 34, Ph.D, 42; LL.D, Alderson-Broaddus Col, 67. Dir. univ. libr, University of Michigan, Ann Arbor, Mich, 53- Other: Mem. bd. dirs, Coun. Libr. Resources, Inc, 58-; pres, Mich. Libr. Asn, 60; mem. exec. cmt, Nat. Book Cmt, 61-; pres, ALA, 63; mem. bd. dirs, Asn. Res. Libr, 64-67. Mem: Asn. Res. Libr; ALA; Mich. Libr. Asn. Consult: 1) Concordia Col, Ft. Wayne, Ind, bldg. plans, with Eero 3aarinen, 55-56; 2) Butler Univ, Indianapolis, Ind, libr. bldg, with Minoru Yamasaki, 59-61; 3) United Nations, New York, N.Y, libr. bldg. plans, with Douglas W. Bryant, Frank B. Rogers & Verner W. Clapp, 60-61; 4) Univ. Toledo, Toledo, Ohio, develop. of libr. program & bldg, 64-; 5) Univ. Chicago, Chicago, Ill, bldg. plans, with Bernard Berelson & Stephen McCarthy, 65. Specialties: 1b, 1e, 1f, 1g; 3a, 3b, 3c, 3d, 3e; 4c; 5a, 5c; 7a, 7b.

WAGNER, DR. ROBERT GEORGE, Feb. 22, 27; Reference Librarian, College of San Mateo, 1700 W. Hillsdale Blvd, San Mateo, Calif. 94402. Home: 2311 Scott St, San Francisco, Calif. 94115. B.S, 50; M.A, 51; Ph.D, 57. Librn, Golden Gate Col, San Francisco, Calif, 54-60; reference librn, Col. San Mateo, San Mateo, Calif, 60- Mem: ALA; Calif. Libr. Asn; Calif. Teachers Asn. Publ: Military Reading, U.S. Army, Fort Ord, Calif, 53. Consult: 1) Ministry of Educ, Teheran, Iran, UNESCO educ. spec. & document. center consult, Oct-Dec, 62. Specialties: 2d (Islamic & Middle East); 7a, 7b.

WALLACE, JAMES OLDHAM, Sept. 22, 17; Librarian, San Antonio College, 1300 San Pedro Ave, San Antonio, Tex. 78212. Home: P.O. Box 13041, San Antonio, Tex. 78213. B.A; M.A, 40; B.S. in L.S, 50. Librn, San Antonio Col, San Antonio, Tex, 50- Other: Mem. exec. bd, ACRL, 60-63, chmn. spec. projects cmt, jr. col. libr. sect, 60-61, chmn. sect, 61-62, mem. cmt, standards, ACRL, 62-65, 67-, mem. nominating cmt, 63; mem. bldg. cmt. col. & univ. bldgs, LAD, 62-64; mem. joint cmt. ALA-Am. Asn. Jr. Cols, ALA, 65- Mem: ALA; Southwest. Libr. Asn; Nat. Soc. Study Educ. Consult: 1) San Antonio Col, San Antonio, Tex, developed program & worked with architect, with W. Edwin Dennis, Jan. 63-68; 2) Hill Jr. Col, Hillsboro, Tex, survey of libr. preliminary to accreditation, Feb. 66; 3) Black Hawk Col, Moline, Ill, bldg, Oct. 66; Nelson Assocs, study of two & four year cols. for Nat. Adv. Cmn. Libr, 67; 5) U.S. Office Educ, Nat. Educ. Asn. Title II libr. grants, 67-68. Specialties: 1b; 2h (jr. cols); 3c; 7a.

WALLACE, SARAH LESLIE, Oct. 28, 14; Publications Officer, Library of Congress, Washington, D.C. 20540. Home: 8705 Jones Mill Rd, Washington, D.C. 20015. A.B, 35; B.S. in L.S, 36. Instructor, Col. St. Catherine, 44-60; admin. asst. in charge of pub. relations & res, Minneapolis Pub. Libr, Minn, 54-57, pub. relations officer, 57-63; publ. officer, Libr. Congress, Wash, D.C, 63- Other: Pub. relations officer, ALA, 60; ed, Quart. Journal of Libr. Congress. Mem: Minn. Libr. Asn; D.C. Libr. Asn; ALA. Publ: Patrons Are People (co-auth & illustrator); Promotion Ideas for Small Public Libraries (auth. & illustrator); Definition: Library, ALA, 61; Friends of the Library (ed), ALA, 62; So You Want to Be a Librarian, Harper & Row, 63; The Library's Public, In: Local Public Library Administration, Municipal Mgt. Series, Int. City Mgr. Asn, 64. Consult: 1) Dakota-Scott Regional Libr, West St. Paul, Minn, report (writing, design & production), 62. Specialties: 6a, 6b, 6c, 6d (bond, millage campaigns; new bldg. campaigns; staff training; Friends orgns); 7c; 9 (publ).

WALLIS, C. LAMAR, Oct. 15, 15; Director of Libraries, Memphis Public Library, 258 S. McLean, Memphis, Tenn. 38104. Home: 4847 Gwynne Rd, Memphis, Tenn. 38117. A.B, 36; M.A, 46; B.L.S, 47. City librn, Richmond, Va, 55-58; dir. libr, Memphis Pub. Libr, 59- Other: Pres, Grad. Libr. Sch. Club, Univ. Chicago, 47; pres, Tex. Libr. Asn, 52; pres-elect, Tenn. Libr. Asn, 68; chmn. legis. cmt, Southeast Libr. Asn, 60-62, chmn. pub. libr. sect, 62-64; secy, Memphis Rotary Club, 64. Mem: ALA; Southeast. Libr. Asn; Tenn. Libr. Asn. Publ: Recommendations for Expanding the Public Library Services, Richmond, Virginia, 56; The Brunswick, Georgia, Old Post Office Building: a Report on Its Adaptability for Use as Brunswick's Public Library, 63; The Friedman Library of Tuscaloosa: a Brief Survey with Recommendations, 64; Libraries in the Golden Triangle: a Study of the Public Library Service of Jefferson and Orange Counties, Texas, 66. Consult: 1) Dyersburg Pub. Libr, Dyersburg, Tenn, advised on plans for remodeling old post office, interior layout and all furniture & equipment, Apr. 65-Feb. 66; 2) Jackson Pub. Libr, Jackson, Tenn, Pub. Libr, Union City, Tenn. & Trenton, Tenn, advised on plans & furnishings for new bldgs, Feb. 66-; 3) Decatur Pub. Libr, Decatur, Ala, advised on plans for new bldg, Mar. 66-; 4) Tex. State Libr, Austin, Tex, surveyed pub. libr. to recommend plan for regional libr, Apr-Aug, 66; 5) Ark. Libr.

KEY TO CONSULTING SPECIALTIES: 1) ARCHITECTURE AND BUILDINGS, 1a) public libraries, 1b) academic libraries, 1c) school libraries, 1d) special libraries, 1e) library interiors, 1f) furnishings, 1g) site and location, 1h) other architectural; 2) COLLECTIONS: SELECTION, EVALUATION, WEEDING, 2a) adults, 2b) young adults, 2c) children, 2d) subject specialty, 2e) O.P. searches, 2f) rare books, 2g) appraisals, 2h) others; 3) TECHNICAL PROCESSES, 3a) cataloging, 3b) classification systems, 3c) acquisitions, 3d) materials processing, 3e) work flow and cost studies, 3f) others, 4) AUTOMATION, 4a) applications of data processing equipment, 4b) information storage and retrieval systems, 4c) systems analysis, 4d) others

Cmn, 506½ Center St, Little Rock, Ark, advised on plans for 21 new pub. libr. & old bldgs. being expanded, May 66- Specialties: 1a, 1e, 1f, 1g; 8b, 8c, 8f.

WASSERMAN, DR. PAUL, Jan. 8, 24; Dean, School of Library & Information Services, University of Maryland, College Park, Md. 20742. Home: 3501 Duke St, College Park Woods, Md. 20740. B.B.A, 48; M.S.L.S, 49; M.S.(econ), 50; Ph.D, 60. Librn. & prof, grad. sch. bus. & pub. admin, Cornell Univ, 53-65; dean, sch. libr. & info. serv, Univ, Md, 65- Mem: Am. Asn. Univ. Prof; Am. Soc. Info. Sci; ALA; D.C. Libr. Asn; Int. Asn. Documentalists; Md. Libr. Asn; SLA. Publ: Information for Administrators, Cornell Univ, 56; Decision-Making: An Annotated Bibliography, Cornell Univ, 58 & Supplement, 58-64; Measurement and Evaluation of Organizational Performance, Cornell Univ, 59; Statistics Sources, Gale Res. Co, 62 & 2nd ed, 65; Management Information Guide Series (ed), Gales Res. Co, 63-; Reader in Library Administration, Microcard, Ed, 68. Consult: 1) Bankers Trust Co, New York, N.Y, analyzed info. serv. & libr. program, July-Aug. 61; 2) Indiana Univ. Grad. Sch. Bus, Bloomington, reviewed libr, info, res. & publ. program, 61-63; 3) Mid. E. Tech, Univ. Ankara, Turkey, studied libr. program, Sept. 63; 4) N.Y. Stock Exchange, New York, studied info. program & serv, Nov. 65-Jan. 66; 5) Walston & Co, New York, planned investment anal. info. serv, Dec. 67-Jan. 68. Specialties: 2d (econ; mgt; bus. admin); 4c; 5b, 5c; 7a; 9 (objective formulation; orgn. & admin. in res. orgns. & acad. programs).

WATKINS, MRS. LILLIAN M, Mar. 18, 04; Consultant, Education & Elementary Libraries, Pasadena City Schools, 351 S. Hudson Ave, Pasadena, Calif. 91109. Home: 2030 E. Orange Grove Blvd, Pasadena, Calif. 91104. B.A, 50; M.S, 55. Supvr. libr. serv, 54-64; consult. educ. & elem. libr. serv, Pasadena City Schs, Pasadena, Calif, 64- Other: Pres, Children & Sch. Librns. Asn; chmn, supvr. & dir, SLACSS; secy, state & south. sect, Instructional Materials Cmt. Mem: Calif. Asn. Sch. Librns; Calif. Asn. Supv. & Curriculum Develop; Nat. Educ. Asn; Calif. Teachers Asn; Sch. Libr. Asn. Calif; Asn. Childhood Educ; Pi Lambda Theta; Alpha Lambda Sigma; Soroptomists; BPW. Publ: Twenty-eight albums of records of children's literature for primary grades (co-auth), Bowmar Records, 63-67; Journal of the West (regional ed), Univ. Okla. Consult: 1) Oxnard Elem. Sch. Dist, 255 Palm Dr, Oxnard, Calif, consult. for planning instructional materials center, May 62; 2) State Dept. Educ, 701 Capital Mall, Sacramento, Calif, planning for title II, May 66. Specialties: 1b, 1c, 1d, 1e, 1f, 1g; 2a, 2b, 2c, 2d (children's literature); 3a, 3b, 3c, 3d, 3e; 5a, 5b, 5c; 6a; 7a, 7b, 7c; 8c, 8d.

WEZEMAN, FREDERICK, May 1, 15; Professor of Library Science & Director of the Library School, University of Iowa, Iowa City, Iowa 52240. B.S, Lewis Inst, 37; M.E, Chicago Teachers Col, 41; B.L.S, Univ. Chicago, 47. Dir, Racine Pub. Libr, Racine, Wis, 47-53; dir, Oak Park Pub. Libr, Oak Park, Ill, 53-55; assoc. prof, libr. sch, Univ. Minn, 55-65; prof. libr. sci. & dir. libr. sch, Univ. Iowa, Iowa City, 66- Mem: ALA; Can. Libr. Asn; SLA; Minn. Libr. Asn. Publ: A Survey of the Public Library, Sioux City Pub. Libr, Sioux City, Iowa, 63; A Survey of the Library Building Needs of the Spencer Public Library, Spencer, Iowa, 64; A Survey of the Public Library, Billings, Montana, Billings Pub. Libr, 64; Building Program—A Working Paper Prepared for the Spencer Library Board, Spencer Pub. Libr, 64; Combination School and Public Libraries in Pennsylvania: A Study with Recommendations, Pa. State Libr, 65; Survey of the Duluth Public Library, Duluth, Minn, 66. Consult: 1) Hopkins Pub. Libr, Hopkins, Minn, survey for future planning, bldg. survey with recommendations, with Robert H. Rohlf, 62; 2) Sioux City Pub. Libr, Sioux City, Iowa, survey of libr, 63; 3) Pa. State Libr, Harrisburg, study of combination sch. & pub. libr. with recommendations, 63-64; 4) Duluth Pub. Libr, Duluth, Minn, study of the pub. libr. including bldg. program & needs, personnel, book collections, branches, financial support, 65-66; 5) Lexington Pub. Libr, Lexington, Ky, report on financial support, serv. program & br. program of the Libr, 66. Specialties: 1a, 1g; 2a, 2b, 2c; 5a, 5b, 5c; 6a, 6b; 7a, 7b, 7c; 8a, 8b, 8c, 8d, 8e, 8f.

WHEELER, DR. HELEN RIPPIER, Feb. 19, 26; Associate Professor, Dept. of Library Science, St. John's University Graduate School, Jamaica, N.Y. 11432. B.A, Barnard Col, 50, M.S, Columbia Univ. Sch. Libr. Serv, 51, Ed.D, Teachers Col, 64; M.A.(educ), Univ. Chicago, 54. Librn, Agnes Russell Center, Columbia Univ. Teachers Col, 56-58; br. head librn. & AV coordinator, Chicago City Jr. Col, 58-61; Latin Am. specialist, Columbia Univ. Libr, 62-64; adjunct asst. prof, grad. libr. sch, Drexel Inst. Tech, 64-65; assoc. prof, grad. sch. libr. studies, Univ. Hawaii, 65-66; assoc. prof, dept. libr. sci, Ind. State Univ, Terre Haute, 66-68; assoc. prof, dept. libr. sci, grad. sch, St. John's Univ, Jamaica, N.Y, 68- Other: Treas, bd. mem. & ed. of Newsletter, Chicago Int. House Asn, 58-61; mem. bibliog. cmt, jr. cols. sect, ACRL, 65-66. Mem: ALA; Am. Asn. Jr. Cols; Nat. Educ. Asn; Hawaii Libr. Asn; Am. Asn. Univ. Prof; SLA; Barnard Alumni Asn; Nat. Orgn. Women; New York Libr. Asn; New York Libr. Club, Nat. Educ. Asn. Publ: Selected 16mm Films and Filmstrips for Junior and Senior High School Library Use, Wilson Libr. Bull, 12/57; Teaching of Library Skills and Attitudes, High Sch. J, 11/59; Library Instruction and the Junior College, Jr.

---

5) PERSONNEL AND RECRUITING, 5a) job evaluation and description, salary recommendations, 5b) recruitment of professionals and management personnel, 5c) administrative organization, 6) PUBLIC RELATIONS, 6a) publications, 6b) publicity programs, 6c) public opinion surveys, 6d) others, 7) SERVICES, 7a) evaluation of current program, 7b) studies of service to special publics, e.g., students, handicapped, aged, etc., 7c) programs for the implementation of new laws, program proposals to governments, 7d) others, 8) COMMUNITY, REGIONAL, STATE PLANNING, 8a) legislative programs, 8b) area analyses, 8c) centralized systems, cooperative arrangements, 8d) development of standards, 8e) state libraries and extension agencies, 8f) regional and statewide surveys, 8g) others, 9) OTHERS.

Col. J, 4/61; What About the Student Library Assistant?, Sch. Activities, 1/64; The Community College Library, A Plan for Action, Shoe String, 65; A Basic Bibliography for the Community College Library, Shoe String, 67. Consult: 1) North. Ill. Univ, De Kalb, NDEA summer inst. for sch. librns, July 65; 2) Honolulu Tech. Sch, Honolulu, Hawaii, libr. transfer & personnel, spring 66; 3) Kauai Tech. Sch. Lihue, Kauai, Hawaii, transfer of libr, Mar. 66; 4) Maui Community Col, Kahului, Maui, Hawaii, transfer of libr, June 66. Specialties: 1b, 1c, 1h (jr. col, community col; instructional materials center); 2b, 2d (Latin Am), 2h (teachers—prfnl; sch; community jr. col); 5b; 7a, 7d (orientation & instruction); 8c; 9 (generally, the areas of the (community) jr. col. sch. libr. & instructional materials center concept; prfnl. educ. collections; orientation & instruction of students & staff).

WHEELER, DR. JOSEPH L, 1884; Consultant on Public Library Problems, Benson, Vt. 05731. A.B, Brown Univ, 06, M.A.(political sci), 07, Litt.D, 36; B.L.S, N.Y. State Libr. Sch, 09, hon. M.L.S, 24; Litt.D, Univ. Md, 34. Dir, Enoch Pratt Libr, Baltimore, Md, 26-45. Other: Pres, Ohio Libr. Asn, 23-24; mem. exec. bd, ALA, 29-33, mem. bd. educ. for librarianship, 31-36, v.pres, 33-34, Lippincott award, 61; mem, Vt. Gov. Adv. Libr. Cmt. Mem: ALA; hon. mem. Vt. Libr. Asn; hon. mem. Md. Hist. Soc; hon. mem. Md. Libr. Asn. Publ: Library and the Community, ALA, 24; The American Public Library Building (with Alfred M. Githens), 41; Progress and Problems in Education for Librarianship, Carnegie Corp, 46; Effective Location of Public Library Buildings, Univ. Ill, 59; Practical Administration of Public Libraries (with Herbert Goldhor), Harpers, 62. Consult: 1) Pub. Libr, Atlanta, Ga, survey for bldg. changes, orgn, opers. & serv, 64-65; 2) San Diego Pub. Libr, survey for regional syst, Mar. 65; 3) Pub. Libr, Sarasota, Fla, survey for new cent. bldg. & for four-county regional syst, Feb. 66; 4) Pub. Libr, Elkhart, Ind, survey of opers, book collections & reader serv, May 66; 5) Pub. Libr, Birmingham, Ala, survey for cent. bldg, June 66. Specialties: 1g, 1h (efficient plan arrangement & econ); 2a; 5c; 6b, 6d (promoting reference serv); 7a, 7d (local hist).

WHITE, DR. LUCIEN W, Nov. 16, 14; Associate Dean of Library Administration, University of Illinois Library, Urbana, Ill. 61801. Home: 514 S. Willis, Champaign, Ill. 61820. A.B, Augustana Col, 35; M.A, Univ. Ill, 44, Ph.D, 47, M.S, 54. Librn, Augustana Col, 54-58; dir. pub. serv. depts, Univ. Ill, Urbana, 58-68, assoc. dean libr. admin, 68- Other: Pres. Alpha chap, Beta Phi Mu, 59-60; pres. Gamma chap, Phi Beta Kappa, 62-63; pres, Ill. Libr. Asn, 63-64. Mem: Ill. Libr. Asn; ALA. Publ: Library Lighting Standards, Wilson Libr. Bull, 12/58; Independent Study and the Academic Library, J. Higher Educ, 1/62; Libraries, United States College and University, In: Encyclopedia International; Books and Reading in a Television Age, Adult Leadership, 1/66; Illinois Junior College Libraries in Perspective, Ill. Libr, 11/67; Seating Achievement in Larger University Libraries, Col. & Res. Libr, 11/67. Consult: 1) Milton Col, Milton, Wis, libr. problems, Nov. 63; 2) Trinity Col, Deerfield, Ill, libr. problems, Aug. 64; 3) East. N.Mex. State Univ, Portales, libr. problems, Mar. 65; 4) Rio Grande Col, Rio Grande, Ohio, libr. problems, July 66; 5) West. Mich. Univ, Kalamazoo, libr. problems, Feb. 67. Specialties: 1b; 2d (acad. & res. libr).

WHITENACK, CAROLYN IRENE, Apr. 10, 16; Professor & Chairman Educational Media, Department of Education, Purdue University, Lafayette, Ind. 47907. Home: 604 Robinson St, West Lafayette, Ind. 47906. A.B, Univ. Ky, 48; M.S, Univ. Ill, 56. Asst. prof. libr. sci. & audiovisual educ, Purdue Univ, Lafayette, Ind, 56-60, assoc. prof, 60-69, prof, 69-, chmn. educ. media, 60- Other: Mem. coun, Am. Asn. Sch. Librns, 55-60; mem, Nat. Educ. Asn-ALA Joint Cmt, 55-60; pres, Ind. Asn. Sch. Librns, 60-61; second v.pres, ALA, 60-61, mem. audiovisual cmt, 61-66; chmn. nominating cmt, 62-63; Nat. Educ. Asn. rep, World Conf. Orgn. of Teaching Profession, Stockholm, Sweden, 62; ALA rep, Int. Fedn. Libr. Asn, Berne, Switzerland, 62. Mem: ALA; Ind. Libr. Asn; Ind. Asn. Sch. Librns; Nat. Educ. Asn; Dept. Audiovisual Instruction; Kappa Delta Pi; Beta Phi Mu; Am. Asn. Univ. Prof. Publ: American Library Association Bulletin (guest ed), 2/61, 2/69; The Changing Role of the Librarian and His Relationship to Educational Media, In: Educational Media in Libraries, Syracuse Univ, 63 & Wilson Libr. Bull, 1/64; New Resources for the School Library Materials Center, In: The School Library Materials Center: Its Resources and Their Utilization, Illini Union Bookstore, 64; School Library Materials Center, Wilson Libr. Bull, 9/64; The Library of the Future (co-auth), Wilson Bull, 11/64; The Educational Media Index, Scholastic Teacher, 1/65. Consult: 1) State Dept. Pub. Instruction, Indianapolis, Ind, div. sch. libr, Title II, 56-; 2) McGraw-Hill, consult. educ. media index, 62-64; 3) Wheaton High Sch, Wheaton, Ill, revise sch. libr. & curriculum, 65; 4) Wabash Valley Educ. Center, Lafayette, Ind, Title III eval, 65-66; 5) Southport High Sch, Indianapolis, Title III Project on community, cultural & resources center, with Nick Fattu & John Moldstad, 66, Princeton Schs, 69. Specialties: 1c; 2b, 2c; 3a; 5a; 7a, 7c; 8a, 8b, 8c, 8d; 9 (programs for media centers).

WIESE, M. BERNICE, Apr. 18, 05; Retired. Home: 245 Rodgers Forge Rd, Baltimore, Md. 21212. A.B, Goucher Col, 26; M.A, Duke Univ, 29; B.S.L.S, Columbia Univ, 48. Dir. libr. serv, Baltimore City Pub. Schs, Baltimore, Md,

---

KEY TO CONSULTING SPECIALTIES: 1) ARCHITECTURE AND BUILDINGS, 1a) public libraries, 1b) academic libraries, 1c) school libraries, 1d) special libraries, 1e) library interiors, 1f) furnishings, 1g) site and location, 1h) other architectural; 2) COLLECTIONS: SELECTION, EVALUATION, WEEDING, 2a) adults, 2b) young adults, 2c) children, 2d) subject specialty, 2e) O.P. searches, 2f) rare books, 2g) appraisals, 2h) others; 3) TECHNICAL PROCESSES, 3a) cataloging, 3b) classification systems, 3c) acquisitions, 3d) materials processing, 3e) work flow and cost studies, 3f) others, 4) AUTOMATION, 4a) applications of data processing equipment, 4b) information storage and retrieval systems, 4c) systems analysis, 4d) others

until 68. Other: Pres, Asn. Sch. Librns. Md, 44-46; secy. bldgs. & equipment sect, LAD, 57-60, mem. adv. cmt, 64-68, mem. adv. cmt, libr. tech. project, 58-61; 2nd v.pres, AASL, 62-63; mem. adv. cmt, Libr. Sch. South. Conn. State Col, 64-; coun, ALA, 64-68; mem. exec. bd, CSD, 64-68, chmn. cmt. books on Asia for Children, 66; Fulbright-Hays lectr. libr. sci, Teachers Training Col, Singapore, 68-69. Mem: Asn. Sch. Librns. Md; Md. Libr. Asn; ALA; AASL. Publ: Teachers and Librarians Work Together, Baltimore Bull. Educ, 11/58; The Principal Evaluates the School Library, Nat. Asn. Sec-Sch. Principals Bull, 11/59; Shortening Process: Centralized Cataloging and Processing Saves Time and Money, Southeast. Librn, fall 61; Centralized Cataloging and Processing in the Baltimore Public Schools—Five Year Report 1956-1961, AASL, 62; School Librarians As an Aid to Comprehensive Education, J. Kemeterian Pelajaran, Kuala-Lumpur, Malaysia, 12/64. Consult: 1) Ministry of Educ, Kuala-Lumpur, Malaysia, libr. consult. to further & expand sch. libr. in Malaysia, May 64-Mar. 65. Specialties: 1c; 2b, 2c; 3b; 7a, 7b; 8d.

WIGHT, DR. EDWARD ALLEN, Aug. 10, 99; Professor Emeritus of Librarianship, Room 425 Library, University of California, Berkeley, Calif. 94720. Home: 986 Creston Rd, Berkeley, Calif. 94708. B.S, Emory Univ, 20; Ph.D, Univ. Chicago, 36. Prof. librarianship, Univ. Calif, Berkeley, 51- Other: Dir. res, Calif. Pub. Libr. Cmn, 58; pres, Asn. Am. Libr. Schs, 60; v.pres, Friends of Berkeley Pub. Libr, 62-64; chmn, libr. develop. & standards cmt, Calif. Libr. Asn, 64. Mem: ALA; Calif. Libr. Asn; Am. Soc. Pub. Admin; Pub. Personnel Asn; Am. Asn. Univ. Prof; West. Govt. Res. Asn. Publ: Public Library Finance and Accounting, ALA 43; Connecticut Library Survey, Conn. State Dept. Educ, Div. Res. & Planning, Hartford, 48; Separation of Professional and Nonprofessional Work in Public Libraries, Calif. Librn, 9 & 12/52; Research in Organization and Administration, Libr. Trends, 10/57; Trends in the Extension of Library Service, Libr. Quart, 1/61; Standards and Stature in Librarianship, ALA Bull, 11/61. Consult: 1) Hayward Pub. Libr, Hayward, Calif, survey of resources, serv. & opportunities for growth, with LeRoy C. Merritt, 54-55; 2) San Bernardino City & County Libr, Calif, study & report of cooperation & functional consolidation of city & county libr, 57-58; 3) Livermore Pub. Libr, Livermore, Calif, gen. survey of pub. libr. planning, 61; 4) Sacramento City & County Libr, Calif, consolidation of Sacramento Pub. Libr, with Ernst & Ernst, 65. Specialties: 3e; 5a, 5c. 5d (position classification); 7a, 7b; 8c. 8e, 8f.

WILLIAMS, EDWIN E, July 13, 13; Associate University Librarian, Harvard University Library, Cambridge, Mass. 02138. Home: 3 Craigie Circle, Cambridge, Mass. 02138. A.B, 32; A.M, 35. Asst. librn. book selection, Harvard Col. Libr, Cambridge, Mass, 56-59, counselor to dir. collections, Harvard Univ. Libr, 59-64, asst. univ. librn, 64-66, assoc. univ. librn, 66- Other: Mem. program eval. & budget cmt, ALA, 63-66; mem. cmt. libr. surveys, ACRL, 65-, chmn, 67-; assoc. ed, Harvard Libr. Bull, 66-67, ed, 68- Mem: ALA; Can. Libr. Asn. Publ: Preliminary Memoranda, Conference on International Cultural, Educational and Scientific Exchanges, Princeton University, November 25-26, 1946 (with Ruth V. Noble): ALA, 47; Farmington Plan Handbook, Asn. Res. Libr, 53; Problems and Prospects of the Research Library (ed), In: Papers and Proceedings of the Monticello Conference of the Association of Research Libraries, Scarecrow, 55; A Serviceable Reservoir: Report of a Survey of the United States Book Exchange, U.S. Book Exchange, 59; Farmington Plan Handbook, rev. & abridged, Asn. Res. Libr, 61; Resources of Canadian University Libraries for Research in the Humanities and Social Sciences: Report of a Survey for the National Conference of Canadian University and Colleges, Nat. Conf. Can. Univs. & Cols, 62. Consult: 1) U.S. Book Exchange, Wash, D.C, gen. survey of opers. & serv. with report, 58-59; 2) Nat. Conf. Can. Univs. & Cols, Ottawa, Can, survey of resources for res. in humanities & social sci. with recommendations, Apr-May 62; 3) Université Laval, Quebec, Que, Can, gen. survey of univ. libr. with written report & follow-up survey, with P.E. Filion, S.J, Oct-Nov. 62 & Nov. 65; 4) N.Y. Pub. Libr, survey for Am. Coun. Learned Socs. of possible serv. to state & city univs, Jan-Feb. 68; 5) Boston Theol. Inst, survey of possibility for cooperation by libr. of seven mem. insts, Aug-Dec. 68. Specialties: 2h (univ. libr).

WILLIAMSON, DR. WILLIAM LANDRAM, Aug. 13, 20; Professor, Library School, University of Wisconsin, 425 Henry Mall, Madison, Wis. 53706. Home: 4714 Regent St, Madison, Wis. 53705. B.A.(hist), Univ. Wis, 41; B.A. in L.S, Emory Univ, 42; M.S, Columbia Univ, 49; Ph.D, Univ. Chicago, 59. Butler librn, Columbia Univ, 54-64; librn, Montclair State Col, N.J, 64-66; lectr, grad. libr. sch, Univ. Chicago, summer 66; prof, libr. sch, Univ. Wis, 66- Other: Chmn, Col. Libr. Div, Tex. Libr. Asn, 50-51; pres, Montclair State Col. chap, Am. Asn. of Univ. Prof, 66. Mem: ALA; Am. Asn. Univ. Prof, N.J. & Wis. Libr. Asn; Archons of Colophon. Publ: Relating the Library to the Classroom, Col. & Res. Libr, 4/53; A Sidelight on the Frontier Thesis: A New Turner Letter, Newberry Libr. Bull, III, 53; Some Notes on Academic Library Buildings (adopted as nat. standard for acad. libr. bldgs), Berita MIPI, Indonesian Coun. Sci, 10/62; William Frederick Poole and the Modern Library Movement, Columbia Univ, 63; book reviews, Libr. Quart. & Col. & Res. Libr. Consult: 1) Govt.

---

5) PERSONNEL AND RECRUITING, 5a) job evaluation and description, salary recommendations, 5b) recruitment of professionals and management personnel, 5c) administrative organization, 6) PUBLIC RELATIONS, 6a) publications, 6b) publicity programs, 6c) public opinion surveys, 6d) others, 7) SERVICES, 7a) evaluation of current program, 7b) studies of service to special publics, e.g., students, handicapped, aged, etc., 7c) programs for the implementation of new laws, program proposals to governments, 7d) others, 8) COMMUNITY, REGIONAL, STATE PLANNING, 8a) legislative programs, 8b) area analyses, 8c) centralized systems, cooperative arrangements, 8d) development of standards, 8e) state libraries and extension agencies, 8f) regional and statewide surveys, 8g) others, 9) OTHERS.

of Indonesia, Djakarta, Indonesia, evaluated & made recommendations on all aspects of col, pub, inst, & govt. libr, Ford Found-State Univ. N.Y. Indonesia project, with A.G.W. Dunningham, 60-62; 2) Md. State Cols. Bd. of Trustees, Baltimore, Md, evaluated three state cols. with recommendations, with Felix E. Hirsch, Mar. 65. Specialties: 2a, 2d (Am. hist; soc. sci); 7a.

WILMER, FLORENCE CONRATH, June 2, 98; Director of Library Services, Catonsville Community College, Catonsville, Md. 21228. Home: 1506 Lochwood Rd, Catonsville, Md. 21228. A.B, Wash. Col, 37; B.S.L.S, Columbia Univ, 38. Dir, U.S. Info. Libr, Johannesburg, S. Africa, 44; lectr, S. Africa, 45; instructor hist, Univ. Baltimore, 46, chmn, dept. hist, 47-53, chmn, faculty libr. cmt, 50-57, dir. libr, 53-57; dir. libr. serv, Catonsville Community Col, Md, 57- Other: Mem. exec. bd, Md. Libr. Asn, 41-42, pres, 43-44, program chmn, learning resources sect, 67-; v.pres, Md. Jr. Col. Asn, 50, pres, 51-52; pres, Md. div, Nat. Women's Party, 50-51. Mem: ALA; ACRL; Md. Libr. Asn; Md. Asn. Jr. Cols; Am. Asn. State & Local Hist; Foreign Policy Asn; Am. Acad. Political Sci; Baltimore Bus. & Prfnl. Women's Coun; Md. Women's Coun; Baltimore Music Club; Columbia Alumni Asn; Wash. Col. Alumni Asn. Publ: Contrib. to prfnl. journals. Consult: 1) Pima County Jr. Col, Tucson, Ariz, space & sequence allotments for preliminary archit. plans, with Oliver Laine & Frank Bowsma, Nov. 67; 2) Eaton-Burnett Jr. Col, 303 E. Fayette St, Baltimore, Md, initial collection, supplies & equipment, personnel, supplying job descriptions & salary recommendations, with James J. Linksz, Jan. 68- Specialties: 1b, 1e, 1f; 2a, 2d (hist); 3c; 5a, 5b, 5c; 7a; 8c, 8d.

WOODWARD, ROBERT C, May 26. 24; Director, Bangor Public Library, Bangor, Maine 04401. Home: 189 Webster Ave, Bangor, Maine 04401. A.B, Bates Col, 48; A.M, Boston Univ, 49. Dir, Dedham Pub. Libr, Mass, 56-62; dir, Bangor Pub. Libr, 62- Other: Treas, Maine Libr. Asn, 63-66; pres, New Eng. Libr. Asn, 64-65. Mem: ALA; New Eng. Libr. Asn; Maine Libr. Asn. Consult: 1) Westwood Pub. Libr, Westwood, Mass, bldg. addition, interior planning & selection of new adminstr, 60-61; 2) Walpole Pub. Libr, Walpole, Mass, bldg. renovation, 60-61; 3) Brewer Pub. Libr, Brewer, Maine, new bldg, 64-66; 4) Husson Col, Bangor, Maine, collection develop, acquisitions & bldg. plans, 64-66; 5) Maine Dept. Educ, State House, Augusta, Maine, survey of high sch. libr. to select demonstration libr. & standards develop, with Ruth Hazelton & James MacCampbell, June-July 66. Specialties: 1a, 1e; 2a, 2d (ref, hist, political sci); 3c; 5a, 5c; 7a; 8a, 8b, 8f.

WOODWARD, RUPERT C, Mar. 4, 18; Director of Libraries, George Washington University Library, Washington, D.C. 20006. B.S, 40; B.S. in L.S, 47; M.A, 61. Chief acquisitions librn, La. State Univ, 55-63; assoc. libr. dir, Tex. A&M Univ, 63-66; dir. libr, George Washington Univ, 67- Other: U.S. del, Conf. on Develop. of Pub. Libr. Serv. in Latin Am, Sao Paulo, Brazil, 51; chmn. binding cmt, Tex. Coun. State Col. Librns, 65-66, chmn. select cmt. on state book contract, 66. Mem: ALA. Publ: Some Considerations in the Automation of a Serials Record, Papers & Proc, Twentieth Biennial Conf, Southwest. Libr. Asn, Little Rock, Ark, 10/64. Consult: 1) Univ. Southwest. La. Libr, Lafayette, survey & recommendations for strengthening the tech. serv. program, Jan. 65; 2) Ford Found, New York, N.Y, survey & advise to the Nat. Engineering Univ, Lima, Peru, Sept-Oct. 66. Specialties: 1b; 2d (gen. Latin Americana), 2e; 3c; 4d (admin. aspects of libr. automation); 5c; 9 (libr. in Latin Am).

Y

YESNER, MRS. BERNICE L, Jan. 10, 24; School Library Consultant, Sunbrook Rd, Woodbridge, Conn. 06525. B.A, Univ. Vt, 45; M.S, South. Conn. State Col, 57. Children's & young adults' librn, Woodbridge Pub. Libr, Woodbridge, Conn, 57-59; sch. librn, Amity Regional Jr. High Sch, Orange, Conn, 59-62; sch. libr. consult. & children's libr. consult, 62-; instructor, Univ. Conn. Continuing Educ. for Women. Other: Chmn. legis. cmt, exec. bd. of Conn. Sch. Libr. Asn, 62-66; mem. state bd, League of Women Voters, Conn, 64-66; chmn. legis. cmt, exec. bd. of New Eng. Sch. Libr. Asn, 65-68; mem. legis. cmt, AASL, 66-69; publicity dir. demonstration elem. sch. libr. project, Conn. Dept. Educ-Conn. Sch. Libr. Asn. Mem: ALA; AASL; New Eng. Sch. Libr. Asn; Conn. Sch. Libr. Asn; Conn. Audio Visual Educ. Asn. Publ: A Report on School Instruction in Library Skills in Connecticut (co-auth), Conn. Sch. Libr. Asn, 64; Connecticut: Sequence of a Success Story, Sch. Libr, 1/65. Consult: 1) Conco Industries, Inc, 30 Water St, West Haven, Conn, libr. layouts, furniture design, 63-; 2) Waterford Pub. Libr, Waterford, Conn, layout & furniture design, 64-65; 3) Ridgefield Schs, Ridgefield, Conn, plans for sch. libr. develop. for syst, remodeling, writing of ESEA Title III grant proposal, 65-66; 4) Salisbury Elem. Sch, Lakeville, Conn, remodeling, plans for new addition, workshops, in-serv. training, 66; 5) McGraw-Hill Text-Film, 330 W. 42nd St, New York, N.Y, sch. libr. consult, cataloging, filmstrip cabinet & package design, filmstrip manual, with Richard Darling, 66- Specialties: 1a, 1c, 1e, 1f; 2b, 2c, 2d (schs: elem, jr. high, high sch); 3a, 3b, 3c, 3d, 3e, 3f (in-serv. training, workshops); 5a, 5b, 5c, 5d (workshops for paraprfnl, clerical & volunteer personnel); 6a, 6b, 6d (sch. libr. demonstration project); 7a, 7c; 8a, 8b, 8c, 8f; 9 (work with firms serving

---

KEY TO CONSULTING SPECIALTIES: 1) ARCHITECTURE AND BUILDINGS, 1a) public libraries, 1b) academic libraries, 1c) school libraries, 1d) special libraries, 1e) library interiors, 1f) furnishings, 1g) site and location, 1h) other architectural; 2) COLLECTIONS: SELECTION, EVALUATION, WEEDING, 2a) adults, 2b) young adults, 2c) children, 2d) subject specialty, 2e) O.P. searches, 2f) rare books, 2g) appraisals, 2h) others; 3) TECHNICAL PROCESSES, 3a) cataloging, 3b) classification systems, 3c) acquisitions, 3d) materials processing, 3e) work flow and cost studies, 3f) others, 4) AUTOMATION, 4a) applications of data processing equipment, 4b) information storage and retrieval systems, 4c) systems analysis, 4d) others

sch, children's & young peoples' libr. to search out the spec. needs for materials & serv).

YOUNG, CAROL, Feb. 16, 12; Library Supervisor, North Platte Public Schools, North Platte, Nebr. 69101. Home: 517 S. Elm, North Platte, Nebr. 69101. A.B.(educ), 48; M.A. (librarianship), 57. Sr. high librn, 56-66; libr. supvr, N. Platte Pub. Schs, 66- Other: Secy, Nebr. Libr. Asn, 65-68. Mem: Nebr. Libr. Asn; ALA. Consult: 1) Nebr. Libr. Cmn, Lincoln, catalogued 2 small town libr, summers 63 & 65. Specialties: 2b, 2c; 3a.

Z

ZIEBOLD, EDNA B, July 9, 09; Director of Library Service, San Diego County Department of Education, 6401 Linda Vista Rd, San Diego, Calif. 92111. Home: 5176 Foothill Blvd, San Diego, Calif. 92109. B.A, Ohio State Univ, 30; B.A.(librarianship), Univ. Wash, 42. Librn. in charge of schs, San Diego County Free Libr, 46-47; dir. libr. serv, San Diego County Dept. Educ, San Diego, Calif, 47- Other: Mem. bd. dirs, AASL, 57-59; pres. San Diego chap, SLA, 66-67. Mem: ALA; Calif. Libr. Asn; SLA. Publ: Harbors of California (co-auth), Melmont, 58; Area Distribution Libraries for Elementary Schools, ALA Bull, 3/59; Sch. Libr. (guest ed), 5/59; How Are We Doing? (contrib, with Margaret Spengler), Calif. J. Elem. Educ, 29: 53-57. Consult: 1) Field Enterprises, Merchandise Mart, Chicago, Ill, bibliog. consult. for World Book Encyclopedia, 60-66; 2) G.P. Putnam's Sons, 200 Madison Ave, New York, N.Y, ed. consult, 64; 3) Grolier, Inc, 575 Lexington Ave, New York, consult. on Book of Knowledge, June 64; 4) Franklin Publ, 367 S. Pasadena Ave, Pasadena, Calif, bibliog. consult. for primary soc. study series, 65; 5) Calif. State Dept. Educ, Sacramento, Calif, consult. to local sch. dist. on ESEA Title II, 66. Specialties: 1c; 2c; 7a, 7b.

ZIMMERMAN, LEE F, Mar. 17, 02; University Librarian Emeritus, University of Idaho, Moscow, Idaho 83843. Home: 213 Crest Dr, Hendersonville, N.C. 28739. B.A, 24; B.S, 29; M.A, 32. Univ. librn, Univ. Idaho, Moscow, 48- Other: Chmn. libr. planning bd, Minn. Libr. Asn, 37-39, mem. nominating cmt, 41-43, chmn, 46; mem. bookbinding cmt, ALA, 38-41, chmn, 40-41, mem. fed. relations cmt, 39-48, mem. libr. projects cmt, 44-45, mem. statist. cmt, 44-48, mem. adult educ. bd, 47-48, mem. coun, 59-63; chmn. reorgn. cmt, Nat. Asn. State Libr, 40-41, v.pres. of asn, 40-41; mem. libr. extension cmt, Pac. Northwest Libr. Asn, 48-50, chmn, 49-50, mem. bibliog. cmt, 48-53, mem. libr. develop. cmt, 50, mem. exec. bd, 52-53, chmn. nominating cmt, 54-55, mem. cmt. on union list of newspapers, 55-57, mem. personnel admin. cmt, 57-58, chmn. col. & univ. div, 60-62; chmn. microfilm cmt, Idaho State Libr. Asn, 49-58, mem. exec. bd, 52-53, v.pres. & preselect, 58-59, pres, 59-60, mem. libr. develop. cmt, 62-64, mem. scholarship cmt, 62-; mem. libr. bldgs. cmt, ACRL, 52-54, mem. cmt. Nat. Libr. Week, 60-61. Mem: Idaho Libr. Asn; Pac. Northwest Libr. Asn; ALA; ACRL. Publ: Appraising Minnesota WPA Library Demonstrations, Libr. J, 2/15/43 & Minn. Libr, 3/43; New Patterns of Library Service, Libr. J, 1/1/46; Services and Functions of the State Library Agency, Idaho Librn, 7/51; Idaho's Ideal, Libr. J, 12/1/56; A Library Renaissance in Idaho, Idaho Libr, 7/59; Pilfering and Mutilating Library Books, Rub-Off, 3/60, The Bookmark, 9/60 & Libr. J, 10/15/61. Consult: 1) Pac. Lutheran Univ, Parkland, Wash, libr. admin, orgn, opers. & serv, Nov. 66. Specialties: 1a, 1b, 1e; 1f, 1g; 2a, 2d (humanities, soc. sci, hist), 2g; 3c, 3d, 3e; 5a, 5b, 5c; 6a, 6b, 6d (projects promotion); 7a, 7b, 7c; 8a, 8b, 8c, 8d, 8e, 8f, 8g (field promotion projects).

---

5) PERSONNEL AND RECRUITING, 5a) job evaluation and description, salary recommendations, 5b) recruitment of professionals and management personnel, 5c) administrative organization, 6) PUBLIC RELATIONS, 6a) publications, 6b) publicity programs, 6c) public opinion surveys, 6d) others, 7) SERVICES, 7a) evaluation of current program, 7b) studies of service to special publics, e.g., students, handicapped, aged, etc., 7c) programs for the implementation of new laws, program proposals to governments, 7d) others, 8) COMMUNITY, REGIONAL, STATE PLANNING, 8a) legislative programs, 8b) area analyses, 8c) centralized systems, cooperative arrangements, 8d) development of standards, 8e) state libraries and extension agencies, 8f) regional and statewide surveys, 8g) others, 9) OTHERS.

SPECIALTY INDEX

ACQUISITIONS

Allen, Kenneth S.
Alvarez, Dr. Robert S.
Anderson, Frank J.
Anderson, Le Moyne W.
Andrews, James C.
Archer, Dr. H. Richard
Ash, Lee
Badten, Jean M.
Beaton, Mrs. Maxine B.
Beatty, William K.
Bitner, Harry
Brinton, Harry
Brown, Alberta L.
Buckley, John
Carrison, Dale K.
Chitwood, Jack
Clark, Mrs. Gertrude M.
Cohen, David
Connolly, Brendan, S.J.
Covey, Dr. Alan D.
Crawford, Helen
Cronin, John W.
Daily, Dr. Jay Elwood
Danton, Dr. J. Periam
Daume, Mrs. Mary R.
Davis, Charlotte D.
Dawson, Dr. John M.
Diehl, Katharine S.
Donohue, Joseph C.
Ebert, Myrl
Ertel, Mrs. Margaret P.
Eshelman, William R.
Fast, Mrs. Elizabeth T.
Filion, Paul-Emile, S.J.
Fitzgerald, Mrs. Louise H.
Frarey, Carlyle J.
Friedlander, Dr. Michel O.
Galvin, Thomas J.
Georgi, Charlotte
Goodbread, Juanita W.
Gorchels, Clarence C.
Gordon, Bernard L.
Gormley, Mark M.
Haas, Elaine
Hamlin, Arthur T.
Harris, Walter H.
Heilmann, Margaret A.
Henderson, Mary J.
Hicks, Warren B.
Hild, Alice P.
Hirsch, Dr. Felix E.
Humphry, James, III
Humphry, John A.
Jackson, Dr. William V.
Jaffarian, Sara
Jansen, Guenter A.
Johnson, Mrs. Barbara C.
Johnson, Leonard L.
Katz, Beatrice
Kopech, Gertrude

Kurth, William H.
Lane, Sister M. Claude, O.P.
Leathers, James A.
Logsdon, Dr. Richard H.
Lucker, Jay K.
McCarthy, Dr. Stephen A.
McCoy, Dr. Ralph E.
McGowan, Frank M.
Maclachlan, Bruce
McNiff, Philip J.
Merritt, Dr. LeRoy C.
Mersky, Roy Martin
Metcalf, Dr. Keyes D.
Miller, Mrs. Melissa
Miller, Dr. Robert A.
Minder, Thomas L.
Minker, Dr. Jack
Mitchell, Eleanor
Moreland, Carroll C.
Morgan, John F.
Murray, Thomas B.
Nelson, Charles A.
Owens, Mrs. Iris
Parsons, Mrs. Mary D.
Raphael, Anne W.
Rateaver, Dr. Bargyla
Ready, William B.
Reichmann, Dr. Felix
Rosenberg, Kenyon C.
Rothines Associates
Rowland, Arthur R.
Rush, N. Orwin
St. John, Francis R.
Samore, Theodore
Schork, Francis W.
Schutze, Gertrude
Shepard, Mrs. Marietta D.
Simmons, Joseph M.
Smith, James LeRoy
Smith, L. Herman
Spyers-Duran, Peter
Stephens, Dr. Irlene R.
Stevens, Nicholas G.
Swank, Dr. Raynard C.
Tanis, Norman Earl
Tauber, Dr. Maurice F.
Taylor, Robert S.
Technical Library Service
Treyz, Joseph H.
Trinkner, Dr. Charles L.
Usher, Mrs. Elizabeth R.
VanJackson, Wallace M.
Van Velzer, Verna J.
Veaner, Allen B.
Voigt, Melvin J.
Voos, Dr. Henry
Vorhies, Eugene
Wagman, Dr. Frederick H.
Wallace, James O.
Watkins, Mrs. Lillian M.
Wilmer, Florence C.
Woodward, Robert C.

Woodward, Rupert C.
Yesner, Mrs. Bernice L.
Zimmerman, Lee F.

See also APPRAISALS OF BOOKS
AND COLLECTIONS, BOOK
COLLECTIONS, OUT-OF-
PRINT BOOK SEARCHES, RARE
BOOKS

ADMINISTRATIVE ORGANIZATION

Ackerman, Page
Allen, Kenneth S.
Anderson, Frank J.
Anderson, Le Moyne W.
Andrews, James C.
Archer, John H.
Ash, Lee
Badten, Jean M.
Baillie, Dr. Stuart
Bartolini, R.P.
Beatty, William K.
Berninghausen, David K.
Berthel, John H.
Bitner, Harry
Blasingame, Ralph
Boaz, Dr. Martha
Brahm, Walter T.
Branscomb, Dr. Lewis C, Jr.
Brinton, Harry
Brodman, Dr. Estelle
Brown, Alberta L.
Bryan, Dr. James E.
Bryant, Jack W.
Burgess, Robert S.
Burke, Dr. John E.
Bury, Peter P.
Butler, Evelyn
Carlson, William H.
Carnovsky, Dr. Leon
Carpenter, Ray L.
Castagna, Edwin
Chait, William
Chapin, Dr. Richard E.
Chen, Dr. John H.M.
Chitwood, Jack
Clarke, Dr. Robert F.
Cole, Doris M.
Connolly, Brendan, S.J.
Covey, Dr. Alan D.
Daily, Dr. Jay Elwood
Danton, Dr. J. Periam
Daume, Mrs. Mary R.
Davis, Charlotte D.
Deahl, Thomas F.
Deale, Henry V.
De Young, Julia M.
Downs, Robert B.
Duke, William R.
Dunlap, Dr. Leslie W.
Eastlick, John T.
Eaton, Dr. Andrew J.

SPECIALTY INDEX

Ebert, Myrl
Edwards, Ida M.
Ertel, Mrs. Margaret P.
Eshelman, William R.
Etchison, Annie L.
Evans, Richard A.
Falgione, Joseph F.
Farber, Evan I.
Filion, Paul-Emile S.J.
Fitzgerald, Dr. William A.
Franklin, Robert D.
Friedlander, Dr. Michel O.
Galick, Mrs. V. Genevieve
Geddes, Andrew
Gelfand, Dr. Morris A.
Geller, William S.
Georgi, Charlotte
Goldstein, Dr. Harold
Goodbread, Juanita W.
Gorchels, Clarence C.
Gosnell, Dr. Charles F.
Grafton, Connie E.
Greer, Dr. Roger C.
Grosch, Audrey N.
Haas, Elaine
Haas, Warren J.
Hamlin, Arthur T.
Harding, Nelson F.
Harnsberger, Therese
Harris, Walter H.
Hart, Dr. Eugene D.
Harvey, Dr. John F.
Heilmann, Margaret A.
Henington, David M.
Henkle, Dr. Herman H.
Heron, David W.
Hicks, Warren B.
Hill, Laurence G.
Hirsch, Dr. Felix E.
Hopp, Dr. Ralph H.
Housel, James R.
Humphry, James, III
Humphry, John A.
Johnson, Mrs. Barbara C.
Johnson, Leonard L.
Jones, Frank N.
Jones, Harold D.
Jones, James V.
Josey, E.J.
Kaser, Dr. David
Katz, Beatrice
Kemper, Dr. Robert E.
Keough, Francis P.
Kuhlman, Augustus F.
Lancour, Dr. Harold
Lane, Sister M. Claude, O.P.
Leopold, Mrs. Carolyn C.
Logsdon, Dr. Richard H.
Lybeck, Pauline
Lyle, Guy R.
McCarthy, Dr. Stephen A.
McConkey, Thomas W.
McCoy, Dr. Ralph E.
McDaniel, Roderick D.
McDiarmid, Dr. Errett W.
McDonough, Roger H.
McElderry, Stanley
McMullan, Theodore N.
McNeal, Dr. Archie L.
McNiff, Philip J.
McPherson, Kenneth F.
Mapp, Edward C.
Marke, Julius J.
Mersky, Roy M.
Metcalf, Dr. Keyes D.
Milczewski, Marion A.
Miller, Dr. Robert A.
Mills, Jesse C.
Mitchell, Eleanor
Molod, Samuel E.
Moreland, Carroll C.
Morgan, John F.
Morin, Wilfred L.
Morse, A. Louis
Muller, Dr. Robert H.
Murphy, Walter H.
Murray, Thomas B.
Nelson Associates, Inc.
Nelson, Charles A.
Oboler, Eli M.
Oltman, Florine A.

Orne, Dr. Jerrold
Palmer, David C.
Parsons, Mrs. Mary D.
Portteus, Elnora M.
Remley, Ralph D.
Rescoe, A. Stan
Rochell, Carlton
Rockwell, Mrs. Jeanette S.
Rod, Donald O.
Rosenberg, Kenyon C.
Roth, Harold L.
Rush, N. Orwin
St. John, Francis R.
Schefter, Joseph A.
Schein, Bernard
Schork, Francis W.
Severance, Robert W.
Shaffer, Kenneth R.
Shank, Dr. Russell
Sheehan, Sister Helen
Shepard, Mrs. Marietta D.
Shepherd, Giles F, Jr.
Simmons, Joseph M.
Simon, Bradley A.
Sinclair, Dorothy
Smith, James L.
Smith, Mrs. June S.
Spyers-Duran, Peter
Stephens, Dr. Irlene R.
Stevens, Nicholas G.
Stewart, David M.
Stoffel, Lester L.
Summers, F. William
Swank, Dr. Raynard C.
Tauber, Dr. Maurice F.
Taylor, Robert S.
Technical Library Service
Trezza, Alphonse F.
Trinkner, Dr. Charles L.
Troke, Mrs. Margaret K.
Usher, Mrs. Elizabeth R.
VanJackson, Wallace M.
Van Velzer, Verna J.
Veit, Dr. Fritz
Vorhies, Eugene
Vreeland, Eleanor P.
Wagman, Dr. Frederick H.
Watkins, Mrs. Lillian M.
Wezeman, Frederick
Wheeler, Dr. Joseph L.
Wight, Dr. Edward A.
Wilmer, Florence C.
Woodward, Robert C.
Woodward, Rupert C.
Yesner, Mrs. Bernice L.
Zimmerman, Lee F.

See also JOB EVALUATION AND DESCRIPTION, PERSONNEL, PLANNING, RECRUITMENT OF PROFESSIONALS AND MANAGEMENT, SYSTEMS ANALYSIS

Adult Collections see BOOK COLLECTIONS: ADULT

APPRAISALS OF BOOKS AND COLLECTIONS

Anderson, Le Moyne W.
Ash, Lee
Bartolini, R.P.
Bevis, Leura D.
Bixler, Paul
Cohen, David
Danton, Dr. J. Periam
Daume, Mrs. Mary R.
Ebert, Myrl
Folcarelli, Ralph J.
Geddes, Andrew
Gordon, Bernard L.
Gosnell, Dr. Charles F.
Hart, Dr. Eugene D.
Holley, Dr. Edward G.
Humphry, James, III
Kuhlman, Augustus F.
McMullan, Theodore N.
McNiff, Philip J.

Mersky, Roy M.
Orne, Dr. Jerrold
Parker, Wyman W.
Reichmann, Dr. Felix
Roth, Harold L.
Rothines Associates
St. John, Francis R.
Samore, Theodore
Schutze, Gertrude
Spyers-Duran, Peter
Stewart, R.C.
Thompson, Donald E.
Thompson, Dr. Lawrence S.
Usher, Mrs. Elizabeth R.
Zimmerman, Lee F.

See also ACQUISITIONS, BOOK COLLECTIONS, OUT OF PRINT BOOK SEARCHES, RARE BOOKS

ARCHITECTURE AND BUILDINGS

ACADEMIC LIBRARIES

Allen, Kenneth S.
Anderson, Frank J.
Anderson, Le Moyne W.
Andrews, James C.
Archer, Dr. H. Richard
Bailey, J. Russell
Baillie, Dr. Stuart
Bean, Donald E.
Benson, William E.
Berninghausen, David K.
Berthel, John H.
Bixler, Paul
Branscomb, Dr. Lewis C, Jr.
Burke, Dr. John E.
Burke, Redmond A, C.S.V.
Butler, Evelyn
Byers, Mrs. Edna H.
Carlson, William H.
Chapin, Dr. Richard E.
Chen, Dr. John H.M.
Cherry, Scott T.
Cohen, Aaron
Coman, Edwin T, Jr.
Connolly, Brendan, S.J.
Covey, Dr. Alan D.
Danton, Dr. J. Periam
Davidson, Dr. Donald C.
Dawson, Dr. John M.
Deale, Henry V.
De Gennaro, Richard
Diehl, Katharine S.
Di Muccio, Sister Mary-Jo
Dix, Dr. William S.
Dunlap, Dr. Leslie W.
Dunn, Dr. Oliver C.
Eaton, Dr. Andrew J.
Ellerbrock, Edward J.
Ellsworth, Dr. Ralph E.
Engley, Donald B.
Eshelman, William R.
Farber, Evan I.
Filion, Paul-Emile, S.J.
Fussler, Dr. Herman H.
Galvin, Hoyt R.
Gelfand, Dr. Morris A.
Gitler, Dr. Robert L.
Goldstein, Dr. Harold
Gorchels, Clarence C.
Gormley, Mark M.
Gosnell, Dr. Charles F.
Greer, Dr. Roger C.
Haas, Elaine
Haas, Warren J.
Hardaway, Elliott
Harlow, Neal
Harvey, Dr. John F.
Healey, James S.
Heiliger, Edward M.
Henkle, Dr. Herman H.
Heron, David W.
Hicks, Warren B.
Hintz, Dr. Carl W.
Hirsch, Dr. Felix E.
Holley, Dr. Edward G.
Hopp, Dr. Ralph H.
Humphry, James, III
Humphry, John A.
Jackson, Dr. William V.

SPECIALTY INDEX

Jesse, William H.
Jones, Frank N.
Jones, Harold D.
Jones, James V.
Kaser, Dr. David
Kuhlman, Augustus F.
Lancour, Dr. Harold
Leggett, Dr. Stanton F.
Library Design Associates
Lucker, Jay K.
Lyle, Guy R.
McAdams, Mrs. Nancy R.
McAnally, Dr. Arthur M.
McCarthy, Dr. Stephen A.
McCoy, Dr. Ralph E.
McDonald, John P.
McDonough, Roger H.
McElderry, Stanley
McKeon, Newton F.
McMullan, Theodore N.
McNeal, Dr. Archie L.
McNiff, Philip J.
McPherson, Kenneth F.
Mapp, Edward C.
Marshall & Brown, Inc.
Mason, Dr. Ellsworth
Metcalf, Dr. Keyes D.
Milczewski, Marion A.
Miles, Paul M.
Miller, J. Gormly
Miller, Dr. Robert A.
Mills, Jesse C.
Mitchell, Eleanor
Moriarty, John H.
Morris, Dr. Raymond P.
Muller, Dr. Robert H.
Murray, Thomas B.
Nelson Associates, Inc.
Oboler, Eli M.
Orne, Dr. Jerrold
Orr, Robert W.
Osborne, Fred Y.
Pease, William A.
Perrine, Richard H.
Poole, Frazer G.
Popecki, Joseph T.
Pullen, Dr. William R.
Ready, William B.
Reason, Dr. Joseph H.
Richards, James H, Jr.
Rockwell, Mrs. Jeanette S.
Rod, Donald O.
Rohlf, Robert H.
Rothines Associates
Rounds, Gertrude W.
Rovelstad, Howard
Rush, N. Orwin
St. John, Francis R.
Samore, Theodore
Scarborough, Ruth E.
Schell, Harold B.
Schneider, Frank A.
Schork, Francis W.
Severance, Robert W.
Shaffer, Kenneth R.
Sheehan, Sister Helen
Shepherd, Giles F, Jr.
Shores, Dr. Louis
Simmons, Joseph M.
Simon, Bradley A.
Skipper, Dr. James E.
Smith, L. Herman
Sprug, Joseph W.
Spyers-Duran, Peter
Stephens, Dr. Irlene R.
Stevens, Nicholas G.
Stone, Dr. C. Walter
Surrency, Erwin C.
Swank, Dr. Raynard C.
Tanis, Norman E.
Tauber, Dr. Maurice F.
Taylor, Robert S.
Technical Library Service
Thompson, Donald E.
Thompson, Dr. Lawrence S.
Trezza, Alphonse F.
Trinkner, Dr. Charles L.
Trotier, Arnold H.
Usher, Mrs. Elizabeth R.
VanJackson, Wallace M.
Veit, Dr. Fritz

Voigt, Melvin J.
Wagman, Dr. Frederick H.
Wallace, James O.
Watkins, Mrs. Lillian M.
Wheeler, Dr. Helen R.
White, Dr. Lucien W.
Wilmer, Florence C.
Woodward, Rupert C.
Zimmerman, Lee F.

PUBLIC LIBRARIES

Alvarez, Dr. Robert S.
Bailey, J. Russell
Baillie, Dr. Stuart
Banister, John R.
Bartolini, R. Paul
Beach, Cecil P.
Bean, Donald E.
Bennett, Gordon L.
Benson, William E.
Boaz, Dr. Martha
Bourne, Philip W.
Brahm, Walter T.
Brinton, Harry
Bryan, Dr. James E.
Bryant, Jack W.
Burns, Lorin R.
Bury, Peter P.
Castagna, Edwin
Cavaglieri, Dr. Giorgio
Chait, William
Chen, Dr. John H.M.
Cherry, Scott T.
Chitwood, Jack
Cochran, Jean D.
Cohen, Aaron
Cole, Mary E.
Coolidge, Coit
Curley, Walter W.
Daume, Mrs. Mary R.
Doms, Keith
Eastlick, John T.
Eisner, Joseph
Ellerbrock, Edward J.
Etchison, Annie L.
Falgione, Joseph F.
Flanders, Frances V.
Franklin, Robert D.
Galvin, Hoyt R.
Garrison, Dr. Guy
Geddes, Andrew
Geller, William S.
Gibson, Frank E.
Goldstein, Dr. Harold
Grafton, Connie E.
Hardaway, Elliott
Hart, Dr. Eugene D.
Healey, James S.
Hellum, Bertha D.
Henderson, John D.
Henington, David M.
Hill, Laurence G.
Holt, Raymond M.
Hope, Arlene
Housel, James R.
Humphry, James, III
Humphry, John A.
Jansen, Guenter A.
Jones, Frank N.
Jones, Wyman
Kantor, David
Keough, Francis P.
Lancour, Dr. Harold
Leathers, James A.
Leggett, Dr. Stanton F.
Library Design Associates
Lute, Harriet
McAdams, Mrs. Nancy R.
McClarren, Robert R.
McConkey, Thomas W.
McDonough, Roger H.
McNiff, Philip J.
McPherson, Kenneth F.
Marshall & Brown, Inc.
Martin, Allie Beth
Miller, Ernest I.
Mills, Jesse C.
Mitchell, Eleanor
Mohrhardt, Charles M.

Molod, Samuel E.
Moran, Virginia L.
Morin, Wilfred L.
Mostar, Roman
Muller, Dr. Robert H.
Munn, R. Russell
Murphy, Walter H.
Mutschler, Herbert F.
Nelson Associates, Inc.
Nielsen, Andre S.
Oliner, Stan
Paine, Clarence S.
Perry, E. Caswell
Peterson, Harry N.
Prideaux, B. Elizabeth
Proctor, Mrs. Margia W.
Putnam, Hamilton S.
Rochell, Carlton
Rockwell, Mrs. Jeanette S.
Rohlf, Robert H.
Roth, Harold L.
Rothines Associates
Rounds, Gertrude W.
Runge, DeLyle P.
St. John, Francis R.
Schmuch, Joseph J.
Schneider, Frank A.
Shaffer, Kenneth R.
Simmons, Joseph M.
Simon, Bradley A.
Smith, Hannis S.
Spyers-Duran, Peter
Stephens, Dr. Irlene R.
Stewart, David M.
Stoffel, Lester L.
Tauber, Dr. Maurice F.
Thomas, Henry
Thompson, Donald E.
Trezza, Alphonse F.
Troke, Mrs. Margaret K.
Ulveling, Dr. Ralph A.
Wallis, C. Lamar
Wezeman, Frederick
Woodward, Robert C.
Yesner, Mrs. Bernice L.
Zimmerman, Lee F.

SCHOOL LIBRARIES

Aceto, Vincent J.
Alexander, Esther M.
Allen, James W.
Allen, Loren H.
Armstrong, Rodney
Badten, Jean M.
Bailey, J. Russell
Baillie, Dr. Stuart
Barber, Raymond W.
Bean, Donald E.
Berry, June
Boaz, Dr. Martha
Buckingham, Betty J.
Buckley, John
Burke, Dr. John E.
Cavaglieri, Dr. Giorgio
Cherry, Scott T.
Chisholm, Dr. Margaret E.
Clark, Rheta A.
Cohen, Aaron
Cohen, David
Cole, Doris M.
Cole, Georgia R.
Connolly, Brendan, S.J.
Crawford, Paul R.
Currie, Dorothy H.
Daume, Mrs. Mary R.
Davies, Ruth A.
Davis, Charlotte D.
Dees, Margaret N.
De Young, Julia M.
Di Muccio, Sister Mary-Jo
Duke, William R.
Dunkley, Grace S.
Edwards, Ida M.
Ellerbrock, Edward J.
Ellsworth, Dr. Ralph E.
Engley, Donald B.
Fitzgerald, Mrs. Louise H.
Folcarelli, Ralph J.
Gilbert, Christine B.
Goodbread, Juanita W.

SPECIALTY INDEX

Gorski, Lorraine K.M.
Hall, Elvajean
Hardaway, Elliott
Harding, Nelson F.
Harnsberger, Therese
Harris, Walter H.
Heilmann, Margaret A.
Hicks, Warren B.
Hild, Alice P.
Housel, James R.
Humphry, John A.
Jacobs, Dr. James W.
Jaffarian, Sara
James, Louise
Johnson, David L.
Johnson, Mrs. Frances K.
Johnson, Leonard L.
Josey, E.J.
Katz, Beatrice
Keough, Francis P.
Lancour, Dr. Harold
Lane, Sister M. Claude, O.P.
Leggett, Dr. Stanton F.
Lembo, Mrs. Diana L.
Leopold, Mrs. Carolyn C.
Library Design Associates
Mack, Mrs. Sara R.
McPherson, Kenneth F.
Mapp, Edward C.
Marshall & Brown, Inc.
Mason, Dr. Ellsworth
Miller, Mrs. Melissa
Mitchell, Eleanor
Moran, Virginia L.
Morse, A. Louis
Murphy, Lavinia E.
Negro, Antoinette
Owens, Mrs. Iris
Parsons, Mrs. Mary D.
Popecki, Joseph T.
Portteus, Elnora M.
Raley, Mrs. Lucille W.
Robertson, Billy O.
Rockwell, Mrs. Jeannette S.
Roth, Harold L.
Rothines Associates
Rounds, Gertrude W.
St. John, Francis R.
Sattley, Helen R.
Schefter, Joseph A.
Schneider, Frank A.
Shapiro, Mrs. Lillian L.
Simon, Bradley A.
Smith, James L.
Spyers-Duran, Peter
Stevens, Nicholas G.
Stone, Dr. C. Walter
Trezza, Alphonse F.
Trinkner, Dr. Charles L.
Watkins, Mrs. Lillian M.
Wheeler, Dr. Helen R.
Whitenack, Carolyn I.
Wiese, M. Bernice
Yesner, Mrs. Bernice L.
Ziebold, Edna B.

SPECIAL LIBRARIES

Allen, Kenneth S.
Anderson, Frank J.
Andrews, James C.
Ash, Lee
Baer, Dr. Karl A.
Bailey, J. Russell
Bean, Donald E.
Beaton, Mrs. Maxine B.
Beatty, William K.
Berry, June
Bertalan, Dr. Frank J.
Boaz, Dr. Martha
Bourne, Philip W.
Brandon, Alfred N.
Brown, Alberta L.
Butler, Evelyn
Casellas, Elizabeth R.
Cavaglieri, Dr. Giorgio
Cherry, Scott T.
Clark, Mrs. Gertrude M.
Cohen, Aaron
Coman, Edwin T, Jr.

Crawford, Helen
Darling, Louise
De Gennaro, Richard
Diehl, Katharine S.
Divett, Dr. Robert T.
Dodd, James B.
Dunlap, Dr. Leslie W.
Ebert, Myrl
Ellerbrock, Edward J.
Etchison, Annie L.
Evans, Richard A.
Friedlander, Dr. Michel O.
Fry, Alderson
Georgi, Charlotte
Gerlach, Dr. Arch C.
Gitler, Dr. Robert L.
Grosch, Audrey N.
Haas, Elaine
Hardaway, Elliott
Henderson, Mary J.
Henkle, Dr. Herman H.
Hopp, Dr. Ralph H.
Humphry, James, III
Humphry, John A.
Johnson, Mrs. Barbara C.
Kinney, Margaret M.
Kopech, Gertrude
Leggett, Dr. Stanton F.
Leondar, Judith C.
Library Design Associates
Lucker, Jay K.
Lybeck, Pauline
McAdams, Mrs. Nancy R.
McGowan, Frank M.
McPherson, Kenneth F.
Marshall & Brown, Inc.
Mersky, Roy M.
Miller, J. Gormly
Miller, Mrs. Melissa
Mills, Jesse C.
Mitchell, Eleanor
Mitchell, Vernon R.
Moreland, Carroll C.
Morgan, John F.
Moriarty, John H.
Morris, Dr. Raymond P.
Mostar, Roman
Oltman, Florine A.
Orton, Floyd E.
Rateaver, Dr. Bargyla
Rescoe, A. Stan
Rockwell, Mrs. Jeanette S.
Rosenberg, Kenyon C.
Roth, Harold L.
Rothines Associates
Rovelstad, Howard
St. John, Francis R.
Schell, Harold B.
Schork, Francis W.
Schutze, Gertrude.
Severence, Robert W.
Shaffer, Kenneth R.
Simmons, Joseph M.
Simon, Bradley A.
Spyers-Duran, Peter
Stephens, Dr. Irlene R.
Surrency, Erwin C.
Tauber, Dr. Maurice F.
Technical Library Service
Usher, Mrs. Elizabeth R.
Vaillancourt, Dr. Pauline M.
Van Velzer, Verna J.
Voigt, Melvin J.
Vormelker, Rose L.
Watkins, Mrs. Lillian M.

SPECIALIZED ASPECTS (see individual biography)

Archer, John H.
Banister, John R.
Berninghausen, David K.
Bloomquist, Harold
Brandon, Alfred N.
Brodman, Dr. Estelle
Burke, Redmond A, C.S.V.
Bury, Peter P.
Cochran, Jean D.
Cohen, Morris L.
Cole, Georgia R.

Coolidge, Coit
Daume, Mrs. Mary R.
Deahl, Thomas F.
Divett, Dr. Robert T.
Eisner, Joseph
Ellerbrock, Edward J.
Ellsworth, Dr. Ralph E.
Folcarelli, Ralph J.
Fry, Alderson
Gitler, Dr. Robert L.
Hamlin, Arthur T.
Harnsberger, Therese
Hellum, Bertha D.
Henderson, John D.
Jacobstein, J. Myron
Jesse, William H.
Johnson, Mrs. Barbara C.
Johnson, Leonard L.
Jordan, Robert T.
Kantor, David
Kurth, William H.
Library Management and Building Consultants, Inc.
Lucker, Jay K.
McClarren, Robert R.
McDaniel, Roderick D.
Marke, Julius J.
Mills, Jesse C.
Montgomery, James W.
Moreland, Carroll C.
Moriarty, John H.
Murphy, Lavinia E.
Murray, Thomas B.
Nesbin, Mrs. Esther W.
Nielsen, Andre S.
Nikas, Mary C.
Osborne, Fred Y.
Pollack, Ervin H.
Portteus, Elnora M.
Rockwell, Mrs. Jeanette S.
Rod, Donald O.
Roth, Harold L.
Spyers-Duran, Peter
Stoffel, Lester L.
Stone, Dr. C. Walter
Troke, Mrs. Margaret K.
Vaillancourt, Dr. Pauline M.
Wheeler, Dr. Helen R.
Wheeler, Dr. Joseph L.

See also FURNISHINGS FOR LIBRARIES, INTERIORS OF LIBRARIES, SITES FOR LIBRARIES

AUTOMATION

SPECIALIZED ASPECTS (see individual biography)

Ballou, Hubbard W.
Berul, Lawrence H.
Buckingham, Betty J.
Buckley, John
Burns, Lorin R.
Chapin, Dr. Richard E.
Cohen, Morris L.
Cranford, Theodore N.
Daily, Dr. Jay E.
Daume, Mrs. Mary R.
Davis, Charlotte D.
Donohue, Joseph C.
Grosch, Audrey N.
Harnsberger, Therese
Heron, David W.
Jones, James V.
Jordan, Robert T.
Kopech, Gertrude
Linford, Arthur J, Jr.
Minker, Dr. Jack
Montgomery, James W.
Orne, Dr. Jerrold
Popecki, Joseph T.
Rateaver, Dr. Bargyla
Ready, William B.
Schafer, Emil
Simon, Bradley A.
Veaner, Allen B.
Voos, Dr. Henry
Woodward, Rupert C.

SPECIALTY INDEX

See also DATA PROCESSING
EQUIPMENT APPLICATIONS,
INFORMATION STORAGE AND
RETRIEVAL SYSTEMS, SYSTEMS ANALYSIS

BOOK COLLECTIONS: SELECTION, EVALUATION, WEEDING

ADULT

Adamovich, Shirley
Alvarez, Dr. Robert S.
Ash, Lee
Bartolini, R. Paul
Bertalan, Dr. Frank J.
Bevis, Leura D.
Bixler, Paul
Boaz, Dr. Martha
Burke, Redmond A, C.S.V.
Bury, Peter P.
Carnovsky, Dr. Leon
Carrison, Dale K.
Castagna, Edwin
Chen, Dr. John H.M.
Chitwood, Jack
Connolly, Brendan, S.J.
Denis, Laurent-G.
Diehl, Katharine S.
Engley, Donald B.
Ertel, Mrs. Margaret P.
Falgione, Joseph F.
Fitzgerald, Dr. William A.
Franklin, Robert D.
Galvin, Thomas J.
Geddes, Andrew
Goldstein, Dr. Harold
Gordon, Bernard L.
Hart, Dr. Eugene D.
Harvey, Dr. John F.
Heilmann, Margaret A.
Hicks, Warren B.
Hill, Laurence G.
Hirsch, Dr. Felix E.
Holley, Dr. Edward G.
Housel, James R.
Humphry, James, III
Humphry, John A.
Jones, Frank N.
Jordan, Robert T.
Kantor, David
Keough, Francis P.
Kinney, Margaret M.
Lancour, Dr. Harold
Lute, Harriet
McCoy, Dr. Ralph E.
Mack, Mrs. Sara R.
McNiff, Philip J.
McPherson, Kenneth F.
Mapp, Edward C.
Martin, Allie B.
Merritt, Dr. LeRoy C.
Metcalf, Dr. Keyes D.
Michniewski, Henry J.
Mills, Jesse C.
Mitchell, Eleanor
Mitchell, Vernon R.
Molod, Samuel E.
Moran, Virginia L.
Morgan, John F.
Morin, Wilfred L.
Nelson Associates, Inc.
Oliner, Stan
Parsons, Mrs. Mary D.
Perry, E. Caswell
Ramirez, William L.
Rateaver, Dr. Bargyla
Reason, Dr. Joseph H.
Reichmann, Dr. Felix
Rescoe, A. Stan
Roth, Harold L.
Rothines Associates
Rush, N. Orwin
St. John, Francis R.
Samore, Theodore
Schmuch, Joseph J.
Schneider, Frank A.
Schutze, Gertrude
Shaw, Thomas S.
Shepard, Mrs. Marietta D.

Simon, Bradley A.
Smith, Mrs. June S.
Stephens, Dr. Irlene R.
Stewart, R.C.
Tanis, Norman E.
Tauber, Dr. Maurice F.
Trinkner, Dr. Charles L.
Troke, Mrs. Margaret K.
Usher, Mrs. Elizabeth R.
VanJackson, Wallace M.
Vormelker, Rose L.
Vreeland, Eleanor P.
Watkins, Mrs. Lillian M.
Wezeman, Frederick
Wheeler, Dr. Joseph L.
Williamson, Dr. William L.
Wilmer, Florence C.
Woodward, Robert C.
Zimmerman, Lee F.

CHILDREN'S

Adamovich, Shirley
Alexander, Esther M.
Anderson, Dorothy J.
Badten, Jean M.
Boaz, Dr. Martha
Buckingham, Betty J.
Chisholm, Dr. Margaret E.
Clark, Rheta A.
Cohen, David
Cole, Doris M.
Cole, Georgia R.
Crawford, Paul R.
Currie, Dorothy H.
Davies, Ruth A.
Davis, Charlotte D.
Dees, Margaret N.
Di Muccio, Sister Mary-Jo
Dunkley, Grace S.
Edwards, Ida M.
Ertel, Mrs. Margaret P.
Fast, Mrs. Elizabeth T.
Field, Mrs. Carolyn W.
Fitzgerald, Mrs. Louise H.
Galfand, Sidney
Gaver, Mary V.
Geddes, Andrew
Gilbert, Christine B.
Goodbread, Juanita W.
Gorski, Lorraine K.M.
Hall, Elvajean
Harding, Nelson F.
Harnsberger, Therese
Harris, Walter H.
Heilmann, Margaret A.
Hild, Alice P.
Hines, Dr. Theodore C.
Holley, Dr. Edward G.
Humphry, John A.
Hurley, Richard J.
Jaffarian, Sara
James, Louise
Johnson, Mrs. Frances K.
Johnson, Leonard L.
Katz, Beatrice
Keough, Francis P.
Lane, Sister M. Claude, O.P.
Lembo, Mrs. Diana L.
Leopold, Mrs. Carolyn C.
Lute, Harriet
Mack, Mrs. Sara R.
McPherson, Kenneth F.
Martin, Allie B.
Merritt, Dr. LeRoy C.
Mitchell, Eleanor
Mitchell, Vernon R.
Molod, Samuel E.
Moran, Virginia L.
Morin, Wilfred L.
Morse, A. Louis
Murphy, Lavinia E.
Nelson Associates, Inc.
Owens, Mrs. Iris
Portteus, Elnora M.
Prideaux, B. Elizabeth
Raley, Mrs. Lucile W.
Rateaver, Dr. Bargyla
Rothines Associates
St. John, Francis R.

Sattley, Helen R.
Simon, Bradley A.
Slocum, Mrs. Betty
Smith, James L.
Smith, Mrs. June S.
Stephens, Dr. Irlene R.
Trinkner, Dr. Charles L.
Vreeland, Eleanor P.
Watkins, Mrs. Lillian M.
Wezeman, Frederick
Whitenack, Carolyn I.
Wiese, M. Bernice
Yesner, Mrs. Bernice L.
Young, Carol
Ziebold, Edna B.

SUBJECT SPECIALISTS (see individual biography)

Aceto, Vincent J.
Adamovich, Shirley
Adams, Scott
Alexander, Esther M.
Anderson, Dorothy J.
Anderson, Frank J.
Andrews, James C.
Ash, Lee
Baer, Dr. Karl A.
Baillie, Dr. Stuart
Ballou, Hubbard W.
Beaton, Mrs. Maxine B.
Beatty, William K.
Berry, John N, III
Bertalan, Dr. Frank J.
Bitner, Harry
Blanchard J. Richard
Blaustein, Albert P.
Bloomquist, Harold
Boaz, Dr. Martha
Bonn, George S.
Brandon, Alfred N.
Brodman, Dr. Estelle
Brown, Alberta L.
Burgess, Robert S.
Burke, Dr. John E.
Burke, Redmond A, C.S.V.
Bury, Peter P.
Butler, Evelyn
Carpenter, Dr. Ray L.
Casellas, Elizabeth R.
Chen, Dr. John H.M.
Chitwood, Jack
Clark, Mrs. Gertrude M.
Cohen, David
Cohen, Morris L.
Coman, Edwin T, Jr.
Connolly, Brendan, S.J.
Crawford, Helen
Crawford, Paul R.
Daily, Dr. Jay E.
Darling, Louise
Daume, Mrs. Mary R.
Davies, Ruth A.
Davis, Charlotte D.
Deahl, Thomas F.
Diehl, Katharine S.
Divett, Dr. Robert T.
Dodd, James B.
Donohue, Joseph C.
Dunlap, Dr. Leslie W.
Ebert, Myrl
Edwards, Ida M.
Engley, Donald B.
Eshelman, William R.
Evans, Richard A.
Farber, Evan I.
Flanders, Frances V.
Fleischman, Al
Friedlander, Dr. Michel O.
Fussler, Dr. Herman H.
Galfand, Sidney
Galvin, Thomas J.
Georgi, Charlotte
Gilbert, Christine B.
Gitler, Dr. Robert L.
Gordon, Bernard L.
Gosnell, Dr. Charles F.
Greer, Dr. Roger C.
Haas, Elaine
Hall, Elvajean

SPECIALTY INDEX

Hamlin, Arthur T.
Harnsberger, Therese
Hellum, Bertha D.
Henderson, Mary J.
Henkle, Dr. Herman H.
Heron, David W.
Hines, Dr. Theodore C.
Hirsch, Dr. Felix E.
Hopp, Dr. Ralph H.
Humphry, James, III
Isley, Doris N.
Jackson, Dr. William V.
Jacobstein, J. Myron
Johnson, Mrs. Barbara C.
Johnson, Leonard L.
Jones, Frank N.
Jones, Harold D.
Josey, E.J.
Kinney, Margaret M.
Kopech, Gertrude
Kurth, William H.
Lane, Sister M. Claude, O.P.
Leondar, Judith C.
Leopold, Mrs. Carolyn C.
Lucker, Jay K.
Lybeck, Pauline
McAdams, Mrs. Nancy R.
McClarren, Robert R.
McGowan, Frank M.
Mack, Mrs. Sara R.
McMullan, Theodore N.
Mapp, Edward C.
Marke, Julius J.
Mason, Dr. Ellsworth
Mersky, Roy M.
Miller, J. Gormly
Mills, Jesse C.
Mitchell, Eleanor
Mitchell, Vernon R.
Montgomery, James W.
Moran, Virginia L.
Moreland, Carroll C.
Morgan, John F.
Moriarty, John H.
Morin, Wilfred L.
Morris, Dr. Raymond P.
Murphy, Lavinia E.
Nelson Associates, Inc.
Oliner, Stan
Oltmen, Florine A.
Orton, Floyd E.
Perreault, Jean M.
Perry, E. Caswell
Pollack, Ervin H.
Portteus, Elnora M.
Raphael, Anne W.
Rateaver, Dr. Bargyla
Reason, Dr. Joseph H.
Redmond, Donald A.
Reichmann, Dr. Felix
Rescoe, A. Stan
Rockwell, Mrs. Jeanette S.
Rosenberg, Kenyon C.
Roth, Harold L.
Rothines Associates
Rowland, Arthur R.
St. John, Francis R.
Samore, Theodore
Sattley, Helen R.
Scarborough, Ruth E.
Schefter, Joseph A.
Schneider, Frank A.
Schutze, Gertrude
Severance, Robert W.
Shank, Dr. Russell
Shaw, Thomas S.
Shepard, Mrs. Marietta D.
Simmons, Joseph M.
Sprug, Joseph W.
Stephens, Dr. Irlene R.
Stern, Dr. William B.
Stewart, R.C.
Surrency, Erwin C.
Technical Library Service
Treyz, Joseph H.
Trinkner, Dr. Charles L.
Usher, Mrs. Elizabeth R.
Vaillancourt, Dr. Pauline M.
VanJackson, Wallace M.
Van Velzer, Verna J.
Voigt, Melvin J.

Voos, Dr. Henry
Vormelker, Rose L.
Wagner, Dr. Robert G.
Wasserman, Dr. Paul
Watkins, Mrs. Lillian M.
Wheeler, Dr. Helen R.
White, Dr. Lucien W.
Williamson, Dr. William L.
Wilmer, Florence C.
Woodward, Robert C.
Woodward, Rupert C.
Yesner, Mrs. Bernice L.
Zimmerman, Lee F.

YOUNG ADULT

Adamovich, Shirley
Alexander, Esther M.
Allen, Loren H.
Anderson, Dorothy J.
Armstrong, Rodney
Badten, Jean M.
Barber, Raymond W.
Berry, June
Boaz, Dr. Martha
Buckingham, Betty J.
Buckley, John
Bury, Peter P.
Carrison, Dale K.
Clark, Rheta A.
Cohen, David
Cole, Doris M.
Cole, Georgia R.
Crawford, Paul R.
Currie, Dorothy H.
Davies, Ruth A.
Davis, Charlotte D.
Dees, Margaret N.
Di Muccio, Sister Mary-Jo
Dunkley, Grace S.
Edwards, Ida M.
Ertel, Mrs. Margaret P.
Fitzgerald, Mrs. Louise H.
Fitzgerald, Dr. William A.
Fleischman, Al
Folcarelli, Ralph J.
Galfand, Sidney
Gaver, Mary V.
Geddes, Andrew
Gilbert, Christine B.
Goodbread, Juanita W.
Gordon, Bernard L.
Gorski, Lorraine K.M.
Harding, Nelson F.
Harnsberger, Therese
Harris, Walter H.
Heilmann, Margaret A.
Hicks, Warren B.
Hild, Alice P.
Holley, Dr. Edward G.
Humphry, John A.
Hurley, Richard J.
Jaffarian, Sara
James, Louise
Johnson, David L.
Johnson, Mrs. Frances K.
Johnson, Leonard L.
Josey, E.J.
Katz, Beatrice
Keough, Francis P.
Kinney, Margaret M.
Lancour, Dr. Harold
Lane, Sister M. Claude, O.P.
Lembo, Mrs. Diana L.
Leopold, Mrs. Carolyn C.
Lindauer, Dinah
Lute, Harriet
McFarland, Kay R.
Mack, Mrs. Sara R.
McNiff, Philip J.
McPherson, Kenneth F.
Mapp, Edward C.
Martin, Allie B.
Merritt, Dr. LeRoy C.
Miller, Mrs. Melissa
Mitchell, Eleanor
Mitchell, Vernon R.
Molod, Samuel E.
Moran, Virginia L.
Morin, Wilfred L.
Morse, A. Louis

Murphy, Lavinia E.
Negro, Antoinette
Nelson Associates, Inc.
Owens, Mrs. Iris
Parsons, Mrs. Mary D.
Portteus, Elnora M.
Prideaux, B. Elizabeth
Raley, Mrs. Lucile W.
Rateaver, Dr. Bargyla
Rothines Associates
St. John, Francis R.
Sattley, Helen R.
Schneider, Frank A.
Shapiro, Mrs. Lillian L.
Simon, Bradley A.
Slocum, Mrs. Betty
Smith, Mrs. June S.
Smith, L. Herman
Stephens, Dr. Irlene R.
Trinkner, Dr. Charles L.
Vreeland, Eleanor P.
Watkins, Mrs. Lillian M.
Wezeman, Frederick
Wheeler, Dr. Helen R.
Whitenack, Carolyn I.
Wiese, M. Bernice
Yesner, Mrs. Bernice L.
Young, Carol

OTHER ASPECTS (see individual biography)

Anderson, Frank J.
Archer, Dr. H. Richard
Ballou, Hubbard W.
Bertalan, Dr. Frank J.
Blasingame, Ralph
Chase, William D.
Clarke, Dr. Robert F.
Danton, Dr. J. Periam
Daume, Mrs. Mary R.
Deahl, Thomas F.
Dix, Dr. William S.
Downs, Robert B.
Farber, Evan I.
Fast, Mrs. Elizabeth T.
Filion, Paul-Emile, S.J.
Galvin, Thomas J.
Gerlach, Dr. Arch C.
Gordon, Bernard L.
Gorski, Lorraine K.M.
Hall, Elvajean
Henkle, Dr. Herman H.
Jackson, Dr. William V.
Jacobstein, J. Myron
Johnson, Mrs. Barbara C.
Johnson, Leonard L.
Jones, Frank N.
Jones, James V.
Kaser, Dr. David
Lyle, Guy R.
McFarland, Kay R.
McKeon, Newton F.
Mapp, Edward C.
Mills, Jesse C.
Nelson, Charles A.
Nesbin, Mrs. Esther W.
Oboler, Eli M.
Pease, William A.
Pullen, Dr. William R.
Rateaver, Dr. Bargyla
Rescoe, A. Stan
Rod, Donald O.
Sheehan, Sister Helen
Shores, Dr. Louis
Simmons, Joseph M.
Simon, Bradley A.
Smith, L. Herman
Stone, Dr. C. Walter
Tauber, Dr. Maurice F.
Treyz, Joseph H.
Wallace, James O.
Wheeler, Dr. Helen R.
Williams, Edwin E.

See also ACQUISITIONS, APPRAISALS OF BOOKS AND COLLECTIONS, RARE BOOKS

Buildings see ARCHITECTURE AND BUILDINGS

SPECIALTY INDEX

CATALOGING

Adamovich, Shirley
Alexander, Esther M.
Andrews, James C.
Ash, Lee
Atherton, Pauline
Badten, Jean M.
Baer, Dr. Karl A.
Beaton, Mrs. Maxine B.
Berrisford, Paul D.
Berul, Lawrence H.
Brinton, Harry
Brown, Alberta L.
Burns, Lorin R.
Carrison, Dale K.
Casellas, Elizabeth R.
Chen, Dr. John H.M.
Clark, Mrs. Gertrude M.
Covey, Dr. Alan D.
Cranford, Theodore N.
Cronin, John W.
Daily, Dr. Jay E.
Dees, Margaret N.
De Young, Julia M.
Dodd, James B.
Edwards, Ida M.
Elrod, J. McRee
Ertel, Mrs. Margaret P.
Fast, Mrs. Elizabeth T.
Fitzgerald, Mrs. Louise H.
Frarey, Carlyle J.
Friedlander, Dr. Michel O.
Galfand, Sidney
Goodbread, Juanita W.
Gormley, Mark M.
Grosch, Audrey N.
Haas, Elaine
Harding, Nelson F.
Harnsberger, Therese
Harris, Walter H.
Heilmann, Margaret A.
Henderson, Mary J.
Henkle, Dr. Herman H.
Herrick, Mary D.
Hild, Alice P.
Hines, Dr. Theodore C.
Hope, Arlene
Humphry, John A.
Jaffarian, Sara
Johnson, Mrs. Barbara C.
Johnson, Leonard L.
Katz, Beatrice
Klempner, Dr. Irving M.
Kopech, Gertrude
Lane, Sister M. Claude, O.P.
Leopold, Mrs. Carolyn C.
Logsdon, Dr. Richard H.
McCarthy, Dr. Stephen A.
Maclachlan, Bruce
Marke, Julius J.
Metcalf, Dr. Keyes D.
Miller, Dr. Robert A.
Minder, Thomas L.
Minker, Dr. Jack
Mitchell, Eleanor
Mitchell, Vernon R.
Moreland, Carroll C.
Morgan, John F.
Morse, A. Louis
Nelson, Charles A.
Orton, Floyd E.
Owens, Mrs. Iris
Perreault, Jean M.
Piternick, George
Portteus, Elnora M.
Raphael, Anne W.
Reichmann, Dr. Felix
Rescoe, A. Stan
Robertson, Billy O.
Rosenberg, Kenyon C.
Rothines Associates
Rowland, Arthur R.
St. John, Francis R.
Samore, Theodore
Schafer, Emil
Schork, Francis W.
Schutze, Gertrude
Simon, Bradley A.
Smith, James L.
Smith, L. Herman

Sprug, Joseph W.
Spyers-Duran, Peter
Stephens, Dr. Irlene R.
Swank, Dr. Raynard C.
Tauber, Dr. Maurice F.
Technical Library Service
Treyz, Joseph H.
Trinkner, Dr. Charles L.
Trotier, Arnold H.
Usher, Mrs. Elizabeth R.
Van Velzer, Verna J.
Voigt, Melvin J.
Voos, Dr. Henry
Vorhies, Eugene
Wagman, Dr. Frederick H.
Watkins, Mrs. Lillian M.
Whitenack, Carolyn I.
Yesner, Mrs. Bernice L.
Young, Carol

SPECIAL ASPECTS & SUBJECTS
(see individual biography)

Adamovich, Shirley
Ballou, Hubbard W.
Buckingham, Betty J.
Clarke, Dr. Robert F.
Cole, Georgia R.
Covey, Dr. Alan D.
Cranford, Theodore N.
Daily, Dr. Jay E.
Dawson, Dr. John M.
Deahl, Thomas F.
De Gennaro, Richard
Elrod, J. McRee
Fast, Mrs. Elizabeth T.
Grosch, Audrey N.
Harnsberger, Therese
Jacobs, Dr. James W.
Jansen, Guenter A.
Johnson, Leonard L.
Jordan, Robert T.
Lembo, Mrs. Diana L.
Miles, Paul M.
Orne, Dr. Jerrold
Orton, Floyd E.
Popecki, Joseph T.
Simon, Bradley A.
Spyers-Duran, Peter
Stephens, Dr. Irlene R.
Tauber, Dr. Maurice F.
Treyz, Joseph H.
Vaillancourt, Dr. Pauline M.
Van Velzer, Verna J.
Voigt, Melvin J.
Voos, Dr. Henry
Yesner, Mrs. Bernice L.

See also CLASSIFICATION SYSTEMS, SYSTEMS ANALYSIS

Children's Collections see BOOK COLLECTIONS: CHILDREN

CLASSIFICATION SYSTEMS

Adamovich, Shirley
Allen, Kenneth S.
Andrews, James C.
Ash, Lee
Atherton, Pauline
Badten, Jean M.
Baer, Dr. Karl A.
Beaton, Mrs. Maxine B.
Brinton, Harry
Brown, Alberta L.
Casellas, Elizabeth R.
Chapin, Dr. Richard E.
Chen, Dr. John H.M.
Clark, Mrs. Gertrude M.
Connolly, Brendan, S.J.
Covey, Dr. Alan D.
Cranford, Theodore N.
Cronin, John W.
Daily, Dr. Jay E.
Dawson, Dr. John M.
Dodd, James B.
Edwards, Ida M.
Elrod, J. McRee
Fast, Mrs. Elizabeth T.
Frarey, Carlyle J.

Friedlander, Dr. Michel O.
Goodbread, Juanita W.
Gorchels, Clarence C.
Gorski, Lorraine K.M.
Haas, Elaine
Harris, Walter H.
Henderson, Mary J.
Henkle, Dr. Herman H.
Herrick, Mary D.
Hild, Alice P.
Hines, Dr. Theodore C.
Holley, Dr. Edward G.
Housel, James R.
Humphry, John A.
Jaffarian, Sara
Johnson, Mrs. Barbara C.
Jordan, Robert T.
Kinney, Margaret M.
Klempner, Dr. Irving M.
Kopech, Gertrude
Lane, Sister M. Claude, O.P.
Leopold, Mrs. Carolyn C.
Logsdon, Dr. Richard H.
Lucker, Jay K.
McCarthy, Dr. Stephen A.
Marke, Julius J.
Minker, Dr. Jack
Mitchell, Eleanor
Mitchell, Vernon R.
Morgan, John F.
Morse, A. Louis
Murray, Thomas B.
Nelson, Charles A.
Owens, Mrs. Iris
Parsons, Mrs. Mary D.
Perreault, Jean M.
Raphael, Anne W.
Reichmann, Dr. Felix
Rescoe, A. Stan
Rosenberg, Kenyon C.
Rothines Associates
Rowland, Arthur R.
St. John, Francis R.
Samore, Theodore
Schaefer, Emil
Schork, Francis W.
Schutze, Gertrude
Simon, Bradley A.
Smith, James L.
Spyers-Duran, Peter
Stephens, Dr. Irlene R.
Swank, Dr. Raynard C.
Tauber, Dr. Maurice F.
Technical Library Service
Treyz, Joseph H.
Trotier, Arnold H.
Usher, Mrs. Elizabeth R.
Van Velzer, Verna J.
Voigt, Melvin J.
Voos, Dr. Henry
Vorhies, Eugene
Wagman, Dr. Frederick H.
Watkins, Mrs. Lillian M.
Wiese, M. Bernice
Yesner, Mrs. Bernice L.

See also CATALOGING, INFORMATION STORAGE AND RETRIEVAL SYSTEMS, SYSTEMS ANALYSIS

DATA PROCESSING EQUIPMENT APPLICATIONS

Allen, Kenneth S.
Anderson, Le Moyne W.
Andrews, James C.
Atherton, Pauline
Bartolini, R. Paul
Berul, Lawrence H.
Bourne, Charles P.
Brahm, Walter T.
Burns, Lorin R.
Chapin, Dr. Richard E.
Chen, Dr. John H.M.
Covey, Dr. Alan D.
Cranford, Theodore N.
Curley, Walter W.
Deahl, Thomas F.
De Gennaro, Richard
Divett, Robert T.

SPECIALTY INDEX

Dodd, James B.
Ellerbrock, Edward J.
Etchison, Annie L.
Friedlander, Dr. Michel O.
Fussler, Dr. Herman H.
Geddes, Andrew
Gorchels, Clarence C.
Grosch, Audrey N.
Haas, Elaine
Harnsberger, Therese
Harvey, Dr. John F.
Healey, James S.
Heiliger, Edward M.
Henderson, Mary J.
Hicks, Warren B.
Hines, Dr. Theodore C.
Humphry, James, III
Jacobs, Dr. James W.
Jansen, Guenter A.
Kemper, Dr. Robert E.
Klempner, Dr. Irving M.
Linford, Arthur John, Jr.
McCoy, Dr. Ralph E.
Marshall & Brown, Inc.
Miller, Mrs. Melissa
Mills, Jesse C.
Minder, Thomas L.
Minker, Dr. Jack
Mitchell, Vernon R.
Mutschler, Herbert F.
Nelson Associates, Inc.
Nelson, Charles A.
Orne, Dr. Jerrold
Parker, Dr. Ralph H.
Perreault, Jean M.
Popecki, Joseph T.
Raphael, Anne W.
Ready, William B.
Robertson, Billy O.
Rosenberg, Kenyon C.
Rothines Associates
St. John, Francis R.
Schafer, Emil
Schork, Francis W.
Schutze, Gertrude
Shank, Dr. Russell
Simon, Bradley A.
Stein, Theodore
Stephens, Dr. Irlene R.
Tauber, Dr. Maurice F.
Technical Library Service
Trinkner, Dr. Charles L.
Voos, Dr. Henry
Vorhies, Eugene

See also AUTOMATION, INFORMATION STORAGE AND RETRIEVAL SYSTEMS, SYSTEMS ANALYSIS

FURNISHINGS FOR LIBRARIES

Aceto, Vincent J.
Allen, James W.
Allen, Kenneth S.
Anderson, Le Moyne W.
Andrews, James C.
Archer, Dr. H. Richard
Armstrong, Rodney
Ash, Lee
Baer, Dr. Karl A.
Bailey, J. Russell
Bartolini, R. Paul
Beach, Cecil P.
Bean, Donald E.
Bennett, Gordon L.
Benson, William E.
Bourne, Philip W.
Brinton, Harry
Brook, John B.
Brown, Alberta L.
Brown, Gerald G.
Bryant, Jack W.
Burke, Dr. John E.
Burke, Redmond A, C.S.V.
Butler, Evelyn
Carlson, William H.
Cavaglieri, Dr. Giorgio
Chen, Dr. John H.M.
Cherry, Scott T.
Chitwood, Jack

Cochran, Jean D.
Coman, Edwin T, Jr.
Coolidge, Coit
Currie, Dorothy H.
Daume, Mrs. Mary R.
Davis, Charlotte D.
Dodd, James B.
Dunn, Dr. Oliver C.
Eastlick, John T.
Eaton, Dr. Andrew J.
Eisner, Joseph
Ellerbrock, Edward J.
Farber, Evan I.
Flanders, Frances V.
Folcarelli, Ralph J.
Galvin, Hoyt R.
Geller, William S.
Gibson, Frank E.
Gorski, Lorraine K.M.
Gosnell, Dr. Charles F.
Grosch, Audrey N.
Haas, Elaine
Hardaway, Elliott
Harnsberger, Therese
Harris, Walter H.
Healey, James S.
Heilmann, Margaret A.
Hellum, Bertha D.
Henington, David M.
Heron, David W.
Hicks, Warren B.
Hild, Alice P.
Hill, Laurence G.
Humphry, James, III
Humphry, John A.
Jansen, Guenter A.
Johnson, Leonard L.
Jones, Wyman
Josey, E.J.
Kantor, David
Keough, Francis P.
Kopech, Gertrude
Kuhlman, Augustus F.
Lane, Sister M. Claude, O.P.
Leathers, James A.
Leggett, Dr. Stanton F.
Leondar, Judith C.
Leopold, Mrs. Carolyn C.
Library Design Associates
McConkey, Thomas W.
McDonald, John P.
McMullan, Theodore N.
McPherson, Kenneth F.
Marshall & Brown, Inc.
Martin, Allie B.
Metcalf, Dr. Keyes D.
Miles, Paul M.
Miller, Mrs. Melissa
Mills, Jesse C.
Mitchell, Eleanor
Mitchell, Vernon R.
Mohrhardt, Charles M.
Morin, Wilfred L.
Mostar, Roman
Murphy, Lavina E.
Murphy, Walter H.
Mutschler, Herbert F.
Nielsen, Andre S.
Nikas, Mary C.
Orne, Dr. Jerrold
Osborne, Fred Y.
Paine, Clarence S.
Perry, E. Caswell
Peterson, Harry N.
Poole, Frazer G.
Popecki, Joseph T.
Portteus, Elnora M.
Proctor, Mrs. Margia W.
Pullen, Dr. William R.
Raley, Mrs. Lucile W.
Rateaver, Dr. Bargyla
Rescoe, A. Stan
Rockwell, Mrs. Jeanette S.
Rod, Donald O.
Rohlf, Robert H.
Rosenberg, Kenyon C.
Roth, Harold L.
Rounds, Gertrude W.
Rovelstad, Howard
Rush, Orwin
St. John, Francis R.

Schell, Harold B.
Schmuch, Joseph J.
Shaffer, Kenneth R.
Shepherd, Giles F, Jr.
Simmons, Joseph M.
Simon, Bradley A.
Smith, Hannis S.
Spyers-Duran, Peter
Stewart, David M.
Surrency, Erwin C.
Tanis, Norman E.
Technical Library Service
Thomas, Henry
Trezza, Alphonse F.
Trinkner, Dr. Charles L.
Troke, Mrs. Margaret K.
Ulveling, Dr. Ralph A.
Usher, Mrs. Elizabeth R.
Van Buren, Martin
VanJackson, Wallace M.
Voight, Edna E.
Wagman, Dr. Frederick H.
Wallis, C. Lamar
Watkins, Mrs. Lillian M.
Wilmer, Florence C.
Yesner, Mrs. Bernice L.
Zimmerman, Lee F.

See also ARCHITECTURE AND BUILDINGS

GOVERNMENT AID PROPOSALS

Aceto, Vincent J.
Adams, Scott
Badten, Jean M.
Baillie, Dr. Stuart
Basche, James R, Jr.
Bertalan, Dr. Frank J.
Blasingame, Ralph
Bloomquist, Harold
Brahm, Walter T.
Brown, Alberta L.
Bryant, Jack W.
Campbell, Henry C.
Castagna, Edwin
Chisholm, Dr. Margaret E.
Chitwood, Jack
Cole, Doris M.
Daume, Mrs. Mary R.
Davis, Charlotte D.
Dees, Margaret N.
Doms, Keith
Duke, William R.
Fast, Mrs. Elizabeth T.
Fitzgerald, Mrs. Louise H.
Folcarelli, Ralph J.
Friedlander, Dr. Michel O.
Galick, Mrs. V. Genevieve
Garrison, Dr. Guy
Geller, William S.
Gibson, Frank E.
Goodbread, Juanita W.
Gordon, Bernard L.
Gosnell, Dr. Charles F.
Harding, Nelson F.
Harnsberger, Therese
Hart, Dr. Eugene D.
Heilmann, Margaret A.
Henderson, John D.
Hicks, Warren B.
Hild, Alice P.
Hines, Dr. Theodore C.
Holt, Raymond M.
Hope, Arlene
Humphry, James, III
Humphry, John A.
Jackson, Dr. William V.
Jaffarian, Sara
Johnson, Mrs. Frances K.
Johnson, Leonard L.
Jones, Harold D.
Kemper, Dr. Robert E.
Kinney, Margaret M.
Klempner, Dr. Irving M.
Lane, Sister M. Claude, O.P.
Lindauer, Dinah
Logsdon, Dr. Richard H.
McConkey, Thomas W.
McDonough, Roger H.
Maclachlan, Bruce

Mersky, Roy M.
Michniewski, Henry J.
Miller, J. Gormly
Molod, Samuel
Morin, Wilfred L.
Morse, A. Louis
Murphy, Lavinia E.
Nelson Associates, Inc.
Nelson, Charles A.
Orne, Dr. Jerrold
Paine, Clarence S.
Palmer, David C.
Prideaux, B. Elizabeth
Raphael, Anne W.
Rescoe, A. Stan
Rochell, Carlton
Rohlf, Robert H.
Rothines Associates
St. John, Francis R.
Schafer, Emil
Schick, Dr. Frank L.
Schneider, Frank A.
Shaffer, Kenneth R.
Shepard, Mrs. Marietta D.
Simon, Bradley A.
Sinclair, Dorothy
Smith, Hannis S.
Smith, Mrs. June S.
Summers, F. William
Trinkner, Dr. Charles L.
Troke, Mrs. Margaret K.
Verschoor, Dr. Irving A.
Vreeland, Eleanor P.
Wallace, Sarah L.
Watkins, Mrs. Lillian M.
Wezeman, Frederick
Whitenack, Carolyn I.
Yesner, Mrs. Bernice L.
Zimmerman, Lee F.

See also LEGISLATIVE PROGRAMS

INFORMATION STORAGE AND RE-
TRIEVAL SYSTEMS

Adams, Scott
Allen, James W.
Allen, Kenneth S.
Allen, Loren H.
Atherton, Pauline
Ballou, Hubbard W.
Berul, Lawrence H.
Bourne, Charles P.
Buckley, John
Burns, Lorin R.
Chen, Dr. John H.M.
Clark, Mrs. Gertrude M.
Cranford, Theodore N.
Daily, Dr. Jay E.
Deahl, Thomas F.
De Gennaro, Richard
Ellerbrock, Edward J.
Etchison, Annie L.
Evans, Richard A.
Friedlander, Dr. Michel O.
Fussler, Dr. Herman H.
Gorchels, Clarence C.
Haas, Elaine
Harnsberger, Therese
Harris, Walter H.
Harvey, Dr. John F.
Hicks, Warren B.
Hines, Dr. Theodore C.
Humphry, James, III
Jacobs, Dr. James W.
Klempner, Dr. Irving M.
Kopech, Gertrude
Leggett, Dr. Stanton
Linford, Arthur J, Jr.
Lucker, Jay K.
Lybeck, Pauline
Marke, Julius J.
Mersky, Roy M.
Miller, Mrs. Melissa
Mills, Jesse C.
Minker, Dr. Jack
Morgan, John F.
Negro, Antoinette
Nelson Associates, Inc.
Nelson, Charles A.
Parker, Dr. Ralph H.

Perreault, Jean M.
Popecki, Joseph T.
Raphael, Anne W.
Rateaver, Dr. Bargyla
Rockwell, Mrs. Jeanette S.
Rosenberg, Kenyon C.
Rothines Associates
St. John, Francis R.
Schafer, Emil
Schutze, Gertrude
Shank, Dr. Russell
Smith, Hannis S.
Stein, Theodore
Stephens, Dr. Irlene R.
Tauber, Dr. Maurice F.
Taylor, Robert S.
Technical Library Service
Voos, Dr. Henry
Vorhies, Eugene

See also AUTOMATION, DATA
PROCESSING EQUIPMENT AP-
PLICATIONS, CATALOGING,
CLASSIFICATION SYSTEMS,
SYSTEMS ANALYSIS

INTERIORS OF LIBRARIES

Aceto, Vincent J.
Allen, James W.
Allen, Kenneth S.
Anderson, Le Moyne W.
Armstrong, Rodney
Ash, Lee
Baer, Dr. Karl A.
Bailey, J. Russell
Bartolini, R. Paul
Beach, Cecil P.
Bean, Donald E.
Beatty, William K.
Bennett, Gordon L.
Benson, William E.
Bourne, Philip W.
Branscomb, Dr. Lewis C, Jr.
Brinton, Harry
Brook, John B.
Brown, Alberta L.
Brown, Gerald G.
Bryant, Jack W.
Burke, Dr. John E.
Burke, Redmond A, C.S.V.
Butler, Evelyn
Cavaglieri, Dr. Giorgio
Chen, Dr. John H.M.
Cherry, Scott T.
Chitwood, Jack
Cochran, Jean D.
Cohen, Aaron
Coman, Edwin T, Jr.
Coolidge, Coit
Covey, Dr. Allan D.
Currie, Dorothy H.
Daume, Mrs. Mary R.
Davis, Charlotte D.
Dodd, James B.
Dunn, Dr. Oliver C.
Eaton, Dr. Andrew J.
Ellerbrock, Edward J.
Engley, Donald B.
Etchison, Annie L.
Falgione, Joseph F.
Farber, Evan I.
Flanders, Frances V.
Folcarelli, Ralph J.
Galvin, Hoyt R.
Geller, William S.
Gibson, Frank E.
Gorski, Lorraine K.M.
Grafton, Connie E.
Haas, Elaine
Haas, Warren J.
Hardaway, Elliott
Harris, Walter H.
Heilmann, Margaret A.
Hellum, Bertha D.
Henderson, John D.
Henington, David M.
Henkle, Dr. Herman H.
Hicks, Warren B.
Hild, Alice P.
Hill, Laurence G.

Humphry, James, III
Humphry, John A.
Jaffarian, Sara
Jansen, Guenter A.
Johnson, Leonard L.
Jones, Frank N.
Jones, Wyman
Kantor, David
Keough, Francis P.
Kopech, Gertrude
Kuhlman, Augustus F.
Lane, Sister M. Claude, O.P.
Leathers, James A.
Leggett, Dr. Stanton F.
Leondar, Judith C.
Library Design Associates
McCoy, Dr. Ralph E.
McDonald, John P.
McMullan, Theodore N.
McNiff, Philip J.
McPherson, Kenneth F.
Marke, Julius J.
Marshall & Brown, Inc.
Martin, Allie B.
Metcalf, Dr. Keyes D.
Miles, Paul M.
Miller, Mrs. Melissa
Mills, Jesse C.
Mitchell, Eleanor
Mitchell, Vernon R.
Morin, Wilfred L.
Mostar, Roman
Murphy, Lavinia E.
Murphy, Walter H.
Mutschler, Herbert F.
Nelson Associates, Inc.
Nielsen, Andre S.
Nikas, Mary C.
Orne, Dr. Jerrold
Paine, Clarence S.
Perry, E. Caswell
Poole, Frazer G.
Popecki, Joseph T.
Proctor, Mrs. Margia W.
Raley, Mrs. Lucile W.
Rateaver, Dr. Bargyla
Rochell, Carlton
Rockwell, Mrs. Jeanette S.
Rod, Donald O.
Rohlf, Robert H.
Rosenberg, Kenyon C.
Roth, Harold L.
Rothines Associates
Rounds, Gertrude W.
Rovelstad, Howard
St. John, Francis R.
Scarborough, Ruth E.
Schmuch, Joseph J.
Shaffer, Kenneth R.
Simon, Bradley A.
Smith, L. Herman
Spyers-Duran, Peter
Stephens, Dr. Irlene R.
Stewart, David M.
Tauber, Dr. Maurice F.
Taylor, Robert S.
Technical Library Service
Thomas, Henry
Trinkner, Dr. Charles L.
Troke, Mrs. Margaret K.
Usher, Mrs. Elizabeth R.
Van Buren, Martin
VanJackson, Wallace M.
Voight, Edna E.
Wagman, Dr. Frederick H.
Wallis, C. Lamar
Watkins, Mrs. Lillian M.
Wilmer, Florence C.
Woodward, Robert C.
Yesner, Mrs. Bernice L.
Zimmerman, Lee F.

See also ARCHITECTURE AND
BUILDINGS

JOB EVALUATION AND DESCRIP-
TION, SALARY RECOMMENDA-
TIONS

Ackerman, Page
Alexander, Esther M.

SPECIALTY INDEX

Allen, Kenneth S.
Anderson, Le Moyne W.
Ash, Lee
Badten, Jean M.
Baer, Dr. Karl A.
Baillie, Dr. Stuart
Beaton, Mrs. Maxine B.
Berry, John N, III
Bertalan, Dr. Frank J.
Boaz, Dr. Martha
Brahm, Walter T.
Branscomb, Dr. Lewis C, Jr.
Brinton, Harry
Brodman, Dr. Estelle
Bryant, Jack W.
Burgess, Robert S.
Bury, Peter P.
Carlson, William H.
Casellas, Elizabeth R.
Chait, William
Chitwood, Jack
Clark, Rheta A.
Cohen, David
Cole, Doris M.
Coman, Edwin T, Jr.
Connolly, Brendan, S.J.
Danton, Dr. J. Periam
Daume, Mrs. Mary R.
Davis, Charlotte D.
De Young, Julia M.
Di Muccio, Sister Mary-Jo
Dodd, James B.
Downs, Robert B.
Eastlick, John T.
Ertel, Mrs. Margaret P.
Eshelman, William R.
Etchison, Annie L.
Falgione, Joseph F.
Fast, Mrs. Elizabeth T.
Fitzgerald, Dr. William A.
Friedlander, Dr. Michel O.
Galick, Mrs. V. Genevieve
Galvin, Thomas J.
Geddes, Andrew
Georgi, Charlotte
Gitler, Dr. Robert L.
Gorchels, Clarence C.
Grafton, Connie E.
Grosch, Audrey N.
Haas, Elaine
Haas, Warren J.
Hamlin, Arthur T.
Harding, Nelson F.
Harnsberger, Therese
Harris, Walter H.
Hart, Dr. Eugene D.
Harvey, Dr. John F.
Heilmann, Margaret A.
Hellum, Bertha D.
Henderson, Mary J.
Henington, David M.
Henkle, Dr. Herman H.
Heron, David W.
Hicks, Warren B.
Humphry, James, III
Humphry, John A.
Jaffarian, Sara
Johnson, Mrs. Barbara C.
Johnson, Leonard L.
Josey, E.J.
Kantor, David
Kemper, Dr. Robert E.
Keough, Francis P.
Kinney, Margaret M.
Kopech, Gertrude
Kuhlman, Augustus F.
Lancour, Dr. Harold
Logsdon, Dr. Richard H.
Lybeck, Pauline
McConkey, Thomas W.
McDiarmid, Dr. Errett W.
McPherson, Kenneth F.
Marke, Julius J.
Mitchell, Eleanor
Molod, Samuel E.
Morse, A. Louis
Muller, Dr. Robert H.
Murphy, Lavinia E.
Murphy, Walter H.
Murray, Thomas B.
Nelson Associates, Inc.

Nelson, Charles A.
Oltman, Florine A.
Owens, Mrs. Iris
Parsons, Mrs. Mary D.
Portteus, Elnora M.
Prideaux, B. Elizabeth
Raley, Mrs. Lucille W.
Redmond, Donald A.
Remley, Ralph D.
Rescoe, A. Stan
Robertson, Billy O.
Rockwell, Mrs. Jeanette S.
Rosenberg, Kenyon C.
St. John, Francis R.
Scarborough, Ruth E.
Schein, Bernard
Schneider, Frank A.
Severance, Robert W.
Shaffer, Kenneth R.
Shank, Dr. Russell
Shapiro, Mrs. Lillian L.
Shepherd, Giles F, Jr.
Simon, Bradley A.
Smith, Mrs. June S.
Spyers-Duran, Peter
Stephens, Dr. Irlene R.
Stewart, David M.
Stoffel, Lester L.
Summers, F. William
Tanis, Norman E.
Tauber, Dr. Maurice F.
Technical Library Service
Trezza, Alphonse F.
Trinkner, Dr. Charles L.
Troke, Mrs. Margaret K.
Usher, Mrs. Elizabeth R.
Van Velzer, Verna J.
Veit, Dr. Fritz
Voos, Dr. Henry
Vorhies, Eugene
Wagman, Dr. Frederick H.
Watkins, Mrs. Lillian M.
Wezeman, Frederick
Whitenack, Carolyn I.
Wight, Dr. Edward A.
Wilmer, Florence C.
Woodward, Robert C.
Yesner, Mrs. Bernice
Zimmerman, Lee F.

See also ADMINISTRATIVE OR-
GANIZATION, PERSONNEL,
RECRUITMENT OF PROFES-
SIONALS AND MANAGEMENT

LEGISLATIVE PROGRAMS, LEGISLA-
TION

Adams, Scott
Alexander, Esther M.
Archer, John H.
Basche, James R, Jr.
Bennett, Gordon L.
Blasingame, Ralph
Brahm, Walter T.
Brown, Alberta L.
Bryant, Jack W.
Campbell, Henry C.
Carlson, William H.
Carpenter, Dr. Ray L.
Castagna, Edwin
Chitwood, Jack
Dees, Margaret N.
Duke, William R.
Engley, Donald B.
Franklin, Robert D.
Galick, Mrs. V. Genevieve
Gibson, Frank E.
Goodbread, Juanita W.
Gosnell, Dr. Charles F.
Grafton, Connie E.
Harnsberger, Therese
Harris, Walter H.
Hellum, Bertha D.
Humphry, James, III
Jackson, Dr. William V.
Jones, Harold D.
Kemper, Dr. Robert E.
Kinney, Margaret M.
Lancour, Dr. Harold
Lane, Sister M. Claude, O.P.

Leathers, James A.
McClarren, Robert R.
McDonough, Roger H.
McElderry, Stanley
McNiff, Philip J.
Marke, Julius J.
Mersky, Roy M.
Miller, J. Gormly
Molod, Samuel E.
Morin, Wilfred L.
Morse, A. Louis
Nelson Associates, Inc.
Nelson, Charles A.
Palmer, David C.
Putnam, Hamilton S.
Raley, Mrs. Lucile W.
Remley, Ralph D.
Rochell, Carlton
Rohlf, Robert H.
St. John, Francis R.
Samore, Theodore
Schick, Dr. Frank L.
Schneider, Frank A.
Shaffer, Kenneth R.
Shapiro, Mrs. Lillian L.
Shepard, Mrs. Marietta D.
Simon, Bradley A.
Smith, Hannis S.
Stephens, Dr. Irlene R.
Summers, F. William
Verschoor, Dr. Irving A.
Vreeland, Eleanor P.
Wezeman, Frederick
Whitenack, Carolyn I.
Woodward, Robert C.
Yesner, Mrs. Bernice L.
Zimmerman, Lee F.

See also GOVERNMENT AID PRO-
POSALS

Library Administration see ADMINIS-
TRATIVE ORGANIZATION

Library Furnishings see FURNISH-
INGS FOR LIBRARIES

Library Interiors see INTERIORS OF
LIBRARIES

Library Services see SERVICES OF
LIBRARIES, SERVICES TO SPE-
CIAL PUBLICS

Location of Libraries see SITES FOR
LIBRARIES

OPINION SURVEYS

Alvarez, Dr. Robert S.
Ash, Lee
Bennett, Gordon L.
Berry, John N, III
Bryant, Jack W.
Burke, Dr. John E.
Bury, Peter P.
Carpenter, Dr. Ray L.
Connolly, Brendan, S.J.
Deahl, Thomas F.
Friedlander, Dr. Michel O.
Gosnell, Dr. Charles F.
Harnsberger, Therese
Hart, Dr. Eugene D.
Housel, James R.
Josey, E.J.
Kemper, Dr. Robert E.
Lancour, Dr. Harold
Logsdon, Dr. Richard H.
McDiarmid, Dr. Errett W.
Mapp, Edward C.
Molod, Samuel E.
Morgan, John F.
Nelson Associates, Inc.
Norton, Alice
Popecki, Joseph T.
Putnam, Hamilton S.
Rice, Cynthia
Richard, St. Clair
Rothines Associates

SPECIALTY INDEX

St. John, Francis R.
Schafer, Emil
Schneider, Frank A.
Simon, Bradley A.
Stephens, Dr. Irlene R.
Trinkner, Dr. Charles L.
Van Velzer, Verna J.
Vreeland, Eleanor P.
Wallace, Sarah L.

See also PUBLIC RELATIONS, SURVEYS

OUT-OF-PRINT BOOK SEARCHES

Allen, Kenneth S.
Anderson, Frank J.
Ash, Lee
Bixler, Paul
Campbell, Henry C.
Eshelman, William R.
Gordon, Bernard L.
Haas, Elaine
Harnsberger, Therese
Holley, Dr. Edward G.
Humphry, James, III
Leopold, Mrs. Carolyn C.
McNiff, Philip J.
Ready, William B.
Richards, James H, Jr.
St. John, Francis R.
Smith, L. Herman
Technical Library Service
Usher, Mrs. Elizabeth R.
Voos, Dr. Henry
Woodward, Rupert C.

See also ACQUISITIONS, APPRAISALS OF BOOKS AND COLLECTIONS, RARE BOOKS

PERSONNEL

SPECIALIZED ASPECTS (see individual biography)

Aceto, Vincent J.
Ackerman, Page
Ash, Lee
Beatty, William K.
Branscomb, Dr. Lewis C, Jr.
Brodman, Dr. Estelle
Bury, Peter P.
Cohen, Morris L.
Daume, Mrs. Mary R.
Donohue, Joseph C.
Fast, Mrs. Elizabeth T.
Gitler, Dr. Robert L.
Goldstein, Dr. Harold
Haas, Elaine
Harnsberger, Therese
Henderson, Mary J.
Jackson, Dr. William V.
Lane, Sister M. Claude, O.P.
McFarland, Kay R.
Negro, Antoinette
Orton, Floyd E.
Rescoe, A. Stan
Shank, Dr. Russell
Shepard, Mrs. Marietta D.
Shores, Dr. Louis
Tauber, Dr. Maurice F.
Technical Library Service
Vaillancourt, Dr. Pauline M.
Van Velzer, Verna J.
Wight, Dr. Edward A.
Yesner, Mrs. Bernice L.

See also ADMINISTRATIVE ORGANIZATION, JOB EVALUATION AND DESCRIPTION, RECRUITMENT OF PROFESSIONALS AND MANAGEMENT

PLANNING: COMMUNITY, STATE AND REGIONAL

CENTRALIZED & COOPERATIVE SYSTEMS

Adams, Scott
Allen, Kenneth S.

Allen, Loren H.
Alvarez, Dr. Robert S.
Anderson, Le Moyne W.
Ash, Lee
Atherton, Pauline
Badten, Jean M.
Basche, James R, Jr.
Beatty, William K.
Berthel, John H.
Berul, Lawrence H.
Blasingame, Ralph
Boaz, Dr. Martha
Brahm, Walter T.
Branscomb, Dr. Lewis C, Jr.
Brinton, Harry
Brown, Alberta L.
Bryant, Jack W.
Buckingham, Betty J.
Campbell, Henry C.
Carlson, William H.
Carpenter, Ray L.
Castagna, Edwin
Chait, William
Chen, Dr. John H.M.
Chitwood, Jack
Cohen, Aaron
Cole, Georgia R.
Cole, Mary E.
Coolidge, Coit
Daume, Mrs. Mary R.
Dees, Margaret N.
De Young, Julia M.
Divett, Robert T.
Dodd, James B.
Downs, Robert B.
Duke, William R.
Eastlick, John T.
Eisner, Joseph
Engley, Donald B.
Falgione, Joseph F.
Fitzgerald, Dr. William A.
Folcarelli, Ralph J.
Galick, Mrs. V. Genevieve
Garrison, Dr. Guy
Geddes, Andrew
Geller, William S.
Georgi, Charlotte
Gibson, Frank E.
Goldstein, Dr. Harold
Gosnell, Dr. Charles F.
Grafton, Connie E.
Greer, Dr. Roger C.
Haas, Warren J.
Hamlin, Arthur T.
Harnsberger, Therese
Harris, Walter H.
Hart, Dr. Eugene D.
Healey, James S.
Hellum, Bertha D.
Henington, David M.
Heron, David W.
Hicks, Warren B.
Hild, Alice P.
Hill, Laurence G.
Hines, Dr. Theodore C.
Holt, Raymond M.
Hope, Arlene
Housel, James R.
Humphry, James, III
Humphry, John A.
Jackson, Dr. William V.
Jacobs, Dr. James W.
Jaffarian, Sara
Johnson, Mrs. Barbara C.
Johnson, David L.
Johnson, Leonard L.
Jordan, Robert T.
Kaser, Dr. David
Kemper, Dr. Robert E.
Keough, Francis P.
Kurth, William H.
Lancour, Dr. Harold
Leathers, James A.
Lute, Harriet
McClarren, Robert R.
McDaniel, Roderick D.
McDiarmid, Dr. Errett W.
McElderry, Stanley
Maclachlan, Bruce
McNiff, Philip J.
Martin, Allie B.

Metcalf, Dr. Keyes D.
Michniewski, Henry J.
Miller, J. Gormly
Miller, Mrs. Melissa
Mills, Jesse C.
Minder, Thomas L.
Molod, Samuel E.
Morin, Wilfred L.
Nelson Associates, Inc.
Nelson, Charles A.
Oliner, Stan
Orne, Dr. Jerrold
Palmer, David C.
Parker, Wyman W.
Popecki, Joseph T.
Prideaux, B. Elizabeth
Raley, Mrs. Lucile W.
Raphael, Anne W.
Ready, William B.
Reichmann, Dr. Felix
Remley, Ralph D.
Rice, Cynthia
Richards, James H, Jr.
Rochell, Carlton
Rohlf, Robert H.
Rothines Associates
St. John, Francis R.
Samore, Theodore
Schafer, Emil
Schneider, Frank A.
Shaffer, Kenneth R.
Shank, Dr. Russell
Shepard, Mrs. Marietta D.
Shepherd, Giles F, Jr.
Simon, Bradley A.
Sinclair, Dorothy
Smith, Hannis S.
Stephens, Dr. Irlene R.
Stewart, David M.
Stoffel, Lester L.
Summers, F. William
Swank, Dr. Raynard C.
Tauber, Dr. Maurice F.
Taylor, Robert S.
Trinkner, Dr. Charles L.
Troke, Mrs. Margaret K.
Verschoor, Dr. Irving A.
Vorhies, Eugene
Wallis, C. Lamar
Watkins, Mrs. Lillian M.
Wezeman, Frederick
Wheeler, Dr. Helen R.
Whitenack, Carolyn I.
Wight, Dr. Edward A.
Wilmer, Florence C.
Yesner, Mrs. Bernice L.
Zimmerman, Lee F.

SPECIALIZED ASPECTS (see individual biography)

Adams, Scott
Bloomquist, Harold
Carpenter, Dr. Ray L.
Daume, Mrs. Mary R.
Fast, Mrs. Elizabeth T.
Isley, Doris N.
Katz, Beatrice
Mersky, Roy M.
Moran, Virginia L.
Rateaver, Dr. Bargyla
Rescoe, A. Stan
Treyz, Joseph H.
Vaillancourt, Dr. Pauline M.
Zimmerman, Lee F.

See also ADMINISTRATIVE ORGANIZATION, PROGRAM EVALUATIONS, SURVEYS, SYSTEMS ANALYSIS

PROGRAM EVALUATIONS

Adams, Scott
Alexander, Esther M.
Allen, James W.
Allen, Kenneth S.
Allen, Loren H.
Alvarez, Dr. Robert S.
Anderson, Le Moyne W.

SPECIALTY INDEX

Archer, John H.
Armstrong, Rodney
Ash, Lee
Atherton, Pauline
Badten, Jean M.
Baer, Dr. Karl A.
Baillie, Dr. Stuart
Barber, Raymond W.
Basche, James R, Jr.
Beach, Cecil P.
Beaton, Mrs. Maxine B.
Beatty, William K.
Bennett, Gordon L.
Berninghausen, David K.
Bertalan, Dr. Frank J.
Berthel, John H.
Bevis, Leura D.
Bitner, Harry
Blasingame, Ralph
Boaz, Dr. Martha
Brahm, Walter T.
Brandon, Alfred N.
Branscomb, Dr. Lewis C, Jr.
Brinton, Harry
Brodman, Dr. Estelle
Bryant, Jack W.
Buckingham, Betty J.
Burke, Dr. John E.
Bury, Peter P.
Carlson, William H.
Carnovsky, Dr. Leon
Carrison, Dale K.
Castagna, Edwin
Chait, William
Chapin, Dr. Richard E.
Chen, Dr. John H.M.
Chitwood, Jack
Clark, Rheta A.
Clarke, Dr. Robert F.
Cochran, Jean D.
Cohen, Aaron
Cohen, David
Cole, Doris M.
Cole, Georgia R.
Cole, Mary E.
Coman, Edwin T, Jr.
Connolly, Brendan, S.J.
Danton, Dr. J. Periam
Darling, Louise
Daume, Mrs. Mary R.
Davies, Ruth A.
Davis, Charlotte D.
Dees, Margaret N.
Denis, Laurent-G.
De Young, Julia M.
Divett, Robert T.
Dix, Dr. William S.
Dodd, James B.
Doms, Keith
Donohue, Joseph C.
Downs, Robert B.
Duke, William R.
Dunlap, Dr. Leslie W.
Eastlick, John T.
Eaton, Dr. Andrew J.
Ebert, Myrl
Edwards, Ida M.
Eisner, Joseph
Engley, Donald B.
Evans, Richard A.
Farber, Evan I.
Fast, Mrs. Elizabeth T.
Fitzgerald, Mrs. Louise H.
Fitzgerald, Dr. William A.
Fleischman, Al
Folcarelli, Ralph J.
Franklin, Robert D.
Friedlander, Dr. Michel O.
Galick, Mrs. V. Genevieve
Galvin, Thomas J.
Gaver, Mary V.
Geddes, Andrew
Gelfand, Dr. Morris A.
Georgi, Charlotte
Gibson, Frank E.
Gilbert, Christine B.
Goldstein, Dr. Harold
Goodbread, Juanita W.
Gorchels, Clarence C.
Gormley, Mark M.
Gosnell, Dr. Charles F.

Greer, Dr. Roger C.
Haas, Elaine
Hamlin, Arthur T.
Harding, Nelson F.
Harlow, Neal
Harnsberger, Therèse
Harris, Walter H.
Hart, Dr. Eugene D.
Healey, James S.
Heilmann, Margaret A.
Hellum, Bertha D.
Henderson, John D.
Henderson, Mary J.
Henington, David M.
Henkle, Dr. Herman H.
Heron, David W.
Hiatt, Dr. Peter
Hicks, Warren B.
Hild, Alice P.
Hill, Laurence G.
Hines, Dr. Theodore C.
Hintz, Dr. Carl W.
Holt, Raymond M.
Hope, Arlene
Hopp, Dr. Ralph H.
Housel, James R.
Humphry, James, III
Humphry, John A.
Jacobs, Dr. James W.
Jaffarian, Sara
James, Louise
Jesse, William H.
Johnson, Mrs. Barbara C.
Johnson, David L.
Johnson, Leonard L.
Jones, Frank N.
Jones, James V.
Josey, E.J.
Kantor, David
Kaser, Dr. David
Katz, Beatrice
Kemper, Dr. Robert E.
Keough, Francis P.
Kinney, Margaret M.
Klempner, Dr. Irving M.
Kopech, Gertrude
Kuhlman, Augustus F.
Kurth, William H.
Lancour, Dr. Harold
Lane, Sister M. Claude, O.P.
Lee, Dr. Robert E.
Lembo, Mrs. Diana L.
Leondar, Judith C.
Logsdon, Dr. Richard H.
Lucker, Jay K.
Lybeck, Pauline
Lyle, Guy R.
McCarthy, Dr. Stephen A.
McClarran, Robert R.
McConkey, Thomas W.
McDaniel, Roderick D.
McDiarmid, Dr. Errett W.
McDonough, Roger H.
McFarland, Kay R.
Mack, Mrs. Sara R.
Maclachlan, Bruce
McPherson, Kenneth F.
Mapp, Edward C.
Marke, Julius J.
Marshall & Brown, Inc.
Martin, Allie B.
Metcalf, Dr. Keyes D.
Michniewski, Henry J.
Miller, J. Gormly
Miller, Mrs. Melissa
Mills, Jesse C.
Minder, Thomas L.
Mitchell, Eleanor
Mitchell, Vernon R.
Molod, Samuel E.
Moreland, Carroll C.
Morgan, John F.
Moriarty, John H.
Morin, Wilfred L.
Morse, A. Louis
Muller, Dr. Robert H.
Murphy, Lavinia E.
Murphy, Walter H.
Negro, Antoinette
Nelson Associates, Inc.
Nelson, Charles A.

Nesbin, Mrs. Esther W.
Oboler, Eli M.
Oltman, Florine A.
Orne, Dr. Jerrold
Owens, Mrs. Iris
Paine, Clarence S.
Palmer, David C.
Parsons, Mrs. Mary D.
Peterson, Harry N.
Popecki, Joseph T.
Prideaux, B. Elizabeth
Putnam, Hamilton S.
Raley, Mrs. Lucile W.
Ramirez, William L.
Rateaver, Dr. Bargyla
Reason, Dr. Joseph H.
Rescoe, A. Stan
Rice, Cynthia
Robertson, Billy O.
Rochell, Carlton
Rockwell, Mrs. Jeanette S.
Rod, Donald O.
Rohlf, Robert H.
Roth, Harold L.
Rothines Associates
St. John, Francis R.
Scarborough, Ruth E.
Schafer, Emil
Schein, Bernard
Schick, Dr. Frank L.
Schmuch, Joseph J.
Schneider, Frank A.
Schork, Francis W.
Schultz, Gertrude
Shaffer, Kenneth R.
Shapiro, Mrs. Lillian L.
Sheehan, Sister Helen
Shepherd, Giles F, Jr.
Shores, Dr. Louis
Simon, Bradley A.
Sinclair, Dorothy
Smith, James L.
Smith, Mrs. June S.
Smith, L. Herman
Stephens, Dr. Irlene R.
Stevens, Nicholas G.
Stewart, David M.
Stoffel, Lester L.
Stone, Dr. C. Walter
Summers, F. William
Swank, Dr. Raynard C.
Tauber, Dr. Maurice F.
Technical Library Service
Thompson, Donald E.
Trinkner, Dr. Charles L.
Troke, Mrs. Margaret K.
Usher, Mrs. Elizabeth R.
VanJackson, Wallace M.
Van Velzer, Verna J.
Veit, Dr. Fritz
Voos, Dr. Henry
Vorhies, Eugene
Wagman, Dr. Frederick H.
Wagner, Dr. Robert G.
Wallace, James O.
Wasserman, Dr. Paul
Watkins, Mrs. Lillian M.
Wezeman, Frederick
Wheeler, Dr. Helen R.
Wheeler, Dr. Joseph L.
Whitenack, Carolyn I.
Wiese, M. Bernice
Wight, Dr. Edward A.
Williamson, Dr. William L.
Wilmer, Florence C.
Woodward, Robert C.
Yesner, Mrs. Bernice L.
Ziebold, Edna B.
Zimmerman, Lee F.

See also PLANNING, SERVICES OF LIBRARIES, SERVICES TO SPECIAL PUBLICS, SURVEYS

PUBLIC RELATIONS

SPECIALIZED ASPECTS (see individual biography)

Alexander, Esther M.
Allen, Kenneth S.

SPECIALTY INDEX

Archer, Dr. H. Richard
Ash, Lee
Berry, John N, III
Daume, Mrs. Mary R.
Fitzgerald, Mrs. Louise H.
Franklin, Robert D.
Goldstein, Dr. Harold
Gordon, Bernard L.
Harnsberger, Therese
Hellum, Bertha D.
Jones, Frank N.
Lane, Sister M. Claude, O.P.
McFarland, Kay R.
Murphy, Lavinia E.
Norton, Alice
Oliner, Stan
Putnam, Hamilton S.
Rateaver, Dr. Bargyla
Richard, St. Clair
Schutze, Gertrude
Stewart, David M.
Technical Library Service
Troke, Mrs. Margaret K.
Vormelker, Rose L.
Wallace, Sarah L.
Wheeler, Dr. Joseph L.
Yesner, Mrs. Bernice L.
Zimmerman, Lee F.

See also OPINION SURVEYS, PUBLICATIONS, PUBLICITY PROGRAMS, SURVEYS

PUBLICATIONS

Allen, James W.
Anderson, Dorothy J.
Anderson, Frank J.
Archer, Dr. H. Richard
Ash, Lee
Beaton, Mrs. Maxine B.
Bennett, Gordon L.
Berry, John N, III
Berry, June
Bevis, Leura D.
Bloomquist, Harold
Brahm, Walter T.
Bryant, Jack W.
Burke, Dr. John E.
Castagna, Edwin
Clarke, Dr. Robert F.
Deale, Henry V.
De Young, Julia M.
Dodd, James B.
Donohue, Joseph C.
Eshelman, William R.
Fitzgerald, Mrs. Louise H.
Friedlander, Dr. Michel O.
Georgi, Charlotte
Gitler, Dr. Robert L.
Goldstein, Dr. Harold
Gosnell, Dr. Charles F.
Grosch, Audrey N.
Harnsberger, Therese
Harris, Walter H.
Hart, Dr. Eugene D.
Harvey, Dr. John F.
Heilmann, Margaret A.
Henington, David M.
Heron, David W.
Humphry, James, III
Kemper, Dr. Robert E.
Lancour, Dr. Harold
Lane, Sister M. Claude, O.P.
Logsdon, Dr. Richard H.
McDiarmid, Dr. Errett W.
Mapp, Edward C.
Marke, Julius J.
Miller, Mrs. Melissa
Mills, Jesse C.
Molod, Samuel E.
Morgan, John F.
Morin, Wilfred L.
Morse, A. Louis
Norton, Alice
Oboler, Eli M.
Oliner, Stan
Paine, Clarence S.
Portteus, Elnora M.
Prideaux, B. Elizabeth
Putnam, Hamilton S.

Raley, Mrs. Lucile W.
Ready, William B.
Richard, St. Clair
Rosenberg, Kenyon C.
Roth, Harold L.
Rothines Associates
St. John, Francis R.
Schneider, Frank A.
Schutze, Gertrude
Shores, Dr. Louis
Simmons, Marion L.
Simon, Bradley A.
Simon, Fannie
Stephens, Dr. Irlene R.
Tanis, Norman E.
Tauber, Dr. Maurice F.
Trinkner, Dr. Charles L.
Van Velzer, Verna J.
Vreeland, Eleanor P.
Wallace, Sarah L.
Watkins, Mrs. Lillian M.
Wezeman, Frederick
Yesner, Mrs. Bernice L.
Zimmerman, Lee F.

See also OPINION SURVEYS, PUBLICITY PROGRAMS, PUBLIC RELATIONS, SURVEYS

PUBLICITY PROGRAMS

Anderson, Dorothy J.
Anderson, Frank J.
Ash, Lee
Bennett, Gordon L.
Berry, John N, III
Bevis, Leura D.
Boaz, Dr. Martha
Bryant, Jack W.
Bury, Peter P.
Chen, Dr. John H.M.
Clarke, Dr. Robert F.
Cohen, David
Cole, Doris M.
Dodd, James B.
Donohue, Joseph C.
Fast, Mrs. Elizabeth T.
Fitzgerald, Mrs. Louise H.
Goldstein, Dr. Harold
Goodbread, Juanita W.
Gosnell, Dr. Charles F.
Harding, Nelson F.
Harnsberger, Therese
Harris, Walter H.
Hart, Dr. Eugene D.
Harvey, Dr. John F.
Henington, David M.
Housel, James R.
Jones, Frank N.
Kemper, Dr. Robert E.
Lancour, Dr. Harold
Logsdon, Dr. Richard H.
Lybeck, Pauline
McDiarmid, Dr. Errett W.
McFarland, Kay R.
Mapp, Edward C.
Mills, Jesse C.
Molod, Samuel E.
Moran, Virginia L.
Morse, A. Louis
Murphy, Lavinia E.
Norton, Alice
Oltman, Florine A.
Paine, Clarence S.
Portteus, Elnora M.
Putnam, Hamilton S.
Raley, Mrs. Lucile W.
Rateaver, Dr. Bargyla
Richard, St. Clair
Robertson, Billy O.
Rosenberg, Kenyon C.
Roth, Harold L.
Rothines Associates
St. John, Francis R.
Schmuch, Joseph J.
Simmons, Joseph M.
Simmons, Marion L.
Simon, Bradley A.
Stewart, David M.
Tauber, Dr. Maurice F.
Vreeland, Eleanor P.

Wallace, Sarah L.
Wezeman, Frederick
Wheeler, Dr. Joseph L.
Yesner, Mrs. Bernice L.
Zimmerman, Lee F.

See also OPINION SURVEYS, PUBLIC RELATIONS, PUBLICATIONS, SURVEYS

RARE BOOKS

Archer, Dr. H. Richard
Ash, Lee
Bartolini, R. Paul
Beatty, William K.
Bevis, Leura D.
Burke, Redmond A, C.S.V.
Crawford, Helen
Diehl, Katharine S.
Georgi, Charlotte
Gordon, Bernard L.
Gosnell, Dr. Charles F.
Henkle, Dr. Herman H.
Holley, Dr. Edward G.
Kinney, Margaret M.
Lane, Sister M. Claude, O.P.
Leopold, Mrs. Carolyn C.
McCoy, Dr. Ralph E.
McMullan, Theodore N.
McNiff, Philip J.
Mersky, Roy M.
Mills, Jesse C.
Parker, Wyman W.
Rateaver, Dr. Bargyla
Reichmann, Dr. Felix
Rescoe, A. Stan
St. John, Francis R.
Samore, Theodore
Stewart, R.C.
Thompson, Dr. Lawrence S.

See also ACQUISITIONS, APPRAISALS OF BOOKS AND COLLECTIONS, BOOK COLLECTIONS, OUT-OF-PRINT BOOK SEARCHES

RECRUITMENT OF PROFESSIONALS AND MANAGEMENT

Aceto, Vincent J.
Ackerman, Page
Allen, Kenneth S.
Anderson, Dorothy J.
Anderson, Frank J.
Anderson, Le Moyne W.
Ash, Lee
Asheim, Dr. Lester
Badten, Jean M.
Baer, Dr. Karl A.
Baillie, Dr. Stuart
Berry, John N, III
Bertalan, Dr. Frank J.
Bevis, Leura D.
Boaz, Dr. Martha
Brahm, Walter T.
Branscomb, Dr. Lewis C, Jr.
Bryant, Jack W.
Burgess, Robert S.
Bury, Peter P.
Carlson, William H.
Chait, William
Cohen, David
Covey, Dr. Alan D.
Danton, Dr. J. Periam
Davis, Charlotte D.
Deahl, Thomas F.
Dees, Margaret N.
Dodd, James B.
Dunlap, Dr. Leslie W.
Eastlick, John T.
Ebert, Myrl
Eshelman, William R.
Etchison, Annie L.
Fast, Mrs. Elizabeth T.
Fitzgerald, Dr. William A.
Friedlander, Dr. Michel O.
Galick, Mrs. V. Genevieve
Geddes, Andrew
Goodbread, Juanita W.
Gorchels, Clarence C.

SPECIALTY INDEX

Grosch, Audrey N.
Haas, Elaine
Hamlin, Arthur T.
Harding, Nelson F.
Harnsberger, Therese
Harris, Walter H.
Harvey, Dr. John F.
Heilmann, Margaret A.
Henkle, Dr. Herman H.
Heron, David W.
Hicks, Warren B.
Hild, Alice P.
Humphry, James, III
Humphry, John A.
Hunt, Donald H.
Johnson, Leonard L.
Kemper, Dr. Robert E.
Lancour, Dr. Harold
Logsdon, Dr. Richard H.
Lybeck, Pauline
McDiarmid, Dr. Errett W.
Marke, Julius J.
Miller, Mrs. Melissa
Mitchell, Eleanor
Molod, Samuel E.
Morin, Wilfred L.
Muller, Dr. Robert H.
Murphy, Lavinia E.
Negro, Antoinette
Nelson Associates, Inc.
Oltman, Florine A.
Portteus, Elnora M.
Raley, Mrs. Lucile W.
Robertson, Billy O.
Rockwell, Mrs. Jeanette S.
Rosenberg, Kenyon C.
St. John, Francis R.
Schein, Bernard
Schneider, Frank A.
Severance, Robert W.
Shank, Dr. Russell
Shepherd, Giles F, Jr.
Simmons, Joseph M.
Simmons, Marion L.
Smith, Mrs. June S.
Spyers-Duran, Peter
Stoffel, Lester L.
Summers, F. William
Tanis, Norman E.
Tauber, Dr. Maurice F.
Technical Library Service
Trinkner, Dr. Charles L.
Troke, Mrs. Margaret K.
Usher, Mrs. Elizabeth R.
Van Velzer, Verna J.
Veit, Dr. Fritz
Vorhies, Eugēne
Vreeland, Eleanor P.
Wasserman, Dr. Paul
Watkins, Mrs. Lillian M.
Wezeman, Frederick
Wheeler, Dr. Helen R.
Wilmer, Florence C.
Yesner, Mrs. Bernice L.
Zimmerman, Lee F.

See also ADMINISTRATIVE ORGANIZATION, JOB EVALUATION AND DESCRIPTION, PERSONNEL

SERVICES OF LIBRARIES

SPECIALIZED SERVICES (see individual biography)

Ash, Lee
Bonn, George S.
Brodman, Dr. Estelle
Bury, Peter P.
Daume, Mrs. Mary R.
Dees, Margaret N.
Dodd, James B.
Donohue, Joseph C.
Dunn, Dr. Oliver C.
Galvin, Thomas J.
Geller, William S.
Gitler, Dr. Robert L.
Harnsberger, Therese
Henderson, Mary J.
Henkle, Dr. Herman H.

Hiatt, Dr. Peter
Hurley, Richard J.
Jesse, William H.
Kantor, David
Lane, Sister M. Claude, O.P.
Lee, Dr. Robert E.
Leondar, Judith C.
Lindauer, Dinah
McFarland, Kay R.
Miller, J. Gormly
Mitchell, Vernon R.
Montgomery, James W.
Moriarty, John H.
Negro, Antoinette
Orne, Dr. Jerrold
Prideaux, B. Elizabeth
Rescoe, A. Stan
Rochell, Carlton
Schutze, Gertrude
Shores, Dr. Louis
Simon, Bradley A.
Stone, Dr. C. Walter
Taylor, Robert S.
Vaillancourt, Dr. Pauline M.
Wheeler, Dr. Helen R.
Wheeler, Dr. Joseph L.

See also PROGRAM EVALUATIONS, SERVICES TO SPECIAL PUBLICS

SERVICES TO SPECIAL PUBLICS: HANDICAPPED, STUDENTS, AGED

Aceto, Vincent J.
Alexander, Esther M.
Allen, Kenneth S.
Armstrong, Rodney
Ash, Lee
Atherton, Pauline
Badten, Jean M.
Beatty, William K.
Berry, June
Bertalan, Dr. Frank J.
Bonn, George S.
Buckingham, Betty J.
Chen, Dr. John H.M.
Chisholm, Dr. Margaret E.
Clarke, Dr. Robert F.
Cole, Doris M.
Connolly, Brendan, S.J.
Daume, Mrs. Mary R.
Davis, Charlotte D.
Duke, William R.
Engley, Donald B.
Fast, Mrs. Elizabeth T.
Fitzgerald, Mrs. Louise H.
Galick, Mrs. V. Genevieve
Galvin, Thomas J.
Gaver, Mary V.
Gibson, Frank E.
Gilbert, Christine B.
Graham, Mae
Hall, Elvajean
Hamlin, Arthur T.
Harnsberger, Therese
Harris, Walter H.
Heron, David W.
Hiatt, Dr. Peter
Hild, Alice P.
Hintz, Dr. Carl W.
Hirsch, Dr. Felix E.
Humphry, John A.
Jaffarian, Sara
Johnson, Mrs. Barbara C.
Johnson, Mrs. Frances K.
Johnson, Leonard L.
Josey, E.J.
Kantor, David
Kemper, Dr. Robert E.
Kinney, Margaret M.
Kuhlman, Augustus F.
Lee, Dr. Robert E.
Lembo, Mrs. Diana L.
Lindhauer, Dinah
Logsdon, Dr. Richard H.
Lucker, Jay K.
Lybeck, Pauline
McCarthy, Dr. Stephen A.
McClarren, Robert R.
McDiarmid, Errett W.

McDonough, Roger H.
Maclachlan, Bruce
Michniewski, Henry J.
Miller, J. Gormly
Miller, Mrs. Melissa
Mitchell, Eleanor
Molod, Samuel E.
Moreland, Carroll C.
Morin, Wilfred L.
Morse, A. Louis
Negro, Antoinette
Nelson Associates, Inc
Nelson, Charles A.
Paine, Clarence S.
Palmer, David C.
Parsons, Mrs. Mary D.
Prideaux, B. Elizabeth
Putnam, Hamilton S.
Raley, Mrs. Lucile W.
Ramirez, William L.
Rateaver, Dr. Bargyla
Roth, Harold Leo
Rothines Associates
St. John, Francis R.
Sattley, Helen R.
Schafer, Emil
Schein, Bernard
Schork, Francis W.
Shaffer, Kenneth R.
Shank, Dr. Russell
Shepherd, Giles F, Jr.
Smith, Mrs. June S.
Stevens, Nicholas G.
Summers, F. William
Swank, Dr. Raynard C.
Tauber, Dr. Maurice F.
Trinkner, Dr. Charles L.
Usher, Mrs. Elizabeth R.
Wagman, Dr. Frederick H.
Wagner, Dr. Robert G.
Watkins, Mrs. Lillian M.
Wezeman, Frederick
Wiese, M. Bernice
Wight, Dr. Edward A.
Ziebold, Edna B.
Zimmerman, Lee F.

See also PROGRAM EVALUATIONS, SERVICES OF LIBRARIES

SITES FOR LIBRARIES

Allen, Kenneth S.
Alvarez, Dr. Robert S.
Anderson, Le Moyne W.
Ash, Lee
Baer, Dr. Karl A.
Bailey, J. Russell
Baillie, Dr. Stuart
Banister, John R.
Bartolini, R. Paul
Beach, Cecil P.
Bean, Donald E.
Bennett, Gordon L.
Berthel, John H.
Bourne, Philip W.
Brahm, Walter T.
Branscomb, Dr. Lewis C, Jr.
Brinton, Harry
Brown, Alberta L.
Bryan, Dr. James E.
Bryant, Jack W.
Burke, Dr. John E.
Burns, Lorin R.
Bury, Peter P.
Butler, Evelyn
Carlson, William H.
Castagna, Edwin
Cavaglieri, Dr. Giorgio
Chait, William
Chen, Dr. John H.M.
Chitwood, Jack
Cochran, Jean D.
Cohen, Aaron
Coman, Edwin T, Jr.
Connolly, Brendan, S.J.
Coolidge, Coit
Covey, Dr. Alan D.
Danton, Dr. J. Periam
Daume, Mrs. Mary R.

Davis, Charlotte D.
Dawson, Dr. John M.
Dodd, James B.
Doms, Keith
Eastlick, John T.
Eaton, Dr. Andrew J.
Eisner, Joseph
Engley, Donald B.
Falgione, Joseph F.
Franklin, Robert D.
Galvin, Hoyt R.
Garrison, Dr. Guy
Geddes, Andrew
Geller, William S.
Gibson, Frank E.
Goldstein, Dr. Harold
Gosnell, Dr. Charles F.
Grafton, Connie E.
Grosch, Audrey N.
Hardaway, Elliott
Harris, Walter H.
Hart, Dr. Eugene D.
Healey, James S.
Hellum, Bertha D.
Henderson, John D.
Henington, David M.
Henkle, Dr. Herman H.
Heron, David W.
Hill, Laurence G.
Holt, Raymond M.
Hope, Arlene
Humphry, James, III
Humphry, John A.
Jansen, Guenter A.
Jesse, William H.
Jones, Wyman
Josey, E.J.
Kantor, David
Keough, Francis P.
Lancour, Dr. Harold
Leathers, James A.
Library Design Associates
McAdams, Mrs. Nancy R.
McCarthy, Dr. Stephen A.
McClarren, Robert R.
McConkey, Thomas W.
McDonough, Roger H.
McNeal, Dr. Archie L.
McNiff, Philip J.
McPherson, Kenneth F.
Marshall & Brown, Inc.
Martin, Allie B.
Metcalf, Dr. Keyes D.
Michniewski, Henry J.
Miles, Paul M.
Miller, Ernest I.
Mills, Jesse C.
Mitchell, Eleanor
Mohrhardt, Charles M.
Morgan, John F.
Morin, Wilfred L.
Mostar, Roman
Muller, Dr. Robert H.
Munn, R. Russell
Murphy, Walter H.
Mutschler, Herbert F.
Nelson Associates, Inc.
Nielsen, Andre S.
Orne, Dr. Jerrold
Paine, Clarence S.
Perry, E. Caswell
Peterson, Harry N.
Poole, Frazer G.
Proctor, Mrs. Margia W.
Rochell, Carlton
Rod, Donald O.
Rohlf, Robert H.
Roth, Harold L.
Rothines Associates
Rovelstad, Howard
Rush, N. Orwin
St. John, Francis R.
Schell, Harold B.
Schmuch, Joseph J.
Shaffer, Kenneth R.
Shepherd, Giles F, Jr.
Simon, Bradley A.
Smith, Hannis S.
Spyers-Duran, Peter
Stephens, Dr. Irlene R.
Stevens, Nicholas G.

Stewart, David M.
Stoffel, Lester L.
Tanis, Norman E.
Tauber, Dr. Maurice F.
Thomas, Henry
Thompson, Donald E.
Trezza, Alphonse F.
Trinkner, Dr. Charles L.
Troke, Mrs. Margaret K.
Ulveling, Dr. Ralph A.
Usher, Mrs. Elizabeth R.
Van Buren, Martin
Wagman, Dr. Frederick H.
Wallis, C. Lamar
Watkins, Mrs. Lillian M.
Wezeman, Frederick
Wheeler, Dr. Joseph L.
Zimmerman, Lee F.

See also ARCHITECTURE AND BUILDINGS

STANDARDS

Alexander, Esther M.
Archer, John H.
Ash, Lee
Atherton, Pauline
Badten, Jean M.
Bartolini, R. Paul
Basche, James R, Jr.
Beatty, William K.
Berninghausen, David K.
Berry, June
Bevis, Leura D.
Blasingame, Ralph
Boaz, Dr. Martha
Brahm, Walter T.
Brinton, Harry
Bryant, Jack W.
Buckingham, Betty J.
Burke, Dr. John E.
Bury, Peter P.
Campbell, Henry C.
Carlson, William H.
Carpenter, Dr. Ray L.
Castagna, Edwin
Chen, Dr. John H.M.
Chitwood, Jack
Clark, Rheta A.
Cohen, Aaron
Cohen, David
Coolidge, Coit
Crawford, Paul R.
Daume, Mrs. Mary R.
Davies, Ruth A.
De Young, Julia M.
Edwards, Ida M.
Falgione, Joseph F.
Fitzgerald, Dr. William A.
Flanders, Frances V.
Folcarelli, Ralph J.
Galick, Mrs. V. Genevieve
Gaver, Mary V.
Gibson, Frank E.
Goldstein, Dr. Harold
Goodbread, Juanita W.
Gosnell, Dr. Charles F.
Grafton, Connie E.
Graham, Mae
Greer, Dr. Roger C.
Harding, Nelson F.
Harnsberger, Therese
Harris, Walter H.
Heilmann, Margaret A.
Henington, David M.
Hicks, Warren B.
Hild, Alice P.
Hintz, Dr. Carl W.
Hirsch, Dr. Felix E.
Holt, Raymond M.
Humphry, James, III
Humphry, John A.
Jackson, Dr. William V.
Jaffarian, Sara
Johnson, Mrs. Barbara C.
Johnson, Mrs. Frances K.
Johnson, Leonard L.
Jones, Frank N.
Jordan, Robert T.
Kantor, David

Kemper, Dr. Robert E.
Keough, Francis P.
Kinney, Margaret M.
Lancour, Dr. Harold
Lane, Sister M. Claude, O.P.
McElderry, Stanley
McNiff, Philip J.
Martin, Allie B.
Michniewski, Henry J.
Miller, Mrs. Melissa
Minder, Thomas L.
Minker, Dr. Jack
Molod, Samuel E.
Morse, A. Louis
Negro, Antoinette
Nelson Associates, Inc.
Nelson, Charles A.
Oboler, Eli M.
Orne, Dr. Jerrold
Owens, Mrs. Iris
Palmer, David C.
Parsons, Mrs. Mary D.
Putnam, Hamilton S.
Raley, Mrs. Lucile W.
Remley, Ralph D.
Robertson, Billy O.
Rohlf, Robert H.
Roth, Harold L.
Rothines Associates
St. John, Francis R.
Samore, Theodore
Schick, Dr. Frank L.
Shapiro, Mrs. Lillian L.
Shores, Dr. Louis
Simon, Bradley A.
Smith, Hannis S.
Smith, L. Herman
Stephens, Dr. Irlene R.
Stewart, David M.
Summers, F. William
Surrency, Erwin C.
Tanis, Norman E.
Trinkner, Dr. Charles L.
Troke, Mrs. Margaret K.
Verschoor, Dr. Irving A.
Vreeland, Eleanor P.
Watkins, Mrs. Lillian M.
Wezeman, Frederick
Wheeler, Dr. Joseph L.
Whitenack, Carolyn I.
Wiese, M. Bernice
Wilmer, Florence C.
Zimmerman, Lee F.

STATE LIBRARIES AND EXTENSION AGENCIES

Archer, John H.
Baillie, Dr. Stuart
Basche, James R, Jr.
Bennett, Gordon L.
Berninghausen, David K.
Blasingame, Ralph
Brahm, Walter T.
Bryant, Jack W.
Campbell, Henry C.
Carlson, William H.
Carpenter, Dr. Ray L.
Cohen, Aaron
Galick, Mrs. V. Genevieve
Garrison, Dr. Guy
Gibson, Frank E.
Goldstein, Dr. Harold
Gosnell, Dr. Charles F.
Grafton, Connie E.
Graham, Mae
Hamlin, Arthur T.
Humphry, James, III
Humphry, John A.
Jackson, Dr. William V.
Kemper, Dr. Robert E.
Lancour, Dr. Harold
Leathers, James A.
McClarren, Robert R.
McDonough, Roger H.
Maclachlan, Bruce
McNiff, Philip J.
Minker, Dr. Jack
Molod, Samuel E.
Morin, Wilfred L.
Murphy, Lavinia E.

SPECIALTY INDEX

Nelson Associates, Inc.
Nelson, Charles A.
Oboler, Eli M.
Orne, Dr. Jerrold
Palmer, David C.
Price, Paxton P.
Putnam, Hamilton S.
Remley, Ralph D.
Rice, Cynthia
Rothines Associates
St. John, Francis R.
Schneider, Frank A.
Simon, Bradley A.
Smith, Hannis S.
Summers, F. William
Swank, Dr. Raynard C.
Tanis, Norman E.
Tauber, Dr. Maurice F.
Verschoor, Dr. Irving A.
Vorhies, Eugene
Wezeman, Frederick
Wight, Dr. Edward A.
Zimmerman, Lee F.

SURVEYS

Aceto, Vincent J.
Adams, Scott
Alexander, Esther M.
Allen, Kenneth S.
Anderson, Frank J.
Ash, Lee
Badten, Jean M.
Basche, James R, Jr.
Beatty, William K.
Bennett, Gordon L.
Berninghausen, David K.
Berry, June
Bertalan, Dr. Frank J.
Bevis, Leura D.
Blasingame, Ralph
Boaz, Dr. Martha
Brahm, Walter T.
Bryant, Jack W.
Burke, Dr. John E.
Bury, Peter P.
Campbell, Henry C.
Carlson, William H.
Carnovsky, Dr. Leon
Carpenter, Dr. Ray L.
Chait, William
Chen, Dr. John H.M.
Chitwood, Jack
Cohen, Aaron
Coman, Edwin T, Jr.
Coolidge, Coit
Crawford, Helen
Crawford, Paul R.
Daume, Mrs. Mary R.
Davis, Charlotte D.
Dawson, Dr. John M.
Denis, Laurent-G.
Dodd, James B.
Downs, Robert B.
Eastlick, John T.
Ebert, Myrl
Edwards, Ida M.
Eisner, Joseph
Engley, Donald B.
Filion, Paul-Emile, S.J.
Fitzgerald, Dr. William A.
Franklin, Robert D.
Galick, Mrs. V. Genevieve
Garrison, Dr. Guy
Gaver, Mary V.
Geddes, Andrew
Geller, William S.
Gibson, Frank E.
Goldstein, Dr. Harold
Goodbread, Juanita W.
Gosnell, Dr. Charles F.
Grafton, Connie E.
Greer, Dr. Roger C.
Haas, Warren J.
Harnsberger, Therese
Harris, Walter H.
Henderson, Mary J.
Henington, David M.
Heron, David W.

Hiatt, Dr. Peter
Hintz, Dr. Carl W.
Holley, Dr. Edward G.
Holt, Raymond M.
Hope, Arlene
Housel, James R.
Humphry, James, III
Humphry, John A.
Jackson, Dr. William V.
Jones, Frank N.
Kemper, Dr. Robert E.
Keough, Francis P.
Lancour, Dr. Harold
Lane, Sister M. Claude, O.P.
Leathers, James A.
McClarren, Robert R.
McCoy, Dr. Ralph E.
McDiarmid, Dr. Errett W.
McDonough, Roger H.
McFarland, Kay R.
McNiff, Philip J.
Martin, Allie B.
Metcalf, Dr. Keyes D.
Michniewski, Henry J.
Milczewski, Marion A.
Miller, Mrs. Melissa
Molod, Samuel E.
Morin, Wilfred L.
Nelson Associates, Inc.
Nelson, Charles A.
Nielsen, Andre S.
Orne, Dr. Jerrold
Paine, Clarence S.
Palmer, David S.
Parker, Wyman W.
Portteus, Elnora M.
Prideaux, B. Elizabeth
Proctor, Mrs. Margia W.
Putnam, Hamilton S.
Rateaver, Dr. Bargyla
Reichmann, Dr. Felix
Remley, Ralph D.
Rescoe, A. Stan
Rice, Cynthia
Rochell, Carlton
Rohlf, Robert H.
Roth, Harold L.
Rothines Associates
St. John, Francis R.
Samore, Theodore
Schein, Bernard
Schick, Dr. Frank L.
Schneider, Frank A.
Shaffer, Kenneth R.
Shank, Dr. Russell
Shepard, Mrs. Marietta D.
Shepherd, Giles F, Jr.
Simon, Bradley A.
Sinclair, Dorothy
Smith, Hannis S.
Stephens, Dr. Irlene R.
Stewart, David M.
Summers, F. William
Swank, Dr. Raynard C.
Tauber, Dr. Maurice F.
Trinkner, Dr. Charles L.
Troke, Mrs. Margaret K.
Verschoor, Dr. Irving A.
Vorhies, Eugene
Vreeland, Eleanor P.
Wallis, C. Lamar
Wezeman, Frederick
Whitenack, Carolyn I.
Wight, Dr. Edward A.
Woodward, Robert C.
Yesner, Mrs. Bernice L.
Zimmerman, Lee F.

See also OPINION SURVEYS, PLANNING, PROGRAM EVALUATIONS, PUBLIC RELATIONS, SYSTEMS ANALYSIS

SYSTEMS ANALYSIS

Anderson, Le Moyne W.
Atherton, Pauline
Berul, Lawrence H.
Bourne, Charles P.

Burns, Lorin R.
Clarke, Dr. Robert F.
Cohen, Aaron
Cranford, Theodore N.
Curley, Walter W.
Daily, Dr. Jay E.
Daume, Mrs. Mary R.
Deahl, Thomas F.
Dodd, James B.
Donohue, Joseph C.
Etchison, Annie L.
Friedlander, Dr. Michel O.
Fussler, Dr. Herman H.
Gorchels, Clarence C.
Gormley, Mark M.
Grosch, Audrey N.
Haas, Elaine
Harnsberger, Therese
Harris, Walter H.
Healey, James S.
Kemper, Dr. Robert E.
Klempner, Dr. Irving M.
Kopech, Gertrude
Kurth, William H.
Leondar, Judith C.
Linford, Arthur J, Jr.
McCoy, Dr. Ralph E.
Maclachlan, Bruce
Marshall & Brown, Inc.
Minder, Thomas L.
Minker, Dr. Jack
Mitchell, Vernon R.
Murphy, Lavinia E.
Nelson, Charles A.
Nelson Associates, Inc.
Parker, Dr. Ralph H.
Raphael, Anne W.
Rosenberg, Kenyon C.
Rothines Associates
St. John, Francis R.
Schafer, Emil
Stein, Theodore
Stephens, Dr. Irlene R.
Taylor, Robert S.
Veaner, Allen B.
Voos, Dr. Henry
Vorhies, Eugene
Wagman, Dr. Frederick H.
Wasserman, Dr. Paul

See also ADMINISTRATIVE ORGANIZATION, AUTOMATION, CLASSIFICATION SYSTEMS, DATA PROCESSING EQUIPMENT APPLICATIONS, INFORMATION STORAGE AND RETRIEVAL SYSTEMS, PLANNING, SURVEYS

TECHNICAL PROCESSES

MATERIALS PROCESSING

Alexander, Esther M.
Allen, Kenneth S.
Anderson, Le Moyne W.
Andrews, James C.
Badten, Jean M.
Banister, John R.
Beaton, Mrs. Maxine B.
Berrisford, Paul D.
Brahm, Walter T.
Brinton, Harry
Brown, Alberta L.
Buckley, John
Carrison, Dale K.
Chen, Dr. John H.M.
Chitwood, Jack
Clarke, Dr. Robert F.
Cohen, David
Connolly, Brendan, S.J.
Cranford, Theodore N.
Cronin, John W.
Curley, Walter W.
Daily, Dr. Jay E.
Daume, Mrs. Mary R.
Dees, Margaret N.
De Young, Julia M.
Diehl, Katharine S.
Dodd, James B.

SPECIALTY INDEX

Elrod, J. McRee
Ertel, Mrs. Margaret P.
Fast, Mrs. Elizabeth T.
Fitzgerald, Mrs. Louise H.
Folcarelli, Ralph J.
Frarey, Carlyle J.
Friedlander, Dr. Michel O.
Galfand, Sidney
Gilbert, Christine B.
Goodbread, Juanita W.
Gormley, Mark M.
Haas, Elaine
Harding, Nelson F.
Harnsberger, Therese
Harris, Walter H.
Healey, James S.
Heilmann, Margaret A.
Henderson, Mary J.
Hicks, Warren B.
Hild, Alice P.
Hill, Laurence G.
Hines, Dr. Theodore C.
Humphry, James, III
Humphry, John A.
Jaffarian, Sara
Jansen, Guenter A.
Johnson, Mrs. Barbara C.
Johnson, Leonard L.
Jones, James V.
Katz, Beatrice
Kemper, Dr. Robert E.
Klempner, Dr. Irving M.
Kopech, Gertrude
Kurth, William H.
Lane, Sister M. Claude, O.P.
Leathers, James A.
Logsdon, Dr. Richard H.
McCarthy, Dr. Stephen A.
Maclachlan, Bruce
Miles, Paul M.
Miller, Mrs. Melissa
Minder, Thomas L.
Minker, Dr. Jack
Mitchell, Eleanor
Moran, Virginia L.
Morgan, John F.
Morse, A. Louis
Nelson Associates, Inc.
Nelson, Charles A.
Owens, Mrs. Iris
Parker, Dr. Ralph H.
Parsons, Mrs. Mary D.
Piternick, George
Raley, Mrs. Lucille W.
Raphael, Anne W.
Reichmann, Dr. Felix
Rescoe, A. Stan
Robertson, Billy O.
Rothines Associates
Rowland, Arthur R.
St. John, Francis R.
Samore, Theodore
Schafer, Emil
Schefter, Joseph A.
Schneider, Frank A.
Schork, Francis W.
Schutze, Gertrude
Sheehan, Sister Helen
Simon, Bradley A.
Slocum, Mrs. Betty
Smith, James L.
Smith, L. Herman
Spyers-Duran, Peter
Stephens, Dr. Irlene R.
Swank, Dr. Raynard C.
Tauber, Dr. Maurice F.
Taylor, Robert S.
Technical Library Service
Treyz, Joseph H.
Trinkner, Dr. Charles L.
Trotier, Arnold H.
Usher, Mrs. Elizabeth R.
Van Velzer, Verna J.
Veaner, Allen B.
Voigt, Melvin J.
Voos, Dr. Henry
Vorhies, Eugene
Wagman, Dr. Frederick H.
Watkins, Mrs. Lillian M.
Yesner, Mrs. Bernice L.
Zimmerman, Lee F.

WORK FLOW AND COST STUDIES

Allen, Kenneth S.
Anderson, Le Moyne W.
Andrews, James C.
Atherton, Pauline
Beatty, William K.
Berul, Lawrence H.
Brahm, Walter T.
Brinton, Harry
Burke, Dr. John E.
Burns, Lorin R.
Bury, Peter P.
Chapin, Dr. Richard E.
Chen, Dr. John H.M.
Clarke, Dr. Robert F.
Covey, Dr. Alan D.
Cranford, Theodore N.
Cronin, John W.
Curley, Walter W.
Daily, Dr. Jay E.
Daume, Mrs. Mary R.
Di Muccio, Sister Mary-Jo
Divett, Dr. Robert T.
Dodd, James B.
Elrod, J. McRee
Fast, Mrs. Elizabeth T.
Fitzgerald, Mrs. Louise H.
Frarey, Carlyle J.
Friedlander, Dr. Michel O.
Goodbread, Juanita W.
Grosch, Audrey N.
Haas, Elaine
Haas, Warren J.
Hamlin, Arthur T.
Harnsberger, Therese
Harris, Walter H.
Healey, James S.
Henderson, Mary J.
Henkle, Dr. Herman H.
Hicks, Warren B.
Hill, Laurence G.
Hines, Dr. Theodore C.
Hope, Arlene
Housel, James R.
Humphry, James, III
Humphry, John A.
Jansen, Guenter A.
Jordan, Robert T.
Kemper, Dr. Robert E.
Keough, Francis P.
Kurth, William H.
Leathers, James A.
Leondar, Judith C.
Logsdon, Dr. Richard H.
Maclachlan, Bruce
Miller, Mrs. Melissa
Minder, Thomas L.
Minker, Dr. Jack
Morin, Wilfred L.
Morse, A. Louis
Muller, Dr. Robert H.
Nelson Associates, Inc.
Nelson, Charles A.
Obeler, Eli M.
Orne, Dr. Jerrold
Parker, Dr. Ralph H.
Piternick, George
Reichmann, Dr. Felix
Robertson, Billy O.
Rosenberg, Kenyon C.
Rothines Associates
St. John, Francis R.
Samore, Theodore
Schafer, Emil
Schefter, Joseph A.
Schneider, Frank A.
Shank, Dr. Russell
Simmons, Joseph M.
Simon, Bradley A.
Smith, James L.
Spyers-Duran, Peter
Stephens, Dr. Irlene R.
Stevens, Nicholas G.
Swank, Dr. Raynard C.
Tauber, Dr. Maurice F.
Taylor, Robert S.
Technical Library Service
Treyz, Joseph H.
Usher, Mrs. Elizabeth R.
Voigt, Melvin J.

Voos, Dr. Henry
Vorhies, Eugene
Wagman, Dr. Frederick H.
Watkins, Mrs. Lillian M.
Wight, Dr. Edward A.
Yesner, Mrs. Bernice L.
Zimmerman, Lee F.

See also CATALOGING, CLASSIFICATION SYSTEMS

Young Adult Collections see BOOK COLLECTIONS: YOUNG ADULT

CONSULTANTS WITH OTHER SPECIALTIES

Ackerman, Page
Allen, Kenneth S.
Archer, John H.
Ash, Lee
Asheim, Dr. Lester
Baillie, Dr. Stuart
Ballou, Hubbard W.
Banister, John R.
Bennett, Gordon L.
Berry, John N, III
Berry, June
Berthel, John H.
Berul, Lawrence H.
Bevis, Leura D.
Bixler, Paul
Blanchard, J. Richard
Blaustein, Albert P.
Bonn, George S.
Brandon, Alfred N.
Burgess, Robert S.
Campbell, Henry C.
Carnovsky, Dr. Leon
Carpenter, Dr. Ray L.
Carrison, Dale K.
Castagna, Edwin
Chen, Dr. John H.M.
Clarke, Dr. Robert F.
Cohen, David
Cole, Georgia R.
Crawford, Paul R.
Currie, Dorothy H.
Daily, Dr. Jay E.
Dalton, Jack
Davidson, Dr. Donald C.
Davies, Ruth A.
Davis, Charlotte D.
Diehl, Katharine S.
Dodd, James B.
Donohue, Joseph C.
Duke, William R.
Evans, Richard A.
Fast, Mrs. Elizabeth T.
Field, Mrs. Carolyn W.
Fitzgerald, Mrs. Louise H.
Franklin, Robert D.
Friedlander, Dr. Michel O.
Galfand, Sidney
Galvin, Thomas J.
Gilbert, Christine B.
Gitler, Dr. Robert L.
Goldstein, Dr. Harold
Gordon, Bernard L.
Gosnell, Dr. Charles F.
Graham, Mae
Gropp, Arthur E.
Grosch, Audrey N.
Haas, Elaine
Hall, Elvajean
Harlow, Neal
Harnsberger, Therese
Harvey, Dr. John F.
Hawken, William R.
Heiliger, Edward M.
Hellum, Bertha D.
Henderson, John D.
Henderson, Mary J.
Hiatt, Dr. Peter
Hines, Dr. Theodore C.
Holt, Raymond M.
Hopp, Dr. Ralph H.
Humphry, John A.
Hurley, Richard J.

SPECIALTY INDEX

Jackson, Dr. William V.
Jacobs, Dr. James W.
Jaffarian, Sara
Johnson, Leonard L.
Jordan, Robert T.
Kemper, Dr. Robert E.
Kopech, Gertrude
Lancour, Dr. Harold
Lane, Sister M. Claude, O.P.
Lee, Dr. Robert E.
Lembo, Mrs. Diana L.
Leondar, Judith C.
Logsdon, Dr. Richard H.
McAnally, Dr. Arthur M.
McCoy, Dr. Ralph E.
Mack, Mrs. Sara R.
Milczewski, Marion A.
Miller, J. Gormly
Minder, Thomas L.
Mitchell, Eleanor
Mitchell, Vernon R.
Morgan, John F.
Morris, Dr. Raymond P.
Morse, A. Louis
Mostar, Roman
Muller, Dr. Robert H.

Murray, Thomas B.
Negro, Antoinette
O'Brien, James M.
Orton, Floyd E.
Peterson, Harry N.
Piternick, George
Pollack, Ervin H.
Portteus, Elnora M.
Price, Paxton P.
Rateaver, Dr. Bargyla
Rescoe, A. Stan
Robertson, Billy O.
Rochell, Carlton
Roth, Harold L.
Rothines Associates
St. John, Francis R.
Sattley, Helen R.
Schafer, Emil
Schefter, Joseph A.
Schick, Dr. Frank L.
Schork, Francis W.
Schutze, Gertrude
Severance, Robert W.
Shank, Dr. Russell
Shepard, Mrs. Marietta D.
Shores, Dr. Louis

Simon, Fannie
Skipper, Dr. James E.
Smith, Hannis S.
Sprug, Joseph W.
Spyers-Duran, Peter
Stephens, Dr. Irlene R.
Stern, Dr. William B.
Stevens, Nicholas G.
Stone, Dr. C. Walter
Swank, Dr. Raynard C.
Tauber, Dr. Maurice F.
Taylor, Robert S.
Technical Library Service
Thompson, Donald E.
Thompson, Dr. Lawrence S.
VanJackson, Wallace M.
Veaner, Allen B.
Veit, Dr. Fritz
Verschoor, Dr. Irving A.
Voos, Dr. Henry
Wallace, Sarah L.
Wasserman, Dr. Paul
Wheeler, Dr. Helen R.
Whitenack, Carolyn I.
Woodward, Rupert C.
Yesner, Mrs. Bernice L.

GEOGRAPHICAL INDEX

ALABAMA
Oltman, Florine A.
Perreault, Jean Michel
Severance, Robert W.

ARIZONA
Covey, Dr. Alan Dale
Munn, R. Russell
Simon, Bradley Alden

CALIFORNIA
Ackerman, Page
Allen, James W.
Alvarez, Dr. Robert S.
Baillie, Dr. Stuart
Blanchard, J. Richard
Boaz, Dr. Martha
Bourne, Charles P.
Coman, Edwin Truman, Jr.
Coolidge, Coit
Cranford, Theodore Nelson
Crawford, Paul Russell
Danton, Dr. J. Periam
Darling, Louise
Davidson, Dr. Donald C.
Davis, Charlotte (Doyle)
Di Muccio, Sister Mary Jo
Dunkley, Grace S.
Edwards, Ida May
Fleischman, Al
Geller, William Spence
Georgi, Charlotte
Gitler, Dr. Robert L(aurence)
Harnsberger, Therese
Harris, Walter H.
Hart, Dr. Eugene D.
Hawken, William R.
Hellum, Bertha D.
Henderson, John D.
Hicks, Warren B.
Holt, Raymond M.
Housel, James R.
Jacobstein, J. Myron
James, Louise
McDaniel, Roderick D.
Miles, Paul M.
Murray, Thomas B.
Nesbin, Mrs. Esther Winter
Osborne, Fred Yantis
Parsons, Mrs. Mary Dudley
Ramirez, William Louis
Raphael, Anne Wagner
Rateaver, Dr. Bargyla
Schafer, Emil
Skipper, Dr. James E.
Smith, L. Herman
Stern, Dr. William B.
Swank, Dr. Raynard C.
Troke, Mrs. Margaret Klausner
Van Velzer, Verna J.
Veaner, Allen B.
Voigt, Melvin J.
Wagner, Dr. Robert George
Watkins, Mrs. Lillian M.
Wight, Dr. Edward Allen
Ziebold, Edna B.

COLORADO
Anderson, Le Moyne W.
Beaton, Mrs. Maxine Bailey
Bennett, Gordon Latta
Eastlick, John Taylor
Ellsworth, Dr. Ralph E.
Sprug, Joseph W.

CONNECTICUT
Ash, Lee
Brahm, Walter T.
Clark, Rheta A.
Engley, Donald B.
Fast, Mrs. Elizabeth T.
Harding, Nelson F.
McDonald, John Peter
Molod, Samuel E.
Morris, Dr. Raymond Philip
Parker, Wyman W.
Yesner, Mrs. Bernice L.

DELAWARE
Dawson, Dr. John M.
Schneider, Frank A.

DISTRICT OF COLUMBIA
Baer, Dr. Karl A.
Burke, Redmond A, C.S.V.
Cronin, John William
Gerlach, Dr. Arch C.
Gropp, Arthur Eric
Jordan, Robert Thayer
Leopold, Mrs. Carolyn Clugston
McCarthy, Dr. Stephen A.
McGowan, Frank M.
Peterson, Harry N.
Poole, Frazer G.
Price, Paxton P.
Reason, Dr. Joseph H.
Rohlf, Robert Henry
Schork, Francis William
Shank, Dr. Russell
Sheehan, Sister Helen
Shepard, Mrs. Marietta Daniels
Wallace, Sarah Leslie
Woodward, Rupert C.

FLORIDA
Beach, Cecil P.
Brinton, Harry
Casellas, Elizabeth Reed (Brannon)
Goldstein, Dr. Harold
Goodbread, Juanita W.
Hardaway, Elliott
Kantor, David
McNeal, Dr. Archie L.
Owens, Mrs. Iris
Runge, DeLyle P.
Rush, N. Orwin
Shores, Dr. Louis
Slocum, Mrs. Betty
Summers, F. William
Trinker, Dr. Charles L.
Trotier, Arnold H.

GEORGIA
Banister, John R.
Byers, Mrs. Edna Hanley
Cochran, Jean D.
Dodd, James Beaupré
Etchison, Annie Laurie
Lyle, Guy R.
Murphy, Walter H.
Nikas, Mary Creety
Pullen, Dr. William R.
Rochell, Carlton
Rowland, Arthur Ray

IDAHO
Oboler, Eli M.

ILLINOIS
Allen, Loren H.
Anderson, Dorothy J.
Andrews, James C.
Asheim, Dr. Lester
Bean, Donald Eckhart
Beatty, William K.
Burns, Lorin R.
Bury, Peter P.
Carnovsky, Dr. Leon
Chitwood, Jack
Dees, Margaret (Nyhus)
Downs, Robert B.
Fussler, Dr. Herman Howe
Henkle, Dr. Herman H.
Jackson, Dr. William Vernon
Johnson, David L.
Library Management & Building
   Consultants, Inc.
Lohrer, Alice
McClarren, Robert R.
McCoy, Dr. Ralph E.
Moreland, Carroll C.
Schefter, Joseph
Simmons, Joseph M.
Smith, James LeRoy
Stoffel, Lester L.
Trezza, Alphonse F.
Veit, Dr. Fritz
White, Dr. Lucien W.

GEOGRAPHICAL INDEX

INDIANA
Bartolini, R. Paul
Cole, Georgia (Rankin)
Dunn, Dr. Oliver C.
Farber, Evan Ira
Hiatt, Dr. Peter
Miller, Dr. Robert A.
Moriarty, John H.
Thompson, Donald Eugene
Whitenack, Carolyn Irene

IOWA
Buckingham, Betty Jo
Dunlap, Dr. Leslie W.
Grafton, C(onnie) Ernestine
Orr, Robert William
Rod, Donald O.
Wezeman, Frederick

KANSAS
Alexander, Esther Mona
Heron, David W.
Lee, Dr. Robert Ellis
Tanis, Norman Earl

KENTUCKY
Thompson, Dr. Lawrence S.

LOUISIANA
Flanders, Frances Vivian
McMullan, Theodore N.
Shaw, Thomas Shuler

MAINE
Adamovich, Shirley
Woodward, Robert C.

MARYLAND
Adams, Scott
Berthel, John H.
Brandon, Alfred N.
Castagna, Edwin
Evans, Richard A.
Graham, Mae
Jacobs, Dr. James Wriley
Leopold, Mrs. Carolyn Clugston
McGowan, Frank M.
Minker, Dr. Jack
Negro, Antoinette
Poole, Frazer G.
Remley, Ralph D.
Rohlf, Robert Henry
Rovelstad, Howard
Wasserman, Dr. Paul
Wiese, M. Bernice
Wilmer, Florence Conrath

MASSACHUSETTS
Archer, Dr. H. Richard
Bloomquist, Harold
Bourne, Philip W.
Bryant, Jack W.
Buckley, John
Connolly, Brendan, S.J.
Curley, Walter W.
De Gennaro, Richard
Galick, Mrs. V. Genevieve
Galvin, Thomas John
Gordon, Bernard L.
Hall, Elvajean
Harwell, Richard
Herrick, Mary Darrah
Hope, Arlene
Jaffarian, Sara
Jones, Frank N(icholas)
Keough, Francis P.
McKeon, Newton F.
McNiff, Philip J.
Metcalf, Dr. Keyes D.
Murphy, Lavinia Ellen
Schmuch, Joseph J.
Shaffer, Kenneth R(aymond)

Taylor, Robert S.
Williams, Edwin E.

MICHIGAN
Brown, Alberta L.
Chapin, Dr. Richard E.
Chase, William D.
Daume, Mrs. Mary Rossiter
De Young, Julia M.
Johnson, Mrs. Barbara Coe
Katz, Beatrice
Miller, Mrs. Melissa
Mohrhardt, Charles M.
Muller, Dr. Robert H.
Spyers-Duran, Peter
Stewart, R.C.
Treyz, Joseph H.
Ulveling, Dr. Ralph
Wagman, Dr. Frederick H.

MINNESOTA
Berninghausen, David Knipe
Berrisford, Paul Dee
Carrison, Dale K.
Grosch, Audrey N.
Hopp, Dr. Ralph H.
McDiarmid, Dr. Errett Weir
Nielsen, Andre S.
Richards, James H, Jr.
Smith, Hannis S.
Smith, Mrs. June Smeck

MISSISSIPPI
Isley, Doris Natelle

MISSOURI
Brodman, Dr. Estelle
Eaton, Dr. Andrew Jackson
Kurth, William H.
Leathers, James A.
Marshall & Brown, Inc.
Parker, Dr. Ralph H.

NEBRASKA
Gibson, Frank E.
Lute, Harriet
Robertson, Billy O'Neal
Young, Carol

NEW HAMPSHIRE
Adamovich, Shirley
Armstrong, Rodney
Putnam, Hamilton S.
St. John, Francis R.

NEW JERSEY
Berul, Lawrence H.
Blasingame, Ralph
Blaustein, Albert P.
Bryan, Dr. James E.
Dix, Dr. William Shepherd
Eshelman, William Robert
Gaver, Mary Virginia
Gorski, Lorraine K.M.
Harlow, Neal
Hines, Dr. Theodore C.
Hirsch, Dr. Felix Edward
Leondar, Judith C.
Lucker, Jay K.
McDonough, Roger H.
McPherson, Kenneth F.
Michniewski, Henry J.
Negro, Antoinette
Palmer, David C.
Roth, Harold Leo
Scarborough, Ruth Ellen
Schein, Bernard
Stephens, Dr. Irlene Roemer
Thomas, Henry
Voos, Dr. Henry

NEW MEXICO
Chisholm, Dr. Margaret E.
Divett, Dr. Robert T.

NEW YORK
Aceto, Vincent John
Atherton, Pauline
Ballou, Hubbard W.
Basche, James R, Jr.
Berry, John N, III
Bitner, Harry
Burgess, Robert S.
Cavaglieri, Dr. Giorgio
Cohen, Aaron
Cohen, David
Cole, Doris M.
Currie, Dorothy H.
Dalton, Jack
Eisner, Joseph
Eshelman, William Robert
Folcarelli, Ralph Joseph
Frarey, Carlyle J.
Friedlander, Dr. Michel O.
Geddes, Andrew
Gelfand, Dr. Morris A.
Gilbert, Christine B.
Gosnell, Dr. Charles F.
Greer, Dr. Roger Clement
Haas, Elaine
Heilmann, Margaret Ayers
Hill, Laurence G.
Hines, Dr. Theodore C.
Humphry, James, III
Humphry, John Ames
Jansen, Guenter A.
Jones, Harold D.
Josey, E.J.
Kaser, Dr. David
Kinney, Margaret Mary
Klempner, Dr. Irving M.
Kopech, Gertrude
Leggett, Dr. Stanton F.
Lembo, Mrs. Diana L.
Lindauer, Dinah
Logsdon, Dr. Richard H.
Lybeck, Pauline
Maclachlan, Bruce
Mapp, Edward Charles
Marke, Julius J.
Mason, Dr. Ellsworth
Miller, (J) Gormly
Montgomery, James W.
Moran, Virginia L.
Morgan, John F
Morin, Wilfred Laurier
Morse, A. Louis
Nelson, Charles A.
Nelson Associates, Inc.
Norton, Alice
O'Brien, James M.
Proctor, Mrs. Margia W.
Reichmann, Dr. Felix
Rice, Cynthia
Richard, St. Clair
Rockwell, Mrs. Jeanette Sledge
Rounds, Gertrude W.
Sattley, Helen R.
Schutze, Gertrude
Shapiro, Mrs. Lillian L.
Shepherd, Giles F, Jr.
Simmons, Marion L.
Simon, Fannie
Stein, Theodore
Stephens, Dr. Irlene Roemer
Tauber, Dr. Maurice F.
Technical Library Service
Usher, Mrs. Elizabeth R.
Vaillancourt, Dr. Pauline M.
Verschoor, Dr. Irving A.
Voigt, Edna E.
Vorhies, Eugene
Vreeland, Eleanor P.
Wheeler, Dr. Helen Rippier

NORTH CAROLINA
Carpenter, Dr. Ray L.
Ebert, Myrl
Ertel, Mrs. Margaret P.
Etchison, Annie Laurie
Galvin, Hoyt R.
Johnson, Mrs. Frances Kennon
Johnson, Leonard L.
Orne, Dr. Jerrold

Van Buren, Martin
Zimmerman, Lee F.

OHIO

Barber, Raymond William
Bixler, Paul
Branscomb, Dr. Lewis Capers, Jr.
Chait, William
Donohue, Joseph Chaminade
Ellerbrock, Edward J.
Franklin, Robert D.
Hamlin, Arthur T.
Heiliger, Edward Martin
Jones, James Victor
Linford, Arthur John, Jr.
Miller, Ernest I.
Pollack, Ervin H.
Portteus, Elnora M.
Rosenberg, Kenyon C.
Sinclair, Dorothy
Vormelker, Rose L.

OKLAHOMA

Bertalan, Dr. Frank J.
Carter, Mrs. Oma
Library Design Associates
McAnally, Dr. Arthur M.
Martin, Allie Beth
Mitchell, Vernon R.

OREGON

Carlson, William H.
Gorchels, Clarence Clifford
Hintz, Dr. Carl W.
Kemper, Dr. Robert E.
Merritt, Dr. LeRoy C.
Prideaux, B. Elizabeth

PENNSYLVANIA

Berul, Lawrence H.
Butler, Evelyn
Cohen, Morris L.
Daily, Dr. Jay Elwood
Davies, Ruth A.
Deahl, Thomas F.
Diehl, Katharine Smith
Doms, Keith
Falgione, Joseph F.
Field, Mrs. Carolyn W.
Galfand, Sidney
Garrison, Dr. Guy
Haas, Warren J.
Harvey, Dr. John Frederick
Hunt, Donald H.
Jackson, Dr. William Vernon
Lancour, Dr. Harold
McConkey, Thomas W.
McFarland, Kay R.
Mack, Mrs. Sara R.

Minder, Thomas L.
Pease, William Artis
Schell, Harold B.
Stevens, Nicholas G.
Stone, Dr. C. Walter
Surrency, Erwin C.

RHODE ISLAND

Healey, James S.
Rothines Associates

SOUTH CAROLINA

Anderson, Frank J.

TENNESSEE

Cole, Mary Elizabeth
Jesse, William H.
Kuhlman, Dr. A(ugustus) F(rederick)
Mills, Jesse C.
Paine, Clarence S.
Perry, E. Caswell
Rescoe, A. Stan
Stewart, David Marshall
Wallis, C. Lamar

TEXAS

Benson, William E.
Burke, Dr. John Emmett
Cherry, Scott T.
Henington, David M.
Holley, Dr. Edward Gailon
Jones, Wyman
Lane, Sister M. Claude, O.P.
McAdams, Mrs. Nancy Reeves
McElderry, Stanley
Mershy, Roy Martin
Perrine, Richard H.
Raley, Mrs. Lucile W.
Wallace, James Oldham

UTAH

Berry, June
Clark, Mrs. Gertrude M.

VERMONT

Adamovich, Shirley
Popecki, Joseph Thomas
Wheeler, Dr. Joseph L.

VIRGINIA

Bailey, J. Russell
Chen, Dr. John H.M.
Clarke, Dr. Robert Flanders
Hurley, Richard J.
Minker, Dr. Jack
Mitchell, Eleanor

Price, Paxton P.
Shank, Dr. Russell
VanJackson, Wallace M.

WASHINGTON

Allen, Kenneth S.
Badten, Jean Margaret
Bevis, Leura Dorothy
Milczewski, Marion A.
Mostar, Roman
Mutschler, Herbert F.
Orton, Floyd Emory

WEST VIRGINIA

Fry, Alderson

WISCONSIN

Brown, Gerald G.
Crawford, Helen
Deale, H(enry) Vail
Fitzgerald, Mrs. Louise H.
Fitzgerald, Dr. William A.
Gormley, Mark McGuire
Samore, Theodore
Schick, Dr. Frank L.
Williamson, Dr. William Landram

WYOMING

Hild, Alice P.
Oliner, Stan

CANADA

Alberta

Duke, William Richard

British Columbia

Elrod, J. McRee
Piternick, George

Ontario

Archer, John H.
Brook, John B.
Campbell, Henry Cummings
Filion, Paul-Emile, S.J.
Henderson, Mary Jane
Ready, William Bernard
Redmond, Donald A.

Quebec

Denis, Laurent-G.
Henderson, Mary Jane

HONDURAS

Parsons, Mrs. Mary Dudley

INDIA

Bonn, George S.
Diehl, Katharine Smith

DATE DUE			
GAYLORD			PRINTED IN U.S.A.